T0198227

Microsoft® Office 365®
PUBLISHER 2019

JOY L. STARKS | MISTY E. VERMAAT

CENGAGE

Australia • Brazil • Mexico • Singapore • United Kingdom • United States

SHELLY CASHMAN SERIES®

**Shelly Cashman Series® Microsoft® Office 365® &
Publisher 2019 Comprehensive**
Joy L. Starks, Misty E. Vermaat

SVP, GM Skills & Global Product Management:
    Jonathan Lau
Product Director: Lauren Murphy
Product Assistant: Veronica Moreno-Nestojko
Executive Director, Content Design: Marah
    Bellegarde
Director, Learning Design: Leigh Hefferon
Learning Designer: Courtney Cozzy
Vice President, Marketing - Science,
    Technology, and Math: Jason R. Sakos
Senior Marketing Director: Michele McTighe
Marketing Manager: Timothy J. Cali
Director, Content Delivery: Patty Stephan
Senior Content Manager: Anne Orgren
Digital Delivery Lead: Laura Ruschman
Designer: Lizz Anderson
Cover image(s): Sergey Kelin/ShutterStock.com
    (Ocean), nikkytok/ShutterStock.com (Crystal),
    INJParin/Shutterstock.com (Marble), Erika
    Kirkpatrick/ShutterStock.com (Driftwood),
    Vladitto/ShutterStock.com (Skyscraper),
    Roman Sigaev/ShutterStock.com (Clouds)

For product information and technology assistance, contact us at
**Cengage Customer & Sales Support, 1-800-354-9706 or
support.cengage.com.**

For permission to use material from this text or product,
submit all requests online at **www.cengage.com/permissions.**

Library of Congress Control Number: 2019911675

Student Edition ISBN: 978-0-357-36002-6
Looseleaf available as part of a digital bundle

Cengage
200 Pier 4 Boulevard
Boston, MA 02210
USA

Cengage is a leading provider of customized learning solutions with employees residing in nearly 40 different countries and sales in more than 125 countries around the world. Find your local representative at **www.cengage.com.**

Cengage products are represented in Canada by Nelson Education, Ltd.

To learn more about Cengage platforms and services, visit **www.cengage.com.**

To register or access your online learning solution or purchase materials for your course, visit **www.cengagebrain.com.**

Printed at CLDPC, USA, 07-22

Microsoft® Office 365®
PUBLISHER 2019

COMPREHENSIVE

Brief Contents

Microsoft **Publisher 2019**

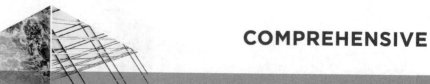

Microsoft® Office 365®
PUBLISHER 2019

COMPREHENSIVE

Contents

Getting to Know Microsoft Office Versions

Cengage is proud to bring you the next edition of Microsoft Office. This edition was designed to provide a robust learning experience that is not dependent upon a specific version of Office.

Microsoft supports several versions of Office:

- **Office 365:** A cloud-based subscription service that delivers Microsoft's most up-to-date, feature-rich, modern productivity tools direct to your device. There are variations of Office 365 for business, educational, and personal use. Office 365 offers extra online storage and cloud-connected features, as well as updates with the latest features, fixes, and security updates.

- **Office 2019:** Microsoft's "on-premises" version of the Office apps, available for both PCs and Macs, offered as a static, one-time purchase and outside of the subscription model.

- **Office Online:** A free, simplified version of Office web applications (Word, Excel, PowerPoint, and OneNote) that facilitates creating and editing files collaboratively.

Office 365 (the subscription model) and Office 2019 (the one-time purchase model) had only slight differences between them at the time this content was developed. Over time, Office 365's cloud interface will continuously update, offering new application features and functions, while Office 2019 will remain static. Therefore, your onscreen experience may differ from what you see in this product. For example, the more advanced features and functionalities covered in this product may not be available in Office Online or may have updated from what you see in Office 2019.

For more information on the differences between Office 365, Office 2019, and Office Online, please visit the Microsoft Support site.

Cengage is committed to providing high-quality learning solutions for you to gain the knowledge and skills that will empower you throughout your educational and professional careers.

Thank you for using our product, and we look forward to exploring the future of Microsoft Office with you!

Using SAM Projects and Textbook Projects

SAM and *MindTap* are interactive online platforms designed to transform students into Microsoft Office and Computer Concepts masters. Practice with simulated SAM Trainings and MindTap activities and actively apply the skills you learned live in Microsoft Word, Excel, PowerPoint, or Access. Become a more productive student and use these skills throughout your career.

If your instructor assigns SAM Projects:

1. Launch your SAM Project assignment from SAM or MindTap.
2. Click the links to download your **Instructions file**, **Start file**, and **Support files** (when available).
3. Open the Instructions file and follow the step-by-step instructions.
4. When you complete the project, upload your file to SAM or MindTap for immediate feedback.

To use SAM Textbook Projects:

1. Launch your SAM Project assignment from SAM or MindTap.
2. Click the links to download your **Start file** and **Support files** (when available).
3. Locate the module indicated in your book or eBook.
4. Read the module and complete the project.

 Open the Start file you downloaded.

Save, close, and upload your completed project to receive immediate feedback.

IMPORTANT: To receive full credit for your Textbook Project, you must complete the activity using the Start file you downloaded from SAM or MindTap.

1 | Creating a Flyer

Objectives

After completing this module, you will be able to:

- Start and exit Publisher
- Choose Publisher template options
- Describe the Publisher window
- Select objects and zoom
- Replace Publisher placeholder and default text
- Check spelling as you type
- Format text and autofit
- Use graphics and insert backgrounds

- Move, align, and resize objects
- Save a publication and print
- Open and modify a publication
- Delete objects
- Create a hyperlink
- Save a print publication as a web publication
- Use Publisher Help

What Is Publisher?

Microsoft Publisher, or Publisher for short, is a full-featured desktop publishing app that helps you create professional-quality publications and marketing materials — including flyers, brochures, advertisements, catalogs, mailing labels, and newsletters — that can be shared easily. Publisher also provides tools that enable you to create webpages and save these webpages directly on a web server. Publisher has many features designed to simplify the production of publications and add visual appeal. Using Publisher, you easily can change the shape, size, and color of text. You also can include borders, shading, tables, images, pictures, charts, and web addresses in publications.

Introduction

To publicize an event, advertise a sale or service, promote a business, or convey a message to the community, you may want to create a flyer and post it in a public location. A **flyer** is a single-page publication, which may be printed on various sizes of paper, announcing personal items for sale or rent (car, boat, apartment); garage or block sales; services being offered (housecleaning, lessons, carpooling); membership, sponsorship, or charity events (civic organization, club); and other messages. Flyers are an inexpensive means of reaching the community, yet many go unnoticed because they are designed poorly. A good flyer, or any publication, must deliver a message in the clearest, most attractive, and most effective way possible. You must clarify your purpose and know your target audience. You need to gather ideas and plan for the printing. Finally, you must edit, proofread, and then publish your flyer. Flyers must stand out to be noticed.

Flyers also can be posted on the web. Electronic bulletin boards, social networking sites, and online auction websites are good places to reach people with flyers, advertising everything from a bake sale to a part-time job opening.

To illustrate the features of Publisher, this book presents a series of projects that create publications similar to those you will encounter in academic and business environments.

Project: Research Study Flyer

The project in this module uses Publisher and a template to create the flyer shown in Figure 1–1. This attractive flyer advertises for participants in a headache research study. The title clearly identifies the purpose of the flyer, using large, bold letters. Below the title, to maintain consistency, the same font is used for the name of the research facility. The graphic or picture is placed to be eye-catching; it represents both the medical and research concepts. The flyer also includes a brief description, website, and phone number. The tear-offs, aligned at the bottom of the flyer, include the phone number for more information. Finally, the font and color schemes support the topic and make the text stand out.

In this module, you will learn how to create the flyer shown in Figure 1–1. You will perform the following general tasks as you progress through this module:

1. Start Publisher and customize the template options, such as choice, color scheme, and font scheme.
2. Navigate the interface and select objects.
3. Format the text in the flyer.
4. Insert graphics in placeholders.
5. Enhance the page by repositioning and aligning objects.
6. After saving and closing a publication, open and revise it.

Starting Publisher

To use Publisher, you must instruct the operating system (i.e., Windows) to start the app. The following section illustrates how to start Publisher.

If you are using a computer or device to step through the project in this module and you want your screen to match the figures in this book, you should change your screen's resolution to 1366 x 768.

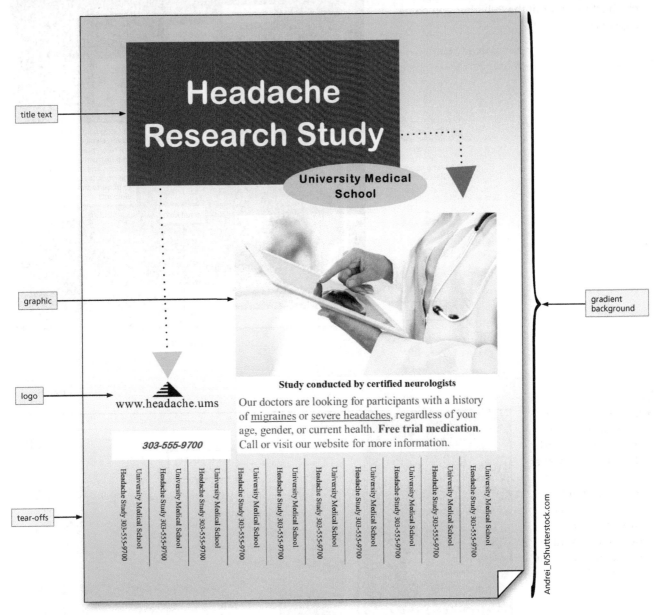

Figure 1–1

To Start Publisher

The following steps, which assume Windows is running, start Publisher based on a typical installation. You may need to ask your instructor how to start Publisher on your computer or device. *Why? You will use Publisher to create the flyer in this module.*

❶

- Click the Start button on the Windows taskbar to display the Start menu.

Q&A | What is a menu?
A **menu** contains a list of related items, including folders, applications, and commands. Each **command** is a menu item that performs a specific action, such as saving a file or obtaining help. A **folder** is a named location on a storage medium that usually contains related documents.

- If necessary, scroll through the list of apps on the Start menu until the Publisher app name appears (Figure 1–2).

Q&A | What if my Publisher app is in a folder?
Click the appropriate folder name to display the contents of the folder.

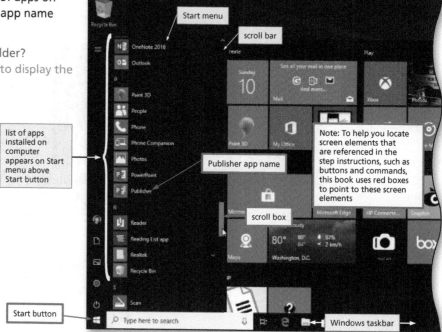

Figure 1–2

②

- Click Publisher on the Start menu to start Publisher and display the Publisher Start screen. If the Publisher window is not maximized, click the Maximize button on its title bar to maximize the window (Figure 1–3).

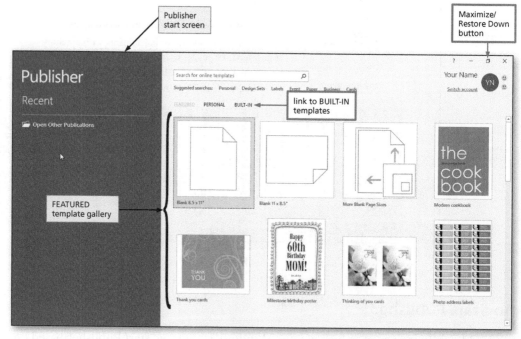

Figure 1–3

Creating a Flyer

BTW
Templates
Choose a template that suits the purpose of the publication, and use headline and graphic placement that attracts your audience. Choose a style that complements the topic.

Publisher provides many ways to begin the process of creating and editing a publication. You can:

- Create a new publication from a template.
- Create a new publication from scratch.
- Create a new publication based on an existing one.
- Open an existing publication.

Choosing the appropriate method depends on your experience with desktop publishing and on how you have used Publisher in the past.

Templates

Because many people find that composing and designing from scratch is a difficult process, Publisher provides templates to assist in publication preparation. Publisher has hundreds of templates to create professionally designed and unique publications. A **template** is a predesigned, preformatted file that contains text formats, themes, placeholder text, headers and footers, and graphics that you can replace with your own information for hundreds of purposes, including creating budgets, flyers, and resumes. Templates help you through the design process by offering you publication options — that you can change accordingly — and preset objects placed in an attractive layout. A template is similar to a blueprint you can use over and over by filling in the blanks, replacing prewritten text as necessary, and changing the art to fit your needs.

Publisher provides three kinds of templates. **Featured templates** (shown in Figure 1–3) are downloaded from Office.com and customized for specific situations. **Built-in templates** are more generic and require no downloading. **Personal templates** are those you have created and saved. In a new installation, you may have no personal templates.

In this first project, as you begin to learn about the features of Publisher, a series of steps is presented to create a publication using a built-in template.

To Select a Built-In Template

When Publisher first starts, recently accessed files display on the left. Blank publications and templates appear on the right in a template gallery. Across the top are ways to search for specific kinds of templates. Built-in templates are organized by publication type (for example, Flyers); within publication type, they are organized by purpose or category (for example, Marketing) and then alphabetically by design type. Publisher groups additional templates into folders. Once you select a built-in template, Publisher displays the **template information pane** on the right, with a larger preview of the selected template, along with some customization options.

The following steps select an event flyer template. *Why? An event flyer template contains many of the objects needed to create the desired flyer.*

- In the Publisher start screen, click the BUILT-IN link to display the built-in templates (Figure 1–4).

Q&A Why does my list of templates look different from what is shown here?
It may be that someone has downloaded additional templates on your system. Or, the resolution on your screen may be different. Thus, the size and number of displayed templates may vary.

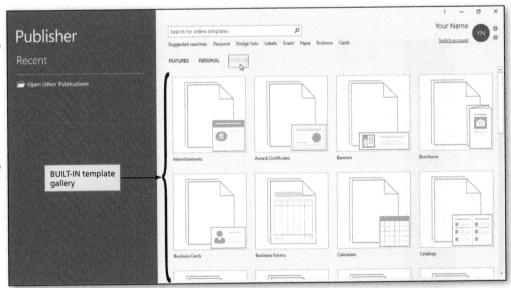

Figure 1–4

2

- If necessary, scroll down to display the desired publication type (in this case, Flyers) (Figure 1–5).

Experiment

- Scroll through the available template types.

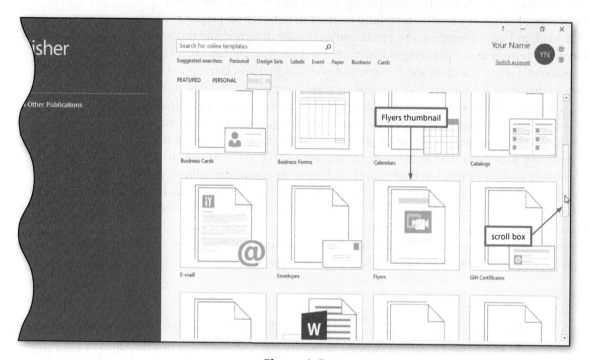

Figure 1–5

3

- Click the Flyers thumbnail to display the Flyer templates and folders of additional templates (Figure 1–6).

Q&A

Can I go back and choose a different category of templates?

Yes, you can click the Back button in the upper-left corner of the template gallery, or you can click Home or Flyers in the navigation trail to move back to those previous locations.

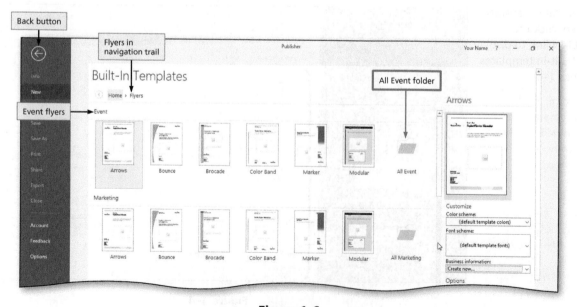

Figure 1–6

4
- Click the All Event folder to open it.
- If necessary, scroll down to display the More Installed Templates area (Figure 1–7).

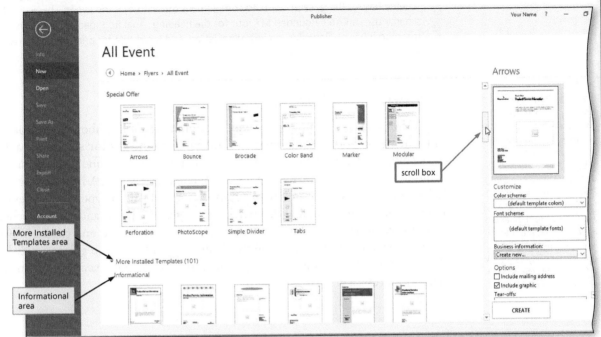

Figure 1–7

5
- Continue scrolling through the More Installed Templates area and then click the Mobile thumbnail in the Informational area to select it (Figure 1–8).

Q&A | Could I use a different template?
You could, but it would not have the same features as the template used in this module.

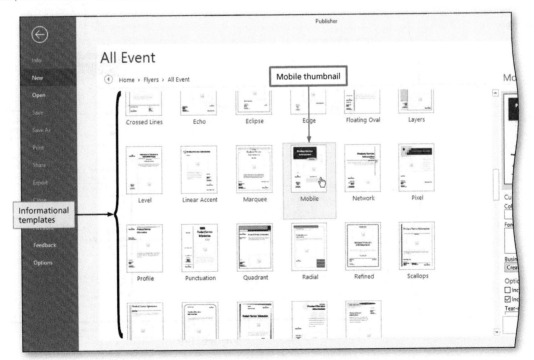

Figure 1–8

Does it make any difference which color scheme and font scheme you use?
Yes. The choice of an appropriate template, font, and color scheme is determined by the flyer's purpose and intended audience. For example, in this Research Study flyer, the Lagoon color scheme has soothing, calm colors to complement the nature of the event. The Galley font scheme uses an Arial Rounded MT font for the heading. Arial Rounded MT is a sans serif font, meaning it has no flourishes on individual letters and is suitable for print publications.

BTW
Font Schemes
Choose a font scheme that gives your flyer a consistent, professional appearance and that characterizes your subject. Make intentional decisions about the font style and type. Avoid common reading fonts such as Arial, Times New Roman, and Helvetica that are used in other kinds of print publications. Flyers are more effective with stronger or unusual font schemes.

Customizing Templates

After you choose a template, you should make choices about the color scheme, font scheme, and other components of the publication. A **color scheme** is a defined set of colors that complement each other when used in the same publication. Each Publisher color scheme provides four complementary colors. A **font scheme** is a defined set of fonts associated with a publication. A **font**, or typeface, is a set of letters, numbers, and symbols that all have the same style and appearance. A font scheme contains one font for headings and another font for body text and captions. Font schemes make it easy to change all the fonts in a publication to give it a new look. Other customization options allow you to choose to include business information, a mailing address, a graphic, or tear-offs.

To Choose Publication Options

The following steps choose customization options for the template. *Why? You typically will want to customize a template with an appropriate font and color scheme, determined by the flyer's purpose and intended audience.*

1

• Click the Color scheme button in the Customize area to display the Color scheme gallery (Figure 1–9).

Q&A What are the individual colors used for in each scheme?
By default, the text will be black, and the background will be white in each color scheme. Publisher uses the first and second scheme colors for major color accents within a publication. The third and fourth colors are used for shading and secondary accents.

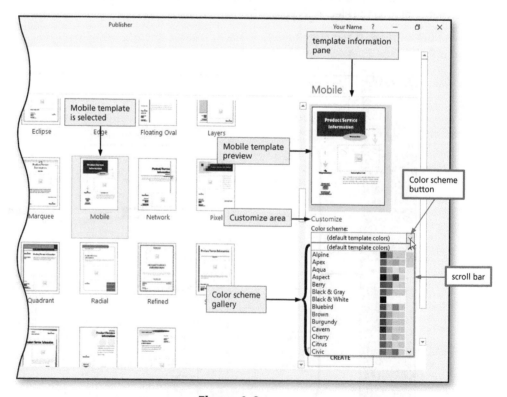

Figure 1–9

2

- Scroll as necessary and then click Lagoon in the Color scheme gallery to select it (Figure 1–10).

Experiment

- Click various color schemes and watch the changes in all of the thumbnails. When you finish experimenting, click Lagoon in the Color scheme gallery.

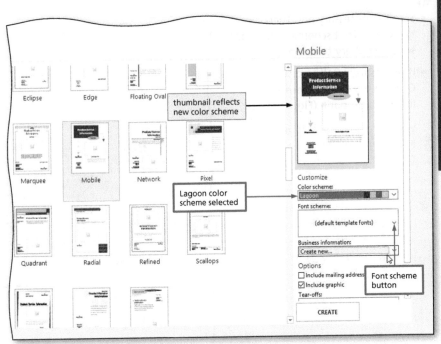

Figure 1–10

3

- Click the Font scheme button in the Customize area to display the Font scheme gallery (Figure 1–11).

Q&A How are the font schemes organized?
The font schemes are organized alphabetically by the generic name of the scheme that appears above each major font in the list.

Experiment

- Click various font schemes and watch the changes in all of the thumbnails.

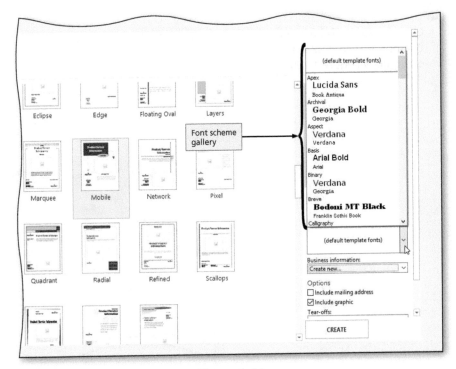

Figure 1–11

4

- Scroll as necessary and then click the Galley font scheme in the Font scheme gallery to select it.

- If necessary, scroll to display the Options area of the template information pane (Figure 1–12).

Q&A What are the three items listed in each font scheme?

The first line is the generic name of the scheme. Below that, both a major font and a minor font are specified. Generally, a major font is used for titles and headings, and a minor font is used for body text. In the Galley font scheme, for example, Galley is the generic name of the scheme, Arial Rounded MT Bold is the major font, and Times New Roman is the minor font.

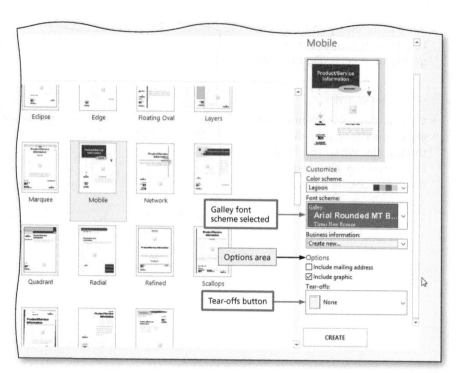

Figure 1–12

5

- Click the Tear-offs button in the Options area to display the Tear-offs gallery (Figure 1–13).

Q&A What are the other kinds of tear-offs?

You can choose to display tear-offs for coupons, order forms, response forms, and sign-up forms.

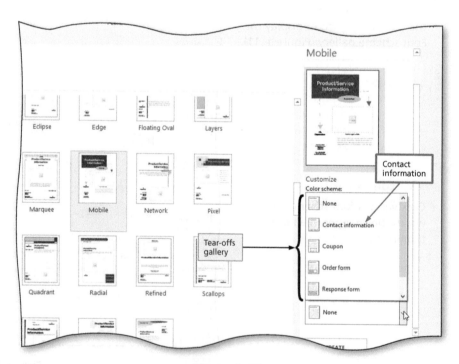

Figure 1–13

6

- Click Contact information in the Tear-offs gallery to select tear-offs that will display contact information (Figure 1–14).

Q&A Should I change the check boxes?
No, the flyer you create in this module uses the default value of no mailing address but includes a graphic.

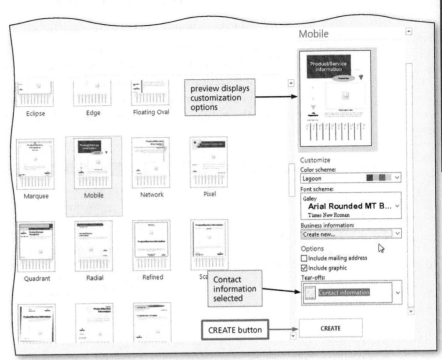

Figure 1–14

7

- Click the CREATE button to create the publication using the selected template and options (Figure 1–15).

Q&A How can I go back if I change my mind?
You can click File on the ribbon and start a new publication, or you can make changes to the template, font scheme, color scheme, and other options by using the ribbon, as you will see in this module.

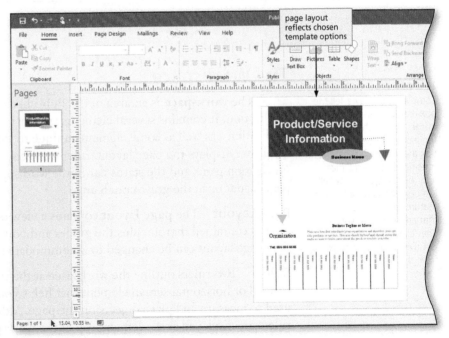

Figure 1–15

The Publisher Window

The Publisher window consists of a variety of components to make your work more efficient and your publications more professional. These include the workspace, ribbon, Mini toolbar, Quick Access Toolbar, KeyTips, and Microsoft Account area. The following sections discuss these components.

When you run Publisher, the default (preset) view is a single-page view, which shows the publication on a mock sheet of paper in the workspace (Figure 1–16).

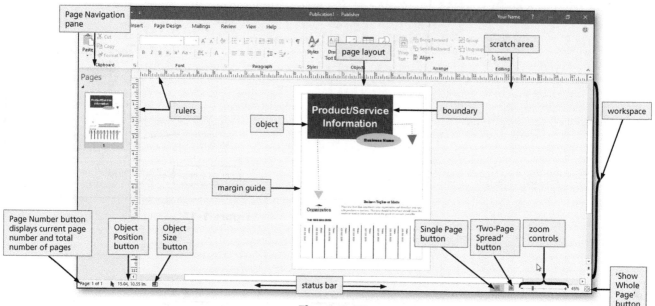

Figure 1–16

The Workspace

The **workspace** is an area of the Publisher window that contains the current publication. It contains several elements similar to the document windows of other applications, as well as some elements unique to Publisher. As you create a publication, Publisher displays the page layout, rulers, objects, guides, scroll bars, the Page Navigation pane, and the status bar in the workspace. You can place objects on the page layout or in the gray scratch area.

Page Layout   The **page layout** contains a view of the publication page, all the objects contained therein, plus the guides and boundaries for the page and its objects. The page layout can be changed to accommodate multipage spreads.

Rulers   Two rulers outline the workspace at the top and left. A **ruler**, which is a vertical or horizontal screen element that helps you measure and place objects, is used to measure and place objects on the page. Although the vertical and horizontal rulers are displayed at the left and top of the workspace, you can move and place them anywhere you need them. You use the rulers to measure and align objects on the page, set tab stops, adjust text frames, and change margins. In addition, the rulers can be hidden to show more of the workspace.

Objects   The elements you want to place in your publication are called **objects**, which include things such as text boxes, WordArt, tear-offs, graphics, pictures, bookmarks, bullets, lines, shapes, and web tools.

Guides and Boundaries   Publisher's page layout displays guides and boundaries of the page and selected objects. A **boundary** is the gray, dotted line surrounding an object. Boundaries are useful when you want to move or resize objects on the page. Boundaries and guides can be turned on and off using the View tab. They do not appear on printed copies. **Margin guides** automatically are displayed in blue at all four margins. Other guides include grid guides, which you can turn on to help organize objects in rows and columns, pink visual layout guides that display as you move objects, and baseline guides that help you align text horizontally across text boxes.

Scroll Bars   You use **scroll bars**, which appear at the right and bottom edges of the workspace, to view publications that are too large to fit on the screen at once. At the right edge of the workspace is a vertical scroll bar. If a publication is too wide to fit in the workspace, a horizontal scroll bar also appears at the bottom of the workspace. On a scroll bar, the position of the **scroll box** reflects the location of the portion of the publication that is displayed in the workspace; you can drag the scroll box or click above or below it to scroll through or display different parts of the publication in the workspace. A **scroll arrow** is a small triangular up or down arrow that is located at each end of a scroll bar; you can click the scroll arrows to scroll through the publication in small increments.

Page Navigation Pane   The **Page Navigation pane** displays all of the current pages in the publication as thumbnails, in a panel on the left side of the workspace. You can click a thumbnail to display that page in the workspace. The Page Navigation pane also displays section buttons.

Status Bar   The **status bar**, which is located at the bottom of the workspace above the Windows taskbar, shows status information about the currently opened publication, the progress of current tasks, and the status of certain commands and keys; it also provides buttons and controls you can use to view the position and size of objects, change the view of a publication, and adjust the size of the displayed publication. As you perform certain commands, various indicators and buttons may appear on the status bar.

The Page Number button allows you to show or hide the Page Navigation pane, and it also displays the current page and number of pages in the publication. A Caps Lock notification will appear next to the Page Number button in the status bar when CAPS LOCK is engaged on the keyboard. The Object Position button helps you line up objects from the left and top margins by displaying the exact position of a selected object. The Object Size button serves as a guideline for resizing objects; it displays the exact size of a selected object. You may choose to have measurements displayed in pixels, picas, points, or centimeters. If no object is selected, the Object Position button displays the location of the pointer. Clicking either button will open the Measurements pane.

The right side of the status bar includes the Single Page, 'Two-Page Spread', and 'Show Whole Page' buttons, as well as the zoom controls. If you right-click the status bar, you can choose which controls to display.

BTW
Ribbon Display Options
Some apps display a 'Ribbon Display Options' button on the title bar with additional ribbon commands, such as Auto-hide.

BTW
AutoSave
Some Office applications include an AutoSave button on the title bar that may be disabled. If you are saving a file on OneDrive, the AutoSave button may be enabled, which allows you to specify whether the app saves the publication as you make changes to it. If AutoSave is disabled (turned off), you need to continue saving changes manually.

The Ribbon

The **ribbon**, which is a horizontal strip located near the top of the Publisher window, below the title bar, is the control center in Publisher that contains tabs of grouped commands that you click to interact with Publisher (Figure 1–17). Each **tab** contains a collection of groups, and each group contains related commands. The ribbon provides easy, central access to the tasks you perform while creating a publication.

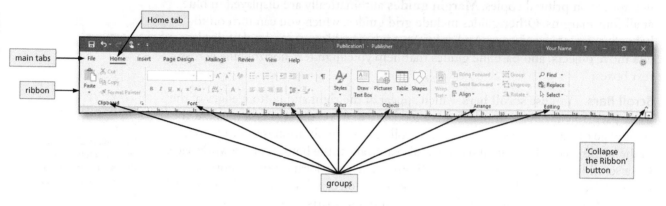

Figure 1–17

When you open a publication or template, the ribbon displays several main tabs, also called default or top-level tabs (that is, File, Home, Insert, Page Design, Mailings, Review, View, and Help). The **Home tab**, also called the primary tab, contains the more frequently used commands. The tab currently displayed is called the **active tab**.

To display more of the publication in the workspace, some users prefer to minimize the ribbon, which hides the groups on the ribbon and displays only the main tabs (Figure 1–18). To minimize the ribbon, click the 'Collapse the Ribbon' button. To use commands on a minimized ribbon, click the tab that you wish to expand. To expand the ribbon, double-click a tab or click the 'Pin the ribbon' button on an expanded tab.

Figure 1–18

Each time you start Publisher, the ribbon appears the same way it did the last time you used Publisher. The modules in this book, however, begin with the ribbon appearing as it did at the initial installation of the software.

In addition to the main tabs, Publisher displays other tabs, called **tool tabs** or contextual tabs, when you perform certain tasks or work with objects such as pictures or tables. If you insert a picture in the publication, for example, the Picture Tools tab and its related subordinate Format tab appear, collectively referred to as the Picture Tools Format tab (Figure 1–19). When you are finished working with the picture and then click elsewhere in the publication, the Picture Tools Format tab disappears from the ribbon. Publisher determines when tool tabs should appear and disappear based on tasks you perform. Some tool tabs, such as the Table Tools tab, have more than one related subordinate tab.

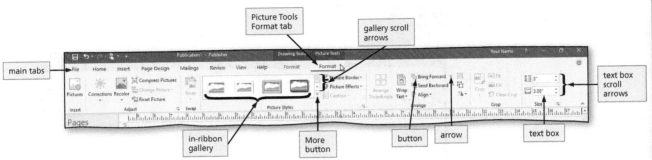

Figure 1–19

Items on the ribbon include buttons, boxes (text boxes, check boxes, etc.), and arrows. Some buttons display both a button and an arrow. When you click the button, the most recent settings are applied. If you click an arrow next to a button, Publisher displays a list, menu, or gallery (shown in Figure 1–19). A **gallery** is a set of choices, often graphical, arranged in a grid or in a list that you can browse through before making a selection. You can scroll through choices in an in-ribbon gallery by clicking the gallery's scroll arrows. Or, you can click a gallery's More button to view more gallery options on the screen at a time. Some buttons and boxes have arrows that, when clicked, also display galleries (Figure 1–20).

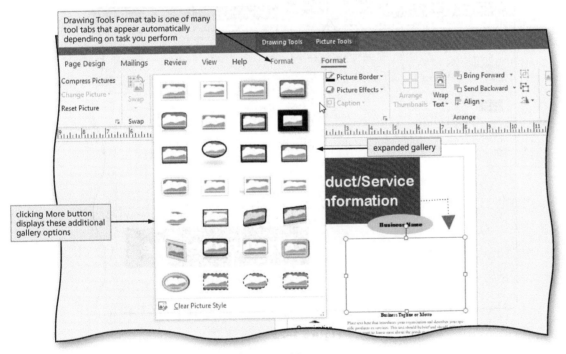

Figure 1–20

Some commands on the ribbon display an image to help you remember their function. When you point to a command on the ribbon, all or part of the command glows in shades of gray, and a ScreenTip appears on the screen. A **ScreenTip** is a label that appears when you point to a button or another on-screen object, which may include the name, purpose, or keyboard shortcut for the object and a link to associated help topics, if any exist (Figure 1–21).

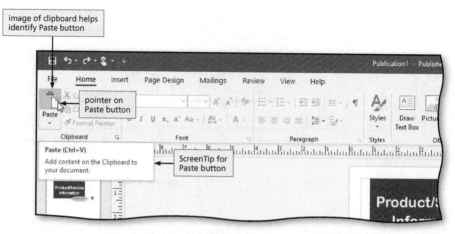

Figure 1–21

Some groups on the ribbon have a small arrow in the lower-right corner, called a **Dialog Box Launcher**, that when clicked, displays a dialog box or a pane with additional options for the group (Figure 1–22). When presented with a dialog box, you make selections and must close the dialog box before returning to the publication. A **pane**, in contrast to a dialog box, is a window that can remain open and visible while you work in the publication and that provides additional options.

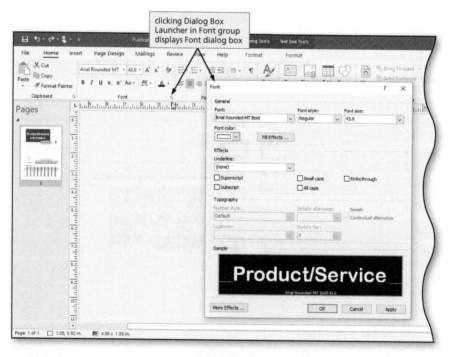

Figure 1–22

The Mini Toolbar and Quick Access Toolbar

The **Mini toolbar**, a small toolbar that appears next to selected text or objects when you right-click, contains the most frequently used text formatting commands (which are those commands related to changing the appearance of text in a publication). If you do not use the Mini toolbar, it disappears from the screen. The buttons, arrows, and boxes on the Mini toolbar vary, depending on whether you are using Touch mode or Mouse mode. To use the Mini toolbar, move the pointer into the Mini toolbar.

All commands on the Mini toolbar also exist on the ribbon. The purpose of the Mini toolbar is to minimize hand or mouse movement. For example, if you want to use a command that currently is not displayed on the active tab, you can use the command on the Mini toolbar instead of switching to a different tab to use the command.

A **shortcut menu**, which appears when you right-click an object, is a list of frequently used commands that relate to the right-clicked object. When you right-click selected text, for example, a shortcut menu appears with commands related to text. If you right-click an item in the page layout, Publisher displays both the Mini toolbar and a shortcut menu.

The **Quick Access Toolbar**, located initially (by default) above the ribbon at the left edge of the title bar, is a customizable toolbar that contains buttons you can click to perform frequently used commands (Figure 1–23). The commands on the Quick Access Toolbar always are available, regardless of the task you are performing. The Touch/Mouse Mode button on the Quick Access Toolbar allows you to switch between Touch mode and Mouse mode. If you primarily are using touch gestures, Touch mode adds more space between commands on menus and on the ribbon so that they are easier to tap. While using touch gestures is a convenient way to interact with Publisher, not all features are supported when you are using Touch mode. If you are using a mouse, Mouse mode will not add the extra space between buttons and commands. The modules in this book show the screens in Mouse mode.

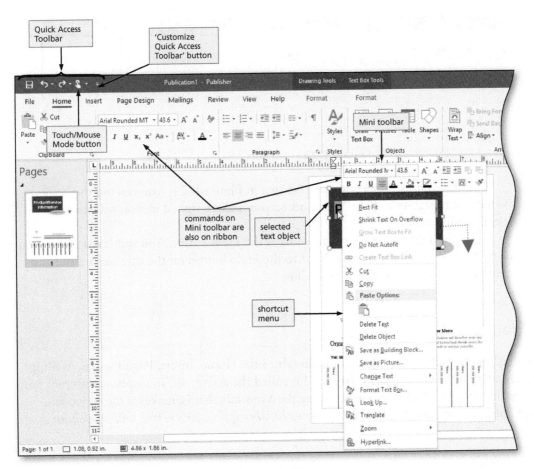

Figure 1–23

You can add other commands to or delete commands from the Quick Access Toolbar so that it contains the commands you use most often. To do this, click the 'Customize Quick Access Toolbar' button on the Quick Access Toolbar and then select the commands you want to add or remove. As you add commands to the Quick Access Toolbar, its length may interfere with the publication title on the title bar. For this reason, Publisher provides an option of displaying the Quick Access Toolbar below the ribbon on the Quick Access Toolbar menu.

Each time you start Publisher, the Quick Access Toolbar appears the same way it did the last time you used Publisher. The modules in this book, however, begin with the Quick Access Toolbar appearing as it did at the initial installation of the software.

KeyTips and the Microsoft Account Area

If you prefer using the keyboard instead of the mouse, you can press ALT on the keyboard to display **KeyTips**, which are labels that appear over each tab and command on the ribbon (Figure 1–24). To select a tab or command using the keyboard, press the letter or number displayed in the KeyTip, which may cause additional KeyTips related to the selected command to appear. For example, to select the Bold button on the Home tab, press ALT, then press H, and then press 1. To remove the KeyTips from the screen, press ALT or ESC until all KeyTips disappear or click anywhere in the Publisher window.

Figure 1–24

In the Microsoft Account area (shown in Figure 1–24), you can use the Your Name link to sign in to your Microsoft account. Once signed in, you will see your account information.

To the right of the Your Name link is the Help button. You will learn more about using Help later in this module. Next to the Help button on the title bar are the clip controls: Minimize, Maximize, and Close.

To Display a Different Tab on the Ribbon

When you start Publisher, the ribbon displays eight main tabs: File, Home, Insert, Page Design, Mailings, Review, View, and Help. Recall that the tab currently displayed is called the active tab. To display a different tab on the ribbon, simply click that tab. The following steps display the View tab, that is, makes it the active tab. *Why? When working with Publisher, you may need to switch tabs to access other options for working with a publication or to verify settings.*

- Click View on the ribbon to display the View tab (Figure 1–25).

Q&A Why did the groups on the ribbon change?
When you switch from one tab to another on the ribbon, the groups on the ribbon change to show commands related to the selected tab.

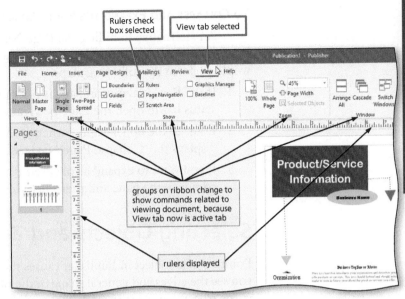

Figure 1–25

- Verify that the Rulers check box (View tab | Show group) is selected. (If it is not selected, click it to display the check mark because you want the rulers to appear on the screen.)

- Click Home on the ribbon to display the Home tab.

Experiment

- Click the other tabs on the ribbon to view their contents. When you are finished, click Home on the ribbon to display the Home tab.

To Hide the Page Navigation Pane

Because the flyer contains only one page, you will hide the Page Navigation pane using the Page Number button on the status bar. **Why?** *Hiding the pane gives you more room on the screen for viewing and editing the flyer.* The following step hides the Page Navigation pane.

- Click the Page Number button on the status bar to hide the Page Navigation pane (Figure 1–26).

Q&A I do not see the Page Navigation pane. What did I do wrong?
It may be that someone has hidden the Page Navigation pane already. The Page Number button opens and closes the Page Navigation pane. Click it again.

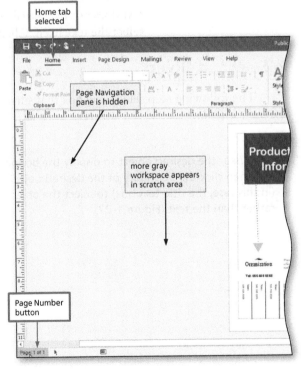

Figure 1–26

Other Ways

1. Click Page Navigation check box (View tab | Show group)

To Collapse and Expand the Page Navigation Pane

An alternative to hiding the Page Navigation pane is to collapse or minimize it, which makes it narrower. If you wanted to collapse the Page Navigation pane, you would perform the following steps.

1. If the Page Navigation pane is not open, click the Page Number button on the status bar to open the Page Navigation pane.

2. Point to the upper-right corner of the Page Navigation pane. When Publisher displays the 'Collapse Page Navigation Pane' button, click it.

3. If you want to expand a collapsed Page Navigation pane, point to the upper-right corner of the pane and then click the 'Expand Page Navigation Pane' button.

Selecting Objects and Zooming

Pointing to an object in Publisher causes the object's boundary to appear, which can help you see the edges and general shape of the object. When you **select** an object by clicking it, the object appears surrounded by a solid **selection rectangle**, which has small squares and circles, called **handles**, at each corner and middle location; these handles let you change the object's size. Many objects also display a **rotation handle**, which is a small circular arrow at the top of a selected object that you can drag to turn the selected object, and an **adjustment handle**, which is a yellow diamond on a selected shape that you can drag to change the shape's proportions without changing the size of the shape. A selected object can be resized, rotated, moved, deleted, or grouped with other objects.

Objects such as photos, clip art, and shapes are easy to select. You simply click them. With other objects such as text boxes, logos, and placeholders, you first must point to them — to display their boundaries — and then click the boundary. Selecting text does not necessarily select the text box object that holds the text; rather, it may select the text itself. Clicking the boundary is the best way to select a text box object.

To Select an Object

The following step selects the box that surrounds the title in the flyer. **Why?** *Before you can edit an object, you first must select it.*

- Point near the desired object to display the boundary and then click the boundary of the desired object (in this case, the title text box) to select the object rather than the text (Figure 1–27).

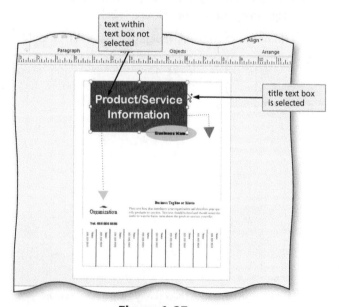

Figure 1–27

Other Ways

1. With no object selected, press TAB until desired object is selected

Zooming

An object that is selected may be too small to edit easily. Publisher provides several ways to **zoom**, or display a view of a publication or an object so that its contents are either enlarged or shrunk. Zoom is used to facilitate viewing and editing and does not change the font size of text; it also does not change the size of an object, such as a picture or a shape.

Table 1–1 shows several zoom methods.

Table 1–1 Zoom Methods

Tool	Method	Result
Function key	To zoom in on an object, press F9 on the keyboard, press F9 again to return to the previous magnification. On some systems, you may have to press FN (FUNCTION)+F9.	Selected object appears centered in the workspace at 100% magnification.
Keyboard shortcut	To zoom to page width, press CTRL+SHIFT+L.	Page layout is magnified as large as possible in the workspace.
Mouse wheel	To change the magnification, press and hold CTRL and then move the mouse wheel down or up.	Page layout appears 20% smaller or larger.
Page Width button	To zoom to page width, click the Page Width button (View tab | Zoom group).	Page layout expands to fill the workspace horizontally.
Ribbon	To use the ribbon, click the View tab. In the Zoom group, click the desired button.	Page layout appears at the selected magnification.
Selected Objects button	To zoom to objects, click the Selected Objects button (View tab | Zoom group).	Selected object is magnified as large as possible to fit on the screen.
Shortcut menu	To zoom in on an object, right-click the object, point to Zoom on the shortcut menu, and then click the desired magnification.	Object appears at selected magnification.
'Show Whole Page' button	To zoom to whole page, click the 'Show Whole Page' button on the status bar.	Page layout is magnified as large as possible in the workspace.
Whole Page button	To zoom to whole page, click the Whole Page button (View tab | Zoom group).	Page layout is magnified as large as possible in the workspace.
Zoom box	To change the magnification, enter a magnification percentage in the Zoom box (View tab | Zoom group).	Page layout appears at the entered magnification.
Zoom arrow	To change the magnification, click the Zoom arrow (View tab | Zoom group) and then click the desired magnification.	Page layout appears at the selected magnification.
Zoom Out button or Zoom In button	To increment or decrement magnification, click the Zoom Out or Zoom In button on the status bar.	Page layout appears 10% smaller or larger with each click.
Zoom slider	To change the magnification of the entire page, drag the Zoom slider on the status bar.	Objects appear at the selected magnification.
100% button	To zoom to page width, click the 100% button (View tab | Zoom group).	Page layout is magnified to 100%.

To Zoom Using a Function Key

When viewing an entire 8½ × 11 inches printed page at the current screen resolution, the magnification is approximately 45%, which makes reading small text difficult. If your keyboard has function keys, you can press F9 to enlarge selected objects to 100% and center them in the Publisher window. Pressing F9 a second time returns the layout to its previous magnification. If you are using touch gestures, you can stretch to zoom in. Alternatively, you can use the zoom controls on the status bar and on the View tab. The following step uses F9 to change the magnification to 100%. **Why?** *Editing small areas of text is easier if you use zooming techniques to enlarge the view of the publication.*

1

- Press F9 on the keyboard to zoom the selected object to approximately 100%. If your mobile device does not display function keys, click the Zoom In button on the task bar several times until your display is magnified to 100% (Figure 1–28).

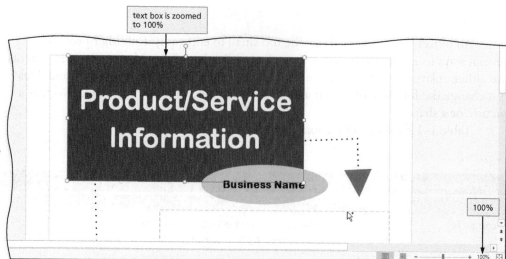

Figure 1–28

Q&A

When I pressed F9, Windows opened a search pane. What should I do?
Your system may have overridden Office functions. Press FN+F9 to zoom to 100% magnification.

What is the best way to zoom?
It really is your personal preference. The Zoom controls on the status bar allow you to change the magnification percentage in 10% increments. The Zoom group on the View tab contains some preset sizes as well as custom sizes of text boxes.

Other Ways

1. Click Zoom arrow (View tab | Zoom group), click desired magnification
2. Click Selected Objects button (View tab | Zoom group)
3. Right-click object, point to Zoom on shortcut menu, click desired magnification on Zoom menu
4. Drag Zoom slider on status bar
5. Click Zoom In button or Zoom Out button on status bar

Selecting and Entering Text

The first step in editing a publication template is to replace its text by typing on the keyboard. You may have to scroll and zoom in the page layout to make careful edits. In a later section of this module, you will learn how to format, or change the appearance of, the entered text.

CONSIDER THIS

While typing text, when should you press ENTER?
As you type, if a word extends beyond the right margin of the text box, Publisher also automatically positions that word on the next line, along with the insertion point. If you press ENTER, Publisher creates a new paragraph. Thus, as you type text in a text box, do not press ENTER when the insertion point reaches the right margin. Instead, press ENTER only in these circumstances:

1. To begin a new paragraph
2. To insert a blank line(s) in a document
3. To terminate a short line of text and advance to the next line
4. To respond to questions or prompts in Word dialog boxes, panes, and other on-screen objects

Text Boxes

Most of Publisher's templates come with text already inserted into text boxes. A **text box** is an object in a publication that is designed to hold text in a specific shape, size, and style. Text boxes also can be drawn on the page using the 'Draw Text Box' button (Home tab | Objects group). Text boxes can be formatted using the ribbon, the Mini toolbar, or the shortcut menu. You can **edit**, or make changes to, many characteristics of a text box, such as font, spacing, alignment, line/border style, fill color, and margins.

As you type, if you make a mistake, you can backspace, or press DELETE as you do in word processing. You also can **undo** an action (such as typing or editing) by clicking the Undo button on the Quick Access Toolbar or by pressing CTRL+Z.

When you create a new text box, it is empty and ready for you to type. In templates, however, Publisher includes two types of text in template text boxes. As you will see in the next steps, placeholder text and default text are selected differently and are used for different purposes.

To Replace Placeholder Text

You use a single click to select **placeholder text**, which is prewritten template text that you replace to customize a publication (such as that in the flyer title). *Why? Clicking once to select text allows you to begin typing immediately without having to select the text and without having to press DELETE.* The following steps select and replace placeholder text.

- Click the title text to select it (Figure 1–29).

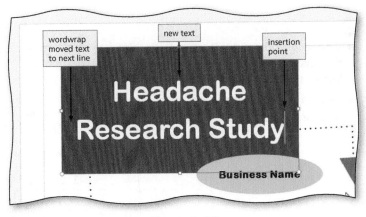

Figure 1–29

- Type `Headache Research Study` (Figure 1–30).

Q&A | What is the blinking vertical bar to the right of the text?
The blinking bar is the insertion point, which indicates where text, graphics, and other items will be inserted in the publication. As you type, the insertion point moves to the right, and when you reach the end of a line, it moves down to the beginning of the next line.

What if I make an error while typing?
Common word processing techniques work in Publisher text boxes. For example, you can press BACKSPACE until you have deleted the text in error and then retype the text correctly.

Why did some of the text move to the next line?
Wordwrap allows you to type words continually without pressing ENTER at the end of each line. As you type, if a word extends beyond the right margin, Publisher automatically positions that word on the next line.

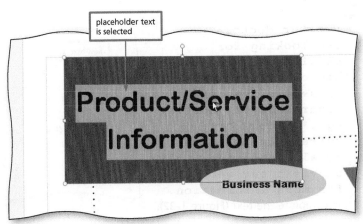

Figure 1–30

3

- Scroll to display the lower portion of the flyer.

- Below the 'Business Tagline or Motto' text box, click the text in the description text box to select the placeholder text (Figure 1–31).

 Q&A Am I skipping the Business Name text box?

The text in the Business Name text box is not selected with a single click. You will edit that text later in the module.

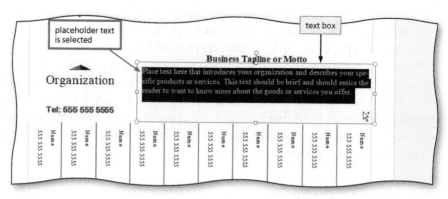

Figure 1–31

4

- Type Our doctors are looking for participants with a history of migraines or severe headaches, regardless of your age, gender, or current health. Free trial medication. Call or visit our website for more information. to complete the text (Figure 1–32).

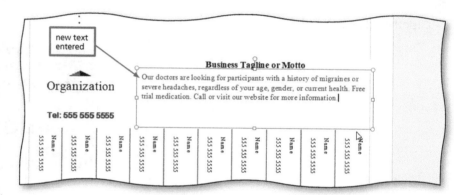

Figure 1–32

5

- On the left side of the flyer, click the text in the phone number text box to select the placeholder text.

- Type 303-555-9700 to replace the text (Figure 1–33).

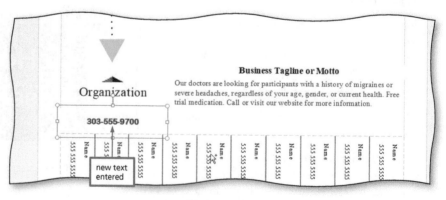

Figure 1–33

To Replace Default Text

In the following steps, you replace the **default text**, or preset text, in other template text boxes. Default text, such as the business name, address, or tag line, is selected by dragging through the text, by double-clicking specific words, or by pressing CTRL+A to select all of the text in the text box. Then, you simply type to replace the selected text. ***Why?*** *Default text is different from placeholder text that is selected with a single click.* The following steps replace default text.

- Scroll to display the upper portion of the flyer.

- Click the text in the Business Name text box to position the insertion point inside the text box (Figure 1–34).

Q&A What is the button that displays the letter, i, inside a blue circle?
It is a smart tag button. If you click it, Publisher offers to fill in the text for you and provides various options. **Smart tag buttons** appear when you point to some screen elements; each one provides a menu of options to help you perform the task at hand.

My business name is different or blank. Did I do something wrong?
No. Someone may have changed the business name during installation. You will replace it in the next steps.

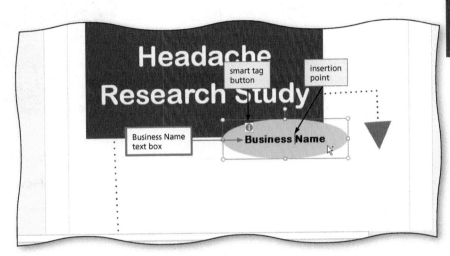

Figure 1–34

2

- Drag through the text in the Business Name text box to select all of the text in the text box (Figure 1–35).

Q&A Could I press CTRL+A to select the text?
Yes, as long as the insertion point is positioned inside the text box, CTRL+A will select all of the text in the text box.

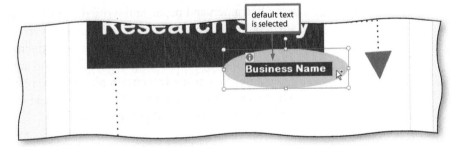

Figure 1–35

3

- Type `University Medical School` to complete the text (Figure 1–36).

Q&A Should I press DELETE before typing?
It is not necessary to press DELETE; the text you type deletes the selected text automatically.

Figure 1–36

Other Ways

1. Select text box, click Select button (Home tab | Editing group), click 'Select All Text in Text Box', type new text

2. Position insertion point in text box, press CTRL+A, type new text

To Deselect an Object

The following step deselects or removes the selection from the object by clicking outside of its boundaries. **Why?** *You may want to view an object without the boundary or insertion point.*

1

- Click outside of the selected object (in this case, the text box) to deselect it (Figure 1–37).

Q&A

Exactly where should I click?
As long as you do not select another object, you can click anywhere in the workspace. You may want to click just to the left of the selection rectangle or in the scratch area.

Figure 1–37

Other Ways

1. Press ESC

Tear-Offs

Across the lower portion of the flyer are contact information tear-offs. **Tear-offs** are small, ready-to-be scored text boxes with some combination of name, phone number, fax, email, or address information. Designed for customer use, tear-offs typically are perforated so that a person walking by can tear off a tab to keep, rather than having to stop, find a pen and paper, and write down the name and phone number. Traditionally, small businesses or individuals wanting to advertise something locally used tear-offs, but more recently, large companies are mass-producing advertising flyers with tear-offs to post at shopping centers, display in offices, and advertise on college campuses.

Publisher tear-offs contain placeholder text and are **synchronized**, which means when you finish editing one of the tear-off text boxes, the others are automatically updated across pages and publications.

To Enter Tear-Off Text

The following steps edit the tear-off text boxes. **Why?** *The tear-offs must contain information to contact the flyer's creator or to request more information.*

1

- Scroll to display the lower portion of the flyer.

- Click the text in one of the tear-off text boxes to select it (Figure 1–38).

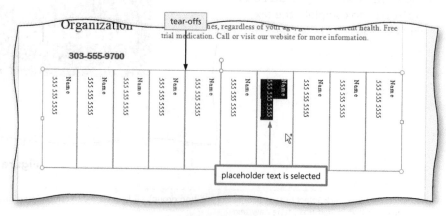

Figure 1–38

2

- Type **University Medical School** and then press ENTER.

- Type **Headache Study 303-555-9700** to complete the tear-off text (Figure 1–39).

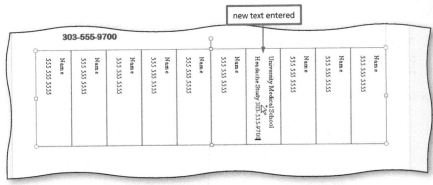

Figure 1–39

3

- Click outside of the text box to synchronize the other tear-offs (Figure 1–40).

Q&A What if I want to make each tear-off different?

Typically, all of the tear-offs are the same, but you can undo synchronization by clicking the Undo button on the Quick Access Toolbar and then entering the text for other tear-offs.

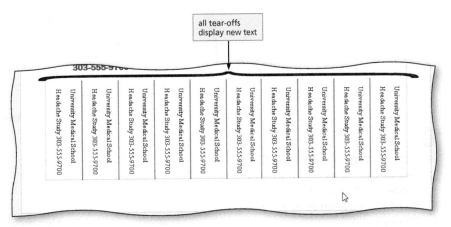

Figure 1–40

Checking the Spelling

As you type text in a publication, Publisher checks your typing for possible spelling errors. Publisher **flags** any potential error in the publication window with a visual alert, usually a red wavy underline. A red wavy underline means the flagged text is not in Publisher's dictionary (because it is a proper name, a slang term, or misspelled). Although you can check the entire publication for spelling errors at once, you also can check these flagged errors as they appear on the screen.

To display a list of corrections for flagged text, right-click the flagged text. Publisher displays a list of suggested spelling corrections on the shortcut menu. A flagged word, however, is not necessarily misspelled. For example, many names, abbreviations, and specialized terms are not in Publisher's main dictionary. In such cases, you instruct Publisher to ignore the flagged words. As you type, Publisher also detects duplicate words while checking for spelling errors. For example, if your publication contains the phrase, to the the store, Publisher places a red wavy underline below the second occurrence of the word, the.

To Check Spelling as You Type

In the following steps, the word, certified, is misspelled intentionally as certfied to illustrate Publisher's check spelling as you type feature. If you are doing this project on a computer, your flyer may contain different misspelled words. *Why? You may have made spelling or typographical errors if your typing was not accurate.*

1

- Click the text in the 'Business Tagline or Motto' text box to position the insertion point inside the text box.

- Drag through the text or press CTRL+A to select all of the text in the text box (Figure 1–41).

Q&A Why does my template list a different business name?
The person who installed Microsoft Office on your computer or network may have set or customized the field.

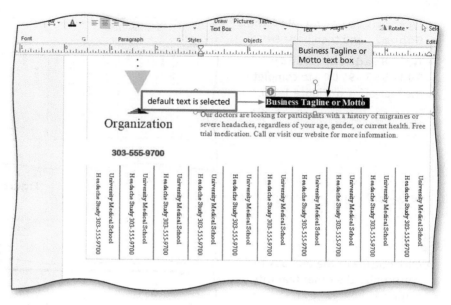

Figure 1–41

2

- Type **Study conducted by certfied neurologists** , misspelling the word, certfied, so that a red wavy underline appears (Figure 1–42).

Q&A What if Publisher does not flag my spelling errors with wavy underlines?
To verify that Publisher will check spelling as you type, click File on the ribbon to open Backstage view and then click Options to display the Publisher Options dialog box. Click Proofing in the left pane and then ensure that the 'Check spelling as you type' check box contains a check mark. Also, ensure the 'Hide spelling and grammar errors' check box does not have a check mark.

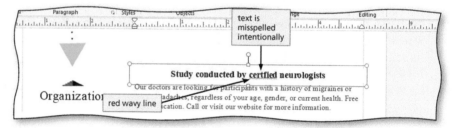

Figure 1–42

3

- Right-click the flagged word (certfied, in this case) to display a shortcut menu that presents suggested spelling corrections and other choices for the flagged word (Figure 1–43).

Q&A What if, when I right-click the misspelled word, my desired correction is not in the list on the shortcut menu?
You can click outside the shortcut menu to close the shortcut menu and then retype the correct word.

What toolbar was displayed when I selected the text?
Recall that the Mini toolbar appears automatically and contains commands related to changing the appearance of text in a publication. If you do not use the Mini toolbar, it disappears from the screen.

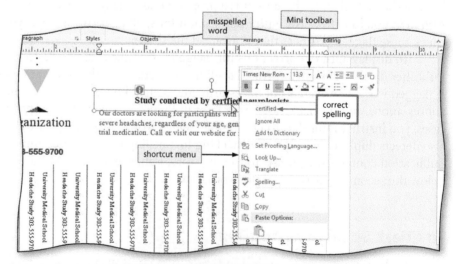

Figure 1–43

4
- Click the correct spelling (in this case, certified) on the shortcut menu to replace the misspelled word with a correctly spelled word (Figure 1–44).

Q&A What if a flagged word actually is a proper name and spelled correctly?
Right-click the word and then click Ignore All on the shortcut menu to instruct Publisher not to flag future occurrences of the same word in this publication.

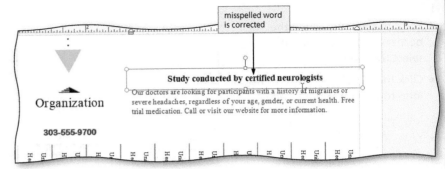

Figure 1–44

Other Ways

1. Click Spelling button (Review tab | Proofing group), click desired commands in Check Spelling dialog box, close Check Spelling dialog box

2. Press F7, click desired commands in Check Spelling dialog box, close Check Spelling dialog box

Autocorrect Options

Publisher assists you by correcting certain kinds of common errors. The **AutoCorrect** feature automatically detects and corrects typing errors. While these options can be turned on or off with the Options command in Backstage view, individual occurrences can be edited with the **AutoCorrect Options button**. This button, one of the smart tags in Publisher, appears below automatically corrected text and lets you undo a correction or specify how Publisher should handle future corrections. A smart tag displays just below or near the text to which it applies. The AutoCorrect Options smart tag first appears as a small blue rectangle below the correction. When you point to the smart tag, it displays a button.

The following AutoCorrect options typically are turned on in an initial installation of Publisher:

- Show AutoCorrect Options button
- Correct TWo INtial CApitals
- Capitalize first letter of sentences
- Capitalize first letter of table cells
- Capitalize names of days
- Correct accidental use of cAPS LOCK
- Replace text as you type
- Automatically use suggestions from the spelling checker

You can create specific exceptions or define your own automatic replacement text by clicking the AutoCorrect Options button (Backstage view | Options | Proofing).

To Use the AutoCorrect Options Button

The next steps edit the template logo. **Why?** *The text of the logo needs to display the research study website.* The default logo is a small picture and the word, Organization, grouped together. To edit one or the other, select the logo first, and then click only the part of the object you wish to edit. Using the AutoCorrect Options button, you will turn off autocorrection for capitalization of the first letter in the web address, because web addresses typically begin with the letters, www.

1

- Point to the logo. When the border is displayed, click it to select the logo.

- Click the placeholder text in the logo to select it (Figure 1–45).

 Q&A My flyer does not contain a logo. What should I do?

It is possible that you have a customized scheme that is overriding your settings. Click the Business Information button (Insert tab | Text group). On the Business Information menu, click 'Edit Business Information'. Choose the custom set and then click DELETE (Business Information dialog box).

Figure 1–45

2

- Type **www.headache.ums** to enter the web address (Figure 1–46).

Q&A Why did Publisher capitalize the first w?

When you typed the period in the web address, Publisher assumed the end of a sentence. Preset AutoCorrect options capitalize the first letter of a sentence. You will fix it in the following steps.

Why did the font size become smaller?

This box automatically adjusts the font size to fit the size of the box. You will learn more about this feature later in the module.

Do I need to address the red wavy line below the web address?

No. When you fix the capitalization of the first letter, Publisher will remove the red wavy line.

Figure 1–46

3

- Move the pointer near the capital W in the web address to display the AutoCorrect Options button (Figure 1–47).

Q&A My web address does not have a capital W. What should I do?

If your web address does not have a capital W, it is possible that someone already has turned that feature off on your system. You can skip to the next section or turn the feature on by doing the following: click File on the ribbon, click Options in Backstage view, click Proofing in the left pane (Publisher Options dialog box), click AutoCorrect Options button (Proofing pane). Make sure the 'Capitalize first letter of sentences' check box displays a check mark.

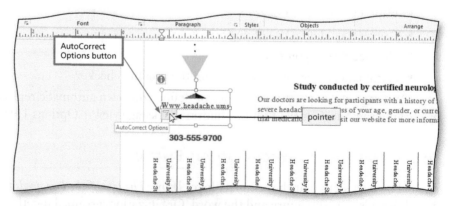

Figure 1–47

- Click the AutoCorrect Options button to display its menu (Figure 1–48).

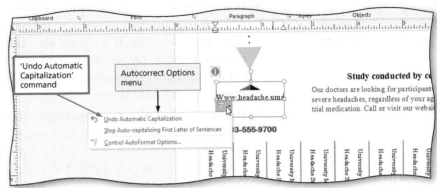

Figure 1–48

5

- Click 'Undo Automatic Capitalization' on the menu to cancel the capitalization of the first letter (Figure 1–49).

Q&A Why did the red wavy line disappear?
By default, Publisher does not flag text that begins with the lowercase letters, www, because it is normally a web address. When it was uppercase, Publisher warned you that it might be the beginning of a sentence with a misspelled word.

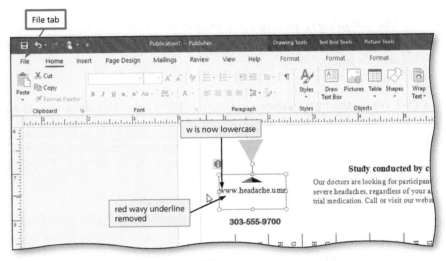

Figure 1–49

Saving a Publication

While you are creating a publication, the computer or mobile device stores it in memory. When you **save** a publication, the computer or mobile device places it on a storage medium such as a hard drive, USB flash drive, or online using a cloud storage service such as OneDrive, so that you can retrieve it later. A saved publication is referred to as a **file**, which is a collection of information stored on a computer, such as a publication, text document, spreadsheet, photo, or song. A **file name** is a unique, descriptive name that identifies the file's content and is assigned to a file when it is saved.

How often should you save a publication?
It is important to save a publication frequently for the following reasons:

- The publication in memory might be lost if the computer or mobile device is turned off or if you lose electrical power while Publisher is running.
- If you run out of time before completing a project, you may finish it at a future time without starting over.

CONSIDER THIS

BTW
Recent List
A list of recently used files
also appears in Backstage
view when you click Open.

When saving a publication, you must decide which storage medium to use:

- If you always work on the same computer and have no need to transport your projects to a different location, then your computer's hard drive will suffice as a storage location. It is a good idea, however, to save a backup copy of your projects on a separate medium in case the file becomes corrupted or the computer's hard drive fails. The publications created in this book are saved on the computer's hard drive.

- If you plan to work on your publications in various locations or on multiple computers or mobile devices, then you should save your publications on a portable medium, such as a USB flash drive. Alternatively, you can save your publications on an online cloud storage service, such as OneDrive.

To Save a Publication for the First Time

The following steps save a publication in the Documents library on your computer's hard drive. *Why? You have performed many tasks while creating this project and do not want to risk losing the work completed thus far, so you should save the file.*

- Click File on the ribbon (shown in Figure 1–49) to open Backstage view (Figure 1–50).

Q&A

What is the purpose of the File tab on the ribbon, and what is Backstage view?
The File tab opens **Backstage view**, which contains commands that let you manage the file and program settings for Publisher. As you click different commands along the left side of Backstage view, the associated screen is displayed on the right side of Backstage view.

What if I accidentally click the File tab on the ribbon?
Click the Back button in Backstage view to return to the Publisher workspace.

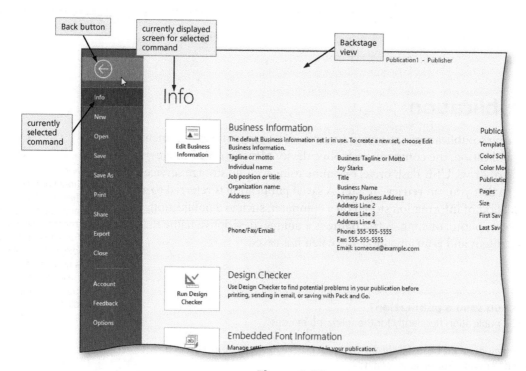

Figure 1–50

2

- Click Save As in Backstage view to display the Save As screen.

- Click This PC in the Save As screen (Figure 1–51).

Q&A What if I wanted to save to OneDrive instead?
You would click OneDrive in the Save As screen.

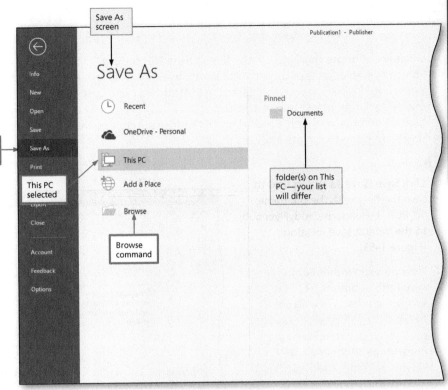

Figure 1–51

3

- Click Browse in the Save As screen to display the Save As dialog box.

Q&A Why does a file name already appear in the File name box in the Save As dialog box?
Publisher automatically suggests a file name the first time you save a publication, usually Publication1 or a similar name. Because the suggested file name is selected in the File name box, you do not need to delete it; as soon as you begin typing, the new file name replaces the selected text.

- Type `SC_PUB_1_HeadacheStudyFlyer` in the File name box to specify the file name for the flyer (Figure 1–52).

Q&A Why are my files, folders, and drives arranged and named differently from those shown in the figure?
The configuration of your computer or mobile device determines how the list of files and folders is displayed and how drives are named. You can change the save location by clicking locations in the Navigation pane.

Do I have to save to the Documents library?
No. You can save to any device or folder. You also can create your own folders by clicking the New folder button shown in Figure 1–52.

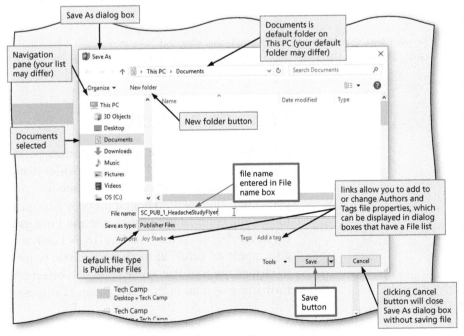

Figure 1–52

What characters can I use in a file name?
The only invalid characters are the backslash (\\), slash (/), colon (:), asterisk (*), question mark (?), quotation mark ("), less than symbol (<), greater than symbol (>), and vertical bar (|).

What are all those characters in the file name in this project?
Some companies require certain rules be followed when creating file names; others allow you to choose your own. While you could have used the file name 'Headache Study Flyer' with spaces inserted for readability, the file names in this book do not use spaces, and all begin with SC (for Shelly Cashman) and PUB (for Publisher) followed by the module number and then a descriptor of the file contents, so that they work with SAM (Skills Assessment Manager), if you are using that platform.

- Click Save (Save As dialog box) to save the flyer with the file name, SC_PUB_1_HeadacheStudyFlyer.pub, to the default save location (Figure 1–53).

How do I know that Publisher saved the publication?
While Publisher is saving your file, it briefly displays a message on the status bar indicating the percentage of the file saved. When the publication appears after saving, the new file name is displayed in the title bar.

What is the .pub at the end of the file name?
Publisher uses the .pub extension to identify Publisher files and applies it automatically. It is similar to the .docx extension used by Microsoft Word.

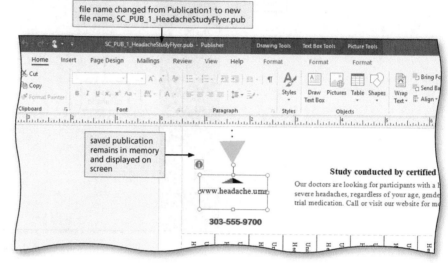

Figure 1–53

Other Ways

1. Press F12, type file name (Save As dialog box), navigate to desired save location, click Save

---

Break Point: If you want to take a break, this is a good place to do so. Exit Publisher. To resume later, start Publisher, open the file called SC_PUB_1_HeadacheStudyFlyer.pub, and continue following the steps from this location forward.

Formatting Text

Although you can format text before you type, many Publisher users enter text first and then format it later. Publisher provides many ways to modify the appearance, or **format**, of selected text or objects. Some formatting options include editing the font, paragraph, alignment, typography, copy fitting, and text effects. The more common formatting commands are shown in the Font group on the Home tab on the ribbon (Figure 1–54) or on the Text Box Tools Format tab. Many of these formatting tools also appear on the Mini toolbar when you point to text. These include the capability to change the font size, color, style, and effects. You will learn more about each of the formatting options in the Font group as you use them.

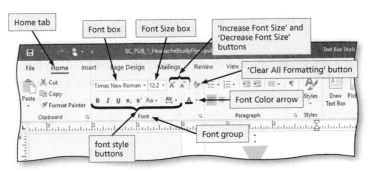

Figure 1–54

A third way to format text involves using the shortcut menu, which appears when you right-click an object or when you press SHIFT+F10. The shortcut menu is a list of frequently used commands that relate to the selected object. If you right-click some items, Publisher displays both the Mini toolbar and a shortcut menu.

How do you know which formats to use in a flyer?

In a flyer template, Publisher uses standard practices of preformatting default text, placeholder text, color, and graphics; however, consider the following formatting suggestions.

- **Increase the font size of characters.** Flyers usually are posted on a bulletin board, on a wall, or in a window. Thus, the font size should be as large as possible so that your audience easily can read the flyer. To give the headline more impact, Publisher template headlines use a font size larger than the font size of the text in the body copy.

- **Change the font of characters.** Use fonts that are easy to read. As is done in the built-in templates, try to use only two different fonts in a flyer; for example, use one font for the headline and another font for all other text. Too many fonts can make a flyer visually confusing.

- **Change the paragraph alignment.** The default alignment for many text boxes in a publication is **left-aligned** — that is, flush at the left margin with uneven right edges. Consider changing the alignment of some of the paragraphs to add interest and variety to the flyer.

- **Highlight key paragraphs with numbers or bullets.** A numbered paragraph is a paragraph that begins with a number. Use numbered paragraphs (lists) to organize a sequence. A bulleted paragraph is a paragraph that begins with a dot or another symbol. Use bulleted paragraphs to highlight important points in a flyer.

- **Emphasize important words.** To call attention to certain words or lines, you can underline them, italicize them, or bold them. Use these formats sparingly, however, because overuse will minimize their effect and make the flyer look too busy.

- **Use color.** Use colors that complement each other and convey the meaning of the flyer. Vary colors in terms of hue and brightness. Headline colors, for example, can be bold and bright. Keep in mind that too many colors can detract from the flyer and make it difficult to read.

Fonts

Characters that appear on the screen are a specific shape and size, determined by the template you choose or the settings you apply. Recall that the font, or typeface, defines the appearance and shape of the letters, numbers, and special characters. The name of the font appears in the Font box (Home tab | Font group). You can leave characters in the default font or change them to a different font. **Font size** specifies the size of the characters and is determined by a measurement system called points. A single **point** is about 1/72 of 1 inch in height. Thus, a character with a font size of 12 is about 12/72, or 1/6, of 1 inch in height. You can increase or decrease the font size of characters in a publication, as well as change the capitalization.

In addition to the common bold, italic, and underline formatting options, Publisher also allows you to apply special text effects and highlights.

Formatting Single versus Multiple Characters and Words

To format a single character, you must select the character. To format a word, however, you simply can position the insertion point in the word to make it the current word and then format the word. Paragraph formatting, such as alignment and bullets, also can be applied without first selecting it; however, if you want to format multiple characters or words, you first must select the words you want to format and then format the selection.

To Bold Text

Bold characters appear somewhat thicker and darker than characters that are not bold. To format text in your flyer, you first will select the text. ***Why?*** *Multiple words must be selected, in order to apply formatting.* The following step adds bold formatting to a sentence in the description.

 1

- Click Home on the ribbon to display the Home tab.

- In the publication, scroll to the description text box and then drag through the text you wish to format (in this case, Free trial medication) to select it.

- With the text selected, click the Bold button (Home tab | Font group) to bold the selected text (Figure 1–55).

Q&A How would I remove a bold format?
You would click the Bold button a second time, or you immediately could click the Undo button on the Quick Access Toolbar, or press CTRL+Z.

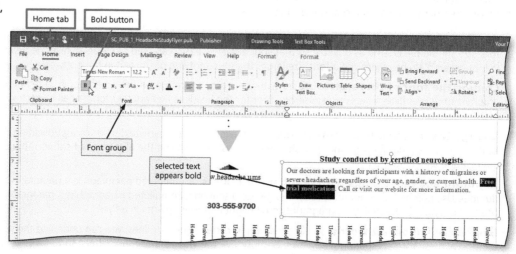

Figure 1–55

Other Ways

1. Click Font Dialog Box Launcher (Home tab | Font group), click Bold in Font style list (Font dialog box), click OK	2. Click Bold button on Mini toolbar	3. Right-click text, point to Change Text on shortcut menu, click Font, click Bold in Font style list (Font dialog box), click OK	4. Press CTRL+B

To Underline Text

Underlines are used to emphasize or draw attention to specific text. **Underlined** text prints with an underscore (_) below each character, including spaces. ***Why?*** *Underlining the spaces between words provides continuity.* The following steps format the text, migraines and severe headaches, with an underline.

 1

- Click the text, migraines, to place the insertion point in the word.

- Click the Underline button (Home tab | Font group) to underline the word.

- Click away from the word to view the underline better (Figure 1–56).

Q&A How can I tell what formatting has been applied to text?

The selected buttons and boxes on the Home tab show formatting characteristics of the location of the insertion point.

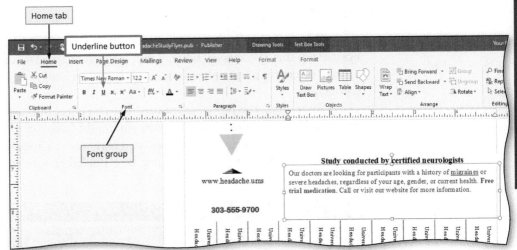

Figure 1–56

2

- Drag through the text, severe headaches, to select it.
- Click the Underline button (Home tab | Font group) to underline the selected text (shown in Figure 1–57).

Other Ways

1. Click Font Dialog Box Launcher (Home tab | Font group), click Underline in Font style list (Font dialog box), click OK
2. Click Underline button on Mini toolbar
3. Right-click text, point to Change Text on shortcut menu, click Font, click Underline in Font Style list (Font dialog box), click OK
4. Press CTRL+U

To Italicize Text

Italic text slants to the right. The following step formats the phone number in italics. *Why? The italicized text draws attention and makes the text stand out.*

- Select the text in the phone number text box.

- With the text selected, click the Italic button (Home tab | Font group) to italicize the selected text (Figure 1–57).

Q&A Why is the Bold button enabled?

The Mobile template displayed the phone number in bold. You are adding italic to the formatting.

selected text is bold by default

selected text appears italicized

previously underlined text

Study conducted by certified neurologists

Our doctors are looking for participants with a history of migraines or severe headaches, regardless of your age, gender, or current health. Free trial medication. Call or visit our website for more information.

www.headache.ums

303-555-9700

Figure 1–57

Other Ways

1. Click Font Dialog Box Launcher (Home tab | Font group), click Italic in Font style list (Font dialog box), click OK
2. Click Italic button on Mini toolbar
3. Right-click text, point to Change Text on shortcut menu, click Font on Change Text submenu, click Italic in Font Style list (Font dialog box), click OK
4. Press CTRL+I

Autofitting Text

Other advanced text formatting commands are located on the Text Box Tools Format tab that is displayed when a text box is selected. You can autofit text, change the text direction, and hyphenate, as well as make changes to the alignment, styles, and typography.

Sometimes, the replacement text that you enter into a template does not fit the same way as the original template text; you might have too much text to fit or too little text to fill the box. In such cases, you may want to **autofit**, or **copy fit**, the text to adjust the way the text fits into the text box. Publisher autofitting choices are listed in Table 1–2.

Table 1–2 Types of Autofitting

Autofitting Option	Result
Best Fit	Shrinks or expands text to fit in the text box, even when the text box is resized
Shrink Text On Overflow	Reduces the point size of text until no text is in overflow
Grow Text Box to Fit	Enlarges text box to fit all of the text at its current size
Do Not Autofit	Leaves text at its original size

To Autofit Text

The following steps autofit the text in the description text box. **Why?** *You want the text to appear as large as possible.*

- Click the text in the description text box and then click Text Box Tools Format on the ribbon to display the Text Box Tools Format tab.

- Click the Text Fit button (Text Box Tools Format tab | Text group) to display the Text Fit menu (Figure 1–58).

Q&A Do I have to select all of the text in a text box in order to autofit it?

No. Because all of the text in the text box is included automatically in autofitting, you do not need to select the text in order to autofit it.

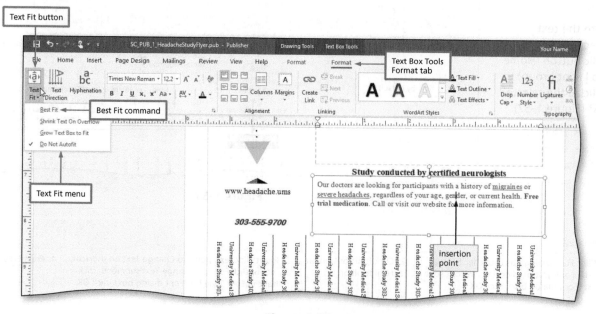

Figure 1–58

2

- Click Best Fit on the Text Fit menu to autofit the text in the text box (Figure 1–59).

Q&A Could I use the 'Increase Font Size' button to make the title larger?
Yes, but you would have to estimate how big to make the text, and future editing might be displayed incorrectly. Autofitting is different from using the 'Increase Font Size' button. With autofitting, the text and any future text is increased or decreased to fit the given size of the text box automatically.

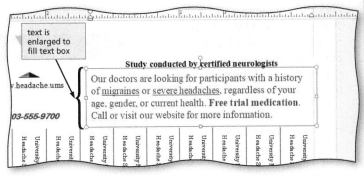

Figure 1–59

Other Ways

1. Right-click text, click Best Fit on shortcut menu

Using Graphics

A **graphic**, also called a graphical image, is a picture, shape, design, graph or chart, diagram, or video. Files containing graphics are available from a variety of sources. For example, a **clip** is a single media file, such as a graphic, a sound, an animation, or a movie that you can add to documents and webpages. You also can insert pictures stored on your computer or storage location or search for pictures on the web. You will learn about other kinds of graphics in future modules.

Many templates have picture placeholders that provide a size and shape to hold selected pictures. A **picture placeholder** has boundaries called the picture frame and a picture icon that is displayed only when you point to it. You can click the picture icon in a template to access the Insert Pictures dialog box; Publisher offers you three choices to locate a picture or graphic: from a file, from an online search, or from your OneDrive account, if you are signed in. In this module, you will insert a picture from a file. In a future module, you will use the online search. You also can insert an empty picture placeholder to reserve space for pictures you want to add later.

BTW
Distributing a Publication
Instead of printing and distributing a hard copy of a publication, you can distribute the Publisher file electronically. Options include sending the publication via email; posting it on cloud storage (such as OneDrive) and sharing the file with others; posting it on social media, a blog, or other website; and sharing a link associated with an online location of the publication. You also can create and share a PDF or XPS image of the publication, so that users can view the file in Acrobat Reader or XPS Viewer instead of in Publisher.

How do you choose appropriate graphics?
If your client or business has not provided you with a graphic, you should look for a graphic that enhances your topic with strong bright colors. Try to coordinate graphic colors and the Publisher color scheme. Perhaps the most important consideration, however, is ownership. Photos and clip art are not always free. Some web clip art galleries might specify royalty-free images for one-time use but not for commercial use (intended to generate profit). For other uses, you must purchase clip art. It is important to read all licensing agreements carefully. The usage of some artwork requires written permission. Copyright laws apply to all images equally; the right of legal use depends on the intended use and conditions of the copyright owner. All images are copyrighted, regardless of whether they are marked as copyrighted.

 CONSIDER THIS

To Use the Picture Placeholder

Many templates contain picture placeholders whose size and shape fit in with the template style. *Why? Publications with pictures attract attention and add a sense of realism; most users want pictures in their publications.* The following steps use the picture placeholder to place a photo that is located in the Data Files. Please contact your instructor for information about accessing the Data Files.

1

- Click the area above the text, Study conducted by certified neurologists, to display the boundary of the picture placeholder and the picture icon (Figure 1–60).

I am not using a mouse. Can I make the boundary visible so that I can see it without pointing to it?

Yes. Tap the Boundaries check box (View tab | Show group) to display the boundaries on all objects.

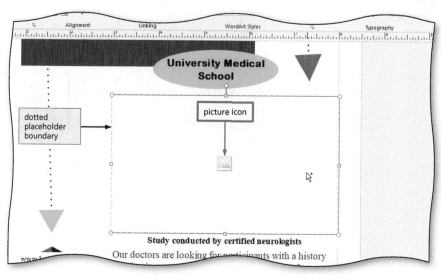

Figure 1–60

2

- Click the picture icon to display the Insert Pictures dialog box (Figure 1–61).

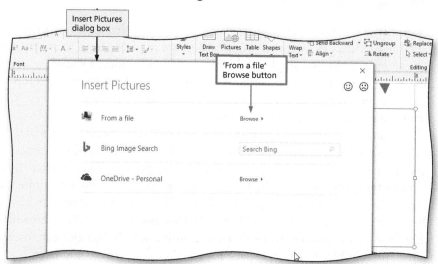

Figure 1–61

3

- Click the 'From a file' Browse button to display the Insert Picture dialog box.

- Navigate to the Data Files and the Module 01 folder. Scroll down in the list, as necessary, to display the file named, Support_PUB_1_Doctor.jpg (Figure 1–62).

Q&A

If I decide not to add a picture, will the placeholder print?

No. Graphic placeholders do not print. Placeholder text will print, however.

Why is my view different?

The default view for graphic files is to display a medium icon. To change the view, click the More options arrow.

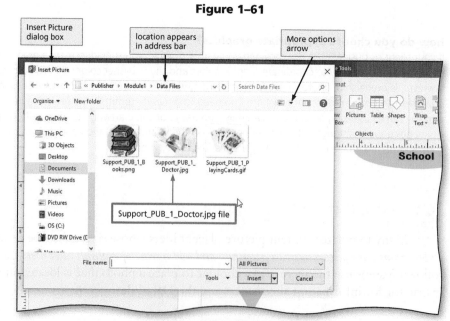

Figure 1–62

4

- Double-click the file named Support_PUB_1_Doctor.jpg to insert the chosen picture into the publication (Figure 1–63).

Q&A How does Publisher decide where to place the picture?

Publisher fills the picture placeholder. If you do not have a picture placeholder selected, Publisher inserts the picture in the middle of the screen, regardless of the magnification or scrolled area.

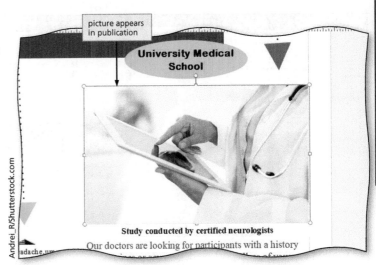

Andrei_R/Shutterstock.com

Figure 1–63

TO INSERT A PICTURE

You do not have to have a picture placeholder to insert pictures into a publication. You can insert both online pictures and those from storage, using the Publisher ribbon. If you wanted to insert a picture without a picture placeholder, you would perform the following steps.

1. Click outside the page layout so that no object is selected.
2. Click Insert on the ribbon to display the Insert tab.
3. Click the Pictures button (Insert tab | Illustrations group) to display the Insert Picture dialog box.
4. Navigate to the location of the desired picture and double-click it to insert the graphic into the publication.

To Change the Background

A **background**, or page fill, is a color, gradient, pattern, texture, picture, or tint that fills the entire page, behind all text and objects on the page layout. Many publications use a background to add interest. *Why? A background eliminates the sometimes harsh glare of a bright white page.* Gradient backgrounds use a progression of color shades to provide a subtle effect. They look more professional than solid colors or pictures. The following steps change the background to a gradient.

1

- Click the 'Show Whole Page' button on the status bar to display the entire page layout.
- Click Page Design on the ribbon to display the Page Design tab.
- Click the Background button (Page Design tab | Page Background group) to display the Background gallery (Figure 1–64).

Figure 1–64

- Click 'Accent 2 Horizontal Gradient' to select a gradient for the background (Figure 1–65).

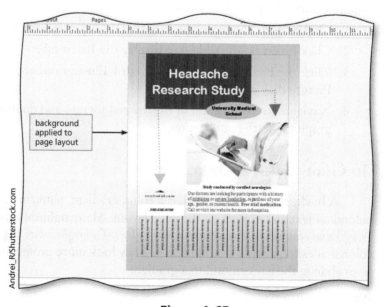

Figure 1–65

Resizing, Moving, and Aligning Objects

Many times, even when using a template, you will want to enhance a page by resizing objects, moving objects around on the page layout, and aligning objects with other objects.

Sometimes pictures and graphics are not the right size. In that case, you need to **resize** them, which means you enlarge or reduce their size. To resize any object in Publisher, select the object and then drag a handle. Recall that a handle is one of several small shapes displayed around an object when the object is selected. Pressing CTRL while dragging (CTRL+drag) keeps the center of the graphic in the same place while resizing. Pressing SHIFT while dragging (SHIFT+drag) maintains the graphic's proportions while resizing. Finally, pressing SHIFT and CTRL while dragging (SHIFT+CTRL+drag) maintains the proportions of the graphic and keeps its center in the same place.

To move an object, it must be selected. The pointer changes to a double two-headed arrow, and you then drag the object to the new location or to the scratch area. If you press and hold SHIFT while dragging, the object moves in a straight line. Pressing CTRL while dragging creates a copy of the object. As you move an object, Publisher displays nonprinting, visual **layout guides** to help you place and align the object to other objects on the page layout. When you **align** an object to another object, its edge or center lines up, either vertically or horizontally. The visual layout guides are pink lines that move from object to object as you drag. Visual layout guides appear when aligning to the left, right, top, bottom, or middle of objects.

If you want to align the text within a text box rather than aligning the text box itself, Publisher provides four alignment options: Align Right, Center, Align Left, and Justify. Justify aligns text on both the left and right, padding the text with extra spaces if necessary. The align tools are on the Home tab in the Paragraph group.

BTW
Moving Text Boxes
Be careful to drag the border of a text box when you want to move it. If you drag the text inside a text box, you may move the text rather than the entire text box object.

To Resize an Object

The following step resizes the logo to make it larger. *Why? Because the logo contains the website address, it should appear as large as possible in the space provided.*

- Scroll as necessary and then select the object to be resized (in this case, the organization logo).

- Press F9 to change the magnification to 100%.

- SHIFT+drag the upper-left sizing handle, up and left, until the status bar displays a size of approximately 2 x 1 inches (Figure 1–66).

Q&A What is a sizing handle?
A **sizing handle** is one of eight small, white circles on the border of a selected object.

Why do I have to use SHIFT while dragging?
Using SHIFT keeps the logo proportional in size as you resize it.

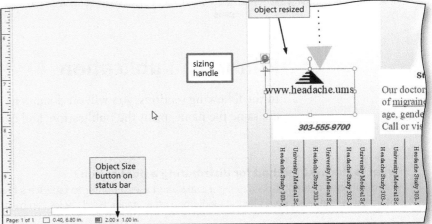

Figure 1–66

Andrei_R/Shutterstock.com

Other Ways

| 1. Enter new width and height in Measurement pane | 2. Enter new width and height (Drawing Tools Format tab \| Size group) | 3. Enter new width and height (Picture Tools Format tab \| Size group) |

To Move an Object

The following steps move the logo from its current location to a location aligned with the template's triangle graphic. **Why?** *Aligning the logo provides consistency.*

1

- If necessary, select the object (in this case, the logo) by clicking its border.

- Drag the object to the right until the vertical pink layout guide appears, indicating that the object is centered with the template triangle graphic (Figure 1–67).

Q&A

When do the layout guides appear?

As you drag an object, when one of its borders or its center aligns with another object on the page, Publisher displays a pink guide showing you the possible alignment.

2

- Release the mouse button, if necessary, to finish moving the object.

- Click the 'Show Whole Page' button on the status bar to view the entire page.

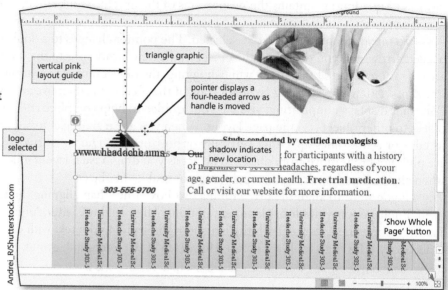

Figure 1–67

Other Ways
1. Select object, press ARROW key
2. Select object, click Object Position button on status bar, enter new x and y coordinates in Measurement pane

Printing a Publication

In the following sections, you will set document properties, save the publication with the same file name, print the publication, and close the publication.

CONSIDER THIS

What is the best method for distributing a publication?

The traditional method of distributing a publication uses a printer to produce a hard copy. A **hard copy**, or **printout**, is information that exists on a physical medium, such as paper. Hard copies can be useful for the following reasons:

- Some people prefer proofreading a hard copy of a publication rather than viewing it on a screen to check for errors and readability.

- Hard copies can serve as a backup reference if your storage medium is lost or becomes corrupted and you need to re-create the publication.

Instead of distributing a hard copy of a publication, users can distribute the publication as an electronic image that mirrors the original publication's appearance. The electronic image of the publication can be sent as an email attachment, posted on a website, or copied to a portable storage medium such as a USB flash drive. Two popular electronic image formats, sometimes called fixed formats, are PDF by Adobe Systems and XPS by Microsoft. In Publisher, you can create electronic image files through the Save As dialog box and the Export, Share, and Print commands in Backstage view. Electronic images of publications, such as PDF and XPS, can be useful, as users can view electronic images of publications without the software that created the original publication (e.g., Publisher). Specifically, to view a PDF file, you use a program called Adobe Reader, which can be downloaded free from Adobe's website. Similarly, to view an XPS file, you use a program called XPS Viewer, which is included in the latest versions of Windows and Internet Explorer.

Sending electronic publications saves paper and printer supplies. Society encourages users to contribute to **green computing**, which involves reducing the electricity consumed and environmental waste generated when using computers, mobile devices, and related technologies, as well as saving paper.

To Change the Document Properties

Publisher helps you organize and identify your files by using **document properties**, which are the details about a file, such as the project author, title, and subject. For example, a class name or document topic can describe the file's purpose or content.

Document properties are valuable for a variety of reasons:

- You can save time locating a particular file because you can view a document's properties without opening the document.

- By creating consistent properties for files that have similar content, you can better organize your documents.

- Some organizations require users to add document properties so that other employees can view details about these files.

The more common document properties are standard and automatically updated properties. **Standard properties** are associated with all Microsoft Office files and include author, title, and subject. **Automatically updated properties** include file system properties, such as the date you create or change a file, and statistics, such as the file size.

You can change the document properties while working with a file in Publisher. When you save the file, Publisher will save the document properties with the file. The following steps change the comment document property. *Why? Adding document properties will help you identify characteristics of the file without opening it.*

1

- Click File on the ribbon to open Backstage view and then, if necessary, click Info in Backstage view to display the Info screen.

Q&A What is the purpose of the Info screen in Backstage view?
The Info screen contains commands that enable you to protect, inspect, and manage versions of a document, as well as view and change document properties.

- Click the Publication Properties button to display its list (Figure 1–68).

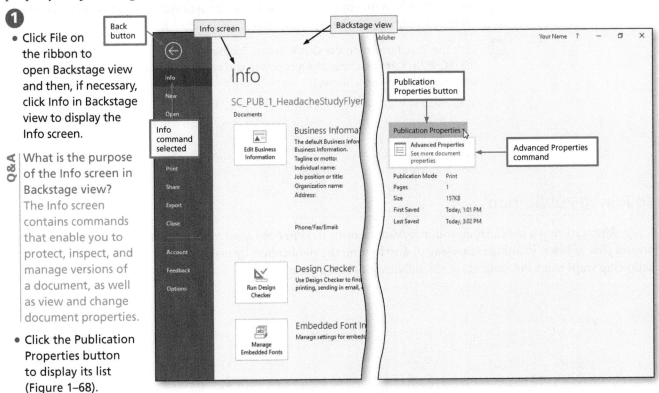

Figure 1–68

2

- Click Advanced Properties to display the SC_PUB_1_HeadacheStudyFlyer.pub Properties dialog box.
- Click the Summary tab.
- Click the Comments text box in the Properties list and then type **CIS 101 Assignment** in the Comments text box (Figure 1–69).

Q&A Why are some of the document properties already filled in?
Depending on previous Publisher settings and where you are using Publisher, your school, university, or place of employment may have customized the properties.

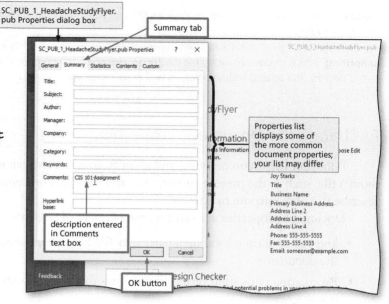

Figure 1–69

3

- Click OK (SC_PUB_1_HeadacheStudyFlyer.pub Properties dialog box) to close the dialog box.
- Click the Back button in the upper-left corner of Backstage view to return to the document window.

To Save a Publication with the Same File Name

It is a good practice to save a publication before printing it, in case you experience difficulties printing. The following step saves the publication again on the same storage location with the same file name.

1 Click the Save button on the Quick Access Toolbar to overwrite the previously saved file (SC_PUB_1_HeadacheStudyFlyer.pub in this case) in the same location it was saved previously (Documents library).

Q&A Why should I save the flyer again?
You have made several modifications to the flyer since you last saved it; thus, you should save it again.

To Print a Publication

After creating a publication, you may want to print it. **Why?** *You want to see how the flyer will appear on a printed piece of paper.* Printing is one way of distributing the publication by using a hard copy or printout. The following steps print the contents of the publication on a printer.

1

- Click File on the ribbon to open Backstage view.

- Click Print in Backstage view to display the Print screen and a preview of the publication (Figure 1–70).

Q&A What if I decide not to print the publication at this time?
Click the Back button in the upper-left corner of Backstage view to return to the Publisher workspace.

My background does not fill the page in the print preview. Did I do something wrong?
No. It may be that your printer cannot print all the way to the edge of the paper. The preview is showing you where the background will be cut off due to the printer margins.

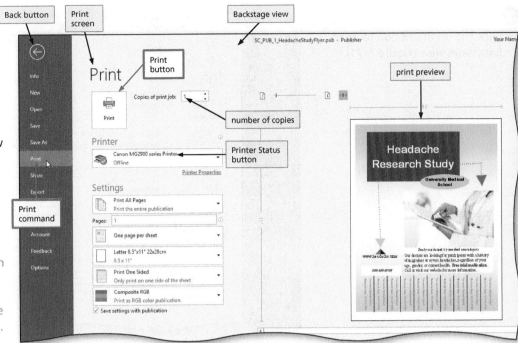

Figure 1–70

Andrei_R/Shutterstock.com

2

- Verify that the selected printer will print the publication. If necessary, click the Printer Status button to display a list of available printer options and then click the desired printer to change the currently selected printer.

Q&A How can I print multiple copies of my publication?
Increase the number in the 'Copies of print job' box in the Print screen.

- Click the Print button in the Print screen to print the publication on the currently selected printer.

- When the printer stops, retrieve the printed publication (shown in Figure 1–1).

Q&A Do I have to wait until my publication is complete to print it?
No, you can print a publication at any time while you are creating it.

Other Ways

1. Press CTRL+P, verify printer settings, click Print button

To Close a Publication

Although you still need to make some edits to this publication, you should close the publication at this time. *Why? You should close a file when you are done working with it or wish to take a break so that you do not make inadvertent changes to it.* The following steps close the current active publication document, SC_PUB_1_HeadacheStudyFlyer.pub, without exiting Publisher.

1

- Click File on the ribbon to open Backstage view (Figure 1–71).

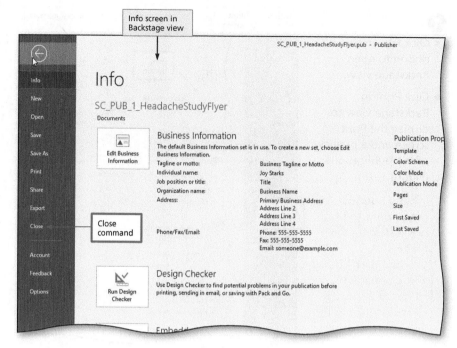

Figure 1–71

2

- Click Close in Backstage view to close the currently open document (SC_PUB_1_HeadacheStudyFlyer. pub in this case) without exiting Publisher (Figure 1–72).

Q&A

What if Publisher displays a dialog box about saving?
Click Save if you want to save the changes, click Don't Save if you want to ignore the changes since the last time you saved, and click Cancel if you do not want to close the document.

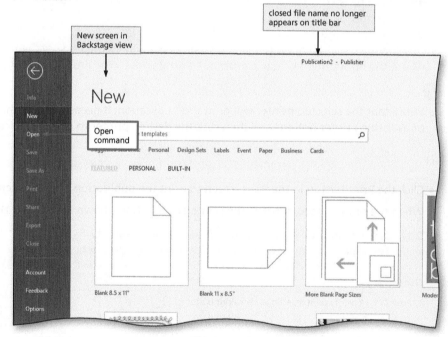

Figure 1–72

Other Ways

1. Press CTRL+F4

Break Point: If you want to take a break, this is a good place to do so. To resume later, start Publisher and continue following the steps from this location forward.

Changing a Publication

After creating a publication, you often will find that you must make changes to it. Changes might be required if the publication contains errors or because of new circumstances. The types of changes made to publications normally fall into three categories: deletions, additions, or modifications.

Deletions Sometimes deletions are necessary in a publication because objects are incorrect or no longer are needed. For example, to place this advertising flyer on a website, the tear-offs no longer are needed. In that case, you would delete them from the page layout.

Additions Additional text, objects, or formatting may be required in a publication. For example, in the SC_PUB_1_HeadacheStudyFlyer.pub flyer, you may want to insert a hyperlink that can be displayed when the flyer is published on the web.

Modifications If you make modifications or edits to text or graphics, normal techniques of inserting, deleting, editing, and formatting apply. Modification also may include copying and pasting.

The **Office Clipboard** is a temporary storage area in a computer's memory that lets you collect up to 24 items (text or objects) from any Office document and then paste these items into almost any other type of document. The Office Clipboard works with the copy, cut, and paste commands:

- To **copy** is the process of selecting text or an object and placing a duplicate of the selected item on the Office Clipboard, leaving the item in its original location in the document. The Copy command (Home tab | Clipboard group) also can be accessed on most shortcut menus or by pressing CTRL+C.
- To **cut** is the process of removing text or an object from a document and placing it on the Office Clipboard. The Cut command (Home tab | Clipboard group) also can be accessed on most shortcut menus or by pressing CTRL+X.
- To **paste** is the process of placing an item stored on the Office Clipboard in the document at the location of the insertion point. The Paste command (Home tab | Clipboard group) also can be accessed on most shortcut menus or by pressing CTRL+V.

In the following sections, you will make changes to the flyer to prepare it for publishing to the web.

BTW
Conserving Ink and Toner
If you want to conserve ink or toner, you can instruct Publisher to print draft quality documents by clicking File on the ribbon to open Backstage view, clicking Options in Backstage view to display the Publisher Options dialog box, clicking Advanced in the left pane (Publisher Options dialog box), scrolling to the Print area in the right pane, placing a check mark in the 'Use draft quality' check box, and then clicking OK. Then, use Backstage view to print the document as usual.

To Open a Recent Publication

Earlier in this module, you saved your publication using the file name, SC_PUB_1_HeadacheStudyFlyer. Publisher maintains a list of the last few publications that have been opened or saved on your computer. The **Recent list** is a list that a program maintains of the last few documents that have been opened or saved on your computer, letting you open them again quickly. It allows you to click the name of the publication to open it, without navigating to the location. The following steps start Publisher and open the SC_PUB_1_HeadacheStudyFlyer file from the Recent list.

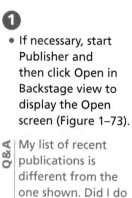

- If necessary, start Publisher and then click Open in Backstage view to display the Open screen (Figure 1–73).

Q&A My list of recent publications is different from the one shown. Did I do something wrong?
No, your list will differ depending on what publications you have opened in the past.

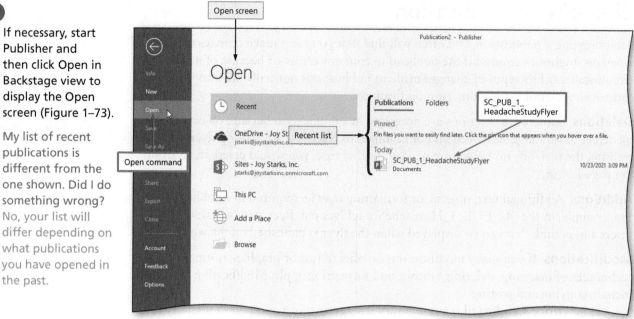

Figure 1–73

2

- In the Recent list, click SC_PUB_1_HeadacheStudyFlyer to open the publication.

Q&A The file does not appear in the Recent list. What should I do?
If the file you wish to open does not appear in the Recent list, click Browse and then navigate to the location of the file to be opened. Double-click the file name to open it.

Can I change the total number of publications listed in the Recent list?
Yes. In Backstage view, click Options to display the Publisher Options dialog box, click Advanced (Publisher Options dialog box), and then in the Display area, change the number in the 'Show this number of Recent Publications' box.

Other Ways
1. Click Open in Backstage view, click Browse, navigate to location of file, double-click file name 2. Press CTRL+O 3. Navigate to file in File Explorer window, double-click file name

To Delete Objects

Templates may display objects in the page layout that you do not wish to use. In those cases, or when you change your mind about including an inserted object, you must delete the object or objects. In order to delete an object, it must be selected. The following steps delete the tear-offs. *Why? If this flyer is displayed on a website, the tear-offs are unnecessary and should be deleted.*

1

- Right-click any one of the tear-offs to select all the tear-offs and display the shortcut menu (Figure 1–74).

My shortcut menu is different from the one shown. Did I do something wrong?
No. Shortcut menus are context sensitive, so they look slightly different if you click the text than if you click the border of the text box.

What do I do if my shortcut menu does not display a Delete Object command?
Click in a slightly different location within the tear-offs.

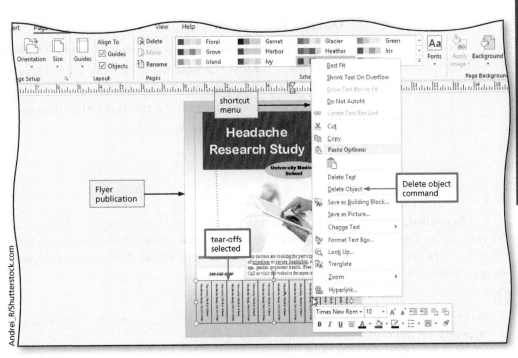

Figure 1–74

2

- Click Delete Object on the shortcut menu to delete the tear-offs (Figure 1–75).

Why did only the text disappear?
You may have selected the text or the boundary of the text box instead of the boundary of the entire object. Select the remaining objects and then press DELETE.

What if I delete an object accidentally?
Press CTRL+Z to undo the most recent step or click the Undo button on the Quick Access Toolbar. The object will reappear in the original location.

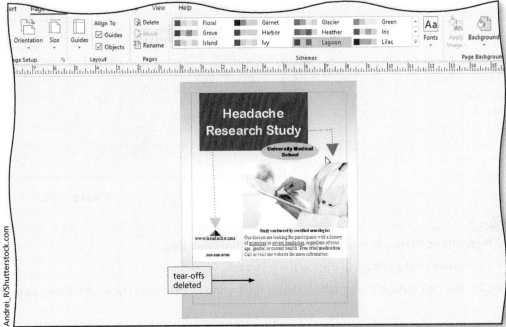

Figure 1–75

Other Ways

1. Select object, press DELETE   2. Select object, press BACKSPACE

To Delete a Text Box

If you wanted to delete a text box, you would follow these steps.

1. Point to the text box until the dotted border is displayed and the pointer changes to a double two-headed arrow.

2. Click the border to select the text box rather than the text.

3. Press DELETE to delete the text box.

To Insert a Hyperlink

A **hyperlink**, or link, is a specially formatted word, phrase, or graphic which, when clicked or tapped, lets you display a webpage on the Internet, another file, an email, or another location within the same file. The following steps create a link to the headache study website. *Why? This version of the flyer will be seen on the web, and users may want to click to register.*

- Select the text you wish to make a hyperlink (in this case, the web address in the logo) and then zoom to 100% (Figure 1–76).

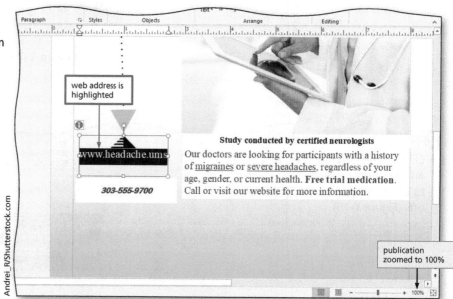

Figure 1–76

- Press CTRL+C to copy the web address to the Office Clipboard.

- Click Insert on the ribbon to display the Insert tab.

- Click the Link button (Insert tab | Links group) to display the Insert Hyperlink dialog box.

- If necessary, click the 'Existing File or Web Page' button in the Link to bar, click the Address box to position the insertion point, and then press CTRL+V to paste the web address from the Office Clipboard. Publisher will add the http:// protocol to the web address (Figure 1–77).

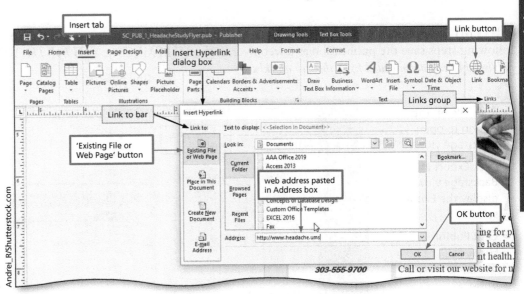

Andrei_R/Shutterstock.com

Figure 1–77

- Click OK (Insert Hyperlink dialog box) to assign the hyperlink (Figure 1–78).

Q&A | How can I tell if it is a hyperlink?
Publisher underlines a hyperlink and uses a purple or blue font for it. When a user hovers over a hyperlink, the pointer will appear as a hand.

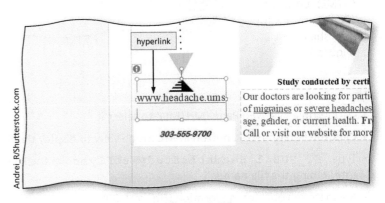

Andrei_R/Shutterstock.com

Figure 1–78

Other Ways

1. Right-click text, click Hyperlink on shortcut menu, enter web address in Address box (Insert Hyperlink dialog box), click OK

2. Press CTRL+K, enter web address in Address box (Insert Hyperlink dialog box), click OK

Creating a Webpage from a Publication

You can create several types of publications with Microsoft Publisher in addition to standard print publications. A **web publication** is one suitable for publishing to the web, containing certain objects, formatting options, hyperlinks, and other features specific to webpages. The following sections create a web version of the flyer that might be posted on a campus website or social networking site.

To Save a Print Publication as a Web Publication

The Export screen in Backstage view includes a group of commands that allow you to save publications as different file types or to package publications for sending to other users. In the following steps, you will export a publication by publishing it to the web. **Publishing HTML**, or **publishing to the web**, is the process of making webpages available to others, for example, on the World Wide Web or on a company's intranet.

A **Hypertext Markup Language (HTML)** file is a file capable of being stored and transferred electronically on a file server in order to display on the web. The **MIME Hypertext Markup Language**

BTW

Web Publications
When converting to a web publication, determine which objects will work effectively on the web and which ones will not, and then modify the publication as necessary. Will the publication be accessible on the web? Is the target audience common web users? If so, determine whether an email or website would be the most efficient means of communication.

(**MHTML**) is a small, single-file HTML format that does not create a supporting folder of resources. The following steps save the publication as a web flyer in the MHTML format. *Why? The MHTML file can be published to and downloaded from the web quickly.*

- Click File on the ribbon to open Backstage view.

- Click Export in Backstage view to display the Export screen.

- Click Publish HTML to display the options.

- Click the 'Web Page (HTML)' button to display options for publishing HTML (Figure 1–79).

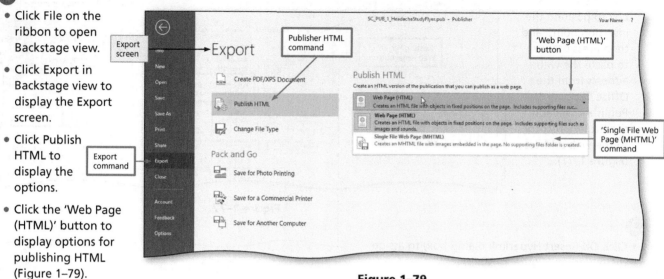

Figure 1–79

- Click 'Single File Web Page (MHTML)' to select it.

- Click the Publish HTML button in Backstage view to display the Save As dialog box.

- Type **SC_PUB_1_HeadacheStudyWebFlyer** in the File name box (Save As dialog box). Do not press ENTER after typing the file name.

- Navigate to your storage location (Figure 1–80).

Q&A

How do I move the dialog box so that it is not covering buttons and parts of the screen I need to access?
In general, you can move dialog boxes by dragging the title bar. You also can resize them to view different parts of your screen.

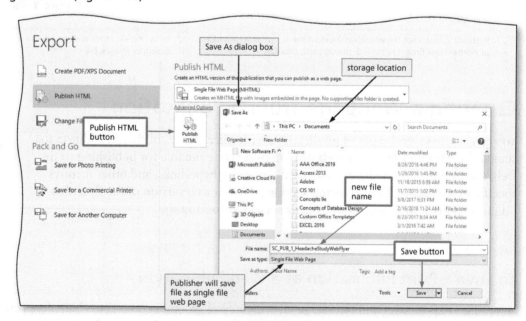

3

- Click Save (Save As dialog box) to save the publication as a single file web page.

Figure 1–80

Other Ways

1. Click Save As in Backstage view, click storage location, enter file name, click 'Save as type' button, click 'Single File Web Page (*.mht;*.mhtml)', click Save (Save As dialog box)

To Preview the Web Publication in a Browser

The following steps preview the web publication. ***Why?*** *Previewing is the best way to test the look and feel of the webpage and to test the hyperlink.* You will open the MHTML file from its storage location.

1

- Click the File Explorer icon on your taskbar to open the File Explorer window. When the File Explorer window opens, navigate to your storage location (Figure 1–81).

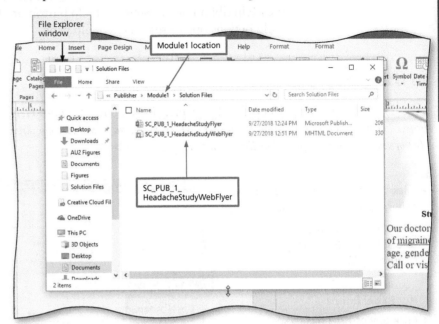

Figure 1–81

2

- Double-click the SC_PUB_1_HeadacheStudyWebFlyer.mht file.

- When the browser window opens, if necessary, maximize the window (Figure 1–82).

Q&A Why does my display look different from what is shown here?
Each brand and version of browser software displays information in a slightly different manner.

Can I click the hyperlink?
You can, but the web address is fictitious. You may see a message saying that the webpage is not found.

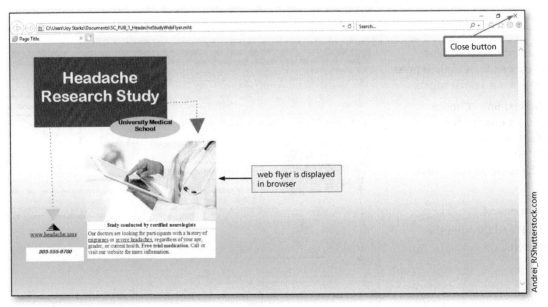

Figure 1–82

3

- Click the Close button on the browser window's title bar and then click the Close button on the File Explorer window's title bar.

Using Publisher Help

At any time while you are using Publisher, you can use Publisher Help to display information about all topics associated with Publisher. You can search for help by using the Help ribbon or by using the Help button on the title bar and in dialog boxes. Both Help options open a searchable Help pane.

To Use the Help Pane

The following steps open the Help pane. *Why? Using Publisher Help, you can search for information based on phrases (such as save a publication or format text) or key terms (such as copy, save, or format). Publisher Help responds with a list of search results displayed as links to a variety of resources.*

1

- Click the Help button (Publisher title bar) to open the Help pane.
- Click the Get Started link to display the list of topics (Figure 1–83).

 Experiment

- Click any of the links to see additional information.

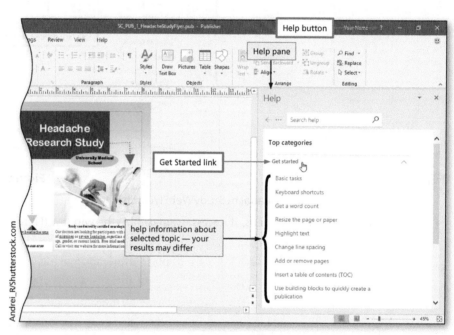

Figure 1–83

2

- In the Search help box, type **autocorrect** and then press ENTER to enter a search topic.
- Click the first link, 'Choose AutoCorrect options for capitalization, spelling, and symbols' to display information about the topic (Figure 1–84).

Experiment

- Scroll and read through the information.

Q&A How do I navigate the Help pane?
You can scroll through the displayed information in the Help pane, click any of the links for additional help, click the Back button on the Help pane to return to a previously displayed screen, or enter search text in the Search help box.

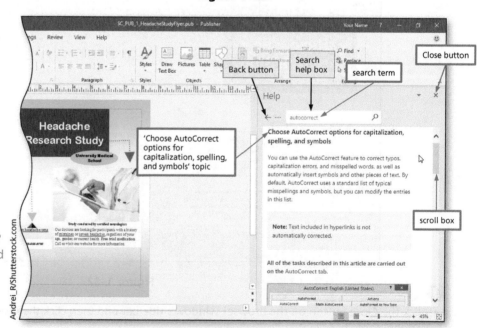

Figure 1–84

3

• When you are finished with the Help pane, click its Close button to close the pane.

Other Ways

1. Press F1

Obtaining Help while Working in Publisher

You can access Help without first opening the Help pane and initiating a search. This can be useful, for example, if you are unsure about how a particular command works or if you are presented with a dialog box that you are not sure how to use.

If you want to learn more about a command, point to its button and wait for the ScreenTip to appear, as shown in Figure 1–85. If the Help icon and 'Tell me more' link appear in the ScreenTip, click the 'Tell me more' link (or press F1 while pointing to the button) to open the Help pane and display a help topic associated with that command.

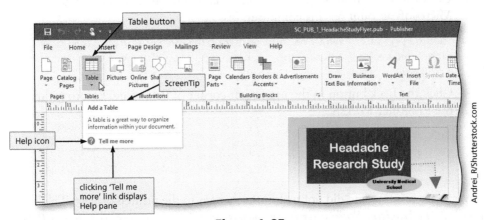

Figure 1–85

Dialog boxes also contain Help buttons, as shown in Figure 1–86. Clicking the Help button or pressing F1 while the dialog box is displayed opens a Help window in a browser that provides information specific to that dialog box, if available.

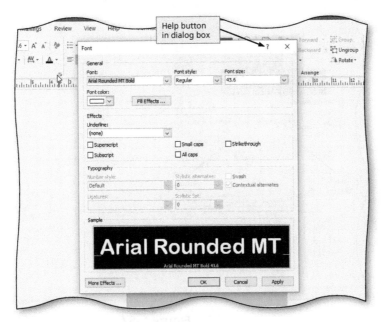

Figure 1–86

To Sign Out of a Microsoft Account

If you are using a public computer or for some other reason wish to sign out of your Microsoft account, you can sign out of the account from the Accounts screen in Backstage view. Signing out of the account is the safest way to ensure that no one else can access online files or settings stored in your Microsoft account. If you wanted to sign out of a Microsoft account from Publisher, you would perform the following steps.

1. Click File on the ribbon to open Backstage view and then click Account to display the Account screen.

2. Click the Sign out link to open the Remove Account dialog box. If a Can't remove Windows accounts dialog box appears instead of the Remove Account dialog box, click OK and skip the remaining steps.

Q&A Why does a Can't remove Windows accounts dialog box appear?
If you signed in to Windows using your Microsoft account, then you also must sign out from Windows rather than signing out from within Publisher. When you are finished using Windows, be sure to sign out at that time.

3. Click the Yes button (Remove Account dialog box) to sign out of your Microsoft account on this computer.

Q&A Should I sign out of Windows after removing my Microsoft account?
When you are finished using the computer, you should sign out of Windows for maximum security.

4. Click the Back button in the upper-left corner of Backstage view to return to the Publisher workspace.

To Exit Publisher

You saved the publication prior to printing and did not make any changes to the printed project. The following step exits Publisher. ***Why?*** *The Headache Study Flyer project now is complete, and you are ready to exit Publisher.*

- Click the Close button in the upper-right corner of the Publisher window to exit Publisher.

- If a Microsoft Publisher dialog box is displayed (Figure 1–87), click Don't Save to retain the original print publication.

Q&A When I exited Publisher, a dialog box did not display. Why not?
If you made changes to your publication since you last saved it, the dialog box shown in Figure 1–87 will appear when you exit Publisher. If you want to save changes before exiting, click Save; if you do not want to save changes, click Don't Save; if you change your mind and do not want to exit Publisher, click Cancel to return to the publication in the Publisher workspace.

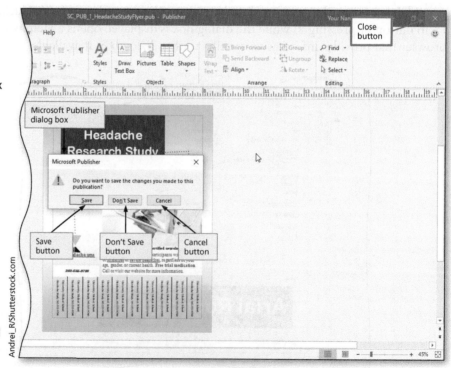

Andrei_R/Shutterstock.com

Figure 1–87

Other Ways

1. Right-click Microsoft Publisher button on Windows taskbar, click Close Window on shortcut menu

Summary

In this module, you learned some basic Publisher techniques as you created a flyer from a template. You learned how to choose a publication template and set font and color schemes. You learned how to enter and edit both placeholder and default text. After creating synchronized tear-offs, you formatted text with bold, underline, and italic. You added a graphic using a picture placeholder. You learned how to delete, resize, move, and align objects. After checking the spelling, you saved the file and reopened it to make revisions, including creating a hyperlink and removing tear-offs in the publication. Finally, you saved a print publication as a web publication.

What decisions will you need to make when creating your next publication?

Use these guidelines as you complete the assignments in this module and create your own publications outside of this class.

1. Select template options.

   a) Select a template that matches your need.

   b) Choose font and color schemes that are appropriate for the flyer's purpose and audience.

2. Choose words for the text.

   a) Replace all placeholder and default text.

   b) Add other objects, as necessary, and delete unused items.

3. Identify how to format various objects in the flyer.

   a) Use bold, underline, and italic for emphasis.

   b) Autofit the text to make the flyer easy to read.

4. Find and insert the appropriate graphic(s).

   a) Resize, move, and align graphics as necessary.

5. Determine whether the flyer will be more effective as a print publication, web publication, or both.

   a) Insert any necessary hyperlinks.

   b) Consider creating a background for a web publication.

CONSIDER THIS: PLAN AHEAD

Apply Your Knowledge

Reinforce the skills and apply the concepts you learned in this module.

Modifying Text and Formatting a Publication

Instructions: Start Publisher. Open the publication, SC_PUB_1–1, in the Data Files. Please contact your instructor for information about accessing the Data Files.

The publication you open is a flyer in which you replace text, delete objects, insert a graphic, (Figure 1-88) and then convert the publication from print to the web.

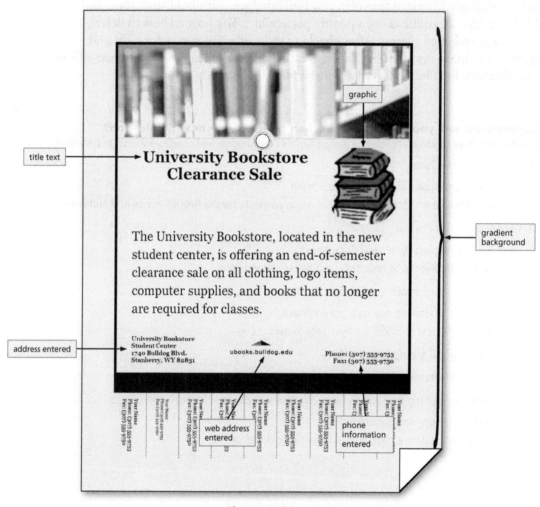

Figure 1–88

Perform the following tasks:

1. Select the headline text and replace it with:

   University Bookstore Clearance Sale

2. Select the body copy text and replace it with:

   The University Bookstore, located in the new student center, is offering an end-of-semester clearance sale on all clothing, logo items, computer supplies, and books that no longer are required for classes.

3. Autofit the text.

4. Select the address text, just above the tear-offs on the left. Zoom to 100%. Replace the text with the following, pressing ENTER at the end of each line except the last.

   University Bookstore

   Student Center

   1740 Bulldog Blvd.

   Stanberry, WY 82831

5. Select the text in the phone number text box in the right portion of the flyer and replace the text with:

   Phone: (307) 555-9753

   Fax: (307) 555-9750

6. Replace the logo text with:

   ubooks.bulldog.edu

7. Use the AutoCorrect options button to change the uppercase U to a lowercase u.

8. Correct any spelling errors.

9. Click the picture icon in the picture placeholder located to the right of the headline text. Navigate to the Data Files and insert the picture named Support_PUB_1_Books.png.

10. Click the Background button (Page Design | Page Background group) and insert the '10% tint of Accent 1' background.

11. Change the publication properties, as specified by your instructor.

12. If requested by your instructor, replace the tear-off text with your name, phone, and email address.

13. Save the file with the file name, SC_PUB_1_UniversityBookstoreFlyer.

14. Delete the tear-offs.

15. Select the web address. Use the Link button (Insert tab | Links group) to convert the web address to a hyperlink.

16. In Backstage view, click Export to display the Export screen.

17. Click Publish HTML to display its options.

18. Click the 'Web Page (HTML)' button and then click 'Single File Web Page (MHTML)' to select it.

19. Click the Publish HTML button and save the publication with the file name, SC_PUB_1_UniversityBookstoreWebFlyer.

20. Submit the revised publications as specified by your instructor.

21. ✸ What other modifications might you make when converting a print publication into a web publication? Why?

Extend Your Knowledge

Extend the skills you learned in this module and experiment with new skills. You may need to use Help to complete the assignment.

Creating a Flyer

Note: To complete this assignment, you will be required to use the Data Files. Please contact your instructor for information about accessing the Data Files.

Instructions: Use Publisher to create a flyer by inserting graphics, drawing text boxes, applying picture styles, and formatting the text. The flyer before modification is shown in Figure 1–89.

Continued >

Extend Your Knowledge *continued*

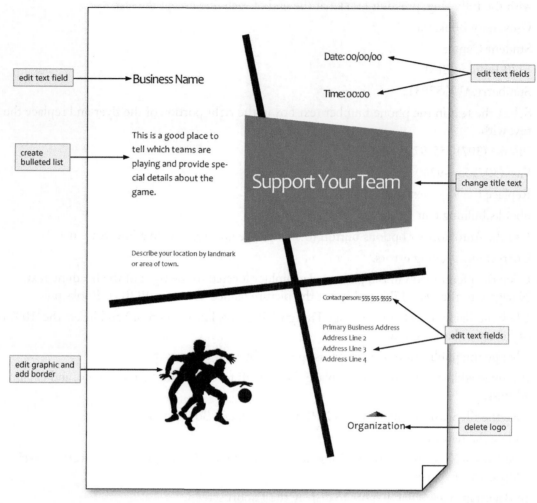

Figure 1–89

Perform the following tasks:

1. Start Publisher.

2. Select the Sports Event Flyer. (*Hint:* Navigate through the BUILT-IN templates, the Flyers folder, and the All Event folder, and then scroll down to the Other area to locate the template.) Use the Wildflower color scheme and the Concourse font scheme. Choose to include no tear-offs.

3. When the template is displayed, if the Page Navigation pane opens, click the Page Number button on the status bar to close it.

4. Use Help to learn about bulleted lists, font sizes, and picture styles.

5. Replace the text with the following:

    Title: Euchre Tournament!

    Business Name: University Math Club Presents:

    Date: 02/09/20

    Time: 3:00 p.m.

    Contact Person: Call: Chang Lee

    Phone Number: (274) 555-9191

    Address: Union Building

           Campus Center

    Describe your location: We will play in the Holiday Room in the Campus Union.

6. Delete the organization logo.

7. Use Help to review bulleted lists. Click the description placeholder text that appears to the left of the heading. Choose a bullet style and type the following, pressing ENTER at the end of each line:

```
Sign up by 02/01/20
Singles or pairs
Prizes awarded
Food provided
```

8. Autofit all text boxes as necessary.

9. Right-click the graphic and then point to Change Picture on the shortcut menu. Click Change Picture on the submenu. Use the Browse button to navigate to the Data Files and then insert the file named Support_PUB_1_PlayingCards.gif. If Publisher places your original graphic in the scratch area, select only it and then delete it.

10. Use Help to learn about picture borders. With the graphic selected, click the More button (Picture Tools Format tab | Picture Styles group) and then select a style with a border from the Picture Styles gallery. Click the Picture Border arrow (Picture Tools Format tab | Picture Styles group) and then click an appropriate color.

11. If requested by your instructor, replace the name, Chang Lee, with your name.

12. Change the publication properties, as specified by your instructor. Save the publication with the file name, SC_PUB_1_CardTournamentFlyer and then print it. Submit it in the format specified by your instructor.

13. ✳ You made several decisions while creating the flyer in this assignment: choosing a bullet style, changing the font size, assigning a border and border color to the picture, and resizing it. What was the rationale behind each of these decisions? What other changes might make the flyer more appealing to its audience?

Expand Your World

Create a solution that uses cloud and web technologies by learning and investigating on your own from general guidance.

Modifying a Publication

Note: To complete this assignment, you will be required to use the Data Files. Please contact your instructor for information about accessing the Data Files.

Instructions: Start Publisher and open the file SC_PUB_1–2 from the Data Files. The file contains a flyer to advertise a school play that you are to modify and post on OneDrive so that the other people involved with the play can contribute their ideas. The flyer before modifications is shown in Figure 1–90.

Perform the following tasks:

1. If necessary, sign in to your OneDrive account.

2. Replace the heading, Promotion Title, with the name of the play, As You Like It.

3. Replace the Business Name with the words, William Shakespeare.

4. Replace the placeholder text, Attention Grabber, with the name of your school.

5. Insert the 'Accent 3 Vertical Gradient' background to the page.

6. If requested to do so by your instructor, change the phone number to your phone number.

Continued >

Expand Your World *continued*

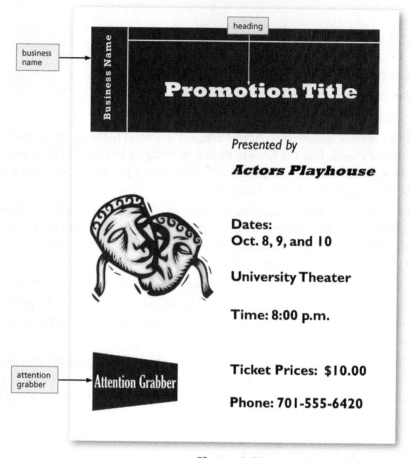

Figure 1–90

7. Save the publication on OneDrive using the file name, SC_PUB_1_TheaterFlyer.

8. Submit the assignment in the format specified by your instructor.

9. Exit Publisher. If necessary, sign out of your OneDrive account.

10. ✳ On what occasions might you save one of your files for school or your job on OneDrive? Do you think using OneDrive enhances collaboration efforts? Why?

In the Lab

Design and implement a solution using creative thinking and problem-solving skills.

Design and Create a Party Flyer

Problem: Your friend manages a local nightclub and is planning a large New Year's Eve party. To help in advertising the party, he has asked you to prepare a flyer.

Perform the following tasks:

Part 1:   Choose an appropriate flyer with a graphic, and choose a color scheme and font scheme. Choose to include no tear-offs. The flyer should contain the headline, Best New Year's Eve Party Ever! Change the business name to The Sage Room. Include the phone number

364-555-2000. Include a reference to Facebook and a link to the nightclub's website, sageroom. biz. The description consists of the following text: As the new year begins and the old year ends, come be our guest at a New Year's Eve Fest! The party begins at 8:00 p.m. The address should be The Sage Room at 229 Center Street in Spring Valley, KY 40002. The motto or tag line should be: Open from 4:00 p.m. to 1:00 a.m. daily. Replace the graphic with an appropriate graphic from the web. Make sure you have the legal right to use the graphic. Enhance the flyer by using fonts, formatting elements (bold, color, underline, italics, etc.), and other page enhancements, such as paragraph alignments and borders. Use the concepts and techniques presented in this module to create and format this flyer. Submit your assignment and answers to the Part 2 critical thinking questions in the format specified by your instructor.

Part 2: ✺ You made several decisions while creating the flyer in this assignment: where to place text, how to format the text (with font, font size, paragraph alignment, underlines, italics, bold, color, etc.) and which page enhancements to add (such as borders and spacing). What was the rationale behind each of these decisions? How did you decide if you had the legal right to use the graphic? How would you recommend distributing this flyer?

2 Publishing a Trifold Brochure

Objectives

After completing this module, you will be able to:

- Discuss advantages of the brochure medium
- Copy and paste with paste options
- Wordwrap text
- Swap pictures using the scratch area
- Use a picture as a background
- Insert and format a shape
- Use stylistic sets
- Edit a form
- Create a transparent text box
- Reset a picture and apply a picture style
- Edit captions and caption styles
- Check the spelling of the entire publication
- Use the Design Checker
- Choose appropriate printing services, paper, and color libraries
- Package a publication for a printing service

Introduction

Whether you want to advertise a service, an event, or a product or merely want to inform the public about a current topic of interest, you might choose a brochure as your promotional publication. A **brochure**, or pamphlet, usually is a high-quality publication with lots of color and graphics, created for advertising purposes. Businesses that may not be able to reach potential clientele effectively through traditional advertising, such as web, newspapers, and radio, can create a long-lasting advertisement with a well-designed brochure.

Brochures come in all shapes and sizes. Colleges and universities produce brochures about their programs. The travel industry uses brochures to entice tourists. Service industries and manufacturers display their products using this visual, hands-on medium.

Project: Museum Brochure

The project in this module shows you how to build the two-page, trifold brochure shown in Figure 2–1. The brochure informs potential visitors about an antique toy museum. Each side of the brochure has three panels. Page 1 (Figure 2–1a) contains the front and back panels, as well as the inside fold. Page 2 (Figure 2–1b) contains a three-panel display that, when opened completely, provides the reader with more details about the museum and a response form.

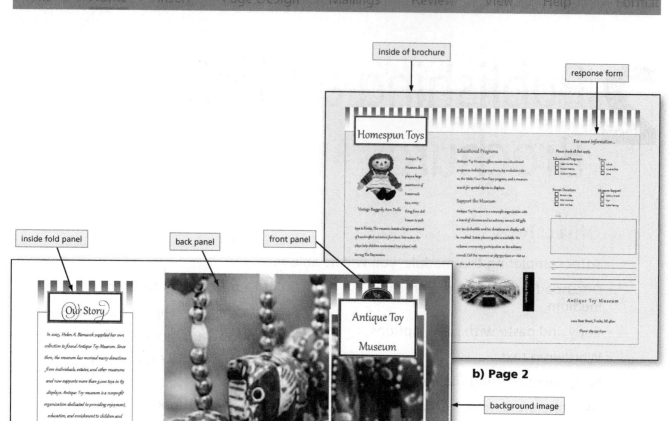

Figure 2–1

BTW

Gatefolds

A gatefold is a four-panel brochure where both ends fold toward the center. Gatefolds, also called foldouts, commonly are used in advertising, for menus, or as inserts in magazines.

On page 1, the front panel contains shapes, text boxes, a graphic, and a background designed to draw the reader's attention and inform the reader of the intent of the brochure. The back panel, which appears in the middle of page 1, contains the name of the museum, the address, phone numbers, and web address. The inside fold, on the left, contains a stylistic heading and information about the museum.

The three inside panels on page 2 contain more information about the museum and a form the reader may use to request more information.

You will perform the following general tasks as you progress through this module:

1. Customize the brochure template options, including color scheme and font scheme.
2. Edit template text and objects.
3. Swap pictures and use picture backgrounds.
4. Create picture styles and shapes.
5. Use stylistic sets to enhance brochure text.
6. Create text box transparency and insert captions.
7. Check the publication for errors.
8. Pack the publication for a printing service.

The Brochure Medium

Professionals commonly print brochures on special paper to provide long-lasting documents and to enhance the graphics. The brochure medium intentionally is tactile. Brochures are meant to be touched, carried home, passed along, and looked at, again and again. Newspapers and flyers usually have short-term readership and are printed on paper that readers throw away or recycle. Brochures, on the other hand, frequently use a heavier stock of paper so that they can stand better in a display rack.

CONSIDER THIS

How do you decide on the purpose, shelf life, and layout of a brochure?
Spend time brainstorming ideas for the brochure. Think about why you want to create one. Decide on the purpose of the brochure. Is it to inform, sell, attract, or advertise an event? Adjust your template, fonts, colors, and graphics to suit that purpose. Brochures commonly have a wider audience than flyers. They need to last longer, so carefully consider whether to add dated material or prices. Create a timeline of effectiveness and plan to have the brochure ready far in advance. Decide how many panels your brochure should have and how often you are going to produce it. If you are working for someone, draw a storyboard and get it approved before you begin actually creating the brochure. Think about alignment of objects, proximity of similar data, contrast, and repetition.

The content of a brochure needs to last longer, too. On occasion, the intent of a brochure is to educate, as would be the case with a brochure on health issues in a doctor's office. More commonly, though, the intent is to market a product or sell a service. Prices and dated materials that are subject to frequent change affect the usable life of a brochure.

Typically, brochures use a great deal of color, and they include actual photos instead of drawings or clip art. Photos give a sense of realism to a publication and show people, places, or objects that are real, whereas images or drawings more appropriately are used to convey concepts or ideas.

Brochures, designed to be in circulation for longer periods as a type of advertising, ordinarily are published in greater quantities and on more expensive paper than are other single-page publications, so they can be more costly. The cost, however, is less prohibitive when brochures are produced **in-house** using desktop publishing software rather than hiring an outside service. The cost per copy is lower when producing brochures in mass quantities.

BTW
How Brochures Differ
Each brochure template produces two pages of graphics, business information text boxes, and story boxes. Brochures are differentiated by the look and feel of the front panel, the location and style of the shapes and graphics, the design of any panel dividers, and the specific kind of decorations unique to each publication set.

BTW
Color Scheme
Choose a color scheme that is consistent with your company, client, or purpose. Do you need color, or will black and white be better? Think about the plan for printing and the number of copies in order to select a manageable color scheme. Remember that you can add more visual interest and contrast by bolding the text in the scheme; however, keep in mind that too many colors can detract from the brochure and make it difficult to read.

BTW
Brochures
Brochures commonly have a wider audience than flyers. They need to last longer. Carefully consider whether to add dated material or prices. Create a timeline of effectiveness and plan to have a brochure ready far in advance.

Table 2–1 lists some benefits and advantages of using the brochure medium.

Table 2–1 Benefits and Advantages of Using the Brochure Medium	
Exposure	An attention-getter in displays
	A take-along document encouraging second looks
	A long-lasting publication due to paper and content
	An easily distributed publication — mass mailings, advertising sites
Information	An in-depth look at a product or service
	An opportunity to inform in a nonrestrictive environment
	An opportunity for focused feedback using forms
Audience	Interested clientele and potential customers
Communication	An effective medium to highlight products and services
	A source of free information to build credibility
	An easier method to disseminate information than a magazine

Creating a Trifold Brochure

Publisher-supplied templates use proven design strategies and combinations of objects, which are placed to attract attention and disseminate information effectively. The options for brochures differ from those of other publications in that they include various page sizes, special kinds of forms, and panel/page layout options.

Making Choices about Brochure Options

For the museum brochure publication, you will use an informational brochure template and make changes to its color scheme, font scheme, page size, and forms. When choosing a template, **page size** refers to the number of panels in the brochure. Form options, which appear on page 2 of the brochure, include an order form, response form, and sign-up form, or no form at all. The **response form** displays check box choices for up to four multiple-choice questions and a comment section. The response form is meant to be detached as a turnaround document.

To Select a Brochure Template

The following steps select the Simple Divider brochure template. *Why? You should use a template until you are more experienced in designing brochures.*

- Start Publisher and then click BUILT-IN to display the built-in templates.
- Click Brochures and then click Marquee in the More Installed Templates Informational section to select the template.
- Click the Color scheme button and then select the Redwood color scheme.
- Click the Font scheme button and select the Calligraphy font scheme.
- Click the Page size button in the Options area and then, if necessary, click 3-panel to choose the number of panels. If necessary, click to remove the check mark in the 'Include customer address' check box.
- If necessary, scroll down and then click the Form button in the Options area. Click Response form to choose the type of form (Figure 2–2).

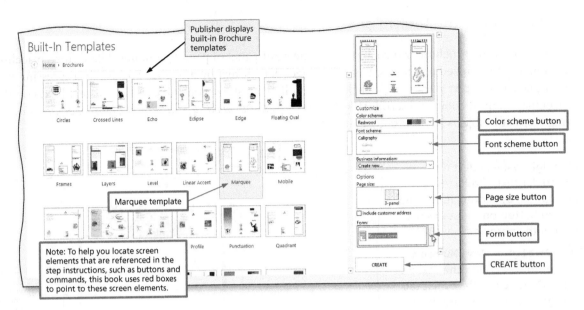

Figure 2–2

2

- Click the CREATE button to create the publication using the selected template and options (Figure 2–3).

Q&A What if I change my mind about the brochure options?

You can choose a different template by using the Change Template button (Page Design tab | Template group) or change the color and fonts schemes using buttons in the Schemes group on the Page Design tab.

3

- Save the publication on your hard drive, OneDrive, or other storage location using the file name, SC_PUB_2_MuseumBrochure.

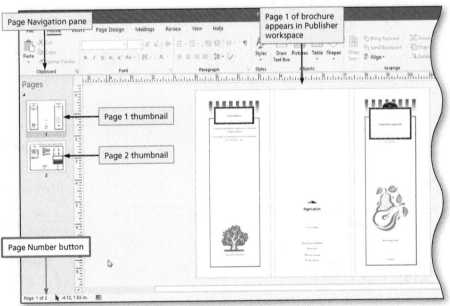

Figure 2–3

To Open and Maximize the Page Navigation Pane

The following step opens the Page Navigation pane to display both pages of the brochure.

1 If the Page Navigation pane is not open, click the Page Number button on the status bar to open the Page Navigation pane. If the Page Navigation pane is minimized, point to the upper-right corner and then click the 'Expand Page Navigation Pane' button to maximize it.

BTW
Touch Mode
Differences
The Office and Windows interfaces may vary if you are using Touch mode. For this reason, you might notice that the function or appearance of your touch screen differs slightly from this module's presentation.

To Edit Objects in the Right Panel

The front of the brochure, which appears in the right panel of page 1, contains default text, placeholder text, and some synchronized text boxes. You must select default text by dragging through it or pressing CTRL+A. You select placeholder text with a single click. In the following steps, you will edit various text boxes on the front panel. You may want to zoom and scroll. *Why? It may be easier to make careful edits at higher magnifications.* The following steps edit objects in the right panel.

1

- In the right panel, select the placeholder text, Product/Service Information, by clicking it. Use the Zoom In button on the status bar to zoom to approximately 130%.

- Type **Antique Toy Museum** to enter the text. Click the Text Fit button (Text Box Tools Format tab | Text group) and then click Best Fit.

- If Publisher displays a Business Name text box below the Antique Toy Museum text box, delete it (Figure 2–4).

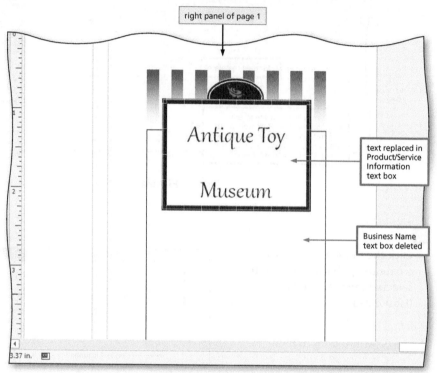

Figure 2–4

2

- Scroll to the lower portion of the right panel and select the Business Tagline or Motto text.

- Type **Where everyone is a kid!** to enter the text.

- Use the Text Fit button (Text Box Tools Format tab | Text group) and the Best Fit command to autofit the text (Figure 2–5).

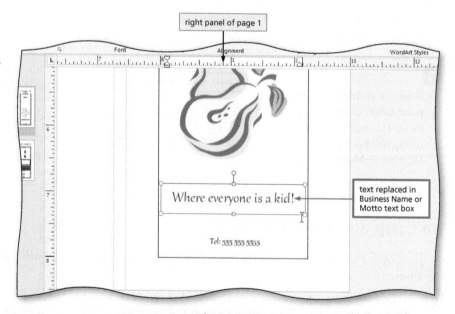

Figure 2–5

To Edit More Text

The following steps edit the telephone number placeholder text.

1 Click the telephone placeholder text to select it. Type **www.toymuseum.org** to replace the text. Use the Text Fit button (Text Box Tools Format tab | Text group) to autofit the text.

2 When Publisher capitalizes the first letter of the web address, point to the W and then click the AutoCorrect Options button. Click 'Undo Automatic Capitalization' on the AutoCorrect options menu (Figure 2–6).

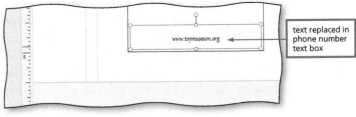

Figure 2–6

To Edit Text in the Middle Panel

When the brochure is folded, the middle panel will appear on the back of the trifold brochure. It contains text boxes for the business address, phone numbers, and email address. The following steps edit the text in the middle panel. As you will see later in the module, because these text boxes are synchronized, editing them also will edit corresponding text boxes on page 2.

1 Scroll as necessary to display the lower portion of the middle panel.

2 Delete the organization logo.

3 Change the Business Name to **Antique Toy Museum** and then use the Text Fit button (Text Box Tools Format tab | Text group) to autofit the text.

4 Drag to select all of the text in the Primary Business Address text box. Do not delete the text. Type **2020 State Street Freelin, MI 48011** to replace the address.

5 Drag to select the phone and fax numbers and the email address text. Do not delete the text. Type **Phone 589-555-6400** to replace the selected text (Figure 2–7).

Experiment

- Click the Page 2 thumbnail in the Page Navigation pane. Verify that synchronization has placed the business name and address in the lower portion of the right panel. When you are finished, click the Page 1 thumbnail in the Page Navigation pane.

BTW
Smart Tags
The AutoCorrect Options button and the Paste Options button are smart tags. Smart tags appear when Publisher has options it can present, such as the Information button that appears as an lowercase i.

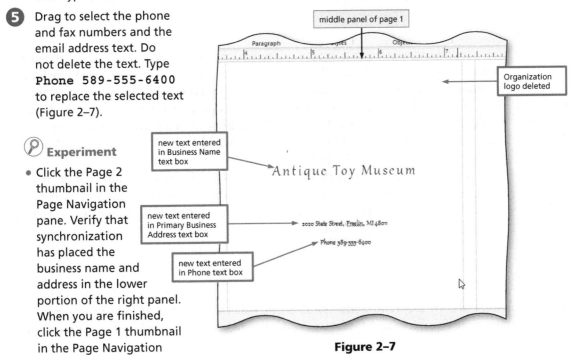

Figure 2–7

Copying, Cutting, and Pasting

In each of the Office 2019 applications, you can store or copy text and objects for later use. The **Office Clipboard** is a temporary storage area that holds up to 24 items (text or graphics) copied from any Office program. The Office Clipboard is different from the **Windows Clipboard** associated with the operating system, which can contain only one item at a time. **Copying** is the process of placing an item on the Office Clipboard; the item also remains in the publication. **Cutting**, by contrast, removes the item from the publication before placing it on the Office Clipboard. The copy and cut functions transfer text or objects to the Windows Clipboard as well as to the Office Clipboard. Cutting is different from deleting. Deleted items are not placed on either clipboard. **Pasting** is the process of copying an item from the Office Clipboard into the publication at the location of the insertion point or selection.

Table 2–2 describes various methods to copy, cut, paste, and delete selected text.

Table 2–2 Copy, Cut, Paste, and Delete

Method	Copy	Cut	Paste	Delete
Shortcut menu	Right-click to display the shortcut menu and then click Copy	Right-click to display the shortcut menu and then click Cut	Right-click to display the shortcut menu and then click Paste	Right-click to display the shortcut menu and then click Delete Text
Ribbon	Click the Copy button (Home tab | Clipboard group)	Click the Cut button (Home tab | Clipboard group)	Click the Paste button (Home tab | Clipboard group)	Not available
Keyboard	Press CTRL+C	Press CTRL+X	Press CTRL+V	Press DELETE or BACKSPACE

In Publisher, you can copy, cut, paste, and delete objects as well as text. If you are copying text, it is advisable to select from the beginning letter of the text and include any ending spaces, tabs, punctuation, or paragraph marks. That way, when you cut or paste, the text will be spaced properly. If you are copying, cutting, pasting, and deleting an object, the object must first be selected. Publisher normally pastes objects from either the Windows Clipboard or the Office Clipboard into the center of the displayed page layout if no object is selected.

The next step in editing the brochure is to include the web address at the bottom of the center panel. One way to enter this information in the brochure is to type it. Because you already typed this information on the right panel, a timesaving alternative would be to copy and paste the text.

To Copy and Paste

In the brochure, you want to copy the website address from one panel to the other. *Why? Copying and pasting reduces errors that might result from retyping information.* The following steps copy and paste the web address.

1

- Scroll until the lower portion of both the right and middle panels are visible.

- Click the web address text box to select it.

- Drag through the text to be copied (the web address in this case).

- Click the Copy button (Home tab | Clipboard group) to copy the selected item in the publication to the Office Clipboard (Figure 2–8).

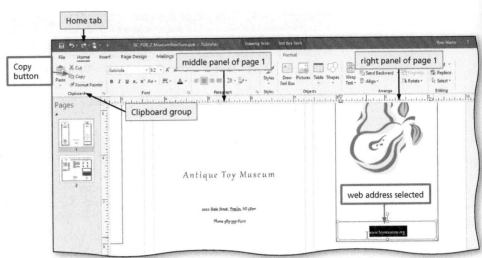

Figure 2–8

2

- Click the phone number text box at the bottom of the center panel and position the insertion point at the end of the phone number. Press ENTER to create a blank line below the phone number text.

- Click the Paste button (Home tab | Clipboard group) to paste the copied item into the text box. Do not press any other keys (Figure 2–9).

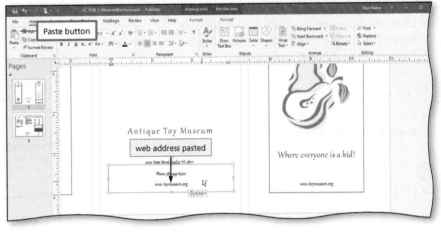

Figure 2–9

Other Ways
1. Right-click selected item, click Copy on shortcut menu, right-click where item is to be pasted, click desired formatting in Paste Options area on shortcut menu
2. Select item, press CTRL+C, position insertion point at paste location, press CTRL+V

Paste Options Button

After you paste, Publisher may display the Paste Options button. Clicking the **Paste Options button** displays the Paste Options menu, which contains buttons representing formatting choices. They also appear when you click the Paste arrow (Home tab | Clipboard group). Table 2–3 describes some of the Paste options when pasting text. Depending on the contents of the Clipboard, you may see different buttons with advanced options for pasting, especially when cutting and pasting graphics.

BTW

Automatic Saving
Publisher can save your publication for you at regular intervals. In Backstage view, click Options and then click Save in the left pane (Publisher Options dialog box). Select the 'Save AutoRecover information every 10 minutes' check box. In the minutes box, specify how often you want Publisher to save files. Do not, however, use AutoRecover as a substitute for regularly saving your work.

Table 2–3 Text Paste Options		
Button	**Option**	**Result**
(Ctrl) ▾	Paste	Pastes the copied content *as is*, without any formatting changes
	'Keep Source Formatting'	Keeps the formatting of the text you copied
	Merge Formatting	Changes the formatting so that it matches the text around it
	'Keep Text Only'	Pastes the copied text as plain unformatted text and removes any styles or hyperlinks

To Select a Paste Option

The following steps select the 'Keep Text Only' paste option. ***Why?*** *The web address should match the font style in the right panel.*

1

- Click the Paste Options button that appears below the pasted information to display the Paste Options menu (Figure 2–10).

 Experiment

- Point to each of the Paste Options buttons to see their ScreenTips.

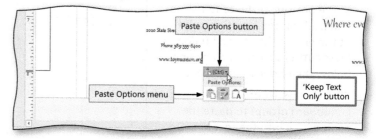

Figure 2–10

2

- Click the 'Keep Text Only' button to paste using the destination formatting (Figure 2–11).

 What does it mean to paste using the destination formatting?

The copied text will be formatted identically to the text in the paste location, including font, font effect, and font size.

Can I change my mind and choose a different paste option?

Yes, you can choose a different paste option — but only before you type anything else. Otherwise, you have to delete and paste again.

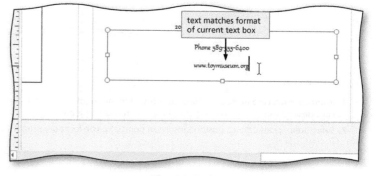

Figure 2–11

Other Ways

1. After pasting, press CTRL to display paste options, click desired paste option
2. Click Paste arrow (Home tab | Clipboard group), click Paste Options button
3. Click Paste Options button on shortcut menu

Typing Paragraphs of Text

When you type paragraphs of text, you will use Publisher's wordwrap feature. Wordwrap allows you to type words in a text box continually without pressing ENTER at the end of each line. When the insertion point reaches the right margin of a text box, Publisher automatically positions the insertion point at the beginning of the next line. As you type, if a word extends beyond the right margin, Publisher automatically positions that word on the next line or hyphenates the word and moves the insertion point.

CONSIDER THIS

How do you decide on a brochure's content?
Gather all the information, such as stories, graphics, logos, colors, shapes, style information, and watermarks. Save copies or versions along the way. If you have to create objects from scratch, have someone else evaluate your work and give you constructive feedback. If you are using forms in your brochure, verify the manner in which the viewer will return the form. Check and double-check all prices, addresses, and phone numbers.

Each time you press ENTER, Publisher inserts a **hard return**, which creates a new paragraph. Thus, as you type text in a text box, do not press ENTER when the insertion point reaches the right margin. Instead, press ENTER only in these circumstances:

- To insert blank lines in a text box
- To begin a new paragraph
- To terminate a short line of text and advance to the next line
- To respond to questions or prompts in Publisher dialog boxes, panes, and other on-screen objects

To view where in a publication you pressed ENTER or SPACEBAR, you may find it helpful to display formatting marks. A **formatting mark**, sometimes called a **nonprinting character**, is a character that appears on screen to indicate the end of a paragraph, a tab, or some other formatting element. Formatting marks appear on the screen, but do not print. For example, the paragraph mark (¶) is a formatting mark that indicates where you pressed ENTER. A raised dot (·) appears where you pressed SPACEBAR. An end-of-field marker (¤) is displayed to indicate the end of text in a text box. Other formatting marks are discussed as they appear on the screen.

To Edit Heading Text in the Left Panel

The left panel appears when the brochure is first opened. It contains text boxes for a heading and summary text. The following steps edit the heading text.

1. Scroll to the top of the left panel on page 1.
2. In the left panel, click to select the Back Panel Heading placeholder text and then type `Our Story` to replace the text.
3. Best fit the text (Figure 2–12).

BTW
Organizing Files and Folders
You should organize and store files in folders so that you easily can find the files later. For example, if you were taking an introductory computer class called CIS 101, a good practice would be to save all Publisher files in a Publisher folder in a CIS 101 folder.

BTW
Brochure Features
Many brochures incorporate newspaper features, such as columns and a masthead, and add eye appeal with logos, sidebars, shapes, and graphics. Small brochures typically have folded panels. Larger brochures resemble small magazines, with multiple pages and stapled bindings.

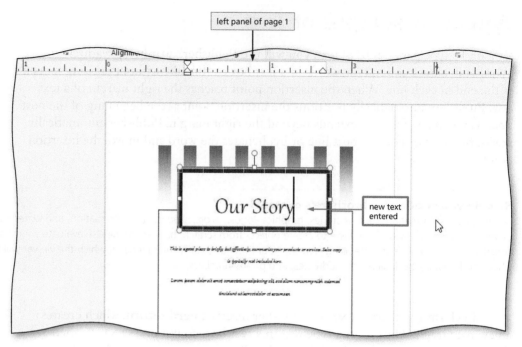

Figure 2–12

To Display Formatting Marks

The following step displays formatting marks, if they do not show already on the screen. *Why? The formatting marks help you see where you pressed ENTER and SPACEBAR, among other actions.*

1

- If it is not selected already, click the Special Characters button (Home tab | Paragraph group) to display formatting marks (Figure 2–13).

 What if I do not want formatting marks to show on the screen?
If you feel the formatting marks clutter the screen, you can hide them by clicking the Special Characters button again. The figures presented in the rest of this module show the formatting marks.

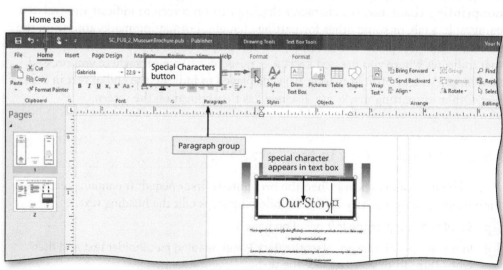

Figure 2–13

Other Ways

1. Press CTRL+SHIFT+Y

To Edit the Font Size

Using Best Fit to autofit text increases or decreases the font size to fit the text box. The **font size** is the size of characters, measured in units called points. The Best Fit option may create many different font sizes in the publication. Design professional recommend a maximum of three or four font sizes per publication and a minimum font size of 10 for regular text. *Why? While there are no hard-and-fast rules, using just a few font sizes keeps the publication from looking too busy or chaotic; a font size of 10 maximizes the readability in print publications for most people.*

The following steps change the font size of text in the middle panel.

1

- In the left panel, select the text below the Our Story heading and zoom to 200%.

- Click the Font Size arrow (Home tab | Font group) to display the Font Size gallery (Figure 2–14).

Q&A Could I use the Font Size arrow on the Text Box Tools tab?
Yes, both Font Size arrows work the same.

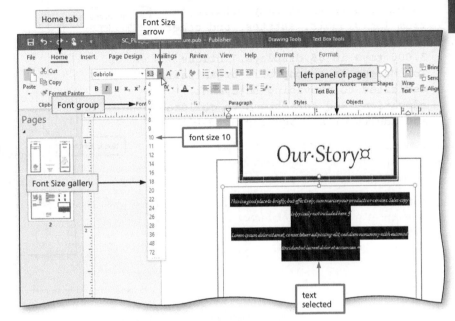

Figure 2–14

2

- Click 10 in the list to change the font size (Figure 2–15).

Q&A Could I use the Best Fit option?
You could; however, to reduce the number of font sizes in the publication overall, choosing a font size from the Font Size gallery is better in this case.

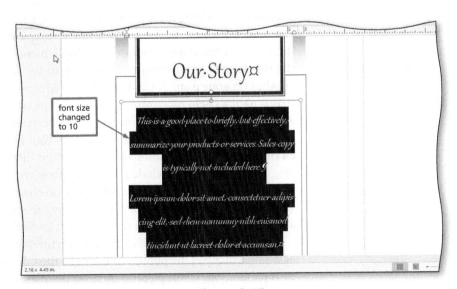

Figure 2–15

Other Ways

1. Select text, click Font Size arrow on Mini toolbar, click desired font size

2. Select text, press CTRL+SHIFT+> or CTRL+SHIFT+<

To Wordwrap Text as You Type

The next step in creating the brochure is to type the text in the left panel. The following step wordwraps the text in the text box. **Why?** *Using wordwrap ensures consistent margins.*

1

- With the text below the heading, Our Story, still selected, type **In 2005, Helen A. Bismarck supplied her own collection to found Antique Toy Museum. Since then, the museum has received many donations from individuals, estates, and other museums and now supports more than 3,000 toys in 65 displays. Antique Toy Museum is a nonprofit organization dedicated to providing enjoyment, education, and enrichment to children and adults of all ages.** (Figure 2–16).

Why isn't the left margin aligned?
The template text was centered, so your replacement text also is centered.

Why does my publication wrap on different words?
Differences in wordwrap relate to your printer. It is possible that the same publication could wordwrap differently if printed on different printers.

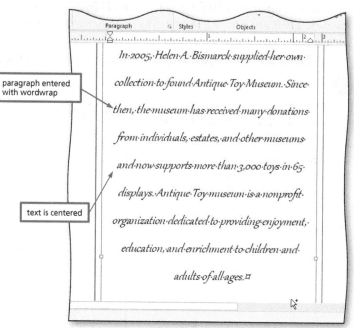

Figure 2–16

Swapping Pictures

BTW
The Ribbon and Screen Resolution
Publisher may change how the groups and buttons within the groups appear on the ribbon, depending on the computer's screen resolution. Thus, your ribbon may look different from the ones in this book if you are using a screen resolution other than 1366 × 768.

In Publisher 2019, you can use the scratch area to manipulate and swap pictures. The scratch area is the gray area that appears outside the publication page. It is used as a temporary holding area; if you are not sure where you want to move an item, you can drag it to the scratch area. When inserting a single picture, you can drag it to the scratch area. When you insert multiple pictures at one time, Publisher arranges the thumbnails or puts them in a column in the scratch area, instead of on top of one another on your page. A **thumbnail** is a reduced-size version of a larger graphic image that is used to help recognize and organize pictures and to save space. If pictures or graphics have been inserted individually into your publication, you can use Publisher's **Arrange Thumbnails** command (Picture Tool Format tab | Arrange group) to reduce all of the pictures to thumbnail size and align them in rows and columns.

Many templates include picture placeholders, each with a picture icon. After the placeholder is replaced with a picture, the icon changes to a **swap icon**. Pictures in the scratch area also have swap icons. You can drag the swap icon to swap pictures with one another, or you can right-click the swap icon to display a shortcut menu with more options.

After you save the publication, the pictures in the scratch area will still be there the next time you open the publication. Unlike the Clipboard, the scratch area is saved with each publication. While pictures increase the file size, the scratch area does not print and contains the same items, regardless of which page of the publication is displayed.

To Insert Multiple Pictures

The following steps insert multiple pictures. **Why?** *Selecting and placing multiple pictures in the scratch area allows you to see what different pictures might look like in the publication.* To complete these steps, you will need to use the photos located in the Data Files. Please contact your instructor for information about accessing the Data Files.

1

- On the status bar, click the 'Show Whole Page' button to display the entire page.
- Click Insert on the ribbon to display the Insert tab.
- Click the Pictures button (Insert tab | Illustrations group) to display the Insert Picture dialog box.
- Navigate to the Data Files.
- One at a time, CTRL+click the files, Support_PUB_2_Mobile.tif, Support_PUB_2_RockingHorse.png, Support_PUB_2_Doll.png, and Support_PUB_2_DisplayRoom.tif to select the four pictures (Figure 2–17).

Q&A Why do I have to use the CTRL key?
CTRL+clicking allows you to select multiple items at once rather than selecting them one at a time.

My file list looks different than the one shown here. Did I do something wrong?
No. Your window probably is set for a different view. Right-click the window, point to View on the shortcut menu, and then click Large icons on the View submenu to match the figures in this book. You may want to enlarge your dialog box by dragging one of its borders.

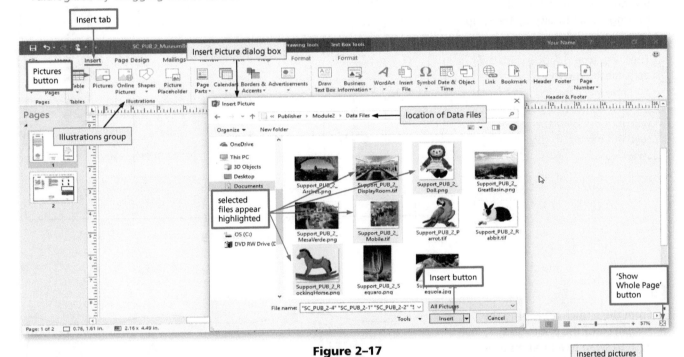

Figure 2–17

2

- Click the Insert button (Insert Picture dialog box) to place the pictures in the scratch area (Figure 2–18).

Q&A My picture appears in the middle of the publication rather than in the scratch area. What did I do wrong?
If you choose just one picture, it is displayed in the middle of the publication. If you select multiple pictures, they appear in the scratch area. You can drag your picture to the scratch area, if necessary.

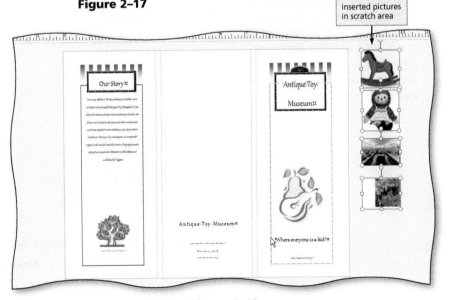

Figure 2–18

To Swap Pictures

When you decide to swap one picture for another, you drag the new picture toward the old picture. When Publisher displays a pink boundary, release the mouse button (or lift your finger away from the screen if you are using touch gestures). When swapping pictures, it is a good idea to swap those that have the same orientation. ***Why?*** *Pictures with the same orientation as the template fit the area better and are not scaled disproportionately.* **Portrait** orientation pictures are taller than they are wide; **landscape** orientation pictures are wider than they are tall. The following steps swap the pictures from the scratch area with the template graphics in the brochure.

1

- Click the scratch area away from the pictures to deselect them.

- In the scratch area, click the photo you wish to use in the brochure (in this case, the picture of the rocking horse) to display the swap icon (Figure 2–19).

Q&A | The swap icon disappeared. Did I do something wrong?
You may have moved the pointer away from the picture. Move the pointer back over the top of the selected picture to display the swap icon.

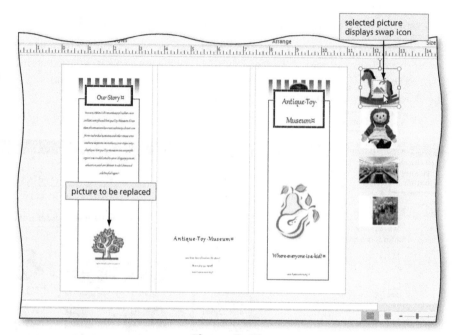

Figure 2–19

2

- From the scratch area, drag the swap icon of the photo you wish to swap to a location over a current graphic on the page. (In this case, drag the picture of the rocking horse to a location over the tree graphic in the left panel.) Do not release the mouse button (Figure 2–20).

Figure 2–20

3

- When the pink boundary is displayed, release the mouse button to swap the pictures (Figure 2–21).

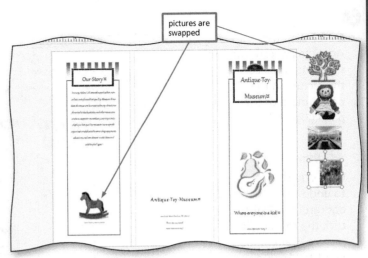

Figure 2–21

Other Ways

1. Select two pictures, click Swap button (Picture Tools Format tab | Swap group)

To Use a Picture as a Background

Many brochures use pictures in the background. **Why?** *A picture adds interest and removes the stark white color around objects in the brochure.* In this brochure, you will apply a picture to the background, using a picture from the scratch area and the shortcut menu. The following steps apply a picture to the background of page 1 of the brochure.

1

- Right-click the picture you wish to use as a background (in this case, the toy mobile picture) to display the shortcut menu.

- Point to 'Apply to Background' on the shortcut menu to display the Apply to Background submenu (Figure 2–22).

Q&A

Will the picture become the background on page 2 as well as on page 1?

No, not unless you navigate to page 2 and apply it there. Each page of a publication has a unique background area.

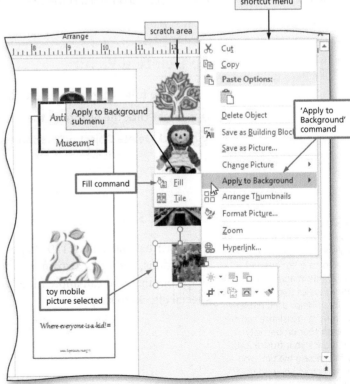

Figure 2–22

2

• Click Fill on the Apply to Background submenu to place the picture in the background of the page (Figure 2–23).

Experiment

• Press CTRL+Z to undo the background. Right-click the toy mobile picture again, point to 'Apply to Background', and then click Tile to view the differences between Fill and Tile. When you are finished, perform Steps 1 and 2 again.

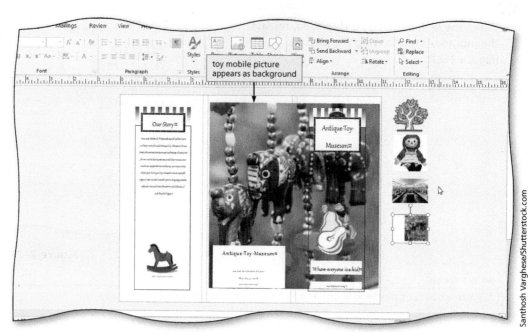

toy mobile picture appears as background

Santhosh Varghese/Shutterstock.com

Figure 2–23

Other Ways

1. Click Background button (Page Design tab | Page Background group), click More Backgrounds in Background gallery, click 'Picture or texture fill' (Format Background dialog box), click File button, navigate to picture, double-click picture, click OK

To Delete a Picture

The following steps delete the picture from the right panel on page 1.

1 Right-click the picture of the pears in the right panel.

2 Click Delete Object on the shortcut menu (shown in Figure 2–22).

Shapes

Publisher has more than 150 shapes that you can use to create logos, graphics, banners, illustrations, and other ornamental objects. You can change the color and weight of shape outlines and can apply fill effects, shadows, reflections, glows, pictures, and other special effects to shapes.

To Insert a Shape

The following steps insert a shape in the lower portion of the middle panel of page 1. *Why? The rectangle will serve as a kind of border to match the borders on the right and left panels.*

- Make sure no text or objects are selected and then display the Insert tab.

- Click the Shapes button (Insert tab | Illustrations group) to display the Shapes gallery (Figure 2–24).

Q&A Why is my gallery different?
Publisher displays the most recently used shapes at the top of the gallery. The recently used shapes on your computer may differ.

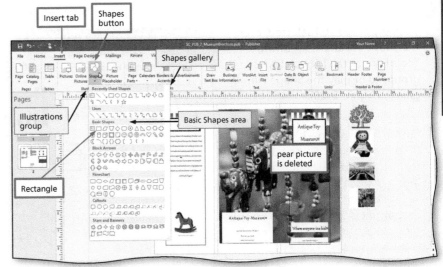

Figure 2–24

- Click the desired shape button (in this case, Rectangle) in the Basic Shapes area to select it.

- Move the pointer into the workspace. Drag to draw a rectangle covering the three text boxes at the bottom of the middle panel (Figure 2–25).

Q&A Why did the rectangle fill with brown?
Brown is the default shape color assigned by the color scheme.

Figure 2–25

Other Ways

1. Click More button (Drawing Tools Format tab | Insert Shapes group), click the desired shape button in gallery, draw rectangle

Santhosh Varghese/Shutterstock.com

To Edit the Shape Fill

The following steps remove the fill color of the shape. *Why? Removing the fill will allow the text to show through.*

1

- With the shape still selected, click the Shape Fill arrow (Drawing Tools Format tab | Shape Styles group) to display the Shape Fill gallery (Figure 2–26).

Q&A Is there a difference between the button and its arrow?
In some cases, yes. Some buttons, such as the Shape Fill button, have both buttons and arrows. When you click the button, the current formatting is applied; when you click the accompanying arrow, Publisher displays a gallery.

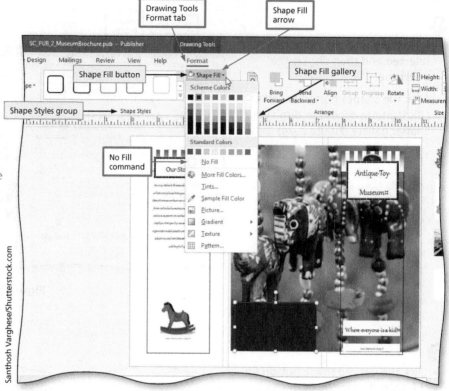

Figure 2–26

2

- Click No Fill in the Shape Fill gallery to remove the fill color (Figure 2–27).

Q&A Is removing the fill color the same as changing it to white?
No. The No Fill command makes the shape transparent; a white fill color would eclipse the text behind it.

Figure 2–27

To Edit the Shape Outline

The following steps change the shape outline color and pattern of the rectangle. *Why? Matching the color and style of the other shapes on page 1 will provide consistency.*

1

- With the shape still selected, click the Shape Outline arrow (Drawing Tools Format tab | Shape Styles group) to display the Shape Outline gallery (Figure 2–28).

🔍 **Experiment**

- Point to different commands in the Shape Outline gallery and look at the choices they offer.

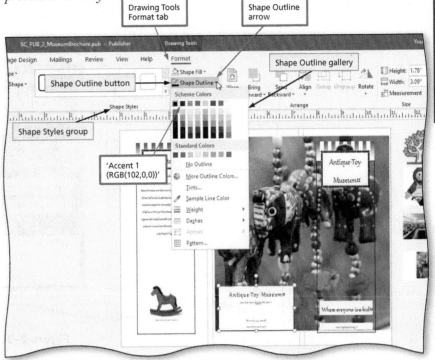

Figure 2–28

2

- Click 'Accent 1 (RGB(102,0,0))' in the Scheme Colors area in the gallery to change the shape color.

- With the shape still selected, click the Shape Outline arrow (Drawing Tools Format tab | Shape Styles group) again.

- Point to Weight to display the Weight gallery (Figure 2–29).

Q&A What is the purpose of the More Lines command?
The command opens the Format Object dialog box, where you can edit the transparency and width and add special effects, such as shadows and bevels, to the shape.

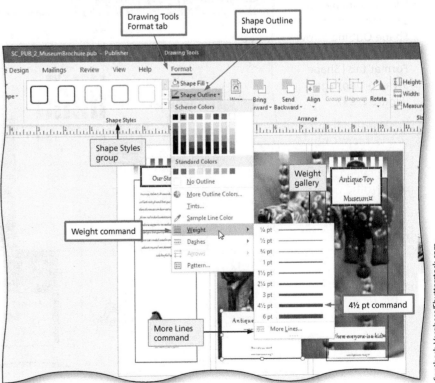

Figure 2–29

3

• Click 4½ pt to select a heavier line (Figure 2–30).

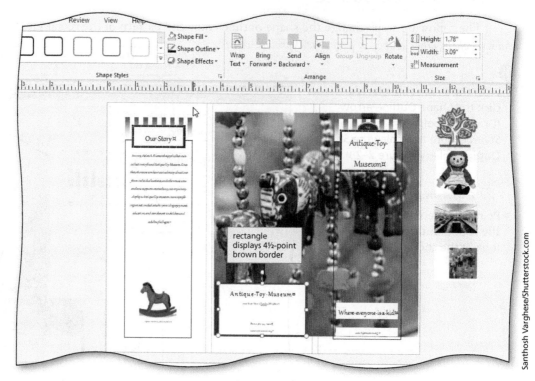

rectangle displays 4½-point brown border

Figure 2–30

4

• With the shape still selected, click the Shape Outline arrow (Drawing Tools Format tab | Shape Styles group) again (Figure 2–31).

Q&A What is the purpose of the 'More Outline Colors' command? The command displays the Color dialog box, where you can fine-tune the colors with standardized colors, a color wheel, or specialized color systems.

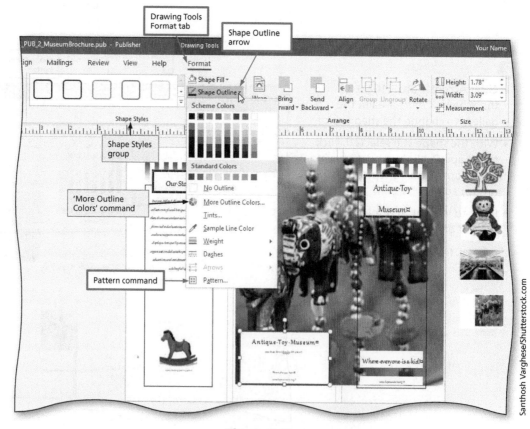

Drawing Tools Format tab

Shape Outline arrow

Shape Styles group

'More Outline Colors' command

Pattern command

Figure 2–31

Santhosh Varghese/Shutterstock.com

- Click Pattern to display the Patterned Lines dialog box.

- In the Pattern area, click the Dotted 90% pattern (Figure 2–32).

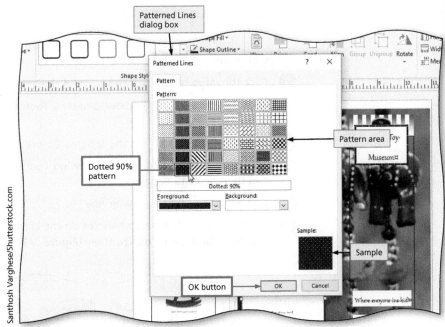

Figure 2–32

Santhosh Varghese/Shutterstock.com

6

- Click OK (Patterned Lines dialog box) to apply the outline. Do not deselect (Figure 2–33).

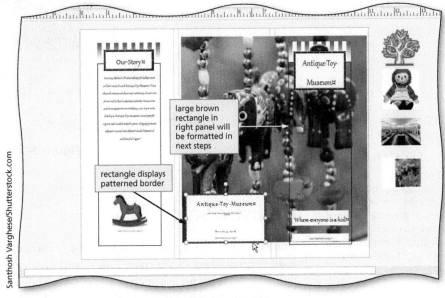

Figure 2–33

Santhosh Varghese/Shutterstock.com

Other Ways

1. To change fill color, click Shape Fill arrow on Mini toolbar, click desired color

2. To change fill color, right-click shape, click Format AutoShape on shortcut menu, click Color button in Fill area, click desired color

3. To change border color or weight, click Shape Outline arrow on Mini toolbar, click desired color

4. To change border color or weight, right-click shape, click Format AutoShape on shortcut menu, click Color arrow or click Width arrow, click choice

To Edit Another Shape

The following steps change the color and weight of the large brown rectangle in the right panel.

1 Click the large brown rectangle in the right panel.

2 Click the Shape Outline arrow (Drawing Tools Format tab | Shape Styles group) to display the gallery.

3 Click 'Accent 5 (White)' in the Scheme Colors area.

4 Click the Shape Outline arrow (Drawing Tools Format tab | Shape Styles group) again and then point to Weight.

5 Click 4½ pt to select a heavier line.

6 If necessary, use the sizing handles on the lower two text boxes to resize the boxes so that they fill the area horizontally (Figure 2–34).

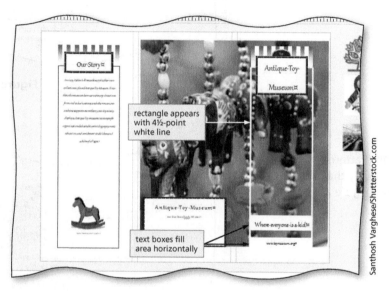

Figure 2–34

Stylistic Sets

Publisher includes a special kind of font feature called a stylistic set. A **stylistic set** is an organized set of alternate letters and glyphs that allow you to change a font's appearance. A **glyph** is a special stroke that appears in text that is not part of the normal font set. Diacritical marks, such as the umlaut (ä) or cedilla (ç), use glyphs.

Besides its regular display, almost every font has three common stylistic sets: bold, italic, and the combination of bold and italic. The letters are displayed in the same font but use a heavier or slanted glyph. Another example with which you may be familiar is a font family that has both serif and sans serif stylistic sets. A **serif** is small line, flourish, or embellishment that crosses the strokes of letters in some fonts. A **sans serif**, meaning without flourish, set has no extra embellishment at the end of characters. Other stylistic sets include alternatives for characters such as e, j, g, or y. The extra characters with accompanying glyphs have to be part of the font set when it is installed. On a typical Publisher installation, only a few font families contain complete stylistic sets. Some fonts, such as Gabriola, allow you to choose a **stylistic alternate** set, which creates a random pattern from among the various stylistic sets available for the current font.

BTW

Stylistic Alternate Sets

If you use a script font that looks like cursive writing, a stylistic alternate can simulate handwriting by using of a set of randomly chosen glyphs with slight differences in appearance.

BTW

Swashes

A swash is an exaggerated serif or glyph that typically runs into the space above or below the next letter. Some swashes can cause an unattractive appearance when used with adjacent descending letters, such as g, j, or y; however, when used correctly, a swash produces a flowing, linear appearance that adds interest to the font.

Typography refers to the art and practice of using specialized effects and fonts, including stylistic sets, drop caps, number styles, and glyphs. Ligatures, stylistic sets, swashes, and stylistic alternates, as well as some alphabetic characters that are not part of the English language, also are created with glyphs.

To Format with a Stylistic Set

The following steps choose a stylistic set for the heading in the left panel. *Why? Stylistic sets add interest and flair to headings.*

1

- Select the text, Our Story, at the top of the left panel.

- Click Text Box Tools Format on the ribbon to display the Text Box Tools Format tab.

- With the text selected, click the Stylistic Sets button (Text Box Tools Format tab | Typography group) to display the Stylistic Sets gallery.

- If necessary, scroll down in the gallery to view more sets (Figure 2–35).

Q&A Do all fonts have fancy stylistic sets?
No, usually only OpenType and scalable fonts contain stylistic sets other than bold and italic.

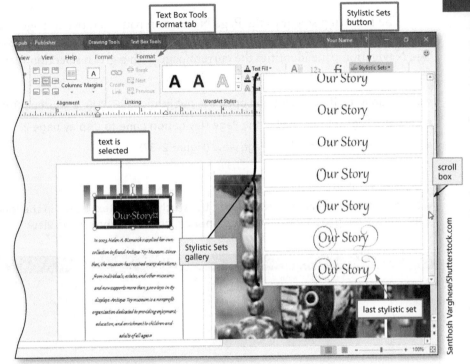

Figure 2–35

2

- Click the desired set (in this case, the last one, at the bottom) to apply the stylistic set to the selected text.

- Click outside the selection to view the formatting (Figure 2–36).

3

- Click the Save button on the Quick Access Toolbar to overwrite the previously saved file.

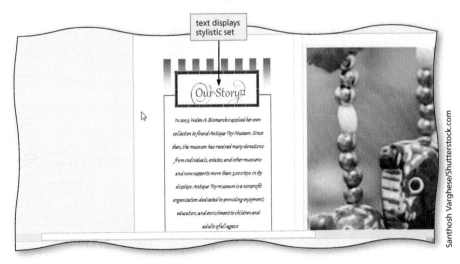

Figure 2–36

Break Point: If you want to take a break, this is a good place to do so. Exit Publisher. To resume later, start Publisher, open the file called SC_PUB_2_MuseumBrochure, and continue following the steps from this location forward.

BTW
OpenType Fonts
Stylistic sets are more common in OpenType fonts. An **OpenType** font is a cross-platform, scalable font format with a wider range of characters than TrueType or PostScript fonts.

Editing the Inside Panels of a Brochure

As you edit the inside panels of the brochure, you will change text, edit the form text boxes, and change the pictures and captions. Headings introduce information about the topic and describe specific products or services. Secondary headings and the stories below them organize topics to make it easier for readers to understand the information.

To Switch to Page 2

The following step uses the Page Navigation pane to move to page 2. *Why? Using the Page Navigation pane is the only way to move among pages by clicking; however, you can instead press F5 and enter the new page number.* The Page Navigation pane identifies the current page with a green selection rectangle.

- Start Publisher, if necessary, and open the publication, SC_PUB_2_MuseumBrochure.
- Click the Page 2 thumbnail in the Page Navigation pane to display page 2.
- If necessary, zoom to Whole Page view (Figure 2–37).

Experiment

- Zoom and scroll on page 2. Notice that the synchronized text boxes in the lower portion of the right panel reflect the edits from page 1. When you are finished, zoom to Whole Page view.

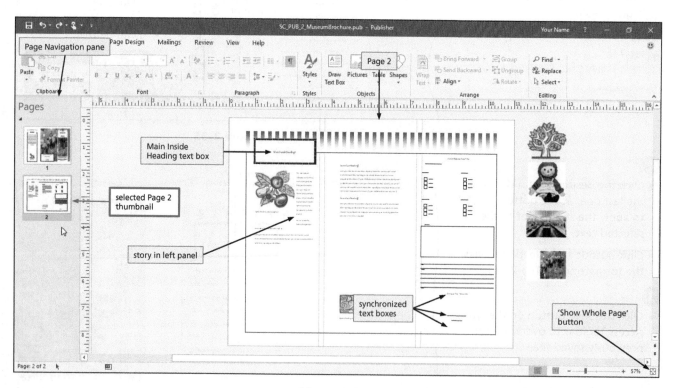

Figure 2–37

Other Ways

1. Press F5, enter page number, click OK

2. Click Next Page button or Previous Page button at bottom of vertical scroll bar

To Edit the Left Panel on Page 2

The following steps edit the text on the left panel of page 2. As you edit the text, zoom and scroll as necessary to view the text.

1 In the left panel of page 2, click the placeholder text in the 'Main Inside Heading' text box to select it.

2 Type `Homespun Toys` to complete the page heading. Use Best Fit to autofit the text.

3 Click the placeholder text for the story in the left panel. Change the font size to 10. Zoom as necessary as you type the story text.

4 Type `Antique Toy Museum displays a large assortment of homemade toys, everything from doll houses to pull-toys to blocks. The museum boasts a large assortment of handcrafted miniature furniture. Interactive displays help children understand toys played with during The Depression.` and then press ENTER to create the first paragraph.

Q&A In the last sentence, my system changed the T in The to lowercase. What should I do?
Point to the letter t. When Publisher displays the AutoCorrect Options button, click it and then click 'Undo Auto Capitalization'.

5 Type `There is something for all interests. The new Machine Room includes fire engines, trucks, tractors, trains, cars, cranes, and earth-moving toys. Our Pretty in Pink room includes dolls from around the world, along with complete toy kitchens.` and then press ENTER to create the second paragraph.

6 Type `Special group programs allow visitors to make toys to take home!` to complete the story (Figure 2–38).

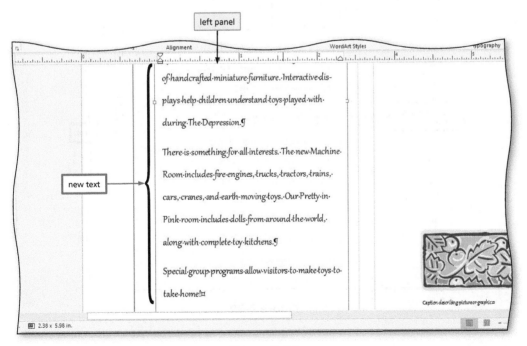

Figure 2–38

To Edit the Middle Panel on Page 2

The following steps edit the text in the middle panel of page 2. As you edit the text, zoom, and scroll as necessary to view the text.

1 In the middle panel of page 2, click the first instance of Secondary Heading placeholder text in the middle panel to select it. Change the font size to 14.

2 Type **Educational Programs** to complete the text.

3 Click the story below the heading to select the placeholder text. Change the font size to 10.

4 Type **Antique Toy Museum offers numerous educational programs, including group tours, toy evolution videos, the Make Your Own Toys program, and a museum search for special objects in displays.** to complete the story.

5 Click the second instance of Secondary Heading placeholder text on the middle panel to select it. Change the font size to 14.

6 Type **Support the Museum** to complete the text.

7 Click the story below the heading to select the placeholder text. Change the font size to 10.

8 Type **Antique Toy Museum is a nonprofit organization with a board of directors and an advisory council. All gifts are tax-deductible and toy donations on display will be credited. Estate planning also is available. We welcome community participation on the advisory council. Call the museum at 589-555-6400 or visit us on the web at www.toymuseum.org.** to complete the story (Figure 2–39).

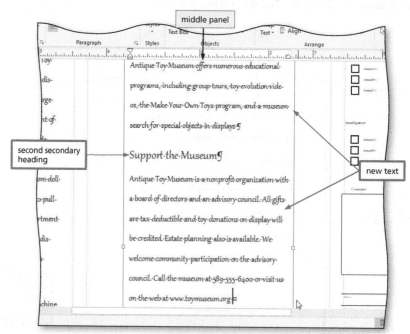

Figure 2–39

Edit Forms

Publisher forms consist of text boxes, graphic boxes, and lines positioned in an attractive and usable format. The check boxes consist of a graphic and a text box grouped together. A **grouped object** consists of more than one object linked together for logical reasons, such as the parts of a masthead or a picture with its caption.

Grouped objects are moved, edited, and formatted together as one. When necessary, grouped objects can be formatted individually by clicking a specific object after selecting the group. They can be ungrouped if you want to move or resize them independently. Alternatively, you can group individual objects if you want to keep them together.

To Edit the Form

A response form displays check box choices for up to four multiple-choice questions and a comment section. The following steps edit the form text boxes and the grouped check boxes in the right panel of page 2. *Why? You must customize the form for the brochure content.*

1

- On the right panel of page 2, click the text in the General Response Form Title text box to select the placeholder text.
- Click the Zoom In button on the status bar to zoom to approximately 230%.
- Change the font size to 14. Type **For more information...** to complete the text. If necessary, drag the lower center sizing handle down until the text is displayed completely.
- Click the instruction text box below the heading to select the placeholder text.
- Change the font size to 10. Type **Please check all that apply.** to finish entering the instruction text (Figure 2–40).

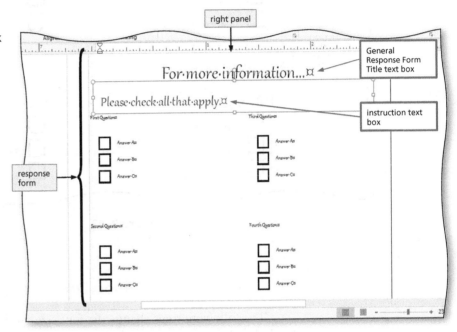

Figure 2–40

2

- If necessary, scroll down to display the check box area.
- Click the First Question heading to select the placeholder text.
- Change the font size to 10. Type **Educational Programs** to change the heading and then click outside the text box to deselect it.
- Repeat the process to replace each of the other three headings shown in Figure 2–41.

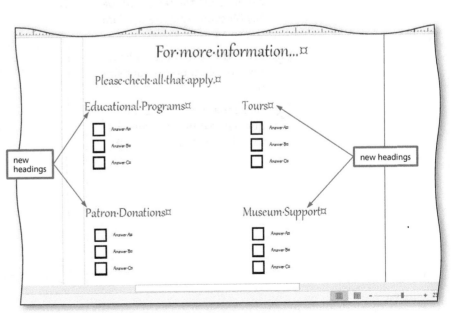

Figure 2–41

- Click the text, Answer A, below the Educational Programs heading in order to select only the placeholder text, not the check box. Do not double-click.

- Change the font size to 6. Type **Make Your Own Toys** to change the placeholder text.

- Repeat the process to edit all of the other check box answers in the form as shown in Figure 2–42.

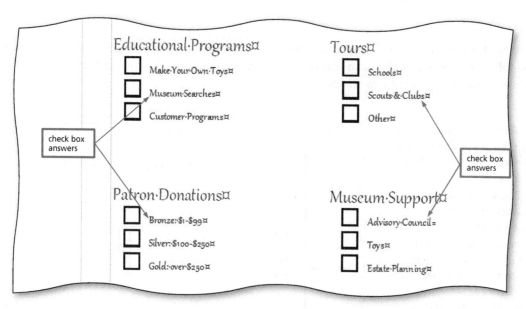

Figure 2–42

Changing the Font Size on Other Text

The following steps change the font size on the text boxes below the form. Recall that these synchronized boxes were updated when you edited the text on page 1.

1 Below the form in the right panel, select the text, Antique Toy Museum. Change the font size to 14.

2 Select the text in the address text box. Change the font size to 10.

3 Select the text in the phone number text box. Change the font size to 10 (Figure 2–43).

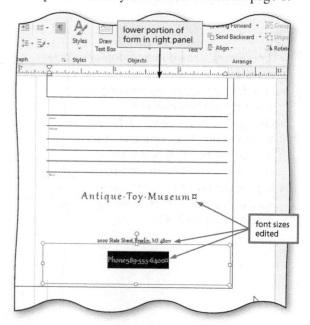

Figure 2–43

To Apply a Background to Page 2

The following steps apply a solid background to page 2.

1 Zoom to Whole Page view, if necessary.

2 With page 2 still displayed in the workspace, click the Background button (Page Design tab | Page Background group).

3 In the Background gallery, click '10% Tint of Accent 1' (Figure 2–44).

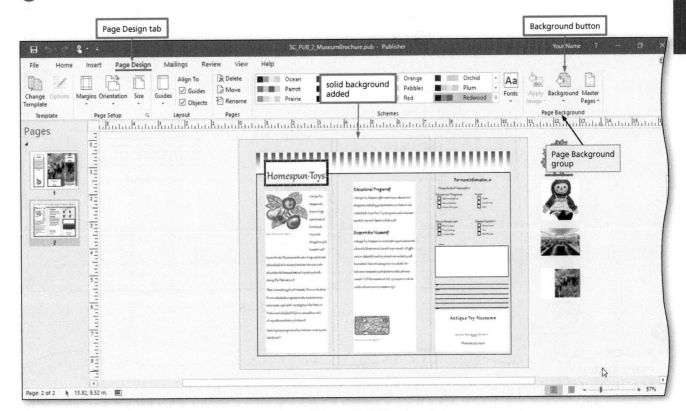

Figure 2–44

Text Box Transparency

Text boxes normally display black text on a white fill or background. Some exceptions are when the color scheme forces the text to be a different color, as it did in the Homespun Toys text box on the left panel of page 2. When you apply a solid background, the text boxes retain their default fill color. If you want to remove the fill color, you must change the transparency. **Transparency** refers to the opacity of an object, which lets you see through the object so that any object behind it is visible. To create transparency, you can choose to remove the fill color by using the Format Text box dialog box or you can use the keyboard shortcut CTRL+T, which toggles between an opaque white background and a transparent background.

BTW
Serif Fonts
Serif fonts are considered Oldstyle when they display a slanted serif. Fonts are considered Modern when they use horizontal serifs.

To Create Transparency in a Text Box

The following steps change the transparency of the text boxes on page 2. *Why? You want the background to show through behind the text.*

1

- Click the border of the large text box in the left panel to select it (Figure 2–45).

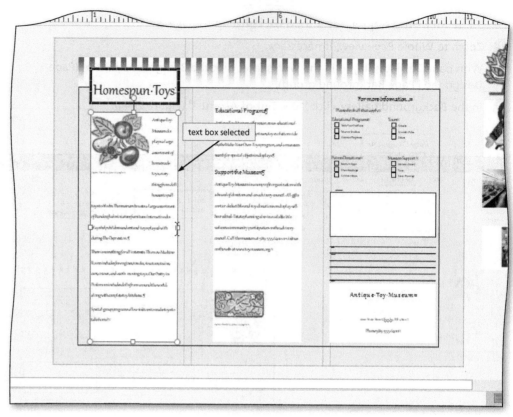

Figure 2–45

2
- Press CTRL+T to make the text box transparent (Figure 2–46).

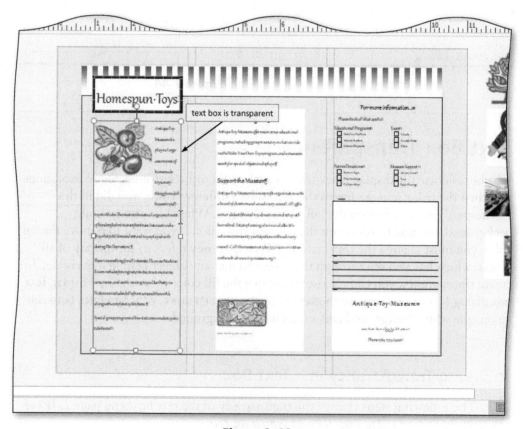

Figure 2–46

3

- Repeat Steps 1 and 2 to apply transparency to all of the text boxes except the Homespun Toys heading and the two captions (Figure 2–47).

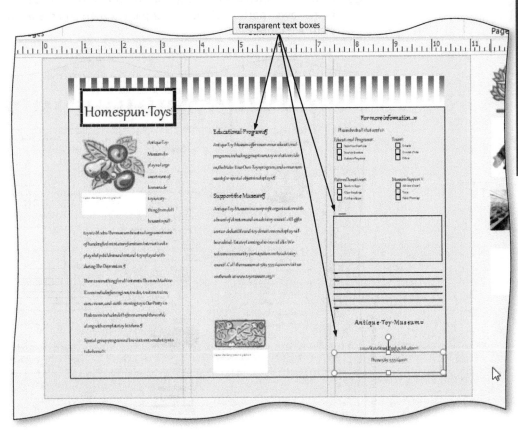

Figure 2–47

Editing Pictures

In Publisher, editing pictures may involve adjusting the pictures by making corrections, recoloring, compressing, or resetting. Publisher also provides **picture styles**, which are collections of formatting options — such as a frame, a rounded shape, and a shadow — that change a picture's overall appearance. The Picture Style gallery has more than 20 picture styles that include a variety of shapes, borders, and scallops. The Picture Tools Format tab on the ribbon contains other options, such as options for adding a border, picture effect, or captions.

To Swap Pictures on Page 2

The following steps swap the pictures on page 2.

1 In the scratch area, click the photo you wish to use in the left panel of the brochure (in this case, the picture of the doll) to display the swap icon.

2 From the scratch area, drag the swap icon of the photo to a location over the graphic in the left panel. When you see a pink boundary, drop the picture.

3 In the scratch area, click the display room picture to display the swap icon.

④ From the scratch area, drag the swap icon of the photo to a location over the graphic in the lower portion of the center pane. When you see a pink boundary, drop the picture (Figure 2–48).

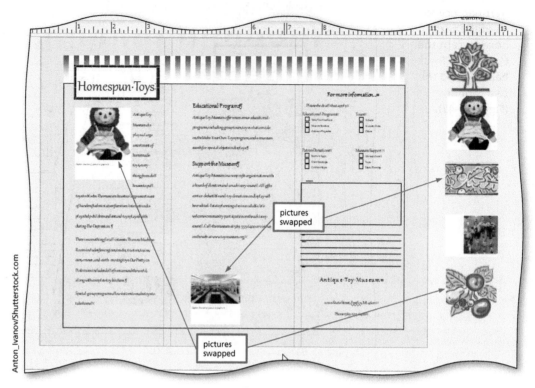

Figure 2–48

To Reset Pictures

If Publisher applies a color scheme to your graphic, or if the picture does not fit correctly in the picture placeholder, you can use the Reset command. *Why? Resetting the picture causes it to revert to its original coloring and better fit it in the placeholder.* The following steps reset the picture of the doll so that the top of the photo no longer appears clipped.

①

- Click the picture of the doll twice to select it without the caption (Figure 2–49).

Q&A How can I tell if I have only the picture selected?
The gray sizing handles indicate the selection.

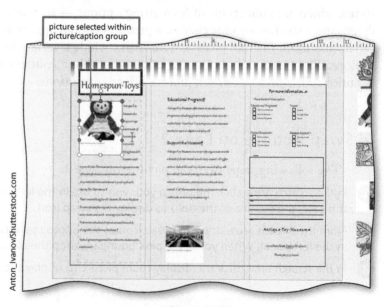

Figure 2–49

2

- Click the Reset Picture button (Picture Tools Format tab | Adjust group) to reset the picture (Figure 2–50).

🔍 **Experiment**

- To see how the picture changed, press CTRL+Z to undo the reset and then press CTRL+Y to redo the reset.

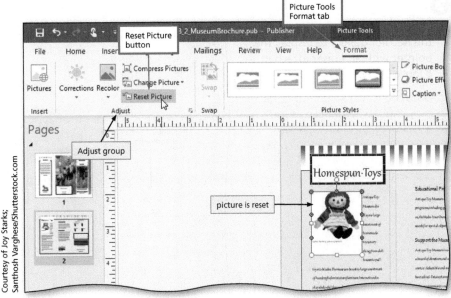

Courtesy of Joy Starks; Santhosh Varghese/Shutterstock.com

Figure 2–50

Other Ways

1. Right-click picture, point to Change Picture on shortcut menu, click Reset picture

To Set a Transparent Color

Publisher allows you to set a transparent color in most graphics. ***Why?*** *Sometimes you do not want to use or see a certain portion of a graphic.* When you set a transparent color, the background shows through behind the chosen color, just as it does when you make the text box transparent. Setting a transparent color is part of the recoloring process that also includes changing the color of the entire graphic to match one of the theme colors or changing the brightness/contrast of the graphic by using the Format Picture dialog box. The picture's original color information remains stored with the image, so you can restore the picture's original colors at any time.

The following steps set a transparent color.

1

- If necessary, select the doll graphic.

- If necessary, display the Picture Tools Format tab.

- Click the Recolor button (Picture Tools Format tab | Adjust group) to display the Recolor gallery (Figure 2–51).

Q&A What does the 'Picture Color Options' command do? The 'Picture Color Options' command displays the Format Picture dialog box, where you can edit settings such as brightness and size.

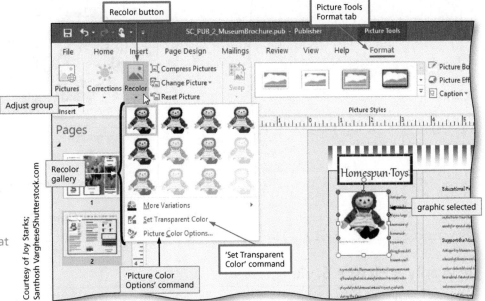

Courtesy of Joy Starks; Santhosh Varghese/Shutterstock.com

Figure 2–51

2

- Click 'Set Transparent Color' in the Recolor gallery to display the pointer with an eraser attached (Figure 2–52).

 Q&A

Does the 'Set Transparent Color' command work on all pictures?

It works on most pictures and some clip art. You cannot create a transparent area in an animated GIF.

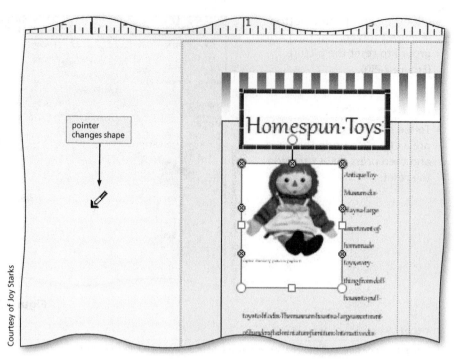

pointer changes shape

Courtesy of Joy Starks

Figure 2–52

3

- Click the white portion on the outside of the doll.

- If the picture seems out of proportion, drag the right-center sizing handle slightly left (Figure 2–53).

Q&A

Can I make another color transparent?

No. In Publisher, only one color per picture can be transparent.

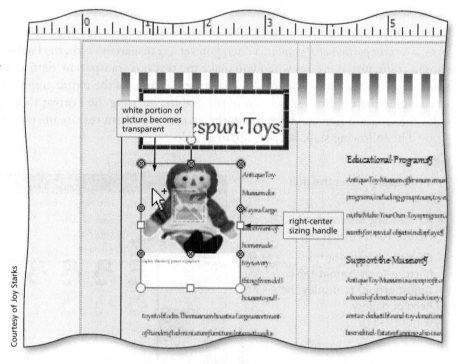

white portion of picture becomes transparent

right-center sizing handle

Courtesy of Joy Starks

Figure 2–53

To Apply a Picture Style

The following steps apply a picture style to the picture in the middle panel on page 2. **Why?** *Picture styles allow you to easily change the basic rectangle format to a more visually appealing style and designer look.*

- Click the desired picture (in this case the picture of the display room in the center panel) twice to select the picture without the caption. Press F9 to zoom to 100%.

- If necessary, click Picture Tools Format on the ribbon to display the Picture Tools Format tab (Figure 2–54).

Anton_Ivanov/Shutterstock.com; Santhosh Varghese/Shutterstock.com

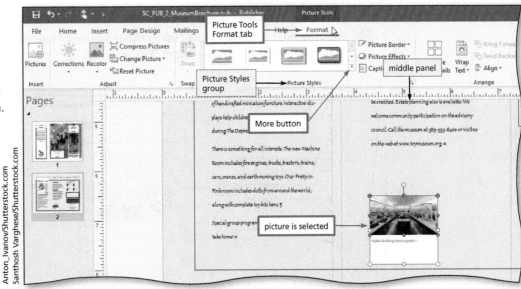

Figure 2–54

- Click the More button (Picture Tools Format tab | Picture Styles group) to display the Picture Styles gallery (Figure 2–55).

Experiment

- Point to each option in the Picture Styles gallery to see a ScreenTip that displays the name of the style.

Anton_Ivanov/Shutterstock.com; Santhosh Varghese/Shutterstock.com

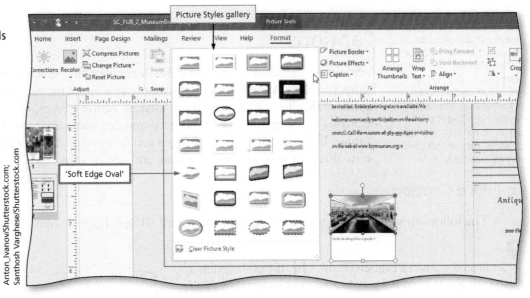

Figure 2–55

❸

- Click 'Soft Edge Oval' in the Picture Styles gallery to apply the selected style to the picture (Figure 2–56).

Anton_Ivanov/Shutterstock.com

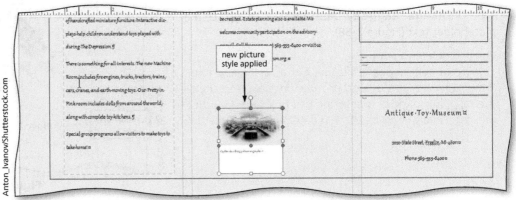

Figure 2–56

To Resize the Picture

The following step resizes the picture in the middle panel.

1 With the picture selected, SHIFT+drag the upper-right sizing handle to better fill the lower portion of the middle panel (Figure 2–57).

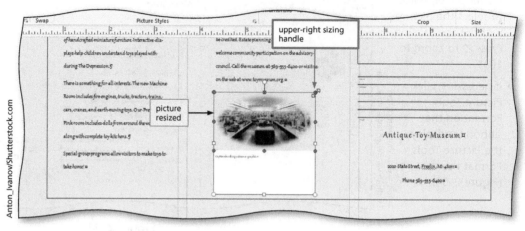

Figure 2–57

BTW
Superscripts and Subscripts
Two special font effects are superscript and subscript. A superscript is a character that appears slightly higher than other text on a line, such as that used in footnotes (reference[1]). A subscript is text that is slightly lower than other text on a line, such as that used in scientific formulas (H_2O).

Captions

A **caption** is explanatory or identification text or a title that accompanies a graphic, figure, or photo. A caption can be as simple as a figure number, as you see in the figures of this book, or a caption can identify people, places, objects, or actions occurring in the graphic. In Publisher templates, some captions already exist near a graphic. In those cases, the caption is a text box grouped with a graphic. If a graphic or photo does not have a caption, you can add one by using the Caption gallery.

To Edit a Caption

The following step edits the text in the captions on page 2. *Why? A caption explains the graphic to the reader.*

1

- Scroll to the desired caption (in this case, the doll caption in the left panel of page 2), and zoom to approximately 230%.

- Click the caption text below the doll photo to select it.

- Change the font size to 12.

- Type **Vintage Raggedy Ann Dolls** to replace the placeholder text (Figure 2–58).

Q&A Can you delete a caption?
Yes, but be sure to delete the text box as well as the text. If the caption is part of a group, click once to select the group, point to the border of the text box, and then click to select it. Finally, press DELETE to delete the caption text box.

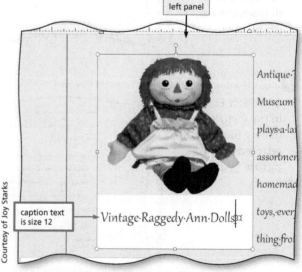

Figure 2–58

To Center Text

As in word processing programs, in Publisher you can change the alignment of the text within a text box. The various options — including Align Left, Center, Align Right, and Justify — apply to the current paragraph.

The following step centers the caption. ***Why?*** *Centering the caption below the picture will give it a more formal, balanced, and symmetrical appearance.* This step also makes the caption text box transparent so that the background color shows through.

- With the insertion point anywhere in the caption, click the Center button (Home tab | Paragraph group) to center the text within the text box.

- Press CTRL+T to create transparency (Figure 2–59).

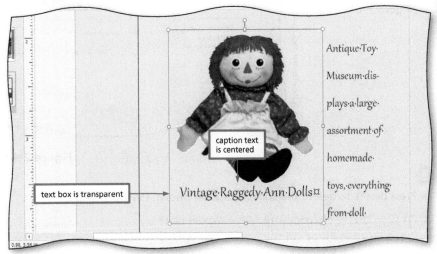

Figure 2–59

Courtesy of Joy Starks

Other Ways
1. Click Center button on Mini toolbar   2. Press CTRL+E

To Ungroup a Caption

Many Publisher templates group or link together the picture and caption in order to make moving them easier. The following steps ungroup the picture and caption. ***Why?*** *When they are ungrouped, the caption text box can be replaced or resized without affecting the picture.*

- Scroll to the lower portion of the middle panel.

- Click the grouped picture and caption (Figure 2–60).

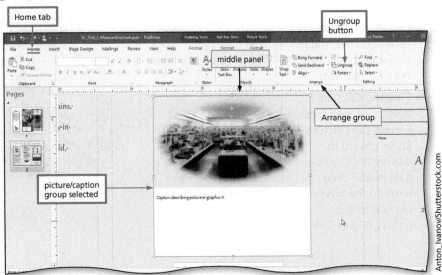

Figure 2–60

Anton_Ivanov/Shutterstock.com

- Click the Ungroup button (Home tab | Arrange group) to ungroup.
- Deselect the group and then select only the caption text box (Figure 2–61).

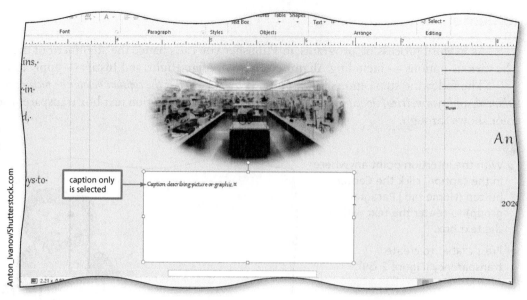

Figure 2–61

- Press DELETE to delete the current caption (shown in Figure 2–62).

Q&A Pressing DELETE did not work. What should I do?
Right-click the border of the current caption text box and then click Cut on the shortcut menu.

Other Ways

1. Select grouped object, press CTRL+SHIFT+G

To Use the Caption Gallery

The following steps use the Caption gallery to add a different, decorative caption to the photo. *Why? A decorative caption adds interest and color.*

- Click the display room picture to select it.
- Click Picture Tools Format on the ribbon to display the Picture Tools Format tab.
- Click the Caption button (Picture Tools Format tab | Picture Styles group) to display the Caption gallery and then scroll to the lower portion of the gallery (Figure 2–62).

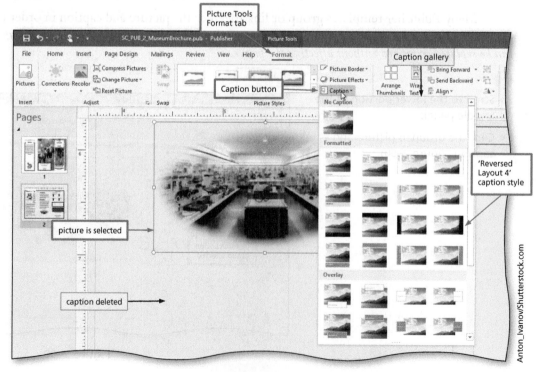

Figure 2–62

2

- Click 'Reversed Layout 4' to apply the caption style to the picture.

- Select the caption text and then type **Machine Room** to enter the caption (Figure 2–63).

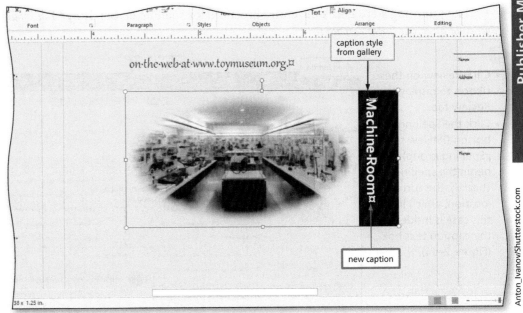

caption style from gallery

on·the·web·at·www.toymuseum.org.¤

new caption

Anton_Ivanov/Shutterstock.com

Figure 2–63

To Edit Another Caption

The following steps edit the caption on page 1 below the rocking horse picture.

1 Click Page 1 in the Page Navigation pane.

2 Scroll to the left panel and zoom as necessary to display the rocking horse picture.

3 Click the caption to select it and then type **We have a large collection of wooden toys!** to complete the caption.

Checking the Publication

You can check a publication for spelling errors as you type, or you can check the entire publication after you have finished editing it. As you check an entire publication for spelling errors, Publisher moves from text box to text box and offers suggestions for words it does not find in its dictionary. Publisher does not look for grammatical errors.

What is the best way to eliminate errors in the brochure?
If possible, proofread the brochure with a fresh set of eyes at least one to two days after completing the first draft. Check repeated elements and special objects, such as watermarks and logos, which need to be placed around, or behind, other objects. Look at text wrapping on every graphic. Ask someone else to proofread the brochure and give you suggestions for improvements. Revise it as necessary and then use the spelling and design checking features of the software.

CONSIDER THIS

A second kind of publication checker is the **Design Checker**, which finds potential design problems in the publication, such as objects hidden behind other objects, text that does not fit in its text box, and pictures that are scaled disproportionately. As with the spelling checker, you can choose to correct or ignore each design problem detected.

BTW
Proper Nouns, Titles, and Headings
If a flagged word is spelled correctly, click the Ignore button to ignore the flag, or click the Ignore All button if the word occurs more than once.

BTW
Storage
Graphic files and fonts require a great deal of storage space but should fit on most USB flash drives. If your USB flash drive is full, have another storage device ready. Publisher will prompt you to insert it.

To Check the Spelling of the Entire Publication

The following steps check the entire brochure for spelling errors. *Why? You should check the spelling on every publication after you finish editing it.*

1
- Click Review on the ribbon to display the Review tab.
- Click the Spelling button (Review tab | Spelling group) to begin the spelling check in the current location, which in this case is inside the caption text box (Figure 2–64).

Q&A
Can I check spelling of just a section of a publication?
Yes, select the text before starting the spelling check.

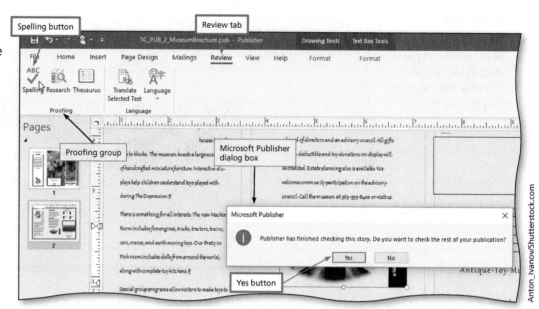

Figure 2–64

2
- When Publisher finishes checking the caption text box, click Yes (Microsoft Publisher dialog box) to tell Publisher to check the rest of the publication. If your publication displays a different error, accept or ignore it, as necessary (Figure 2–65).

Q&A
What does the Options button do?
When you click the Options button (Check Spelling dialog box), Publisher displays the Publisher Options dialog box, where you can edit settings such as AutoCorrect, spelling rules, and dictionaries.

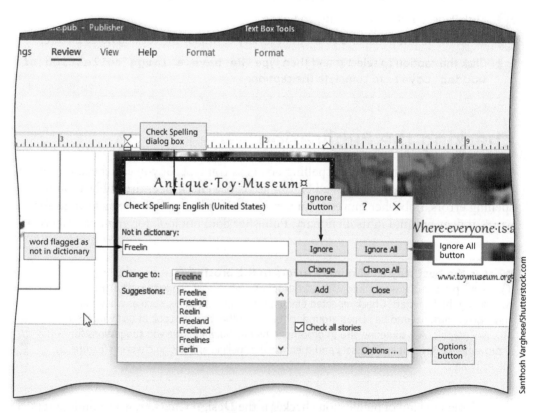

Figure 2–65

- Click the Ignore All button (Check Spelling dialog box) to ignore the flagged word each time it occurs (in this case, Freelin, the name of the city).

Q&A Could I click the Ignore button?
You could, but because this is a proper name that occurs more than once, it is faster to click the Ignore All button.

- If Publisher flags any other words, choose the correct spelling in the Suggestions list, click the Change button, and then continue the spelling check until the next error is identified, or the end of the publication is reached.

- When the Microsoft Publisher dialog box is displayed, indicating that the spelling check is complete, click OK to close the dialog box.

Other Ways

1. Press F7	2. Right-click flagged word, click Spelling on shortcut menu

To Run the Design Checker

The following steps run the Design Checker. *Why? The Design Checker troubleshoots and identifies potential design problems in the publication.*

1

- Click File on the ribbon to open Backstage view and, by default, display the Info screen (Figure 2–66).

Q&A Will the Design Checker fix the problems automatically?
In some cases, you will have the option of choosing an automatic fix for the issue; in other cases, you will have to fix the problem manually.

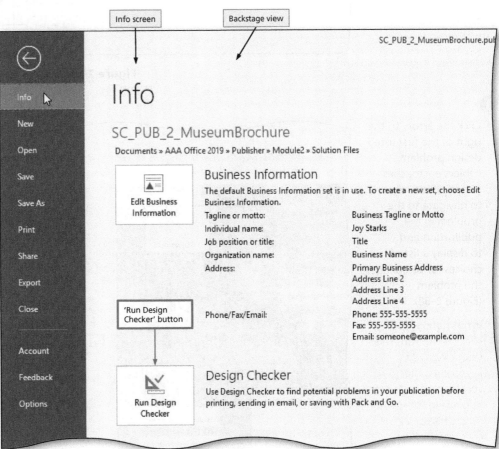

Figure 2–66

2

- Click the 'Run Design Checker' button in the Info screen to open the Design Checker pane (Figure 2–67).

Q&A What are the links at the bottom of the Design Checker pane?

You can click the 'Design Checker Options' link to specify the order in which the Design Checker checks the pages of your publication or to specify which kinds of design issues to include. The second link offers tips from the Publisher Help system about using the Design Checker.

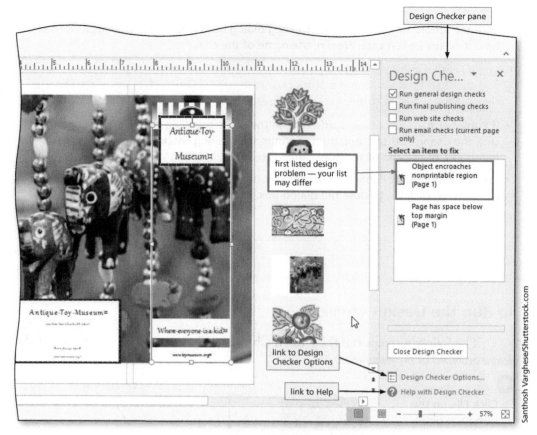

Figure 2–67

3

- Click the arrow to the right of the first listed design problem, 'Object encroaches nonprintable region', to navigate to the problem in the publication and to display a list of choices for resolving the problem (Figure 2–68).

Q&A What happens if I click 'Never Run this Check Again'?

If you click the command, Publisher will not look for that kind of error in the current publication.

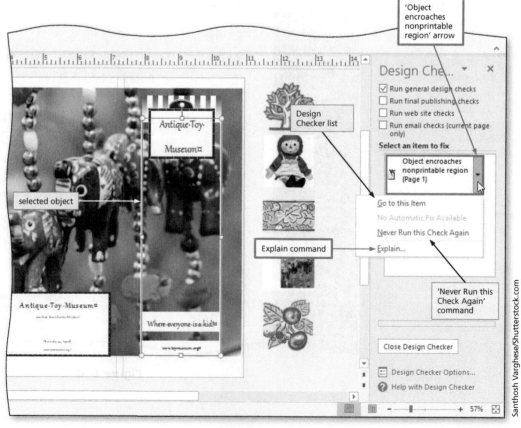

Figure 2–68

4

- Click Explain to view references on the problem in the Help pane (Figure 2–69).

🔍 **Experiment**

- Click the applicable link in the Help pane to read more about the problem.

Q&A | What is the listed design problem?

A small amount of space appears between the margin of the page and the object closest to the margin. This is intentional and was part of the template, but the Design Checker notes the problem for your information. Publication objects may be close to the printable area margin. Although Design Checker provides this warning, the brochure will print correctly.

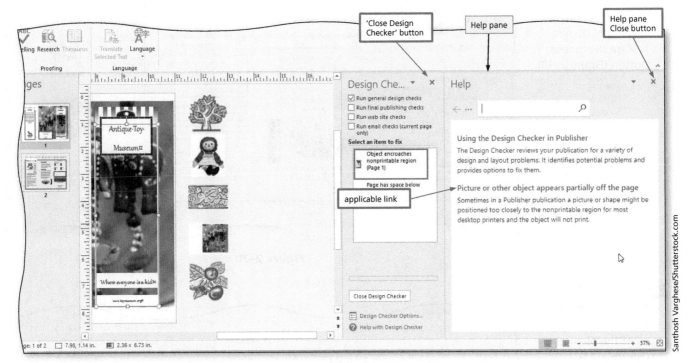

Figure 2–69

5

- Fix any issues not related to space or pictures. Click the Close button in the Help pane.

- Click the 'Close Design Checker' button in the Design Checker pane (shown in Figure 2–69) to close the Design Checker pane and return to the publication.

Q&A | How do I fix a picture that is not scaled proportionally?

If you have made changes such as changes to picture styles or transparency in a picture, Publisher will flag the picture. If it truly is not scaled proportionally, when you click the error, the resulting menu will display an enabled 'Fix Rescale Picture' command, which you can click.

Clearing the Scratch Area

Several pictures remain in the scratch area. While leaving them there will not cause a design or printing problem, keeping them there does increase the file size. It is a good idea to remove them if you are sure you will not be using those pictures again in this publication. You can select multiple objects by dragging around them and then pressing DELETE.

To Select Multiple Objects by Dragging around Them

The following steps select all of the pictures in the scratch area. **Why?** *Selecting them all will make deleting quicker.*

• In the scratch area, drag, starting above and to the left of the first thumbnail, moving down and to the right, to include all of the pictures in the selection rectangle. Do not release the mouse button (Figure 2–70).

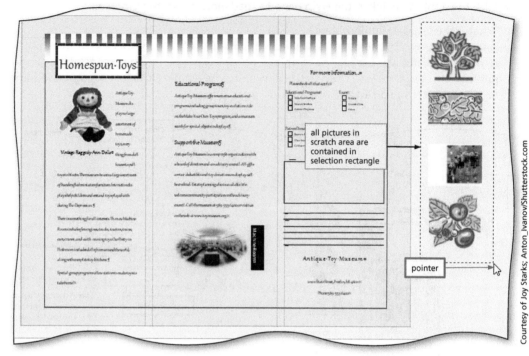

Figure 2–70

• Release the mouse button to select all of the pictures (Figure 2–71).

Q&A Besides grouping the pictures for quick deletion, is there any other reason I might select them all? Grouping pictures helps when you need to arrange the pictures into thumbnails. You also can copy grouped pictures easily from one publication to another.

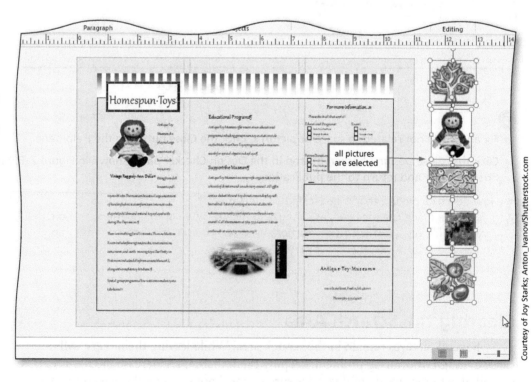

Figure 2–71

- Press DELETE to remove the pictures from the scratch area.
- Click the Save button on the Quick Access Toolbar to overwrite the previously saved file.

> **Other Ways**
>
> 1. CTRL+click each object in the scratch area , press DELETE

Break Point: If you want to take a break, this is a good place to do so. Exit Publisher. To resume later, start Publisher, open the file called SC_PUB_2_MuseumBrochure, and continue following the steps from this location forward.

Previewing and Printing

When you work with multipage publications, it is a good idea to preview each page before printing. In addition, if you decide to print on special paper or print on both sides of the paper, you must adjust certain settings on the Print screen in Backstage view.

> **BTW**
>
> **View Multiple Sheets Grid**
>
> In multipage publications, you can use the View Multiple Sheets grid to choose how the pages display in the print preview. For example, choosing 5 × 2 in the grid causes Publisher to display 5 pages vertically (high) and 2 pages across (wide), for a total display of 10 pages.

To Preview Multiple Pages and Print

Previewing both pages in the publication is an important step in getting it ready for outside printing. The following steps preview what the printed copy will look like and then print the brochure on both sides. *Why? Printing on both sides gives you the opportunity to check your panels and folds and to view the brochure as your readers will view it.* If your printer does not have the capability to print double-sided, follow your printer's specifications to print one side of the brochure, turn the paper over, and then print the reverse side.

- Start Publisher, if necessary, and display page 1 of the brochure.
- Click File on the ribbon to open Backstage view.
- Click Print in Backstage view to display the Print screen.
- Click the 'View Multiple Sheets' button to display the View Multiple Sheets gallery (Figure 2–72).

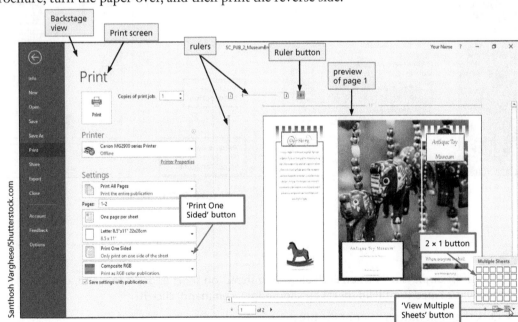

Santhosh Varghese/Shutterstock.com

Figure 2–72

Q&A | What are the rulers in the Print gallery?
Publisher displays rulers at the top and left of the print preview to help you verify the size of the printed page. You can turn off the ruler display by clicking the Ruler button.

2

- Click the '2 × 1' button to display the pages above one another.
- Verify the printer name that appears on the Printer Status button will print a hard copy of the publication. If necessary, click the Printer Status button to display a list of available printer options and then click the desired printer to change the currently selected printer.
- Click the 'Print One Sided' button to display the list of options (Figure 2–73).

Q&A

If the brochure has only two pages, why do all of those preview grids exist?

Publisher allows for more pages in every kind of publication so that you have the option to add them. If you click a button in the grid for more than two pages — either horizontally or vertically — the size of the preview is reduced.

Is this the best way to preview the brochure?

Viewing two full pages with intensive graphics and text may give you a good overview of the publication; however, this type of preview is not a substitute for checking the publication for errors by reading the content carefully and using the spelling and design checking tools.

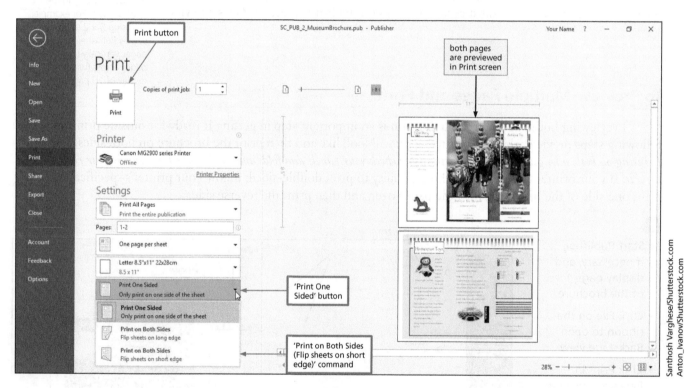

Figure 2–73

3

- If your list displays a 'Print on Both Sides (Flip sheets on short edge)' command, click it; or, if your list displays a 'Manual 2 Sided Print (Flip sheets on short edge)' command, click it.
- Click the Print button to print the brochure.
- When the printer stops, retrieve the printed publication.

Other Ways

1. Press CTRL+P, choose settings, click Print button (Print screen)

Printing Considerations

When a business needs mass quantities of publications, it generally **outsources**, or submits its publications to an outside printer, for duplicating. Preparing a publication for outside printing requires special considerations.

How do you make wise professional printing choices?
Make a firm decision that quality matters and then consult with several commercial printers ahead of time. Get prices, color modes, copies, paper, and folding options in writing before you finish your brochure. Brochures are most effective on heavier paper, with strong colors and a glossy feel. Together with the commercial printer, select a paper that is going to last. Check to make sure the commercial printer can accept Microsoft Publisher 2019 files.

If you start a publication from scratch, it is best to set up the publication for the type of printing you want before you place objects on the page. Otherwise, you may be forced to make design changes at the last minute. You also may set up an existing publication for a printing service. In order to provide you with experience in setting up a publication for outside printing, this project guides you through the preparation steps — even if you are submitting this publication only to your instructor.

You need to consider various advantages and limitations as you think about printing options, such as whether to use a copy shop or commercial printer. You may have to make some trade-offs when deciding on the best printing option. Table 2–4 shows some of the questions you can ask yourself when considering printing options.

BTW
Distributing a Document
Instead of printing and distributing a hard copy of a document, you can distribute the document electronically. Options include sending the document via email; posting it on cloud storage (such as OneDrive) and sharing the file with others; posting it on a social networking site, blog, or other website; and sharing a link associated with an online location of the document. You also can create and share a PDF or XPS image of the document, so that users can view the file in Acrobat Reader or XPS Viewer instead of in Publisher.

Table 2–4 Choosing a Printing Option			
Consideration	**Questions to Answer**	**Desktop Option**	**Professional Options**
Color	Is the quality of photos and color a high priority?	Low to medium quality	High quality
Convenience	Do I want the easy way?	Very convenient and familiar	Time needed to explore different methods, unfamiliarity
Cost	How much do I want to pay?	Printer supplies and personal time	High-resolution color/high quality is expensive; however, the more you print, the less expensive the per-copy price
Quality	How formal is the purpose of my publication?	Local event; narrow, personal audience	Business, marketing, professional services
Quantity	How many copies do I need?	1 to 10 copies	10 to 500 copies: use a copy shop; 500+ copies: use a commercial printer
Turnaround	How soon do I need it?	Immediate	Rush outside printing is probably an extra cost

Paper Considerations

Professional brochures are printed on a high grade of paper to enhance the graphics and create longer-lasting documents. Grades of paper are based on weight. Desktop printers commonly use **20-lb. bond paper**, which is a lightweight paper intended for writing and printing. A commercial printer might use 60-lb. glossy or linen paper.

BTW
Printer Memory
Some printers do not have enough memory to print a wide variety of images and colors. In these cases, the printer prints up to a certain point on a page and then stops — resulting in only the top portion of the publication printing. Check with your instructor to see if your printer has enough memory to work with colors.

The finishing options and their costs are important considerations that may take additional time to explore. **Glossy paper** is a coated paper, produced using a heat process involving clay and titanium. **Linen paper**, with its mild texture or grain, can support high-quality graphics without the shine and slick feel of glossy paper. Users sometimes choose special paper stock, such as cover stock, card stock, or text stock. This textbook is printed on 45-lb. blade-coated paper. **Blade-coated paper** is coated and then skimmed and smoothed to create the pages you see here.

These paper and finishing options may seem burdensome, but they are becoming conveniently available to desktop publishers. Local office supply stores have shelf after shelf of various types of paper specifically designed for laser and ink-jet printers. Some of the paper you can purchase has been prescored for specific folding.

Color Considerations

When printing colors, Publisher uses a color scheme called RGB. **RGB** stands for the three colors — red, green, and blue — used to print the combined colors of your publication. RGB provides the best color matching for graphics and photos. Desktop printers may convert the RGB specifications to CMYK, which stands for cyan, magenta, yellow, and key (black). Professional printers, on the other hand, can print your publication using color scheme processes, or **libraries**. These processes include black and white, spot color, and process color.

In **black-and-white printing**, the printer uses only one color of ink (usually black, but you can choose a different color if you want). You can add accent colors to your publication by using different shades of gray or by printing on colored paper. Your publication can have the same range of subtleties as a black-and-white photo.

A **spot color** is used to accent a black-and-white publication. Newspapers, for example, may print their masthead in a bright, eye-catching color on page 1 but print the rest of the publication in black and white. **Spot-color printing** uses semitransparent, premixed inks typically chosen from standard color-matching guides, such as Pantone. Choosing colors from a **color-matching library** helps ensure high-quality results, because printing professionals who license the libraries agree to maintain the specifications, control, and quality.

In a spot-color publication, each spot color is **separated** on its own plate and printed on an offset printing press. The use of spot colors has become more creative in the past few years. Printing services use spot colors of metallic or florescent inks, as well as screen tints, to provide color variations without increasing the number of color separations and cost. If your publication includes a logo with one or two colors, or if you want to use color to emphasize line art or text, consider using spot-color printing.

Process-color printing or four-color printing means your publication can include color photos and any color or combination of colors, using a print shop's CMYK process-color library.

Process-color printing is the most expensive proposition; black-and-white printing is the cheapest. Using color increases the cost and time it takes to process the publication. When using either the spot-color or the process-color method, the printer first must output the publication to film on an **image setter**, which is an output device that re-creates the publication on film or photographic paper. The film then is used to create color printing plates. A **printing plate** is thin paper or a metal sheet used in printing that transfers one of the colors in a publication onto paper in an offset process. Publisher can print a preview of these individual sheets showing how the colors will separate before you take your publication to the printer.

A newer printing technology called **digital printing** uses toner instead of ink to reproduce a full range of colors. Digital printing does not require separate printing plates. Digital printing usually is less expensive than offset printing without sacrificing quality significantly.

Special Paper

Printing a brochure on a high grade of paper results in a professional look. Heavier paper stock helps a brochure stand up better in display racks, although any paper will suffice. **Brochure paper** is a special paper with creases that create professional-looking folds and with a paper finish that works well with color and graphics.

To Print on Special Paper

If you have special paper, you would perform the following steps to choose that special paper before printing. See your instructor for assistance in choosing the correct option for your printer.

1. Open Backstage view and then click Print to display the Print screen.
2. Click the Printer Properties link below the Printer Status box to display your printer's Properties dialog box.
3. Find the paper or quality setting and then choose the paper.
4. Click OK in the Printer Properties dialog box to return to Backstage view.

Packing the Publication for the Printing Service

The publication file can be packed for the printing service in two ways. The first way is to give the printing service the Publisher file in Publisher format using the Pack and Go wizard. The second way is to save the file in a format called Encapsulated PostScript. Both of these methods are discussed in the following sections. Alternatively, some printing services will take a Publisher document in its native format (.pub) without any packing; however, in that case, the printing service may not have the exact fonts that you used, and will need to substitute different ones.

To Use the Pack and Go Wizard

The **Pack and Go wizard** is a Publisher feature that guides you through the steps to collect and pack all the files the printing service needs and then compresses the files. *Why? Publisher checks for and embeds the TrueType fonts used in the publication, in case the printing service does not have those fonts available.* The following steps use the Pack and Go Wizard to ready the publication for submission to a commercial printing service. These steps create a compressed, or zipped, folder on your storage device.

- Click File on the ribbon to open Backstage view.
- Click Export in Backstage view to display the Export screen.
- In the Pack and Go area, click 'Save for a Commercial Printer'.

BTW
Subsetting
A file prepared for submission to a commercial printer includes all fonts used in the publication. If you use only a small number of characters from a font, such as for drop caps or for headlines, you can instruct Publisher to embed only the characters you used from the font. Embedding only part of a font is called subsetting. The advantage of font subsetting is that it decreases the overall size of the file. The disadvantage is that it limits the ability of the printing service to make corrections. If the printing service does not have the full font installed on its computer, corrections can be made only by using the characters included in the subset.

- Click the 'Pack and Go Wizard' button to start the Pack and Go wizard.
- Click the Browse button (Pack and Go Wizard dialog box) and then navigate to your storage location (Figure 2–74).

Q&A Should I save my file first?

You do not have to save it again; however, if you plan to store the publication on a storage device other than the one on which you previously saved the brochure, save it again on the new medium before starting the Pack and Go wizard.

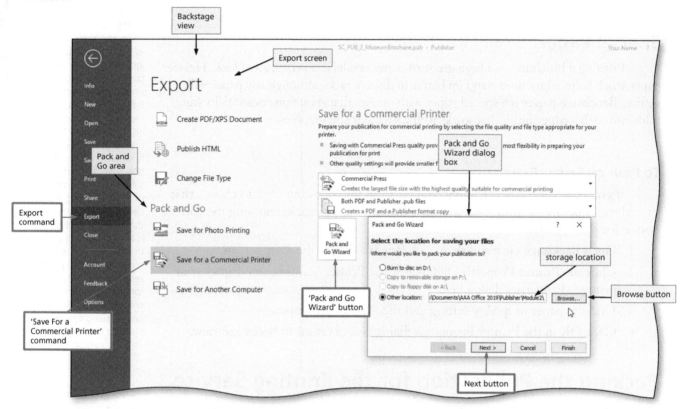

Figure 2–74

②

- Click the Next button (Pack and Go Wizard dialog box). If Publisher displays another Pack and Go Wizard dialog box with a Next button, click the Next button.

- When the final Pack and Go Wizard dialog box is displayed, remove the check mark in the 'Print a composite proof' check box (Figure 2–75).

Q&A What if I make a change to the publication after using the Pack and Go Wizard?

The file is saved in a compressed format on your storage location with the same file name as your Publisher file. If you make changes to the publication after packing the files, be sure to use the Pack and Go Wizard again so that the changes are part of the packed publication.

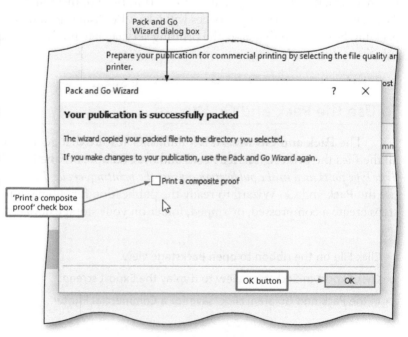

Figure 2–75

- Click OK to close the Pack and Go Wizard dialog box.
- Because the brochure now is complete, exit Publisher. If a Microsoft Publisher dialog box appears, click Don't Save to exit Publisher.
- Sign out of your Microsoft Account, if necessary.

Summary

In this module, you learned how to make choices about brochures and brochure templates as you edited headings and other text boxes. You used a stylistic set for the headings. You copied and pasted using special paste options, and you displayed formatting marks as the text wrapped in paragraphs. You made text boxes transparent. You also swapped pictures, reset them, and set a transparent color. After applying a picture style, you edited all captions and used the caption gallery. Finally, you checked the spelling and the design of the publication before packing it for a printing service.

What decisions will you need to make when creating your next publication?
Use these guidelines as you complete the assignments in this module and create your own publications outside of this class.

1. Decide on the purpose, shelf life, and layout.

    a) Select a template that suits your needs.

    b) Choose font and color schemes that are appropriate for the brochure's purpose and audience.

2. Create the brochure.

    a) Replace all placeholder and default text.

    b) Copy and paste text when possible to avoid introducing new errors.

    c) Edit forms.

    d) Use appropriate pictures with captions.

    e) When you swap pictures, when possible, ensure that they fit in the space.

3. Identify how to format various objects in the brochure.

    a) Copy formats and adjust font sizes for consistency.

    b) Apply transparency to text boxes and pictures where appropriate.

    c) Use stylistic sets to enhance the brochure.

4. Proofread and check the publication.

    a) Read the brochure.

    b) Ask another person to read it.

    c) Use the spelling checker feature.

    d) Use the Design Checker.

5. Plan for printing and packing.

    a) Choose appropriate printing options.

    b) Consult with a commercial printing service.

    c) Use the Pack and Go wizard.

CONSIDER THIS: PLAN AHEAD

Apply Your Knowledge

Reinforce the skills and apply the concepts you learned in this module.

Swapping Graphics

Note: To complete this assignment, you will be required to use the Data Files. Please contact your instructor for information about accessing the Data Files.

Instructions: Start Publisher. Open the file called SC_PUB_2-1.pub in the Data Files. The publication contains a map of the United States with places for you to insert pictures from your recent trip out west. You produce the collage shown in Figure 2–76.

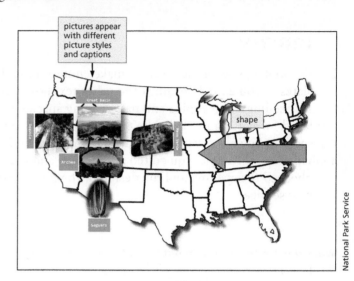

Figure 2–76

Perform the following tasks:

1. Click the Pictures button (Insert tab | Illustrations group). Navigate to the Data Files. CTRL+click the figures named, Support_PUB_2_Arches.png, Support_PUB_2_MesaVerde.png, Support_PUB_2_GreatBasin.png, Support_PUB_2_Sequoia.jpg, and Support_PUB_2_Saguaro.png. Click the Insert button to insert the multiple pictures into the publication.

2. One at a time, swap the pictures for the empty picture placeholders, outlined in light gray. Arrange the pictures on the page layout as shown in Figure 2–76. Reset any picture as necessary.

3. If instructed to do so, substitute your own picture for one of the pictures.

4. One at a time, choose a different caption style for each picture by clicking the Caption button (Picture Tools Format tab | Picture Styles group) and applying a caption style. Use the captions, Sequoia, Great Basin, Mesa Verde, Arches, and Saguaro. Center each caption.

5. If a caption is displayed too far away from the picture, ungroup the picture and caption and move the caption closer to the picture.

6. One at a time, choose a different picture style for each picture by clicking the More button (Picture Tools Format tab | Picture Styles group) and applying a picture style.

7. Use the Shapes button (Insert tab | Illustrations group) to insert a Left Arrow shape, as shown in Figure 2–76. Edit the shape fill and change the color to 'Hyperlink (Dark Blue), Lighter 60%'.

8. Check the spelling of your publication and use the Design Checker.

9. Save the publication with the file name, SC_PUB_2_VacationPhotos.

10. Preview the publication as you print a copy.

11. Pack the publication by using the Pack and Go wizard.

12. Submit the revised document in the format specified by your instructor.

13. ✳ Do you think using different styles and captions on each picture makes the publication look cluttered? Why or why not? What kind of banner or headline might be appropriate across the top?

Extend Your Knowledge

Extend the skills you learned in this module and experiment with new skills. You may need to use Help to complete the assignment.

Creating a Brochure from Scratch

Note: To complete this assignment, you will be required to use the Data Files. Please contact your instructor for information about accessing the Data Files.

Instructions: Start Publisher. You are to start from scratch and create a brochure advertising an exotic pet boarding service. You will set the color and font scheme, create panel guides, insert images, and add other formatting to the brochure.

Perform the following tasks:

1. Click BUILT-IN and then click Brochures. Scroll to the Blank Sizes area and then click the Letter (Landscape) thumbnail.

2. Choose the Field color scheme and the Paper font scheme. Click the CREATE button to display the blank page in the workspace.

3. Maximize the window, if necessary. If necessary, click the Special Characters button (Home tab | Paragraph group) to display special characters.

4. Use Help to read about creating guides and then perform the following tasks:

   a. To create panel guides, move your pointer over the vertical ruler until you see the pointer change to a split horizontal bar (⬍). Drag from the vertical ruler into the publication to create a nonprinting guide, stopping at 3⅝" as measured on the horizontal ruler. Drag another guide from the vertical ruler into the publication, stopping at 7⅜".

   b. In the Page Navigation pane, right-click the Page 1 thumbnail and then click 'Insert Duplicate Page' on the shortcut menu. You will leave page 2 blank for future content.

   c. If necessary, click the Page 1 thumbnail in the Page Navigation pane to return to page 1 in the brochure.

   d. Save the publication on your storage device with the file name, SC_PUB_2_ExoticBoardingBrochure.

5. Insert the pictures, Support_PUB_2_Background.png, Support_PUB_2_Parrot.tif, and Support_PUB_2_Rabbit.tif.

6. Right-click the background shape that has green and gold shapes, point to 'Apply to Background' on the shortcut menu, and then click Fill to fill the background with the graphic.

7. To create the right panel, which serves as the front of the brochure, do the following:

   a. Drag the parrot to the right panel. Position it approximately in the upper center portion of the right panel. Resize the picture to approximately 2 × 2.5 inches. Click the More button (Picture Tools Format | Pictures Styles), and choose an appropriate picture style, such as 'Simple Frame Black'. Deselect the picture. If the parrot is not displayed completely, click the Reset Picture button (Picture Tools Format tab | Adjust group).

   b. Click the 'Draw Text Box' button (Home tab | Objects group). Drag to create a text box at the top of the right panel and make the text box approximately 1½" tall. Stay within the

Continued >

Extend Your Knowledge *continued*

margin and guides. Type **Exotic Boarding** to enter the text. Right-click the text and then click Best Fit on the shortcut menu.

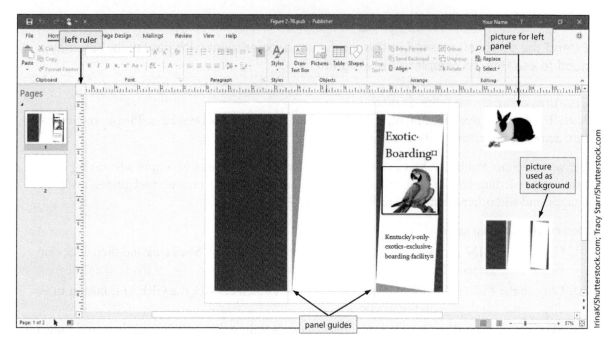

Figure 2–77

c. Click the 'Draw Text Box' button (Home tab | Objects group). Drag to create another text box in the lower portion of the right panel, approximately the same size as the previous text box. Change the font size to 20. Type **Kentucky's only exotics-exclusive boarding facility** to enter the text in the text box (Figure 2–77).

8. To create the left panel:

a. Drag the rabbit to the left panel. Position it in the upper portion of the panel. Resize the picture approximately to fill the area between margins of the left panel. Click the Recolor button (Picture Tools Format tab | Adjust group) and then click Set Transparent color. Click the white portion around the rabbit to make it transparent.

b. Add a caption to the rabbit picture. Type **The food is always fresh!** in the caption text box. Select the text, change the font size to 16, and center the text.

c. Create a larger text box below the rabbit, approximately 5 inches high, filling the green area left to right. If necessary, change the font to Constantia. Change the font color to white and the font size to 16. Type the following text, allowing Publisher to wrap the text:

In addition to our standard boarding, we offer luxury suites to give your exotic pets the full resort experience.

Press ENTER twice and then type the following, pressing ENTER at the end of each line.

Services include:

Daily grooming

Daily out-of-cage playtime

Daily email updates

Daily morning/bedtime treats

Daily foraging toy

Nail trim, if needed

9. To create the middle panel of page 1:

    a. Create another text box in center portion of the center panel. Change the font size to 16. Type the following, centering each line, and pressing ENTER at the end of each line:

```
Exotic Boarding

1492 Harrison

Mission, KY 40029

Phone (502) 555-1492

exoticboarding.com
```

    b. Click the Online Pictures button (Insert tab | Illustrations group) and use the search term, Kentucky outline. As you choose a graphic, read the specific license for any image you plan to use, even for educational purposes, to ensure that you have the right to use the image.

    c. Make the image transparent. Move and resize the image as necessary.

    d. If requested by your instructor, replace the graphic with the state outline from your home state, and use your address in the text box.

10. Check the brochure for spelling errors and design errors and fix them as necessary. Delete any pictures in the scratch area. Save the file again.

11. Preview the publication by using the Print screen in Backstage view. If possible, print the publication on special brochure paper.

12. ✳ When would you use a template instead of creating a brochure from scratch? Would formatting the font before you type be easier than selecting text and formatting it afterward?

Expand Your World

Create a solution that uses cloud and web technologies by learning and investigating on your own from general guidance.

Creating a Webpage with a Brochure Link

Instructions: If you do not have a OneDrive account, create one. Start Publisher and open one of your brochures. Save the brochure on OneDrive. You would like to create a webpage with a link to download one of your brochures stored on the cloud, because many company websites include a link to download a print copy of various brochures.

Perform the following tasks:

1. Start the Notepad app or other text editor app on your computer. Enter the code from Figure 2–78, leaving the ninth line blank, as shown in Figure 2–78. (*Hint:* Use TAB to indent the appropriate lines.)

```
SC_PUB_2_MyWebpage.html - Notepad

File  Edit  Format  View  Help

<!DOCTYPE html>
<html lang ="en">
        <head>
                <meta charset="utf-8" />
                <title>My Webpage</title>
        </head>
        <body>

                <h1>Download my brochure here</h1>

        </body>              blank line
</html>
```

Figure 2–78

Continued >

Expand Your World *continued*

2. If requested to do so by your instructor, change the words, My Webpage, to your name in line five.

3. Save the file on your storage device, using SC_PUB_2_MyWebpage.html as the file name. Do not close the text editor window.

4. Start a browser and navigate to your OneDrive account.

5. Right-click the stored brochure file to display the shortcut menu and then click Embed. When prompted, click the Generate button (Embed dialog box). When OneDrive displays the HTML code, press CTRL+C to copy the highlighted code.

6. Go back to the text editor window and position the insertion point on line nine. Press CTRL+V to paste the code into the file. If necessary, click Format on the menu bar and then click Word Wrap to enable the feature. Save the HTML file again and then close the window.

7. To view your webpage, open a File Explorer window and then navigate to the location of your saved HTML file. Double-click the SC_PUB_2_MyWebpage.html file. If the browser asks permission to run the ActiveX content, click the 'Allow blocked content' button.

8. Submit the assignment in the format specified by your instructor.

9. ✺ Does your school provide a brochure about its program? Can you download the brochure from the school's website? Do you think it still is useful or beneficial to have a hard copy of the brochure? Why or why not?

In the Lab

Design and implement a solution using creative thinking and problem-solving skills.

Creating a Youth Soccer League Brochure

Problem: Your brother helps manage a recreational youth soccer league. He has asked you to create a brochure about the league's preseason sign-up.

Part 1:   Use the Ascent Event brochure template to create a brochure announcing the Youth Soccer League. Pick an appropriate color and font scheme and include a sign-up form. Type **Preseason Sign-Up** as the brochure title. Type **Youth Soccer League** to replace the Business Name text. Type your address and phone number in the appropriate text boxes. Delete the logo. Replace all graphics with sports icons or graphics. Edit the captions to suit the images. The league commissioner will send you content for the stories at a later date. Edit the sign-up form event boxes as shown in Table 2–5. Use appropriate font sizes.

Table 2–5 Sign-Up Form Check Box Content		
Age Group	**Play Format**	**Price**
U6: 6 years old and younger	4 v 4	$35.00
U8: 8 years old and younger	7 v 7	$35.00
U10: 10 years old and younger	9 v 9	$50.00
U12: 12 years old and younger	9 v 9	$50.00
U14: 14 years old and younger	11 v 11	$50.00
U16: 16 years old and younger	11 v 11	TBA

Part 2:   ✺ On a separate piece of paper, create a table similar to Table 2–1 in this module, listing the type of exposure, information, audience, and purpose of the communication. Turn in the table with your printout.

3 Designing a Newsletter

Objectives

After completing this module, you will be able to:

- Describe the advantages of using the newsletter medium and identify the steps in its design process
- Edit a newsletter template
- Set page options
- Edit a masthead
- Import text files
- Navigate pages
- Continue a story across pages and insert continued notices

- Customize the ribbon
- Use Publisher's Edit Story in Microsoft Word feature
- Insert and edit marginal elements
- Revise a newsletter
- Apply decorative drop caps
- Check hyphenation in stories
- Create a template with property changes

Introduction

Desktop publishing is becoming an increasingly popular way for businesses of all sizes to produce their printed publications. The desktop aspects of design and production make it easy and inexpensive to produce high-quality publications in a short time. **Desktop publishing** (DTP) encompasses performing all publishing tasks from a desk, including the planning, designing, writing, and layout, as well as printing, collating, and distributing. With a personal computer and a software program, such as Publisher, you can create a professional publication from your computer without the cost and time of using a professional printing service.

Project: Energy Newsletter

Newsletters provide a popular way for offices, businesses, schools, and other organizations to distribute information to their clientele. A **newsletter** usually is a double-sided, multipage publication with newspaper features, such as columns and a masthead, and the added eye appeal of sidebars, pictures, and other graphics.

Newsletters have several advantages over other publication media. Typically, they are cheaper to produce than brochures. Brochures, designed to be in circulation longer as a type of advertising, are published in greater quantities and on more expensive paper than newsletters, making brochures more costly. Newsletters also differ from brochures in that newsletters commonly have a shorter shelf life, making newsletters a perfect forum for information with dates. Newsletters are narrower and more focused in scope than newspapers; their eye appeal is more distinctive. Many companies distribute newsletters to interested audiences; however, newsletters also are becoming an integral part of many marketing plans to widen audiences because they offer a legitimate medium by which to communicate services, successes, and issues.

The project in this module uses a Publisher newsletter template to produce the Anchor Steady newsletter shown in Figure 3–1. This monthly publication informs

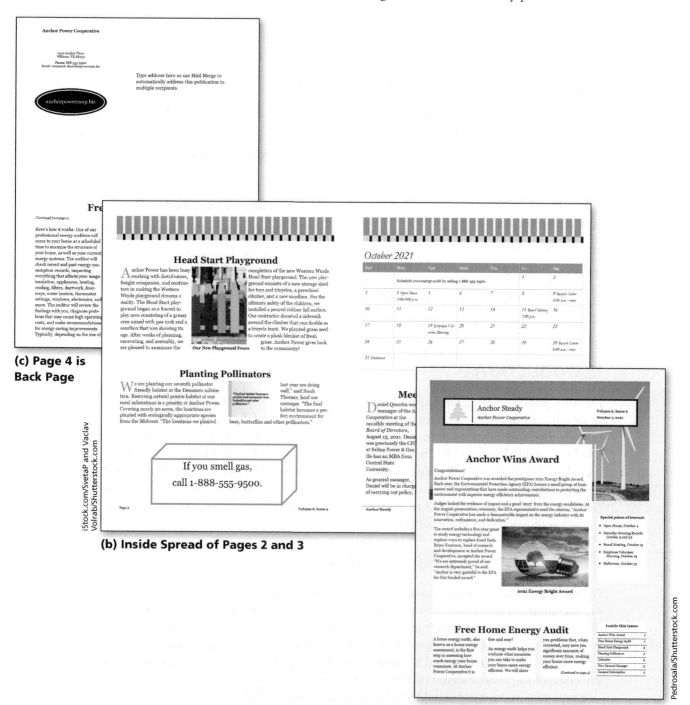

(c) Page 4 is Back Page

(b) Inside Spread of Pages 2 and 3

(a) Page 1

iStock.com/SvetaP and Vaclav Volrab/Shutterstock.com

Pedrosala/Shutterstock.com

Figure 3–1

readers about the Anchor Power Cooperative. The company's four-page newsletter contains a masthead, headings, stories, sidebars, pull-quotes, a calendar, and graphics.

You will perform the following general tasks as you progress through this module:

1. Select a newsletter template and edit publication options.
2. Import text from files and connect stories across pages.
3. Use continued notices.
4. Customize the ribbon.
5. Edit using Microsoft Word, when necessary.
6. Insert marginal elements.
7. Apply drop caps and hyphenation.
8. Create a template and change properties.

How do you decide on the purpose and audience of a newsletter?

Designing an effective newsletter involves a great deal of planning in order to deliver a message in the clearest, most attractive, and most effective way possible. Spend time brainstorming ideas for the newsletter with other members of the organization. Determine why you want to create a newsletter in the first place and what message you want to convey. Remember that newsletters both communicate and educate. Identify the scope of the newsletter and whether you want the topic to be general in nature or more specific — perhaps about only one aspect of the organization. Use the phrase, "I want to tell <audience> about <topic> because <purpose>." Decide on one purpose, and adjust your plans to match that purpose.

As you decide on your audience, ask yourself these questions:

• Who will be reading the stories?
• What are the demographics of this population? That is, what are their characteristics, such as gender, age, educational background, and heritage?
• Why do you want those people to read your newsletter?

Decide if the audience is a local or broader audience, interested clientele, patrons, employees, prospective customers, or family members. Keep in mind the age of your readers and their backgrounds, including both present and future readers.

Benefits and Advantages of Newsletters

Table 3–1 lists some benefits and advantages of using the newsletter medium.

Table 3–1 Benefits and Advantages of Using a Newsletter	
Purpose	**Benefits and Advantages**
Exposure	A publication easily distributed via office mail, by bulk mail, or electronically A pass-along publication for other interested parties A coffee-table reading item in reception areas
Education	An opportunity to inform in a nonrestrictive environment A directed education forum for clientele Increased, focused feedback that is unavailable in most advertising
Contacts	A form of legitimized contact A source of free information to build credibility An easier way to expand a contact database than other marketing tools
Communication	An effective medium to highlight the inner workings of a company A way to create a discussion forum A method to disseminate more information than with a brochure
Cost	An easily designed medium using desktop publishing software An inexpensive method of mass production A reusable design using a newsletter template

Publisher's newsletter templates include stories, graphics, sidebars, and other elements typical of newsletters using a rich collection of intuitive design, layout, typography, and graphic tools. Because Publisher takes care of many of the design issues, using a template to begin a newsletter gives you the advantage of proven layouts with fewer chances of publication errors.

Newsletter Design Choices

Publisher's many design-planning features include more than 100 different newsletter templates from which you may choose, each with its own set of design, color, font, and layout schemes. Each newsletter template produces four pages of stories, graphics, page numbers, and other objects in the same way. The difference is the location and style of the shapes and graphics, as well as the specific kind of decorations unique to each publication set. A **publication set** is a predefined group of shapes, designed in patterns to create a template style. A publication set is constant across publication types; for example, the Bars newsletter template has the same shapes and style of objects as does the Bars brochure template. A publication set helps in branding a company across publication types.

Another choice you have when making decisions about newsletter design is how the pages will be organized and ultimately printed. A one-page spread displays and prints the pages individually in portrait mode, which means the printed pages would need to be stapled or bound in some way. A two-page spread displays the first and last pages individually but displays the middle pages as two facing pages, similar to a book format. If you have special newsletter paper, such as 11 × 17, the pages print landscape, so you can fold the newsletter. Other print sizes are available as built-in templates, listed within the Blank Pages section. In the workspace, a two-page spread makes it easier to see how the pages will look when open. Stories and figures spanning a two-page spread rarely need notices about continuation. In a two-page spread, the page on the left is called a **verso page**. The page on the right is called a **recto page**.

Because newsletters sometimes are mailed, Publisher can reserve a place on the last page to place a customer address or, more likely, a label. An 8½ × 11-inch newsletter commonly is folded in half before being mailed.

BTW

Publisher Help
At any time while using Publisher, you can find answers to questions and see information about various topics through Publisher Help. Used properly, this form of assistance can increase your productivity and reduce your frustrations by minimizing the time you spend learning how to use Publisher.

BTW

The Ribbon and Screen Resolution
Publisher may change how the groups and buttons within the groups appear on the ribbon, depending on the computer's screen resolution. Thus, your ribbon may look different from the ones in this book if you are using a screen resolution other than 1366 × 768.

To Choose a Newsletter Template and Options

The following steps choose a newsletter template and change its options.

1 Start Publisher and then click BUILT-IN to display the built-in templates.

2 Scroll as necessary and then click the Newsletters thumbnail to display the newsletter templates.

3 Scroll to the section labeled More Installed Templates and then click Fading Frame to choose the template.

4 Click the Color scheme button in the template information pane. Scroll as necessary and then click Prairie to choose the color scheme.

5 Click the Font scheme button, scroll as necessary, and then click Archival to choose the font scheme.

6 Do not click the Business information button because it is not used in this publication.

7 Click the Page size button in the Options area and then, if necessary, click 'Two-page spread' to choose how the template will display.

8 If necessary, scroll down in the template information pane and click to display a check mark in the 'Include customer address' check box (Figure 3–2).

9 Click the CREATE button to create the publication based on the template settings.

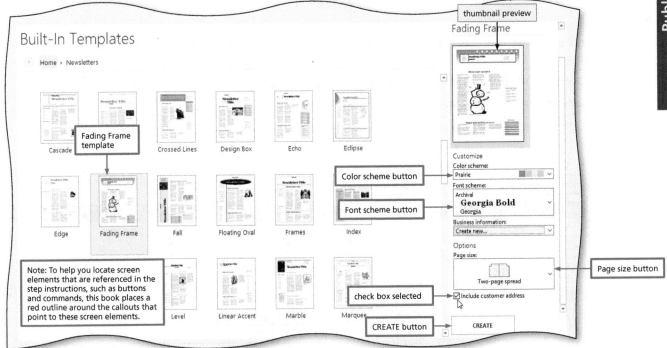

Figure 3–2

To Set Publisher Display Settings

It is helpful to display formatting marks, which indicate where in the publication you pressed ENTER, SPACEBAR, and other keys. The following steps display formatting marks and open the Page Navigation pane to display all of the pages of the newsletter.

1 If the Special Characters button (Home tab | Paragraph group) is not selected already, click it to display formatting marks on the screen.

2 If the Page Navigation pane is not open, click the Page Number button on the status bar to open the Page Navigation pane. If the Page Navigation pane is minimized, click the 'Expand Page Navigation Pane' button to maximize it.

How do you decide about options for the layout and printing?
Choosing a layout and printing options before you even write the stories is a daunting, yet extremely important, task. The kind of printing process and paper you will be using will affect the cost and, therefore, the length of the newsletter. Depending on what you can afford to produce and distribute, the layout may need more or fewer stories, graphics, columns, and sidebars. Base your decisions on content that will be repeated in future newsletters.

Make informed decisions about the kind of alignment you plan to use. Choose the paper size and determine how columns, a masthead, and graphics will affect your layout. Decide what kinds of features in the newsletter should be close to each other. A consistent look and feel with simple, eye-catching graphics normally is the best choice for the publication set. Plan to include one graphic with each story. Because newsletters usually are mass produced, collated, and stapled, you should make a plan for printing and decide if you are going to publish it in-house or externally. Choose a paper that is going to last until the next newsletter.

CONSIDER THIS

To Set Page Options

Publisher newsletters can display one, two, or three columns of story text, or you can mix the format. **Why?** *Changing the number of columns in a story or mixing the format adds visual interest.* Inside pages also can display calendars and forms. The following steps select page options for the various pages in the newsletter.

- With page 1 of the newsletter displayed in the workspace, click Page Design on the ribbon to display the Page Design tab.
- Click the Options button (Page Design tab | Template group) to display the Page Content dialog box.
- Click the Columns button to display its list (Figure 3–3).

Q&A Does the column choice affect the objects down the right side of the newsletter page?

No, the number of columns that you choose will be displayed in the stories only, and the choice affects only the current page.

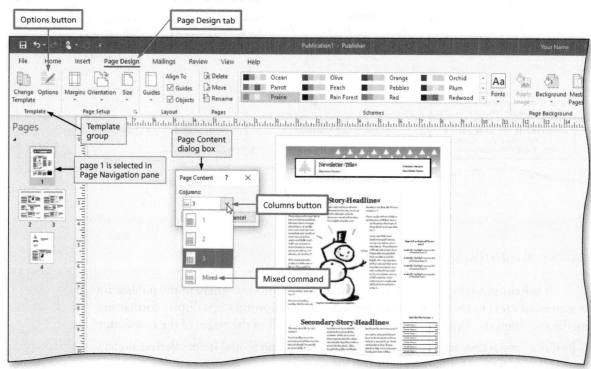

Figure 3–3

- Click Mixed in the Columns list to choose a mixed number of columns for the stories on page 1.
- Click OK (Page Content dialog box) to change the options for the page (Figure 3–4).

Q&A Is one choice better than another one?

No, it is a personal or customer preference. Longer stories may need to be continued at different places, depending upon how many columns of text you have. The more columns you have, the more white space is created on the page.

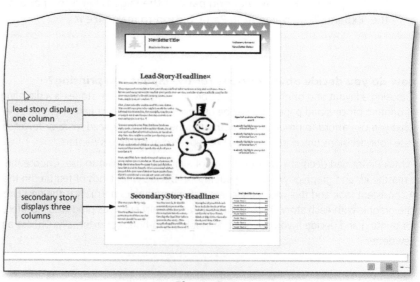

Figure 3–4

3

- In the Page Navigation pane, click the 'Page 2 and Page 3' thumbnail to display the pages in the workspace.

- Click the Page Design tab and then click the Options button (Page Design tab | Template group) to display the Page Content dialog box.

- Click the 'Select a page to modify' button to display its list (Figure 3–5).

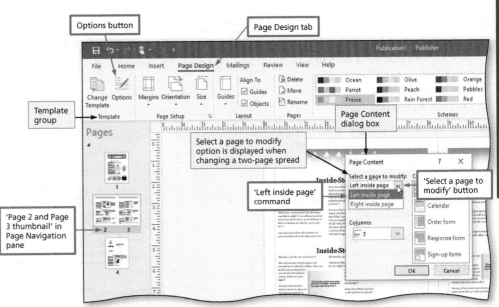

Figure 3–5

4

- If necessary, click 'Left inside page' to choose the verso page.

- Click the Columns button to display its list (Figure 3–6).

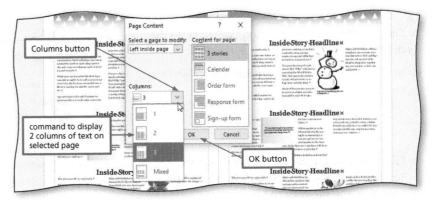

Figure 3–6

5

- Click 2 in the Columns list to choose a two-column format for the stories on page 2.

- Click OK (Page Content dialog box) to close the dialog box (Figure 3–7).

Q&A Can I move pages around in my newsletter?
Yes, you can right-click in the Page Navigation pane and then choose Move on the shortcut menu. Publisher will display a dialog box, allowing you to specify which page to move and the new location.

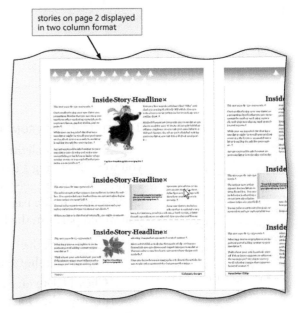

Figure 3–7

6

- Click the Page Design tab and then click the Options button (Page Design tab | Template group) to display the Page Content dialog box again.

- Click the 'Select a page to modify' button and then click 'Right inside page' to choose the recto page.

- Click the Columns button and then click 2 in the Columns list to choose two columns.

- In the Content for page area, click Calendar to insert a calendar on the recto page (Figure 3–8).

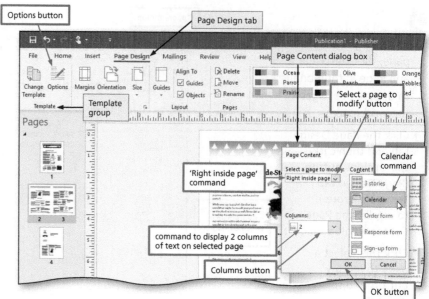

Figure 3–8

7

- Click OK (Page Content dialog box) to close the dialog box.

Q&A My calendar looks different. Did I do something wrong?

No. The calendar option uses the current month on your system. Any month is acceptable for this project.

- Click the Save button on the Quick Access Toolbar, browse to the storage location, and then save the file with the file name, SC_PUB_2_EnergyNewsletter (Figure 3–9).

Q&A Should I change the options for the back page?

No. You will edit those objects individually later in the module.

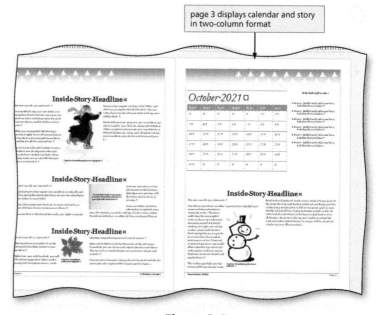

Figure 3–9

BTW

Organizing Files and Folders
You should organize and store files in folders so that you easily can find the files later. For example, if you were taking an introductory computer class called CIS 101, a good practice would be to save all Publisher files in a Publisher folder in a CIS 101 folder.

TO DELETE PAGES FROM A NEWSLETTER

Not all newsletters are four pages long. Some will have more or fewer pages. If you were designing a newsletter with only two pages, it would be best to delete pages 2 and 3 because page 4 already is formatted to be a back page in most templates. Pages 2 and 3 have inside page numbers and graphics. If you wanted to delete pages 2 and 3, you would perform the following steps.

1. Right-click the 'Page 2 and Page 3' thumbnail in the Page Navigation pane to display the shortcut menu.

2. Click Delete on the shortcut menu to delete pages 2 and 3. When Publisher displays the Delete Page dialog box for confirmation, select the Both pages option button and then click OK (Delete Page dialog box).

To Add Pages to a Newsletter

If you wanted to add extra pages to a newsletter, you would perform the following steps.

1. Right-click the 'Page 2 and Page 3' thumbnail in the Page Navigation pane to display the shortcut menu.
2. Click Insert Page on the shortcut menu to insert a new page. Follow the directions in the Insert Newsletter Pages dialog box to insert either a left-hand page, a right-hand page, or both, and then click OK (Insert Newsletter Pages dialog box).

Editing the Masthead

Most newsletters contain a masthead similar to those used in newspapers. A **masthead** is a box or section printed in each issue that lists information such as the name, publisher, location, volume, and date. The Publisher-designed masthead included in the Fading Frame newsletter publication set contains several text boxes and colors that create an attractive, eye-catching graphic to complement the set.

To Edit the Masthead

The following steps edit text in the masthead, including the volume and issue number. *Why? Publications typically use volume numbers to indicate the number of years the publication has been in existence. The issue number indicates its sequence. Volume numbers and issue numbers do not necessarily correlate to the calendar year and month. Schools, for example, sometimes start in the fall with Volume 1, Issue 1.*

❶

- Click the Page 1 thumbnail in the Page Navigation pane to change the display to page 1.
- Click the text, Newsletter Title, to select it and then zoom to 150%.
- Type **Anchor Steady** to replace the text. Right-click the text and then click Best Fit on the shortcut menu (Figure 3–10).

Q&A Why does my font look different? Publisher replaces the selected text with the font from the publication set. Your font may differ from the one shown.

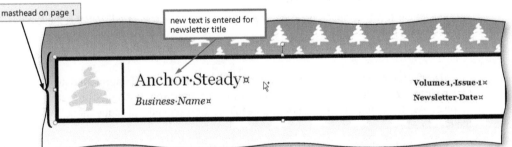

Figure 3–10

❷

- Click the default text in the Business Name text box and then press CTRL+A to select all of the text.
- Type **Anchor Power Cooperative** to replace the text (Figure 3–11).

Figure 3–11

3

- Click the placeholder text in the Newsletter Date text box to select it.

- Type `October 1, 2021` to replace the text.

- Click the placeholder text in the Volume 1, Issue 1 text box to select it.

- Type `Volume 6, Issue 2` to replace the text (Figure 3–12).

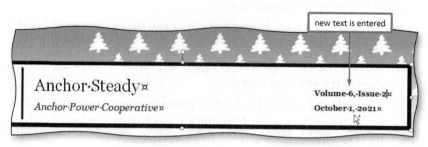

Figure 3–12

Newsletter Text

Newsletter content may come to you, as the desktop publisher, in various ways. Authors may submit their stories in email or as attachments. Others may post a Microsoft Word document or a graphic on the company's common storage drive. Still other authors may handwrite their stories or record them on a recording device. In those cases, you will have to type the story yourself.

CONSIDER THIS

How do you gather topics and research stories?

Gather credible, relevant information in the form of stories, pictures, dates, figures, tables, and discussion threads. Plan far enough ahead so that you have time to take pictures or gather graphics for each story — even if you end up not using them. Stay organized; keep folders of information and store pictures and stories together. If you have to write a story from scratch, gather your data, do your research, and have an informed reader go over your content.

The same principles of audience, purpose, and topic apply to individual stories, just as they do for the newsletter as a whole. Evaluate your sources for authority, timeliness, and accuracy. Be especially wary of information obtained from the web. Any person, company, or organization can publish a webpage on the Internet. Answer these questions about the source:

- Authority: Does a reputable institution or group support the source? Is the information presented without bias? Are the author's credentials listed and verifiable?

- Timeliness: Is the information up to date? Are the dates of sources listed? What is the last date that the information was revised or updated?

- Accuracy: Is the information free of errors? Is it verifiable? Are the sources clearly identified?

Identify the sources for your text and graphics. Notify all writers of important dates, and allow time for gathering the data. Make a list for each story: include the author's name, the approximate length of the story, the electronic format, and associated graphics. Ask the author for suggestions for headlines. Consult with colleagues about other graphics, features, sidebars, and the masthead.

Acknowledge all sources of information; do not plagiarize. Not only is plagiarism unethical, it also is considered an academic crime that can have severe consequences, such as failing a course or being expelled from school.

When you summarize, paraphrase (rewrite information in your own words), present facts, give statistics, quote exact words, or show a map, chart, or other graphical image, you must acknowledge the source. Information that commonly is known or accessible to the audience constitutes **common knowledge** and does not need to be acknowledged. If, however, you question whether certain information is common knowledge, you should document it — just to be safe.

Publisher allows users to import text and graphics from many sources, from a variety of different programs, and in many different file formats. Publisher uses the term, **importing**, to describe inserting text or objects from any other source into the Publisher workspace. Publisher uses the term, **story**, when referring to text that is contained within a single text box or a chain of linked text boxes. Each newsletter template provides **linked text boxes**, or text boxes whose text flows from one to another. In the templates, two or three text boxes may be linked automatically; however, if a story is too long to fit in the linked text boxes, Publisher will offer to link even more text boxes for easy reading.

Replacing Placeholder Text Using an Imported File

Publisher suggests that 175 to 225 words will fit in the space allocated for the lead story. The story is displayed in a two-column text box format that connects, or links, the running text from one text box to the next. Publisher links text boxes according to your settings, and it displays arrow buttons to navigate to the next and previous text boxes.

This edition of *Anchor Steady* contains several stories, some of which have been typed previously and stored using Microsoft Word, as they might be in a business setting. The stories, located in the Data Files, are ready to be used in the newsletter. Please contact your instructor for information about accessing the Data Files. You will type the final story yourself. Each story will include a **headline**, which is a short phrase printed at the top of a story, usually in a bigger font than the story. A headline summarizes the story.

BTW
Touch Mode Differences
The Office and Windows interfaces may vary if you are using Touch mode. For this reason, you might notice that the function or appearance of your touch screen differs slightly from this module's presentation.

To Edit the Lead Story Headline

The following steps edit the Lead Story Headline placeholder text.

1 Click the placeholder text, Lead Story Headline, on page 1 to select it.

2 Type **Anchor Wins Award** to replace the text (Figure 3–13).

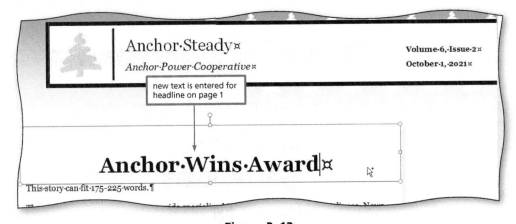

Anchor·Steady¤

Anchor·Power·Cooperative¤

Volume·6,·Issue·2¤

October·1,·2021¤

new text is entered for headline on page 1

Anchor·Wins·Award¤

This·story·can·fit·175-225·words.¶

Figure 3–13

To Import a Text File

The following steps import a text file to replace the Publisher-supplied placeholder text for the lead story. *Why? Importing the story prevents typographical errors that might be introduced by typing the text.* To complete these steps, you will be required to use the Data Files. Please contact your instructor for information about accessing the Data Files.

1

- Scroll down to display the story below the headline. Zoom to approximately 100%.

- Click the placeholder text in the story to select it (Figure 3–14).

🔎 **Experiment**

- Read the placeholder text to learn about design suggestions related to newsletter publications.

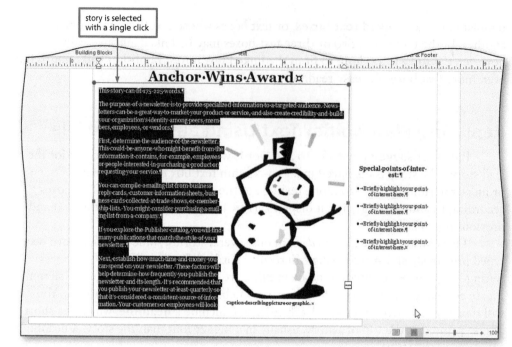

Figure 3–14

2

- Display the Insert tab.

- Click the Insert File button (Insert tab | Text group) to display the Insert Text dialog box.

- Navigate to the location of the file to be opened (in this case, the Module 03 folder in the Publisher Data Files) (Figure 3–15).

Q&A What kinds of text files can Publisher import?

Publisher can import files from most popular applications. If you click the 'All Text Formats' button (Insert Text dialog box), you can see a list of specific file types.

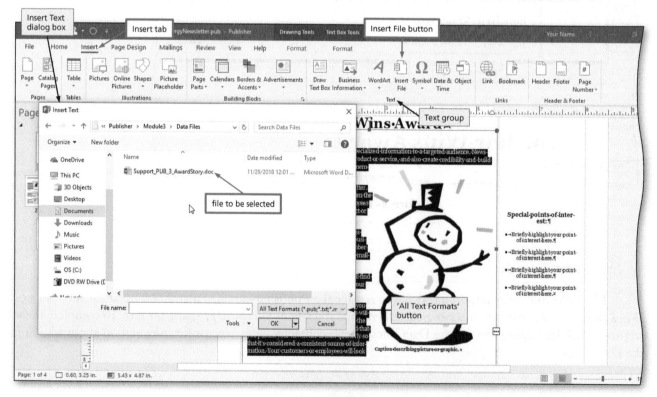

Figure 3–15

3

- Double-click the file named Support_PUB_3_AwardStory. doc to insert the text into the newsletter (Figure 3–16).

Q&A

Why is this file stored in the .doc format instead of the .docx format?
The .docx format sometimes produces an Office file validation error, especially on networked drives.

Why did Publisher display the Converting dialog box before my text appeared?
While Publisher is importing the story, you may see a message saying Publisher is converting this file. Wait until the process is complete before you continue to edit.

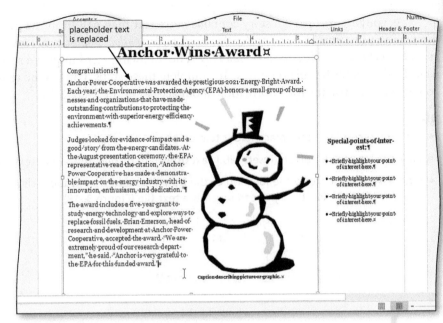

Figure 3–16

Other Ways

1. Right-click story, point to Change Text on shortcut menu, click Text File on Change Text submenu, click file name, click OK (Insert Text dialog box)

To Edit the Secondary Story Headline

The following steps edit the Secondary Story Headline placeholder text.

1 Scroll down on page 1 and then click the placeholder text, Secondary Story Headline, to select it.

2 Type **Free Home Energy Audit** to replace the text (Figure 3–17).

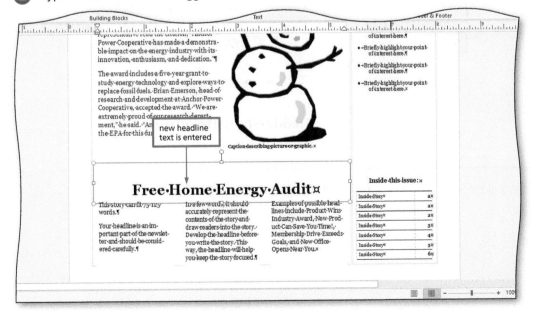

Figure 3–17

To Continue a Story across Pages

As you import text, if a story contains more text than will fit in the default text box, Publisher displays a message to warn you. ***Why?*** *You then have the option to allow Publisher to connect, or* **autoflow**, *the text to another available text box or to flow the text manually.* The following steps import a story and continue it from page 1 to page 2 using Publisher dialog boxes. To complete these steps, you will be required to use the Data Files. Please contact your instructor for information about accessing the Data Files.

- Click the secondary story placeholder text on page 1 to select it.
- Click the Insert File button (Insert tab | Text group) to display the Insert Text dialog box.
- If necessary, navigate to the location of the Data Files and then double-click the file named Support _PUB_3_AuditStory.doc to insert the text file (Figure 3–18).

Q&A

Why did Publisher display a dialog box and move to page 2?
The story was too large to fit in the space provided on page 1. Publisher moved to the first available text box with default or placeholder story text.

What do the three autoflow dialog box buttons do?
If you click Yes, as you will do here, Publisher will insert the rest of the text in the currently selected text box. If you click No, Publisher will move to the next story text box and ask again. If you click Cancel, you will have to flow the text manually.

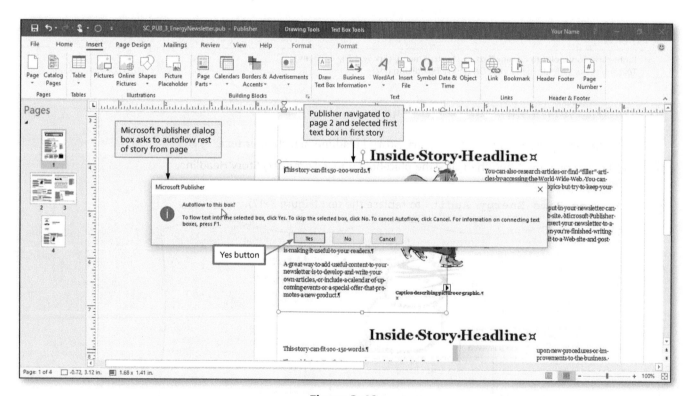

Figure 3–18

2

- In the Microsoft Publisher dialog box, click Yes to autoflow the story to the selected text box (Figure 3–19).

Q&A What if I have no more spare text boxes in which to flow the text?
Publisher will ask if you want new text boxes created. If you answer yes, Publisher automatically will create a new page with new text boxes.

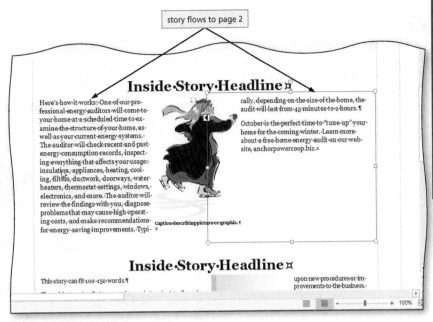

Figure 3–19

To Follow a Story across Pages

Publisher provides a way to move quickly back and forth through a continued story. ***Why?*** *While reading and editing the story, you may forget where the rest of the story is located or want to jump to its location quickly.* The following steps use the Next and Previous buttons to follow the story from text box to text box, across pages.

1

- Click the Page 1 thumbnail in the Page Navigation pane and navigate to the Free Home Energy Audit story at the bottom of the page.

- Click the third text box in the story to display the Previous and Next buttons (Figure 3–20).

Q&A Do all text boxes have Previous and Next buttons?
No. Only text boxes that contain a linked story display the buttons.

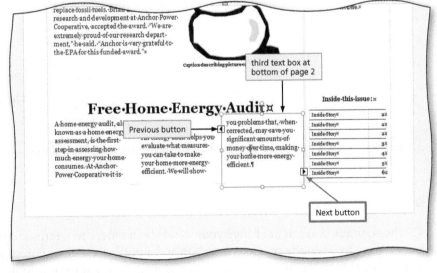

Figure 3–20

● Click the Next button to move to the rest of the story — the first text box at the top of page 2 (Figure 3–21).

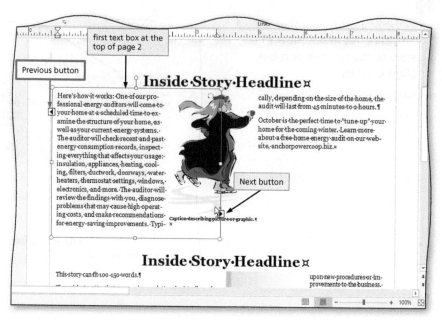

Figure 3–21

● Click the Previous button to move back to the first part of the story — the third text box at the bottom of page 1 (Figure 3–22).

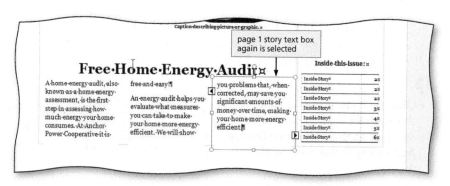

Figure 3–22

Other Ways

1. Select text box, click Previous or Next button (Text Box Tools Format tab | Linking group)

To Break a Text Box Link

Sometimes, you might change your mind about where to continue a story. In that case, you have two choices. You can undo the previous insertion and autoflow again, or you can break the connection and create a manual one. When you break a connection, the extra text that cannot fit in the text box is placed in the **overflow area**. *Why? Unlike the Clipboard, the overflow area is maintained when you save the publication, allowing you to access it at any time.* The following step breaks the connection between the story at the bottom of page 1 and its continuation at the top of page 2 and then places the extra text in the overflow area.

● If necessary, navigate to page 1 and the story at the bottom of the page and click the third column in the story to select the text box.

● Display the Text Box Tools Format tab.

- Click the Break button (Text Box Tools Format tab | Linking group) to break the connection to the rest of the story (Figure 3–23).

Q&A Where is the rest of the story now? Publisher places it in an overflow area, as indicated by the 'Text in Overflow' button in Figure 3–23. The text box on page 2 becomes blank.

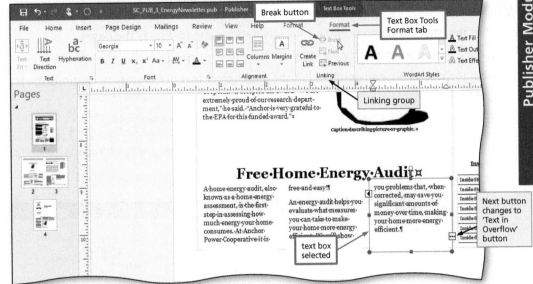

Figure 3–23

To Manually Continue the Story across Pages

The following steps manually move the text from the overflow area to another text box. *Why? You cannot see the text while it is in overflow.*

1

- If necessary, select the text box that displays the 'Text in Overflow' button.
- Click the 'Text in Overflow' button to display the pitcher-shaped pointer (Figure 3–24).

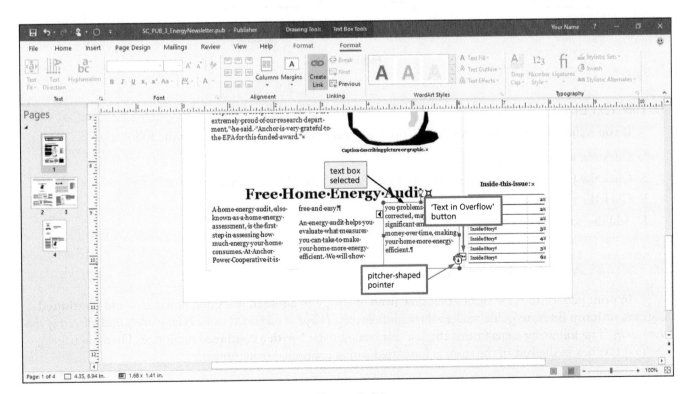

Figure 3–24

2

- Click the Page 4 thumbnail in the Page Navigation pane to display the pages.

- Scroll as necessary to display the story at the bottom of page 4.

- With the pitcher-shaped pointer, click the placeholder text in the story to continue the Free Home Energy Audit text (Figure 3–25).

Q&A What if I change my mind and want to continue to a different text box?

You can click the Undo button on the Quick Access Toolbar, or you can click the last column of the story on page 1 and then click the Break button (Text Box Tools Format tab | Linking group). You then can click the 'Text in Overflow' button again.

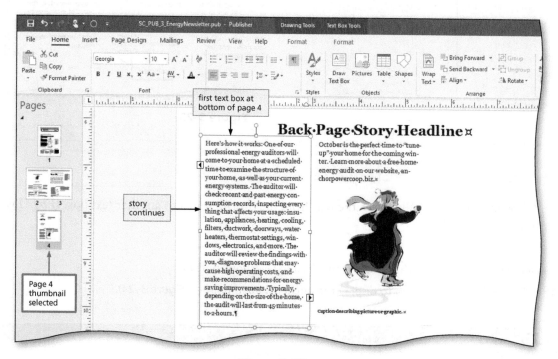

Figure 3–25

TO LINK TEXT BOXES

If you wanted to link text boxes that do not have text in overflow, you would do the following.

1. Click the first text box to select it.

2. Click the Create Link button (Text Box Tools Format tab | Linking group).

3. Click the new text box.

4. Add the continued notices.

To Format with Continued Notices

In print publications for stories that flow from one page to another, it is good practice to add **continued notices**, or **jump lines**, to guide readers through the story. *Why? A continued notice helps readers find the rest of the story easily.* The following steps format the last text box on page 1 with a continued on notice. Then, on page 3, the first text box in the rest of the story is formatted with a continued from notice.

1

- Click the Page 1 thumbnail in the Page Navigation pane and then navigate to the bottom of the page.

- Right-click the third column of text in the lead story to display the shortcut menu (Figure 3–26).

Q&A Will Publisher ask me what page number to use?
No, the placement of the notices and the page numbering are automatic.

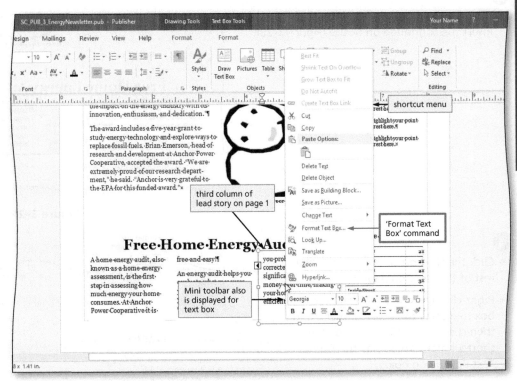

Figure 3–26

2

- Click 'Format Text Box' on the shortcut menu to display the Format Text Box dialog box.

- Click the Text Box tab to display the Text Box sheet.

- Click to display a check mark in the 'Include "Continued on page…"' check box (Figure 3–27).

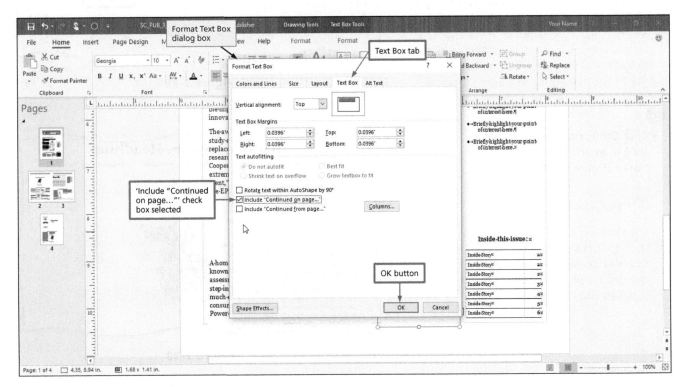

Figure 3–27

● Click OK (Format Text Box dialog box) to insert the continued on notice (Figure 3–28).

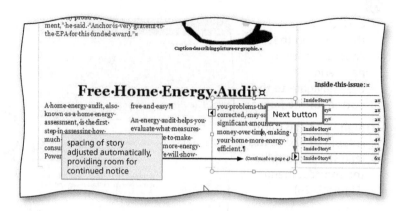

Figure 3–28

● Click the Next button to move to the rest of the story on page 4.

● Right-click the text in the first text box to display the shortcut menu and then click 'Format Text Box' on the shortcut menu to display the Format Text Box dialog box.

● If necessary, click the Text Box tab (Format Text Box dialog box) to display the Text Box sheet.

● Click to display a check mark in the 'Include "Continued from page…"' check box (Figure 3–29).

Q&A What do I do if my dialog box is covering up the text box?
The setting changes will take place when you click OK. If you want to see both the dialog box and the text box, you can drag the title bar of the dialog box to a better location.

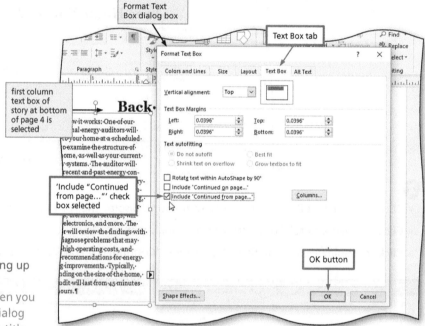

Figure 3–29

● Click OK (Format Text Box dialog box) to insert the continued from notice (Figure 3–30).

⊘ Experiment

Use the Next and Previous buttons to move between the linked text boxes on pages 1 and 4. Examine the continued notices with the supplied page numbers.

Figure 3–30

Other Ways

1. Select text box, click Text Dialog Box Launcher (Text Box Tools Format tab | Text group), click Text Box tab, click 'Include "Continued on page…"' or 'Include "Continued from page…"'

To Edit the Headlines for the Continued Story

The following step edits the inside headline for the continued story.

1 Click the Back Page Story Headline placeholder text to select it and then type **Free Home Energy Audit** to replace the text (Figure 3–31).

Figure 3–31

To Edit Page 2

The following steps edit the headline and import the text for two stories on page 2 and delete the third story to make room for later content. To complete these steps, you will be required to use the Data Files. Please contact your instructor for information about accessing the Data Files.

1 Scroll to display the top portion of page 2 and then click the Inside Story Headline placeholder text above the first story to select it. Recall that the first story text box is blank because of the autoflow change.

2 Type **Head Start Playground** to replace the selected headline.

3 Click inside the empty story text box to position the insertion point.

4 Click the Insert File button (Insert tab | Text group) to display the Insert Text dialog box.

5 If necessary, navigate to the Data Files and then double-click the file named Support_PUB_3_PlaygroundStory.doc to insert the text file.

6 Repeat Steps 1 through 5 for the second story on page 2. Use the text, Planting Pollinators, as the headline. Insert the text file named Support_PUB_3_PollinatorsStory.docx for the story.

7 Zoom to approximately 100% to display both stories and headlines (Figure 3–32).

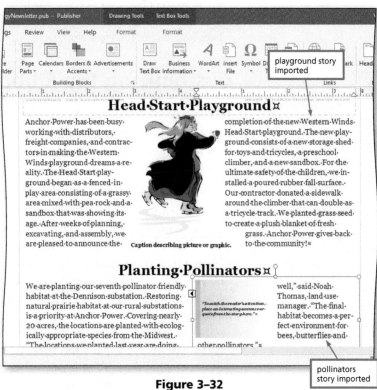

Figure 3–32

To Delete Objects on Page 2

The following steps remove the headline, story, and graphic on page 2. You will fill that area later in the module.

① Navigate to the bottom of page 2.

② Beginning in the margin, drag around the outside of the template headline, story, graphic, and caption objects to select them all.

③ Press DELETE to delete the selected objects (Figure 3–33).

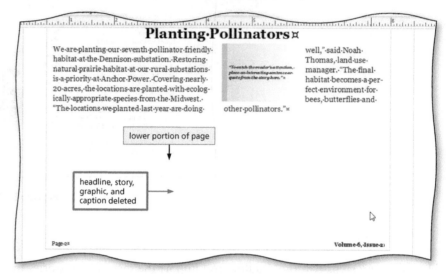

Figure 3–33

④ Click the Save button on the Quick Access Toolbar to save the file again with the same file name and in the same location.

Break Point: If you want to take a break, this is a good place to do so. Exit Publisher. To resume later, start Publisher, open the file called SC_PUB_3_EnergyNewsletter, and continue following the steps from this location forward.

BTW

Text in Overflow
The overflow area is an invisible storage location within a publication that holds extra text. You can move text out of overflow and back into a publication by one of several means: flowing text into a new text box, autofitting text, enlarging the text box, changing the text size, changing the margins within the text box, or deleting some of the text in the text box.

Customizing the Ribbon

It is easy to **customize**, or personalize, the ribbon the way that you want it. You can:

- Create custom groups and custom tabs to contain frequently used commands.
- Rearrange or rename buttons, groups, and tabs to fit your work style.
- Rename or remove buttons and boxes from an existing tab and group.
- Add new buttons to a custom group or to the Quick Access Toolbar.

When you add new buttons to the ribbon, you may choose from a list that includes commands that you may use elsewhere in Publisher, such as those on shortcut menus, commands from Backstage view, or other commands that are not on the ribbon. Or, you can create a new button that executes a command or set of commands that you record. In this module, you will create a custom group on the Review tab and add a command that is not currently on the ribbon. The command will appear as a button in the new custom group.

You can customize the ribbon in all of the Microsoft Office applications, but the customizations are application specific. The changes you make to the Publisher ribbon will not change the ribbon in any other Microsoft Office application. When you no longer need the customization, it can be removed individually, or the entire ribbon can be reset to its default settings by removing all customizations.

To Customize the Publisher Ribbon

The following steps add the 'Edit Story in Microsoft Word' button to a new group on the Review tab on the ribbon. *Why? The Review tab has empty space to hold custom groups. The other tabs are full. Adding a custom group to one of the other tabs would compress the existing groups, which might make it more difficult to locate buttons and boxes.*

1

- Click File on the ribbon to open Backstage view and then click Options to display the Publisher Options dialog box.

- Click Customize Ribbon in the left pane (Publisher Options dialog box) to display the options for customizing the ribbon in the right pane.

- Click the 'Choose commands from' button to view the list of commands (Figure 3–34).

Q&A Why are some commands not on the ribbon?

Publisher is a powerful program with many commands. Including all of the available commands on the ribbon would be overwhelming to many users. Publisher includes the more frequently used or popular commands in its default set.

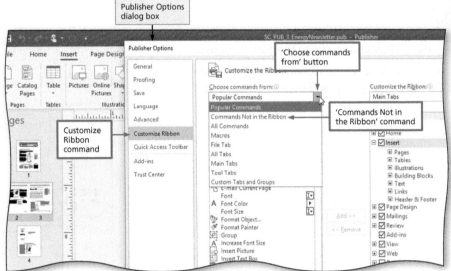

Figure 3–34

2

- Click 'Commands Not in the Ribbon' to display the list.

- Click the command you want to add (in this case, the 'Edit Story in Microsoft Word' command).

- Click Review in the Main Tabs list to select the destination tab and then click the New Group button to create a custom group.

- Click the Add button to add the chosen command to the new group (Figure 3–35).

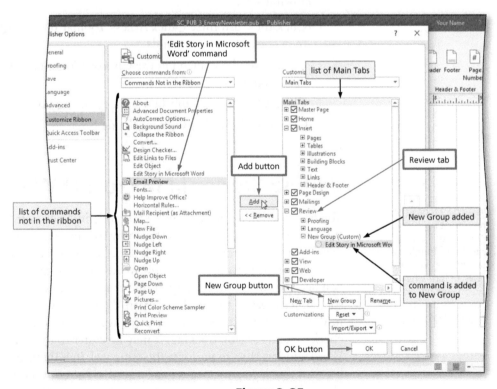

Figure 3–35

Q&A

Q&A

Can I add more than one command to the ribbon?
Yes, but you have to add them one at a time.

Do I have to add commands to a new group?
Yes. Commands can be added only to custom groups. The default tabs and groups cannot be changed.

3

- Click OK (Publisher Options dialog box) to close the dialog box and to create the custom group.
- Click Review on the ribbon to display the Review tab and its new group and button (Figure 3–36).

Q&A

Can I rename the custom group?
Yes, you can rename any group or command by clicking the Rename button in the Publisher Options dialog box. As you rename, you can choose a custom icon for the command.

Why is the new button dimmed?
The button becomes active when the insertion point is inside a text box where editing in Word would be logical.

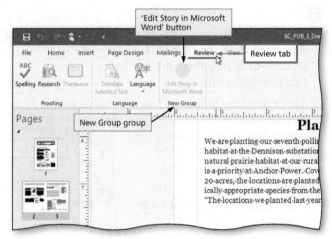

Figure 3–36

Other Ways

1. Right-click ribbon, click 'Customize the Ribbon' on shortcut menu, choose or create groups, add commands, click OK (Publisher Options dialog box)

TO ADD A BUTTON TO THE QUICK ACCESS TOOLBAR

If you wanted to add a button to the Quick Access Toolbar, you would perform the following steps.

1. Click the Customize Quick Access Toolbar button (Quick Access Toolbar) and then click More Commands.

2. Click desired command in the Choose Commands From list (Publisher Options dialog box).

3. Click Add button (Publisher Options dialog box).

4. Click OK (Publisher Options dialog box).

Editing Stories in Microsoft Word

You have seen that you can edit text directly in Microsoft Publisher or import text from a previously stored file. A third way to edit text is to use Microsoft Word as your editor. Publisher provides an easy link between the two applications.

If you need to edit only a few words, it is faster to continue using Publisher. If you need to edit a longer story or one that is not available on your storage device, it sometimes is easier to edit the story in Word. Many users are accustomed to working in Word and want to take advantage of available Word features, such as grammar checking and revision tracking. It may be easier to drag and drop paragraphs in a Word window than to perform the same task in a Publisher window, especially when it involves moving across pages in a larger Publisher publication. Editing your stories in Word allows you to manipulate the text using the full capabilities of a word processing program.

While you are editing a story in Word, you cannot edit the corresponding text box in Publisher; Publisher displays a gray box instead of the text. When you close Word, control returns to Publisher, and the text appears.

Occasionally, if you have many applications running, such as virus protection and other memory-taxing programs, Publisher may warn you that you are low on computer memory. In that case, exit the other applications and try editing the story in Word again.

To Edit a Story Using Microsoft Word

The following steps use Microsoft Word in conjunction with Publisher to create the text on page 3 of the newsletter. *Why? Some people find it easier to edit stories using Microsoft Word.* Microsoft Word version 6.0 or later must be installed on your computer for this procedure to work.

1
- If necessary, navigate to page 3 and then scroll to display the story in the lower portion of page 3.
- Click the placeholder text in the story to select it.
- If necessary, display the Review tab (Figure 3–37).

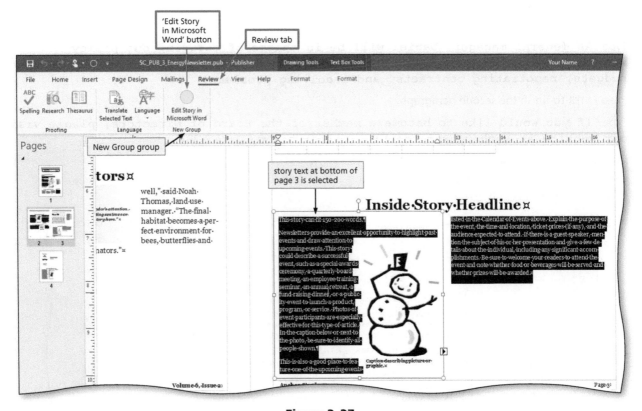

Figure 3–37

2
- Click the 'Edit Story in Microsoft Word' button (Review tab | New Group group) to start the Word program. Maximize the window, if necessary.
- Press CTRL+A to select all of the text, change the font size to 12, and then type `Daniel Quentin was chosen general manager of the Anchor Power Cooperative at the monthly meeting of the Board of Directors, August 13, 2021. Daniel was previously the CFO at Salina Power & Gas. He has an MBA from Central State University.` to replace the placeholder text.

- Press ENTER to finish the first paragraph (Figure 3–38).

Why are my formatting marks not showing in Microsoft Word?

It is possible that someone has turned off formatting marks. Click Word's 'Show/Hide ¶' button (Word Home tab | Paragraph group) to show or hide them.

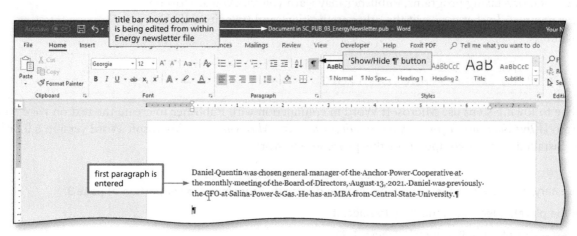

Figure 3–38

❸

- Type **As general manager, Daniel will be in charge of carrying out policy, managing revenue and expenses, helping with long-range planning, developing new budgets, negotiating contracts, and resolving problems.**

- Press ENTER to finish the second paragraph.

- Type **If you would like to become a member of the Board of Directors, please visit our website at anchorpowercoop.biz.** to finish the text (Figure 3–39).

Why are my fonts different?

Usually, the Word text displays the same formatting as the previous text in Publisher. Your display may differ, depending on available fonts.

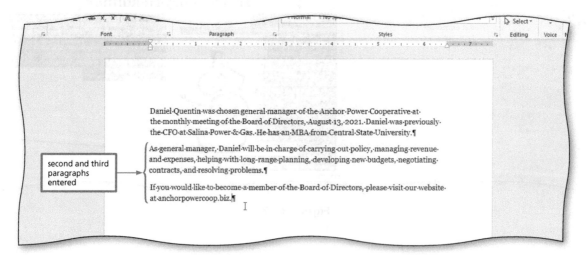

Figure 3–39

To Format while Editing in Microsoft Word

The following step uses CTRL on the keyboard to select multiple sections of nonadjacent text and format them in Microsoft Word. *Why? You cannot select nonadjacent text in Publisher.*

- Drag to select the words, Board of Directors, in the first paragraph.
- CTRL+drag to select the words, Board of Directors, in the third paragraph.
- Click the Italic button (Home tab | Font group) on the Word ribbon (Figure 3–40).

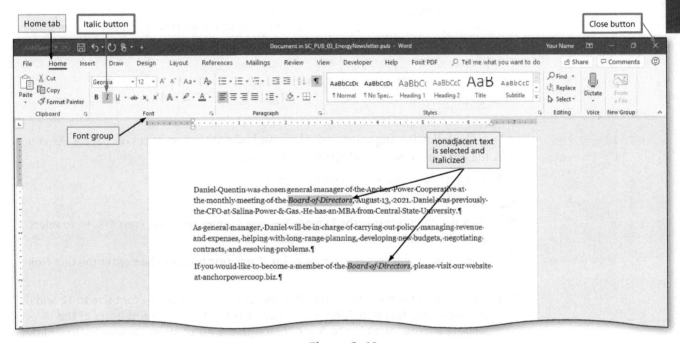

Figure 3–40

To Exit Word and Return to Publisher

The following steps exit Word and return to Publisher. *Why? You must exit Word in order to edit the text box in Publisher.*

- Click the Close button on the title bar of the Document in SC_PUB_3_EnergyNewsletter.pub - Word window to exit Word (Figure 3–41).

Q&A Why do I see only gray lines instead of the text?
Starting Microsoft Word from within Microsoft Publisher is a drain on your computer's memory and on the refresh rate of your screen. Try navigating to page 1 and then back to page 3 to refresh the screen.

2
- Select the text in the headline for the story and then type **Meet Our New General Manager** as the new headline.

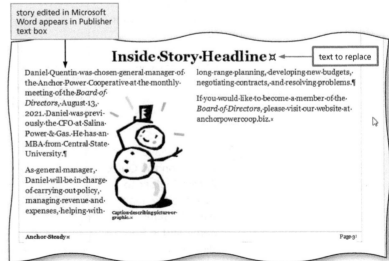

Figure 3–41

To Edit Objects on Page 4

Table 3–2 lists text for the other objects on page 4.

Table 3–2 Text for Page 4	
Location	**Text**
Business Name	Anchor Power Cooperative
Primary Business Address	2500 Anchor Plaza Willison, NE 68052
Phone, Fax, Email text box	Phone: 888-555-9500 Email: comments@anchorpowercoop.biz
Attention getter	anchorpowercoop.biz
Organization logo	<delete>
Business Tagline or Motto	<delete>
Mail Merge instructions text box	<leave as is>

The following steps delete the logo and edit other text boxes on page 4. As you edit the text boxes, zoom and scroll as necessary.

1 Navigate to the upper portion of page 4.

2 Edit the Business Name if necessary.

3 Click the default text in the Primary Business Address text box. Press CTRL+A to select all of the text. Enter the text from Table 3–2.

4 Select the default text in the Phone, Fax, Email text box and then enter the text from Table 3–2.

5 Select the text in the attention getter and delete it. Change the font size to 12 and then enter the text from Table 3–2. If Publisher capitalizes the first letter of the website address, point to the A and then click the AutoCorrect Options button. Click 'Undo Automatic Capitalization' in the list.

6 Select the Organization logo and delete it.

7 Select the Business Tagline or Motto text box and delete it (Figure 3–42).

Q&A Should I delete the Mail Merge text box in the upper-right portion of the page? No. It will serve as a placeholder for the energy company to use when it eventually mails the printed publication to clients.

8 Click the Save button on the Quick Access Toolbar to save the file again with the same file name and in the same location.

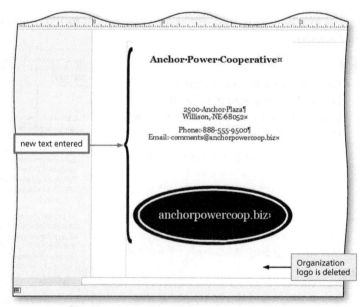

new text entered

Organization logo is deleted

Figure 3–42

Marginal Elements

Publisher newsletter templates include marginal elements and layout features to make the newsletter more attractive and to add interest to the page. A **sidebar**, or breakout, is a small piece of text, set off with a box or graphic and positioned adjacent to the body of a document. It contains auxiliary information that is not vital for understanding the main text but usually adds interest or additional information. Tables of contents, art boxes, and bulleted points of interest are examples of sidebars. A newsletter **table of contents**, or margin table, usually is a narrow, short list that is used to refer readers to specific pages or to present listed or numeric items in the margin area. A **pull-quote**, or **pullout**, is an excerpt from the main story used to highlight the concepts within the story or to attract readers. Pull-quotes, like sidebars, can be set off with a box or graphic. Graphics, shapes, and borders also are used sometimes as marginal elements.

To Edit Sidebars

The energy newsletter template includes two sidebars on page 1. The first one is a table of contents. The second is a bulleted list about special points of interest. *Why? Some newsletters use a sidebar table as an index to locate stories in longer newsletters; sidebars also are used to break up a page with lots of text and attract readers to inside pages. Other newsletters use sidebar tables to display numerical data and lists.* Table 3–3 lists the text for the sidebars that you will edit in the following steps.

Table 3–3 Text for Sidebars		
Inside this issue:	Anchor Wins Award	1
	Free Home Energy Audit	1
	Head Start Playground	2
	Planting Pollinators	2
	Calendar	3
	New General Manager	3
	General Information	4
Special points of interest:	• Open House, October 4	
	• Saturday Morning Recycle <soft return> October 9 and 23	
	• Board Meeting, October 15	
	• Employee Volunteer <soft return> Morning, October 19	
	• Halloween, October 31	

BTW

Bullets and Soft Returns
If you are editing a bulleted list, a soft return will not repeat the bullet. This is ideal for short phrases and lists within a single bullet.

- Navigate to the lower portion of page 1.
- Locate the Inside this issue sidebar and then click Inside Story in the first row select it. Zoom as necessary (Figure 3–43).

Q&A
Do I have to edit the lower sidebar first?
No. You can edit them in any order.

What are the dotted gray lines in the table?
Publisher displays dotted gray lines to indicate the size of each cell in the table. A **cell** is the text box located where a table column and table row intersect. The lines do not print.

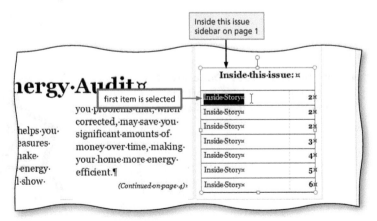

Figure 3–43

2

- Type **Anchor Wins Award** to replace the text and then press TAB. Complete the table with the data from Table 3–3. Use TAB to move from cell to cell (Figure 3–44).

Q&A Could I click the next cell instead of pressing TAB?
You could click the cell, but you then would need to select the page number and type to replace it. Pressing TAB both advances to and selects the data in the next cell.

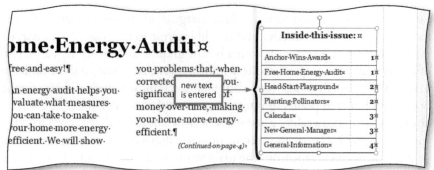

Figure 3–44

To Use a Soft Return

The following steps edit the Special points of interest sidebar. The sidebar contains a bulleted list placeholder. As you replace bulleted text, Publisher creates a hard return each time you press ENTER. A hard return creates a new paragraph and new bullet with appropriate paragraph spacing. Sometimes, however, you do not want a new bullet. *Why? A longer, two-line bullet should not display a second bullet graphic.* In this case, when you want a new line, you can use a **soft return**, also called a **manual line break**. To create a soft return, you press SHIFT+ENTER. There may be other times to use a soft return, such as in a title or heading, to prevent hyphens, or to balance a two-line heading.

1

- Navigate to the Special points of interest sidebar and then click the bulleted list to select it. Zoom as necessary (Figure 3–45).

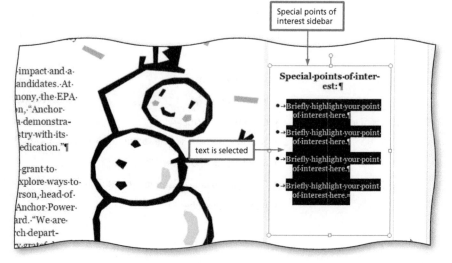

Figure 3–45

2

- Type **Open House, October 4** and then press ENTER to insert the first bulleted item (Figure 3–46).

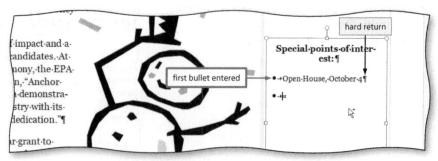

Figure 3–46

- Type **Saturday Morning Recycle** to create the beginning of the second bullet.

- Press SHIFT+ENTER to create a soft return (Figure 3–47).

What is the symbol that appeared at the end of the line?
Publisher displays the curved arrow, or manual line break symbol, when you press SHIFT+ENTER so that you can see the keystroke and differentiate it from a paragraph mark or hard return. The symbol does not print.

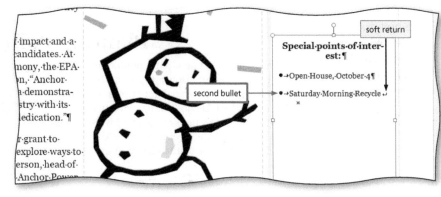

Figure 3–47

- Type **October 9 and 23** and then press ENTER to finish the bulleted item. Complete the bulleted list with the data from Table 3–3.

- Select the text in the heading and change the font size to 8.2 to match the font size of the bulleted list (Figure 3–48).

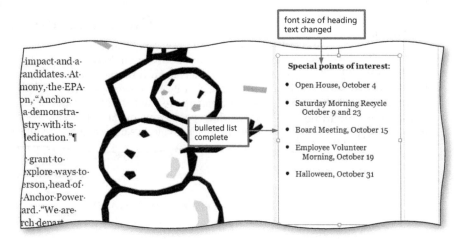

Figure 3–48

To Edit a Pull-Quote

People often make reading decisions based on the size of the story. Using a pull-quote brings a small portion of the text to their attention. *Why? Pull-quotes invite the reader to read the story; they also are useful for breaking the monotony of long columns of text and for adding visual interest.* The following steps insert a pull-quote using function keys to copy and paste the quote from the story.

- Navigate to the second story, Planting Pollinators, on page 2.

- Drag to select the text in the last sentence in the second column.

- Press CTRL+C to copy the sentence to the Clipboard (Figure 3–49).

How should I choose the text for the pull-quote?
Layout specialists say pull-quotes should summarize the intended message in one or two sentences.

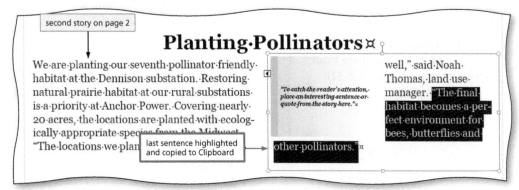

Figure 3–49

2

- Click to select the pull-quote placeholder text in the second column in the story (Figure 3–50).

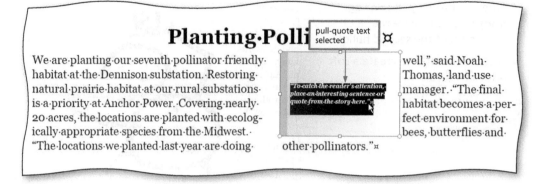

Figure 3–50

3

- Press CTRL+V to paste the sentence from the Clipboard.

- Click the Paste Options button and then click the 'Keep Text Only' button to accept the destination formatting (Figure 3–51).

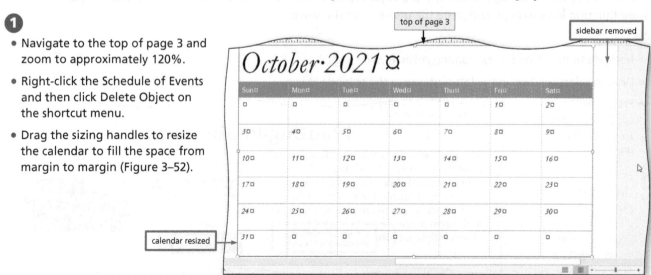

Figure 3–51

Q&A

How would I insert a pull-quote if one did not exist?

Click the Page Parts button (Insert tab | Building Blocks group) to display the Page Parts gallery. Choose a pull-quote in the Pull Quotes area. When the pull-quote appears in the publication, move it to the desired location and then edit the text.

To Edit the Calendar

The following steps edit the calendar on page 3. On the right side of the calendar is a bulleted list similar to the one on page 1. On the left side is a table of dates. Each date is a text box that you can edit. You will delete the bulleted list and then resize and edit the calendar. *Why? You want users to see events on specific dates.*

1

- Navigate to the top of page 3 and zoom to approximately 120%.

- Right-click the Schedule of Events and then click Delete Object on the shortcut menu.

- Drag the sizing handles to resize the calendar to fill the space from margin to margin (Figure 3–52).

Figure 3–52

- Click the 'Draw Text Box' button (Insert tab | Text group) and then drag a text box across Monday through Thursday in the first row of the calendar.

- If necessary, change the font size to 10. Type **Schedule your energy audit by calling 1-888-555-9500.** in the text box (Figure 3–53).

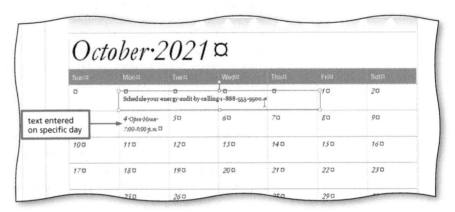

text entered in next text box

Figure 3–53

- Click just to the right of 4 in the calendar.

- Change the font size to 10. Press SPACEBAR and then type **Open House 7:00-9:00 p.m.** to create the entry box (Figure 3–54).

text entered on specific day

Figure 3–54

4

- Repeat the process to complete the calendar events by entering the following.

- On October 9, type **Recycle Center 8:00 a.m.-noon** to enter the event.

- On October 15, type **Board Meeting 7:00 p.m.** to enter the event.

- On October 19, type **Employee** and then press SHIFT+ENTER to create a soft return.

- Type **Volunteer Morning** to complete the text.

- On October 30, type **Recycle Center 8:00 a.m.-noon** to enter the event.

- On October 31, type **Halloween** (Figure 3–55).

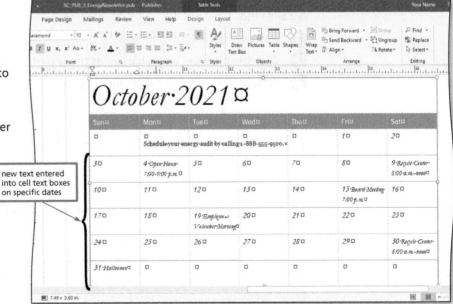

new text entered into cell text boxes on specific dates

Figure 3–55

Using Graphics in a Newsletter

Marginal elements and stories in newsletters often contain graphics and pictures. Most graphic designers employ a simple technique for deciding how many graphics are too many: they hold the publication at arm's length and glance at it. Then, closing their eyes, they count the number of things they remember. Remembering more than five graphics indicates too many; fewer than two indicates too few. Without question, graphics can make or break a publication. The world has come to expect them. Used correctly, graphics enhance the text, attract the eye, and brighten the look of the publication. If you use graphics from the web, make sure you review the copyright licenses to ensure you can comply with copyright restrictions.

CONSIDER THIS

How do you decide on the best layout?
As you insert graphics and arrange stories, follow any guidelines from the authors or from the company for which you are creating the newsletter. Together, determine the best layout for visual appeal and reliable dissemination of content. Make any required changes. Print a copy and mark the places where sidebars and pull-quotes would make sense. Verify that all photos have captions.

In newsletters, you should use photos as true-to-life representations for stories about employees, services, and products. Drawings, on the other hand, can explain, instruct, entertain, or represent images for which you have no picture. The careful use of graphics can add flair and distinction to your publication.

To Delete the Banner

The following steps delete the banner on page 1 in preparation for adding a page background.

1. Navigate to the top of page 1.
2. Click the blue and white banner at the top of the page to select it.
3. Press DELETE to delete the banner (Figure 3–56).

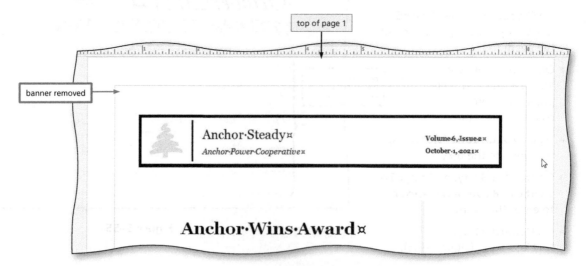

Figure 3–56

To Insert Pictures for the Newsletter

The following steps insert multiple pictures. To complete these steps, you will need to use the photos located in the Data Files. Please contact your instructor for information about accessing the Data Files.

1 Click Insert on the ribbon to display the Insert tab.

2 Click the Pictures button (Insert tab | Illustrations group) to display the Insert Picture dialog box.

3 Navigate to the Data Files.

4 One at a time, CTRL+click the Support_PUB_3_Windmills.tif, Support_PUB_3_EnergyAudit.tif, Support_PUB_3_Lightbulb.tif, Support_PUB_3_Playground.tif, and Support_PUB_3_Manager.tif files to select the five pictures.

5 Click the Insert button (Insert Picture dialog box) to place the pictures in the scratch area.

6 Deselect the pictures (Figure 3–57).

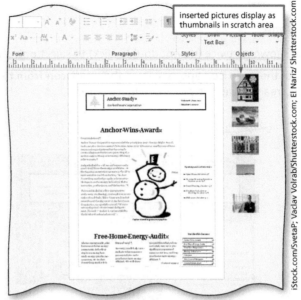

Figure 3–57

To Apply a Page 1 Background

The following steps use one of the pictures as a background for page 1.

1 Right-click the windmill picture to display the shortcut menu.

2 Point to 'Apply to Background' on the shortcut menu to display the Apply to Background submenu.

3 Click Fill on the Apply to Background submenu to place the picture in the background of the page (Figure 3–58).

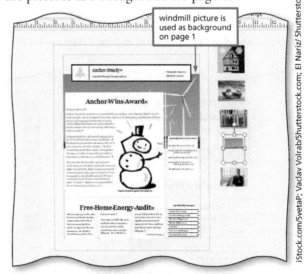

Figure 3–58

To Reformat a Picture

The following steps replace the picture on page 1 and reformat its size and proportions. ***Why?*** *Many times, the picture you want to use in a publication is not the same size as the placeholder.* In the case of the picture on page 1, you need to change the size of the picture, move it to an appropriate location on the page, and reset its proportions.

- Zoom to approximately 70%.

- Click the picture of the snowman twice (do not double-click) to select only the picture.

- Point to the picture until the swap icon appears. Drag the swap icon from the newsletter to the picture of the lightbulb in the scratch area to swap the pictures (Figure 3–59).

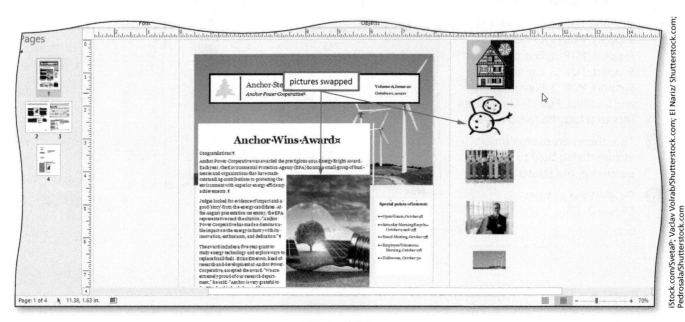

Figure 3–59

2
- Right-click the lightbulb picture to display the shortcut menu (Figure 3–60).

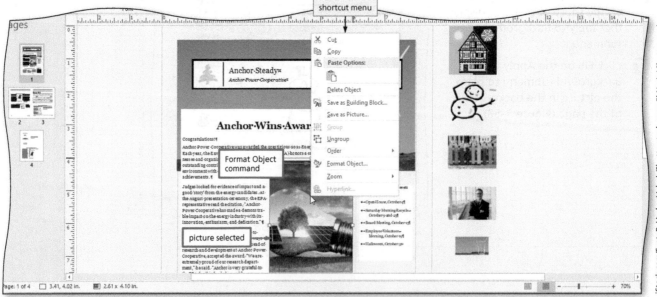

Figure 3–60

③

- Click Format Object on the shortcut menu to display the Format Object dialog box.

- Click the Size tab to display the Size sheet.

- In the Height box, select the text and then type **2.3** to set the new height. In the Width box, select the text and then type **3** to set the new width (Figure 3–61).

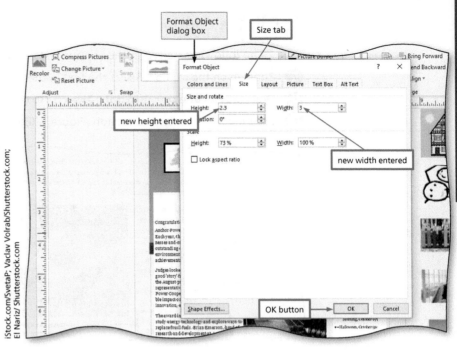

Figure 3–61

④

- Click OK (Format Object dialog box).

- Drag the picture to a location in the lower-right corner of the story.

- Click the Reset Picture button (Picture Tools Format tab | Adjust group) to rescale the picture proportionally (Figure 3–62).

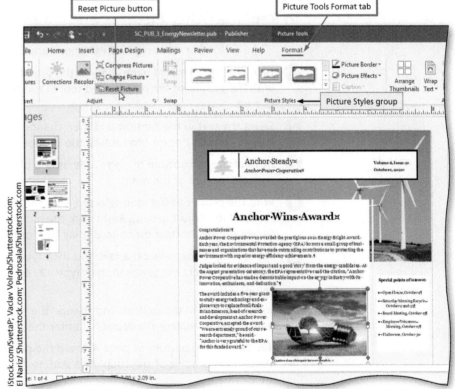

Figure 3–62

Other Ways

1. Select picture, enter size using Measurements pane, click Reset Picture button (Picture Tools Format tab | Adjust group)

To Edit the Caption

The following steps edit the caption for the lightbulb picture.

1 Zoom in on the caption. Select the text in the caption and change the font size to 10.

2 Type `2021 Energy Bright Award` to complete the caption.

3 Press CTRL+E to center the caption (Figure 3–63).

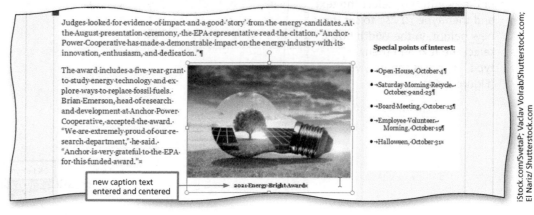

Judges·looked·for·evidence·of·impact·and·a·good·'story'·from·the·energy·candidates.·At·the·August·presentation·ceremony,·the·EPA·representative·read·the·citation,·"Anchor·Power·Cooperative·has·made·a·demonstrable·impact·on·the·energy·industry·with·its·innovation,·enthusiasm,·and·dedication."¶

The·award·includes·a·five-year·grant·to·study·energy·technology·and·explore·ways·to·replace·fossil·fuels.·Brian·Emerson,·head·of·research·and·development·at·Anchor·Power·Cooperative,·accepted·the·award.·"We·are·extremely·proud·of·our·research·department,"·he·said.·"Anchor·is·very·grateful·to·the·EPA·for·this·funded·award."¤

Special points of interest:

●→Open·House,·October·4¶

●→Saturday·Morning·Recycle,·October·9·and·23¶

●→Board·Meeting,·October·15¶

●→Employee·Volunteer·Morning,·October·19¶

●→Halloween,·October·31¤

new caption text entered and centered → 2021·Energy·Bright·Award¤

Figure 3–63

To Replace Other Pictures and Captions

The following steps replace other pictures and captions in the newsletter.

1 Navigate to the top of page 2. Swap the placeholder graphic of the couple ice skating with the picture of the playground fence. You do not have to reformat or reset the picture.

2 Select the text in the caption and then change the font size to 10. Type `Our New Playground Fence` to replace the caption. Center the caption.

3 Navigate to the bottom of page 3. Swap the placeholder graphic of the snowman with the picture of the man.

4 With the picture of the man selected, click the Reset Picture button (Picture Tools Format tab | Adjust group). Right-click the picture of the man and then click Format Object on the shortcut menu to display the Format Object dialog box.

5 In the Height box, select the text and then type `2.3` to set the height. In the Width box, select the text and then type `3` to set the width. Click OK (Format Object dialog box).

6 Select the text in the caption and change the font size to 10. Type `Daniel Quentin` to replace the caption. Center the caption.

7 Navigate to the bottom of page 4. Swap the picture of the energy house with the placeholder graphic of the couple ice skating. You do not have to reformat or reset the picture.

8 Select the text in the caption and change the font size to 10. Type `Schedule your audit today.` to replace the caption. Press CTRL+R to right-justify the caption. Move the picture and caption to the right margin.

9 Click the Save button on the Quick Access Toolbar to save the file again with the same file name and in the same location.

To Insert an Accent Bar

An accent bar is a graphic element in a rectangular shape that can be used to add visual interest, to create a banner, or to insert a graphic separation in a publication. The following steps replace the current banners on pages 2 and 3 with a bar from the Borders & Accents gallery. *Why replace the current banner? Sometimes the template banner does not match the theme of the newsletter.* In the case of this energy newsletter, the blue color from the color scheme is appropriate, but the energy company does not want to portray snowy trees, as the current banner does.

1

- Navigate to page 2. Zoom to 100%.

- Click the banner at the top of the page to select it. Press DELETE to delete the banner.

- Click Insert on the ribbon to display the Insert tab.

- Click the 'Borders & Accents' button (Insert tab | Building Blocks group) to display the gallery (Figure 3–64).

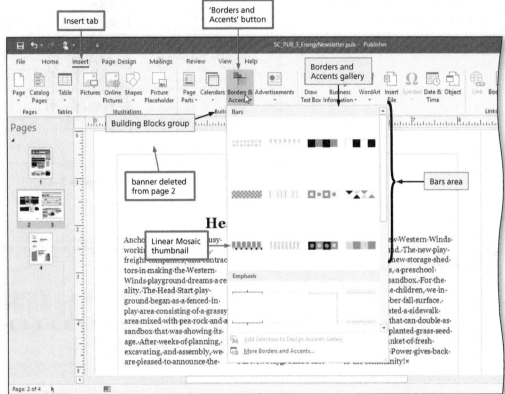

Figure 3–64

2

- In the Bars area, click the Linear Mosaic thumbnail to insert it into the publication (Figure 3–65).

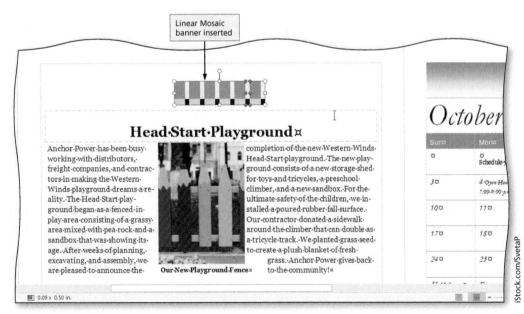

Figure 3–65

3

- Drag the graphic to the upper-left corner of the page, within the margins.

- Drag the lower-right sizing handle to the right margin until the graphic is approximately 1-inch tall and fills the area between margins (Figure 3–66).

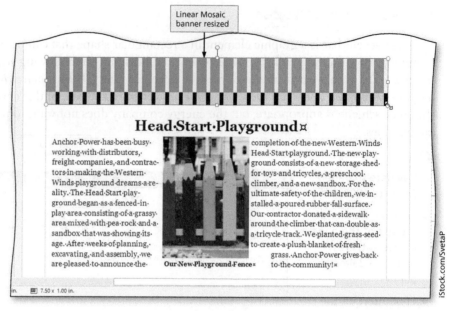

Figure 3–66

 4

- Repeat Steps 1 through 3 to replace the banner on page 3 (Figure 3–67).

Q&A What is the difference between a banner and an accent bar?
They are very similar. Both can be headings; however, a banner usually is on page 1 and may include text.

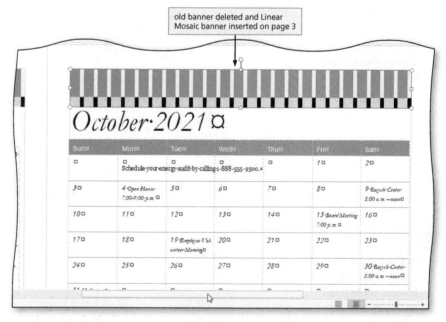

Figure 3–67

To Create a Shape with Text

Why? *Adding text to a shape can create an interesting graphic effect.* Text within a shape moves with the shape; if you created a separate text box, that would not be true. The following steps create a shape and add text to it at the bottom of page 2.

1

- Navigate to the lower part of page 2.
- Click the Shapes button (Insert tab | Illustrations group) to display the Shapes gallery (Figure 3–68).

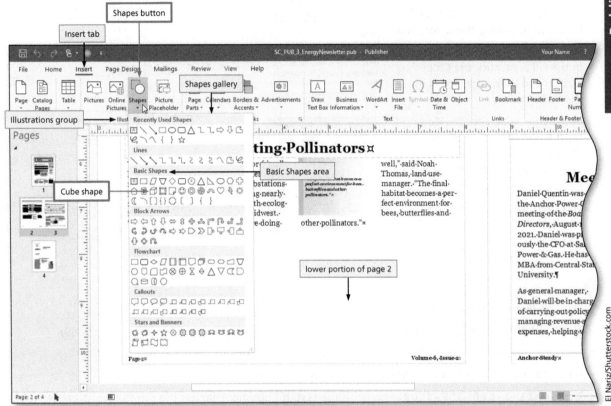

Figure 3–68

2

- In the Basic Shapes area, click Cube.

- Drag to create a cube at the bottom of the page, approximately 5 inches wide and 2 inches tall.

- Right-click the shape to display the shortcut menu (Figure 3–69).

Q&A Why is the cube blue?
Default colors for shapes come from the chosen color scheme.

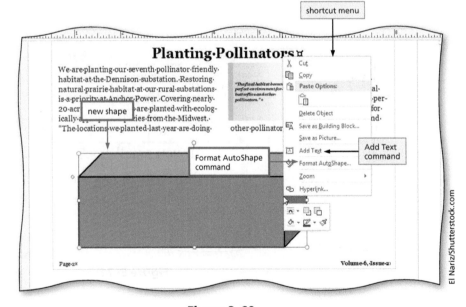

Figure 3–69

③

- Click Format AutoShape on the shortcut menu to display the Format AutoShape dialog box.

- If necessary, click the Colors and Lines tab to display the Colors and Lines sheet.

- In the Fill area, click the Color button and then click No Fill in the Color gallery.

- In the Line Area, click the Color button and then click 'Accent 1 (RGB(51,153,255))' (second color in first row) to change the line color.

- Select the text in the Width box and then type 4 to set the width of the shape (Figure 3–70).

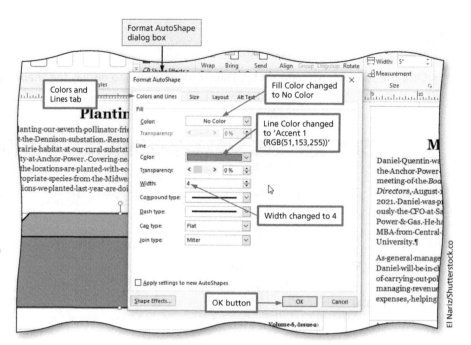

Figure 3–70

④

- Click OK (Format AutoShape dialog box) to format the cube.

- Right-click the shape again and then click Add Text on the shortcut menu (shown in Figure 3–69).

- Set the font size to 24. Press CTRL+E to center the insertion point.

- Type **If you smell gas,** and then press ENTER to complete the first line of text.

- Type **call 1-888-555-9500.** to finish the text. If Publisher changes the c in the word, call, to a capital letter, edit the letter or use the AutoCorrect Options button to fix it (Figure 3–71).

◄ Q&A | Can I add text to all shapes?
No. Some shapes, such as lines, connectors, and some freeform drawings, have no room for text.

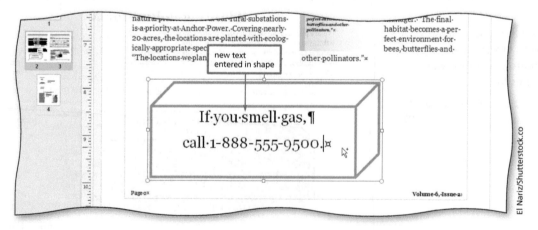

Figure 3–71

Other Ways

1. Create shape, click Edit Text button (Drawing Tools Format tab | Insert Shapes group), type text

To Center the Shape on the Page

Why? *It is a good idea to align every element on the page either with a margin or another object; that way, the element does not look random or ill placed.* Pink visual layout guides help you identify alignments as you move objects. The following steps center the shape horizontally on the page.

1

- At the bottom of page 2, drag the cube shape toward the center and bottom of the page until you see the pink layout guides (Figure 3–72).

Q&A What do the pink layout guides indicate?
The vertical pink line shows the center of the shape aligned with the center of the page. The horizontal pink link shows the bottom of the shape aligned with the bottom of the story on page 3.

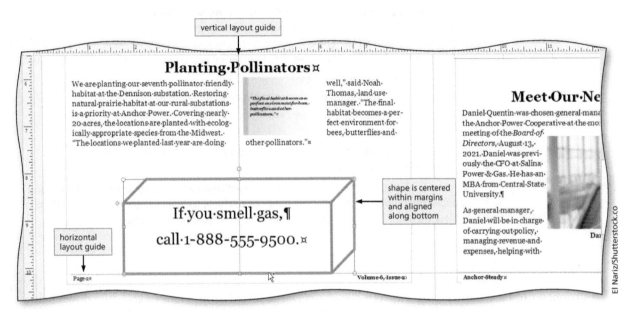

Figure 3–72

2

- Release the mouse button to place the shape.

Other Ways
1. Select shape, click Align button (Drawing Tools Format tab | Arrange group), click 'Relative to Margin Guides' on Align menu, click Align button again, click desired alignment on Align menu

To Remove Pictures from the Scratch Area

The following steps remove pictures from the scratch area, as they no longer are needed.

1 Click the 'Show Whole Page' button on the status bar.

2 In the scratch area, drag around all of the thumbnails to select them.

3 Press DELETE to remove the pictures from the scratch area.

4 Click the Save button on the Quick Access Toolbar to save the file again with the same file name and in the same location.

Break Point: If you want to take a break, this is a good place to do so. Exit Publisher. To resume later, start Publisher, open the file called SC_PUB_3_EnergyNewsletter, and continue following the steps from this location forward.

BTW
Deleting Objects
If you think even a remote possibility exists that you might use an object again, do not delete it. Simply drag it to the scratch area. That way, it is saved with the publication but will not appear on the page layout itself, and it will not print. When you are certain that you no longer will need an object, delete it to reduce the size of your Publisher file.

Revising a Newsletter

Once you complete a publication, you may find it necessary to make changes to it. Before submitting a newsletter to a customer or printing service, you should proofread it. While **proofreading**, you look for grammatical errors and spelling errors. You want to be sure the layout, graphics, and stories make sense. If you find errors, you must correct, make changes to, or edit the newsletter. Other readers, perhaps customers or editors, may want to proofread your publication and make changes (such as moving text) or adding embellishments (such as a drop cap). You also should check how Publisher has hyphenated your stories.

CONSIDER THIS

How should you proofread and revise a newsletter?

As you proofread the newsletter, look for ways to improve it. Check all grammar, spelling, and punctuation. Be sure the text is logical and transitions are smooth. Where necessary, add text, delete text, reword text, and move text to different locations. Ask yourself these questions:

- Does the title suggest the topic?
- Does the first line of the story entice the reader to continue?
- Is the purpose of the newsletter clear?
- Are all sources acknowledged?
- Are there any other graphics that will add purpose or interest to the story without overwhelming the page?

The final phase of the design process is a synthesis involving proofreading, editing, and publishing. Publisher offers several methods to check for errors in your newsletter. None of these methods is a replacement for careful reading and proofreading.

To Create a Drop Cap

A dropped capital letter, or **drop cap**, is a decorative, large initial capital letter extending down below the other letters in the line. If the text wraps to more than one line, the paragraph typically wraps around the dropped capital letter. The following steps create a dropped capital letter A to begin the word, Anchor, in the story on page 2. **Why?** *A drop cap will set off the paragraph and draw the reader's eye toward the beginning of the story.*

- Navigate to page 2 and then click to the left of the letter, A, at the beginning of the first story to position the insertion point. Zoom to approximately 120%.

- Display the Text Box Tools Format tab.

- Click the Drop Cap button (Text Box Tools Format tab | Typography group) to display the Drop Cap gallery (Figure 3–73).

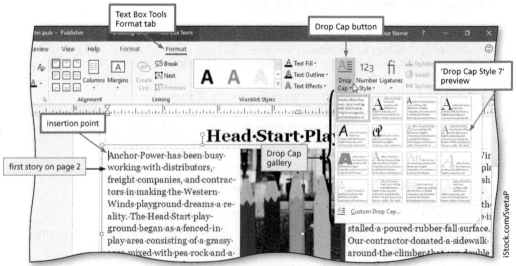

Figure 3–73

iStock.com/SvetaP

2

- Click the 'Drop Cap Style 7' preview to select it (Figure 3–74).

 Will this drop cap look inconsistent with the other fonts on the page?

The drop cap is in the same font as the body text to match the rest of the paragraph's characters.

Figure 3–74

To Customize a Drop Cap

The Drop Cap dialog box allows you to customize the drop cap. You can format the number of lines in the drop cap or even change it to an **up cap**, in which case the larger letter extends up above the rest of the text. You also can change the font, font style, and color of the text.

Once you create a customized style, it is added to the Drop Cap gallery for the current publication. *Why?* *Publisher makes it available to use in other portions of the publication, if desired.* The following steps change the drop cap size to two lines.

1

- With the insertion point still positioned before the desired letter (in this case, the A of Anchor), click the Text Box Tools Format tab and then click the Drop Cap button (Text Box Tools Format tab | Typography group) again to display the Drop Cap gallery (Figure 3–75).

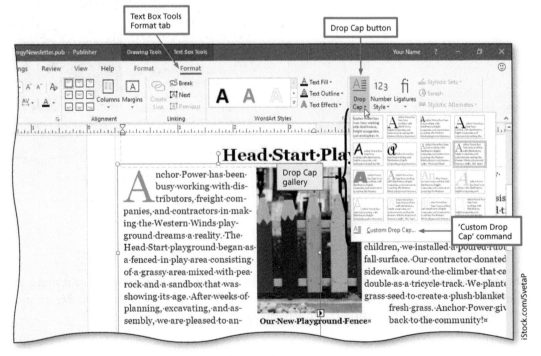

Figure 3–75

- Click 'Custom Drop Cap' at the bottom of the gallery to display the Drop Cap dialog box.

- Click the 'Size of letters' down arrow until the height of the drop cap is 2 lines high (Figure 3–76).

Experiment

- Change other settings in the Drop Cap dialog box and watch the contents of the Preview area change. When you are finished experimenting, return all options to the settings in Figure 3–76.

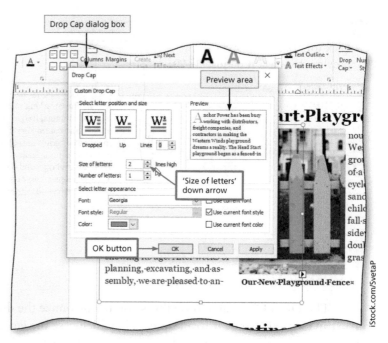

Figure 3–76

- Click OK (Drop Cap dialog box) to apply the formatting (Figure 3–77).

Q&A Is a drop cap limited to a single letter?
No, you can format up to 15 contiguous letters and spaces as drop caps at the beginning of each paragraph.

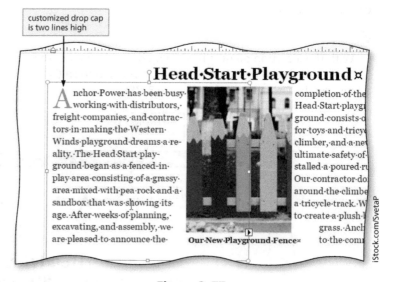

Figure 3–77

To Reuse a Customized Drop Cap

Anytime you use a special feature in a multipage publication, it is a good idea to use it more than once when possible. **Why?** *That way, your feature does not look like an afterthought or a mistake but like a conscious design decision.* The following steps use the customized drop cap again for a second story.

- Navigate to the second story on page 2.

- Position the insertion point before the letter, W, in the word, We, at the beginning of the story.

- Click the Drop Cap button (Text Box Tools Format tab | Typography group) to display the Drop Cap gallery (Figure 3–78).

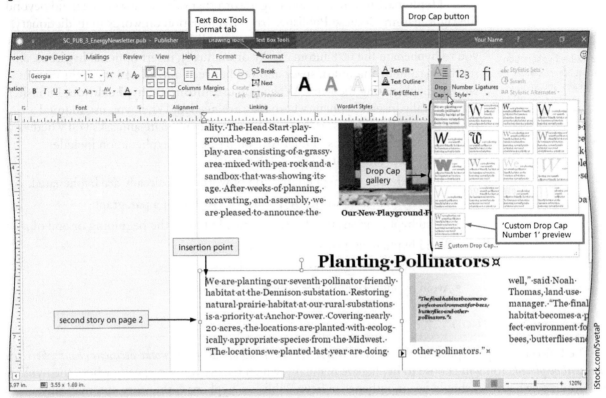

Figure 3–78

2

- Click 'Custom Drop Cap Number 1' in the gallery to apply the recently created drop cap.

3

- Navigate to the story on page 3. Repeat Steps 1 and 2 to create a drop cap for the letter D in Daniel (Figure 3–79).

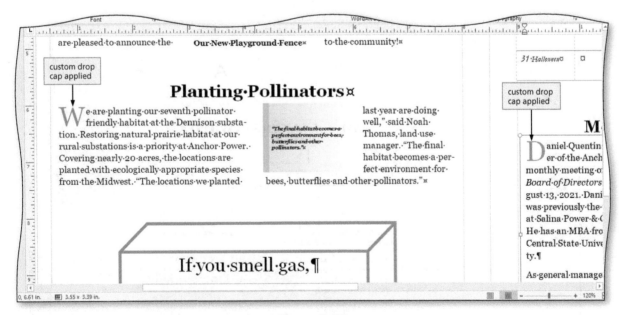

Figure 3–79

BTW
Choosing a Different Hyphenation Location
When using the Hyphenation dialog box, Publisher shows all the possible hyphenation locations at appropriate syllable breaks (shown in Figure 3-81). The current choice is highlighted in blue. You can choose to hyphenate at one of the other places in the word by clicking the hyphen and then clicking the Yes button.

Hyphenation

Hyphenation refers to splitting a word that otherwise would extend beyond the right margin. Because Publisher bases hyphenation on words in its dictionary, it is a good idea to review the hyphenation. Publisher's hyphenation feature allows you to hyphenate the text automatically or manually, insert optional **hyphens**, and set the maximum amount of space allowed between a word and the right margin without hyphenating the word. When you use **automatic hyphenation**, Publisher automatically inserts hyphens where they are needed. When you use **manual hyphenation**, Publisher searches for the text to hyphenate and asks you whether you want to insert the hyphens in the text. Some rules for hyphenation include:

- Hyphenate only at standard syllable breaks.
- Do not change the hyphen location of words that already are hyphenated.
- Avoid hyphenating words in the first or last line of a paragraph.
- Avoid hyphenations that leave only two letters at the beginning or end of a line.
- Avoid hyphenating two lines in a row.
- Avoid hyphenating a line across text boxes or pages.
- Avoid hyphenating proper nouns.

To Check Hyphenation

The following steps hyphenate the stories. *Why? Hyphenating allows you to make decisions about where the hyphens will be placed.* You will choose to hyphenate manually, which means you can specify where the hyphen should occur, or whether it should occur, rather than have Publisher hyphenate the story automatically.

- Navigate to page 1 and click the first column of the lead story.
- Display the Text Box Tools Format tab.
- Click the Hyphenation button (Text Box Tools Format tab | Text group) to display the Hyphenation dialog box (Figure 3–80).

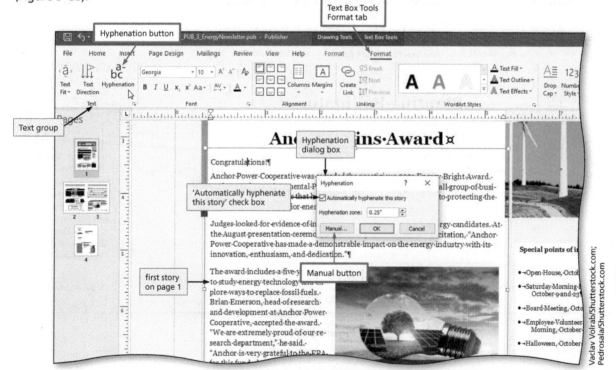

Figure 3–80

Q&A What is the hyphenation zone?
The **hyphenation zone** is the maximum amount of space Publisher allows between a word and the right margin without hyphenating the word. To reduce the number of hyphens, increase the hyphenation zone. To reduce the ragged edge of the right margin, decrease the hyphenation zone.

②

- If necessary, click to remove the check mark in the 'Automatically hyphenate this story' check box.
- Click the Manual button (Hyphenation dialog box) to hyphenate the story manually and to display the first hyphenation choice (Figure 3–81).

Q&A Why is the text already hyphenated?
The default value is automatic hyphenation. Publisher hyphenates after the standard syllables.

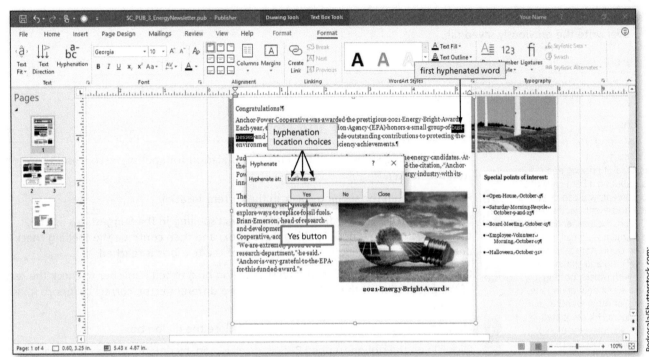

Figure 3–81

③

- Click the Yes button because the location of this text and the suggested hyphenation follow the rules.
- Publisher highlights the next hyphenation suggestion for the word, innovation (Figure 3–82).

④

- Click the No button because this word is on the last line of the third paragraph and it results in two-character hyphenation.

Q&A My hyphenation stopped on a different word. What should I do?
Because of differences in fonts and resolutions, your computer may stop at a different word. Use the rules discussed in this module to evaluate your word and choose the correct hyphenation.

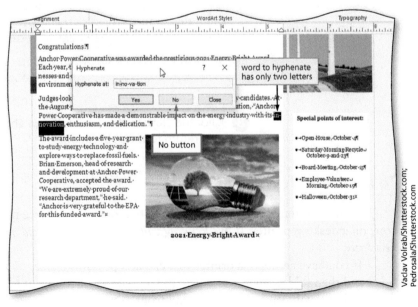

Figure 3–82

- Continue to click the Yes or No button (Hyphenation dialog box) using the hyphenation rules listed previously.
- Click OK when the hyphenation for the story is complete.
- One at a time, repeat Steps 1 through 3 for the other stories and sidebars in the publication, adjusting the hyphens as necessary.

Q&A What sort of hyphenation issues might I find?
You may have to choose to hyphenate at a different location by clicking the hyphen in the Hyphenation dialog box. You may find the hyphenation correct, in which case you will click the Yes button. Or, you may decide not to hyphenate because it would create two hyphens in a row.

- When you are finished hyphenating all of the stories, click the Save button on the Quick Access Toolbar to overwrite the previously saved file.

Other Ways

1. Press CTRL+SHIFT+H, choose settings, click OK (Hyphenation dialog box), make hyphenation choices, click OK (Microsoft Publisher dialog box)

BTW
Distributing a Document
Instead of printing and distributing a hard copy of a document, you can distribute the document electronically. Options include sending the document via email; posting it on cloud storage (such as OneDrive) and sharing the file with others; posting it on a social networking site, blog, or other website; and sharing a link associated with an online location of the document. You also can create and share a PDF or XPS image of the document so that users can view the file in Acrobat Reader or XPS Viewer instead of in Publisher.

To Check the Spelling and Design

The following steps check the entire publication for spelling errors and then run the Design Checker.

1. Press F7 to begin the spelling check in the current location.
2. If Publisher flags any words, choose the correct spelling in the Suggestions list, click the Change button (Check Spelling dialog box) and then continue the spelling check until the next error is identified or the end of the text box is reached.
3. Click the Yes button (Microsoft Publisher dialog box) to tell Publisher to check the rest of the publication. If the publication displays a different error, correct or ignore it, as necessary.
4. Click OK (Microsoft Publisher dialog box) to close the dialog box.
5. Click File on the ribbon to open Backstage view and, by default, display the Info screen.
6. Click the 'Run Design Checker' button to display the Design Checker pane.
7. If your publication has problems other than objects near the margin, point to an error in the Select an item to fix list (Design Checker pane). When an arrow appears on the right side of the error, click the arrow and then click 'Go to this Item' on the menu. Fix or ignore the flagged item, as necessary.

Q&A I have an object not visible error. What should I do?
Your story may have an unfilled text box. You can delete it or leave it alone. It will not print.

8. Click the Close button in the Design Checker pane to close the Design Checker pane and return to the publication.

To Print the Newsletter

While it often is cheaper in business situations to outsource newsletter printing, you may want to print a copy on a desktop printer. **Why?** *Printing will allow you to proofread more easily and also assess the look and feel of the newsletter.*

If you have access to a printer that can accept **tabloid** size, 17 × 11.5-inch paper, you can print double-sided and then fold the paper to create the newsletter. If you want to print double-sided on 8.5 × 11-inch paper, the newsletter will print on the back and front of two pages that you then can staple. The following steps make choices about printing the newsletter.

1

- Navigate to page 1.
- Click File on the ribbon to open Backstage view and then click Print to display the Print screen.
- In the Settings area, click the 'One page per sheet' button to display its list (Figure 3–83).

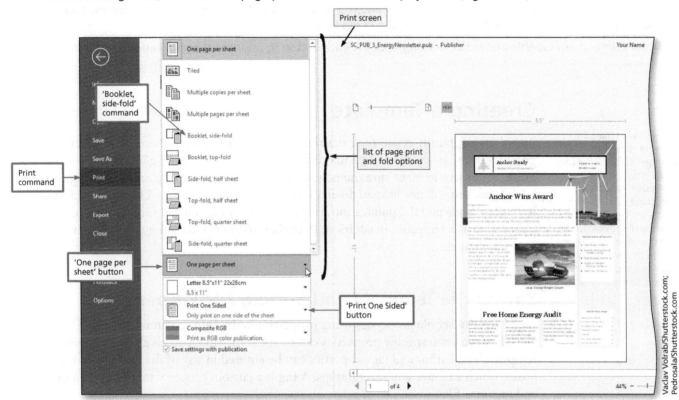

Figure 3–83

2

- Click 'Booklet, side-fold' to specify how the newsletter will print.
- Click the 'Print One Sided' button and then click the appropriate manual or duplex print setting (Figure 3–84).

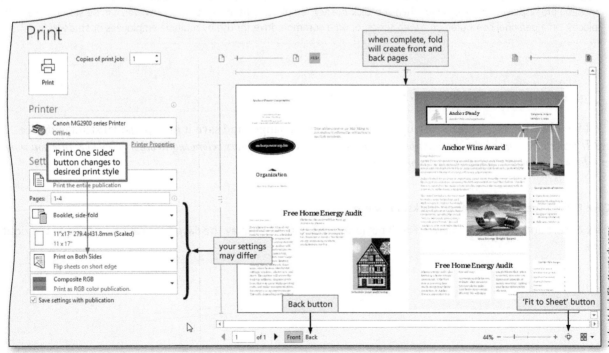

Figure 3–84

Experiment

• Click the Back button to see the inside two-page spread. If necessary, click the 'Fit to Sheet' button on the Print screen taskbar.

3

• If the printer is capable of handling oversized paper and you have access to 17 × 11.5-inch paper, load the paper into the printer and then click the Print button in the Print screen.

• If your printer is not capable of oversize printing, click the Back button to return to the publication workspace.

Creating a Template

Newsletters typically retain their masthead, color scheme, font scheme, and other graphics from issue to issue. In a first issue, you must make design choices and implement them to make sure the newsletter is displayed correctly, and reviewing that takes time. You will not have to do all of that for subsequent issues. Once the decisions have been made and the publication has been distributed, you can reuse the same publication as a template. In addition, Publisher allows you to add it to the templates on your computer.

Saving the Template and Setting File Properties

You can set file properties using properties in the Info screen in Backstage view; however, two specific properties can be set at the time you save a publication or template. The author and tag properties can be entered in any of the Save As dialog boxes, which can save you several steps. A **tag** is a custom property that helps you find and organize files.

CONSIDER THIS

Where should a company store its templates?

On a business computer, for an organization that routinely uses templates, templates should be saved in the default location. Publisher stores templates within the program data in a folder named Custom Office Templates. Templates stored in the default location are displayed in the catalog when you click the My Templates button. Templates, however, can be stored in several places: on a personal computer, on a web server, or on a common drive for use by multiple employees or students.

To Create a Template with Property Changes

The following steps create a template with property changes and save it on a personal storage device. *Why? It is not recommended to save templates on lab computers or computers belonging to other people because you may not want others to use your templates due to privacy issues.*

1

• Click File on the ribbon to open Backstage view.

• Click Export and then click 'Change File Type' in the left pane to display the Save Publication options in the right pane.

• Click Template in the Publisher File Types area to save the file as a Publisher template (Figure 3–85).

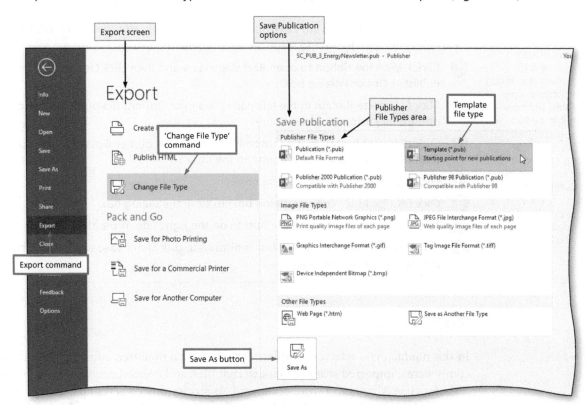

Figure 3–85

②

• Click the Save As button to display the Save as Template dialog box.

• Type **SC_PUB_3_EnergyNewsletterTemplate** to change the name of the publication. Do not press ENTER.

• Navigate to your preferred storage location.

• Click the Tags text box and then type **monthly newsletter** to add the tag words (Figure 3–86). The current text in the Tags text box will disappear as you start to type. Publisher will add a semicolon to the end of the tag.

 Can I make the newsletter template read-only so that users will have to save updates with a different file name?

Yes. After saving, open the File Explorer window. Right-click the file name, click Properties on the shortcut menu, and then place a check mark in the Read-only check box (Publication Properties dialog box | General tab).

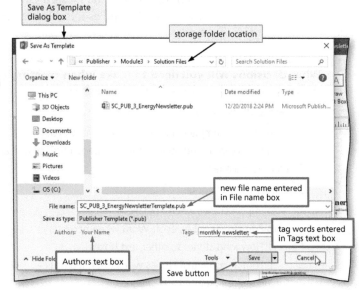

Figure 3–86

③

• Click the Save button (Save As Template dialog box) to save the template.

Other Ways

1. In Backstage view, click Save As, choose location, enter name of newsletter, click 'Save as type' button, click Publisher Template, click Save button (Save As dialog box)

BTW
**Conserving Ink
and Toner**
If you want to conserve ink
or toner, you can instruct
Publisher to print draft-
quality documents by clicking
File on the ribbon to open
Backstage view and then
clicking Print in the Backstage
view to display the Print
screen. Click the Printer
Properties link and then,
depending on your printer,
click the Quality button and
then click Draft in the list.
Click OK to close the Printer
Properties dialog box and
then click the Print button
as usual.

To Remove All Ribbon Customization and Exit Publisher

When working in a lab environment, it is advisable to remove the ribbon customization. The following steps remove all ribbon customization.

1 Click File on the ribbon to open Backstage view and then click Options to display the Publisher Options dialog box.

2 Click Customize Ribbon in the left pane (Publisher Options dialog box) to display the options for customizing the ribbon.

3 Click the Reset button in the Customizations area (Publisher Options dialog box) and then click 'Reset all customizations' in the list.

4 Click Yes (Microsoft Office dialog box).

5 Click OK (Publisher Options dialog box) to close the dialog box.

6 To exit Publisher, click the Close button on the right side of the title bar.

7 If a Microsoft Publisher dialog box is displayed, click Don't Save so that any changes you have made are not saved.

Summary

In this module, you selected template options for a newsletter, edited the masthead components, imported stories from external files, and created original stories using the 'Edit Story in Microsoft Word' command. As stories flowed across pages, you inserted continued notices. You edited sidebars, pull-quotes, and the calendar. In revising the newsletter, you applied decorative drop caps, hyphenated the stories, checked the spelling, and ran the Design Checker. Finally, you saved the newsletter both as a Publisher file and as a Publisher template that the company can edit each month.

CONSIDER THIS: PLAN AHEAD

What decisions will you need to make when creating your next newsletter?
Use these guidelines as you complete the assignments in this module and create your own publications outside of this class.

1. Decide on the layout.

   a) Select a template and options that match your need.

   b) Set columns and options for each page purpose and audience.

2. Edit the masthead.

3. Gather the text content.

   a) Import stories when possible.

   b) Edit stories in Microsoft Word when necessary.

   c) Flow long stories to other text boxes.

   d) Format continued stories with continued notices.

4. Create and edit marginal elements.

5. Insert other elements, such as advertisements.

6. Edit graphics and captions.

7. Revise as necessary.

   a) Proofread and check the publication.

   b) Run a hyphenation check.

8. Create a template for future use.

Apply Your Knowledge

Reinforce the skills and apply the concepts you learned in this module.

Creating a Newsletter

Note: To complete this assignment, you will be required to use the Data Files. Please contact your instructor for information about accessing Data Files.

Instructions: Start Publisher. You will produce the fractions newsletter shown in Figure 3–87.

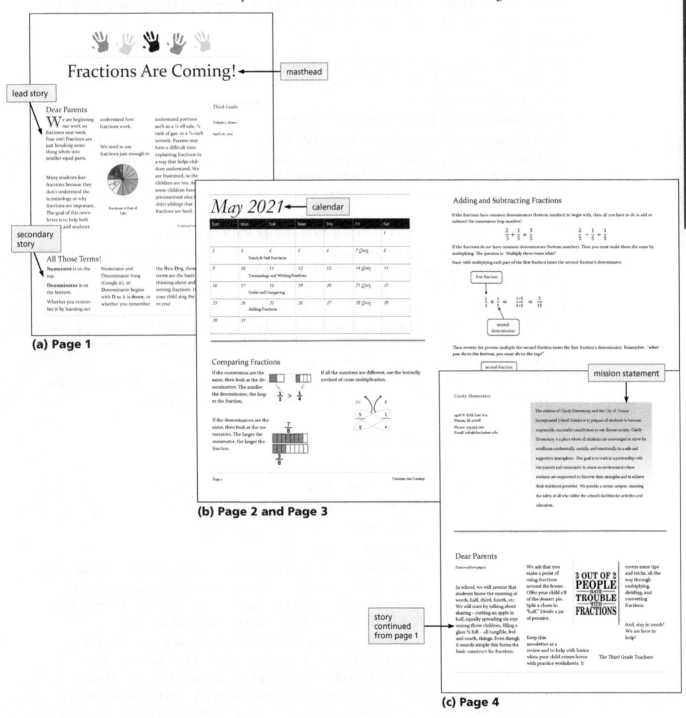

(a) Page 1

(b) Page 2 and Page 3

(c) Page 4

Figure 3–87

Continued >

Apply Your Knowledge *continued*

Perform the following tasks:

1. Click BUILT-IN and then click Newsletters.

2. Choose the Kid Stuff newsletter template, the Garnet color scheme, and the Paper font scheme. Set the Page size to Two-page spread.

3. Create the publication. Navigate to page 2. Use the Options button (Page Design tab | Template group) to choose to include a calendar and a 2-column format on the left inside page. The date of your calendar may differ. Click the Options button (Page Design tab | Template group) again for the right-inside page, and include 3 stories and a 1-column format.

4. To edit page 1:

   a. Edit the masthead as shown in Figure 3–87a. Below the masthead, on the right, change the business name to Third Grade. Change the date to April 26, 2021. Do not change the volume and issue numbers.

   b. For the lead story, use Dear Parents as the headline.

   c. Click the story to select it. Click the Insert File button (Insert tab | Text group). Import the story, Support_PUB_3_DearParentsStory.doc, from the Data Files. When Publisher wants to continue the story, click the No button in each dialog box until you get to the Back Page Story on page 4; then, click the Yes button. Change the title of the Back Page Story to Dear Parents.

   d. Press CTRL+A to select all of the story and then change the font size to 12.

   e. Return to page 1 and right-click the right-most column of the imported story and then click 'Format Text Box' on the shortcut menu. Click the Text Box tab and then place a check mark in the 'Include "Continued on page…"' check box. Click OK (Format Text Box dialog box).

   f. Click the Next button that displays at the end of the text box to move to page 4. Right-click the left-most column of the imported story and then click 'Format Text Box' on the shortcut menu. In the Text Box sheet, place a check mark in the 'Include "Continued from page…"' check box. Click OK (Format Text box dialog box).

   g. Return to page 1 and the beginning of the story. Create a drop cap on the first letter of the story, W. Use Drop Cap Style 6. If necessary, change to a two-line drop cap.

   h. Insert the following graphics:

      Support_Pub_3_LeadStoryPicture.png

      Support_Pub_3_ComparingButterfly.png

      Support_Pub_3_ComparingNumerators.png

      Support_Pub_3_ComparingDenominators.png

      Support_Pub_3_TroublePicture.png

      Support_PUB_3_AddSubtractFractions.png

   i. Point to the imported picture of the pie graph. When Publisher displays the swap icon, swap the picture with the placeholder picture on page 1. If necessary, reset the picture so it is proportional and then resize. Change the caption so that it reads: Fractions: A Part of Life. Move the picture and caption below the text in the second column of the story.

   j. Click anywhere in the lead story text and then click the Hyphenation button (Text Box Tools format tab | Text group) to display the Hyphenation dialog box. Remove the check mark from the 'Automatically hyphenate this story' check box. Click the Manual button (Hyphenation dialog box) to hyphenate the story manually and to display the first hyphenation choice. Click Yes or No, as appropriate, using the rules discussed earlier in this module, in the section titled Hyphenation.

   k. Delete the Special points of interest sidebar.

l. Edit the Inside this issue sidebar with the rows shown below and then delete the text in the unused rows of the sidebar.

Calendar	2
Comparing Fractions	2
Adding & Subtracting	3
Contact Information	4
Mission Statement	4

5. If necessary, customize the ribbon to display the 'Edit Story in Microsoft Word' button (Review tab | New Group group). (*Hint:* Refer to the section in this module titled To Edit a Story Using Microsoft Word.)

6. To edit the secondary story:

   a. For the secondary story on page 1, click the headline and then type `All Those Terms!` as the new text.

   b. Click the placeholder text of the story. Click the 'Edit Story in Microsoft Word' button (Review tab | New Group). When Word is running, press CTRL+A to select all of the text. Change the font size to 12. Type the following text, pressing ENTER at the end of each paragraph except the last:

   `Numerator is on the top.`

   `Denominator is on the bottom.`

   `Whether you remember it by learning our Numerator and Denominator Song (Google it), or Denominator begins with D so it is down, or whether you remember the Nice Dog, those terms are the basis for thinking about and writing fractions. Have your child sing the song to you!`

   c. Bold the term, Numerator, in the first sentence and the word, Denominator, in the second sentence. Also bold the first letter of Nice and the first letter of Dog.

   d. Exit Word to return to Publisher. Hyphenate the second story as you did the first (in Step 4j).

7. To edit page 2:

   a. Delete the Schedule of Events sidebar. Resize the calendar to fill the blank space left by the sidebar. Add four text boxes to the calendar, one for each week, with text as follows:

   Touch and Feel Fractions

   Terminology and Writing Fractions

   Order and Comparing

   Adding Fractions

   b. Add the word, Quiz, to each Friday on the calendar.

   c. At the bottom of page 2, change the headline to read, Comparing Fractions. Click the placeholder story text to select it and then import the story named Support_PUB_3_ ComparingFractions. Delete the placeholder graphic and caption. Move the three graphics shown in Figure 3–87b to the story and resize them. (*Hint:* If a graphic does not display after you move it, click the Bring Forward button (Picture Tools Format tab | Arrange group).)

7. To edit page 3:

   a. Navigate to page 3 and zoom to whole page or 45%. Select the text in the first Inside Story headline. Type `Adding and Subtracting Fractions` to replace the headline.

   b. Start dragging in the margin and continue to drag around all objects except the first story headline to select them. Delete the objects.

   c. Move the text-based graphic from the scratch area to the blank space on page 3. Resize the graphic to fill the entire page.

Continued >

Apply Your Knowledge *continued*

8. To edit page 4:

   a. In the top half of the page, change the Business Name to Clardy Elementary.

   b. Change the address to 1428 N. 67th East Ave., Donna, IA 50008.

   c. Change the phone number to 515-555-1217. Delete the fax number.

   d. Change the email address to info@clardyelem.edu.

   e. Delete the Business Tagline or Motto, the attention getter, and the Organization logo.

   f. In the story in the upper-right part of page 4, import the story named Support_PUB_3_MissionStatement.doc. Hyphenate the story.

   g. Use the swap technique to swap the 3 out of 2 people sign with the dinosaur graphic. Delete the caption.

9. If requested by your instructor, change other text and graphics, such as the special points of interest, table of contents sidebar, and stories on page 3. Use your name and address at the top of page 4.

10. Delete any pictures remaining in the scratch area. Check the spelling in the newsletter. Use the Design Checker to fix any errors in the newsletter. Save the file with the file name, SC_PUB_3_FractionsNewsletter.pub.

11. Remove the ribbon customization. (*Hint:* Refer to the section titled To Remove All Ribbon Customization and Exit Publisher, earlier in this module.)

12. Submit the publication in the format specified by your instructor.

13. ✳ Do you think adding three graphics to the story on page 2 makes it look too busy? Why or why not? Would you rather type the story in Step 6b in Publisher or Word? Why?

Expand Your Knowledge

Extend the skills you learned in this module and experiment with new skills. You may need to use Help to complete the assignment.

Customizing the Publisher Ribbon

Instructions: Start Publisher. Open the newsletter SC_PUB_3_EnergyNewsletter.pub, which you created in this project. If you did not create the publication, see your instructor for ways to complete this assignment. You are to create a new group Mailings tab to mail publications as PDFs. You may need to use Help to complete this assignment.

Perform the following tasks:

1. Click File on the ribbon to open Backstage view and then click Options to display the Publisher Options dialog box.

2. Click Customize Ribbon in the left pane (Publisher Options dialog box) to display the options for customizing the ribbon in the right pane.

3. In the list of Main tabs on the right, click the plus sign next to Mailings to display the current tabs and to select it. At the bottom of the Publisher Options dialog box, click the New Group button. When Publisher displays the new group, click the Rename button to display the Rename dialog box. Name the new tab Send as PDF.

4. Click the 'Choose commands from' button and then click 'Commands Not in the Ribbon' in the list.

5. Scroll in the list and then click 'Send Publication as PDF Attachment'. Click the Add button to add it to the Send as PDF (Custom) group.

6. With the new button selected, click the Rename button and choose an icon in the Rename dialog box. You can keep the name of the button the same. Click OK (Rename dialog box). Click OK (Publisher Options dialog box).

7. When Publisher displays the publication again, click the Mailings tab to view the new group. Press PRT SC (or similar key) on the keyboard to capture a screenshot of the new tab.

8. Click the 'Send Publication as PDF Attachment' button (Mailings tab | Send as PDF group) to start your email program (Figure 3–88).

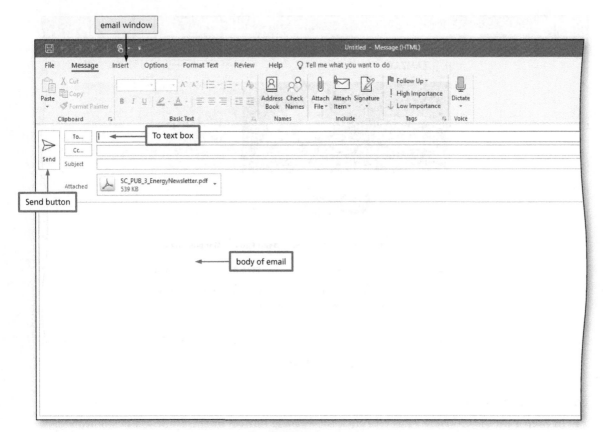

Figure 3–88

9. In the To text box, type your email address (or your instructor's email address, if told to do so).

10. In the body of the email, press CTRL+V to paste the screenshot. Right-click the screenshot and then click Crop on the Mini toolbar. Drag the cropping handles until only the ribbon is displayed so that you can display your customization.

11. Click the Send button.

12. If you are in a lab environment, remove all customization to the ribbon and to return it to its original state.

13. Exit Publisher.

14. ✸ Why do you think Publisher Help recommends sending newsletters as PDF attachments? What issues might arise if you send the Publisher file in the .pub format?

Expand Your World

Create a solution that uses cloud and web technologies by learning and investigating on your own from general guidance.

Converting Files

Instructions: Start a browser and navigate to zamzar.com (Figure 3–89). You would like to explore converting your newsletter to formats other than the .pub Publisher format. While Publisher has many formats in the Save As type list, a cloud service may offer even more choices.

Figure 3–89

Perform the following tasks:

1. In Step 1 on the Convert Files tab, click the Browse button or the Choose Files button (depending on your browser) and then navigate to one of your completed newsletters.

2. In Step 2, click the 'Convert files(s) to:' box and choose a conversion format, such as html or an e-book format.

3. In Step 3, enter your email address.

4. In Step 4, click the Convert button to send the converted file to your email. If you receive a message indicating the conversion is about to happen, click OK.

5. When you receive the email from Zamzar, click the link provided and then click the Download Now button. Your browser should direct you to save the download.

6. If your download is a compressed file, right-click the zipped file to display a shortcut menu. Click Extract or Extract All to extract the file.

7. Open the converted file.

8. Submit the assignment in the format specified by your instructor.

9. ✳ What format might you use to post your newsletter on the web? Would an HTML file be better than a download link? Why or why not? When might you convert to a PDF format?

In the Lab

Design and implement a solution using creative thinking and problem-solving skills.

Publisher Newsletter Analysis

Note: To complete this assignment, you will be required to use the Data Files. Please contact your instructor for information about accessing the Data Files.

Problem: Use a copy of a newsletter that you regularly receive or obtain one from a friend, an organization, or a school. Using the principles in this module, analyze the newsletter.

Part 1: Start Publisher. Open the publication, SC_PUB_3-1.pub, from the Data Files. Use the skills you learned in editing sidebars to fill in each of the empty cells in the table as it applies to your selected newsletter. The topics to look for are listed below:

- Purpose
- Audience
- Paper
- Distribution
- Font and color scheme
- Consistency
- Alignment
- Repeated elements
- Continued notices and ease of navigation
- Sidebars, pull-quotes, patterns, etc.
- Print the publication and attach a copy of the newsletter. Submit both to your instructor.

Part 2: After looking at each of the elements in the table with respect to the newsletter you chose, list five ways could you improve the newsletter.

4 | Creating a Custom Publication from Scratch

Objectives

After completing this module, you will be able to:

- Create a custom publication size
- Create color and font schemes
- Manipulate and duplicate shapes
- Flip and rotate objects
- Resize using exact dimensions
- Create a building block
- Make picture corrections

- Snap and nudge
- Use WordArt
- Create a custom bullet
- Create text boxes and change borders
- Apply fills and outlines
- Apply and delete customizations

Introduction

Customizing publications and tailoring them to a specific organization, with font schemes, color schemes, page dimensions, and margins allows desktop publishers to be more creative and provide made-to-order publications for their clients. The process of developing a publication that communicates a company brand and specific requirements entails careful analysis and planning. Coordinating design choices with the customer and gathering necessary information will help you determine the design and style that will be most successful in delivering the company's message. Whether you are creating a publication from scratch or using a template, many settings and preferences can be customized and saved. Once saved, a publication can be reused, resulting in increased productivity and continuity across publications.

Project: Mailer

Module 4 uses Publisher to create a mailer. **Mailers** commonly are smaller, single-page publications used for advertising and marketing. Mailers include information about the organization, pictures, contact information, and other pertinent information with many colors and eye-catching graphics. Mailers also may include coupons. The mailer created in this module advertises specials and coupons for a sandwich shop named That Sandwich Place and includes graphics, bulleted items, and WordArt. The completed publication is shown in Figure 4–1.

Figure 4–1

To illustrate some of the customizable features of Microsoft Publisher, this project presents a series of steps to create the mailer with a customized color scheme that uses the company colors: gray, red, and pink. A customized font scheme will include the Britannic Bold font for the heading and a secondary font, Arial, for the body text.

The graphics combine clip art with shapes and fills, repeating the color scheme. With a solid color in the background, a picture is edited and repurposed as a reusable building block for the company. Finally, a WordArt object and a bulleted list provide the text content, as shown in Figure 4–1. Coupons appear on the left.

You will perform the following general tasks as you progress through this module:

1. Customize the publication by editing the page size, margins, font schemes, and color schemes.
2. Edit graphics.
3. Create and use building blocks.
4. Edit and format text with line spacing, text effects, and gradient fills.
5. Use WordArt.
6. Change paragraph formatting and create bulleted lists.
7. Create a coupon advertisement.
8. Apply customizations.
9. Delete customizations.

Custom-Sized Publications

Publications come in a variety of sizes and shapes. Customers and designers do not always want to use one of the preset sizes, such as 8½ × 11. In such a case, you may want to create a **custom-sized publication** with specific dimensions, orientation, and margins. Custom-sized publications are used for everything from newspaper advertisements to greeting cards to bulletins.

What steps should you take when creating a custom publication?
Define the purpose of the publication. Choose a font scheme and color scheme to match the customer's logo or company colors. Define which pieces of business information you plan to use. Does the proposed publication fulfill the need? If you are working from scratch, look at similar publication templates. Choose margins and a paper size that will help standardize the publication with others used in the industry.

BTW
Blank Publications
If you want Publisher to start with a blank publication rather than the list of templates each time you start the program, do the following: click File to open Backstage view and then click Options. Click General in the left pane (Publisher Options dialog box) and then remove the check mark in the 'Show the New template gallery when starting Publisher' check box.

CONSIDER THIS

To Select a Blank Publication

When you first start Publisher, the template gallery displays a list of featured and built-in templates, as well as blank publications. Most users select a publication template and then begin editing. It is not always the case, however, that a template will fit every situation. Sometimes you want to think through a publication while manipulating objects on a blank page, trying different shapes, colors, graphics, and effects. Other times you may have specific goals for a publication, such as size or orientation, that do not match any of the templates. For these cases, Publisher provides **blank publications** with no preset objects or design, which allow you to start from scratch.

The following steps select a blank print publication.

❶ Start Publisher.

❷ Click the 'Blank 8.5 × 11"' thumbnail in the template gallery to create a blank publication in the Publisher window.

❸ If the Publisher window is not maximized, click the Maximize button on the title bar.

❹ If the Special Characters button (Home tab | Paragraph group) is not selected already, click it to display formatting marks on the screen.

❺ If the Page Navigation pane is open, click the Page Number button on the status bar to close the Page Navigation pane (Figure 4–2).

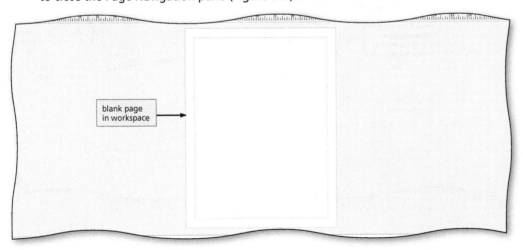

blank page
in workspace

Figure 4–2

To Create a Custom Page Size

The following steps create a new custom page size. **_Why?_** _The customer has requested a mailer that measures 7.75 × 5 inches._ Publisher and other Office applications use the term **page setup** to refer to the process of changing the document margins, orientation, and size, among other settings.

1

• Click Page Design on the ribbon to display the Page Design tab.

• Click the Size button (Page Design tab | Page Setup group) to display the Size menu, which lists standard page sizes and options for other sizes (Figure 4–3).

Q&A How does the 'Create New Page Size' command differ from the Page Setup command?

When you choose the 'Create New Page Size' command, you can name and save the settings. A new thumbnail will appear in the template gallery every time you start Publisher, which allows you to reuse the page size for other publications. The Page Setup command affects only the current publication.

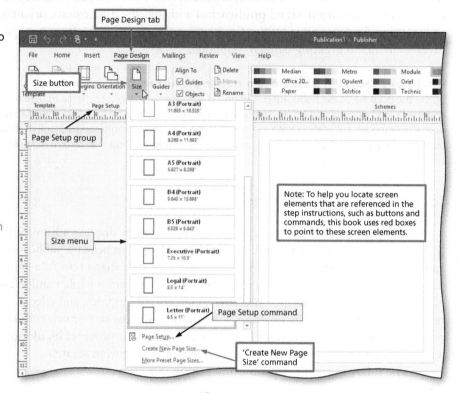

Figure 4–3

2

• Click 'Create New Page Size' at the bottom of the Size menu to display the Create New Page Size dialog box.

• In the Name text box (Create New Page Size dialog box), type **Mailer** to name the custom size.

• Click the Layout type button to display the list of layouts (Figure 4–4).

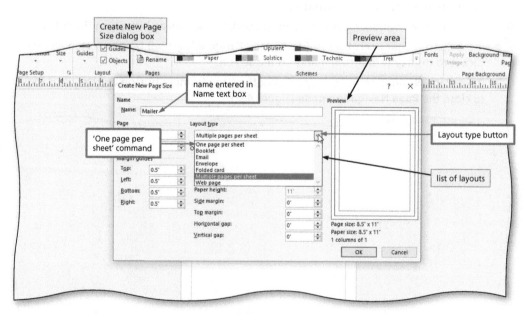

Figure 4–4

Experiment

- One at a time, click each of the layout types in the list to view additional settings that may appear. Note how the preview changes.

3

- Click 'One page per sheet' to display the settings associated with single publications on a sheet of paper.

- Select the text in the Width box and then type **7.75** to set the width for the publication.

- Select the text in the Height box and then type **5** to set the height for the publication.

- One at a time, select the text in each of the four Margin guides boxes and type **0.25** to change the margin on each side of the publication (Figure 4–5).

Q&A Why are the margins set to 0.25?
Many desktop printers cannot print all the way to the edge of the paper, and leaving a little space frames the content.

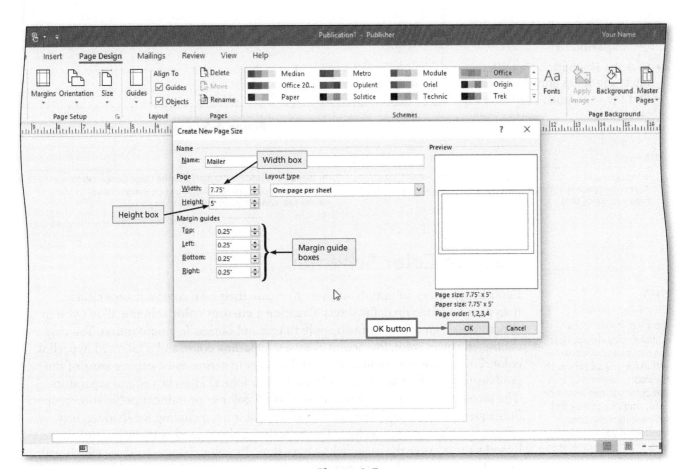

Figure 4–5

4

- Click OK (Create New Page Size dialog box) to save the page size and margins.

- Zoom to 100% if necessary (Figure 4–6).

Q&A Where will the custom layout be saved?

The saved layout will appear in the template gallery when you first start Publisher or when you click File on the ribbon and then click New. To view custom sizes in the template gallery, click the 'More Blank Page Sizes' thumbnail.

 **Experiment**

- Click the Size button (Page Design tab | Page Setup group) to verify that the new page size has been saved.

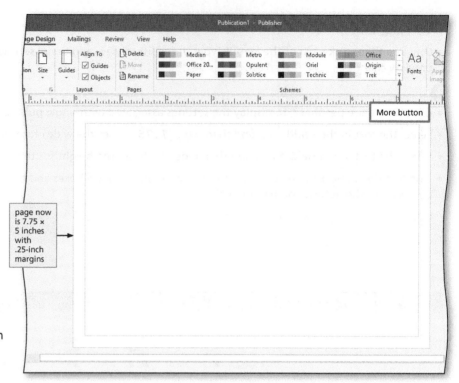

Figure 4–6

Other Ways

1. In template gallery, click 'More Blank Page Sizes' thumbnail, click 'Create new page size' thumbnail, enter values, click OK (Create New Page Size dialog box)

2. To change margins, click Margins button (Page Design tab | Page Setup group), click Custom Margins, enter margin values on Margin Guides tab, click OK (Layout Guides dialog box)

Custom Color Schemes

Publisher provides an option for users to create their own color schemes rather than use one of the predefined sets. Creating a **custom color scheme** allows you to choose your own colors that will apply to text and objects in a publication. You may choose one main color, five accent colors, a hyperlink color, and a followed hyperlink color. The main color commonly is used for text in major, eye-catching areas of the publication. The first accent color is used for graphical lines, boxes, and separators. The second accent color typically is used as fill color in prominent publication shapes. Subsequent accent colors may be used in several ways, including for shading, text effects, and alternate font colors. The hyperlink color is used as the font color for hyperlink text. After the user clicks a hyperlink, its color changes to show which path, or trail, the user has clicked previously.

Once created, the name of the custom color scheme appears in the list of color schemes. The chosen colors also will appear in the galleries related to shapes, fills, and outlines. A **gallery** is a set of choices, often graphical, arranged in a grid or in a list. You can scroll through choices in a gallery by clicking the gallery's scroll arrows. Some buttons and boxes have arrows that, when clicked, also display a gallery.

To Create a New Color Scheme

The mailer will use the accent colors gray, red, and pink, as well as a black main color for text. *Why? The customer wants to emulate the colors associated with his restaurant.* The following steps create a custom color scheme.

1
- Click the More button (Page Design tab | Schemes group) (shown in Figure 4–6) to display the Schemes gallery (Figure 4–7).

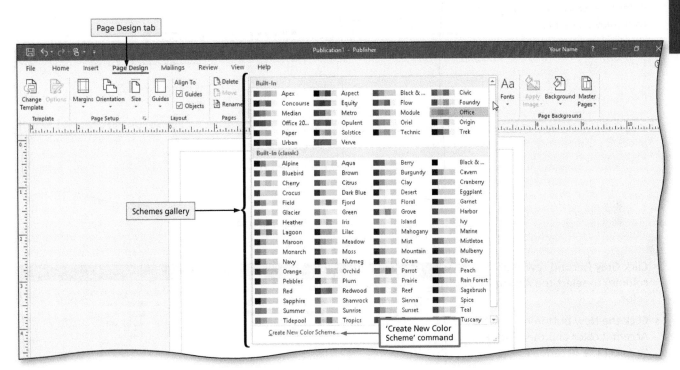

Figure 4–7

2
- Click 'Create New Color Scheme' to display the Create New Color Scheme dialog box.

- Type **That Sandwich Place** in the 'Color scheme name' text box (Create New Color Scheme dialog box) to assign the color scheme the same name as the company (Figure 4–8).

Q&A What if I do not enter a name for the modified color scheme?
Publisher assigns a name that begins with the word, Custom, followed by a number (i.e., Custom 8).

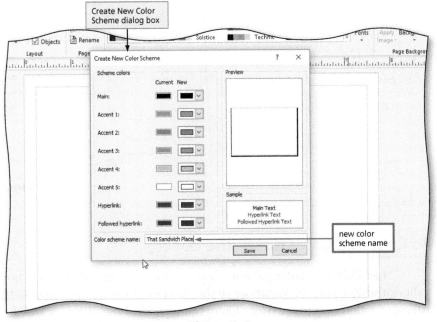

Figure 4–8

3

- In the Scheme colors area, click the New button next to the Accent 1 color to display a gallery of color choices (Figure 4–9).

🔍 **Experiment**

- Point to each color in the gallery to display its name.

Q&A Why is this color gallery different from others?

This color gallery is a general palette of colors. It does not display the typical accent colors across the top because you are choosing the accent colors in this dialog box.

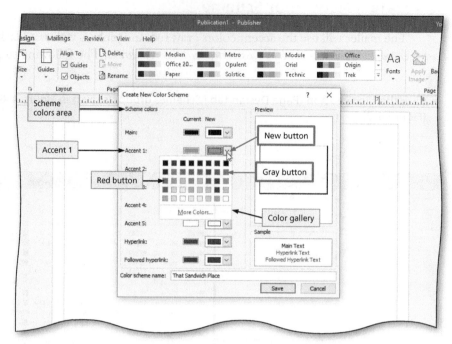

Figure 4–9

4

- Click Gray (second row, eighth column) to select the Accent 1 color.

- Click the New button next to the Accent 2 color and then click Red to select the Accent 2 color.

- Do not close the Create New Color Scheme dialog box (Figure 4–10).

Q&A Can I delete a color scheme once I create it?

Yes. To delete a color scheme, first display the list of color schemes, right-click the custom color scheme, and then click Delete Scheme on the shortcut menu.

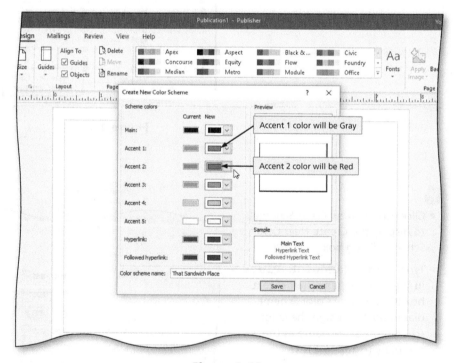

Figure 4–10

To Choose a Color Not in the Gallery

Most Publisher color galleries display approximately 40 common colors. For example, in the Font Color gallery, the 40 colors are variations of the chosen color scheme. Some galleries also display recently used colors. All color galleries display a More Colors command. **Why?** *When clicked, the command allows the user to choose from other Standard colors, Custom colors, and PANTONE colors.* The following steps choose a color from the Standard color sheet (Colors dialog box).

①

- In the Create New Color Scheme dialog box, click the New button associated with Accent 3 to display the color gallery (Figure 4–11).

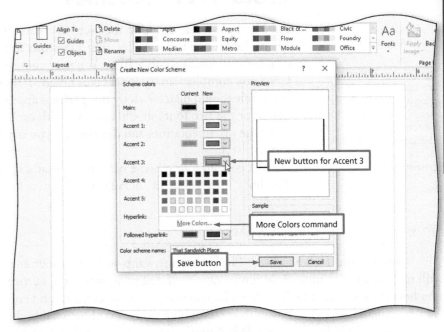

Figure 4–11

②

- Click More Colors in the color gallery to display the Colors dialog box.

- If necessary, click the Standard tab and then click the desired color (in this case, the medium pink color in the fifth row from the bottom and fourth from the right) (Figure 4–12).

⊘ **Experiment**

- Click each of the tabs in the Colors dialog box to see the types of colors and color systems from which you can choose.

③

- Click OK (Colors dialog box) to select the chosen color.

- Click the Save button (Create New Color Scheme dialog box) to save the new color scheme.

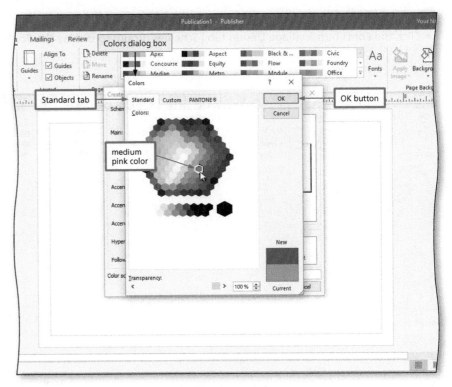

Figure 4–12

Other Ways

1. In any color gallery, click More Colors, click desired color, click OK (Colors dialog box)

Custom Font Schemes

Publisher provides an option for users to create their own font schemes rather than use any of the predefined sets. Creating a **custom font scheme** allows you to choose your own fonts to use in a publication. You may choose one heading font and one body font. Choosing complementary fonts takes practice. In general, either the heading font and body font should match exactly but perhaps appear in different sizes or styles (such as italics) or the two fonts should contrast with each other dramatically in features such as size, type ornamentation, and direction. **Type ornamentation** refers to serif, structure, form, or style.

A custom font scheme has a name that will appear in the font scheme gallery. The body font will be the default font for new text boxes.

To Create a New Font Scheme

Because the That Sandwich Place company wants to portray flair and quality, a customized font scheme will include the Britannic Bold font, a sans-serif design, in which the vertical lines are clearly thicker than the horizontals. Britannic Bold has a high degree of stroke contrast and commonly is used for headings, advertisements, and signs rather than continuous body text. The Arial body font provides a nice contrast with the Britannic Bold heading font. *Why? Arial is a sans-serif, TrueType font and is easily legible in print publications.* **TrueType** refers to scalable fonts that produce high-quality characters on both computer screens and printers. The following steps create a new font scheme.

- Click the Fonts button (Page Design tab | Schemes group) to display the Fonts gallery (Figure 4–13).

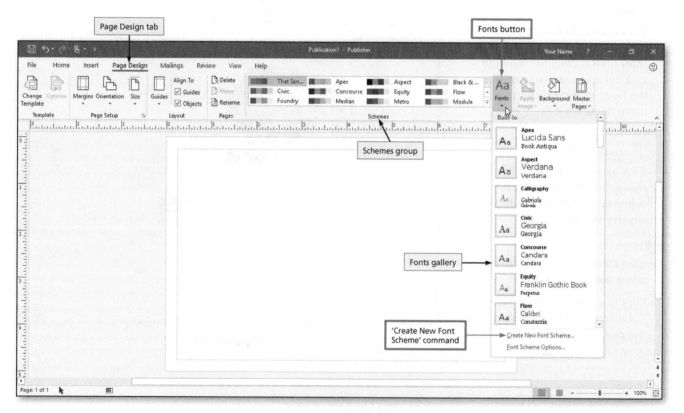

Figure 4–13

- Click 'Create New Font Scheme' in the Fonts gallery to display the Create New Font Scheme dialog box.

- Type **That Sandwich Place** in the 'Font scheme name' text box (Create New Font Scheme dialog box) to name the font scheme with the same name as the company (Figure 4–14).

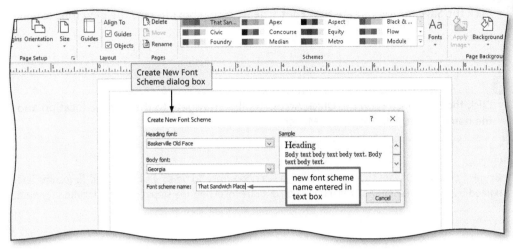

Figure 4–14

- Click the Heading font arrow to display the list of fonts (Figure 4–15).

Experiment

- Click different fonts and watch the Sample box change. When you are finished, click the Heading font arrow again.

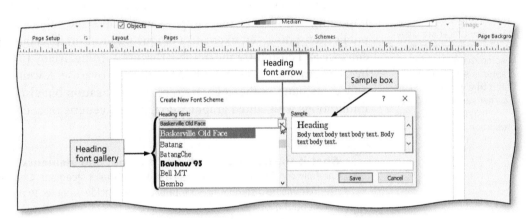

Figure 4–15

- Scroll as necessary and then click Britannic Bold to select the heading font.

- Click the Body font arrow, scroll as necessary, and then click Arial to select the body font (Figure 4–16).

Q&A

Can I delete a font scheme once I create it?
Yes. To delete a font scheme, display the list of font schemes, right-click the custom font scheme, and then click Delete Scheme on the shortcut menu. You also can rename or duplicate the scheme.

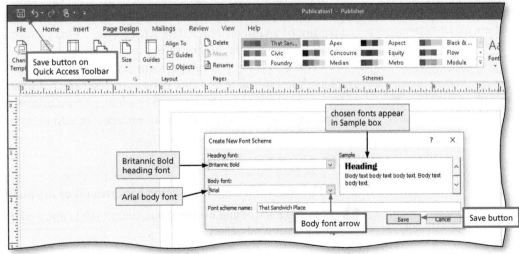

Figure 4–16

5

- Click the Save button (Create New Font Scheme dialog box) to save the new font scheme.

Q&A | Where is the new font scheme stored?
Each font scheme that you create will appear at the top of the gallery, alphabetized by name.

6

- Click the Save button on the Quick Access Toolbar. Navigate to the storage location and then save the file with the file name, SC_PUB_4_RestaurantMailer.

Break Point: If you want to take a break, this is a good place to do so. Exit Publisher. To resume later, start Publisher, open the file named SC_PUB_4_RestaurantMailer.pub and continue following the steps from this location forward.

Editing Graphics

BTW

Using the CTRL Key
When you CTRL+drag a sizing handle, the graphic is resized, keeping the center of the graphic in the same place. This is true whether you use a corner handle to resize or a side handle to change the proportion.

You insert graphics or pictures into publications by choosing them online or by importing them from a file. Graphics and shapes add value and visual flair to publications; however, to create a unique publication for a business, it is good to enhance and customize the graphic through editing. Many times, customers are bored by stock graphics and clip art because of their overuse. A well-edited graphic not only contributes to the uniqueness of the publication but also adds a personal touch. Publications with edited graphics do not look generic or computer generated.

CONSIDER THIS

What is the best way to choose a layout and elements?
Carefully consider the necessary elements and their placement. Choose margins and a paper size that will help standardize the publication. Decide whether to add dated material or prices. Think about alignment of elements and proximity of similar data. Create appropriate contrast or repetition when using fonts and colors.

If you are working for someone, draw a storyboard and get it approved before you begin. If you need to create objects from scratch, have someone else evaluate your work and give you constructive feedback.

BTW

Scaling
The term, **scaling**, when it applies to graphics, means changing the vertical or horizontal size of the graphic by a percentage. Scaling can create interesting graphic effects. Caricature drawings and intentionally distorted photographs routinely use scaling. When used for resizing, scaling is appropriate to make graphics fit in tight places.

In the following sections, you will apply a background; insert, change and duplicate a shape; and then insert a picture. The main graphic for That Sandwich Place is a picture of a sandwich on a dark background. This picture will be edited and framed to create a reusable graphic for future use.

With Publisher, you can perform several types of adjustments or edits on graphics. You can rotate and flip; correct or reset the color; set a transparent color; resize or change the proportion; add borders, picture effects, and captions; and — if it is a drawing, curve, or clip art — you can erase or edit certain portions of the graphic.

To Change the Background

The following steps change the background of the publication.

1 Click the Background button (Page Design tab | Page Background group) to display the Background gallery.

2 In the Solid Backgrounds area, click '10% Tint of Accent 2' to apply a background color (Figure 4–17).

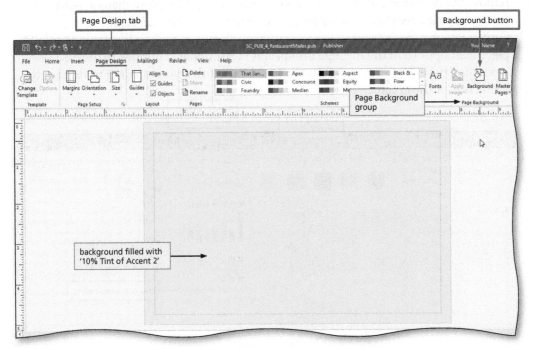

Figure 4–17

To Insert a Block Arc Shape

The following steps insert a shape.

1 Display the Insert tab.

2 Click the Shapes button (Insert tab | Illustrations group) to display the Shapes gallery. In the Basic Shapes area, click the Block Arc shape.

3 On the publication page, drag a shape approximately 7.25 inches wide and .75 inches tall (Figure 4–18).

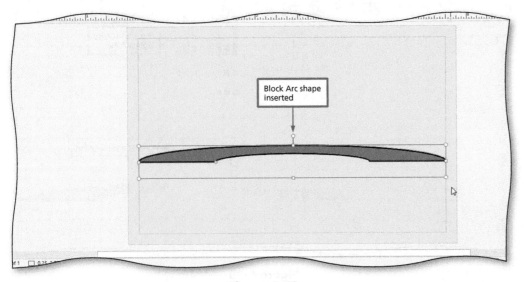

Figure 4–18

To Manipulate a Shape

The following steps remove the border and then recolor and reshape using the yellow, diamond-shaped adjust handle. **Why?** *You want to manipulate the shape to be thicker and not have the black default border.*

The Drawing Tools Format tab provides several ways to manipulate shapes, including formatting options in the Shape Styles group, placement options in the Arrange group, and measurements options in the Size group. In addition, many shapes display yellow, diamond-shaped adjust handles that you can drag to reshape the characteristics or exaggerate one side of the graphic.

- With the shape selected, click the Shape Outline button (Drawing Tools Format tab | Shape Styles group) to display the Shape Outline gallery (Figure 4–19).

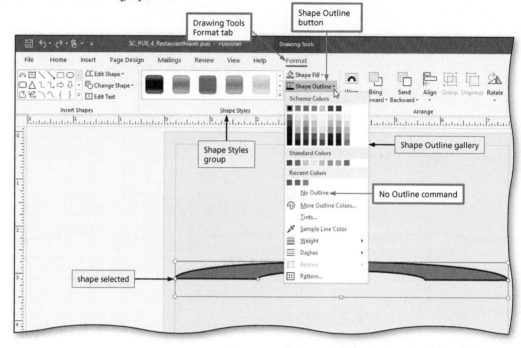

Figure 4–19

- Click No Outline to remove the border.
- Click the Shape Fill button (Drawing Tools Format tab | Shape Styles group) to display the Shape Fill gallery (Figure 4–20).

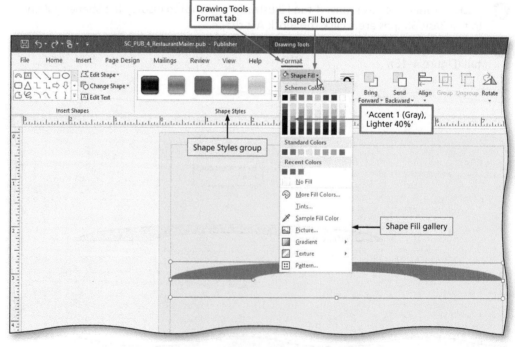

Figure 4–20

- Click 'Accent 1 (Gray), Lighter 40%' to change the color of the shape.

- Drag the yellow adjust handle down approximately 0.25 inches (Figure 4–21).

Q&A

What does the adjust handle do? Unlike the regular sizing handles that change the overall size of a shape, an adjust handle edits the thickness and angle of the shape at the handle's location.

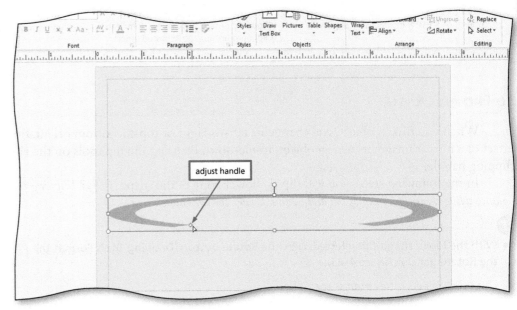

Figure 4–21

Other Ways

1. Right-click shape, click Format AutoShape on shortcut menu, in Color and Lines sheet click Line Color arrow, click No Outline, click Fill Color arrow, click color choice, click OK (Format AutoShape dialog box)

To Duplicate the Shape

While you can use copy and paste methods to create a copy of the shape, Publisher has a shortcut to create a duplicate. The pointer displays a small plus sign as you create the duplicate. The following step duplicates the shape. *Why? You want an exact copy to provide balance on the top and bottom of the mailer.*

- With the shape still selected, CTRL+drag the shape to create a duplicate.

- Drag one copy to a location approximately 1 inch from the top of the mailer. Drag the other to the bottom margin (Figure 4–22).

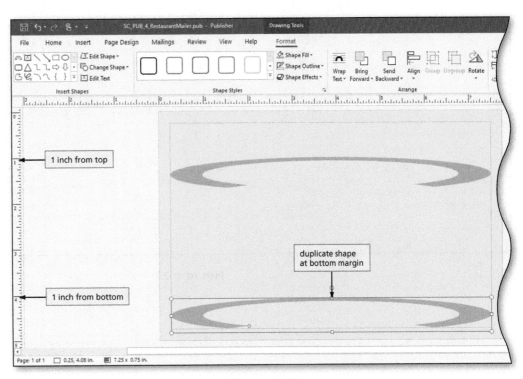

Figure 4–22

Other Ways

1. Right-click object, click Copy, right-click object, click Paste, move pasted object	2. Select shape, click Copy (Home tab | Clipboard group), click Paste (Home tab | Clipboard group), move pasted object	3. Select shape, press CTRL+C, press CTRL+V, move pasted object

To Flip an Object

When you **flip** an object, you change its left-to-right or top-to-bottom orientation. You can create the effect of a mirror image or turn an object upside-down by using the flip tools on the ribbon; Publisher has no flipping handle.

In the following steps, you will flip the lower copy of the shape. *Why? Flipping the lower shape will provide balance while creating a kind of top and bottom border for the mailer.*

- With the lower shape still selected, click the Rotate button (Drawing Tools Format tab | Arrange group) to display the Rotate gallery (Figure 4–23).

Q&A Can I flip objects other than shapes?
Yes, you can flip most objects, including pictures and text boxes.

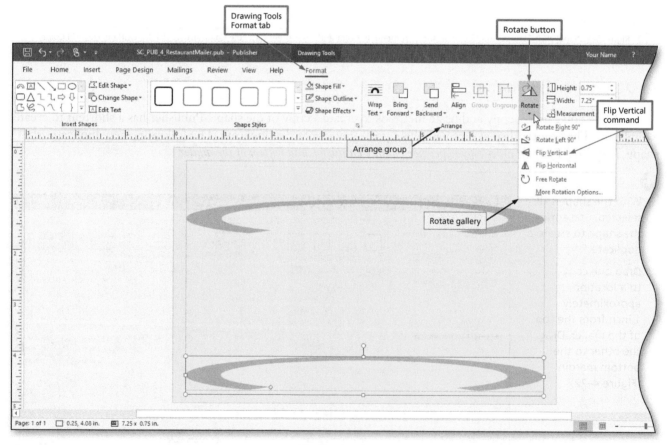

Figure 4–23

2

- Click Flip Vertical to flip the shape (Figure 4–24).

℗ Experiment

- Click the Rotate button again and click different commands on the Rotate gallery to see how they work. When you are done, click Flip Vertical.

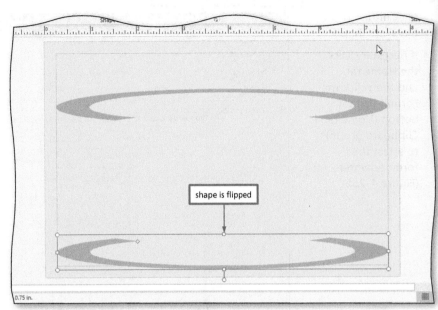

Figure 4–24

To Insert a Trapezoid Shape

The following steps insert a shape.

1 Display the Insert tab.

2 Click the Shapes button (Insert tab | Illustrations group) to display the Shapes gallery. In the Basic Shapes area, click the Trapezoid shape.

3 Drag to create a trapezoid shape in the center of the publication between the two other shapes (Figure 4–25).

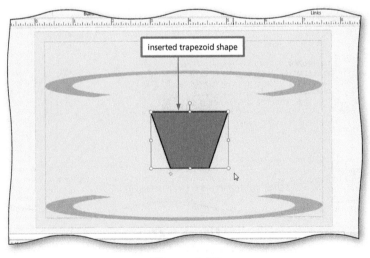

Figure 4–25

To Use the Format Painter with Shapes

You can use the format painter to copy formatting with shapes in the same manner as you do with text. The following steps copy the formatting of the block arc shape and apply it to the trapezoid using the format painter. **Why?** *Using the format painter is faster and more accurate than repeating all of the previous formatting changes.*

1

- Click either of the block arc shapes.

- If necessary, click the Home tab and then click the Format Painter button (Home tab | Clipboard group) to select the format painter (Figure 4–26).

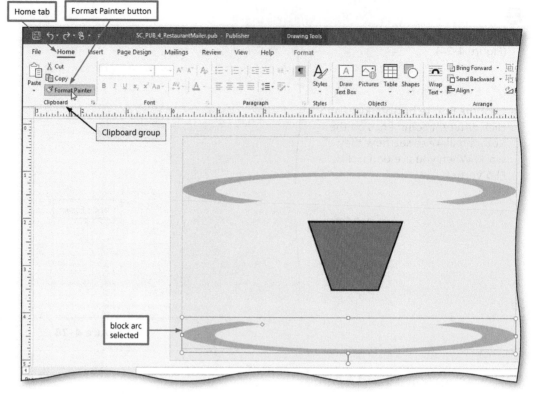

Figure 4–26

2

- Click the trapezoid to copy the formatting (Figure 4–27).

Q&A

Did the format painter copy the manipulations made earlier using the yellow diamond-shaped handle? No. The format painter copied only the outline and fill, and it would have copied any applied shape styles or shape effects.

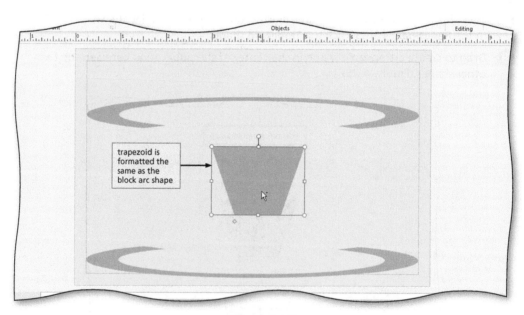

Figure 4–27

To Rotate a Shape

When you **rotate** an object, you turn it so that the top of the object faces a different direction. For example, a picture of a person could be rotated to look like that person is standing on his or her head. The Rotate button on the Drawing Tools Format tab and on other tabs contains commands to rotate and flip in specific directions and percentages. Each selected object in Publisher displays one or more rotation handles used to rotate the object freely. To rotate in 15-degree increments, hold down SHIFT while dragging a rotation handle. To rotate an object on its base, hold down CTRL and drag the rotation handle; the object will rotate in a circle by pivoting around the handle. You can enter other rotation percentages using the Rotate button (Drawing Tools Format tab | Arrange group).

In the following steps, you will rotate the trapezoid. *Why? A trapezoid on its side will serve as the background for the coupons.*

1

- With the trapezoid selected, click the Rotate button (Drawing Tools Format tab | Arrange group) to display the Rotate gallery (Figure 4–28).

Q&A Can I rotate objects other than shapes?
Yes, you can rotate all objects, including shapes, text boxes, and tables. Rotate buttons also appear on multiple tabs on the ribbon.

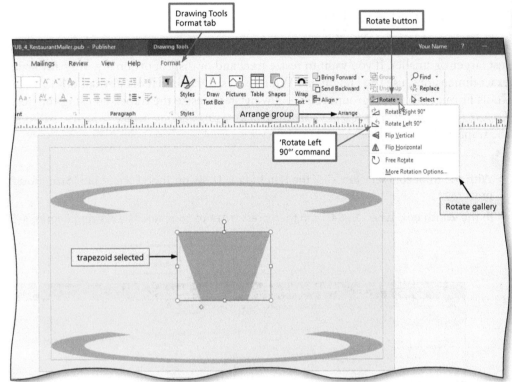

Figure 4–28

2

- Click 'Rotate Left 90°' in the Rotate gallery to rotate the trapezoid (Figure 4–29).

Q&A Could I have used the rotation handle to rotate the trapezoid?
Yes, but sometimes it is difficult to rotate to exact degree settings.

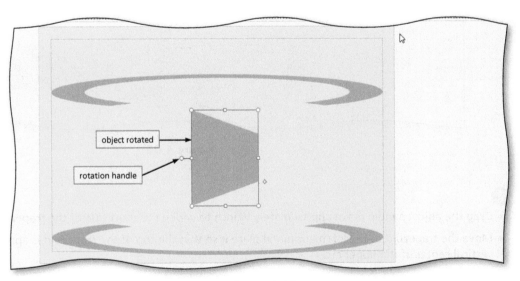

Figure 4–29

Other Ways

1. Drag rotation handle	2. Right-click object, click Format AutoShape on shortcut menu, click Size tab (Format AutoShape dialog box), enter rotation percentage, click OK	3. Click Object Size button (status bar), enter rotation percentage in Measurement pane

To Resize Using Exact Dimensions

If you want to resize an object proportionally, SHIFT+drag a sizing handle; the object appears the same, just larger or smaller. If you want to resize freehand or disproportionately, drag any sizing handle. To resize using exact dimensions, use the Height and Width boxes (Drawing Tools Format tab | Arrange group) or (Picture Tools Format tab | Size group). The following steps resize the trapezoid using the height and width boxes. *Why? Entering exact measurements is more precise than dragging a sizing handle.* You also will reshape, move, and duplicate the trapezoid.

- With the trapezoid selected, click the Height box (Drawing Tools Format tab | Size group), type **3.57** and then press TAB.
- In the Width box, type **1.64** and then press ENTER to complete the resizing (Figure 4–30).

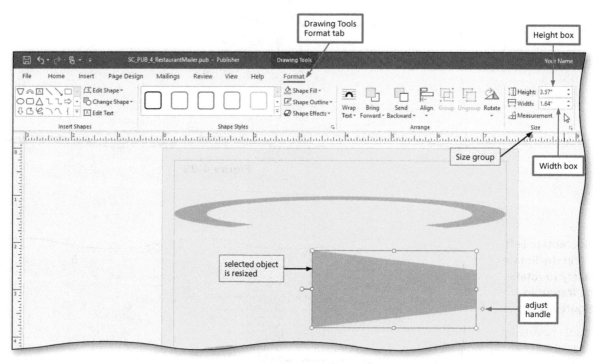

Figure 4–30

- Drag the adjust handle down approximately ⅛ inch to widen the short side of the trapezoid slightly.
- Move the trapezoid to the left margin and place it so that the top of the trapezoid is approximately even with the vertical center of the upper arc.

- CTRL+drag to create a copy of the trapezoid and move it down so that the bottom of the trapezoid is approximately even with the vertical center of the lower arc (Figure 4–31).

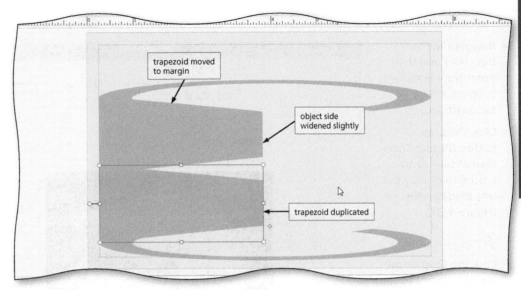

Figure 4–31

Other Ways

1. Click Object Size button (Publisher status bar), enter dimensions in Measurements pane
2. Click Measurement button (Drawing Tools Format tab | Size group), enter dimensions

Building Blocks

Building blocks are graphical elements that you can insert in a publication; they include advertisement items, business information components, calendars, design accents, and page parts. You also can create your own building blocks and add them to the Building Block Library. The **Building Block Library** displays folders of building block components. When saving a building block, you can enter a title, description, and keywords to help you find the building block later. You also can choose the gallery and category in which you wish to save.

    Alternatively, you can save edited graphics on your storage device as pictures. Saving a graphic as a picture allows you to use that graphic in other applications, whereas building blocks are available only in Publisher.

BTW
Building Block Categories
In the Create New Building Block dialog box, you cannot change the gallery list, but you can enter a new category and save your graphic to that new category. Once you click OK, the new category will appear each time you access the Building Block Library.

To Crop an Object

    The following steps open a picture and **crop**, or trim away, part of the picture *Why? The picture has more background than is necessary for this publication.* After choosing the Crop tool, cropping handles display on the sides and corners of the picture. A **cropping handle** is a small black handle that you drag to crop a picture. These handles are similar to resizing handles, but when they are dragged, the edge of the picture is cropped. To crop one side, drag the side cropping handle on that side. To crop evenly on two sides at once, hold down CTRL as you drag a side cropping handle. To crop all four sides evenly, press CTRL+SHIFT while you drag a corner cropping handle.

    To complete these steps, you will be required to use the Data Files. Please contact your instructor for information about accessing the Data Files.

- Display the Insert tab.

- Click the Pictures button (Insert tab | Illustrations group) to display the Insert Picture dialog box.

- Navigate to the Data Files and then insert the file named Support_PUB_4_ Sandwich.jpg.

- Click the Crop button (Picture Tools Format tab | Crop group) to display the cropping handles (Figure 4–32).

Experiment

- Click the Crop arrow and then point to 'Crop to Shape' to see the options for cropping. Click the Crop button to return to a regular crop.

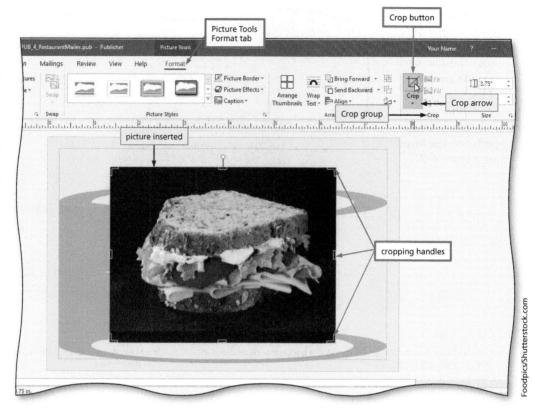

Figure 4–32

2

- CTRL+SHIFT+drag the lower-right corner cropping handle toward the center until most of the background is removed and all of the sandwich is still visible.

- Drag other side cropping handles until all four sides display the same minimal amount of background (Figure 4–33).

 What is gray area around the picture?
The gray area shows the part of the picture that has been cropped.

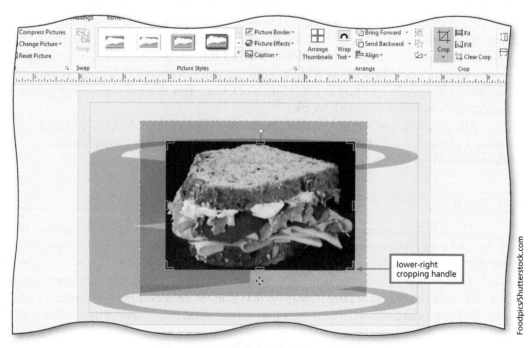

Figure 4–33

3
- Click the Crop button again (Picture Tools Format tab | Crop group) to turn off the cropping handles and to display the cropped picture (Figure 4–34).

🔎 **Experiment**

- Click the Clear Crop button (Picture Tools Format tab | Crop group) to see what happens when you clear the crop. Click the Undo button (Quick Access Toolbar) to undo the Clear Crop command.

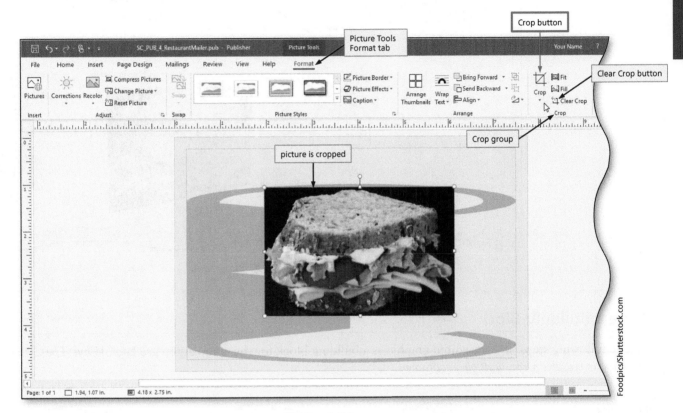

Figure 4–34

Other Ways

1. Right-click picture, click Format Picture on shortcut menu, in Picture sheet enter crop amounts, click OK (Format Picture dialog box)

To Add a Picture Style

The following steps format the picture. To complete these steps, you will be required to use the Data Files. Please contact your instructor for information about accessing the Data Files.

1 With the picture selected, click the More button (Picture Tools Format tab | Picture Styles group) to display the Picture Styles gallery.

2 Click 'Bevel Perspective Left, White' in the Picture Styles gallery to apply the selected style to the picture (Figure 4–35).

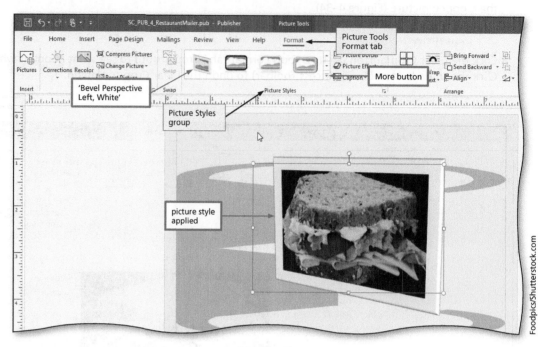

Figure 4–35

To Save a Building Block

The following steps save the edited graphic as a building block for the company to use later. *Why? The graphic becomes reusable across multiple publications.*

- Right-click the desired graphic or object (in this case, the cropped picture with the picture style) to display a shortcut menu (Figure 4–36).

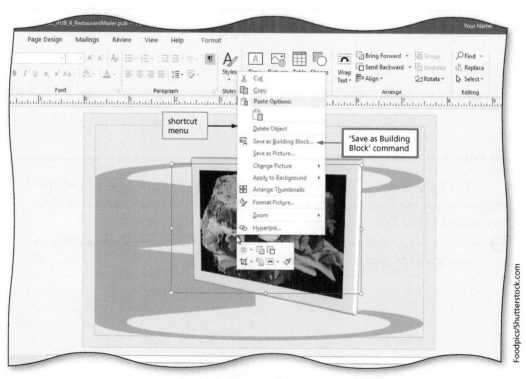

Figure 4–36

- Click 'Save as Building Block' to display the Create New Building Block dialog box.

- If necessary, select any text in the Title text box and then type **That Sandwich Place Graphic** in the Title text box.

- Press TAB to move to the Description text box and then type **This graphic is our signature sandwich with frame.** to enter the description.

- Click the Keywords text box and then type **sandwich, frame** to enter the keywords (Figure 4–37).

❸

- Click OK (Create New Building Block dialog box) to save the building block.

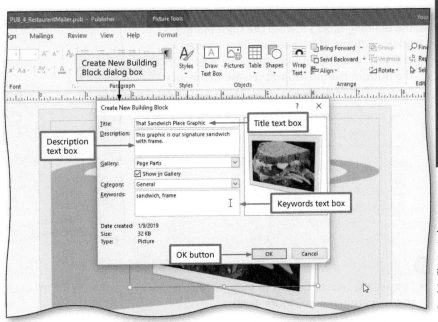

Figure 4–37

Other Ways

1. Click Page Parts button (Insert tab | Building Blocks group), click 'Add Selection to Page Parts Gallery' (Page Parts Gallery), enter information (Create New Building Block dialog box), click OK

TO SAVE THE GRAPHIC AS A PICTURE

If you wanted to use the graphic in another application, such as Microsoft Word or Microsoft PowerPoint, you would perform the following steps to save the graphic as a picture on your storage device.

1. Right-click the object and then click 'Save as Picture' on the shortcut menu to display the Save As dialog box.

2. Type the name of the graphic in the File name box.

3. Navigate to your storage location.

4. Edit property tags as desired and then click the Save button (Save As dialog box) to save the graphic as a picture.

To Snap an Object to the Margin Guide

The following steps snap the building block to the margin. *Why? Snapping is a magnet-like alignment that occurs between object borders and margin guides and helps align objects with margins.*

Publisher 2019 provides snapping behavior that has been improved compared to previous versions. As you drag an object toward another object's edge, midline, or guide, the object you are dragging acts almost "sticky" when it aligns; the dragging process slows. Snapping is an easy way to align objects with the margin or with other objects, and snapping is more accurate than moving to an approximate location.

1

- Drag the border of the object (in this case, the building block) toward the right margin guide until the blue snapping lines appear and then drag down until the graphic touches the bottom margin. Do not release the mouse button (Figure 4–38).

Q&A How can I place objects more precisely?
You can use the Measurements pane, or you can right-click the object and then click Format Object on the shortcut menu. The Format Object dialog box contains a Layout tab on which you can enter the precise measurements in the 'Position on page' text boxes.

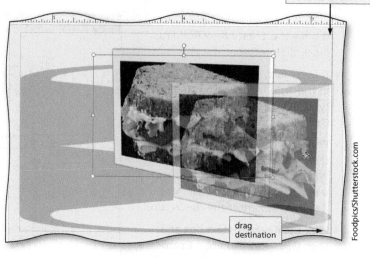

Figure 4–38

2

- Release the mouse button to snap the object to the margin guide (Figure 4–39).

Q&A Will the object snap if I have turned off margin guides?
Yes. If the guides are hidden, objects will still snap to the guides, and the guides will appear as the objects come into alignment.

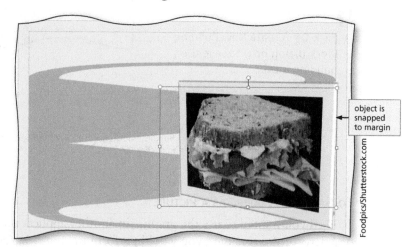

Figure 4–39

To Nudge an Object

Sometimes you need to fine-tune the location of a graphic or text box. You can **nudge** to move a graphic a small amount in one direction by using the arrow keys. The following steps nudge the building block.

1

- With the building block still selected, press ARROW keys until the picture touches the trapezoids with approximately the same amount of room above and below the trapezoids (Figure 4–40).

2

- Click the Save button on the Quick Access Toolbar.

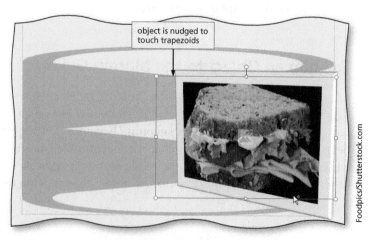

Figure 4–40

Break Point: If you want to take a break, this is a good place to do so. Exit Publisher. To resume later, start Publisher, open the file named SC_PUB_4_RestaurantMailer and continue following the steps from this location forward.

WordArt

WordArt is a gallery of formatted, decorative text styles used to create fancy text effects. A WordArt object actually is a graphic, not text. Publication designers typically use WordArt to create eye-catching headlines, banners, or watermark images. Most designers agree that you should use WordArt sparingly and, at most, only once per page, unless you are trying to achieve some kind of special effect or illustration.

WordArt has its own tab on the ribbon that is displayed only when a WordArt object is selected. On the WordArt tab, you can change a variety of settings, such as the fill, outline, warp, height, and alignment, as well as edit the color, shape, and shape effect.

BTW

WordArt Spelling
Keep in mind that WordArt objects are drawing objects; they are not Publisher text. Thus, if you misspell the contents of a WordArt object and then check spelling in the publication, Publisher will not flag the misspelled word(s) in the WordArt text.

To Insert a WordArt Object

The following steps add a WordArt object at the top of the mailer. *Why? While a formatted text box might create a suitable effect, using WordArt increases the number of special effect possibilities and options.*

1
- If necessary, deselect any selected objects on the page and display the Insert tab.
- Click the WordArt button (Insert tab | Text group) to display the WordArt gallery (Figure 4–41).

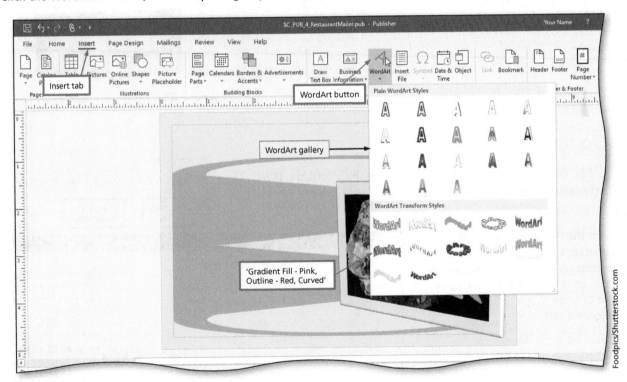

Figure 4–41

Foodpics/Shutterstock.com

● Click the desired style (in this case, 'Gradient Fill - Pink, Outline - Red, Curved') in the WordArt gallery to select it and display the Edit WordArt Text box.

● Type **That Sandwich Place** in the Text text box (Edit WordArt Text dialog box) to enter the text to appear in the WordArt object.

● Click the Font box, scroll as necessary, and then click Britannic Bold in the Font list.

● If necessary, click the Size arrow, scroll as necessary, and then click 36 in the Size list (Figure 4–42).

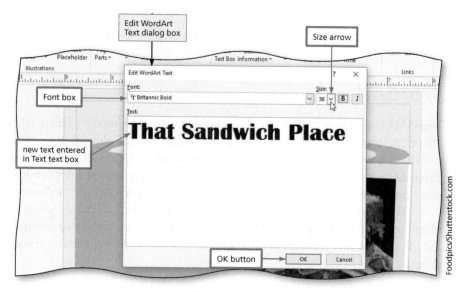

Figure 4–42

● Click OK to close the Edit WordArt Text dialog box and insert the WordArt object.

● Drag the WordArt object to the top margin (Figure 4–43).

Q&A Should I try to center the WordArt?

No. You will center it later in the module.

Figure 4–43

To Change the WordArt Shape

The following steps change the shape of the WordArt. **Why?** *The owner of That Sandwich Place prefers a shape that more closely matches the arc graphic.*

● With the WordArt object still selected, click the 'Change Shape' button (WordArt Tools Format tab | WordArt Styles group) to display the Change Shape gallery (Figure 4–44).

Q&A Could I use the WordArt Styles gallery to choose a different shape?

No. The gallery contains combinations of shapes, color outlines, and fills. Here you want to change only the shape.

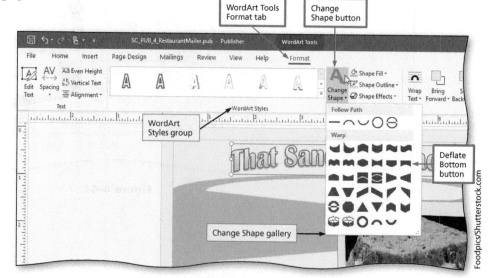

Figure 4–44

- Click the Deflate Bottom button (row 2, column 6) in the Warp area in the Change Shape gallery to select it (Figure 4–45).

Figure 4–45

Text Boxes

In a new, blank publication, if you start typing text, Publisher creates a large text box that fills the page. By creating a text box yourself, you can create a specific size and location and then format the text separately from the rest of the publication. By default, text inside text boxes is single-spaced within paragraphs and double-spaced between paragraphs.

To Draw a Text Box

The following step draws a text box in the scratch area. *Why? You cannot type directly in the publication or in the scratch area without first creating a text box.* After formatting the text, you will move it in front of the gray trapezoid to create a coupon. Customers exchange coupons for discounts when purchasing a product. Some coupons offer rebates or free items to attract customers. Wide distribution of coupons often is accomplished by sending small printed documents through mail, magazines, newspapers, and newsletters. More recently, however, coupons are distributed as electronic tags collected through preferred customer cards via the Internet and mobile devices, such as smartphones.

- Display the Home tab.

- Click the 'Draw Text Box' button (Home tab | Objects group).

- In the scratch area, drag a text box approximately 3.25 inches wide and 1.3 inches tall. Publisher will display the Text Box Tools tab (Figure 4–46).

Q&A What are the default font settings for text boxes?
The text is black, the alignment is left justified, and the font is the body font of the font scheme. The margins within the text box are set to 0.04 inches. All of the settings can be changed.

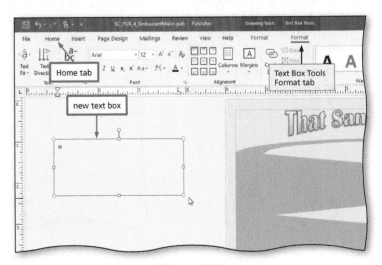

Figure 4–46

Other Ways

1. Click 'Draw Text Box' button (Insert tab | Text group)

BTW
Background
Transparency
If a shape or text box has white
in the background, you may
want to remove it so that the
objects behind show through.
Select the shape or text box
and then press CTRL+T to make
the object transparent.

Bulleted Lists

A **bulleted list** is a series of lines (or paragraphs), each beginning with a bullet character. When you click the Bullets button (Home tab | Paragraph group), Publisher displays the Bullets gallery, which is a list of commands and thumbnails that show different bullet styles. You can choose a standard bullet character (•) and adjust its size and how far the text is indented. You also can customize the bullet by choosing a different character or symbol.

To Create a Custom Bullet

The following steps create a bulleted list using a custom character. **Why?** *The owner of That Sandwich Place wants the bullet to look like a sandwich.*

1

• With the insertion point inside the text box, click the Bullets button (Home tab | Paragraph group) to display the Bullets gallery (Figure 4–47).

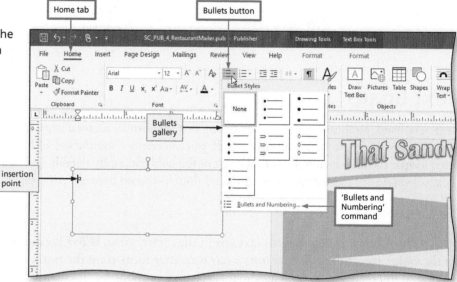

Figure 4–47

2

• Click 'Bullets and Numbering' in the Bullets gallery to display the Bullets and Numbering dialog box.

• Click any Bullet character other than a blank one (Figure 4–48).

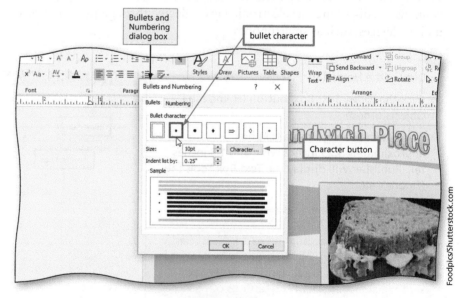

Figure 4–48

Foodpics/Shutterstock.com

3

- Click the Character button (Bullets and Numbering dialog box) to display the Bullet Character dialog box.

- Click the Font arrow (Bullet Character dialog box) to display the Font list (Figure 4–49).

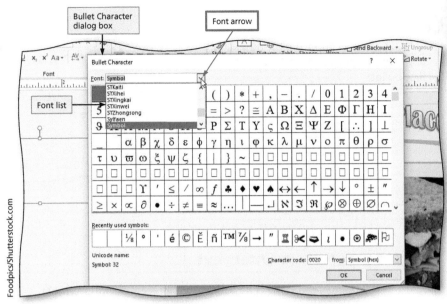

Foodpics/Shutterstock.com

Figure 4–49

4

- Scroll as necessary and then click 'Segoe UI Emoji' in the list.

- Scroll down approximately halfway and then click the sandwich shape, character code 1F354 (Figure 4–50).

Q&A Could I enter the character code to find the character faster?
Yes.

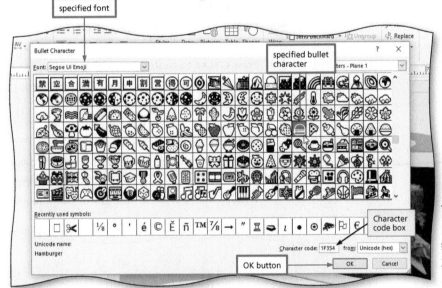

Foodpics/Shutterstock.com

Figure 4–50

5

- Click OK (Bullet Character dialog box) to choose the symbol and return to the Bullets and Numbering dialog box.

- Click the Size up arrow until it says 16pt to enter the size.

- Click the 'Indent list by' up arrow until it displays 0.45" indentation (Figure 4–51).

Q&A What does pt stand for?
The letters pt stand for **point**, which is a physical measurement equal to approximately 1/72 of an inch. Therefore, the bullet will be approximately 0.22 inches square.

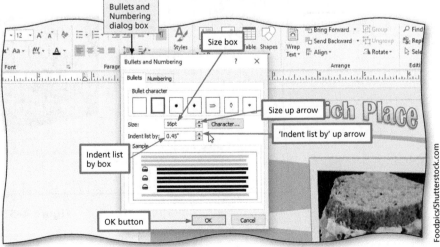

Foodpics/Shutterstock.com

Figure 4–51

• Click OK (Bullets and Numbering dialog box) to apply the settings (Figure 4–52) and insert the first bullet.

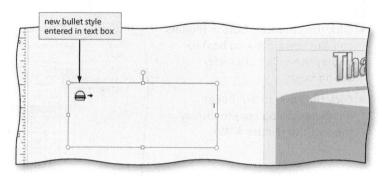

new bullet style entered in text box

Figure 4–52

To Enter Text

The following steps enter bulleted text.

1 With the insertion point in the text box, click the Font Size arrow (Home tab | Font group) and then click 16 in the Font Size list.

2 Click the Font Color button (Home tab | Font group) and click Red in the Standard Colors area.

3 Press CTRL+E to center.

4 Type the following text, pressing ENTER after each line but the last one:
$5 OFF
with purchase of
$30 or more

5 If necessary, change the uppercase W to lowercase.

6 Drag the text box to a location in front of the upper trapezoid and click the 'Show Whole Page' button on the status bar (Figure 4–53).

text is centered and bulleted

'Show Whole Page' button

Foodpics/Shutterstock.com

Figure 4–53

To Create a Second Coupon

The following steps copy the coupon and change the text.

1 CTRL+SHIFT+drag the coupon down to a location in front of the second trapezoid.

2 Change the text to:
FREE DESSERT
with purchase of
combo meal

3 Click the Save button on the Quick Access Toolbar to save the file again with the same file name and in the same location (Figure 4–54).

Figure 4–54

To Change a Text Box Border

The following steps change the border of the text box from no line to a dashed line. *Why? A dashed line will help suggest perforation and indicate that the area is a coupon.*

1
- Click the border of the upper text box to select it.

- Click the Shape Outline button (Drawing Tools Format tab | Shape Styles group) to display the Shape Outline gallery.

- Point to Dashes to display the Dashes submenu (Figure 4–55).

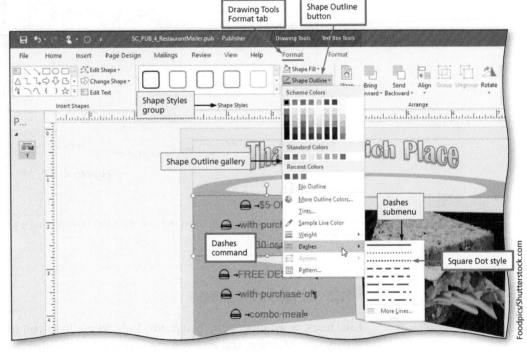

Figure 4–55

2

- Click Square Dot on the submenu and then deselect to display a dotted line around the text box (Figure 4–56).

Figure 4–56

3

- Repeat steps 1 and 2 for the lower text box (Figure 4–57).

Figure 4–57

Other Ways

1. Right-click text box, click 'Format Text Box' on shortcut menu, in Colors and Lines sheet click Dash Type button, click desired dash type, click OK (Format Text Box dialog box)

Fills and Outlines

Like many word processing programs, Publisher allows you to format text with a large variety of font, color, and line spacing choices. In Publisher, you can **fill** or paint text with a color or with a special effect. You also can apply effects to the **outline** around the text, which is similar to adding a border or stroke around each letter. The larger the text, the more dramatic the outline.

Table 4–1 displays the fill effects for text. Table 4–2 displays the outline effects for text.

Table 4–1 Text Fill Effects

Fill Effect	Settings	Result
No fill	None	Text is transparent (best used over a solid color)
Solid fill	Color button Transparency slider	Text appears with a solid color (default setting)
Gradient fill	Preset gradients button Type button Direction button Angle arrows Gradient stops Color button Position arrows Transparency slider and arrows Rotate with shape check box	Gradual progression of colors and shades

Table 4–2 Text Outline Effects

Fill Effect	Settings	Result
No fill	None	Text displays fill effect or default settings with no outline
Solid fill	Color button Transparency slider Width arrows Compound type Dash type button Cap type button Join type button	Outline appears as a solid color at specified width and type settings
Gradient fill	Preset gradients button Type button Direction button Angle arrows Gradient stops Color button Position arrows Transparency slider and arrows Width button Compound type button Dash type button Cap type button Join type button	Outline appears with gradual progression of colors and shades at specified width and type settings

BTW

Shapes

Determining what shape to use with pictures is an important decision. Consider the choice of shape that will work with your picture. If your picture is square, you can insert it into a circle, but you may lose some of the edges, or your picture may be distorted slightly. If your picture is rectangular, however, an oval shape may be interesting and aesthetically pleasing. If you want to focus on the center of your picture, a star shape may help direct the viewer's attention.

Other text effects include shadows, reflections, glows, and bevels, each with a wide variety of settings and styles.

To Align Text and Format

Publisher allows you to align text in any one of many different places by using buttons on the Text Box Tools Format tab in the Alignment group. While word processing programs such as Microsoft Word have only four alignment buttons (Left, Center, Right, and Justify), Publisher has nine because all text appears inside text boxes; therefore, you can align text in three ways (Left, Center, and Right) along the top, center, and bottom of text boxes.

The following steps center align the text along the top of the text box. *Why? Placing the text at the highest point possible in the text box will prevent the text from overlapping the bulleted list once the text box is moved to its final position.*

1

- Display the Home tab.

- Click the 'Draw Text Box' button (Home tab | Objects group).

- In the scratch area, drag a text box approximately 1.64 inches wide and .39 inches tall.

- Click the 'Align Top Center' button (Text Box Tools Format tab | Alignment group) to change the alignment of the text in the text box (Figure 4–58).

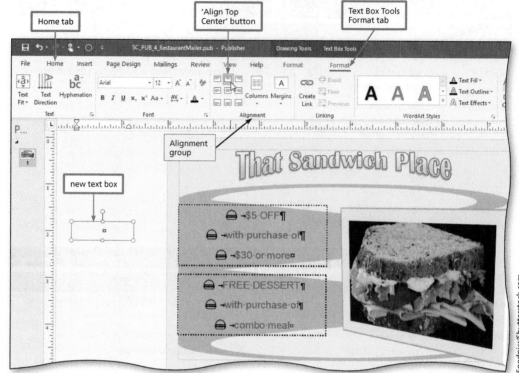

Figure 4–58

2

- If necessary, change the font to Arial, and change the font size to 10.

- Type **Offer Expires 5/31** to complete the text (Figure 4–59).

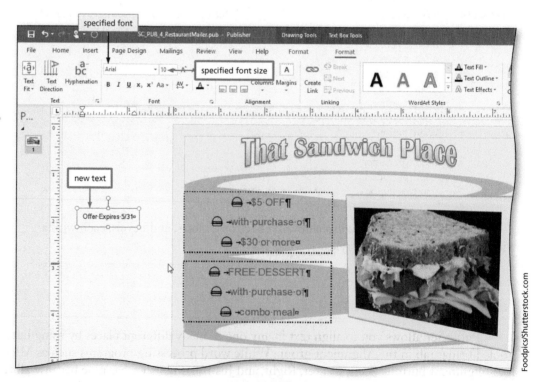

Figure 4–59

To Outline Text

The following steps outline the text in red. *Why? A red outline will enhance the text and make it stand out more than a red font alone would.*

- Select the text in the text box.
- Click the Text Outline button (Text Box Tools Format tab | WordArt Styles group) to display the Text Outline gallery (Figure 4–60).

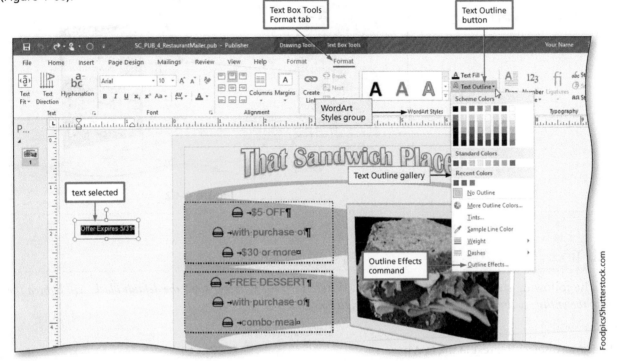

Figure 4–60

- Click Outline Effects to display the Format Shape dialog box.
- Click the Solid line option button and then click the Color button to display the Color gallery (Figure 4–61).

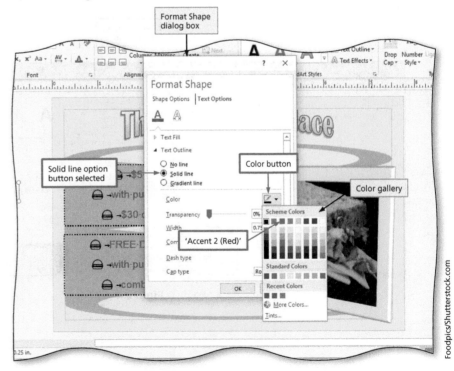

Figure 4–61

● Click 'Accent 2 (Red)' in the Color gallery to change the outline color.

● Click the Width down arrow until 0.5 pt is displayed in the Width box (Figure 4–62).

● Click OK (Format Shape dialog box).

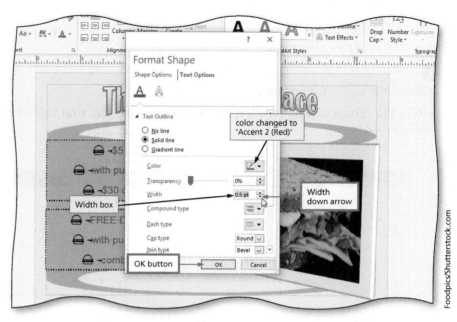

Figure 4–62

To Fill Text

The following steps fill the text with white. *Why? A white fill, rather than the default black, will lighten the inside of the outline so that it is more visible in this small font size.*

● If necessary, select the text in the text box.

● Click the Text Fill button (Text Box Tools Format tab | WordArt Styles group) to display the Text Fill gallery (Figure 4–63).

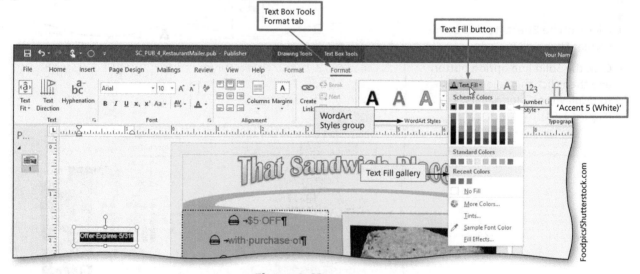

Figure 4–63

②
- Click 'Accent 5 (White)' to change the fill color.
- Click outside of the selected text to view the filled text (Figure 4–64).

Q&A How is this outlined and filled text different from just changing the font color to red?
The outline is heavier than a regular font. Changing the text fill creates the stroked effect desired for this project.

Figure 4–64

To Rotate a Text Box

The following steps rotate the Offer Expires text box.

① If necessary, select the text box.

② Click the Rotate button (Drawing Tools Format tab | Arrange group) to display the Rotate gallery and then click 'Rotate Left 90°' to rotate the object (Figure 4–65).

Figure 4–65

To Move and Duplicate

The following steps move the text box and create a duplicate.

① Drag the text box to the left edge of the upper coupon.

2 CTRL+drag downward to create a copy for the lower coupon (Figure 4–66).

Figure 4–66

Other Ways

1. Point to the rotation handle; when rotation pointer appears, SHIFT+drag object
2. Right-click object, click Format Text Box on shortcut menu, click Size tab (Format Picture dialog box), enter rotation percentage, click OK
3. Click Object Size button on status bar, enter rotation percentage in Measurement pane

---

Aligning Objects

In desktop publication applications, the Home tab alignment tools refer to the text inside the text box in which you are working; however, in most cases, you can align objects — such as a text box itself — with margin guides, ruler guides, and grid guides; or you can align objects relative to one another so that the placement of an object is based on the placement of another object or group of objects or along the margins. You also can center objects relative to the margins on the page.

Many align commands are accessed via the Align button in the Arrange group on the Drawing Tools Format tab. To align objects manually, simply drag an object and look for the pink alignment guides. Objects can be aligned based on their edges or their midlines.

To Create an Address Text Box

The following steps create a text box and insert the company address and phone number.

1 In the scratch area, drag a text box approximately 2.5 inches wide and .60 inches tall. Click the Drawing Tools Format tab and verify the height and width in the Size group.

2 In the text box, press CTRL+E to center.

3 Type **275 Oak Street in Middlebury** and then press ENTER.

BTW

Fitting Graphics
The Fit button (Picture Tools Format tab | Crop group) places the entire, original graphic within the cropping handle dimensions, even if that means creating a disproportional image. The Fill button (Picture Tools Format tab | Crop group) places the original graphic within the cropping handles and maintains proportions, which sometimes means a slight cropping occurs if the cropping handle dimensions are not the same shape as the original. The Clear Crop button (Picture Tools Format tab | Crop group) resets the graphic to its original size and dimension with no cropping. The commands become enabled after an initial crop.

4 Type `223-555-9700` to complete the text (Figure 4–67).

Figure 4–67

Foodpics/Shutterstock.com

To Align Objects

The following steps align a text box in the center of the publication relative to the right and left margins, using an Align command. **Why?** *Using an Align command guarantees correct placement.*

1

- Drag the new text box to a location near the bottom center of the mailer.

- Click the Align button (Drawing Tools Format tab | Arrange group) to display the Align menu (Figure 4–68).

Q&A

The phone number appears in the margin. Is that okay? Yes. Because the mailer is smaller than a normal piece of paper, printers will have no trouble printing that text.

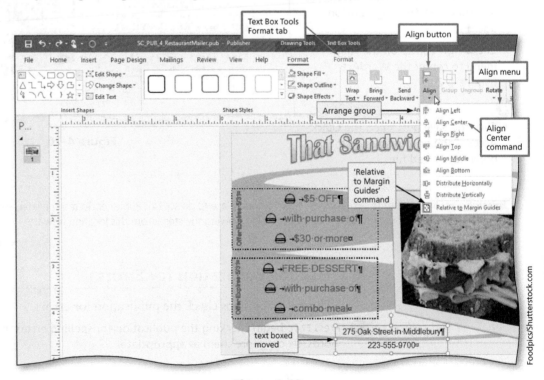

Figure 4–68

Foodpics/Shutterstock.com

2

- If the Align commands are dimmed, click 'Relative to Margin Guides' to allow Publisher to align objects and then click the Align button again.

- Click Align Center on the Align menu to center the text box relative to the left and right margins (Figure 4–69).

Figure 4–69

3

- Select the WordArt at the top of the mailer.

- Click the Align button (WordArt Tools Format tab | Arrange group).

- If the Align commands are dimmed, click 'Relative to Margin Guides' on the Align menu to allow Publisher to align objects and then click the Align button again.

- Click Align Center on the Align menu to center the WordArt (Figure 4–70).

4

- Click the Save button on the Quick Access Toolbar to overwrite the previously saved file.

Figure 4–70

Break Point: If you want to take a break, this is a good place to do so. Exit Publisher. To resume later, start Publisher, open the file called SC_PUB_4_RestaurantMailer.pub and continue following the steps from this location forward.

To Check the Publication for Errors

The following steps check the publication for errors.

1 Press F7 to begin checking the publication for spelling errors. If Publisher flags any words, fix or ignore them as appropriate.

2 When Publisher displays a dialog box asking if you want to check the rest of your publication, click Yes.

3 When the spelling checker is complete, click OK.

4 Click File on the ribbon to open Backstage view and, by default, display the Info screen.

5 Click the 'Run Design Checker' button.

6 If Publisher displays an error about a text box being partially off the page, select the text box and then slowly nudge it up until the error disappears.

7 Ignore any errors related to the picture. If the Design Checker identifies any other errors, fix them as necessary.

8 Close the Design Checker pane.

9 Print the mailer, if instructed to do so.

10 Click the Save button on the Quick Access Toolbar to save the file again with the same file name and in the same location.

To Close a Publication without Exiting Publisher

The following steps close the publication without exiting Publisher.

1 Click File on the ribbon to open Backstage view.

2 Click Close to close the publication without exiting Publisher and to return to the template gallery.

Using Customized Sizes, Schemes, and Building Blocks

Earlier in this module, you created a custom blank page for a 7.75 × 5-inch mailer, a customized font scheme, a customized color scheme, and a graphic that you stored as a building block. These customizations are meant to be used again. They also can be deleted if you no longer need them.

In the following sections, you will open and access the customizations as if you were going to create a second publication for the same company. You then will delete them.

To Open a Customized Blank Page

The following steps open a customized blank page. *Why? The previously stored page size was saved in the custom area.*

BTW

Conserving Ink and Toner
If you want to conserve ink or toner, you can instruct Publisher to print draft quality documents by clicking File on the ribbon to open Backstage view and then clicking Print in Backstage view to display the Print screen. Click the Printer Properties link and then, depending on your printer, click the Print Quality button and choose Draft in the list. Close the Printer Properties dialog box and then click the Print button as usual.

1

- With Publisher running, if necessary, click File on the ribbon to open Backstage view and then click New to display the template gallery in the New screen (Figure 4–71).

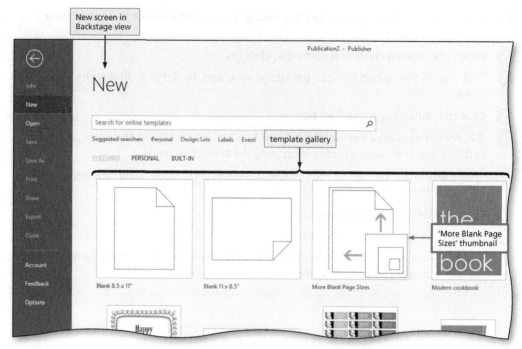

Figure 4–71

2

- Click the 'More Blank Page Sizes' thumbnail to view the Standard and Custom page sizes (More Blank Page Sizes gallery).

- Click the Mailer thumbnail in the Custom area to select it (Figure 4–72).

Q&A Why do my thumbnails look different?
The custom sizes on your computer will differ depending on the users and previous customizations.

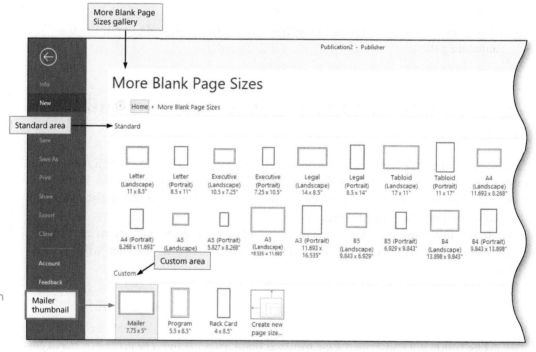

Figure 4–72

Other Ways

1. Click 'Choose Page Size' button (Page Design tab | Page Setup group), click custom size

To Apply Customized Color and Font Schemes

The following steps apply customized color and font schemes. *Why? Your publication colors and fonts need to adhere to company schemes.*

- Click the Color scheme button (template information pane) and then scroll to the top of the list (Figure 4–73).

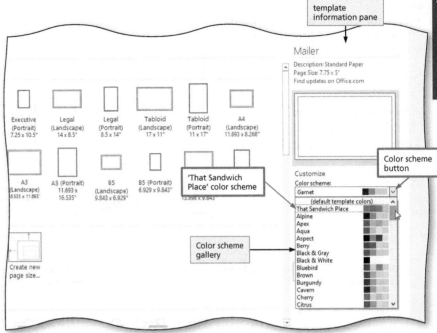

Figure 4–73

2

- Click the 'That Sandwich Place' color scheme to select it.

- Click the Font scheme button (template information pane) and then scroll to the top of the list (Figure 4–74).

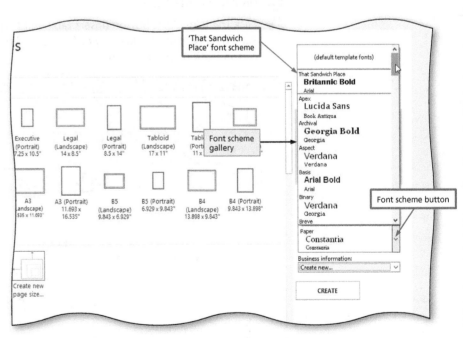

Figure 4–74

3
- Click the 'That Sandwich Place' font scheme to select it (Figure 4–75).

4
- Click the CREATE button (template information pane) to create the publication.

🔍 **Experiment**
- Type a few words and watch Publisher create a page-sized text box. Delete the text box after you are done.

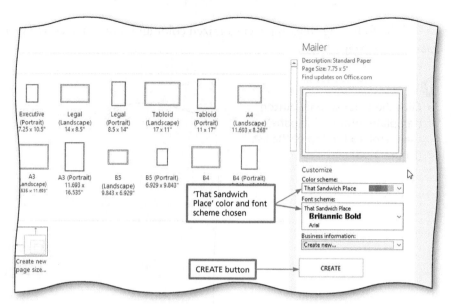

Figure 4–75

Other Ways

1. Click More button (Page Design tab | Schemes group), click custom color scheme

2. Click Fonts button (Page Design tab | Schemes group), click custom font scheme

To Insert a Saved Building Block

The following steps insert the building block that you created earlier in this module.

1 Display the Insert tab.

2 Click the Page Parts button (Insert tab | Building Blocks group) to display the Page Parts gallery. Your display may differ, depending on previous users and previous customizations (Figure 4–76).

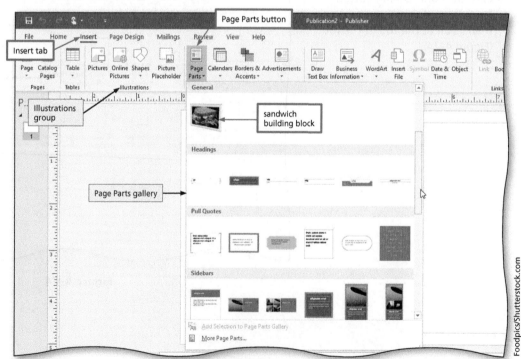

Figure 4–76

Click the desired building block — in this case the sandwich graphic — to insert it into the publication.

Deleting Customizations

In laboratory environments, where many students work on the same computers throughout the day, it is a good idea to delete content you have created that is stored on the computer. You also might want to delete customization and content for companies with which you no longer do business.

To Delete Content from the Building Block Library

The following steps delete the That Sandwich Place graphic from the Building Block Library. *Why? Many graphics are proprietary or copyrighted. It is a good idea to delete them when you no longer need them.* Deleting from the library does not delete the graphics from saved publications.

1

- Display the Insert tab.
- Click the Page Parts button (Insert tab | Building Blocks group) to display the Page Parts gallery.
- Right-click the sandwich building block to display a shortcut menu (Figure 4–77).

Experiment

- Click Edit Properties on the shortcut menu and view the Edit Building Block Properties dialog box and its fields of information that Publisher saves. When finished, click OK to close the dialog box and then right-click the graphic again to display the shortcut menu.

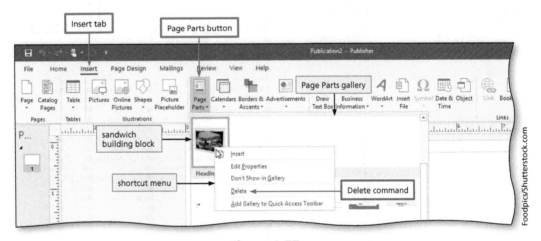

Figure 4–77

- Click Delete on the shortcut menu to delete the graphic.
- If Publisher displays a dialog box asking if you want to delete the building block permanently, click the Yes button.

To Delete the Custom Color Scheme

The following steps delete the That Sandwich Place color scheme from Publisher's list of color schemes. *Why? If you are working in a lab environment, you should delete all custom schemes.* Deleting the color scheme does not change the colors in previously created publications.

1

- Display the Page Design tab to display the color schemes.

- Click the More button (Page Design tab | Schemes group) to display the Color Scheme gallery (Figure 4–78).

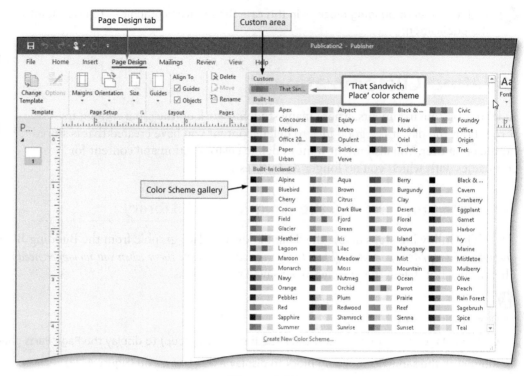

Figure 4–78

2

- Right-click the 'That Sandwich Place' color scheme in the Custom area to display the shortcut menu (Figure 4–79).

Q&A How does the 'Add Gallery to Quick Access Toolbar' command work?

The Quick Access Toolbar appears above the ribbon on the Publisher title bar. It contains buttons for commonly used commands and settings, and it is customizable. Click the 'Add Gallery to Quick Access Toolbar' command to add a button on the right side of the toolbar. When you click that button, Publisher sets your color scheme automatically.

2

- Click Delete Scheme on the shortcut menu to delete the color scheme.

- When Publisher displays a dialog box asking if you want to delete the color scheme, click Yes.

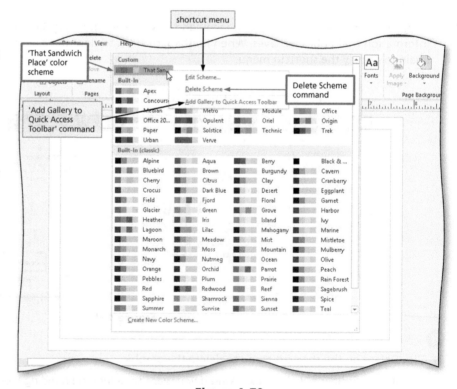

Figure 4–79

Other Ways

1. Right-click custom scheme name (Page Design tab | Schemes group), click Delete Scheme on shortcut menu, click Yes (Microsoft Publisher dialog box)

To Delete the Custom Font Scheme

The following steps delete the 'That Sandwich Place' font scheme from the list of font schemes. **Why?** *You no longer need to use the font scheme.* Deleting the font scheme does not change the fonts in previously created publications.

- Click the Fonts button (Page Design tab | Schemes group) to display the Fonts gallery.
- Right-click the 'That Sandwich Place' font scheme in the Fonts gallery to display a shortcut menu (Figure 4–80).

Q&A How does the 'Update Scheme from Publication Styles' command work?
If you change the font in some of your text boxes and like it better than the original one specified in the font scheme, you can click the 'Update Scheme from Publication Styles' command to change the font scheme permanently.

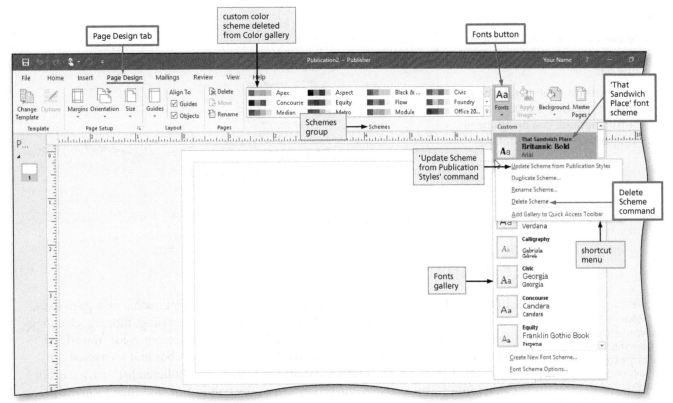

Figure 4–80

- Click Delete Scheme on the shortcut menu to delete the font scheme.
- When Publisher displays a dialog box asking if you want to delete the building block, click Yes.

To Delete the Custom Page Size

The following steps delete the customized blank page size named Mailer. Deleting the page size does not change the size of previously created publications. **Why?** *Publisher does not go back and change settings in a saved publication.*

- Click the Size button (Page Design tab | Page Setup group) to display the Size gallery.
- Right-click Mailer to display the shortcut menu (Figure 4–81).

- Click Delete on the shortcut menu to delete the page size.
- When Publisher displays a dialog box asking if you want to delete the size permanently, click Yes.

- To exit Publisher, click the Close button on the right side of the title bar.
- If a Microsoft Publisher dialog box is displayed, click the Don't Save button because you do not need to save this blank publication.

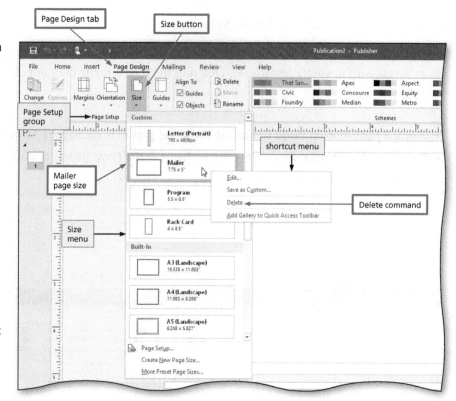

Figure 4–81

Other Ways

1. In template gallery, right-click custom template, click Delete on shortcut menu

Summary

BTW

Desktop Publishing
Advances in desktop publishing, combined with the convenience and quality of desktop printers, have created a surge in the popularity of programs such as Microsoft Publisher 2019. Some businesses that once used programs such as Adobe InDesign and QuarkXPress are switching to Publisher because of the intuitive commands provided by Windows, the more than 3,000 templates, the easy learning curve, and the integration with other Office applications.

In this module, you learned how to customize Publisher by creating new page sizes, color schemes, and font schemes. You edited graphics by rotating, flipping, changing the proportions, selecting a correction, and setting a transparent color. You added a graphic to the Building Block Library. You created a text box and formatted the text with a gradient. You created a WordArt object and a bulleted list with a custom bullet. You added a coupon advertisement to the publication and then formatted and duplicated it. Finally, you opened a blank publication and first used all of the customizations and then deleted the customized building blocks, color schemes, font schemes, and page sizes.

What decisions will you need to make when creating your next custom publication?

Use these guidelines as you complete the assignments in this module and create your own publications outside of this class.

1. Decide on the customization.

    a) Create a custom page size.

    b) Create a custom color scheme.

    c) Create a custom font scheme.

2. Choose your graphics.

    a) Edit and format pictures and clip art to create custom graphics.

3. Save reusable graphics as building blocks.

4. Create headings and text.

    a) Change the line spacing as necessary.

    b) Wrap text.

    c) Apply text effects.

    d) Align and distribute objects.

    e) Create bulleted lists.

5. Use WordArt sparingly.

6. Insert shapes for emphasis and interest.

    a) Use color, gradient, and picture fills as necessary.

    b) Crop pictures to shapes as needed.

7. Delete customizations in lab settings.

Apply Your Knowledge

Reinforce the skills and apply the concepts you learned in this module.

Creating a Bookmark from Scratch

Instructions: Start Publisher. You are to create a page size, color scheme, font scheme, and bulleted text for grade school teachers to use as a punchable bookmark. (Teachers punch a hole in each category as students complete that specific kind of book.) You produce the bookmark publication shown in Figure 4–82.

Perform the following tasks:

1. In Backstage view, click New and then click the 'Blank 8.5 × 11'' thumbnail in the template gallery.

2. To create a custom page size:

   a. Click the Size button (Page Design tab | Page Setup group) and then click 'Create New Page Size' on the Size menu. In the Name text box (Create New Page Size dialog box), type **Bookmark** to name the custom size.

   b. Click the Layout type button and then click 'One page per sheet'.

   c. Set the width to 2.75 and the height to 9.

   d. Click OK (Create New Page Size dialog box) to save the page size.

   e. Click the Margins button (Page Design tab | Page Setup group) and then choose None in the Margins gallery.

3. To create a custom color scheme:

   a. Click the More button (Page Design tab | Schemes group) and then click 'Create New Color Scheme'.

   b. Type **Bookmark** in the Color scheme name text box (Create New Color Scheme dialog box).

   c. In the Scheme colors area, click the New button next to Accent 1 color and then click Sky Blue.

   d. Click the New button next to the Accent 2 color and then click Red.

   e. Click the Save button (Create New Color Scheme dialog box) without changing any of the other colors.

4. To create a custom font scheme:

   a. Click the Fonts button (Page Design tab | Schemes group) and then click 'Create New Font Scheme'.

   b. Type **Bookmark** in the Font scheme name text box (Create New Font Scheme dialog box).

   c. Select Century Schoolbook as the heading font and Comic Sans MS as the body font.

   d. Click the Save button (Create New Font Scheme dialog box).

5. To create shapes with fills and outlines:

   a. Click the Shapes button (Insert tab | Illustrations group) and then click Rectangle. Draw a rectangle that fills the entire page.

   b. Click the More button (Drawing Tools Format tab | Shape Styles group) and then click 'Diagonal Gradient – Accent 1' to create a fill.

Figure 4–82

   c. Click the Shape Outline button and choose the color Main (Black) in the Scheme Colors area. Click the button again, point to Weight in the gallery, and then click 2¼ on the submenu.

   d. Click the Shapes button (Insert tab | Illustrations group) and then click 'Rectangle: Rounded Corners' in the Basic Shapes area. Drag a rounded rectangle beginning approximately ½ inch from the top of the bookmark page. The rounded rectangle should be 2.64 inches wide and 8 inches tall. (*Hint:* Use the boxes in the Size group on the Drawing Tools Format tab.) Nudge the rounded rectangle so it does not touch any side.

   e. Click the Shape Fill arrow (Drawing Tools Format tab | Shape Styles group) and then click No Fill in the gallery.

   f. Click the Shape Outline arrow (Drawing Tools Format tab | Shape Styles group) and then click 'Accent 2 (Red)' in the Scheme Colors area.

6. Draw a text box across the top of the bookmark page approximately .5 inches tall. Change the font to Century Schoolbook and the font size to 26, and then type **Read Widely** as the text. Center and bold the text.

7. Right-click the rounded rectangle and then click Add Text on the shortcut menu. Change the font size to 20. Click the Paragraph Dialog Box Launcher and then type **18** in the After paragraphs box (Paragraph dialog box). Click OK.

8. Click the Bullets button (Home tab | Paragraph group) and then click any bullet style.

9. To create the bulleted icons:

   a. In the text box, type **Realistic** and then press SHIFT+ENTER to create a soft return (↵).

   b. Type **Fiction** to complete the text. Do not press ENTER.

   c. Select the text.

   d. Click the Bullets button again (Home tab | Paragraph group) and then click 'Bullets and Numbering'. Click the Character button (Bullets and Number dialog box | Bullets sheet).

   e. When Publisher displays the Character dialog box, change the font to Segoe UI Emoji. In the Character code box, if necessary, select any preexisting text, type 1F4D6, and then click OK (Character dialog box).

   f. In the Bullets and Numbering dialog box, change the font size to 20 and the indent to 0.5. Click OK (Bullets and Numbering dialog box).

   g. Press END to position the insertion point at the end of the last line and then press ENTER to begin the next bulleted item.

10. Repeat Steps 9a through 9f with the text and character codes shown in Table 4–3. Do not press ENTER after the last bulleted item.

Table 4–3 Character Codes for Bullets	
Text	**Character Code**
Science ↵ Fiction	1F6F8
Mystery	1F50D
Poetry	1F3B5
Biography	1F935
Auto-↵ biography	2712
Traditional ↵ Literature	1F934
Fantasy	1F984
Information	24BE

Continued >

Apply Your Knowledge *continued*

11. One at a time, select each genre text and choose any font color, which also will change the bullet graphic.

12. Select the rounded rectangle and the Read Widely text box. Center align them within the margin.

13. Click the Shapes button (Insert tab | Illustrations group) and then click Line in the Shapes gallery. SHIFT+drag to create a straight line across the rounded rectangle, below the words Realistic Fiction, to separate it from the next bullet. Change the line to your choice of dotted lines.

14. CTRL+SHIFT+drag a duplicate line and place it between the next two categories. Continue creating duplicate lines until each reading genre is separated as shown in Figure 4–82.

15. Save the file with the file name, SC_PUB_4_Bookmark, and submit it in the format required by your instructor.

16. If requested by your instructor, create a second page that will print on the back of the bookmark. Insert a textbox with a space for a user's name. Rotate the text box left 90°.

17. Delete all customizations as described in the module.

18. ✳ Do the colors added in Step 11 improve the bookmark? Why or why not?

Extend Your Knowledge

Extend the skills you learned in this module and experiment with new skills. You may need to use Help to complete the assignment.

Editing Graphics

Note: To complete this assignment, you will be required to use the Data Files. Please contact your instructor for information about accessing the Data Files.

Instructions: Start Publisher. Open the publication, SC_PUB_4-1.pub, from the Data Files. You are to edit the graphic so that it appears as shown in Figure 4–83.

vectomaker studio/Shutterstock.com

Figure 4–83

Perform the following tasks:

1. Use Help to learn more about recoloring graphics and changing 3-D settings.
2. Zoom to 100% and select the graphic. Click the Recolor button (Picture Tools Format tab | Adjust group), point to More Variations, and then click Hyperlink (Blue) in the Scheme colors.
3. Crop the eagle to remove the white space around its head as much as possible.
4. Flip the eagle so that it faces the other way.
5. Use the 'Save as Picture' command to save the eagle graphic as a PNG file on your storage device, with the file name, SC_PUB_4_EagleGraphic.
6. Delete the eagle graphic from the publication.
7. Draw a hexagon shape, approximately 4 inches square. (*Hint:* If you press SHIFT while dragging a shape, the proportions are maintained.)
8. Click the Shape Fill button (Drawing Tools Format tab | Shape Styles group) and then click Picture to display the Select Picture dialog box. Choose the 'From a file' option, navigate to your storage location, and then select the file, SC_PUB_4_EagleGraphic.png.
9. Change the shape outline to red.
10. Right-click the shape and click Format AutoShape on the shortcut menu. Click the Compound Type button (Format AutoShape dialog box) and then click 6pt multi-line at the bottom of the list.
11. Click the Shape Effects button (Format AutoShape dialog box), scroll down, and expand the Glow area. Click the Presets button and choose 'Accent 2, 8 pt glow'. Click the Color button and then click Red. Expand the 3-D Format area. For the bottom bevel, enter a width and height of 1.1. Enter a depth of 36. Expand the 3-D Rotation area, click the Presets button, and then choose 'Off Axis 1, Right'. Click OK (Format Shape dialog box). Click OK (Format AutoShape dialog box).
12. Save the revised publication with the file name, SC_PUB_4_EagleComplete, and then submit it in the format specified by your instructor.
13. ☀ Why do you think the instructions ask you to save the graphic as a picture (a .png file) in Step 5? What other things would you add to the file to make it usable as letterhead?

Expand Your World

Create a solution that uses cloud and web technologies by learning and investigating on your own from general guidance.

Choosing Colors

Instructions: Locate a picture with your school colors or the web address (URL) of your school logo. The picture should be in the .gif, .png, or .jpg format. The web address might be something like www.myschool.edu/logo.gif. Start a browser and navigate to www.imagecolorpicker.com (Figure 4–84). The website may differ slightly from what is shown in Figure 4–84.

Continued >

Expand Your World *continued*

Source: imagecolorpicker.com

Figure 4–84

Perform the following tasks:

1. Scroll down on the webpage to see the various choices. If you have the web address of your school logo, type it in the 'URL to Image' text box. If you have a picture, click the 'Upload your image' button, browse to and open the image, and then click the Submit Query button (File upload dialog box).

2. When the image is displayed, click the main color of the image. Write down the RGB codes. Click two other prominent colors in the logo and write down their RGB codes.

3. Start Publisher and create a blank publication. Click the More button (Page Design tab | Schemes group) to display the Color Schemes gallery. Click 'Create New Color Scheme' in the Color Schemes gallery to display the Create New Color Scheme dialog box. Enter a name for your new color scheme.

4. Click the New button next to the Accent 1 color and then click the More Colors button to display the Colors dialog box. Click the Custom tab and enter the RGB numbers. Click OK (Colors dialog box).

5. Repeat Step 4 for the Accent 2 and Accent 3 colors.

6. Save the color scheme. Use the color scheme to create a shape, WordArt, or text fill.

7. Submit the assignment in the format specified by your instructor.

8. If you are working in a lab environment, delete any customizations.

9. ✳ In what other situations might you want to search for exact colors? Make a list of companies that might copyright their logo and its colors. Do you know of any colors that commonly are referred to by a company name, such as "Facebook blue"?

In the Lab

Design and implement a solution using creative thinking and problem-solving skills.

Creating a Fill and Border Sampler

Problem: You decide to create a sample of various kinds of shape fills to show to prospective customers at your desktop publishing business.

Part 1: Open a blank publication and change the margins to .5 inches. Create a rectangle shape 2 inches wide and 1.5 inches tall. Duplicate the shape 14 times to create a total of 15 rectangles. Move the rectangles to create 5 rows of 3 each, starting approximately 1 inch from the top. Align the tops of each row, and align each column on the left. One at a time, fill the shapes. Use at least one of each of the following: no fill with an outline, a fill with no outline, a picture fill, a gradient fill, a texture fill, a pattern fill, a shadow outline, a BorderArt background, a dashed outline, a heavy outline, and one special effect. Insert a WordArt shape across the top that says, My Fill & Border Sampler, as a heading.

Part 2: ✳ Do you think adding text to each rectangle, noting the various settings, would improve the usability of this publication? Why or why not?

5 | Using Business Information Sets

Objectives

After completing this module, you will be able to:

- Design letterhead
- Create a logo
- Fill a shape with a picture and crop it
- Create a business information set
- Insert business information fields into a publication
- Use the Measurement pane to position and scale objects
- Create and apply a new text style
- Wrap text
- Apply the read-only attribute to a publication

- Insert an automatically updated date and time
- Add a numbered list and increase the indent
- Create and print an envelope
- Create a certificate
- Create and print business cards
- Publish a portable PDF/XPS file
- Embed fonts in a publication

Introduction

Incorporating personal information unique to a business, an organization, or an individual user expands the possibilities for using Publisher as a complete application product for small businesses. Business information sets, which include pieces of information such as a name, an address, a motto, or even a logo can be inserted automatically and consistently across all publications. Publisher allows you to insert, delete, and save multiple business information sets and apply them independently.

Using business information sets is just one way that people expand Publisher's capabilities. Some users create large text boxes and use Publisher like a word processor. Others create a table and perform mathematical and statistical operations or embed charts as they would with a spreadsheet. Still others create a database and use Publisher for mass mailings, billings, and customer accounts. Publisher's capabilities make it an efficient tool in small business offices — without the cost and learning curve of some of the high-end dedicated application software.

How do you make decisions about letterhead components?

Work with the customer to design a letterhead that matches the color and font schemes of the company, if any. Decide on placement of vital information, page size, and white space. Discuss a plan for printing. Will the customer send the letterhead out for commercial printing or print copies in-house? Will users want to type directly on the Publisher letterhead? Define user-friendly features, such as an automatic date and an easy-to-use text box for typing letters.

Project: Letterhead and Business Cards

Storing permanent information about a business facilitates the customization of publications, such as letterhead, business cards, and other office-related publications. A **business information set** is a group of customized information fields about an individual or an organization that can be used to generate information text boxes across publications. Many of the Publisher templates automatically create business information text boxes to incorporate data from the business information set. Publications created from scratch also can integrate a business information set by including one or more pieces in the publication. For example, you can save your name, address, and telephone number in a business information set. Whenever you need that information, you can insert it in a publication without retyping it.

To illustrate some of the business features of Microsoft Publisher, this project presents a series of steps to create a business information set. You will use the business information set in a letterhead, an envelope, a certificate, and a business card. You also will create a logo and a portable file for easy viewing and embed fonts in the Publisher file for editing on a different computer. The project creates publications for a fire department and its fire chief, as shown in Figure 5–1.

You will perform the following general tasks as you progress through this module:

1. Create a business letterhead and a logo.
2. Create and use a business information set.
3. Use the Measurement pane.
4. Create and apply a new style.
5. Customize business letterhead for ease of use.
6. Create other publications, including an envelope, a certificate, and business cards.
7. Create portable files.
8. Embed fonts.

Creating Letterhead

In many businesses, **letterhead** refers to preprinted paper with pertinent facts about the company and blank space to contain the text of the correspondence. Letterhead, typically used for official business communication, is an easy way to convey company information to the reader and quickly establish a formal and legitimate mode of correspondence. The company information may be displayed in a variety of

Stock Vector/Shutterstock.com

Figure 5–1

places — across the top, down the side, or split between the top and bottom of the page. Although most business letterhead is 8½ × 11 inches, other sizes are becoming more popular, especially with small agencies and not-for-profit organizations.

Generally, it is cost-effective for companies to outsource the printing of their letterhead; however, designing the letterhead in-house and then sending the file to a commercial printer saves design consultation time, customization, and money. Black-and-white or spot-color letterhead is more common and less expensive than composite or process color. Businesses sometimes opt not to purchase preprinted letterhead because of its expense, color, or the limited quantity required. In those cases, companies design their own letterhead and save it as a file. In some cases, businesses print multiple copies of their blank letterhead and then, using application software, prepare documents to print on the letterhead paper.

BTW

Logos

The Building Block Library contains many logo styles from which you may choose, or you can create a logo from a picture, from a file, or from scratch. Although Publisher's logo styles are generic, commercial logos typically are copyrighted. Consult with a legal representative before you commercially use materials bearing clip art, logos, designs, words, or other symbols that could violate third-party rights, including trademarks.

To Open a Letterhead Template

The following steps open a letterhead template and apply color and font schemes.

1 Start Publisher.

2 In the template gallery, click BUILT-IN to display the BUILT-IN templates.

③ Scroll as necessary and then click the Letterhead thumbnail within the BUILT-IN templates to display the Letterhead templates.

④ In the section labeled More Installed Templates, click the Quadrant thumbnail to choose the template.

⑤ Click the Color scheme button in the template information pane. Scroll as necessary and then click Wildflower to choose the color scheme.

⑥ Click the Font scheme button, scroll as necessary, and then click Data to choose the font scheme.

⑦ If necessary, click to display a check mark in the Include logo check box (Figure 5–2).

⑧ Click the CREATE button to create the publication based on the template settings.

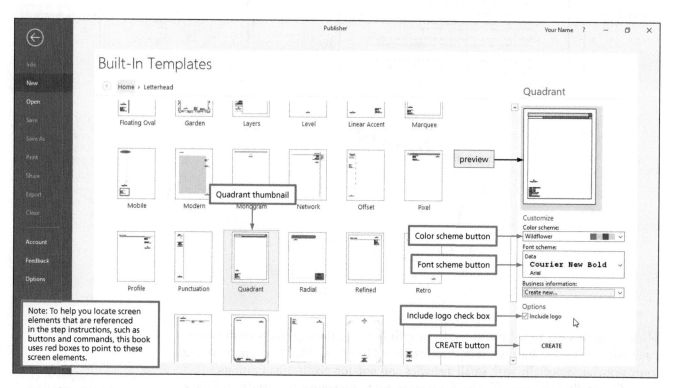

Figure 5–2

To Set Publisher Display Settings

The following steps display formatting marks and special characters and then hide the Page Navigation pane.

① If the Publisher window is not maximized, click the Maximize button on the title bar.

② If the Special Characters button (Home tab | Paragraph group) is not selected already, click it to display formatting marks on the screen.

③ If the Page Navigation pane is open, click the Page Number button on the status bar to close the pane because this is a single-page publication.

Creating a Logo

With the basic letterhead created, you now are ready to create a customized logo for the fire department. To create a logo for Adams County Fire & Rescue, you will crop a picture, save it, fill a shape with a picture, and then combine the pictures and save the logo. Many types of publications use logos to identify and distinguish the page. A **logo** is a recognizable symbol that identifies a person, a business, or an organization. Logos may be composed of a name, a picture, or a combination of text, symbols, and graphics.

To Crop a Picture

The following steps open a picture and crop it. To complete these steps, you will be required to use the Data Files. Please contact your instructor for information about accessing the Data Files.

1. Zoom to 100% and scroll to display the top portion of the letterhead.

2. Display the Insert tab.

3. Click the Pictures button (Insert tab | Illustrations group) to display the Insert Picture dialog box.

4. Navigate to the Data Files and then insert the file named Support_PUB_5_Badge.png. In the publication, drag the badge to the scratch area and resize it to be approximately 5 × 5 inches.

5. Click the Crop button (Picture Tools Format tab | Crop group) to display the cropping handles.

6. Drag the upper-left corner cropping handle toward the center until the border is removed and less white space appears at the top.

7. Drag the lower-right corner cropping handle toward the center until the border is removed and less white space appears at the bottom (Figure 5–3).

Q&A What is the purpose of the Fit and Fill buttons (Picture Tools Format tab | Crop group)? The Fit and Fill buttons are used with picture placeholders. If your picture is larger or smaller than the placeholder, Publisher allows you quickly to resize the picture to fit (in the case of larger pictures) or fill (in the case of smaller pictures) the placeholder while maintaining the original aspect ratio.

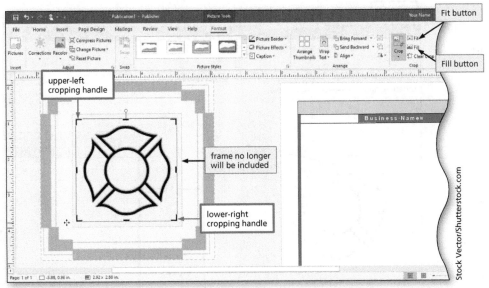

Figure 5–3

8. Click the Crop button (Picture Tools Format tab | Crop group) again to turn off the cropping handles.

Shape Fills

Every shape in the Shapes gallery can be filled, except for the lines and braces. You can fill a shape with solid color, and you also can fill shapes with pictures and other types of formatting. The Shape Styles gallery (Drawing Tools Format tab) displays many preset fills and outlines; however, the Shape Fill button (Drawing Tools Format tab | Shape Styles group) displays a gallery with various ways to customize the fill, as outlined in Table 5–1.

Table 5–1 Ways to Fill a Shape		
Shape Fill	**Display**	**Result**
Color	Displays Color gallery	Fills with a solid color
More Fill Colors	Displays Colors dialog box	Fills with chosen solid color
Tints	Displays Fill Effects dialog box	Fills with a tint or shade of a chosen color
Sample Fill Color	Changes the pointer to an eyedropper	Fills with color that is clicked
Picture	Displays Insert Pictures dialog box	Fills with a picture from storage or an online picture, clipped or cropped to the shape
Gradient	Displays Gradient gallery	Fills with chosen gradient
Texture	Displays Texture gallery	Fills with chosen texture
Pattern	Displays Format Shape dialog box	Fills with chosen pattern using foreground and background color
Crop to Shape	Accessed via the Crop arrow, displays Shape gallery	Crops or clips displayed picture to the desired shape

The Drawing Tools Format tab appears only when you are working with shapes, graphics, or clip art. It normally does not appear when you are working with a picture; however, another way to use shapes is to **crop to shape**, also called clipping. When you **crop to shape**, you display the picture first and then crop it to the desired shape using the Crop arrow (Picture Tools Format tab | Crop group). You also can right-click a shape and insert text with the Add Text command on the shortcut menu.

To Fill a Shape with a Picture

The following steps create a circle shape and fill it with a picture. **Why?** *Filling is an easy way to change the shape of a picture.* To complete these steps, you will be required to use the Data Files. Please contact your instructor for information about accessing the Data Files.

- Display the Insert tab.
- Click the Shapes button (Insert tab | Illustrations group) to display the Shapes gallery (Figure 5–4).

Q&A I do not see a circle in the Shapes gallery, so how do I create one?

To create a circle, you must click the oval and then SHIFT+drag in the publication. To create a square, select a rectangle and then SHIFT+drag in the publication.

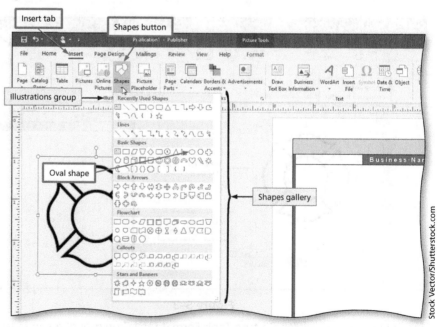

Figure 5–4

2

- Click the Oval shape in the Basic Shapes area.

- In the scratch area, SHIFT+drag downward to create a circle approximately 1.4 × 1.4 inches, as shown in Figure 5–5.

- If necessary, move the badge to the left.

Q&A Why is the circle filled with red? Publisher uses the Accent 1 color from the color scheme to fill shapes.

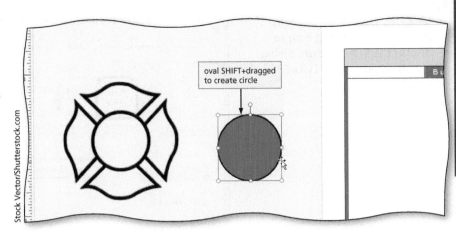

Figure 5–5

3

- With the circle selected, if necessary, display the Drawing Tools Format tab.

- Click the Shape Fill button (Drawing Tools Format tab | Shape Styles group) to display the Shape Fill gallery (Figure 5–6).

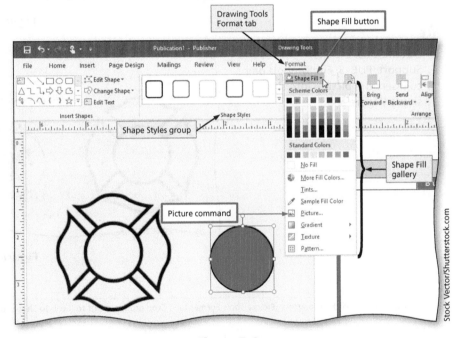

Figure 5–6

4

- Click Picture in the Shape Fill gallery to display the Insert Pictures dialog box (Figure 5–7).

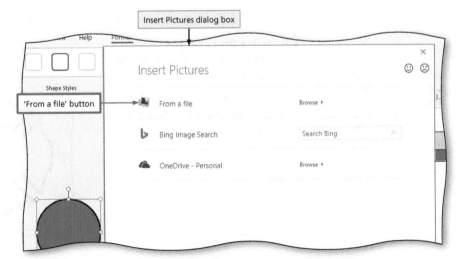

Figure 5–7

● Click the 'From a file' button
(Insert Pictures dialog box) to
display the Select Picture dialog
box. Navigate to the Data Files
(Figure 5–8).

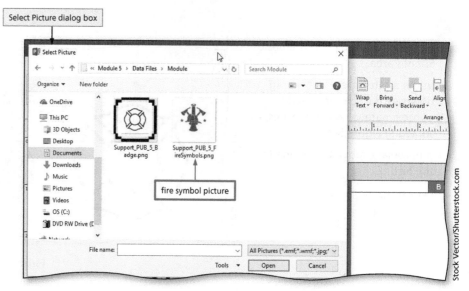

Figure 5–8

● Double-click the file,
Support_PUB_5_FireSymbols.png,
to insert the picture into the
shape (Figure 5–9).

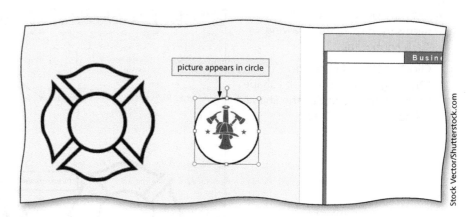

Figure 5–9

Other Ways

1. Insert picture, click Crop arrow (Picture Tools Format tab | Crop group), point to 'Crop to Shape' on Crop menu, select shape

---

To Group

BTW
**Rotating while
Cropping**
You can rotate a picture
while using the crop tool
by dragging the green
rotation handle. To rotate in
15-degree increments, hold
down SHIFT while dragging
the handle.

The following steps group the badge with the circle.

❶ Select the circle graphic and
drag it to a position over the
badge, as shown in Figure 5–10.

❷ Select both graphics and then
press CTRL+SHIFT+G to group
them.

Figure 5–10

To Save Grouped Objects as a Picture

The following steps save the grouped pictures as a new picture on your storage device. *Why? Saving them as a new picture allows you to use it in many other apps, in other Publisher publications, and in business information sets.*

1

- Right-click the grouped pictures to display a shortcut menu (Figure 5–11).

Q&A Are grouped graphics the only kind of object you can save as a picture?
No. You can save any object as a picture, including shapes, tables, text boxes, and clip art.

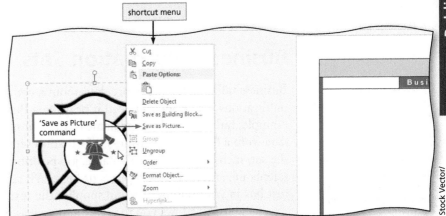

Figure 5–11

2

- Click 'Save as Picture' on the shortcut menu to display the Save As dialog box.
- Type **SC_PUB_5_FireLogo** in the File name box to name the file.
- Navigate to your storage device (Figure 5–12).

Experiment

- Click the 'Save as type' button (Save As dialog box) to see the different kinds of file formats that are available.

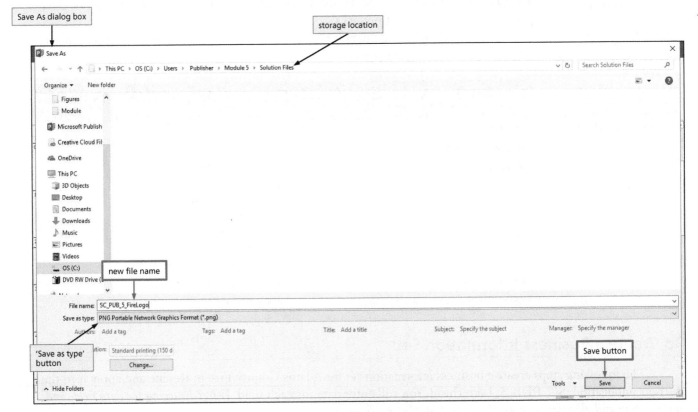

Figure 5–12

- Edit property tags as desired and then click the Save button (Save As dialog box) to save the graphic as a picture.
- Delete the grouped graphic from the scratch area.

Business Information Sets

BTW
Business Information Sets
Using different business information sets allows you to maintain alternate information about your business; a second or related business, such as a major supplier or home business; an outside organization for which you maintain information, such as scouting or sports; and your personal home or family information.

Business information sets store data about a company. This data then is used in publications whenever you need it or when a Publisher template incorporates it. For example, rather than type the name of the company multiple times, you can insert the data from a field in the business information set. A **field** is a specific component in the set, such as an individual's name, job position or title, organization name, address, telephone, email address, tagline, or logo. When you insert a field, Publisher places a text box in your publication and supplies the text.

Publisher allows you to create and save as many different business information sets as you want. If you have more than one set saved, you can choose the set you need from a list. The sets are stored within the Publisher application files on your computer. When you create a new publication, the business information set used most recently populates the new publication. When Publisher first is installed, the business information is generic, with words such as Title and Business Name. In a laboratory situation, the business information set may be populated with information about your school that was provided when Microsoft Office 2019 was installed.

BTW
Previous Business Information Set
If other people have used the computer you are working on, it is possible that other business information sets appear in your list. If you need to delete a business information set, click the leftmost button in the Select a Business Information set area (shown in Figure 5–17), select the set, and then click the Delete button (Business Information dialog box).

If you edit a text box within a publication that contains personal information, you change the set for that publication only unless you choose to update the set. To affect changes for all future publications, you edit the business information set itself. You can edit the stored business information set at any time — before, during, or after performing other publication tasks.

Table 5–2 displays the data for each of the fields in the business information set that you will create in this project.

Table 5–2 Data for the Business Information Set	
Field	**Data**
Individual name	Joel Larson
Job or position or title	Fire Chief
Organization name	Adams County Fire & Rescue
Address	Adams County Fire & Rescue 3600 Augusta Avenue Donelson, MI 48011
Phone, fax, and e-mail	Phone: 906-555-3600 Fax: 906-555-3601 Email: jlarson@adamscofr.com
Tagline or motto	All Hands, Always Ready
Business information set name	Fire & Rescue

To Create a Business Information Set

The following steps create a business information set for Adams County Fire & Rescue and apply it to the current publication, SC_PUB_5_Letterhead. You will enter data for each field. *Why? Entering the data fields and saving them will allow you to reuse the content in other publications.*

①

- Display the Insert tab.

- Click the Business Information button (Insert tab | Text group) to display the Business Information menu, which lists business information fields and commands (Figure 5–13).

Q&A Why does my screen look different?
If you have any saved business information sets on your computer, your menu may contain other data in each field.

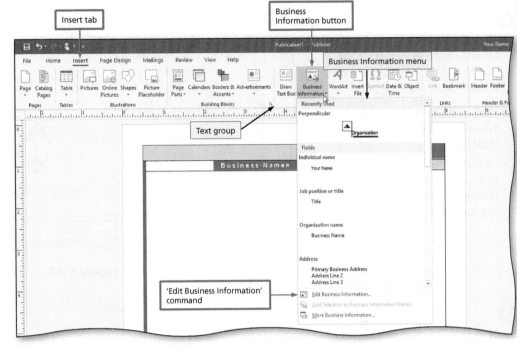

Figure 5–13

②

- Click 'Edit Business Information' on the Business Information menu to display the Create New Business Information Set dialog box (Figure 5–14).

Q&A Why does the Individual name text box already have a name in it?
The person or company that installed Publisher may have supplied data for the business information set. You will replace the data in the next step.

How do you use the other commands on the Business Information menu?
The 'Add Selection to Business Information Gallery' command allows you to add selected text and graphics as a Publisher building block. The 'More Business Information' command opens the Building Block Library, from which you can add objects to your publication.

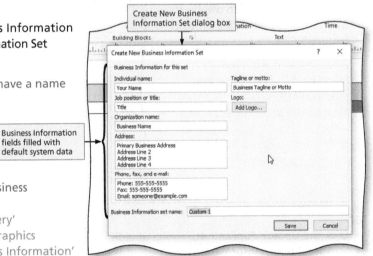

Figure 5–14

③

- Enter the data from Table 5–2, pressing TAB to advance from one field to the next (Figure 5–15).

Q&A How do I delete data after it is inserted in a field?
In the Create New Business Information Set dialog box, you can select the text in the field and then press DELETE. To remove a business information field while editing a publication, you simply delete the text box from the publication itself; however, this does not delete it permanently from the set. You can remove entire business information sets after they are stored; you will see how to do this later in this module.

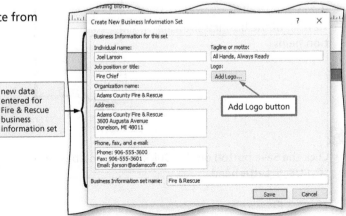

Figure 5–15

4

- Click the Add Logo button (Create New Business Information Set dialog box) to display the Insert Picture dialog box.

- Navigate to the storage location you used previously to save the logo file.

- Double-click the desired file (in this case, SC_PUB_5_FireLogo.png) (Insert Picture dialog box) to insert the logo (Figure 5–16).

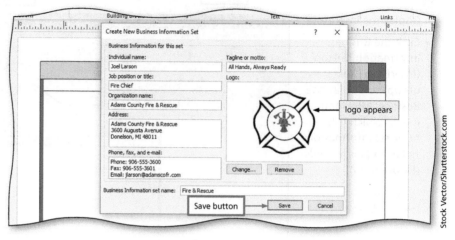

Figure 5–16

5

- Click the Save button (Create New Business Information Set dialog box) to save the business information set and to display the Business Information dialog box (Figure 5–17).

Does saving the business information set also save the publication?
No, you are saving a separate, internal data file that contains only the data in the fields.

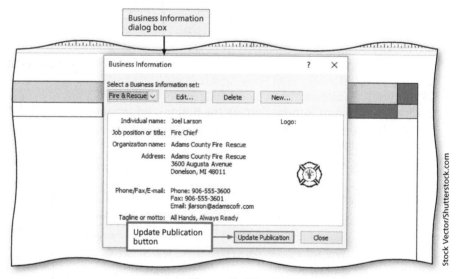

Figure 5–17

6

- Click the Update Publication button (Business Information dialog box) (Figure 5–18).

Experiment

- Zoom and scroll as necessary to view all of the business information fields.

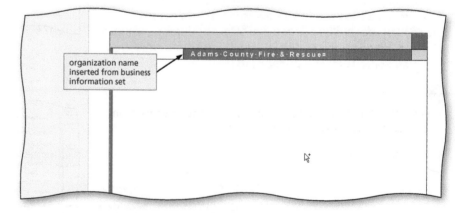

Figure 5–18

7

- Click the Save button on the Quick Access Toolbar. Browse to your storage location. Save the file with the file name, SC_PUB_5_Letterhead.

Other Ways

1. In template gallery, click Business Information button in Customize area in template information pane, click Create New in the Business information area, enter field data, click Save

TO CHANGE THE BUSINESS INFORMATION SET OF AN EXISTING PUBLICATION

If you wanted to apply a different business information set to a publication, you would perform the following tasks.

1. Open a publication.
2. Display the Insert tab.
3. Click the Business Information button (Insert tab | Text group) to display the Business Information menu.
4. Click 'Edit Business Information' on the Business Information menu to display the Business Information dialog box.
5. Click the leftmost button in the Select a Business Information set area to display the available business information sets.
6. Click the business information set you wish to use.
7. Click the Update Publication button (Business Information dialog box).

Break Point: If you want to take a break, this is a good place to do so. Exit Publisher. To resume later, start Publisher, open the file called SC_PUB_5_Letterhead.pub, and continue following the steps from this location forward.

To Insert a Business Information Field

When you insert an individual field, Publisher places either a text box with the information in the center of the screen with a preset font and font size or a picture box with the logo. You then may position the field and format the text as necessary. *Why? Publisher uses the default formatting. Applied formatting affects the current publication only.* The following steps insert a field, in this case the tagline or motto, from the business information set into the current publication.

①

- Zoom to approximately 120%, scroll to the lower portion of the page layout, and display the Insert tab.
- Click the Business Information button (Insert tab | Text group) to display the Business Information menu (Figure 5–19).

 Experiment

- Scroll through the various information fields and commands on the menu to see the kinds of fields and components that you might insert.

Q&A When would I use the other components, such as those in the Contact Information area?
Content Information components are similar to building block items that can be inserted as objects into the current publication. Contact Information components are populated with appropriate business information fields from the current set.

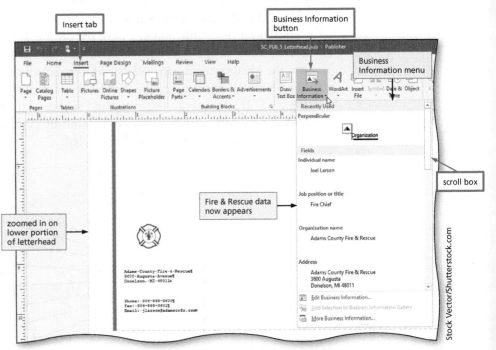

Figure 5–19

②

• Scroll as necessary and then click the desired field (in this case, the Tagline or motto field) to insert it into the publication (Figure 5–20).

◁ My field inserted in the middle of the letterhead. Did I do
Q&A something wrong?

No. Publisher inserts business information fields in the center of the screen. You will adjust the position later in the module.

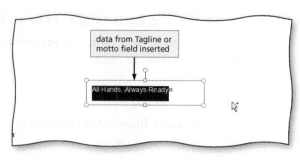

Figure 5–20

To Create a Business Information Set from a Publication

If you have typed business information manually into a letterhead, you still can save it as a business information set. To do so, you would perform the following steps. If you currently are performing the steps in this module, do not perform these steps until you are finished because creating a business information set from a publication overwrites the current business information set.

1. Choose a letterhead template and create the publication.
2. Click the text in the Business Name text box and then type the name of the business.
3. To add the field to the current business information set, which will overwrite the current information, click the information smart tag and then click 'Save to Business Information Set' to save the data.
4. Repeat Steps 2 and 3 for the address, phone, tagline (if it exists), and logo.

Using the Measurement Pane

To place and scale objects precisely, rather than estimating by dragging and resizing, you use the **Measurement pane** to enter the exact values for the horizontal position, vertical position, width, and height of the object. The Measurement pane not only sets the location and size of an object, it also sets the angle of rotation. If the object is text, the Measurement pane offers additional character spacing or typesetting options. The Measurement pane can be displayed as a floating toolbar with eight text boxes (Figure 5–21). It also can be moved and anchored to one of the four sides of the workspace. Entries can be typed in each box by clicking the appropriate arrows. If no object is selected, the boxes will be disabled.

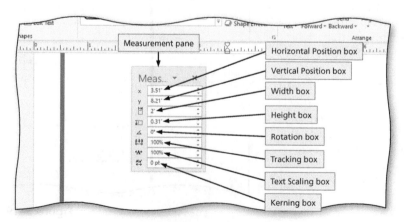

Figure 5–21

Table 5–3 lists the text boxes on the Measurement pane that are used to edit the position, size, and rotation of an object. The first five text boxes edit the location and position of objects on the page layout.

Table 5–3 Measurement Pane Settings		
Box Name	**Specifies**	**Default Unit of Measurement**
Horizontal Position	Horizontal distance from the left edge of the page to the upper-left corner of the object	Inches
Vertical Position	Vertical distance from the top of the page to the upper-left corner of the object	Inches
Width	Width of the object	Inches
Height	Height of the object	Inches
Rotation	Rotation of the object counterclockwise from the original orientation	Degrees
Tracking	General spacing between all selected characters	Percentages
Text Scaling	Width of selected characters	Percentages
Kerning	Spacing between two selected characters to improve readability	Points

To Open the Measurement Pane

The following step opens the Measurement pane. *Why? You can choose the exact size and location of any object by using the Measurement pane.*

- Display the Drawing Tools Format tab.
- Click the Measurement button (Drawing Tools Format tab | Size group) to open the Measurement pane.
- If necessary, drag the pane's title bar toward the status bar and let it snap into an anchored position (Figure 5–22).

Q&A Does the Measurement pane always appear at the bottom of the workspace?
No. It is a floating toolbar and can be placed anywhere on the screen or docked to any of the four sides of the workspace.

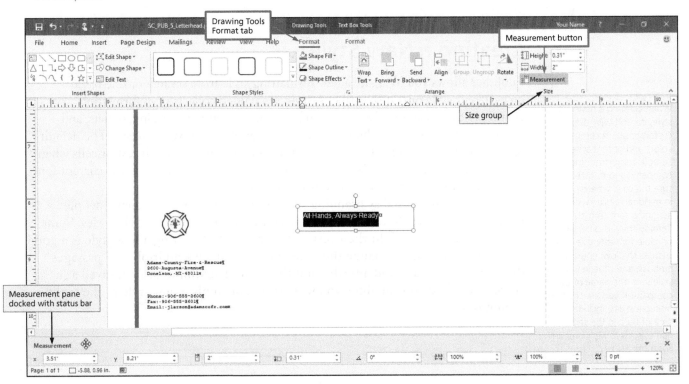

Figure 5–22

Other Ways	
1. Click Object Position button on status bar	2. Click Object Size button on status bar

To Position Objects Using the Measurement Pane

The following step positions and scales the motto precisely using the Measurement pane. *Why? The customer has asked that the Fire & Rescue tagline appear more prominently at the bottom of the letterhead.*

- With the Tagline or motto text box selected, in the Measurement pane, select the text in the Horizontal Position box and then type **5** to replace it. Press TAB to advance to the next text box.

- Type **9.75** in the Vertical Position box and then press TAB.

- Type **2.75** in the Width box and then press TAB.

- Type **0.5** in the Height box and then press ENTER to finish editing the exact place and size of the object (Figure 5–23).

Q&A

Should I change the value in the Rotation box?

No. A zero value is appropriate for an object that should appear straight up and down.

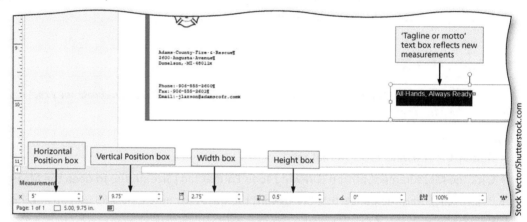

Figure 5–23

Creating a New Style

BTW

Styles

When creating a new text style, consult with the customer about company colors and/or font schemes. Sample colors from the company logo to make sure the colors match. Keep in mind reusability when assigning font formats. Remind the customer of possible formatting features, such as shadow, engrave, emboss, and others. Save the style with the name of the company. If you are creating multiple styles, include the type of data in the style name, such as My Company Footnote Style.

Publisher allows you to create a new formatting style from scratch or one based on a current style or text selection. A **style** is a named collection of formatting characteristics, including font, font size, font color, character spacing, bullets, and shadows, among other attributes. Styles can be applied to text or objects. The default style in Publisher is called the **Normal style**, and it is applied to all text or cells when you start the program. The Normal style includes the body font from the current font scheme in a black font color with left-justified alignment.

Styles can be used as branding for a business; for example, many people recognize the James Bond font. It has become a brand for the movie series. Some companies even copyright their text styles or brands. Creating a new style is a good idea when you want to change those defaults or you have multiple text passages that must be formatted identically, and the desired attributes are not saved as a current style. For this module, you will create and apply a new style to the tagline or motto.

To Sample a Font Color

The first step in creating a new style will be to choose a font color. You will sample the red color in the logo. ***Why?*** *The font color of your new style will match the logo in all publications.* A **sample** lets you copy an element's color and apply it elsewhere. When you sample a color, the pointer changes to an eyedropper; then, any color that you click in the publication is added to all color galleries, just below the color scheme palette. The following steps sample the font color.

- With the text still selected, display the Text Box Tools Format tab, if necessary.

- Click the Font Color arrow (Text Box Tools Format tab | Font group) to display the Font Color gallery (Figure 5–24).

Q&A Does it make a difference whether I use the Font Color arrow on the Home tab or on the Text Box Tools Format tab?
You may use either one. Typically, when you select text, Publisher automatically displays the Text Box Tools Format tab, so using the Font Color arrow would be quicker.

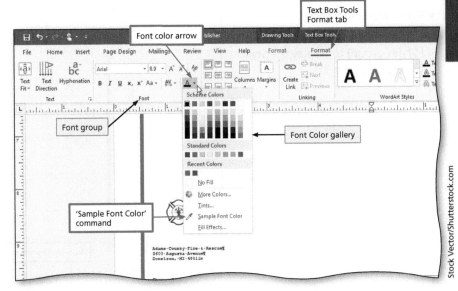

Figure 5–24

- Click 'Sample Font Color' in the Font Color gallery to display the eyedropper pointer (Figure 5–25).

Q&A Could I just click the red color in the color palette?
You could; however, sampling from the logo itself will ensure no change to the style if someone changes the color scheme later.

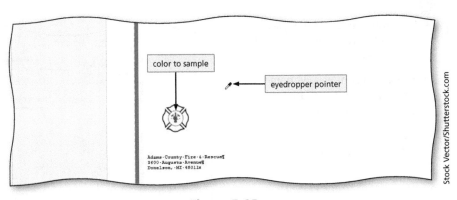

Figure 5–25

- Click the red color in the logo to pick up the color and apply the sampled color to the selected text.

- Click outside the text to deselect it and view the result (Figure 5–26).

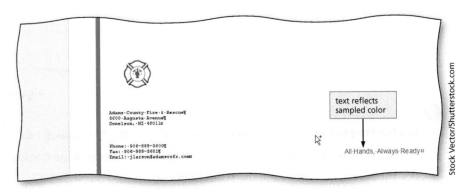

Figure 5–26

To Create a New Style

The following steps display the New Style dialog box to create a new style. *Why? Using a style sometimes is easier than using the format painter.*

1

- Select the text, All Hands, Always Ready, again.

- Display the Home tab.

- Click the Styles button (Home tab | Styles group) to display the Styles gallery (Figure 5–27).

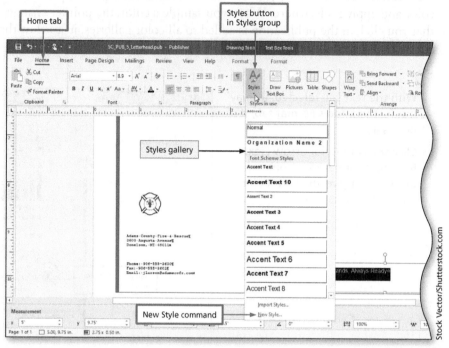

Figure 5–27

2

- Click New Style in the Styles gallery to display the New Style dialog box.

- In the 'Enter new style name' text box, type **Fire & Rescue** to name the style (Figure 5–28).

Q&A

Why did the name also appear in the 'Style for the following paragraph' box?
Publisher assumes you will want to use the same style for subsequent paragraphs. If you want to change that setting, you can click the 'Style for the following paragraph' arrow (New Style dialog box) and then click a different style.

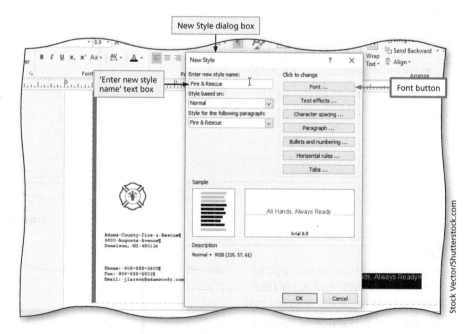

Figure 5–28

3

- Click the Font button (New Style dialog box) to display the Font dialog box.

- Click the Font arrow (Font dialog box) and then select the Monotype Corsiva font in the Font list.

- Click the Font style button and then click Bold Italic in the Font style list.

- Type **20** in the Font size box to set the font size (Figure 5–29).

Stock Vector/Shutterstock.com

Experiment

- Click the More Effects button (Font dialog box) to display the Format Text Effects dialog box. Explore the many settings. Close the Format Text Effects dialog box without changing the settings.

Q&A Why should I choose Monotype Corsiva?

Monotype Corsiva is a font that contrasts nicely with the Arial font in the font scheme. It displays swashes and glyphs that make the letters flow from one to another.

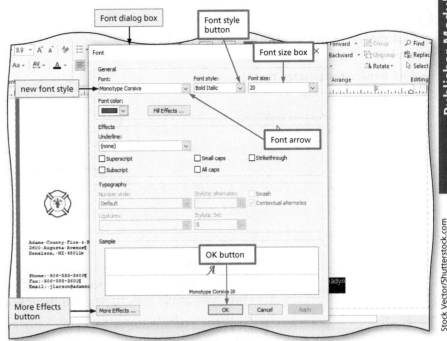

Figure 5–29

4

- Click OK (Font dialog box) to close the Font dialog box.
- Click OK (New Style dialog box) to close the New Style dialog box.

To Apply the New Style

New styles are stored in the publication in which they are created. *Why? Publisher assumes you will want to use the style again in the same publication; however, you can import styles from one publication to another.* The following steps apply the new style to the entire tagline.

- If necessary, select the text, All Hands, Always Ready.
- Click the Styles button (Home tab | Styles group) to display the Styles gallery.
- Scroll to display the 'Fire & Rescue' style (Figure 5–30).

Q&A Can I edit or rename a style?

Yes. Click the Styles button (Home Tab | Styles group), right-click the style name, and then click Modify or Rename on the shortcut menu.

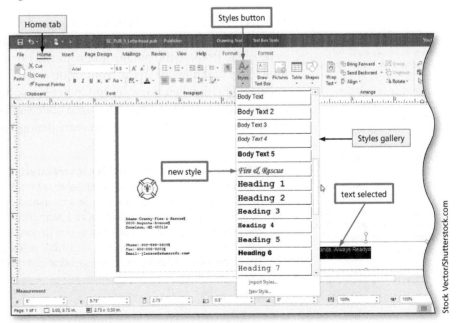

Figure 5–30

● Click the 'Fire & Rescue' style in the Styles list to apply it to the text.

● Click outside the selected text to view the change (Figure 5–31).

Q&A Could I use the format painter to copy the formatting attributes?
Yes. You can edit the formatting either way.

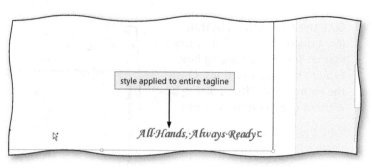

style applied to entire tagline

All Hands, Always Ready

Figure 5–31

TO IMPORT STYLES

Because styles are publication specific, if you want to use a style in a different publication, you would have to perform the following steps to import the style.

BTW
AutoFit Text
Some Publisher template and business information set text boxes, such as titles, mastheads, and taglines, are preset to 'Shrink Text On Overflow'. To change the autofit settings, right-click the text box and then choose the style on the shortcut menu.

1. Click the Styles button (Home tab | Styles group) to display the Styles gallery.

2. Click Import Styles in the Styles gallery.

3. Navigate to the publication that contains the desired style (Import Styles dialog box).

4. When a Publisher dialog box appears, asking if you wish to make changes to the Normal style, click the No button (Microsoft Publisher dialog box).

5. As Publisher goes through each of the font styles, click the No button until you see the desired style. In that case, click the Yes button (Microsoft Publisher dialog box).

Customizing the Letterhead for Interactivity

BTW
VBA
VBA, or Visual Basic for Applications, is a program that allows designers to write code in Publisher to customize the user experience further. For example, if you want to remind users to save the file with a different file name, you can include message box code. You also can position the insertion point, select objects, and create buttons — all of which are displayed when the user opens the publication.

When creating publications that are designed to be edited by others or publications with which users must interact, it is important to make the publication as user-friendly as possible. Prepare the publication with the novice user in mind. Always place the interactive components in the front or on top of other objects in the publication. Use updatable fields when possible, and insert blank lines or tabs to help users know where to type. You also can create customized code to place the insertion point, turn on and off certain Publisher features, and create dialog box reminders for the user.

CONSIDER THIS

Why do you need to consider interactivity?
Your publications will be most beneficial to others if you make them as user-friendly as possible. Think about the times you have opened templates or files and had to find the pointer, navigate to a field, figure out the formatting, and worry about how to save the file. You should mitigate those problems as much as possible as you design templates and files that will be used over and over. Business sets, building blocks, updatable fields, interactive components, and preset margins, lines, and tabs will help users create publications quickly and efficiently.

To Create a Text Box for Users

To make the letterhead more functional for the firehouse, the following steps insert a large text box in which users can type their text.

1 Click the 'Show Whole Page' button on the status bar and then click the scratch area so that no object is selected.

2 Click the 'Draw Text Box' button (Home tab | Objects group) to select it.

3 Drag to create a large rectangular text box that fills the center of the letterhead, as shown in Figure 5–32. The text box will overlap the logo.

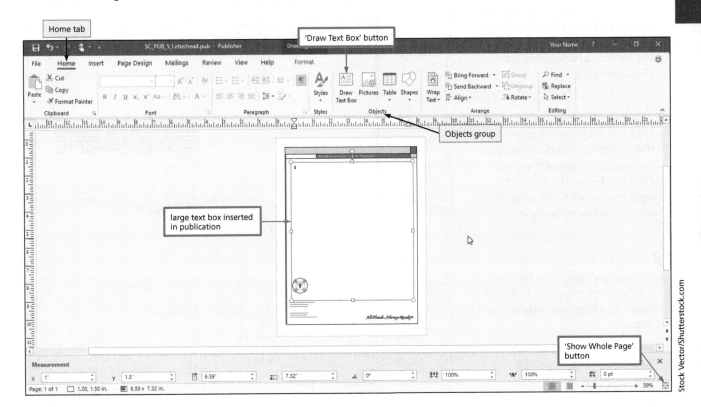

Figure 5–32

To Use the Paragraph Dialog Box

The default line and paragraph settings are determined by the font or style used; however, in general, the default line spacing for text boxes is greater than 1 because Publisher accommodates the largest character of the font family and adds an additional amount of space for the text box margin. The default spacing after paragraphs varies. The Paragraph dialog box allows you to change line spacing, indentation, and alignment with more settings than are available on the ribbon. In Publisher, **line spacing** refers to the amount of vertical space between each line of text within a paragraph. **Paragraph spacing** refers to the space, measured in points, that appears directly above and below a paragraph. **Indentation** refers to how far the first line is from the margin; it does not change subsequent lines in the paragraph. **Alignment** refers to the how text wraps at the margin.

The following steps change the font size to 12 and set the paragraph spacing to insert one blank line when the user presses ENTER. *Why? Many business letters use a font size of 12, and a single blank line between paragraphs makes the text easy to read.*

1

- Press F9 to zoom the text box to 100% and then display the Home tab.

- Click the Font Size arrow (Home tab | Font group) and then click 12 in the Font Size gallery to change the font size.

- Click the Paragraph Dialog Box Launcher (Home tab | Paragraph group) to display the Paragraph dialog box. If necessary, click the Indents and Spacing tab (Figure 5–33).

 Experiment

- Click the Alignment button (Paragraph dialog box) and view the various Alignment styles. Click the Preset button in the Indentation area and view the various Indentation styles.

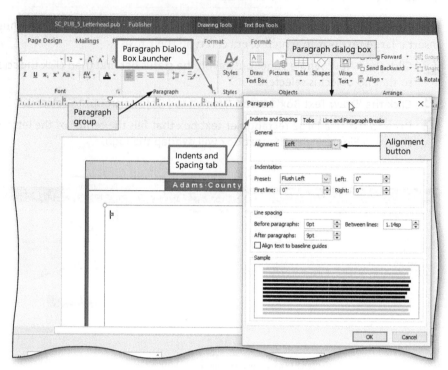

Figure 5–33

2

- If necessary, select the text in the Between lines box and then type **1.14sp** to enter the line spacing.

- Select the text in the After paragraphs box. Type **12** to change the paragraph spacing after each paragraph (Figure 5–34).

Q&A Can I use the arrow keys associated with the boxes in the Paragraph dialog box?
Yes, the up and down arrows change the value in the boxes one point at a time.

3

- Click OK (Paragraph dialog box) to save the settings.

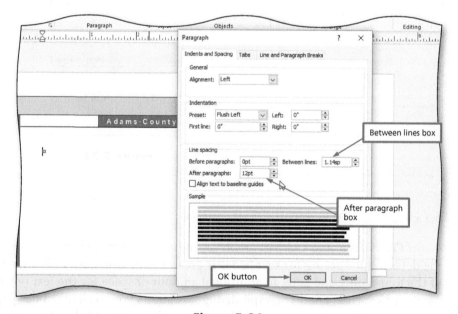

Figure 5–34

Other Ways

1. Right-click text box, point to Change Text on shortcut menu, click Paragraph on Change Text submenu, enter settings, click OK (Paragraph dialog box)

Text Wrapping

Wrapping refers to how objects wrap themselves around other objects on the page. Typically, text wrapping is used when wrapping text boxes around pictures; however, it also is used when wrapping text boxes with other text boxes and objects. Wrapping tightly means that very little space appears around the margins of the object, so text can be placed very close to the object. Wrapping loosely means more space appears between the text and the object. Some pictures wrap differently than others. Some clip art, for example, has internal **wrapping points** that allow you to create nonrectangular wraps when you choose to wrap tightly.

Table 5–4 defines the various Wrap Text options.

Table 5–4 Wrap Text Options	
Option	Result
None	Text does not wrap. It is displayed either behind or in front of the graphic, depending upon which object is in front.
Square	Text wraps around the graphic, creating a rectangular white border between the text and graphic.
Tight	Text wraps very closely around the graphic, creating a narrow white border between the text and graphic. Depending on the wrapping points of the graphic itself, the border may not be rectangular.
Top and Bottom	Text is displayed above and below the graphic, leaving horizontal white space across the text box on either side of the graphic.
Through	Depending on the type of graphic, text is displayed through the graphic or around it, based on wrapping points.
In Line with Text	Text is displayed above graphic. Subsequent lines of text are displayed in line with the bottom of the graphic, leaving horizontal white space across the text box.
Edit Wrap Point	Wrapping points are displayed for customized wrapping solutions.

To Set the Text Wrapping

The following steps set the text wrapping of the logo so that text will appear to the side of the logo. *Why? Text running over the top of the logo would be difficult to read.*

1

- With the text box selected, scroll to the lower portion of the letterhead and then display the Drawing Tools Format tab.

- Click the Send Backward button (Drawing Tools Format tab | Arrange group) to send the text box behind the logo.

- Select the logo (Figure 5–35).

Q&A I cannot select the logo. What should I do?
Click in the text box area and try sending it backward again.

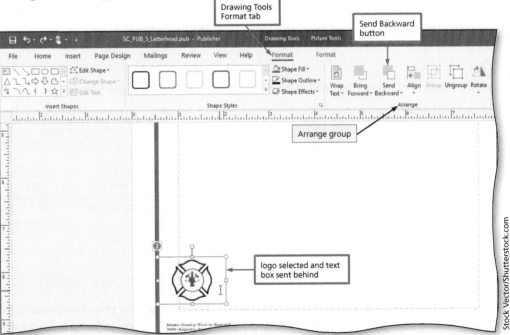

Figure 5–35

● Display the Home tab.

● Click the Wrap Text button (Home tab | Arrange group) to display the Wrap Text gallery (Figure 5–36).

Experiment

● Click 'Edit Wrap Points' in the Wrap Text gallery to view the wrapping points. Click the Undo button on the Quick Access Toolbar to undo the setting. Click the Wrap Text button again.

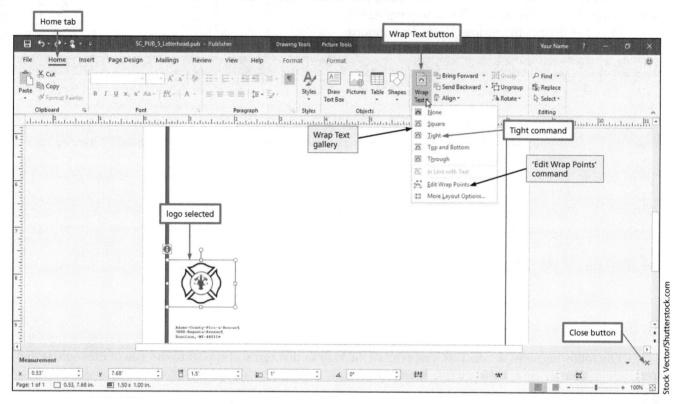

Figure 5–36

● Click Tight in the Wrap Text gallery to have the text wrap around the picture.

Q&A What changed?

Because you have yet to type any text, you will not see a change in text wrapping.

Other Ways

1. Click Wrap Text button (Picture Tools Format tab | Arrange group), click desired wrapping style

2. Click Text Dialog Box Launcher (Text Box Tools Format tab | Text group), click Layout tab, click desired wrapping style, click OK (Format Text Box dialog box)

3. Right-click text box, click 'Format Text Box' on shortcut menu, click Layout tab, click desired wrapping style, click OK (Format Text Box dialog box)

To Insert an Automatic Date

Publisher and other Microsoft Office applications can access your computer's stored date and time. You can retrieve the current date and/or time and display it in a variety of formats. In addition, you can choose to update the date and time automatically each time the file is accessed. ***Why?*** *Whenever the user opens the letterhead to prepare a new letter, the date will be current.* The following steps insert an automatic date.

1

- Close the Measurement pane by clicking its Close button (shown in Figure 5–36) to give yourself more room in the workspace.
- Scroll to the top of the page and click inside the large text box.
- Display the Insert tab.
- Click the 'Date & Time' button (Insert tab | Text group) to display the Date and Time dialog box.

Experiment

- Scroll in the Available formats list to view the various ways that Publisher can insert the date or time.

- Click the second format in the Available formats list to select it.
- Click the Update automatically check box so that it contains a check mark (Figure 5–37).

 What does the Default button do?
When you click the Default button, the current settings for date and time are chosen automatically every time you insert the date or time.

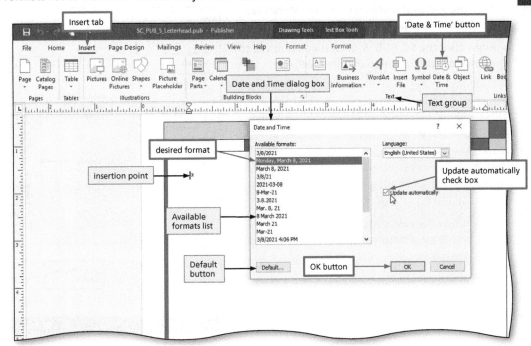

Figure 5–37

2

- Click OK (Date and Time dialog box) to close the dialog box.
- Press ENTER twice to create a blank line after the date (Figure 5–38).

 Why is my date different?
Checking the Update automatically check box (Date and Time dialog box) causes Publisher to access your computer's system date. The publication will display your current date.

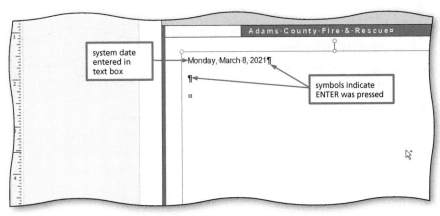

Figure 5–38

3

- Click the Save button on the Quick Access Toolbar to save the file with the same file name in the same location.
- Click File on the ribbon to open Backstage view.
- Click Close to close the publication without exiting Publisher and return to the template gallery.

To Set the Read-Only Attribute

Once a generic letterhead is created, it is a good idea to change the file's attribute, or classification, to read-only. With a **read-only** file, you can open and access the file normally, but you cannot make permanent changes to it. *Why? With a read-only file, users will be forced to save the publication with a new file name, which keeps the original letterhead intact and unchanged for the next user.*

While you can view system properties in Publisher 2019, you cannot change the read-only attribute from within Publisher. Setting the read-only attribute is a function of the operating system. Therefore, the following steps set the read-only attribute to true using File Explorer and the Properties dialog box.

1

- Click the File Explorer button on the Windows 10 taskbar. Navigate to your storage location.

- Right-click the SC_PUB_5_Letterhead.pub file to display a shortcut menu (Figure 5–39).

 I see multiple SC_PUB_5_Letterhead.pub file names. Which one should I choose?
Choose the top or most recent one in the list. It is possible that another person has created the file using your computer, which would result in multiple listings. Your file should be the most recent and should appear at the top of the list, provided that you saved the document recently.

Why is my shortcut menu different?
You may have different programs installed on your computer that affect the shortcut menu.

Figure 5–39

2

- Click Properties on the shortcut menu to display the Properties dialog box.

- If necessary, click the General tab in the Properties dialog box to display its settings.

- Verify that the file is the one you previously saved on your storage device by looking at the Location information.

- Click to place a check mark in the Read-only check box in the Attributes area (Figure 5–40).

What is the difference between applying a read-only attribute and creating a Publisher template?
Publisher templates do not prevent users from saving over the template with the same file name, which would destroy the default settings and user text box features. The read-only attribute keeps the file unchanged and the same for every user.

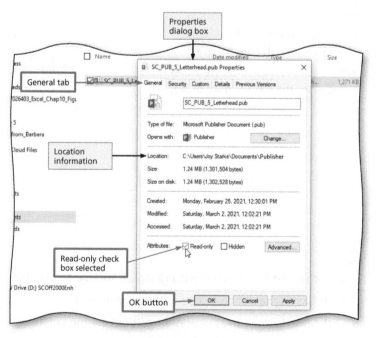

Figure 5–40

3
- Click OK to close the Properties dialog box and apply the read-only attribute.

Using the Custom Letterhead Template

In this project, you will open the letterhead file in Publisher, type the text of their letter, and then save the finished product with a new file name, thus preserving the original letterhead file.

To Open a Publication from the Recent List

Publisher maintains a list of the last few publications that have been opened or saved on your computer. The following steps open the SC_PUB_5_Letterhead.pub publication from the Recent list.

1 If necessary, click the Publisher app button on the taskbar to return to Publisher and the template gallery.

2 Click Open to display the Open screen and recent publications.

3 Click the SC_PUB_5_Letterhead.pub file in the Recent Publications list to open the file.

4 Click the center of the letterhead to place the insertion point in the main text box.

5 Zoom to 150% and scroll to the top of the letterhead, if necessary (Figure 5–41).

BTW
Using Read-Only Files
Read-only files can be deleted and moved, but Windows will prompt you with a dialog box asking you to confirm that you want to move or delete a read-only file.

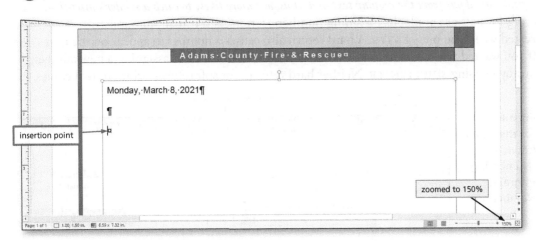

Figure 5–41

To Type the Beginning of the Letter

The following step enters the first part of the text of a letter.

1 Type the first part of the letter as shown in Figure 5–42, which includes the greeting and the first three paragraphs. Press ENTER only to complete a paragraph.

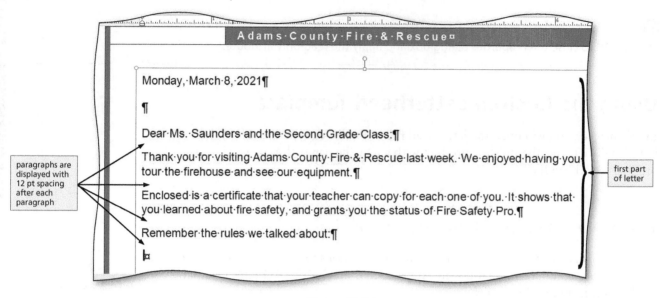

Figure 5–42

To Create a Numbered List

A **numbered list** is a series of paragraphs, each beginning with a sequential number that may be followed by a separator character, such as a period or parenthesis. The following steps create a numbered list. ***Why?*** *Numbered lists make paragraphs stand out from the regular text and, thus, are more likely to catch a reader's attention.* Several different numbering formats are available, including numbers, letters, and roman numerals.

A hard return is created when you press ENTER. A hard return also causes a number to appear on the next line in a numbered list. If you wanted to create a new line within a numbered list without assigning a new number, you would use a soft return by pressing SHIFT+ENTER. Neither hard returns nor soft returns print on hard copies.

1

- With the insertion point still positioned at the end of the typed text on a blank line (shown in Figure 5–42), click the Numbering button (Home tab | Paragraph group) to display the Numbering gallery (Figure 5–43).

Q&A What is the 'Bullets and Numbering' command?
That command displays the Bullets and Numbering dialog box, where you can change the format, the separator, the number with which to start, and the indentation.

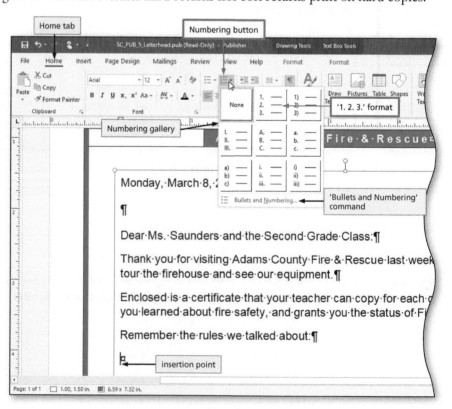

Figure 5–43

②

- Click the '1. 2. 3.' format in the Numbering gallery to insert the numeral 1 followed by a period and tab (Figure 5–44).

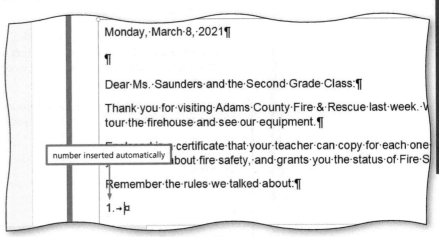

Figure 5–44

③

- Type the paragraphs shown in Figure 5–45. At the end of each paragraph, press ENTER to create a blank line (Figure 5–45).

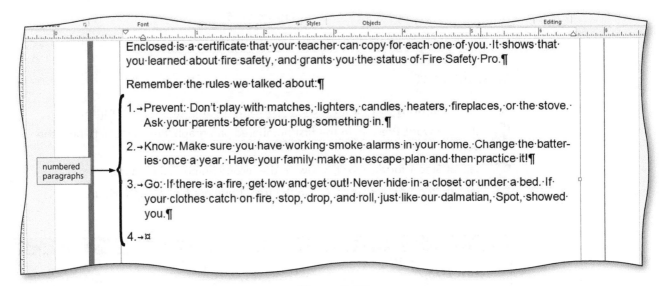

Figure 5–45

④

- Click the Numbering arrow (Home tab | Paragraph group) to display the Numbering gallery and then click None to turn off numbering and remove the numeral 4 that was automatically inserted.

- Type the final paragraph and signature block, as shown in Figure 5–46. Press ENTER twice at the end of the paragraph. Press ENTER four times after the word, Sincerely, to leave room for a signature.

◄ | Why did the signature line indent?
Q&A | The end of the letter wrapped around the graphic, as you directed it to earlier in the module.

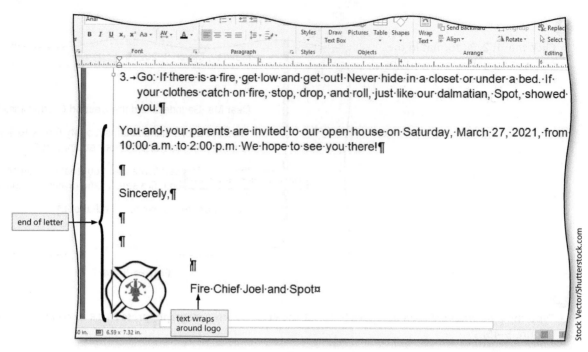

Figure 5–46

To Bold Text

The following steps bold the key words in the numbered paragraphs.

1 Click the word, Prevent, in the first numbered paragraph. Press CTRL+B to bold the word.

2 Repeat Step 1 for the word, Know, in the second numbered paragraph.

3 Repeat Step 1 for the word, Go, in the third numbered paragraph (Figure 5–47).

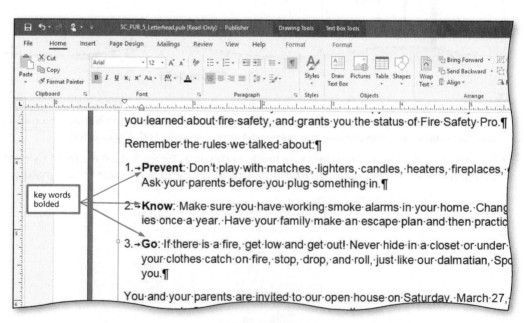

Figure 5–47

To Increase the Indent

The 'Increase Indent Position' and 'Decrease Indent Position' buttons (Home tab | Paragraph group) move paragraphs further away from or closer to the margin of the text box. The following steps increase the indent for the numbered paragraphs. **Why?** *Indenting the paragraphs will further delineate them and make the three key points easy to find on the page.*

1

- Select the three numbered paragraphs by dragging down the left side of the text box.
- Click the 'Increase Indent Position' button (Home tab | Paragraph group) to indent the paragraphs (Figure 5–48).

Q&A How far does it indent the paragraphs?

By default, it moves the paragraph .5 inches every time you click the button.

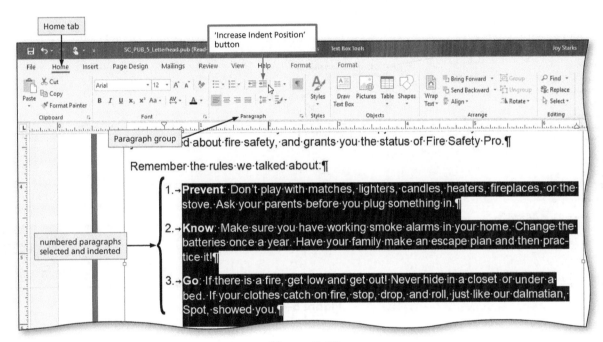

Figure 5–48

2

- Press F7 to check spelling. Correct any errors.

Other Ways

1. Select text, click 'Increase Indent Position' button on Mini toolbar
2. Right-click text, point to Change Text on shortcut menu, click Paragraph on Change Text submenu, enter settings, click OK (Paragraph dialog box)

To Save the Letter

To illustrate the read-only properties of the letter, you will try to save the publication in the same place with the same file name, SC_PUB_5_Letterhead. **Why?** *Because you have changed the publication to read-only, Publisher will generate an error message. You then will choose a new file name and save the file.* The following steps save the file with a new file name.

1

- Click the Save button on the Quick Access Toolbar to display the Save As dialog box. Do not navigate to another location.

- Click the Save button (Save As dialog box) to display the Confirm Save As dialog box (Figure 5–49).

Q&A What would happen if the file were not read-only?
Clicking the Save button would save the edited letter, replacing the custom template.

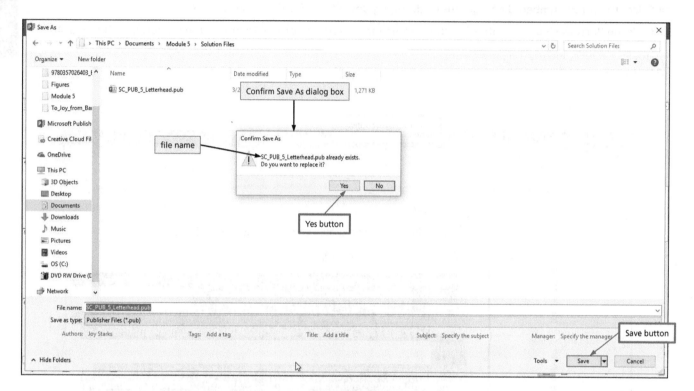

Figure 5–49

2

- Click the Yes button (Confirm Save As dialog box) to try to save the file. A Save As dialog box is displayed as a warning (Figure 5–50).

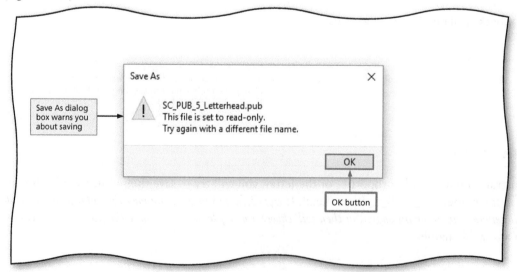

Figure 5–50

- Click OK to return to the Save As dialog box.
- Click the File name box, select or delete the previous file name, and then type `SC_PUB_5_SaundersLetter` as the new file name (Figure 5–51).

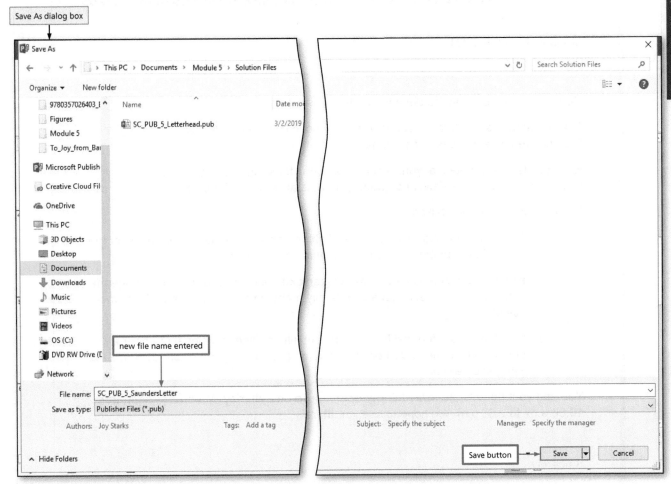

Figure 5–51

- Click the Save button (Save As dialog box) to save the file with the new file name.
- Print a hard copy of the letter, if instructed to do so. When the printer stops, retrieve the hard copy (Figure 5–52).

❺

- Click File on the ribbon to open Backstage view.
- Click Close to close the publication without exiting Publisher and to return to the template gallery.

Adams County Fire & Rescue

Monday, March 8, 2021

Dear Ms. Saunders and the Second Grade Class:

Thank you for visiting Adams County Fire & Rescue last week. We enjoyed having you tour the firehouse and see our equipment.

Enclosed is a certificate that your teacher can copy for each one of you. It shows that you learned about fire safety, and grants you the status of Fire Safety Pro.

Remember the rules we talked about:

1. **Prevent**: Don't play with matches, lighters, candles, heaters, fireplaces, or the stove. Ask your parents before you plug something in.
2. **Know**: Make sure you have working smoke alarms in your home. Change the batteries once a year. Have your family make an escape plan and then practice it!
3. **Go**: If there is a fire, get low and get out! Never hide in a closet or under a bed. If your clothes catch on fire, stop, drop, and roll, just like our dalmatian, Spot, showed you.

You and your parents are invited to our open house on Saturday, March 27, 2021, from 10:00 a.m. to 2:00 p.m. We hope to see you there!

Sincerely,

Fire Chief Joel and Spot

Adams County Fire & Rescue
3600 Augusta Avenue
Donelson, MI 48011

Phone: 906-555-3600
Fax: 906-555-3601
Email: jlarson@adamscofr.com

All Hands, Always Ready

Stock Vector/Shutterstock.com

Figure 5–52

Break Point: If you want to take a break, this is a good place to do so. Exit Publisher. To resume later, start Publisher, and continue following the steps from this location forward.

Envelopes

Envelopes are manufactured in a variety of sizes and shapes. The most common sizes are #6 personal envelopes, which measure $3\frac{5}{8} \times 6\frac{1}{2}$ inches, and #10 business envelopes, which measure $4\frac{1}{8} \times 9\frac{1}{2}$ inches. You can customize the page layout to instruct Publisher to print envelopes for invitations, cards, and mailers or to merge an address list with an envelope template to avoid using labels.

Although the majority of businesses outsource the production of their preprinted envelopes, most desktop printers have an envelope-feeding mechanism that works especially well for business envelopes. Check your printer's documentation for any limitations on the size and shape of envelopes. For testing purposes, you can print a test envelope on $8\frac{1}{2} \times 11$-inch paper, if necessary.

To Create an Envelope

The following steps use the template gallery to produce a business-sized envelope for Adams County Fire & Rescue. *Why? The template automatically uses information from the business information set created earlier in this project.*

- With the template gallery still displayed, click BUILT-IN and then click Envelopes to display the available templates.

- If necessary, scroll to the More Installed Templates area and then click the Quadrant thumbnail.

- If necessary, choose the Wildflower color scheme and the Data font scheme.

- If necessary, click the Business information button and then click 'Fire & Rescue' to select the business information set.

- Click the Page size button to display the list of page sizes (Figure 5–53).

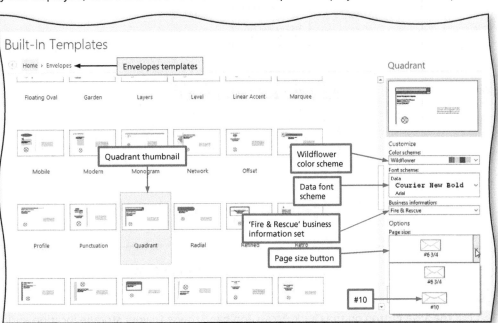

Figure 5–53

2

- Click #10 to choose a business-size envelope.

- If necessary, click to display a check mark in the Include logo check box (Figure 5–54).

Q&A What if I want a different size envelope?
In the template gallery, scroll to the Blank Sizes area and choose the size from the list. Otherwise, you could change the size by using the Size button (Page Design tab | Page Setup group).

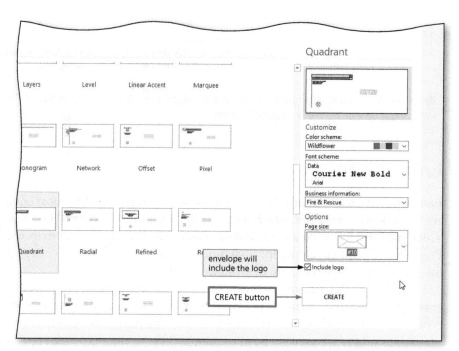

Figure 5–54

3

- Click the CREATE button to display the envelope with the specified settings (Figure 5–55).

Q&A Why does a different number appear on my title bar after the word, Publication?
The number will vary, depending on how many publications you have opened or created during the current Publisher session.

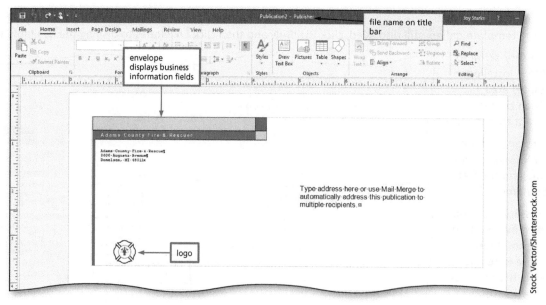

Figure 5–55

4

- Click the Save button on the Quick Access Toolbar. Browse to your storage location and then save the file with the file name, SC_PUB_5_Envelope.

To Address the Envelope

The envelope is ready to use. The following steps fill in the name and address on this envelope.

1 Click the placeholder text in the address text box to select it.

2 Type the following address, pressing ENTER at the end of each line except the last one (Figure 5–56):

```
Ms. Marie Saunders and class
Reagan Elementary
174 Stanley Blvd.
Donelson, MI 48011
```

Q&A Could I use a mailing label instead of typing the address?
Yes, you can delete the text box and use a mailing label. Publisher has the capability to create mailing labels and perform a mail merge.

Did the font size change as I was typing?
It might have changed. The text box is set for Best Fit, so when you typed the fourth line, Publisher might have reduced the font size slightly so that everything appeared in the text box.

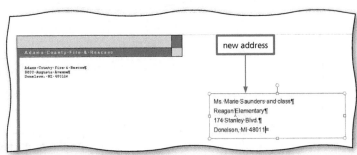

Figure 5–56

To Set Options and Print the Envelope

The following steps print a hard copy of the envelope with special settings. *Why? Most of the time, you must adjust the settings when printing envelopes.*

1

- Open Backstage view and then click Print to display the Print screen.

- Verify that the printer listed on the Printer Status button will print a hard copy of the publication.

- Click the Tiled button to display the options (Figure 5–57).

Q&A Why is the envelope displayed across two pages?
The default value for page settings is to place the publication on an 8½ × 11-inch piece of paper. The envelope will not fit, so Publisher tiles it until you change the setting.

Figure 5–57

2

● Click Envelope in the list (Figure 5–58).

Q&A What does the 'Save settings with publication' check box do?
If the check box is selected and the publication is saved, you will save time by not having to choose those settings each time you want to print.

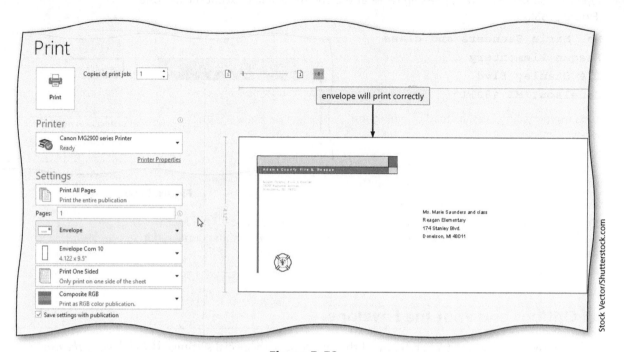

Figure 5–58

3

● If instructed to do so, click the Print button in the Print screen to print the envelope on the currently selected printer. Otherwise, click the Close button to close the publication without saving and without exiting Publisher. If Publisher displays a dialog box that asks you to save the publication again, click the Save button to save the envelope print settings along with the envelope.

Award Certificates

An award **certificate** commonly is a single-page publication presented in recognition of an achievement. Publisher has several certificate templates; many others are available online. The certificates have many uses, such as for attendance, for accomplishments, as gift certificates, or in completion of a regimen or coursework.

To Create and Edit an Award Certificate

The following steps use the template gallery to produce an award certificate for Adams County Fire & Rescue. *Why? The fire chief wants to give each student recognition for visiting the firehouse and listening to the fire safety presentation.*

1

● With the template gallery still displayed, click BUILT-IN and then click Award Certificates to display the available templates.

● Click the **Celtic Knotwork** thumbnail.

- If necessary, choose the Wildflower color scheme and the Data font scheme in the Customize area.
- If necessary, click the Business information button and then click 'Fire & Rescue' to select the business information set (Figure 5–59).

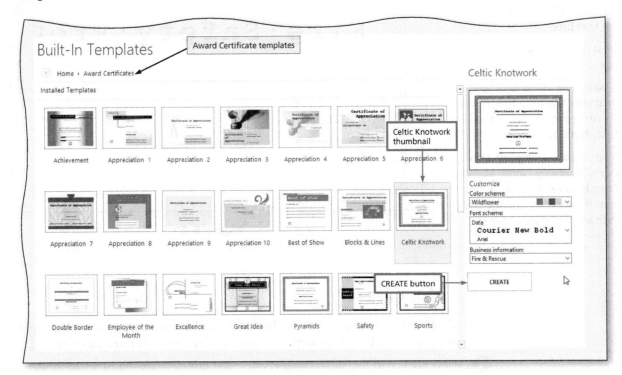

Figure 5–59

2

- Click the CREATE button.
- When Publisher displays the certificate, zoom to 100%.
- Select the text in the Certificate of Appreciation text box. Type **Fire Safety Pro** to replace the text.
- Right-click the text and then click Best Fit on the shortcut menu (Figure 5–60).

Figure 5–60

• Point to the 'Name of Recipient' box to display its border and then click the border to select the text box.

• Press DELETE to delete the text box.

• If necessary, zoom to 100% and then click the placeholder text in the 'in recognition of valuable contributions to' text box.

• Type **upon completion of Fire Safety Day at the firehouse** to replace the text. If necessary, change the U to lowercase (Figure 5–61).

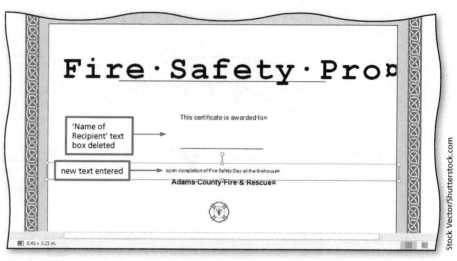

Figure 5–61

To Edit Font Sizes

Desktop publishing professionals recommend using no more than three font sizes on a page. The following steps edit font sizes in the certificate for consistency.

1 Select the text in the 'upon completion…' text box. Change the font size to 12. Change the font size of the 'Adams County…' text box to 12.

2 Click the placeholder text in the 'This certificate is awarded to' text box to select it. Change the font size to 12.

3 Change the font size for each Signature and Date text box to 8 (Figure 5–62).

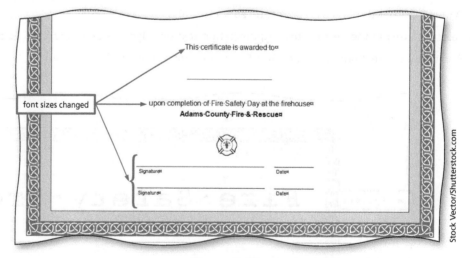

Figure 5–62

To Complete the Certificate

The following steps make final edits to the certificate. To complete these steps, you will be required to use the Data Files. Please contact your instructor for information about accessing the Data Files.

1 Click the 'Show Whole Page' button on the taskbar and then drag the logo to a position at the right-center of the certificate and resize it so that it is slightly larger.

2 Insert the picture named Support_Pub_5_Signature.png from the Data Files. Drag the picture to a location on the bottom signature line.

3 Insert a text box above the Date line and then insert the current date. Change the font to size 12 (Figure 5–63).

4 Click the Save button on the Quick Access Toolbar. Browse to your storage location and then save the file with the file name, SC_PUB_5_Certificate.

5 Print the certificate if instructed to do so.

6 Close the publication without exiting Publisher. If Publisher displays a dialog box that asks you to save the publication again, click the No button.

Figure 5–63

Break Point: If you want to take a break, this is a good place to do so. You can exit Publisher now. To resume later, start Publisher, and continue following the steps from this location forward.

Business Cards

Another way companies are reducing publishing costs is by designing their own business cards. A **business card** is a small publication, 3½ × 2 inches, typically printed on heavy stock paper. It usually contains the name, title, business, and address information for an employee, as well as a logo, distinguishing graphic, or color to draw attention to the card. Many employees want their telephone, cell phone number, and other information on their business cards in addition to their email and web addresses, so that colleagues and customers can reach them quickly.

Business cards can be saved as files to send to commercial printers or to be printed by desktop color printers on perforated paper.

To Create a Business Card

Because the business information set contains information about Adams County Fire & Rescue and its fire chief, using a Publisher business card template is the quickest way to create a business card. *Why? Not only does the template set the size and shape of a typical business card, it also presets page and printing options for easy production.*

The following steps use the template gallery to produce a business card for the fire chief at Adams County Fire & Rescue.

• With the template gallery still displayed, click BUILT-IN and then click the Business Cards thumbnail.

• If necessary, scroll to the More Installed Templates area and then click the Quadrant thumbnail.

• If necessary, choose the Wildflower color scheme, the Data font scheme, and the 'Fire & Rescue' business information set.

• If necessary, place a check mark in the Include logo check box (Figure 5–64).

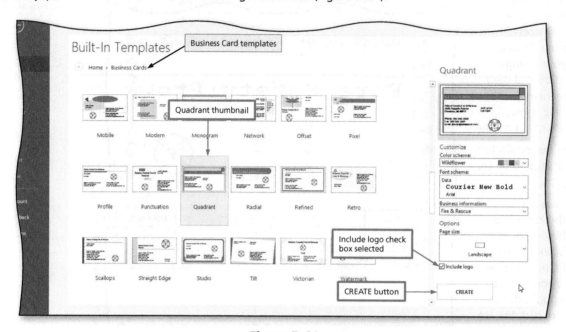

Figure 5–64

• Click the CREATE button to create the business card.

• Select the text in the Business Name text box and change the font size to 10.

• One at a time, select the text in the Name text box and the Title text box and change the font size to 10.

• One at a time, select the text in the Address text box and the Phone text box and change the font size to 6 (Figure 5–65).

Figure 5–65

• Click the Save button on the Quick Access Toolbar. Browse to your storage location. Save the file with the file name, SC_PUB_5_BusinessCard.

To Print the Business Card

The following steps change settings in the Print screen. ***Why?*** *You have the choice of printing multiple business cards per sheet or only one card per sheet. Layout options allow you to set specific margins to match specialized business card paper.*

- Open Backstage view and then click Print to display the Print screen.
- If necessary, verify the printer name that appears on the Printer Status button will print a hard copy of the publication.
- If necessary, click the Pages button to display the Pages list and then click 'Multiple copies per sheet' to select the option.
- If necessary, type   8   in the 'Copies of each page' box.

Experiment

- Type   10   in the 'Copies of each page' box. Look at the print preview and make sure all 10 business cards will print completely. If they will not, change the number back to 8.
- Click the Layout Options button to display the Layout Options dialog box.
- If you are using special paper, change the settings to match your paper. If you are using plain paper, change the numbers to match those shown in Figure 5–66, if necessary.

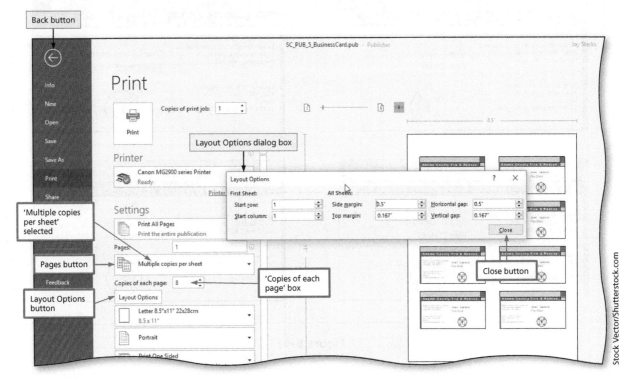

Figure 5–66

- Click the Close button (Layout Options dialog box) to close the dialog box.
- If instructed to do so, click the Print button in the Print screen to print the business cards on the currently selected printer (Figure 5–67). Otherwise, click the Back button in Backstage view to return to the publication.

Figure 5–67

Stock Vector/Shutterstock.com

Other Ways

1. Press CTRL+P, set options in Print screen, click Print button

To Set Publication Properties

Because you also plan to send the business cards to a commercial printer, it is important to set publication properties. Publication properties are set in the Info screen in Backstage view. The following steps set publication properties.

1 Open Backstage view and, by default, display the Info screen.

2 Click the Publication Properties button in the right pane of the Info screen and then click Advanced Properties to display the properties dialog box for your publication. If necessary, click the Summary tab.

3 Type **Business Card** in the Title text box.

4 If necessary, type **Joel Larson** in the Author text box.

5 Type **Adams County Fire & Rescue** in the Company text box (Figure 5–68).

6 Click OK (Publication Properties dialog box) to save the settings.

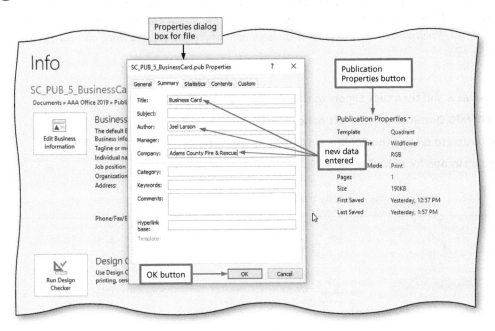

Figure 5–68

Creating Portable Files

The final step is to create a portable file of the business card for document exchange among computers. Publisher offers two choices: PDF or XPS. **PDF** stands for **Portable Document Format,** a flexible file format based on the PostScript imaging model that is cross-platform and cross-application. PDF files accurately display and preserve fonts, page layouts, and graphics. The content in a PDF file can be viewed by everyone, using a free viewer available on the web. **XPS** stands for **XML Paper Specification** and is also a format that preserves document formatting and enables file sharing. XPS is Microsoft's portable format and is similar to PDF. When an XPS file is viewed online or printed, it retains exactly the format that you intended.

CONSIDER THIS

Why do you need to create portable files?

You might have to distribute your artwork in a variety of formats for customers, print shops, webmasters, and as email attachments. The format you choose depends on how the file will be used, but portability is always a consideration. The publication might need to be used with various operating systems, monitor resolutions, computing environments, and servers.

It is a good idea to discuss with your customer the types of formats he or she might need. It usually is safe to begin work in Publisher and then use the Save As command or Print command to convert the files. PDF is a portable format that can be read by anyone using a free reader, which is available on the web. The PDF format is platform- and software-independent. Generally, PDF files are virus free and safe as email attachments.

To Publish in a Portable Format

The following steps publish the business card in a portable format using high-quality settings and maintaining document properties. *Why? You might want to create a portable file for an outside printing service or to display your publication on the web. Publisher allows you to set additional options for quality, graphics, and document properties when creating portable files.*

1

- If necessary, open Backstage view and then click Export to display the Export screen.
- If necessary, click 'Create PDF/XPS Document' in the left pane.
- Click the 'Create PDF/XPS' button to display the Publish as PDF or XPS dialog box.
- If necessary, navigate to your storage location (Figure 5–69).

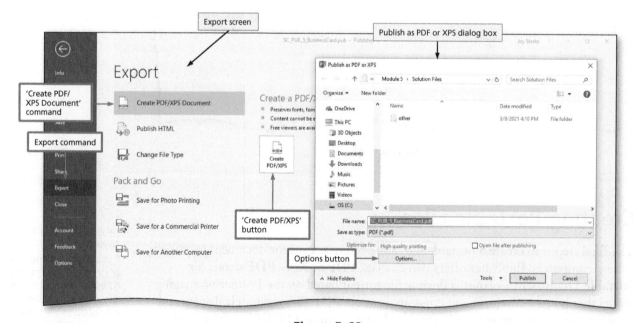

Figure 5–69

2

- Click the Options button or Change button (Publish as PDF or XPS dialog box) to display the Publish Options dialog box.
- If necessary, in the Specify how this publication will be printed or distributed area, click 'High quality printing' (Publish Options dialog box).
- If necessary, in the Include non-printing information area, click both check boxes to select them.

- Do not change any of the other default values (Figure 5–70).

 Experiment

- Click each choice in the Specify how this publication will be printed or distributed box to view the description that displays below the box, along with other settings. When you are done, click 'High quality printing'.

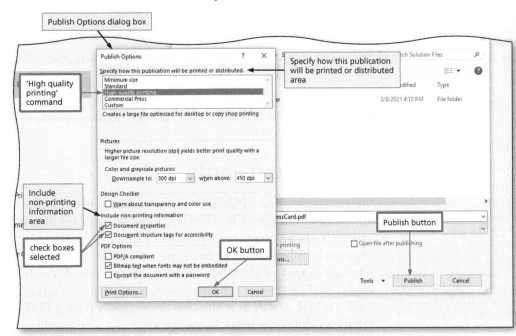

Figure 5–70

3

- Click OK (Publish Options dialog box) to close the dialog box.

- Click the Publish button (Publish as PDF or XPS dialog box) to create the portable file.

- When the PDF file opens, maximize the window if necessary (Figure 5–71).

Q&A My portable file did not open. What should I do?
Open a File Explorer window, navigate to your storage location, and then double-click the PDF or XPS file.

Why does my display look different?
Your computer may not have the same PDF reader installed. If no PDF reader is installed, the file may open in an XPS reader.

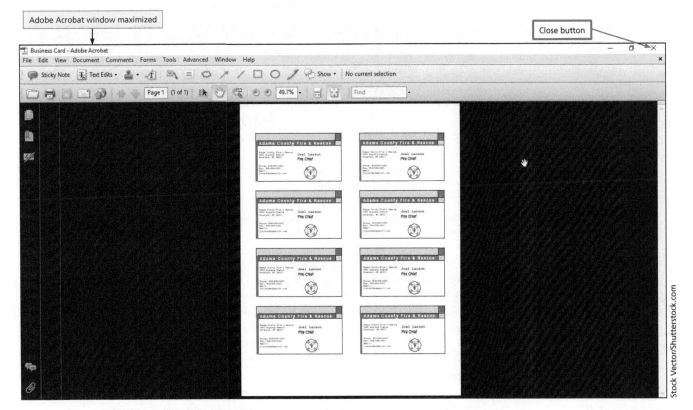

Figure 5–71

Stock Vector/Shutterstock.com

• Click the Close button on the PDF or XPS title bar to close the display of the portable file.

Other Ways

1. In Backstage view, click Save As, specify save location, click 'Save as type' button (Save As dialog box), click PDF (*.pdf) in the Save as type list, click Options or Change button, select options, click OK (Publish Options dialog box), click Save button (Save As dialog box)

Embedding Fonts

BTW

Distributing a Document

Instead of printing and distributing a hard copy of a document, you can distribute the document electronically. Options include sending the document via email; posting it on cloud storage (such as OneDrive) and sharing the file with others; posting it on social media, a blog, or other website; and sharing a link associated with an online location of the document. You also can create and share a PDF or XPS image of the document, so that users can view the file in Acrobat Reader or XPS Viewer instead of in Publisher.

If you plan to send a Publisher file to a professional printing service or to other users, they may or may not have the same fonts available on their computers as you do on yours. Thus, any fonts unique to your printer or new font styles that you created may have to be substituted. When the publication is opened, Publisher usually displays a dialog box that informs the user of the substitution. Publisher tries to find a similar font based on the text ornamentation, but with a font substitution, your publication will not look exactly as it did. One option is to create a PDF or XPS as you did earlier in the module, which would maintain the look of the publication; however, the PDF or XPS user cannot make significant changes to the design. If you want to preserve your font settings and create a fully editable file, you should **embed**, or include, the fonts with the publication. Optionally, you can embed a **subset** of a font, which means embedding only the specific characters you used in the publication.

Most common fonts, such as Times New Roman, do not have to be embedded because most users already have that font. In general, TrueType fonts can be embedded only if their licensing allows embedding; however, all of the TrueType fonts that are included in Publisher allow licensed embedding.

Embedding fonts increases the file size of a publication, so you may want to limit the number of fonts or subsets that you embed; however, embedding fonts is one of the best ways to ensure that a font is always available.

Table 5–5 displays some of Publisher's embedding options.

Table 5–5 Type of Embedding

Type of Embedding	Kinds of Fonts (If Any)	Advantages	Restrictions
Full font embedding		The recipient does not need the same font to view or edit the file.	You must own the embedded font by owning your printer or by purchasing the font. Fully embedded fonts create a large file size.
	Print and preview fonts	Viewable fonts are embedded in the publication.	The recipient cannot edit the publication.
	Licensed, installable fonts	Embedded fonts, licensed as installable, may be installed permanently for use in other publications and programs.	No restrictions exist.
	Licensed, editable fonts	Embedded fonts that are licensed as editable are available for use in other publications and programs.	The publication with the editable fonts must remain open in order for the recipient to use the font.
	TrueType fonts	TrueType fonts include permissions defined by the original publisher of the font that detail when and how the font may be embedded.	The TrueType fonts can be applied to a publication only if the embedded fonts are installed on the local computer.
Subset font embedding		The recipient does not have to own the font to view it.	Only the characters that you use in the publication are included in the font family. Subset font embedding creates a file that is larger than one with no embedding but smaller than one with full font embedding.
No font embedding		File size does not change.	The recipient needs to have the same fonts installed or must accept a substitution.
Save as PDF or XPS		Fonts, layout, and design are maintained.	Recipient has limited editing capabilities.

To Embed Fonts

The following steps embed the fonts with the business card. ***Why?*** *Because other workers at Adams County Fire & Rescue may want to use this file to create their own business cards, you will embed all of the characters, rather than just a subset, in the heading font.* In order to keep the file size slightly smaller, you will not embed the common system fonts that most users have (in this case, Times New Roman).

- With the SC_PUB_5_Business Card still displayed in the workspace, click the File tab to open Backstage view and, by default, display the Info screen.
- Click the 'Manage Embedded Fonts' button to display the Fonts dialog box.
- Click to place a check mark in the 'Embed TrueType fonts when saving publication' check box (Fonts dialog box).
- If necessary, click to place a check mark in the 'Do not embed common system fonts' check box (Figure 5–72).

Q&A What will users see when they open the file?
A dialog box will verify that some fonts were embedded and allow the user to substitute those if necessary.

What does the Embed/Don't Embed button do?
If you own the font but do not want others to use it, you can click to select the specific font in the list and then click the Don't Embed button. In that case, the Embed Font column will display a no, and the button will change to the Embed button. You must select a specific font in the list to enable the button.

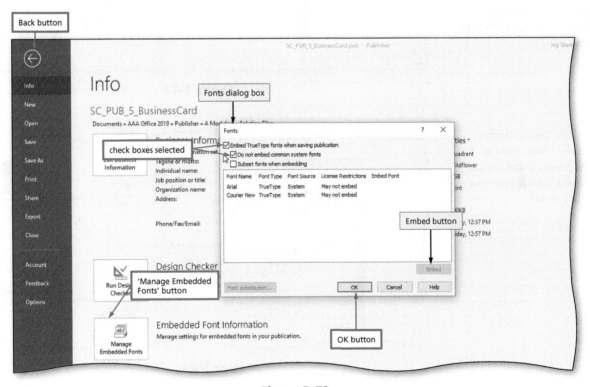

Figure 5–72

- Click OK (Fonts dialog box) to close the dialog box.
- Click the Back button (Backstage view) to return to the publication.
- Click the Save button on the Quick Access Toolbar to save the file again with the same file name.

To Delete the Business Information Set

The following steps delete the Fire & Rescue business information set. *Why? Others who work on your computer may not want to use the business information set. Deleting the business information set does not delete the information from saved publications.*

- Display the Insert tab.

- Click the Business Information button (Insert tab | Text group) to display the Business Information menu.

- Click 'Edit Business Information' on the Business Information menu to display the Business Information dialog box.

- If necessary, click the leftmost button in the Select a Business Information set area and then click 'Fire & Rescue' to select the set (Figure 5–73).

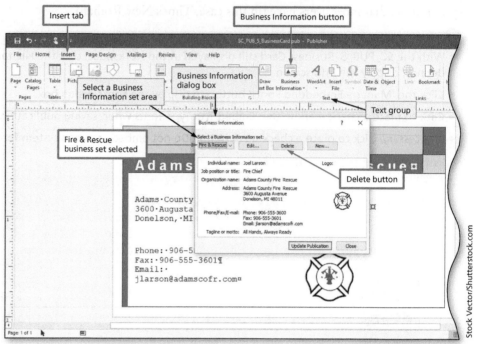

Figure 5–73

- Click the Delete button (Business Information dialog box) to delete the business information set (Figure 5–74).

Q&A Will this delete the fields from the current business card?
No. It will delete only the set. All publications containing that data will remain unchanged.

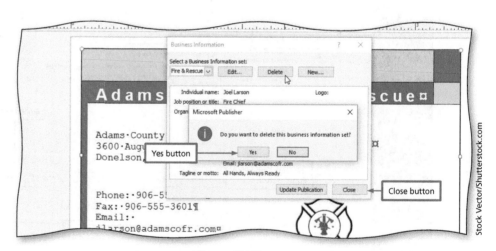

Figure 5–74

- When Publisher displays a dialog box asking you to confirm the deletion, click the Yes button.

- Click the Close button (Business Information dialog box) to close the dialog box.

- To exit Publisher, click the Close button on the right side of the title bar. If a Microsoft Publisher dialog box is displayed, click the Don't Save button so that any changes you have made are not saved.

Summary

In this module, you learned how to create a logo and cropped and filled a shape with a picture. To personalize and customize the publication further, you created a business information set with its many components and then used the business information set to create a letterhead. You created a new style and applied it to text in the letterhead and used the Measurement pane for exact placement and scaling. After adding a customized text box with an automatic date, you saved the letterhead as a read-only file. As you prepared a letter using the new letterhead, you created a numbered list. Finally, you used the business information set to create an award certificate, an envelope, and a business card. You created a portable file using the business card and embedded fonts in preparation for an outside printer.

CONSIDER THIS: PLAN AHEAD

What decisions will you need to make when creating your next business publications?
Use these guidelines as you complete the assignments in this module and create your own publications outside of this class.

1. Gather the business information from the customer.

   a) Create a business information set, including appropriate fields and a logo, if applicable.

   b) Create any necessary text styles.

2. Create letterhead.

   a) Use business information fields or type business information text.

   b) Create an automatic date and a user-friendly text box for future use.

   c) Set the read-only attribute.

3. Create certificates.

   a) Choose an appropriate template.

   b) Edit text boxes as necessary.

4. Create envelopes.

   a) Use business information sets when possible.

   b) Include a location for addresses or future labels.

   c) Set publication properties.

5. Create business cards.

   a) Insert a tagline or motto.

   b) Set publication properties.

6. Publish portable files.

   a) Proofread and check the publication.

   b) Save as PDF or XPS.

Apply Your Knowledge

Reinforce the skills and apply the concepts you learned in this module.

Customizing Letterhead

Note: To complete this assignment, you will be required to use the Data Files. Please contact your instructor for information about accessing the Data Files.

Instructions: Start Publisher. Open the publication, SC_PUB_5-1.pub, from the Data Files. The publication is a letterhead that contains default business information fields. You will create a new business information set, publish the file in a portable format, and create an envelope. Figure 5–75 shows the completed letterhead and envelope.

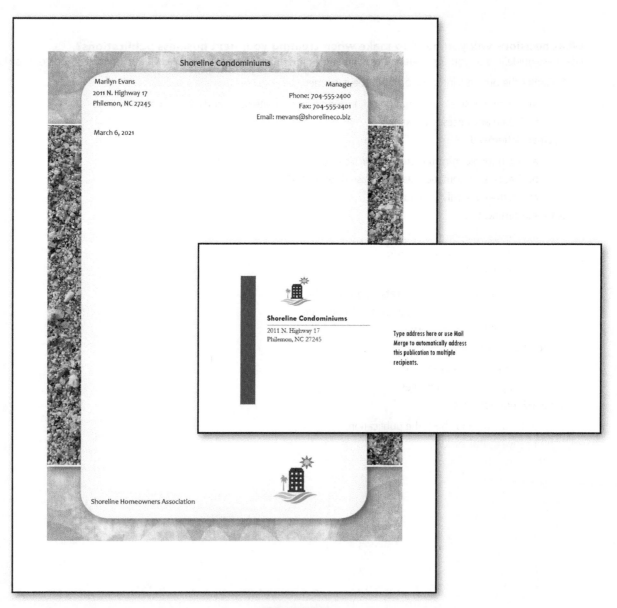

Figure 5–75

Perform the following tasks:

1. Click the Business Information button (Insert tab | Text group) and then click 'Edit Business Information' on the Business Information menu. Click the New button (Business Information dialog box).
2. Enter the information from Table 5–6 and then insert the logo file. The picture for the logo is available in the Data Files. If instructed to do so, use your email address in the business information set.

Table 5–6 Business Information Data	
Field Name	**Company Data**
Individual name	Marilyn Evans
Job position or title	Manager
Organization name	Shoreline Condominiums
Address	2011 N. Highway 17 Philemon, NC 27245
Phone, fax, and email	Phone: 704-555-2400 Fax: 704-555-2401 Email: mevans@shorelineco.biz
Business information set name	Shoreline Condominiums
Tagline or motto	Shoreline Homeowners Association
Logo	Support_PUB_5_CondoLogo.png

3. Click the Save button (Create New Business Information Set dialog box) to save the business information set with the company's name, Shoreline Condominiums.
4. Click the Update Publication button (Business Information dialog box) to change the fields in the current letterhead.
5. Click the Business Information button (Insert tab | Text group) and scroll as necessary to insert the logo.
6. With the logo selected, click the Measurement button (Drawing Tools Format tab | Size group) to display the Measurement pane.
    a. Select the text in the Horizontal Position box and then type 6 to replace it. Press TAB to advance to the next box.
    b. If necessary, select the text and then type 8.75 in the Vertical Position box and then press TAB.
    c. If necessary, type 1.5 in the Width box and then press TAB.
    d. Type 1 in the Height box and then press ENTER.
    e. Close the Measurement pane.
7. Change the text wrapping on the logo to Square.
8. Draw a large text box, approximately 5.5 by 7.5 inches, to fill the main part of the letterhead. Click inside the textbox and then click the 'Date & Time' button (Insert tab | Text group) to display the Date & Time dialog box. Choose the third date format, and choose to update it automatically.
9. Open Backstage view and then click Save As. Save the publication using the file name, SC_PUB_5_CondoLetterhead.
10. To publish the letterhead as a PDF in order to send it to a commercial printer, open Backstage view and then click Export to display the Export screen. Click the 'Create PDF/XPS' button in the Export screen to display the Publish as PDF or XPS dialog box. Navigate to your storage location.

Continued >

Apply Your Knowledge *continued*

11. Click the Options button (Publish as PDF or XPS dialog box) to display the Publish Options dialog box. If necessary, in the Specify how this publication will be printed or distributed area, click 'High quality printing' in the list. If necessary, in the Include non-printing information area, click both check boxes to select them. Do not change any of the other default values.

12. Click OK (Publish Options dialog box) to close the dialog box. Click the Publish button (Publish as PDF or XPS dialog box) to create the portable file. View the PDF (or XPS) file and then close the Adobe Reader (or XPS Reader) window.

13. Close the letterhead publication. Set the Read-only attribute using the File Explorer window, as discussed in the module.

14. Start Publisher. Click BUILT-IN, click the Envelopes thumbnail, and then choose the Straight Edge envelope template in size #10. Use the Trek color scheme and the Modern font scheme. If necessary, choose the Shoreline Condominiums business information set. Click the CREATE button to display the publication in the Publisher workspace.

15. Change the company name text to font size 14. Change the address text to font size 12.

    If directed by your instructor to do so, insert your name and address in the 'Type address here' text box.

16. Print the envelope with appropriate printer settings.

17. If you are working in a lab situation, click the Business Information button (Insert tab | Text group) and then click 'Edit Business Information' on the business Information menu. Click the Delete button (Business Information dialog box) and then click the Yes button (Microsoft Publisher dialog box) to delete the Shoreline Condominiums business information set. Click the Close button (Business Information dialog box).

18. Save the envelope with the file name, SC_PUB_5_CondoEnvelope, and then exit Publisher.

19. Submit the files as specified by your instructor.

20. ✳ When would it be more advantageous to send the letterhead out for printing rather than just type text in the template and print it on a desktop printer? If a company uses preprinted letterhead, how does it create content? Would an advantage be gained by running the paper through the printer and just using a Publisher text box with proper dimensions, or do you think most companies use a copy machine?

Extend Your Knowledge

Extend the skills you learned in this module and experiment with new skills. You may need to use Help to complete the assignment.

Adding Styles to the Quick Access Toolbar

Note: To complete this assignment, you will be required to use the Data Files. Please contact your instructor for information about accessing the Data Files.

Instructions: Open the publication named SC_PUB_5-2.pub from the Data Files. You will add the Styles button to the Quick Access Toolbar, apply styles to the publication, and then remove the button from the Quick Access Toolbar.

Perform the following tasks:

1. Use Help to learn more about customizing the Quick Access Toolbar.

2. If necessary, click the Page Number button on the status bar to open the Page Navigation pane.

3. Right-click the Styles button (Home tab | Styles group) to display the shortcut menu.

4. Click 'Add to Quick Access Toolbar' on the shortcut menu to add the Styles button to the Quick Access Toolbar (shown in Figure 5–76).

5. Select the text on Page 1 of the thank-you card. Click the Styles button on the Quick Access Toolbar and then choose the Hometown Insurance style.

6. Click the 'Page 2 and Page 3' thumbnail in the Page Navigation pane to display the inside pages in the Publisher workspace.

7. Select the text on page 2 (in the upper portion of the page layout). Click the Styles button on the Quick Access Toolbar and then choose the Heading 4 style, if necessary.

8. Select the text on page 3 (in the lower portion of the page layout). Click the Styles button on the Quick Access Toolbar and then choose the 'Body Text 5' style.

9. Click the page 4 thumbnail in the Page Navigation pane to display the back page in the Publisher workspace.

10. Select the text on page 4 of the thank you card. Click the Styles button on the Quick Access Toolbar and then choose the Hometown Insurance style.

11. If instructed to do so, draw a text box and insert your name and address on Page 4.

12. Click the 'Customize Quick Access Toolbar' button on the right side of the Quick Access Toolbar to display the shortcut menu and then click More Commands to display the Publisher Options dialog box and, by default, the Quick Access Toolbar settings.

13. Click the Styles button in the Customize Quick Access Toolbar list (Figure 5–76).

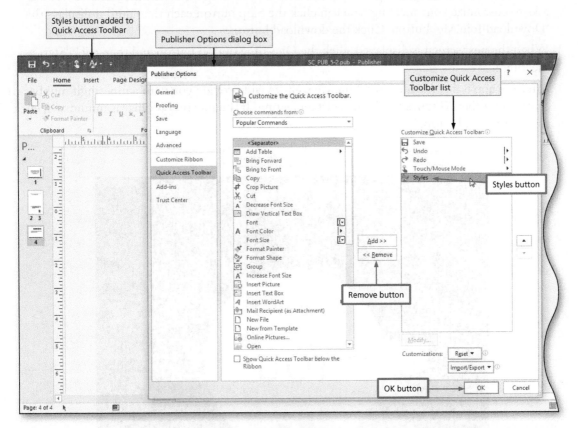

Figure 5–76

14. Click the Remove button (Publisher Options Dialog box) to remove the Styles button from the Quick Access Toolbar. Click OK to return to the publication.

15. Save the revised publication with the file name, SC_PUB_5_InsuranceThankYou, and then submit it in the format specified by your instructor.

Continued >

Extend Your Knowledge *continued*

16. Exit Publisher.

17. ✳ Would you consider adding the Styles button to the Quick Access Toolbar on a permanent basis? Why or why not? What other features do you use so often that you might want to add them to the Quick Access Toolbar?

Expand Your World

Create a solution that uses cloud and web technologies by learning and investigating on your own from general guidance.

Sharing Ideas

Problem: You work online from home as a desktop publisher for a business. You would like to discuss with a coworker your ideas for new company letterhead, but it has become tedious and time-consuming sending files back and forth. You decide to try a free screen-sharing program.

Instructions:

1. Start a browser and navigate to http://join.me. Click the Get Started button, which requires an email address and password to create a free account. (If you already have an account, you can click the 'Host a Free Meeting' button and then skip to Step 3.) When the Join.Me website asks to customize your meeting, you can click the Skip button each time until it displays the 'Download Join.Me' button. Click the download button.

2. When the next screen is displayed, click the One-time option button and then click 'Start a meeting'.

3. After the app is downloaded, the Join.Me website will provide you with a nine-digit number to share with others (Figure 5–77) and start a meeting. If the meeting toolbar is minimized, click the Participant button.

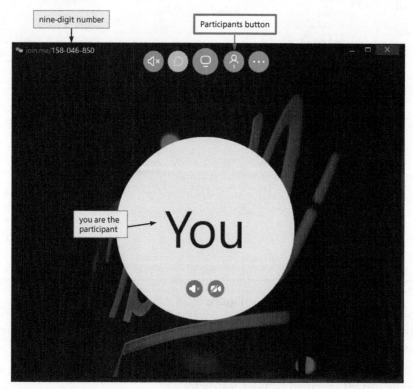

Figure 5–77

4. Contact another student in your class or a friend, and ask him or her to navigate to the Join.Me website and click the Join Meeting button to enter the number. (No download is required for others to view your screen; they need just the nine-digit number.)

5. Once the user has joined you, start Publisher and demonstrate how to create a simple letterhead.

6. When you are finished, click the Exit button.

7. Write a paragraph about your experience with the screen-sharing program. Include several advantages and disadvantages for collaborating in this manner.

8. Submit the assignment in the format specified by your instructor.

9. ✸What other screen-sharing programs have you heard about or used? What are the advantages to a web-based, free service, such as Join.Me? Do you think screen sharing is an important tool in business? Why or why not?

In the Lab

Design and implement a solution using creative thinking and problem-solving skills.

Creating a New Style

Problem: The Simply Soup restaurant would like you to create a text style that management can import into all of the restaurant's current publications. Simply Soup also wants to use this text style in an upcoming menu change.

Part 1: Start Publisher. Using a blank page, create a text box with the name of the restaurant as text. Create a new style using the Harlow Solid Italic font or a decorative italic font on your computer. Use a 48-point, bright green font. Save the style with the name, Simply Soup. Create another text box with your name in it and then apply the new style. Embed all possible fonts and then save the publication for the restaurant to use. Print a copy for your instructor.

Part 2: ✸ Can you think of several companies that have distinct formatting for the business name? How is branding the text different from branding a logo? Search the web for third-party providers of specific font styles, such as the James Bond font or the IBM font. Write a brief report on your findings. Include information about the vendor, pricing, downloading, and copyrights.

6 Working with Publisher Tables

Objectives

After completing this module, you will be able to:

- Change page orientation
- Apply shape effects
- Create tables and enter data
- Apply table formats
- Select table rows, columns, and cells
- Insert and delete rows and columns in tables
- Merge, split, and divide cells diagonally
- Resize and align tables and cells

- Format tables with borders
- Create a multipage calendar
- Use a master page
- Edit BorderArt
- Apply font effects
- Embed an Excel table in a Publisher publication
- Use Excel tools on the Publisher ribbon to format a table

Introduction

A table is a good way to present a large amount of data in a small, organized space. Tabular data, or data that can be organized into related groups and subgroups, is presented best in rows and columns with appropriate headings. A well-defined, descriptive table will have three general characteristics. First, the data will be meaningful: it will relate closely to the purpose of the publication. The data in a table will support or provide evidence of any analyses or conclusions. Second, a table will be unambiguous: it will have clear labels, titles, headings, legends, or footnotes. The purpose of the table will be clear, and the scale will be well defined. Third, a table should be efficient so that the reader quickly can understand the data and its presentation in order to draw conclusions and apply the data to a particular situation. An efficient table is formatted appropriately and read quickly.

While many tables are created using Microsoft Excel, Publisher tables are formatted easily and fit well in many kinds of publications. Readers can understand the purpose of a publication table and promptly retrieve the important information. As you will learn in this module, many of Excel's features can be embedded for use in Publisher tables.

Project: Table, Calendar, and Excel Functionality

The decision to use a table in a publication is based on a need to organize a large amount of information in an easily recognizable format and to reduce the amount of text necessary to explain the situation. From tables of content to bank rate tables to timetables, you may need to display text, graphics, dates, or color in many different tabular ways. Publisher allows you to create tables from scratch or use tables that already are organized for specific purposes.

In this project, you will create three different publications that incorporate tables for the Print Pack Go company, as shown in Figure 6–1. Print Pack Go provides custom graphic design, high-quality printing, and reliable shipping choices. The first publication will be a work schedule (Figure 6–1a) prepared using a table to indicate hours and days for employees. The second publication will be a promotional calendar that Print Pack Go wants a promotional calendar that the company can send out to steady customers and give to potential ones (Figure 6–1b). Finally, a letter to a prospective customer (Figure 6–1c) will contain an embedded table with formulas and formatting.

You will perform the following general tasks as you progress through this module:

1. Employ reusable parts, such as business information sets, building blocks, and logos.
2. Apply shape effects, such as glows, reflections, and 3-D effects.
3. Insert and format tables.
4. Create a calendar.
5. Use master pages to insert objects that will appear on every page.
6. Add BorderArt to help outline pages and tables.
7. Embed or link a table for advanced formatting.
8. Use Excel functionality within Publisher.

Reusable Parts

The manager at Print Pack Go wants several publications, including a work schedule, a calendar, and a letter with price quotes, for potential customers. Certain objects will be repeated in all the publications — including the color and font scheme, the business information set, and the name of the company in a WordArt object — to serve as a recognizable branding.

CONSIDER THIS

Why should you create reusable objects for branding?

Creating reusable components, such as business sets, logos, and a stylistic company name, helps create a positive perception of a company and creates identifiable branding. A brand identity should be communicated in multiple ways with frequency and consistency throughout the life of a business. Sometimes a brand is as simple as golden arches; other times it is a stylistic font that identifies a popular soda, no matter what the language. Developing and marketing a brand takes time and research. When desktop publishers are asked to help with brand recognition, they can suggest reusable colors, fonts, schemes, logos, business information sets, graphics, and other tools to assist the company in creating a customer-friendly, consistent brand.

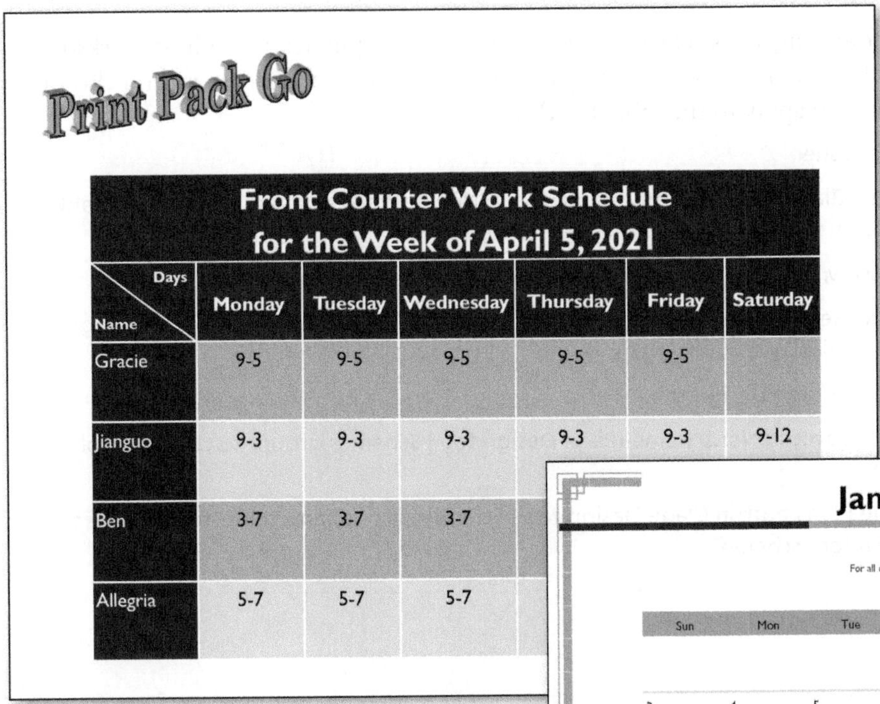

a) Formatted Table

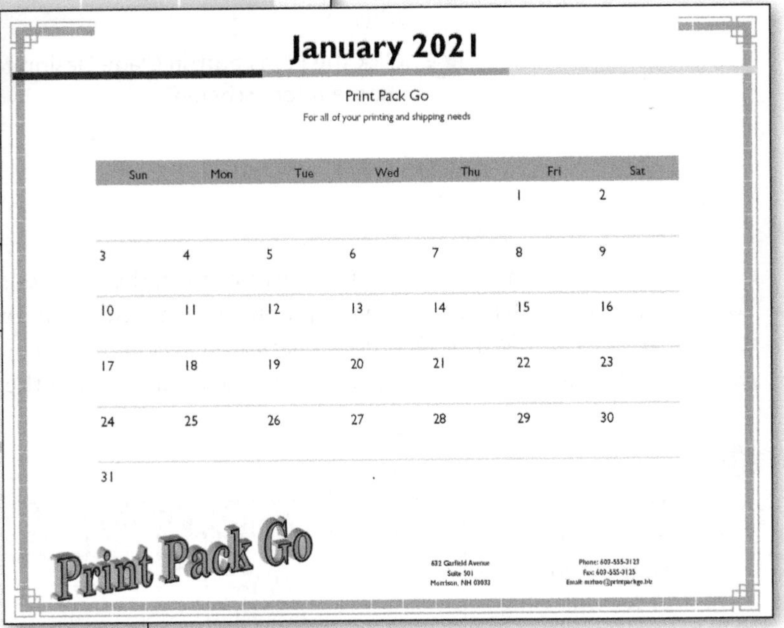

b) Calendar with BorderArt

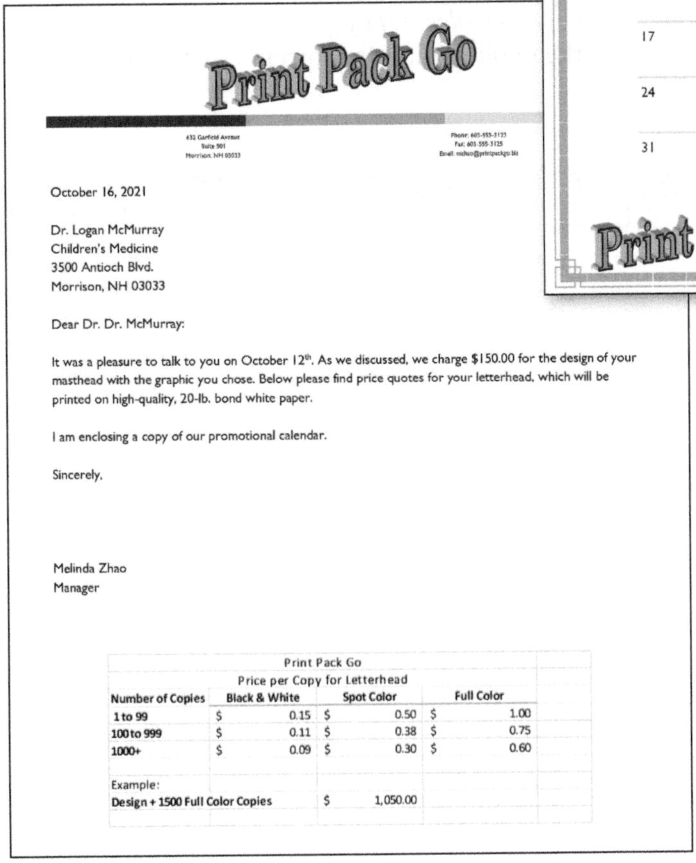

c) Letter with Embedded Table

Figure 6–1

To Select a Blank Publication and Adjust Settings

The following steps select an 8.5 × 11 blank print publication, adjust workspace settings, such as the Page Navigation pane display and special characters, and choose schemes that will apply to the table for Print Pack Go.

1   Start Publisher.

2   Click the 'Blank 8.5 x 11"' thumbnail in the New template gallery to create a blank publication in the Publisher window.

3   If necessary, collapse the Page Navigation pane.

4   If it is not selected already, click the Special Characters button (Home tab | Paragraph group) to display formatting marks.

5   Display the Page Design tab.

6   Click the Cavern color scheme (Page Design tab | Schemes group) to choose a color scheme.

7   Click the Fonts button (Page Design tab | Schemes group) and then click Solstice to choose a font scheme.

To Change the Page Orientation

When a publication is in **portrait orientation**, the short edge of the paper is the top of the publication. You can instruct Publisher to lay out a publication in **landscape orientation**, which is a page that is wider than it is tall. *Why? The table will show more information horizontally, so the long edge of the paper needs to be at the top of the publication.* The following steps change the page orientation of the publication from portrait to landscape.

1

• Click the Orientation button (Page Design tab | Page Setup group) to display the Orientation menu (Figure 6–2).

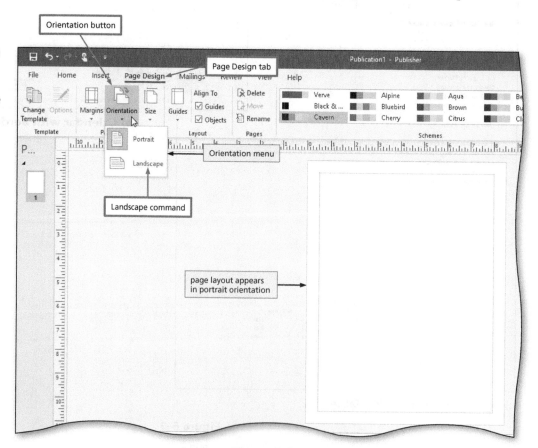

Figure 6–2

2

- Click Landscape on the Orientation menu to change the orientation of the page (Figure 6–3).

Could I have chosen a template with landscape orientation?
Yes, if you know in advance that you want landscape orientation, choose one of the landscape orientation templates. If you already have created objects, use the 'Change Page Orientation' button (Page Design tab | Page Setup group).

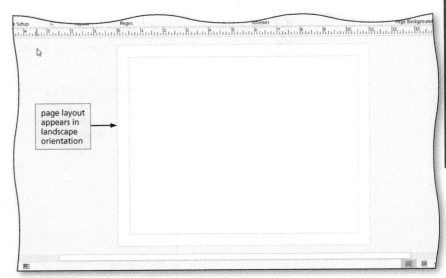

page layout appears in landscape orientation

Figure 6–3

Creating a Business Information Set

Table 6–1 displays the data for each of the fields in the business information set that you will create in this project. Because you will be creating a graphical representation for the logo, you will leave that field blank.

Table 6–1 Data for Business Information Fields	
Fields	**Data**
Individual name	Melinda Zhao
Job position or title	Manager
Organization name	Print Pack Go
Address	632 Garfield Avenue Suite 501 Morrison, NH 03033
Phone, fax, and e-mail	Phone: 603-555-3123 Fax: 603-555-3125 Email: mzhao@printpackgo.biz
Tagline or motto	For all of your printing and shipping needs
Logo	<none>
Business information set name	Print Pack Go

To Create a Business Information Set

The following steps create a business information set for Print Pack Go, which will be used in multiple publications.

1 Display the Insert tab.

2 Click the Business Information button (Insert tab | Text group) to display the Business Information menu.

3 Click 'Edit Business Information' to display the Business Information dialog box. If a New button is displayed, click the New button (Business Information dialog box) to display the Create New Business Information Set dialog box.

4　Enter the data from Table 6–1, pressing TAB to advance from one field to the next (Figure 6–4).

5　Click the Save button (Create New Business Information Set dialog box).

6　Click the Update Publication button (Business Information dialog box).

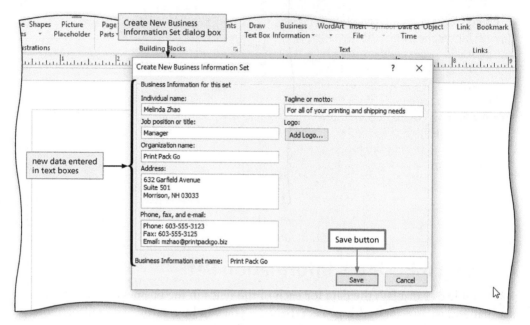

Figure 6–4

To Insert and Format a WordArt Object

The following steps insert a WordArt object to use branding.

1　Zoom to 100% and, if necessary, display the Insert tab.

2　Click the WordArt button (Insert tab | Text group) to display the WordArt gallery.

3　Click the 'Fill - None, Outline - Red' preview in the Plain WordArt Styles area of the WordArt gallery to select it.

4　In the Text text box (Edit WordArt Text dialog box), type **Print Pack Go** to enter the text.

5　Click the Font arrow (Edit WordArt Text dialog box) and then click Century Schoolbook or a similar font.

6　If necessary, click the Size arrow (Edit WordArt Text dialog box) and then click 36 to choose a 36-point font size.

7　Click OK (Edit WordArt Text dialog box) to close the dialog box and insert the WordArt object.

8　Click the Shape Fill arrow (WordArt Tools Format tab | WordArt Styles) and then click 'Accent 4 (RGB (204, 204, 204))' (fourth color in first row) to fill the WordArt with a gray color.

9　Click the Shape Outline arrow (WordArt Tools Format tab | WordArt Styles group) and then click 'Accent 1 (RGB (102, 51, 51))' (second color in first row) to outline the WordArt with a brown color.

10　Click the Shape Outline arrow (WordArt Tools Format tab | WordArt Styles group), point to Weight in the Shape Outline gallery to display the Weight submenu, and then click 1½ pt on the Weight submenu to change the outline weight (Figure 6–5).

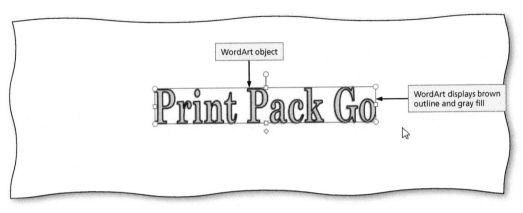

Figure 6–5

Shape Effects

Shape effects change the design and style of a shape or WordArt and other objects.
Shape effects are applied in a way similar to text effects. Many new shape effects are
available in Publisher 2019, including advanced shadows, reflections, glow, soft edges,
bevels, and 3-D rotations, as shown in Table 6–2.

Table 6–2 Shape Effects			
Effect	**Description**	**Gallery Options**	**Adjustable Settings**
Shadow	Semitransparent shading is added to the shape to create the illusion of a shadow and give the shape depth.	Outer Inner Perspective	Transparency Size Blur Angle Distance
Reflection	A replicated shadow with matching borders is added to the shape to create the appearance of a reflection.	Variations	Transparency Size Blur Distance
Glow	Color and shading are added around all sides of the shape so that it seems to glow for decorative emphasis.	Glow Variations	Color Size Transparency
Soft Edges	The edges of a shape are blurred inward a certain amount to make the border less harsh.	Point values	Size
Bevel	Shading and artificial shadows are used to emulate a 3-D beveled edge or contour, which frames the shape.	Bevel	Top Bottom Depth Contour Material Lighting
3-D Rotation	An angle's shape is rotated and backfilled with a shadow effect to apply parallel, perspective, and oblique 3-D effects.	Parallel Perspective	X Rotation Y Rotation Perspective

BTW
WordArt
Design experts recommend
using WordArt sparingly.
As a rule, use WordArt as
decoration rather than to
convey information. Use
only one WordArt object per
publication.

A Shape Effects button is available on both the Drawing Tools Format tab
and the WordArt Tools Format tab. The Picture Tools Format tab displays a similar
Picture Effects button. You will use the 3-D Rotation tool in the next series of steps to
add a 3-D effect to the WordArt.

To Apply a Shape Effect

The following steps format the WordArt object with the 3-D Rotation shape effect. **Why?** *The 3-D effect provides the perception of depth and adds interest to the publication.*

- Scroll the workspace to the right so that objects on the screen will be visible when the gallery is displayed in the next step.

- If necessary, select the shape (in this case, the WordArt object) and then click the Shape Effects button (WordArt Tools Format tab | WordArt Styles group) to display the Shape Effects gallery.

Experiment

- Point to each of the commands, one at a time, and view the choices in each gallery.

- Point to the desired shape effect (in this case, 3-D Rotation) to display the gallery (Figure 6–6).

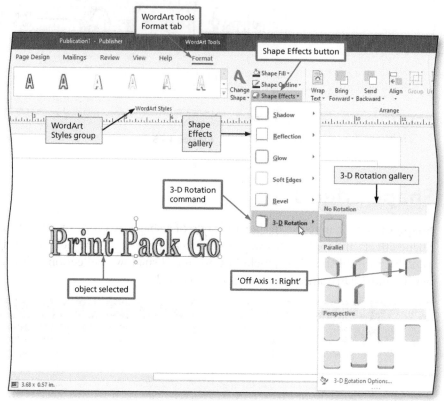

Figure 6–6

2

- Click 'Off Axis 1: Right' in the 3-D Rotation gallery to format the shape (Figure 6–7).

Figure 6–7

Other Ways

1. Click the WordArt Styles Dialog Box Launcher (WordArt Tools Format tab | WordArt Styles group), click Shape Effects button (Format WordArt dialog box | Colors and Lines sheet), click desired effect, click Presets button, click desired thumbnail, click OK (Format Shape dialog box), click OK (Format WordArt dialog box)

To Fine-Tune a Shape Effect

The following steps make changes to the shape effect by adjusting specific settings. *Why? In this case, you have decided that the 3-D effect is too thick, and you want to reduce its depth.*

1

- With the WordArt shape still selected, click the Shape Effects button (WordArt Tools Format tab | WordArt Styles group) to display the Shape Effects gallery.

- Point to 3-D Rotation to display its gallery (Figure 6–8).

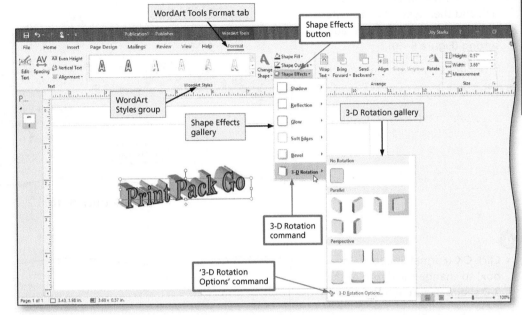

Figure 6–8

2

- Click '3-D Rotation Options' in the gallery to display the Format Shape dialog box for this shape.

- If necessary, drag the title bar of the dialog box to position it so that it does not cover the WordArt shape (Figure 6–9).

Experiment

- Scroll through the choices in the Format Shape dialog box and click various effects to look at their settings.

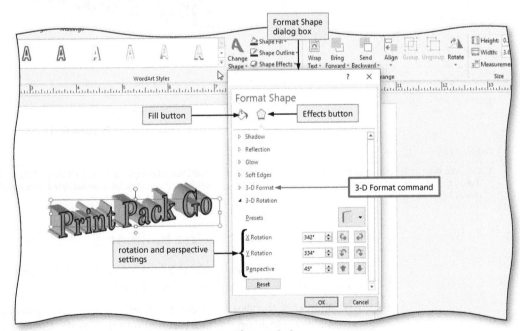

Figure 6–9

Q&A | What does the Fill button at the top of the Format Shape dialog box do?
The Fill button causes Fill settings to appear. The default value is a gray, solid fill for the 3-D effect. You can change the color, type of fill, and apply gradients.

- Click 3-D Format (Format Shape dialog box) to expand the area.

- Select the text in the Depth Size box and then type **12** to enter a value smaller than the default setting (Figure 6–10).

Q&A What does a smaller value do to the shape?

The smaller the value, the thinner the shadowing behind the object, which creates the illusion of a narrower 3-D depth.

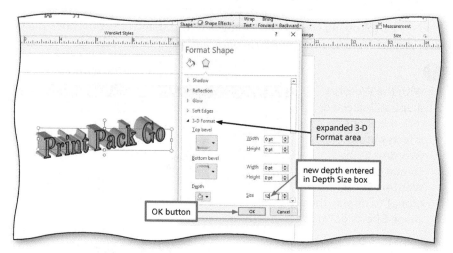

Figure 6–10

- Click OK (Format Shape dialog box) to change the depth of the 3-D shape (Figure 6–11).

Q&A What other options might I change when using a 3-D Rotation shape effect?

In the 3-D Rotation area, the X Rotation box changes the width of the rotation; the Y Rotation box changes the height of the rotation. The Perspective option makes a change only if you chose one of the preset perspective styles.

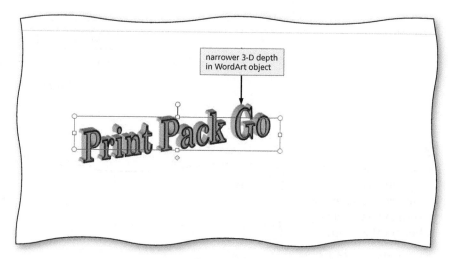

Figure 6–11

Other Ways

1. Click WordArt Styles Dialog Box Launcher (WordArt Tools Format tab | WordArt Styles group), click Shape Effects button (Format WordArt dialog box | Colors and Lines sheet), click desired effect, choose desired settings, click OK (Format WordArt dialog box), click OK (Format Object dialog box)

To Add an Object to the Building Block Library

The following steps add the formatted WordArt object to the Building Block library so that you can use it in multiple publications.

1 Right-click the WordArt object to display a shortcut menu and then click 'Save as Building Block' on the shortcut menu to display the Create New Building Block dialog box.

2 Type **Print Pack Go** to replace the text in the Title text box.

3 Press TAB to move to the Description text box and then type **WordArt brand to use in all publications** to insert a description.

4 Click the Keywords text box and then type `logo, brand, print, pack, go` to enter keywords (Figure 6–12).

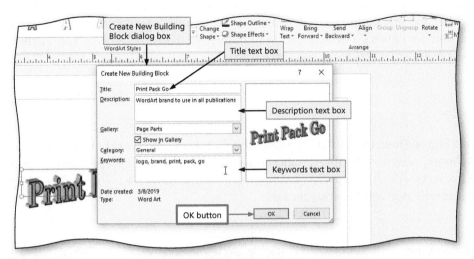

Figure 6–12

5 Accept all other default settings and then click OK (Create New Building Block dialog box) to close the dialog box.

6 To prepare for inserting a table on the page, drag the WordArt object to the scratch area.

7 Save the publication on your desired save location using the file name, SC_PUB_6_WorkSchedule.

Using Tables

The next step is to create a table listing the days, employees, and hours for the company (shown in Figure 6–1a). A Publisher **table** is a collection of contiguous text boxes that are displayed in rows and columns. The intersection of a row and a column is called a **cell**, and cells are filled with text or graphical data. Within a table, you easily can rearrange rows and columns, change column widths and row heights, merge or divide cells, and insert diagonal lines. You can format the cells to give the table a professional appearance, using elements such as preset formats, shading, and cell diagonals. You also can edit the inner gridlines and outer border of a table. For these reasons, many Publisher users create tables rather than using large text boxes with tabbed columns. Tables allow you to enter data in columns as you would for a schedule, price list, resume, or table of contents.

When should you use tables?
Use tables to present numerical and tabular information in an easy-to-digest format. Work with the customer to design a table that is clear and concise. Make sure the table heading and the row and column headings employ standard wording and measurements. Format the table for easy reading. Use recognizable labels for each row and column. Use standard scales and measures. Make sure the readers do not have to spend a lot of time to identify the purpose of the table and grasp the data they are seeking. Use borders, colors, fonts, and alignment to delineate the rows and/or columns.

CONSIDER THIS

The first step in creating a table is to insert an empty table in the publication. When inserting a table, you must specify the number of columns and rows you expect to use. The number of columns and rows is called the **dimension** of the table. In Publisher, the first number in a dimension is the number of columns, and the second is the number of rows. For example, in Publisher, a 2 × 3 (pronounced "two by three") table consists of two columns and three rows.

To Insert an Empty Table

When you click the Table button (Insert tab | Tables group), Publisher presents a grid of rows and columns from which you can choose, as well as the Insert Table command. The following steps insert an empty table with eight columns and five rows. *Why? The numbers are an estimate of how many you will need. If necessary, you can add more columns and insert more rows after creating the table.*

1

- Display the View tab and then click the Whole Page button (View tab | Zoom group) to display the entire page.

- Display the Insert tab.

- Click the Table button (Insert tab | Tables group) to display the Table gallery (Figure 6–13).

Q&A What does Publisher show in the Table gallery?
The gallery displays a grid of clickable squares. The squares represent the columns and rows.

Where will the table be inserted?
Publisher inserts the table in the center of the workspace window.

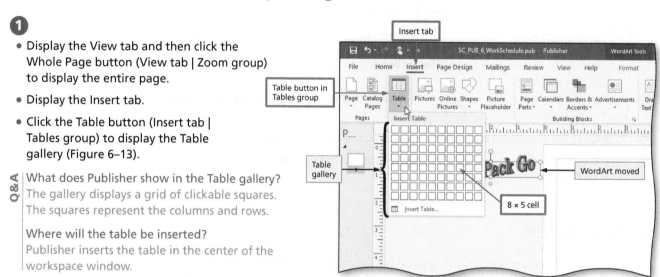

Figure 6–13

2

- In the grid, click the 8 × 5 cell to create a table with eight columns and five rows (shown in Figure 6–14).

Q&A What are the small symbols in the table cells?
Each table cell has an **end-of-cell mark**, which is a formatting mark that assists you with selecting and formatting cells. Formatting marks do not print on a hard copy. The end-of-cell marks currently are left-aligned, that is, positioned at the left edge of each cell.

Other Ways

1. Click Table button (Insert tab | Tables group), click Insert Table, enter number of rows and columns (Create Table dialog box), click OK

To Apply a Table Format

You may have noticed that the ribbon now displays two new tabs. *Why? When working with tables, the Table Tools Layout tab offers buttons and commands that help you in inserting, deleting, merging, and aligning rows, columns, and cells; the Table Tools Design tab provides formatting, border, and alignment options.*

The Table Format gallery (Table Tools Design tab | Table Formats group) allows you to format a table with a variety of colors and shading. The following steps apply a table format to the table in the publication.

1

• If necessary, click the table to select it and then click the Table Tools Design tab (Figure 6–14).

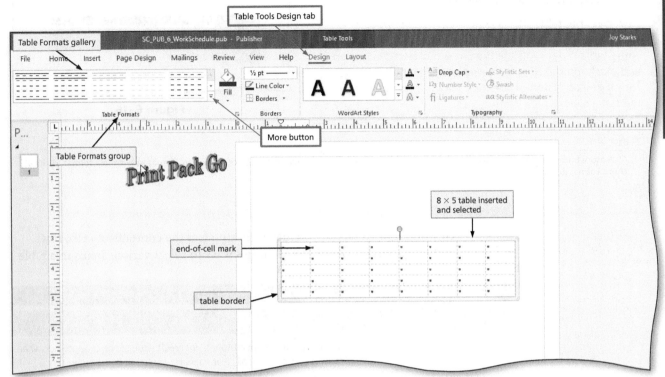

Figure 6–14

2

• Click the More button in the Table Formats gallery (Table Tools Design tab | Table Formats group) to expand the gallery (Figure 6–15).

Q&A My gallery looks different. Did I do something wrong?
No. Depending on your screen resolution, your gallery choices may differ.

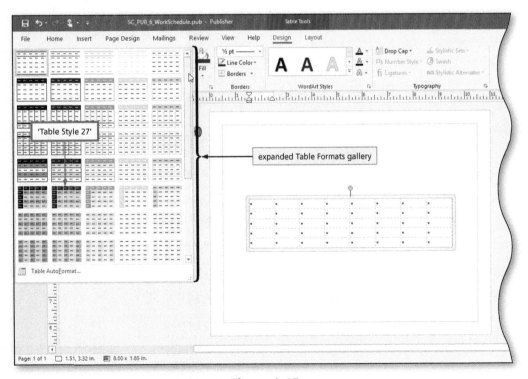

Figure 6–15

● Click 'Table Style 27' in the Table Format gallery to apply the selected style to the table (Figure 6–16).

◄| How does the table style adjust when I add rows and
Q&A| columns?
Some table styles replicate the pattern correctly when you add a column but do not alternate colors when you add a row. If you add rows or columns, you may need to reapply the table style.

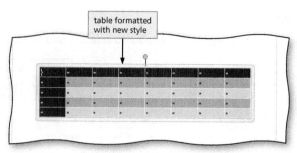

table formatted with new style

Figure 6–16

Other Ways

1. Click More button in Table Formats gallery (Table Tools Design tab | Table Formats group), click Table AutoFormat, select table format, click OK (Auto Format dialog box)

Selecting Table Contents

When working with tables, you may need to select the contents of cells, rows, columns, or the entire table. Table 6–3 identifies ways to select various items in a table.

Table 6–3 Selecting Items in a Table	
Item to Select	**Action**
Cell	If you are using a mouse, point to the upper-left edge of the cell and click when the pointer changes to a small, solid, upward-angled pointing arrow.
	Or, position the insertion point in the cell, click the Select button (Table Tools Layout tab | Table group) and then click Select Cell in the Select gallery.
	Or, right-click the cell, point to Select on the shortcut menu, and then click Select Cell on the Select submenu.
Column	If you are using a mouse, point above the column and click when the pointer changes to a small, solid, downward-pointing arrow.
	Or, position the insertion point in the column, click the Select button (Table Tools Layout tab | Table group), and then click Select Column in the Select gallery.
	Or, right-click the column, point to Select on the shortcut menu, click Select Column on the Select submenu.
Row	If you are using a mouse, point to the left of the row and click when the pointer changes to a right-pointing block arrow.
	Or, position the insertion point in the row, click the Select button (Table Tools Layout tab | Table group), and then click Select Row in the Select gallery.
	Or, right-click the row, point to Select on the shortcut menu, and then click Select Row on the Select submenu.
Multiple cells, rows, or columns adjacent to one another	Drag through cells, rows, or columns.
	Or, select first cell and then hold down SHIFT while selecting the next cell, row, or column.
Next cell	Press TAB.
Previous cell	Press SHIFT+TAB.
Table	Click somewhere in the table, click the Select Table button (Table Tools Layout tab | Table group), and then click Select Table on the Select Table gallery.
	Or, right-click the table, point to Select on the shortcut menu, and then click Select Table on the Select submenu.

To Delete a Column

The following steps delete the eighth column. **Why?** *You previously estimated how many columns you would need. You now realize that you need only seven columns.* Deleting a column also deletes any text or graphics in the column cells.

- If necessary, position the insertion point anywhere in the column that you wish to delete (in this case, the eighth column).

- Click Table Tools Layout on the ribbon to display the Table Tools Layout tab.

- Click the Delete button (Table Tools Layout tab | Rows & Columns group) to display the Delete menu (Figure 6–17).

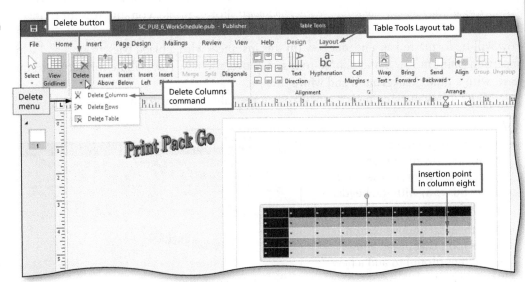

Figure 6–17

Q&A How would I delete just the data in the column?

Drag to select the cells in the column and then press DELETE. Or, right-click the selection and then click Delete Text on the shortcut menu.

- Click Delete Columns on the Delete menu to delete the current column (Figure 6–18).

Q&A How would I delete more than one column?

You could delete them one at a time, or you could select multiple cells, rows, and columns and then Once they are selected, you use the Delete button (Table Tools Layout tab | Rows & Columns group) to delete them.

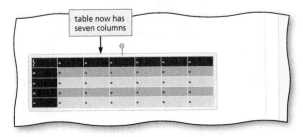

Figure 6–18

Other Ways

1. Right-click cell, point to Delete on shortcut menu, click Delete Columns (Delete submenu)

To Delete a Row

If you wanted to delete a row in a table rather than a column, you would perform the following steps.

1. Position the insertion point in the row that you want to delete.

2. Click the Delete button (Table Tools Layout tab | Rows & Columns group) and then click Delete Rows; or, right-click cell, point to Delete on the shortcut menu, click Delete Rows on the Delete submenu.

To Insert a Row

The next step is to insert a new row. You can insert a row at the end of a table by positioning the insertion point in the bottom-right corner cell and then pressing TAB. You cannot use TAB to insert a row at the beginning or middle of a table. Instead, you use the Insert Above or Insert Below buttons. Where you place the insertion point is important before you decide to insert above or below the current location. ***Why?*** *A new row takes on the formatting of the row that contains the insertion point.* For example, you might want to insert a new row in the table between the first and second rows. If you place the insertion point in row 1 and choose to insert below, the new row will be formatted as a header row (in this instance, with a black background and white text). If you place the insertion point in row 2 and choose to insert above, the new row will be formatted to match the data cells (in this case, with a plum background and white text).

The following step inserts a new row in the table using the ribbon.

- Position the pointer somewhere in the first row of the table because you want to insert a row above this row, with the header formatting.

- Click the Insert Above button (Table Tools Layout tab | Rows & Columns group) to add a new heading row.

- Click elsewhere in the table to remove the selection of the new row (Figure 6–19).

 **Experiment**

- On the Table Tools Layout tab, point to each of the buttons in the Rows & Columns group to view the ScreenTips. In addition, look at the pictures on the buttons themselves, which will help you identify each function.

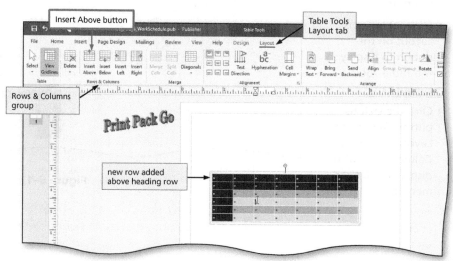

Figure 6–19

Other Ways

1. Right-click row, point to Insert on shortcut menu, click appropriate Insert command

TO INSERT A COLUMN

If you wanted to insert a column in a table rather than a row, you would perform the following steps.

1. Position the insertion point in the column to the left or right of where you want to insert the column.

2. Click the Insert Left button (Table Tools Layout tab | Rows & Columns group) to insert a column to the left of the current column, or click the Insert Right button (Table Tools Layout tab | Rows & Columns group) to insert a column to the right of the current column. Or, you could right-click the column, point to Insert on the shortcut menu, and click Insert Left or Insert Right on the Insert submenu.

To Resize the Table

The following steps resize the table. ***Why?*** *Making the table as large as possible allows for more information in each of the cells and accommodates larger font sizes, which are appropriate for publications intended for posting.*

1

- Using the rulers as a guide, drag the border of the table up and left, to a location approximately 2 inches from the top of the page and 1 inch from the left.

- Using the mouse, point to the lower-right corner of the table border. (Figure 6–20).

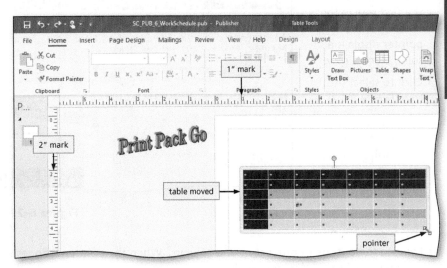

Figure 6–20

2

- When the pointer changes to a double-headed arrow, drag down and to the right until the table border snaps to the lower-right corner margin guides.

- Drag the WordArt object to a location just within the top and left margins.

- Zoom to approximately 60%, if necessary (Figure 6–21).

 What do I do if I have no mouse?
You can resize the table by using the Measurement pane. Tap the Object Size button on the status bar to open the Measurement pane and then enter 9.27" in the Width text box and 6" in the Height text box.

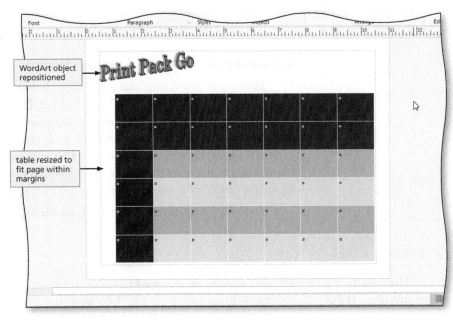

Figure 6–21

Other Ways

1. Right-click table, click Format Table on shortcut menu, enter size of table in Size and rotate area in Size sheet (Format Table dialog box), click OK

To Select a Row

The following step selects the first row. *Why? The row needs to be selected before you can apply formatting.*

1

- Point to the left of the first row in the table until the pointer displays a solid, black arrow.

- Click to select the row (Figure 6–22).

Q&A Why did the cells turn a different color?
In Publisher, the selection highlight reverses the color scheme.

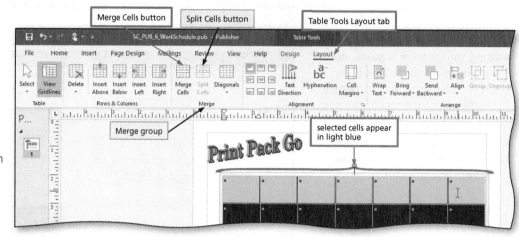

Figure 6–22

Experiment

- Point to the outside of other rows and columns. When the pointer changes to a solid arrow, click to select the row or column. Select the first row again.

Other Ways

1. Drag through all cells in row
2. Right-click cell, click Select on shortcut menu, click Select Row on Select submenu
3. Click cell, click Select button (Table Tools Layout tab | Table tab), click Select Row

To Change Row Heights and Column Widths

When you first create a table, all the columns have the same width, and all the rows have the same height. When you drag a border, the current column or row changes size; all the other columns or rows remain the same, increasing or decreasing the overall size of the table. If you SHIFT+drag a border, the table remains the same size; the rows or columns on either side of the border change size. The only limitation is when changing the row height; you can decrease the height only down to the current font size. If you wanted to change the height of a row or width of a column, you would perform the following step.

1. Drag the bottom border of a row or the right border of a column.

To Merge Cells

The cells in the heading area need to be changed in order to accommodate the desired content, in a process called merging. *Why? The area will hold the table title.* The following step merges multiple cells into a single cell.

1

- With the first row still selected, click the Merge Cells button (Table Tools Layout tab | Merge group) to merge the seven cells into one cell.

- Click elsewhere in the table to view the merged cells (Figure 6–23).

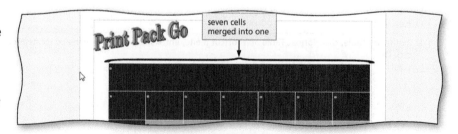

Figure 6–23

To Split Cells

Sometimes, you may want to split a merged cell back into multiple cells. If you wanted to split cells, you would perform the following steps.

1. Position the insertion point in the cell to split.
2. Click the Split Cells button (Table Tools Layout tab | Merge group) (shown in Figure 6–22).

To Create a Cell Diagonal

The following steps create a cell diagonal to accommodate headings for both the column and row in the same cell. A **cell diagonal** is a line that splits the cell diagonally, creating two triangular text boxes. Commonly used for split headings or multiple entries per cell, the cell diagonal can be slanted from either corner.

- Click the first cell in row 2.
- Display the Table Tools Layout tab.
- Click the Diagonals button (Table Tools Layout tab | Merge group) to display the Diagonals menu (Figure 6–24).

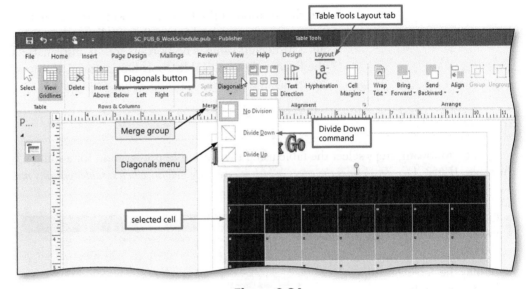

Figure 6–24

- Click Divide Down on the Diagonals menu to create a diagonal in the cell.
- Click outside the table to deselect the cell (Figure 6–25).

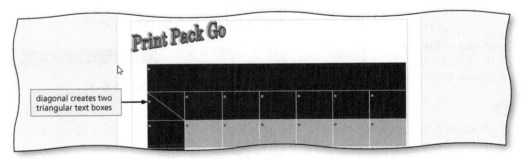

Figure 6–25

To Remove a Diagonal

Sometimes, you may want to remove a previously placed diagonal in a cell. If you wanted to remove the diagonal, you would perform the following steps.

1. Position the insertion point in either side of the diagonal cell.
2. Click the Diagonals button (Table Tools Layout tab | Merge group) to display the Diagonals menu and then click No Division on the Diagonals menu.

Table Borders

In addition to applying a table style and changing columns and rows, you can customize a table by adding borders. As opposed to a page border, a table **border** is the line that is displayed along the edge of a cell, row, or column. It is good practice to format and create borders in the following order:

1. Make your selection. Publisher allows you to add borders to individual cells, rows, columns, or the entire table.

2. Set the weight of the border. The default value is 1/2 pt, but you can change the weight to various point values; the higher the point value, the thicker the border.

3. Set the color of the border. The shades of the color scheme colors display in a palette, but all colors are available.

4. Set the location of the border, choosing from individual borders, inside or outside borders on multiple cells, cell diagonals, all borders, or no border at all. The default value is no borders for an unformatted table. When you click the Borders button (Table Tools Design tab | Borders group) and choose a location, all weight and color settings are applied.

To Select a Table

The following steps select the table using the ribbon in preparation for adding a border on the outside of the table. *Why? A border defines the edges, which is especially helpful when a table contains multiple background colors.*

- Click to position the insertion point in the table.

- Display the Table Tools Layout tab.

- Click the Select button (Table Tools Layout tab | Table group) to display the Select menu (Figure 6–26).

Figure 6–26

- Click Select Table to select the table (shown in Figure 6–27).

Other Ways

1. Right-click table, point to Select on shortcut menu, click Select Table on Select submenu

To Change the Line Weight

The following steps change the weight of the border on all cells in the table. *Why? A thicker border will be more visible if the table is printed or posted online.*

- Display the Table Tools Design tab.

- With the desired portions of the table selected (in this case, the entire table), click the Line Weight button (Table Tools Design tab | Borders group) to display the Line Weight menu (Figure 6–27).

- Click 1 ½ pt on the Line Weight menu to increase the size of the border.

Q&A Nothing seemed to happen. Did I do something wrong?
The default setting is No borders, so the weight setting will not be visible until you choose a location in subsequent steps.

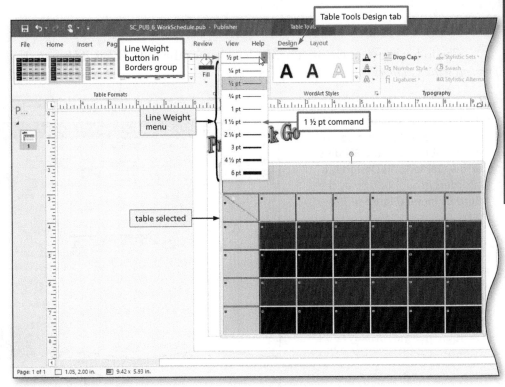

Figure 6–27

Other Ways

1. Right-click table, click Format Table on shortcut menu, click Colors and Lines tab (Format Table dialog box), click desired border preset, enter weight in Width box, click OK

To Change the Border Color

The following steps change the border color. **Why?** *A white color will make the borders stand out more.*

- With the desired portions of the table selected (in this case, the entire table), click the Line Color button (Table Tools Design tab | Borders group) to display the Line Color gallery (Figure 6–28).

- Click 'Accent 5 (White)' as the color (shown in Figure 6–30).

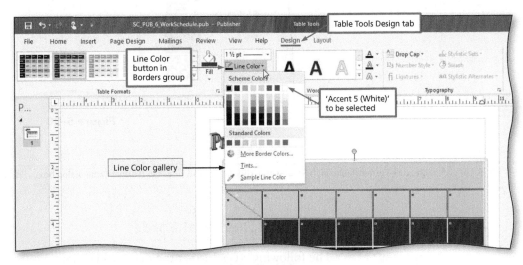

Figure 6–28

Other Ways

1. Right-click table, click Format Table on shortcut menu, click Colors and Lines tab (Format Table dialog box), click desired border preset, click Color button in Line area, select color, click OK

To Add Borders

The following steps choose a border location for the cells. *Why? Adding the border to the table will cause the previous setting changes to appear.*

● With the desired portions of the table selected (in this case, the entire table), click the Borders arrow (Table Tools Design tab | Borders group) to display the Borders menu (Figure 6–29).

Q&A

What happens if I click the Borders button instead of the Borders arrow?

If you click the Borders button, Publisher applies the previous border setting to the current selection. If you point to the button, Publisher displays the current settings as a ScreenTip.

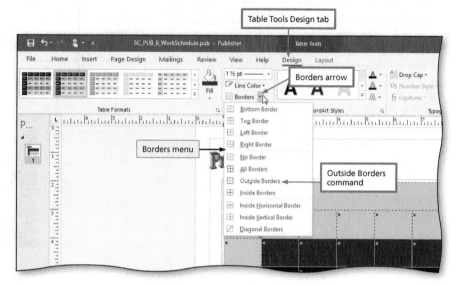

Figure 6–29

● If necessary, click Outside Borders on the Borders menu to add an outside border to the selection.

● Click outside the table to view the borders (Figure 6–30).

Q&A

Does the border appear all the way around the table?

No. The Borders command applies to the cells only, not the entire table.

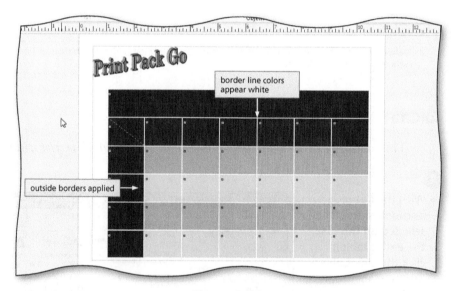

Figure 6–30

Other Ways

1. Right-click table, click Format Table on shortcut menu, click Colors and Lines tab (Format Table dialog box), click desired border preset, click OK

To Format the Diagonal Border

The following steps format the diagonal border.

● Drag to select both sides of the cell containing the diagonal border.

● Click the Borders arrow (Table Tools Design tab | Borders group) to display the Borders menu. If Diagonal Borders is selected, click Diagonal Borders to turn it off.

③ Click the Line Color button (Table Tools Design tab | Borders group) and then click 'Accent 1 (White)' on the Line Color menu to choose white as the color.

④ Click the Borders arrow (Table Tools Design tab | Borders group) to display the Borders menu and then click Diagonal Borders to add a diagonal border to the selection.

⑤ Click outside the selection to view the diagonal border (Figure 6–31).

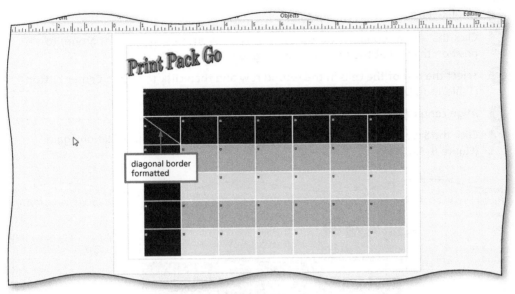

Figure 6–31

To Edit Cell Alignment

As with text box alignment, Publisher offers a variety of options for aligning text within a cell, both vertically and horizontally. The Alignment group on the Table Tools Layout tab also includes options for changing the text direction, applying hyphenation, and specifying cell margins. The following step edits the cell alignment. **Why?** *Aligning the text properly will make the table easier to read.*

①

• Click the left side of the cell containing the diagonal border to position the insertion point.

• Display the Table Tools Layout tab.

• Click the 'Align Bottom Left' button (Table Tools Layout tab | Alignment group) to position the insertion point in the lower-left corner of the cell (Figure 6–32).

Q&A How can I tell if it worked?
Notice the end-of-cell mark positioned in the lower-left corner of the cell. This indicates that text will appear at that position.

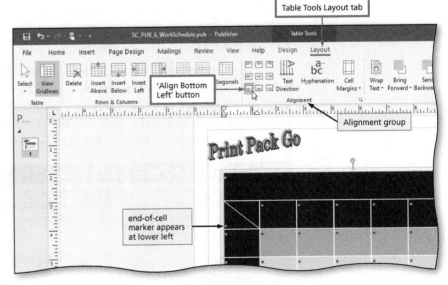

Figure 6–32

To Align and Format Other Cells

The following steps align the other cells in the table.

1 Click the right side of the cell containing the diagonal border to position the insertion point.

2 Display the Home tab and change the font color to 'Accent 5 (White)'.

3 Display the Table Tools Layout tab.

4 Click the 'Align Top Right' button (Table Tools Layout tab | Alignment group) to position the text at the top and right-aligned.

5 Select the rest of the cells in the second row and then click the Align Center button (Table Tools Layout tab | Alignment group).

6 Align center the cell in the first row.

7 Click the Save button on the Quick Access Toolbar to save the publication again (Figure 6–33).

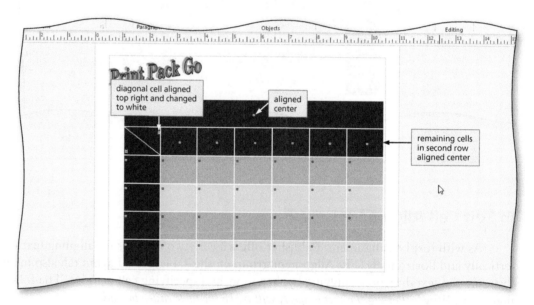

Figure 6–33

Entering Data in Tables

The next step is to enter text in the table cells. To place text in a cell, you click the cell and then type. To advance from one cell to the next, press TAB. When you are at the rightmost cell in a row, press TAB to move to the first cell in the next row. To move up or down within the table, use the arrow keys or simply click the desired cell.

Table 6–4 displays the data for the work schedule table.

Table 6–4 Data for the Work Schedule Table						
Front Counter Work Schedule for the Week of April 5, 2021						
Name/Days	Monday	Tuesday	Wednesday	Thursday	Friday	Saturday
Gracie	9-5	9-5	9-5	9-5	9-5	
Jianguo	9-3	9-3	9-3	9-3	9-3	9-12
Ben	3-7	3-7	3-7	3-7		9-5
Allegria	5-7	5-7	5-7	5-7	5-7	12-5

To Enter Data in a Table

The following steps enter data in the table. As you enter data, be careful when pressing ENTER. *Why?* *ENTER is used to begin a new paragraph within a cell. You cannot add new rows or columns by pressing ENTER. Pressing* SHIFT+ENTER, *however, creates a new line within the cell without the extra spacing adding for a new paragraph.*

- Click the left side of the cell containing the diagonal border.
- Change the font size to 14.
- Type **Name** to complete the text.
- Press TAB to move to the next cell.
- Change the font to size 14 and click the Bold button (Home tab | Fonts group). Type **Days** to complete the text in the diagonal cells (Figure 6–34).

Q&A How do I edit cell contents if I make a mistake?
Click in the cell and then correct the entry.

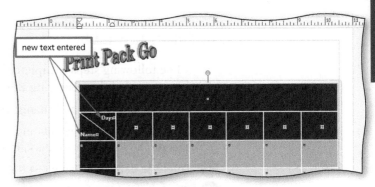

Figure 6–34

- Select the rest of the cells in the second row.
- Change the font size to 18.
- Type the days of the week, Monday through Saturday, in the cells to the right of the diagonal cell.
- If necessary, SHIFT+drag the right border of the Wednesday column to the right so that the word does not wrap and hyphenate. Adjust any other column widths to prevent hyphenation (Figure 6–35).

Q&A Why are my row headings bold?
The table format you selected includes bold headings.

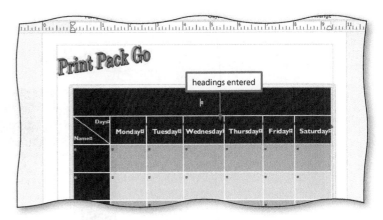

Figure 6–35

- Click the cell in the top row and change the font size to 28.
- Type **Front Counter Work Schedule** and then press SHIFT+ENTER to move to the next line.
- Type **for the Week of April 5, 2021** to complete the heading (Figure 6–36).

Q&A Why would I perform the formatting before entering the text?
Formatting first saves keystrokes. You do not have to go back and select to add the formatting.

What if I have more data than will fit in a cell?
By default, the data you enter in a cell wraps just as text wraps between the margins of a text box. You can turn off that feature by clicking to remove the check mark in the 'Grow to Fit Text' check box (Table Tools Layout tab | Size group).

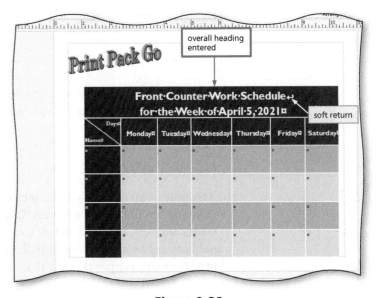

Figure 6–36

Deleting Table Data

To delete the contents of a cell, select the cell contents and then press DELETE or BACKSPACE. You also can drag and drop or cut and paste the contents of cells. To delete an entire table, select the table, click the Delete button (Table Tools Layout tab | Rows & Columns group), and then click Delete Table on the Delete menu.

To Finish the Table

The following steps complete the table by changing the font size, changing the cell alignment, and then entering the rest of the data.

1 Select all empty cells and change the font size to 18.

2 Select all empty cells in columns 2 through 7. Align Top Center the columns and change the font color to black, if necessary.

3 Enter the data from Table 6–4 (Figure 6–37).

4 Check the publication for spelling errors, ignoring personal names.

5 Click the Save button on the Quick Access Toolbar to save the publication again. Close the file.

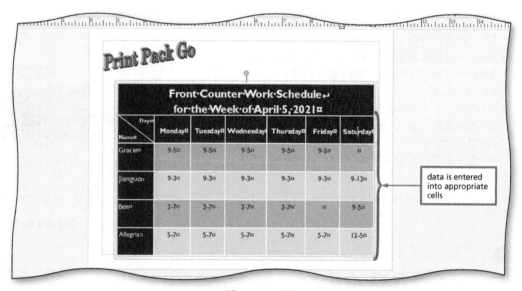

Figure 6–37

Break Point: If you want to take a break, this is a good place to do so. Exit Publisher. To resume later, start Publisher and continue following the steps from this location forward.

Calendars

The next series of steps creates a calendar. Publisher can format a calendar with any combination of months and year. Calendar cells, like table cells, can be formatted with colors, borders, text, and styles. You can create calendars as independent, stand-alone publications or insert them as building blocks in other publications. Calendars are used for many purposes other than just presenting dates. Information that changes from day to day can be presented as text in a calendar, such as school lunches, practice schedules, homework assignments, or appointments and meetings. Colors and graphics are used in calendars to display holidays, special events, reminders, and even phases of the moon.

CONSIDER THIS

Why do companies create promotional pieces?
A **promotional piece**, or **promo**, is an inclusive term for a publication or an article that includes advertising and marketing information for a product or service known to and purchased by customers and clients. Companies create promotional pieces that will increase company recognition. Make sure that promotional pieces are useful to customers.

Including calendars in a publication can date the material because the publication may not be useful after the calendar date has passed. Companies should consider carefully whether to include calendars in publications.

To Create a Calendar

The following steps create a 12-month calendar. *Why? Print Pack Go wants to use a calendar as a promotional piece.*

1

- Click Built-In in the New screen (Backstage view) to display the built-in templates.
- Click the Calendars thumbnail to display the calendar templates.
- Click the Level calendar template to select it.
- If necessary, click the Color scheme button in the Customize area and then click Cavern in the list to choose a color scheme.
- If necessary, click the Font scheme button and then click Solstice in the list to choose a font scheme.
- If necessary, click the Business information button and then click 'Print Pack Go' to select it.
- If necessary, scroll to display the remaining settings (Figure 6–38).

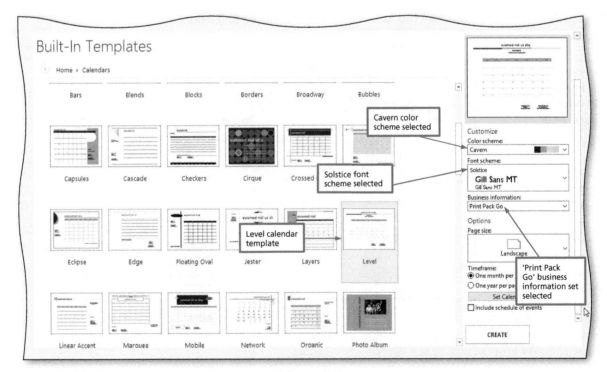

Figure 6–38

2

- If necessary, click the Page size arrow in the Options area and then click Landscape in the list to choose landscape orientation.

- If necessary, click the 'One month per page' option button to select it.

- Click the 'Set Calendar Dates' button to display the Set Calendar Dates dialog box.

- Click the Start date button (Set Calendar Dates dialog box) to display the list of months (Figure 6–39).

Q&A How can I create a one-month calendar?

To create just one month on one page, use the same month and date in both the Start date and End date boxes (Set Calendar Dates dialog box).

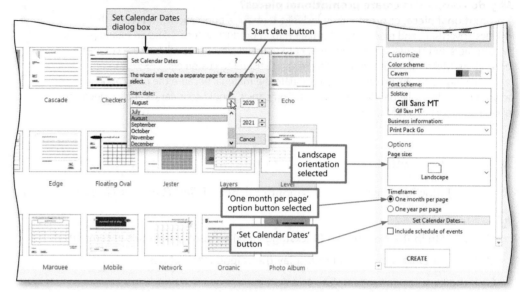

Figure 6–39

3

- Scroll as necessary and then click January to select the starting month.

- If necessary, click the up or down arrow on the Start date year box (Set Calendar Dates dialog box) until 2021 is displayed.

- Click the End date button and then click December to choose the ending month.

- If necessary, click the up or down arrow on the End year box until 2021 is displayed (Figure 6–40).

Q&A What kind of object is the year box with the up and down arrows?

Microsoft refers to this as a numerical up and down box. Such boxes commonly are used for fixed data in a sequential list from which the user can choose. You also can type in a numerical up and down box.

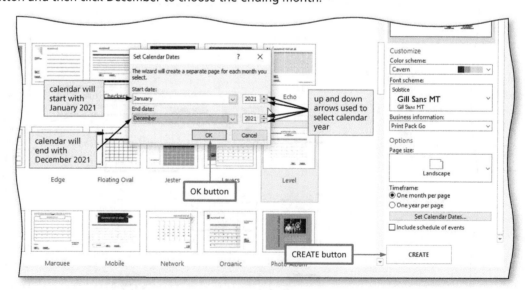

Figure 6–40

4

- Click OK (Set Calendar Dates dialog box) to set the dates and close the dialog box.

- Click the CREATE button in Backstage view to create the calendar (Figure 6-41).

Q&A Why do so many thumbnails appear in the Page Navigation pane? Because you selected January through December, Publisher created 12 pages, one for each month.

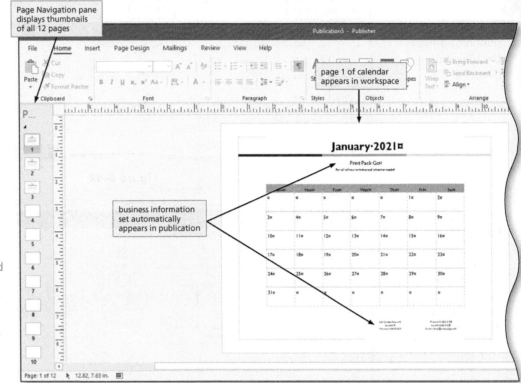

Figure 6–41

5

- Save the publication on your desired save location using the file name, SC_PUB_6_Calendar.

Master Pages

A **master page** is a background area that is repeated across all pages of a publication. Similar to the header and footer areas in traditional word processing software, a master page requires you to enter the information or insert the objects only once to synchronize them across all pages. The master page is the ideal place for a watermark, a page border, or repeating graphics. When you access the master page, Publisher displays a new tab (shown in Figure 6–43).

Each publication starts with one master page. If you have a multipage publication, you can choose to use two different master pages for cases such as facing pages in a book; in those circumstances, you might want different graphics in the background of each page. If you want to display master page objects only on certain pages, the Apply To button (Master Page tab | Master Page group) provides several options. This is useful for cases such as background images on every page except the title page in a longer publication or a watermark on the inside of a brochure but not on the front. In the calendar publication, you will create a page border and use the building block you created earlier in the module.

To View the Master Page

The following steps view the master page. *Why? The master page is a special page that cannot be accessed via the Page Navigation pane.*

1

- Click View on the ribbon to display the View tab (Figure 6-42).

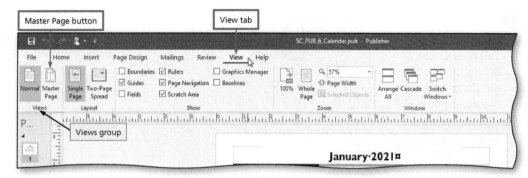

Master Page button

View tab

Views group

January·2021¤

Figure 6–42

2

- Click the Master Page button (View tab | Views group) to access the master page and to display the Master Page tab on the ribbon (Figure 6–43).

Q&A Why is the scratch area a different color?
Publisher uses a different color to remind you that you are not in the regular publication window. This helps you remember to close the master page before continuing with the other objects in the publication.

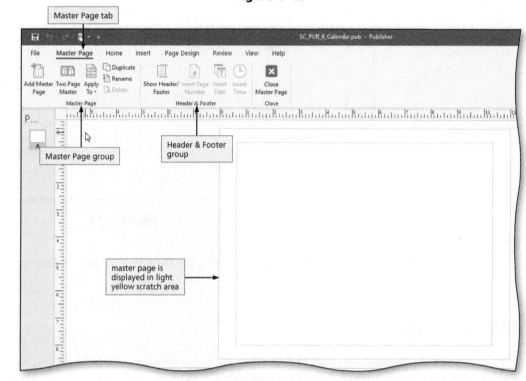

Master Page tab

Master Page group

Header & Footer group

master page is displayed in light yellow scratch area

Figure 6–43

Other Ways

1. Click the Master Pages button (Page Design tab | Page Background group), click 'Edit Master Pages' on Master Pages menu

2. Press CTRL+M

BorderArt

BorderArt is a group of customizable graphical borders, such as patterns, hearts, apples, balloons, or decorative shapes, that can be added as an edge or a border to a shape, a text box, or the entire page. BorderArt makes the page margins stand out and adds interest to the page. Placing BorderArt on a master page causes the border to appear on every page of the publication.

To Add BorderArt

The following steps create a rectangle shape on the master page and apply BorderArt. *Why? BorderArt creates a page border for each page of the calendar.*

1

- Display the Insert tab.

- Click the Shapes button (Insert tab | Illustrations group) and then click the Rectangle shape.

- Drag to draw a rectangle that fills the area within the margins.

- Right-click the shape to display a shortcut menu (Figure 6–44).

Q&A Should I allow for a margin around the rectangle?
No. The company will send out this publication for professional printing and binding. Most professional printers can print right to the edge of the page.

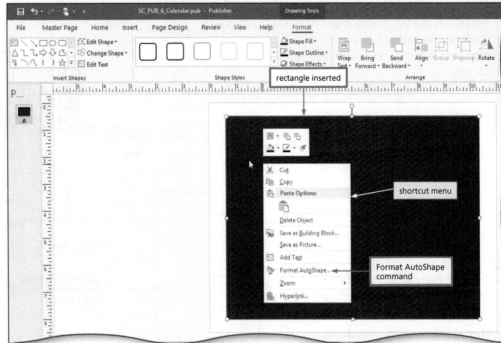

Figure 6–44

2

- Click Format AutoShape on the shortcut menu to display the Format AutoShape dialog box.

- If necessary, click the Colors and Lines tab (Format AutoShape dialog box). Click the Color button in the Fill area to display the Color gallery (Figure 6–45).

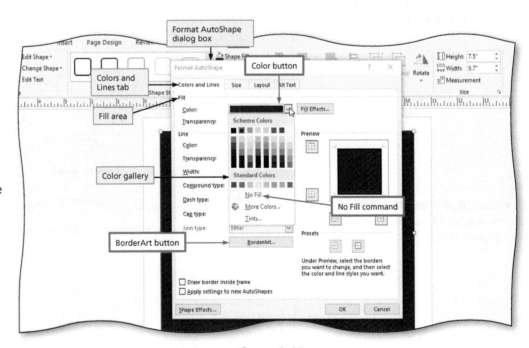

Figure 6–45

3

- Click No Fill in the Color gallery to create a shape without any fill color.

- Click the BorderArt button to display the BorderArt dialog box.

- Scroll as necessary in the Available Borders area and then click the Twisted Line border to select it and display it in the Preview area.

- If necessary, click the 'Stretch pictures to fit' option button to select it (Figure 6–46).

Experiment

- Scroll to view all the available borders in the list. Notice that some are repeating square elements and others use special corners.

 Q&A Could I use one of my own pictures as a BorderArt? Yes, you can click the Create Custom button (BorderArt dialog box) and then navigate to your storage location.

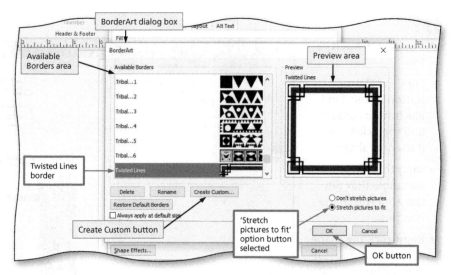

Figure 6–46

4

- Click OK (BorderArt dialog box) to return to the Format AutoShape dialog box.

- Click the Color button in the Line area and then choose 'Accent 2 (RGB (155, 153, 204))' (third color in first row).

- Select the text in the Width text box and then type **30 pt** to enter the width (Figure 6–47).

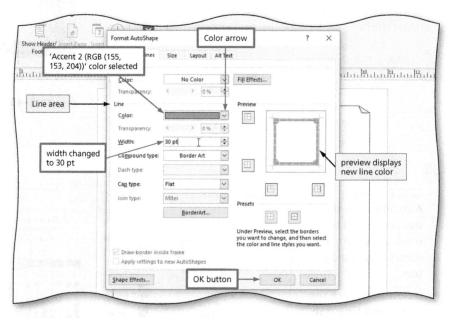

Figure 6–47

5

- Click OK (Format AutoShape dialog box) to apply the border (Figure 6–48).

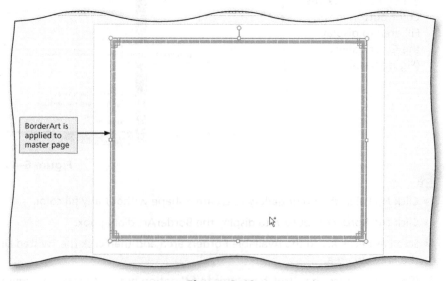

Figure 6–48

To Insert a Building Block

The following steps insert the Print Pack Go building block on the master page. *Why? Placing the building block on the master page will cause it to appear on each page of the calendar.*

- Display the Insert tab.
- Click the Page Parts button (Insert tab | Building Blocks group) to display the Page Parts gallery (Figure 6–49).

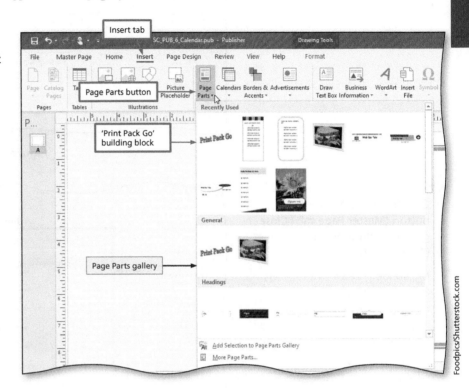

Figure 6–49

2

- Click the 'Print Pack Go' building block in the Page Parts gallery to insert the graphic on the master page.
- Drag the graphic to the lower-left corner of the master page so that it almost touches the decorative border (Figure 6–50).

Experiment

- Click the Color Options button to view the choices for the building block.

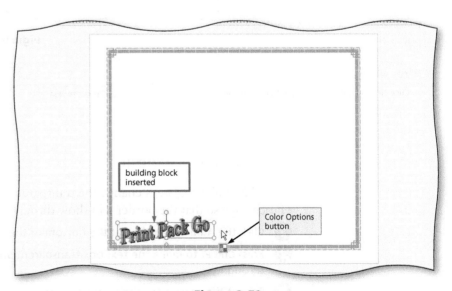

Figure 6–50

Foodpics/Shutterstock.com

To Close the Master Page

The following steps close the master page and return to the regular page layout and Publisher workspace. *Why? You are finished with the background elements and need to work on the calendar pages.*

- Click Master Page on the ribbon to display the Master Page tab (Figure 6–51).

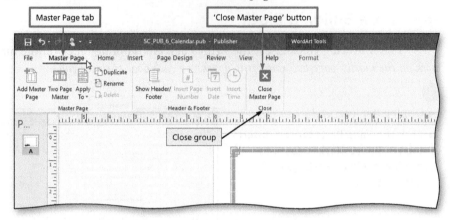

Figure 6–51

- Click the 'Close Master Page' button (Master Page tab | Close group) to close the master page (Figure 6–52).

Q&A

My building block overlaps the calendar. What should I do?
Open the master page again and move the building block slightly down and to the left.

What else could I add to the master page?
You could add a background effect, headers, footers, or any text or graphics that you want to appear on every page of the publication.

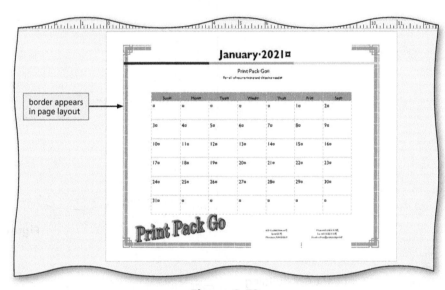

Figure 6–52

Other Ways

1. Click Normal button (View tab | Views group)   2. Press CTRL+M

To Finish the Calendar

The following steps change the transparency on the two text boxes at the bottom of each page so that the border will show through.

1. Click the Address text box at the bottom of the January 2021 calendar to select it.

2. Press CTRL+T to make the text box transparent and allow the BorderArt to show through.

3. Repeat the process for the Phone text box.

4. Click the Page 2 thumbnail in the Page Navigation pane. Repeat Steps 1 through 3 to change the text boxes.

5 Repeat the process for each page in the calendar (Figure 6–53).

6 Click the Save button on the Quick Access Toolbar to save the file with the same file name in the same location.

7 Close the file without exiting Publisher.

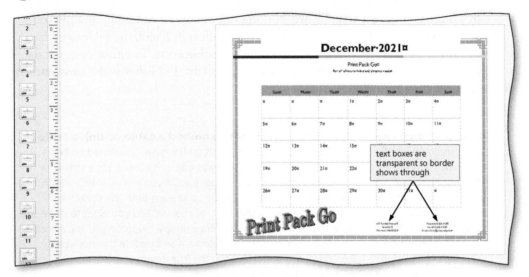

December·2021¤

Print·Pack·Go¤

text boxes are transparent so border shows through

Figure 6–53

To Save the Calendar Pages as Images

If you wanted to send the calendar or another publication to a professional printer with each page as a separate image, you would perform the following steps.

1. Click File to open Backstage view and then click Export to display the Export screen.
2. Click the 'Save for Photo Printing' button to display the Save for Photo Printing screen.
3. Click the 'JPEG Images for Photo Printing' button and then choose either the JPEG or the TIFF file format.
4. Click the 'Save Image Set' button to display the Choose Location dialog box.
5. Click the New folder button (Choose Location dialog box). Type the name of the new folder, such as Calendar Pages, and then press ENTER.
6. Click the Select Folder button (Choose Location dialog box) to save the publication pages as images.

Break Point: If you want to take a break, this is a good place to do so. Exit Publisher, if necessary. To resume later, start Publisher and continue following the steps from this location forward.

Using Excel Tables

In this module, you will integrate Microsoft Excel when you create a Publisher table. An **Excel-enhanced table** uses Excel tools to enhance Publisher's table formatting capabilities; it takes advantage of Excel functionality to add items such as totals, averages, charts, and other financial functions. You can paste, create, or insert an Excel-enhanced table into a Publisher publication. Two types of Excel-enhanced tables are available: embedded and linked.

BTW

Conserving Ink and Toner
If you want to conserve ink or toner, you can instruct Publisher to print draft quality documents by clicking File on the ribbon to open Backstage view, and then clicking Print in the Backstage view to display the Print screen. Click the Printer Properties link, and then, depending on your printer, click the Print Quality button and choose Draft in the list. Close the Printer Properties dialog box and then click the Print button as usual.

BTW
External Files
When using files or objects created by others, do not use the source document unless you are certain it does not contain a virus or other malicious content. Use antivirus software to verify that any files you use are free of viruses and other potentially harmful programs.

BTW
Distributing a Document
Instead of printing and distributing a hard copy of a document, you can distribute the document electronically. Options include sending the document via email; posting it on cloud storage (such as OneDrive) and sharing the file with others; posting it on social media, a blog, or other website; and sharing a link associated with an online location of the document. You also can create and share a PDF or XPS image of the document, so that users can view the file in Acrobat Reader or XPS Viewer instead of in Publisher.

An **embedded** table uses Excel data and can be manipulated with some Excel functionality; however, the data becomes part of the Publisher publication and must be edited with Publisher running. Publisher displays Excel tabs on the ribbon to help you edit an embedded table. On the other hand, a **linked** table is connected permanently to an Excel worksheet; it is updated automatically from the Excel worksheet. When you edit a linked table, you actually are working in Excel, with full functionality. You can edit a linked table in Excel or Publisher. If you edit it in Excel, the table is updated automatically the next time you open the Publisher publication. In either case, the data you use from the Excel file is called the **source** document. Publisher is the **destination** document.

CONSIDER THIS

How should you make the decision whether to embed a table or link a table?
The decision on whether to embed or link a table depends on the data. You would embed a table when you want a static, or unchanging, table that you edit in Publisher. For example, a table from last year's sales probably is not going to change; thus, if you embed it into a Publisher brochure about the company's sales history, it will look the same each time you open the publication. You would link a table when the data is likely to change, and you want to make sure the publication reflects the current data in the Excel file. For example, suppose you link a portion or all of an Excel worksheet to a Publisher investment statement and update the worksheet quarterly in Excel. With a linked table, any time you open the investment statement in Publisher, the latest update of the worksheet will be displayed as part of the investment statement; in other words, the most current data always will appear in the statement.

The process of integrating an Excel table can be performed in one of three ways: you can create an embedded table from scratch, you can paste an embedded or linked table, or you can insert an embedded or linked table from a file.

In this project, you will create a letter and insert an embedded table. You then will format the Excel-enhanced table.

To Create the Letterhead

The following steps create a letterhead that Print Pack Go will use to send a letter and table to the Print Pack Go managers.

1. Click Built-In in the New screen in Backstage view to display the built-in templates.

2. Click the Letterhead thumbnail to display the letterhead templates.

3. If necessary, click the Level template to select it.

4. If necessary, click the Color scheme button in the Customize area and then click Cavern in the list to choose a color scheme.

5. If necessary, click the Font scheme button and then click Solstice in the list to choose a font scheme.

6. If necessary, click the Business information button and then click 'Print Pack Go' to select it.

7. If necessary, click to remove the check mark in the Include logo check box (Figure 6–54).

8. Click the CREATE button to create the letterhead.

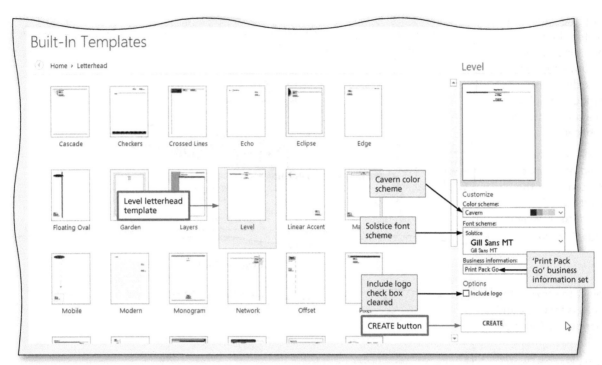

Figure 6–54

To Format the Letterhead

The following steps format the letterhead. *Why? You need to customize the publication and insert the Print Pack Go building block.*

- Zoom to 120% and scroll to the top of the page.

- Delete the business name text box that displays Print Pack Go.

- Drag around the remaining objects on the page to select them (Figure 6–55).

Q&A I am having trouble selecting by dragging. What should I do?
You can SHIFT+click the graphic and each of the text boxes to select the multiple items.

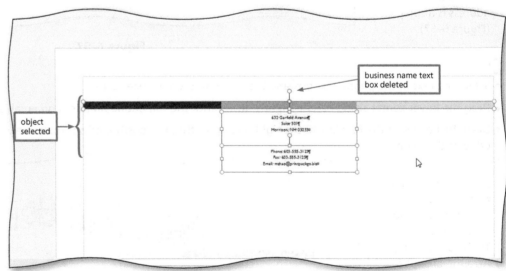

Figure 6–55

- SHIFT+drag the selection down to approximately 1.5 inches from the top of the page.

Q&A Why am I holding down SHIFT while I drag?
SHIFT moves the selection in a straight line.

- Display the Insert tab.

- Click the Page Parts button (Insert tab | Building Blocks group) and then click the 'Print Pack Go' graphic to insert it into the publication.

- SHIFT+drag the building block to the center of the page, just above the decorative line (Figure 6–56).

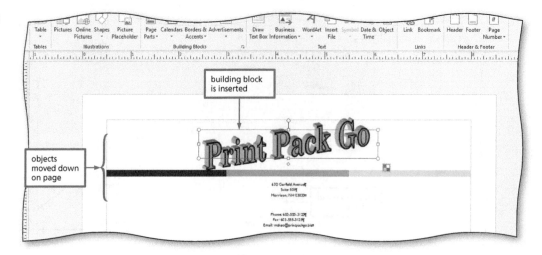

Figure 6–56

❸

- Select the text in the address text box and change the font size to 10.

- SHIFT+drag the text box to the left until it is approximately 1 inch from the left edge of the paper.

- Drag the lower-center sizing handle slightly down until the full address is displayed (Figure 6–57).

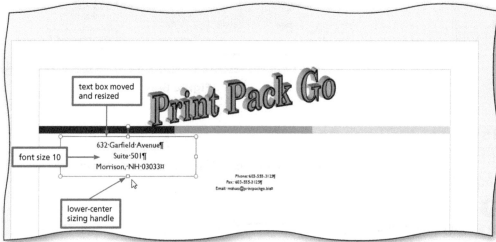

Figure 6–57

❹

- Select the text in the phone text box and then change the font size to 10.

- Drag the lower-center sizing handle slightly down until the full phone number and email address are displayed.

- Drag the border of the text box to the right and up so that it is positioned approximately 1 inch from the right edge of the paper.

- Select both the address and phone text boxes and then click the Align button (Drawing Tools Format tab | Arrange group) to display the Align menu. Click Align Top (Figure 6–58).

❺

- Save the publication on your desired save location using the file name, SC_PUB_6_QuoteLetter.

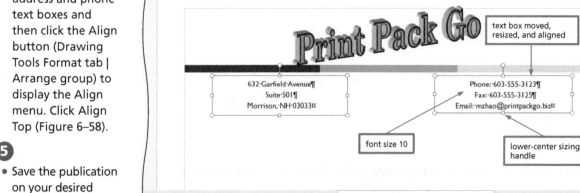

Figure 6–58

To Format the Body of the Letter

The following steps create a text box and enter text for the body of the letter.

1 Zoom to Whole Page view.

2 Click the 'Draw Text Box' button (Insert tab | Text group) and then drag to create a text box in the center of the page.

3 Click the Measurement button (Drawing Tools Form tab | Size group) to open the Measurement pane.

4 Type `.5` for the left (x), `2.5` for the right (y), `7.25` for the width, and `5.25` for the height in the Measurement pane.

5 Click inside the text box, if necessary, and set the font size to 12 pt.

6 Click the Paragraph Dialog Box Launcher (Home tab | Paragraph group) to display the Paragraph dialog box.

7 If necessary, change the After paragraphs setting to 6pt (Figure 6–59).

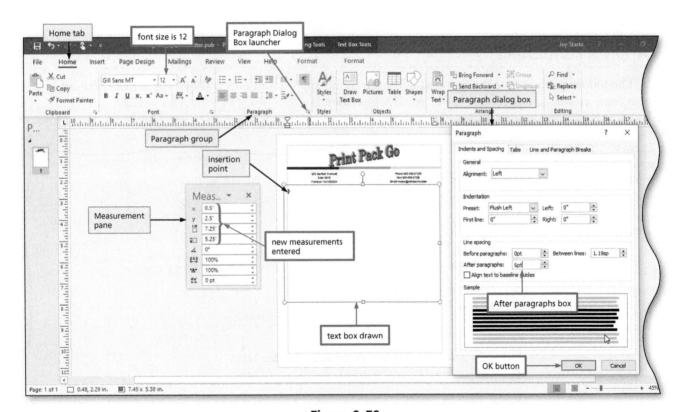

Figure 6–59

8 Click OK (Paragraph dialog box) to close the dialog box. Close the Measurement pane.

Font Effects

Font effects are predefined formatting options that provide more choices than the more commonly used bold, underline, and italic formats. For example, you can apply a **superscript** font effect so that text or a number is raised slightly above the normal baseline of text. Superscripts are used for abbreviations, footnotes, and other cases where you want a raised number. Conversely, you can apply a **subscript** font effect to create small numbers placed below the normal text baseline, such as those used in scientific and chemical notations.

Table 6–5 lists the font effects for Publisher, along with a sample and description for each one.

Table 6–5 Font Effects		
Effect	**Sample**	**Description**
All Caps	ALL CAPS	All uppercase letters, as when using CAPS LOCK
Small Caps	SMALL CAPS	All uppercase letters, displayed at the same height as normal lowercase letters
Strikethrough	~~Strikethrough~~	Each letter has a hyphen through it
Subscript	H_2O	Smaller-sized letter or number printed slightly below the baseline
Superscript	Superscript[47]	Smaller-sized letter or number printed slightly above the baseline
Underline	Double dash wavy	Various types of underlines besides the standard underscore character

To Apply a Font Effect

The following steps type the first part of the letter and apply a font effect. **Why?** *The author of the letter wants to create an ordinal number (i.e., the th should be superscript).*

- Zoom to 150% and scroll to the top of the text box.

- Type the first part of the letter as shown in Figure 6–60.

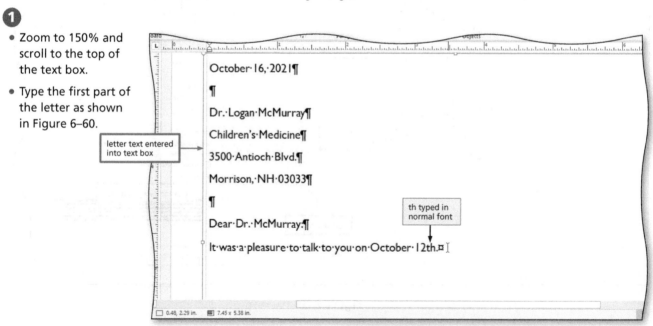

letter text entered into text box

October·16,·2021¶

¶

Dr.·Logan·McMurray¶

Children's·Medicine¶

3500·Antioch·Blvd.¶

Morrison,·NH·03033¶

¶

Dear·Dr.·McMurray:¶

It·was·a·pleasure·to·talk·to·you·on·October·12th.¤

th typed in normal font

0.48, 2.29 in.   7.45 x 5.38 in.

Figure 6–60

- Select the letters th after the date.

- Click the Font Dialog Box launcher (Home tab | Font group) to display the Font dialog box.

- Click to display a check mark in the Superscript check box (Figure 6–61).

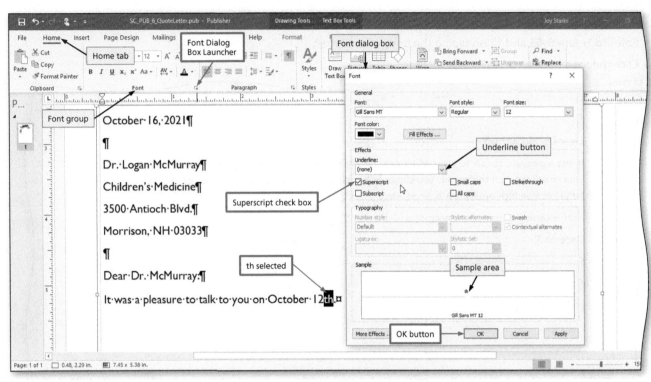

Figure 6–61

 Experiment

- One at a time, click the other font effects and look at the preview in the Sample area. Click the Underline button to see a list of additional underline choices. When you are done, turn off all font effects except the superscript.

3

- Click OK (Font dialog box) and then click away from the selection to view the superscript (Figure 6–62).

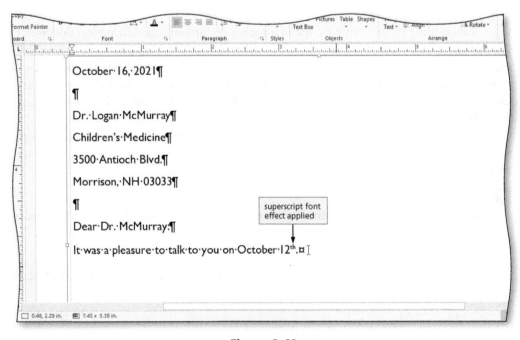

Figure 6–62

4

- Refer to Figure 6–63 and finish typing the body of the letter.
- Click the Save button (Quick Access Toolbar).

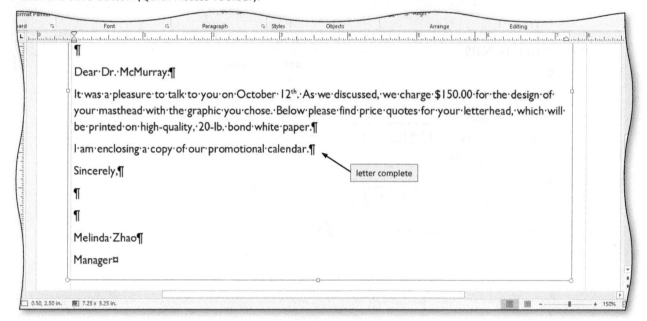

Figure 6–63

Other Ways

1. Select text, press CTRL+SHIFT++   2. Click Superscript button (Home tab | Font group)

To Create an Embedded Table

Embedding means using a copy of a source document in a destination document without establishing a permanent link. Embedded objects can be edited; however, changes do not affect the source document. For example, if a business embedded an Excel worksheet into its Publisher electronic newsletter that contained updatable fields, users viewing the publication in Publisher could enter their personal data into the embedded table and recalculate the totals. Those users would not need access to the original Excel worksheet. *Why?* *Publisher embeds the necessary Excel commands.*

The following steps create an embedded table showing the prices of various copies. You will retrieve the values from an Excel file. To complete these steps, you will be required to use the Data Files. Please contact your instructor for information about accessing the Data Files.

 1

- Zoom to Whole Page view and then scroll to the right of the page layout to display more of the scratch area in the Publisher workspace. If necessary, deselect any selected object.

- Display the Insert tab.

- Click the Object button (Insert tab | Text group) to display the Insert Object dialog box (Figure 6–64).

Q&A | Why should I insert the table in the scratch area?
It is easier to work with tables outside the publication and then move them to the page layout after editing.

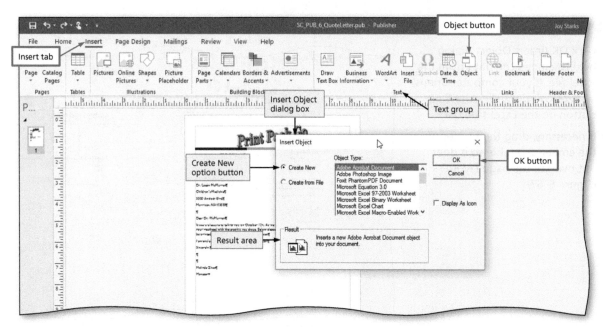

Figure 6–64

 Experiment

- Scroll through the list of object types to view the different kinds of documents and graphics that you can embed. Click the object types to read a description in the Result area.

2

- Click the 'Create from File' option button to select it (Insert Object dialog box) (Figure 6–65).

Q&A What does the Create New option button do?
You would click the Create New option button if you wanted to create an embedded table or another object from scratch.

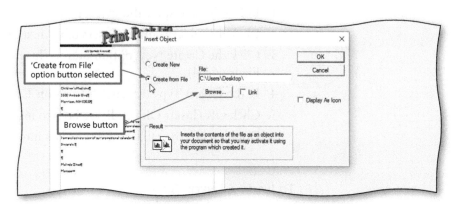

Figure 6–65

3

- Click the Browse button to display the Browse dialog box.

- Navigate to the location of the Data Files on your computer.

- Double-click the Excel file named Support_PUB_6_CopyPrices.xlsx (Browse dialog box) to select the file and return to the Insert Object dialog box (Figure 6–66).

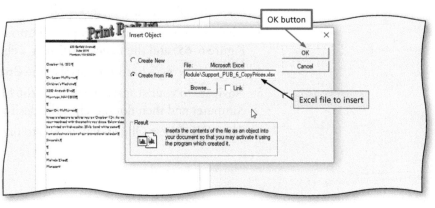

Figure 6–66

4

- Click OK (Insert Object dialog box) to embed the data from the Excel file. If your computer opens an Excel window, click the Close button on the Excel title bar.
- If necessary, drag the border of the embedded table so it does not overlap the page layout (Figure 6–67).

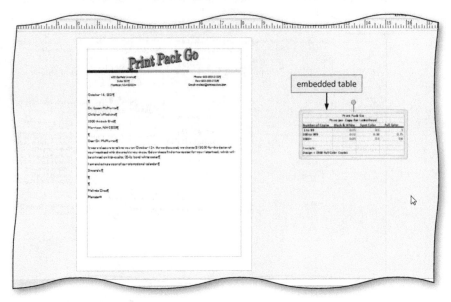

Figure 6–67

To Create an Embedded Table from Scratch

If you wanted to create an embedded table from scratch, you would perform the following steps.

1. In Publisher, display the Insert tab.
2. Click the Object button (Insert tab | Text group).
3. Click the Create New option button (Insert Object dialog box) (shown in Figure 6–64).
4. In the Object Type list, click 'Microsoft Excel Worksheet'.
5. Click OK (Insert Object dialog box) to insert the table.
6. Double-click the table and insert data into each cell.

To Insert a Linked Table

If you wanted to create a linked table, you would perform the following steps.

1. In Publisher, display the Insert tab.
2. Click the Object button (Insert tab | Text group).
3. Click the 'Create from File' option button (Insert Object dialog box) (shown in Figure 6–65) and then click to display a check mark in the Link check box.
4. Click the Browse button to display the Browse dialog box.
5. Navigate to your storage location or the location of the Data Files on your computer and then double-click the desired Excel file (Browse dialog box).
6. Click OK (Insert Object dialog box) to link the data from the Excel file.

To Copy and Paste an Embedded Table

If you wanted to copy and paste from an Excel worksheet to create an embedded table, you would perform the following steps.

1. Start Microsoft Excel 2019.
2. Select the cells to include in the embedded table and then press CTRL+C to copy them.
3. Start Microsoft Publisher 2019.
4. Click the Paste arrow (Home tab | Clipboard group) and then click Paste Special in the gallery.
5. Click the Paste option button (Paste Special dialog box) and then click New Table in the As box.
6. Click OK (Paste Special dialog box) to embed the table.

To Copy and Paste a Linked Table

If you wanted to copy and paste from an Excel worksheet to create a linked table, you would perform the following steps.

1. Start Microsoft Excel 2019.
2. Select the cells to include in the embedded table and then press CTRL+C to copy them.
3. Start Microsoft Publisher 2019.
4. Click the Paste arrow (Home tab | Clipboard group) and then click Paste Special in the gallery to display the Paste Special dialog box.
5. Click the Paste Link option button.
6. Click OK (Paste Special dialog box) to link the table.

To Edit an Embedded Table

When you double-click an embedded object, most Microsoft apps activate a subset of the source application commands on a ribbon that appears in the destination application. *Why? The embedded features allow you to edit the object without starting the source app.*

Each Excel cell reference in the following steps represents the intersection of a column (indicated by a capital letter) and a row (indicated by a number). For example, the first cell in column A is cell A1, the third cell in column B is cell B3, and so forth.

Specifically, in the following steps you will enter some text in the Excel cells and use Excel commands to format numerical data in the accounting number format that includes a dollar sign ($), commas where necessary, and two decimal places.

- Zoom in on the table.
- Double-click the table to display the Excel tabs on the Publisher ribbon.
- If the formula bar is not displayed, click View on the ribbon and then click the Formula Bar check box (View tab | Show group).

• Click cell A8 to select it. Type **Example:**   to enter the text (Figure 6–68).

Q&A

What happened to the Publisher tabs?

Publisher displays Excel functionality while you are working in an embedded table. When you click outside the table, the Publisher tabs will reappear.

How do I tell Excel I am done with a specific cell?

You can press ENTER, click the Enter button on the formula bar, or simply click another cell.

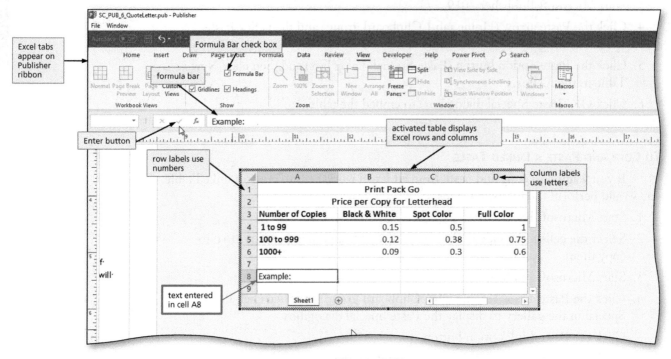

Figure 6–68

2

• Click cell A9 to select it.

• Click the Bold button (Excel Home tab | Font group) and then type **Design + 1500 Full Color Copies** to enter text (Figure 6–69).

Q&A

My text ran over into the next cell. Did I do something wrong?

No. As long as there is nothing in the adjacent cell, it is acceptable for the text to run over. If you have a column of consistently long entries, you could widen the column by dragging the column border in the column header row.

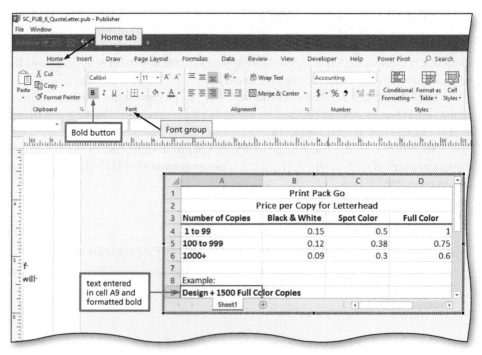

Figure 6–69

- Select cells B4 through D6 by dragging through them.
- Click the 'Accounting Number Format' button (Excel Home tab | Number group) to apply dollar signs and two decimal places to the data (Figure 6–70).

- Click cell C9 and apply the accounting number format.

Q&A The formatting is not showing up in cell C9. Did I do something wrong?
No. The formatting will show up as soon as you enter a value or sum in the cell in the next series of steps. Excel allows you to format empty cells.

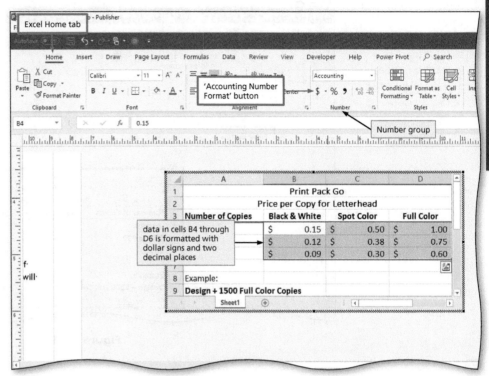

Figure 6–70

To Perform Math in an Embedded Table

The following steps create a formula in the embedded table. ***Why?*** *Publisher does not contain commands that can perform mathematical calculations, so you must use an Excel formula or function.* In Excel, a **formula** is a math sentence that calculates a value using cell references, numbers, and arithmetic operators such as +, -, *, and /. A formula begins with an equal sign. As you type a formula, instead of typing numbers, you can type a cell reference if the number is located somewhere in the embedded table. A **cell reference** is the column letter and row number location that identifies the required cell, such as A1.

In addition to typing formulas, you can insert functions. A **function** is a named operation that replaces the action of an arithmetic expression. For example, if you want to add a column or row of numbers, you can click the AutoSum button (Excel Home tab | Editing group) to activate the SUM function and generate a total. When you click the AutoSum button, the values to add appear in a **marquee**, or dotted flashing border. After a sum is created, you can repeat the pattern and duplicate the procedure in a process called **replication**. Excel displays a special fill handle to help with replication.

- Click cell C9 to position the insertion point.
- Type `= 150+(D6*1500)` to enter the formula (Figure 6–71).

Q&A What is the formula calculating?
The formula adds the design fee of $150.00 to the cost of the copies. The copies are calculated by multiplying the number of copies (1500) by the price in cell D6. The parentheses indicate order of precedence. The multiplication will take place first, then the addition.

Q&A

Why is D6 in a different color in the formula?
Each time you enter a cell reference, Excel color codes it and highlights the cell in the same color to help you locate the data.

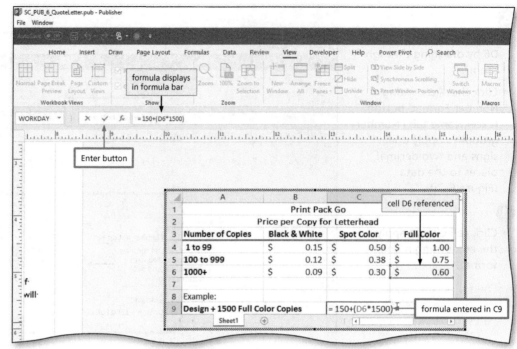

Figure 6–71

2

- Click the Enter button on the formula bar (Figure 6–72).

Q&A

How can I find out more about formulas and functions?
You can click the Search button on the ribbon and then type `functions` in the Search box. Click the Get help link to learn about many mathematical functions that will help you with formulas that are more complex.

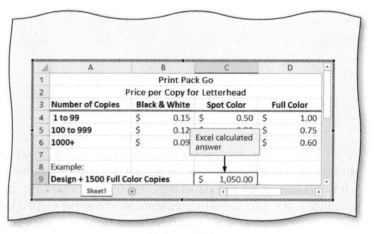

Figure 6–72

To Move and Position the Table

The following steps move and reposition the embedded table.

1 Click outside the table to display the table border.

2 Zoom to 80%. Scroll as necessary to view both the letter and the table.

3 Drag the border of the table to position the table in the lower portion of the letter. Resize the table as necessary to fill the area, as shown in Figure 6–73.

4 Click the Save button on the Quick Access Toolbar to save the file with the same file name in the same location.

5 Check the publication for spelling errors and design errors. If instructed to do so, print the publication.

6 Click the Close button on the Publisher title bar to exit Publisher.

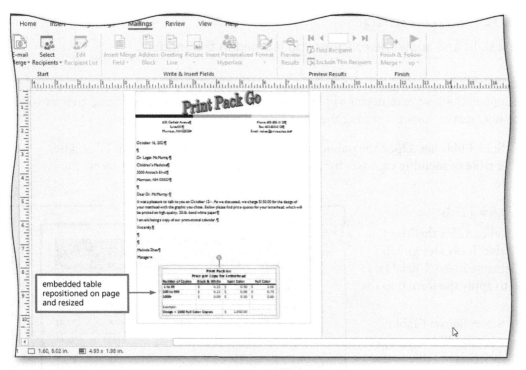

embedded table repositioned on page and resized

Figure 6–73

Summary

In this module, you learned how to use tables to present data in efficient and meaningful ways. You formatted a WordArt object to assist in branding a company; created and formatted tables and data, including the use of table styles, merging, and cell diagonals; created a calendar with a page border on the master page; and used font styles in a letter and embedded data from Excel into a Publisher publication. You also used the Excel-enhanced tools to format the table and perform calculations.

What decisions will you need to make when creating your next custom publication?

Use these guidelines as you complete the assignments in this module and create your own publications outside of this class.

1. Choose reusable objects.
    a) Use business information sets.
    b) Use building blocks.
    c) Create new objects.
2. Apply shape effects sparingly.
3. Create tables.
    a) Create and format a table.
    b) Enter data.
    c) Add table borders.
4. Create a calendar.
5. Use a master page for repeating items across pages.
6. Apply BorderArt to make pages or tables stand out.
7. If you need added functionality, embed an Excel table.
    a) Embed tables for static data edited in Publisher.
    b) Link tables when you want both Publisher and Excel to change and to use the full functionality of Excel.

CONSIDER THIS: PLAN AHEAD

Apply Your Knowledge

Reinforce the skills and apply the concepts you learned in this module.

Formatting a Table

Note: To complete this assignment, you will be required to use the Data Files. Please contact your instructor for information about accessing the Data Files.

Instructions: Start Publisher. Open the publication, SC_PUB_6-1, from the Data Files. The publication is a table of monthly expenses for a youth camping club. Figure 6–74 shows the formatted table.

Perform the following tasks:

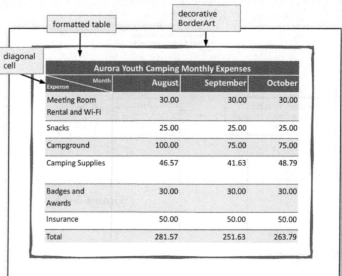

1. Click the table. Click the More button (Table Tools Design tab | Table Formats group). Click 'Table Style 24' to apply the format to the table.

2. Click the Select button (Table Tools Layout tab | Table group) and then click Select Table in the Select gallery to select the entire table. Display the Home tab. Change the font size to 18. Select the first row and change the font size to 20.

3. Click anywhere in the first row of the table. Click the Insert Above button (Table Tools Layout tab | Rows & Columns group) to insert a row above row 1.

Figure 6–74

4. With the new row still selected, click the Merge Cells button (Table Tools Layout tab | Merge group) to merge the cells in the new row. Type **Aurora Youth Camping Monthly Expenses** to enter a title. Format the font size to be 20. If necessary, format the text to be white.

5. Center the title. For each of the column headings, click the 'Align Center Right' button (Table Tools Layout tab | Alignment group). Right-align the numerical data.

6. To create headings:

   a. Click the first cell in the second row. Click the Diagonals button (Table Tools Layout tab | Merge group) and then click Divide Down in the gallery to create a cell with a diagonal.

   b. Click in the left side of the split cell. Change the font size to 14. Type **Expense** and then click the 'Align Bottom Left' button (Table Tools Layout tab | Alignment group) to change the heading alignment.

   c. Click the right side of the split cell. Change the font size to 14. Change the font color to white and then press CTRL+B to make the text bold. Type **Month** and then click the 'Align Top Right' button (Table Tools Layout tab | Alignment group) to change the heading alignment.

7. To format a diagonal:

   a. Select both halves of the diagonal cell.

   b. Click the Line Weight button (Table Tools Design tab | Borders group) and then choose 2 ¼ pt in the gallery.

c. Click the Line Color button (Table Tools Design tab | Borders group) and then click 'Accent 5 (White)' in the gallery to choose white as the color.

d. Click the Borders arrow (Table Tools Design tab | Borders group) to display the Borders gallery and then, if Diagonal Borders is not selected, click Diagonal Borders to add a white diagonal border to the selection.

8. To format other borders:

a. Select the first two rows of the table.

b. Click the Line Weight button (Table Tools Design tab | Borders group) and then choose 1 ½ pt in the gallery.

c. Click the Line Color button (Table Tools Design tab | Borders group) and choose 'Accent 5 (White)' color.

d. Click the Borders arrow (Table Tools Design tab | Borders group) and choose All Borders.

9. To create BorderArt:

a. Right-click the border of the table and then click Format Table on the shortcut menu.

b. In the Colors and Lines sheet, click the BorderArt button (Format Table dialog box).

c. Select the Handmade border and then click OK (BorderArt dialog box).

d. Click the Line Color button (Format Table dialog box) and then click 'Accent 3 (Green)' (fourth color in first row). Click OK (Format Table dialog box).

10. If any of the text is hyphenated, drag the column border on the right side slightly right to remove the hyphen.

11. Click the border of the table and then drag to align the table so that it is centered both horizontally and vertically relative to the margins. (*Hint:* Click the Align button (Table Tools Layout tab | Arrange group) and make choices from there.)

12. If directed to do so by your instructor, draw a text box in the lower-right corner of the page and enter your name.

13. Open Backstage view and then click Save As to display the Save As dialog box. Save the publication on your storage device using the file name, SC_PUB_6_MonthlyExpenses.

14. Check the publication for spelling errors and design errors. Print the publication with appropriate printer settings.

15. Submit the file as specified by your instructor.

16. ✺ Look at the totals in the table. Are you sure they are correct? How do you know? If the table were embedded or linked to Excel, what tools, commands, or functions would you have used to enhance or check the table?

Extend Your Knowledge

Extend the skills you learned in this module and experiment with new skills. You may need to use Help to complete the assignment.

Adding an Excel Chart to a Publication

Note: To complete this assignment, you will be required to use the Data Files. Please contact your instructor for information about accessing the Data Files.

Continued >

Extend Your Knowledge *continued*

Instructions: Start Publisher and open a blank 8.5 × 11-inch publication. You will create a table and a 3-D column chart of the 10 most populous counties in Indiana, as shown in Figure 6–75.

Perform the following tasks:

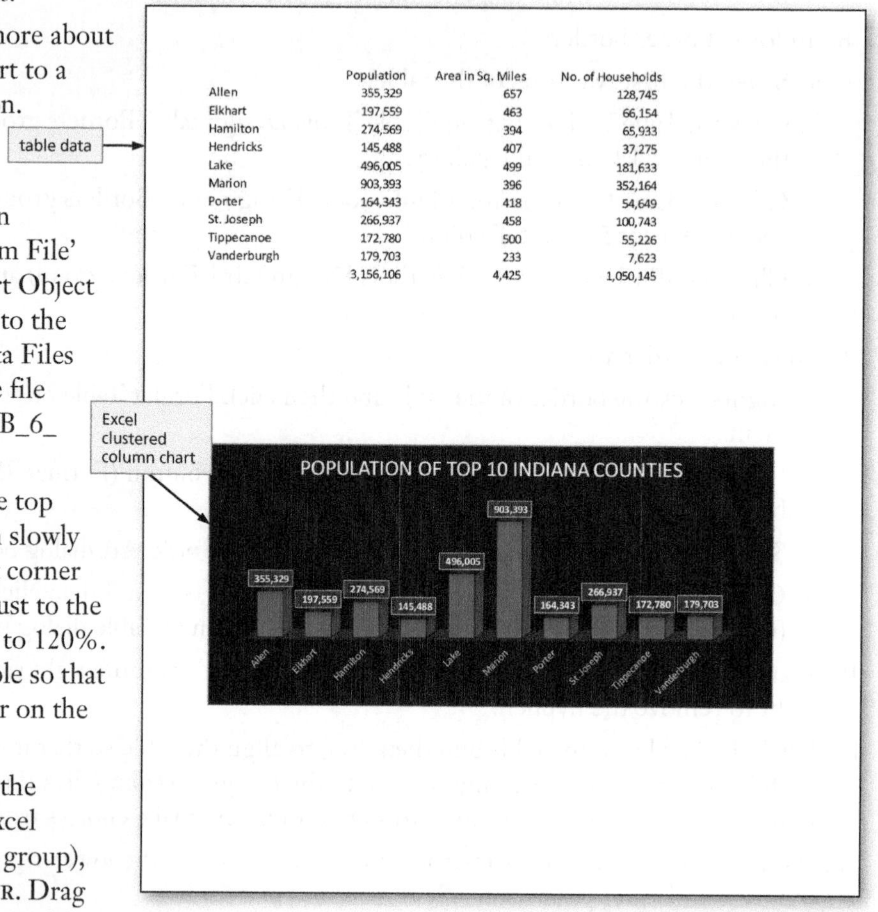

1. Use Help to learn more about adding an Excel chart to a Publisher publication.

2. Click the Object button (Insert tab | Text group) and then click the 'Create from File' option button (Insert Object dialog box). Browse to the location of your Data Files and double-click the file named Support_PUB_6_ Top10Counties.xlsx.

3. Drag the table to the top of the page and then slowly drag the lower-right corner of the table border just to the right margin. Zoom to 120%. Double-click the table so that the Excel tabs appear on the Publisher ribbon.

4. Click cell B12, click the AutoSum button (Excel Home tab | Editing group), and then press ENTER. Drag the lower-right corner of the selection rectangle to the right to replicate the SUM function to cells C12 and D12.

table data

Excel clustered column chart

Figure 6–75

5. Drag to select cells B2 through D12. Click the Comma Style button (Excel Home tab | Number group) to add commas to the numbers. Click the Decrease Decimal button (Excel Home tab | Number group) twice to remove the decimal places.

6. Drag to select cells A1 through B11. Display the Excel Insert tab. Click the 'Insert Column or Bar Chart' button (Excel Insert tab | Charts group) to display the gallery and then click '3-D Clustered Column' to add the chart to the publication.

7. Drag the chart to a location below the numbers. With the chart still selected, point to each part of the chart, labels, data columns, and legend to identify the various parts of the chart.

8. Display the Excel Chart Tools Design tab. Click the Style 6 button (Chart Tools Design tab | Chart Styles group).

9. Select the text in the chart title, change the font size to 18 if necessary, and then type **Population of Top 10 Indiana Counties** to replace the text.

10. Drag a side sizing handle to increase the width of the chart to approximately 6 inches, as measured on the horizontal ruler.

11. Click the table above the chart. Display the Excel View tab. Click to remove the check mark in the Gridlines check box (Excel View tab | Show group).

12. Click the scratch area to return to the Publisher ribbon. Change the publication properties as specified by your instructor. Check the publication for spelling errors and design errors.

13. Save the revised publication with the file name, SC_PUB_6_Top10Counties. Print the publication and then submit it in the format specified by your instructor.

14. Exit Publisher.

15. ⊛ In reviewing the available types of charts and graphs, what other type of chart might make sense for the data in the table? Would a pie chart be a good choice? Why or why not?

Expand Your World

Create a solution that uses cloud and web technologies by learning and investigating on your own from general guidance.

Formatting a Table from the Web

Instructions: The National Park Service maintains data on average temperature and precipitation in the national parks. You are to copy one of the National Park Service's tables, paste it into Publisher, and format it appropriately.

Perform the following tasks:

1. Start a browser and navigate to https://www.nps.gov/pore/planyourvisit/weather.htm. The webpage displays information for California locations, including Bear Valley National Park. Scroll as necessary to display the first table. Drag through all the table cells and then copy.

2. Start Publisher and open a blank 11 × 8.5-inch publication.

3. Click the Paste arrow (Home tab | Clipboard group) and then click Paste Special on the menu. When Publisher displays the Paste Special dialog box, if necessary, click New Table and then click OK (Paste Special dialog box). (*Hint:* Web tables sometimes display all black cells until formatted.)

4. Click the More button (Table Tools Design tab | Table Formats group) and then click Table Style 18 (Figure 6–76).

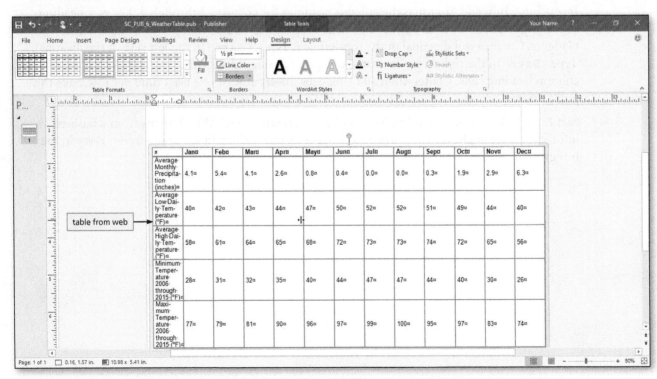

Figure 6–76

Continued >

Expand Your World *continued*

5. Because the table should display tourist season only, use the Delete button on the Table Tools Layout tab to remove the columns for January, February, March, November, and December.

6. Point to the border between columns 1 and 2. When the pointer changes to a double-headed arrow, drag to the right to widen the column to approximately 3 inches wide. Point to the table border. When the pointer changes to a four-headed arrow, drag the border of the table to center the table on the page approximately.

7. Click the WordArt button (Insert tab | Text group) and then click 'Fill - Light Orange, Outline - Orange' in the gallery. Type **Bear Valley Weather** and then click OK (Edit WordArt text dialog box) to insert the WordArt object. Move the WordArt object above the table. Apply a 3-D rotation effect of your choice to the WordArt with a depth size of 20.

8. Save the file on your storage device with the file name, SC_PUB_6_WeatherTable.

9. Submit the assignment in the format specified by your instructor.

10. ❋ What are some of the challenges in using tables from the web? How did you overcome them in this exercise?

In the Lab

Design and implement a solution using creative thinking and problem-solving skills.

Using a Master Page

Problem: The owners of Aurora Kitchen Store would like you to create a master page that they can use as a background for an upcoming brochure. They also would like to see what a schedule might look like of their cooking and baking classes.

Part 1:   Create a blank 11 × 8.5-inch publication. Go to the master page. Add a rectangle with a light blue gradient background that fills the page. Choose an appropriate BorderArt style. Create a WordArt object with a 3-D Rotation shape effect that contains the word, Aurora. Return to the publication. Create a table of four columns and five rows. Select an appropriate table style. Insert June, July, and August as the column headings for columns 2 through 4. For row headings, beginning with row 2, enter Air Frying, Cake Decorating, Skillet Comparison, and Kitchen Gadgets. Create a cell diagonal in the top-left cell. Type **Class** in the left side of the diagonal. Type **Days** in the right side. Format and align each side. Change the border color on the row and column heading cells. Center-align all blank cells. Insert at least one class time per row. Save the publication.

Part 2:   ❋ What kind of publications might use a master page? Which items from a business information set might be appropriate for a master page? Which items would have to stay in the foreground? Why?

7 Advanced Formatting and Merging Publications with Data

Objectives

After completing this module, you will be able to:

- Create a watermark
- Explain character spacing techniques
- Kern and track characters
- Use the Measurement pane to edit character spacing
- Differentiate among tab styles
- Set a tab stop and enter tabbed text
- Produce a main publication to be used as a form letter
- Use the Mail Merge wizard to create form letters

- Create and edit a data source
- Use grouped field codes
- Select, sort, and filter records in a data source
- Insert individual field codes and preview results
- Recolor and compress graphics
- Merge a publication with an Excel database
- Print selected records

Introduction

Whether you want individual letters sent to everyone on a mailing list, personalized envelopes for a mass mailing, an invoice sent to all participants, or a printed set of mailing labels to apply to your brochures, you can use Publisher to maintain your data and make the task of mass mailing and merged publication creation easier.

Merged publications, such as form letters, should be timely and professional looking yet, at the same time, personalized. Used regularly in both business and personal correspondence, a **form letter** is a form of correspondence that has the same basic content no matter to whom it is sent; however, items such as name, address, city, state, and ZIP code change from one form letter to the next. Thus, form letters are personalized to the addressee. An individual is more likely to open and read a personalized letter or email message than a standard Dear Sir or Dear Madam message. With word processing and database techniques, it is easy to generate individual, personalized documents for a large group and include features unique to desktop publishing. A **data source** or **data file** is a mail merge file with the unique data for individual people or items. The file may contain only a list of names and addresses, or it also may include paths to pictures, product part numbers, postal bar codes, participant purchase history, accounts receivable, email addresses, and a variety of additional data that you may use in a merged publication.

Project: Merging Form Letters and Bib Sheets

The project in this module begins with letterhead from the Charity 5K Race Foundation and creates a form letter with merged fields for each registrant from a Publisher mailing list, as shown in Figure 7–1. The letter, formatted with a graphic watermark (Figure 7–1a), will be mailed along with an enclosed bib sheet, or runner's ID that typically is pinned on the runner's shirt, that displays a unique registration number (Figure 7–1b).

form letter with merged field codes

bib sheet merged with category and runner numbers

watermark

a) Form Letter

b) Merged Bib Sheet

Figure 7–1

You will perform the following general tasks as you progress through this module:

1. Create a watermark.
2. Change the character spacing, such as tracking, kerning, and scaling.
3. Set and use tabs.
4. Use the Mail Merge wizard to create a data source.
5. Insert field codes in a form letter.
6. Edit the data source and sort.
7. Adjust graphics by editing the color brightness, contrast, and compression.
8. Create a bib sheet to merge with an Excel database.

BTW

The Ribbon and Screen Resolution
Publisher may change how the groups and buttons within the groups appear on the ribbon, depending on the computer or mobile device's screen resolution. Thus, your ribbon may look different from the ones in this book if you are using a screen resolution other than 1366 × 768.

To Start Publisher and Open a File

The following steps start Publisher and open a file. To complete these steps, you will be required to use the Data Files. Please contact your instructor for information about accessing the Data Files.

1 Start Publisher. Click the 'Open Other Publications' link in the left pane of the Publisher screen to display the Open screen.

2 Use the Browse button to navigate to the location of the file to be opened.

3 Double-click the file named SC_PUB_7-1.pub to open the selected publication in the Publisher window.

4 If the Publisher window is not maximized, click the Maximize button on the Publisher title bar to maximize it.

5 If the Special Characters button (Home tab | Paragraph group) is not selected already, click it to display formatting marks on the screen (Figure 7–2).

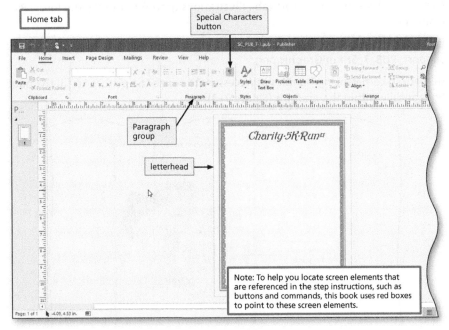

Figure 7–2

Watermarks

A **watermark** is a semitransparent graphic that is visible in the background on a printed page. In Publisher, you create watermarks by placing text or graphics on the master page. A master page is a background area similar to the header and footer area in traditional word processing software. Each publication starts with one master page. If you have a multipage publication, you can choose to use two different master pages for cases such as facing pages in a book; you might want different graphics in the background of each page. If you want to display master page objects only on certain pages, the Apply To button (Master Page tab | Master Page group) provides several options. This is useful for cases in which background images appear on every page except the title page in a longer publication or a watermark that appears on the inside of a brochure but not on the front.

CONSIDER THIS

How do you use watermarks?

As graphics that are visible in the background on some publications, watermarks may be translucent; others can be seen on the paper when held up to the light. Other times the paper itself has a watermark when it is manufactured. Watermarks are used for both decoration and identification, as well as to provide security solutions to prevent document fraud. Creating a watermark on the master page causes the watermark to repeat on each page of the publication. A master page can contain anything that you can put on a publication page, as well as headers, footers, page numbers, date and time, and layout guides that can be set up only on a master page.

To Insert and Place the Watermark Graphic

The following steps insert the graphic that will be used for the watermark on the master page. To complete these steps, you will be required to use the Data Files. Please contact your instructor for information about accessing the Data Files.

1 Press CTRL+M to access the master page.

2 Display the Insert tab.

3 Click the Pictures button (Insert tab | Illustrations group) to display the Insert Picture dialog box.

4 If necessary, navigate to the Data Files and insert the picture named Support_PUB_7_5KRunGraphic.png.

5 SHIFT+drag corner sizing handles as necessary to resize the picture to fill the page horizontally within the margins (Figure 7–3).

graphic inserted on master page

Figure 7–3

To Change the Transparency of a Graphic

The following steps change the transparency of the graphic. **Why?** *The downloaded graphic is too dark for a watermark; text inserted over parts of the graphic would be difficult to read.*

1

- Right-click the graphic to display a shortcut menu (Figure 7–4).

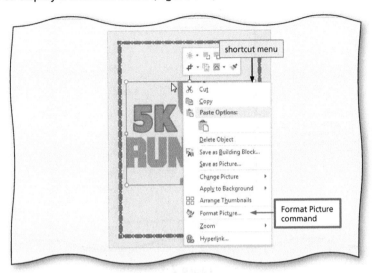

Figure 7–4

2

- Click Format Picture on the shortcut menu to display the Format Picture dialog box.

- In the Transparency area (Format Picture dialog box), drag the Transparency slider to 85% (Figure 7–5).

Q&A What does the transparency percentage signify?

A 100% transparency appears white. A 0% transparency displays the picture in its original, full-color state.

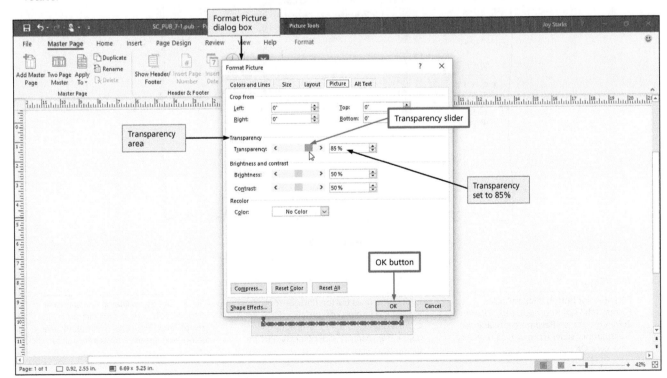

Figure 7–5

* Click OK to close the dialog box and apply the transparency to the graphic (Figure 7–6).

Q&A | What else could I add to the master page?
You could add a background effect, headers, footers, or any text or graphics that you want to appear on every page of the publication.

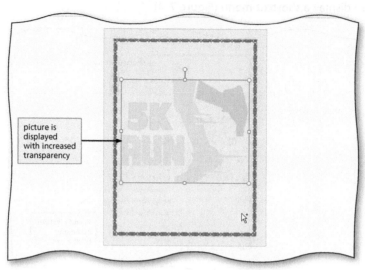

picture is displayed with increased transparency

Figure 7–6

* Press CTRL+M to close the master page.

* Click File to open Backstage view and then click Save As. Browse to your storage location. Save the file with the file name, SC_PUB_7_5KRunLetter (Figure 7–7).

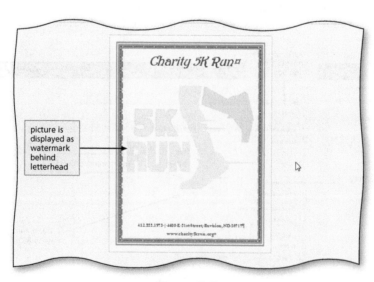

picture is displayed as watermark behind letterhead

Charity 5K Run

Figure 7–7

Other Ways

1. Click Recolor button (Picture Tools Format tab | Adjust group), click 'Picture Color Options' on Recolor menu, adjust Transparency slider (Format Picture dialog box), click OK

2. Click Corrections button (Picture Tools Format tab | Adjust group), click 'Picture Corrections Options' in Corrections gallery, adjust Transparency slider (Format Picture dialog box), click OK

3. Click Picture Styles Dialog Box Launcher (Picture Tools Format tab | Picture Styles group), click Picture tab (Format Picture dialog box), adjust Transparency slider, click OK

Spacing between Characters

Sometimes you need to fine-tune the spacing between characters on the page. For instance, you may want to spread characters apart for better legibility. Other times, you may want to move characters closer together for space considerations without changing the font or font size. Or, you may be using a font that employs **proportional spacing**, which uses different widths for different characters. For example, in a proportionally spaced font, the letter i is narrower than the letter m. This book uses a proportionally spaced font, as do most other books, newspapers, and magazines.

The opposite of proportional spacing is **monospacing**, where every letter is the same width. Older printers and monitors were limited to monospaced fonts because of the dot matrix used to create the characters. Now, almost all printers, with the exception of line printers, are capable of printing with either proportionally spaced or monospaced fonts. Because most fonts use proportional spacing, the scaling, tracking, and kerning features in Publisher provide you with many ways to make very precise character spacing adjustments.

Scaling, or **text scaling**, refers to the process of shrinking or stretching text. It changes the width of individual characters in text boxes. The WordArt toolbar has a button for scaling; however, scaling can be applied to any text box by using the Measurement pane, as well.

Tracking, or **character spacing**, refers to the adjustment of the general spacing between all selected characters. Tracking text compensates for the spacing irregularities caused when you make text much larger or much smaller. For example, smaller type is easier to read when it has been tracked loosely. Tracking maintains the original height of the font and overrides adjustments made by justification of the margins. Tracking is available only if you are working on a print publication. It is not available with web publications.

Kerning, or **track kerning**, is a form of tracking related to pairs of characters that can appear too close together or too far apart, even with standard tracking. Kerning can create the appearance of even spacing and is used to fit text into a given space or to adjust line breaks. For instance, certain uppercase letters, such as T, V, W, and Y, often are kerned when they are preceded or followed by a lowercase a, e, i, o, or u. With manual kerning, Publisher lets you choose from normal, expanded, and condensed kerning for special effects. Text in smaller point sizes usually does not need to be kerned unless the font contains many serifs.

You can adjust the spacing between characters and the size of characters using the lower three boxes in the Measurement pane, as described in Table 7–1. Some spacing specifications also can be applied using the ribbon or through dialog boxes.

BTW
Scaling Graphics
Scaling, when it applies to graphics, means changing the vertical or horizontal size of a graphic by a percentage. Scaling can create interesting graphic effects. For example, a square graphic could become a long, thin graphic suitable for use as a single border if the scale height were increased to 200% and the scale width were reduced to 50%. Caricature drawings and intentionally distorted photographs routinely use scaling. When used for resizing, scaling is appropriate to make a graphic fit in tight places.

BTW
Kerning
The term, kerning, comes from the typesetting era, when publishers actually shaved off part of the metal letters (called types or sorts) to allow for subsequent letters to be placed closer. The edge above the shaved-off part was called a kern.

Table 7–1 Character Spacing Tools in the Measurement Pane		
Box Name	**Specifies**	**Preset Unit of Measurement**
Tracking	General space between characters	Percent
Text Scaling	Width of characters	Percent
Kerning	Subtle space between paired characters	Point size

In the following sections, you will kern and track text that appears at the top and bottom of the letterhead.

To Kern Character Pairs

The following steps kern character pairs in the heading on the page. *Why? Some letters look better when kerned, especially when using large font sizes.*

1

- Click the Object Size button on the status bar to open the Measurement pane. If necessary, drag the Measurement pane so that it floats on the left of the page.

- Drag to select the letters, Ch, in the word, Charity, and then zoom to 100% (Figure 7–8).

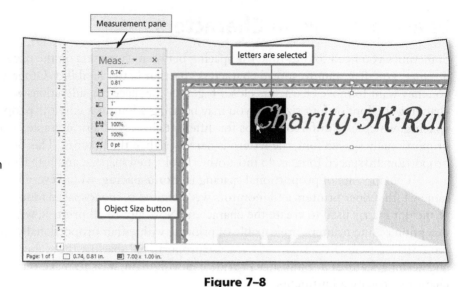

Figure 7–8

2

- Drag through the text in the Kerning box in the Measurement pane, type 2 to replace the value, and then press ENTER to move the letters further apart (Figure 7–9).

◢ How is kerning measured?
Q&A When you enter a value in the Kerning box (Measurement pane), it changes the points between characters. A point is approximately equal to 1/72nd of an inch. The higher the number, the further apart the characters will appear. A negative number will move the characters closer together.

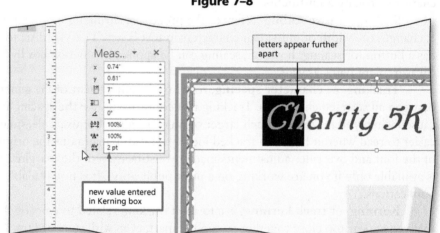

Figure 7–9

3

- Select the letters, ty, in the word, Charity.

- Drag through the text in the Kerning box (Measurement pane), type -2 as the new value, and then press ENTER to move the letters closer together (Figure 7–10).

- Select the letters, Ru, in the word, Run.

- Drag through the text in the Kerning box (Measurement pane), type -2 as the new value, and then press ENTER to move the letters closer together (Figure 7–10).

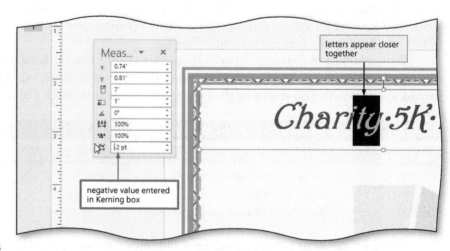

Figure 7–10

Other Ways

1. Right-click selected text, point to Change Text on shortcut menu, click Character Spacing on Change Text submenu, enter kerning settings (Character Spacing dialog box), click OK

2. To increase kern, press CTRL+SHIFT+RIGHT BRACKET (])

3. To decrease kern, press CTRL+SHIFT+LEFT BRACKET (])

To Track Characters

The following steps track the small text at the bottom of the page more loosely. *Why? Small text is harder to read when the letters are very close together.* Publisher has five predefined tracking sizes: Very Tight, Tight, Normal, Loose, and Very Loose.

● Scroll to the bottom of the page, click the text in the text box, and then press CTRL+A to select all of the text.

● Click the Character Spacing button (Home tab | Font group) to display the Character Spacing menu (Figure 7–11).

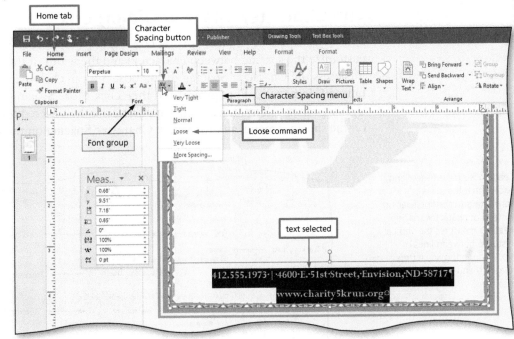

Figure 7–11

● Click Loose in the Character Spacing menu to track the text more loosely (Figure 7–12).

Q&A How can I tell if the text changed?
You can click the Undo button (Quick Access Toolbar) and then click the Redo Button (Quick Access Toolbar) to see the before and after effects of tracking.

How is tracking measured?
Tracking is a percentage of how much space is inserted between characters. Tight tracking reduces the percentage. Loose tracking increases the percentage. When you choose Very Loose, the text is tracked 125%.

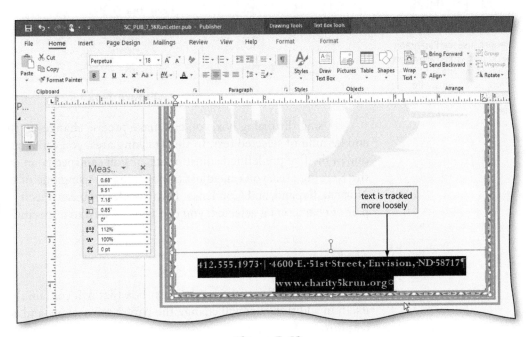

Figure 7–12

Other Ways

1. Enter tracking setting in Tracking box in Measurement pane

2. Right-click text, point to Change Text on shortcut menu to display Change Text submenu, click Character Spacing on Change Text submenu, enter tracking settings (Character Spacing dialog box), click OK

The Character Spacing Dialog Box

The Character Spacing dialog box (Figure 7–13) provides even more ways to customize the spacing between characters and the width of the characters themselves. To access the Character Spacing dialog box, you can click the Character Spacing button (Home tab | Font group) and then click More Spacing on the Character Spacing menu. Alternatively, you can right-click the selected text, point to Change Text on the shortcut menu, and then click Character Spacing on the Change Text submenu.

BTW

Leading
Leading is similar to tracking, except that it applies formatting to the line spacing instead of character spacing. Leading measures the vertical distance between lines of text — ignoring any letters that descend below the line.

BTW

Paragraph Dialog Box
To make vertical spacing changes, use the Paragraph dialog box, which allows you to adjust the line spacing before paragraphs, after paragraphs, and between lines.

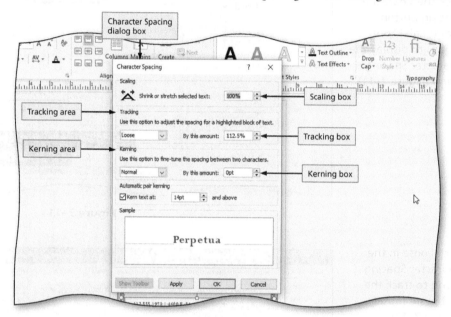

Figure 7–13

Using the dialog box, you can make precise changes to the scaling, tracking, and kerning of selected text. In the Tracking area, you can adjust the tracking by using one of the five predefined adjustments, or you can specify an exact percentage. In the Kerning area, you can adjust the tracking by using one of three predefined kerns: Normal, Expand, and Condense. If you prefer, you can specify an exact point value. If a pair of characters is selected, you can apply a kern to a specific font size.

To Create a Text Box

The following steps create a text box that will contain the body text of the letter itself. In addition, you will change the paragraph spacing and set the font size in the text box.

1. Click the 'Show Whole Page' button on the status bar to display the whole page.

2. If necessary, display the Home tab and then click the 'Draw Text Box' button (Home tab | Objects group). Drag to draw a large text box in the middle of the page.

3. Set the font size to 12.

④ Click the Paragraph Dialog Box Launcher (Home tab | Paragraph group) to display the Paragraph dialog box. If necessary, click the Indents and Spacing tab to display the Indents and Spacing sheet.

⑤ In the Line spacing area (Paragraph dialog box), select the text in the After paragraphs box and then type 0 to replace the text. Click OK to change the settings and close the dialog box.

⑥ Use the Measurement pane to enter the following settings: Horizontal Position 1", Vertical Position 2", Width 6.5", and Height 6.25" (Figure 7–14).

⑦ Close the Measurement pane.

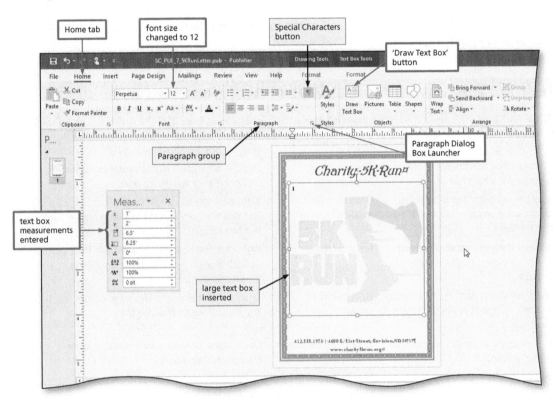

Figure 7–14

BTW
Displaying Rulers
To turn the rulers on or off, press CTRL+R or click the Rulers check box (View tab | Show group).

Working with Tabs and the Ruler

The **ruler** appears above the Publisher workspace and contains buttons, markers, margins, and measurements to help you place text and objects. Publisher uses tabs and markers to help position tab stops, margins, and indentations within text boxes. A **tab**, or **tab stop**, is a horizontal location inside a text box designated by a tab stop marker on the Publisher ruler. A **tab stop marker** appears darkened on the ruler as a straight line, an L-shaped marker, or a T-shaped marker. A **margin marker** appears as either a gray pentagon or a gray rectangle on the ruler. Margin markers set and indicate margins on the left and right of a text box. A **'First Line Indent' marker** allows you to change the left margin for only the first line in a paragraph. The typing area within the text box boundaries appears in light gray on the ruler; the rest of the ruler is a darker gray. Numbers on the ruler represent inches, but inches can be changed to centimeters, picas, pixels, or points. The **tab selector** is located at the left end of the ruler. It displays an icon representing the alignment of the text at the tab stop (Figure 7–15).

BTW
Tabs vs. Indents
Sometimes it is difficult to determine whether to use tab stops or indents. Use tab stops when you want to indent paragraphs as you go or when you want a simple column. When the tab stop is positioned for a long passage of text, using TAB to indent the first line of each paragraph is inefficient because you must press it each time you begin a new paragraph. In these cases, it is better to use an indent because it automatically carries forward when you press ENTER.

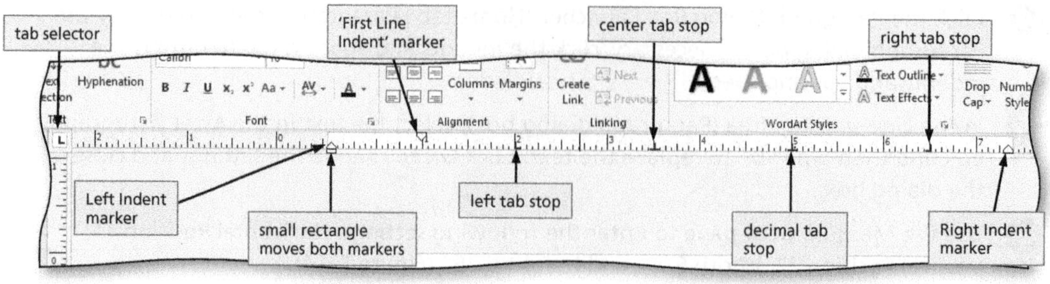

Figure 7–15

Table 7–2 explains the functions of the markers and buttons on the ruler, as well as how to modify them.

Table 7–2 Ruler Tools

Tool Name	Description	How to Change	Other Ways
'First Line Indent' marker	A downward-pointing pentagon that indicates the position at which paragraphs begin	Drag to desired location	Double-click margin marker, enter location in First line box (Paragraph dialog box)
Left Indent marker	An upward-pointing pentagon that indicates the left position at which text wraps	Drag to desired location	Double-click margin marker, enter location in Left box (Paragraph dialog box)
Move both markers	A small rectangle used to move both the Left Indent marker and the 'First Line Indent' marker at the same time	Drag to desired location	Right-click text box, click 'Format Text Box', click Text Box tab (Format Text box dialog box), enter text box margins
Object margins	Gray indicates the area outside the object margin; white indicates the area inside the object margin	Resize object	Right-click text box, click 'Format Text Box', click Size tab (Format Text box dialog box), enter height and width
Right Indent marker	An upward-pointing pentagon that indicates the rightmost position at which text wraps to the next line	Drag to desired location	Double-click margin marker, enter location in Right box (Paragraph dialog box)
Tab selector	Displays the current alignment setting: left, right, center, or leader	Click to toggle choice	Double-click tab stop marker, select alignment (Paragraph dialog box)
Tab stop marker	Displays the location of a tab stop	Click to create; drag to move	Double-click ruler, set tab stop location (Paragraph dialog box)

BTW

Units of Measurement

If you want to change the unit of measurement on the ruler, open Backstage view and then click Options in the left pane to display the Publisher Options dialog box. Click Advanced in the left pane and then click the 'Show measurements in units of' arrow. Choose the preferred unit of measurement and then click OK (Publisher Options dialog box).

You can drag markers to any place on the ruler within the text box boundaries. You can click a marker to display a dotted line through the publication, which allows you to see in advance where the marker will be set. Markers are paragraph specific, which means that when you set the tabs and indents, they apply to the current paragraph. Once the tabs and indents are set, however, pressing ENTER carries the markers forward to the next paragraph.

The Special Characters button (Home tab | Paragraph group) shown in Figure 7–14 makes nonprinting characters visible to help you format text passages, including tab characters (→), end-of-paragraph marks (¶), and end-of-frame marks (¤).

Setting Tabs

Publisher offers two ways to set tabs. With a text box selected, you can choose the type of tab you want by clicking the tab selector button until the appropriate icon is displayed. You then can click at the desired tab location on the ruler to place the icon.

A second way to set tabs in a text box is by using the Tabs sheet in the Paragraph dialog box (Figure 7–16). You can access the Paragraph dialog box by double-clicking the ruler or by clicking the Paragraph Dialog Box Launcher (Home tab | Paragraph group).

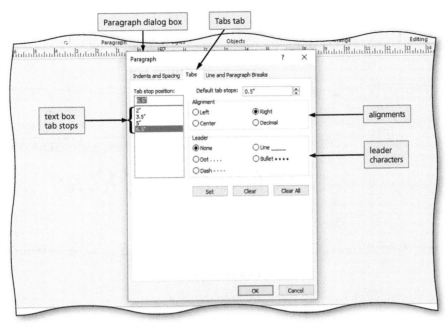

Figure 7–16

With tab stops, you can align text to the left, right, center, or at a decimal character. In addition, Publisher can insert special leading characters before a tab, such as dashes, dots, or lines. Table 7–3 lists the types of tab alignments and their common uses.

Table 7–3 Types of Tab Alignments

Name	Icon	Action	Purpose
Left tab	L	Text begins at tab stop and is inserted to the right	Used for most tabbing
Right tab	⅃	Text begins at tab stop and is inserted to the left	Used for indexes, programs, and lists
Center tab	⊥	Text is centered at the tab stop as it is typed	Used to center a list within a column
Decimal tab	⊥.	Aligns numbers or text based on a decimal point, independent of the number of digits	Used for aligning currency amounts in a list
Leader tab	⊥.	Text begins at tab stop and is inserted to the left; space preceding the tab is filled with chosen character: dot, dash, line, or bullet	Used for tables of contents, printed programs, bulletins, etc.

The tab stop alignment can be changed by clicking the Paragraph Dialog Box Launcher (Home tab | Paragraph group), by double-clicking an existing marker, or by clicking the tab selector on the ruler until it displays the type of tab that you want. The leader character can be changed only through the Paragraph dialog box.

To Set a Tab Stop

The following step uses the horizontal ruler to set or insert a tab stop at the 3.25" position in the form letter text box. *Why? The standard modified block format of letter writing displays the date beginning at the center of the letter, horizontally.*

BTW

Leader Tabs
A **leader tab** is a type of right tab in which the blank space to the left of the number is filled with a specific character. Customized via the Tabs dialog box, a leader repeats the character from the previous text or tab stop to fill in the tabbed gap. For example, a printed musical program might contain the name of the composition on the left and the composer on the right. Using a leader tab, that space in between could be filled by dots or periods to help the viewer's eye follow across to the corresponding composer.

BTW

Default Tabs
Default tabs are set every .5 inches in a text box; default tabs do not display markers.

BTW

Leader Tab Characters
Available leader tab character styles include None, Dot, Dash, Line, and Bullet.

1

- With the insertion point located in the main text box of the form letter, press F9 to zoom to 100%.

- Click the horizontal ruler at the 3.25" mark to create a left tab stop. Move the pointer so that you can view the tab stop marker (Figure 7–17).

Is the tab always a left-aligned tab?
Left-aligned is the default tab setting. If you want to change the tab type, click the tab selector until you see the tab type you want and then click the ruler at the tab stop location.

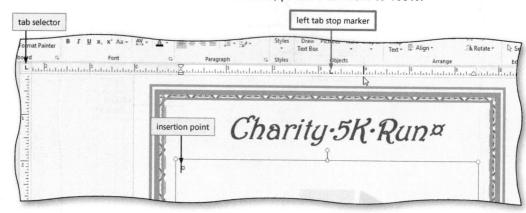

Figure 7–17

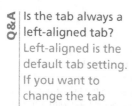 **Experiment**

- Click the Paragraph Dialog Box Launcher (Home tab | Paragraph group) and then click the Tabs tab (Paragraph dialog box) to view the tab setting. Click the Close button.

Other Ways

1. Click Paragraph Dialog Box Launcher button (Home tab | Paragraph group), click Tabs tab (Paragraph dialog box), type tab stop position in Tab stop position text box, click OK

To Enter Tabbed Text

The following steps enter tabbed text. *Why? Pressing TAB will move the insertion point to the 3.25" tab stop in the center of the letter so that the date can be entered in the correct position for a block format letter.*

1

- Press TAB to move the insertion point to the tab stop (Figure 7–18).

How do I delete a tab?
To delete a tab, drag the tab marker from its location on the ruler to the tab selector and drop it there or drag it straight down off the ruler. Or, you can click the Paragraph Dialog Box Launcher (Home tab | Paragraph group) and then click the Tabs tab (Paragraph dialog box). Select the tab stop location and click the Clear button.

Figure 7–18

- Display the Insert tab on the ribbon.
- Click the 'Date & Time' button (Insert tab | Text group) to display the Date and Time dialog box.
- Click the third available format and then click the Update automatically check box to place a check mark in it (Figure 7–19).

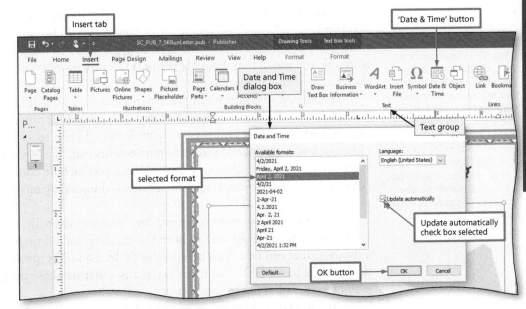

Figure 7–19

- Click OK (Date and Time dialog box) to insert the current date at the tab stop.
- Press ENTER twice to insert a blank line (Figure 7–20).

Q&A Why is my date different?
Publisher inserts the current date; your display should reflect the current date (the date you create this publication).

Figure 7–20

4

- Click the Save button on the Quick Access Toolbar to overwrite the previously saved file.

Break Point: If you want to take a break, this is a good place to do so. You can exit Publisher now. To resume later, start Publisher, open the file called SC_PUB_7_5KRunLetter.pub and continue following the steps from this location forward.

Merging Data into Publications

The process of generating an individualized publication for mass mailing involves creating a main publication and a data source. The main publication contains the constant or unchanging text, punctuation, space, and graphics, embedded with variables or changing values from the data source. A data source or database is a file

BTW
Tab Stop Alignment
The tab stop alignment can be changed by clicking the Paragraph Dialog Box Launcher (Home tab | Paragraph group), by double-clicking an existing marker, or by clicking the tab selector on the ruler until it displays the type of tab that you want.

BTW
**Formatting
Numerical Fields**
If you have numerical data
in your data source, you can
format the numbers even
before previewing the results.
Click the field code in the
publication, click the Format
button (Mailings tab | Write
& Insert Fields group), and
then click Format Currency or
Format Number. A dialog box
will appear that allows you
to make choices about the
numbering formats.

where you store all addresses or other personal information for participants, friends and family members, or merchants with whom you do business. The term **database** generically describes a collection of data, organized in a manner that allows easy access, retrieval, and use of that data. **Merging** is the process of combining the contents of a data source with a main publication.

Personalized contact with your participants can result in increased revenue. Addressing participants by name and remembering their preferences is the kind of personal attention that builds participant loyalty. When retail establishments keep close track of participants' interests, participants usually respond by returning and spending more time and money there. When you include content in a mailing that addresses your participants' specific interests, the participants are more likely to pay attention and respond.

Publisher allows users to create data sources internally, which means it could be beneficial to use Publisher as both the creating and editing tool. Publisher creates a database that can be edited independently by using Microsoft Access; however, you do not need to have Microsoft Access or any other database program installed on your system to use a Publisher data source.

If you plan to import, or bring in, data from another application, Publisher can accept data from a variety of other formats, as shown in Table 7–4.

BTW
Zero Point
You can CTRL+drag or
CTRL+click the tab selector
to change the publication's
zero point or **ruler origin**.
The zero point, at 0 inches
on the ruler, is useful for
measuring the width and
height of objects on the page
without having to add or
subtract from a number other
than zero. To change the
ruler back, double-click the
tab selector.

Table 7–4 Data Formats

Data Format	File Extension
Any text files, such as those generated with WordPad, TextPad, or Notepad where tabs or commas separate the columns, and paragraph marks separate the rows	.txt, .prn, .csv, .tab, and .asc
Microsoft Access files	.ade, .adp, .mdb .mde, .accdb, and .accde
Microsoft Data Access and OLE DB (provider for Oracle) files	.dbf
Microsoft Data Link files	.udl and .od
Microsoft Excel files	.xls and .xlsx
Microsoft Office address list file	.mdb
Microsoft Office list shortcuts	.ols
Microsoft Outlook contacts lists	.pst
Microsoft Publisher address lists	.mdb
Microsoft Word files	.doc, .docx, and .docm
ODBC file DSNs	.dsn
SQL Server and Office database connections	.odc
Webpage creation apps	.htm, .html, .asp, .mht, .mhtml

Creating a Data Source

A data source is a file that contains the data that changes from one merged publication to the next. As shown in Figure 7–21, a data source often is shown as a table that consists of a series of rows and columns. Each row is called a **record**. The first row of a data source is called the **header record** because it identifies the name of each column. Each row below the header row is called a **data record**. Data records contain the text that varies in each copy of the merged publication. The data source for this project contains five data records; you will edit the data source and add a sixth record later. In this project, each data record identifies a different person who has registered for a race. Thus, the six form letters will be generated from this data source.

Each column in the data sources is called a **data field**. A data field represents a group of similar data. Each data field must be identified uniquely with a name, called a **field name**. For example, First Name is the name of the data field (column) that contains the first names of those who registered for the 5K run. In this project, the data source contains nine data fields with the following field names: Title, First Name, Last Name, Address Line 1, Address Line 2, City, State, ZIP Code, and Category.

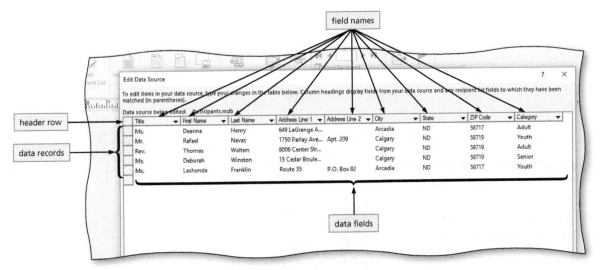

Figure 7–21

CONSIDER THIS

How do you know what to include in a data source?

When you create a data source, you need to determine what fields it should contain. That is, you need to identify the data that will vary from one merged publication to the next. Following are a few important points about fields:

- For each field, you may be required to create a field name. Because data sources often contain the same fields, some programs create a list of commonly used field names that you may use.

- Field names must be unique; that is, no two field names may be the same.

- Fields may be listed in any order in the data source. That is, the order of fields has no effect on the order in which they will print in the main publication.

- Organize fields so that they are flexible. For example, break the name into separate fields: title, first name, and last name. This arrangement allows you to customize fields.

In Publisher, data sources sometimes are called **recipient lists** or **address lists**. Publisher allows you to create as many data sources as you like, providing a customizable interface in which to enter the data.

To Use the Mail Merge Wizard

A **wizard** is a tool that guides you through the steps of a process or task by asking a series of questions or presenting options. The following steps begin the process of creating a data source by using the Mail Merge wizard. ***Why?*** *The Mail Merge wizard opens a pane with steps to create a data source and a form letter.*

①

- Click Mailings on the ribbon to display the Mailings tab.

- Click the Mail Merge arrow (Mailings tab | Start group) to display the Mail Merge menu (Figure 7–22).

Q&A What is the difference between a mail merge and an email merge?
They use different fields, leading to different kinds of publications. An email merge uses fields common to email correspondence, such as To, From, and Subject, whereas a mail merge uses fields such as address, city, and state. Both need to connect to recipient lists or data files.

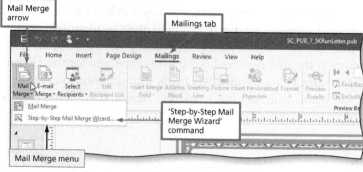

Figure 7–22

②

- Click 'Step-by-Step Mail Merge Wizard' on the Mail Merge menu to open the Mail Merge pane.

- Click the 'Type a new list' option button (Mail Merge pane) to select it (Figure 7–23).

Q&A My pane looks different. Did I do something wrong?
No. Your pane may display a different font or resolution.

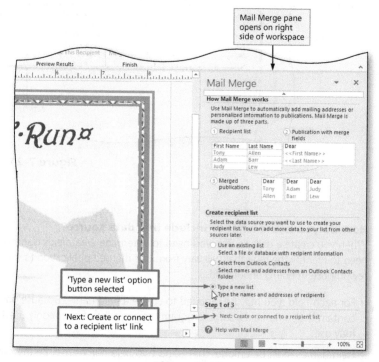

Figure 7–23

③

- Click the 'Next: Create or connect to a recipient list' link at the bottom of the pane to display the New Address List dialog box (Figure 7–24).

Q&A Can I use other tabs and ribbon commands while the Mail Merge pane is open?
Yes, the pane will remain open in the workspace while you edit the form letter.

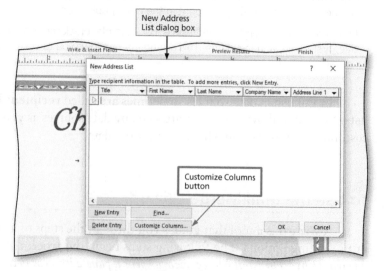

Figure 7–24

To Customize Data Source Fields

Publisher provides a list of 13 commonly used field names. This project uses 8 of the 13 field names supplied by Publisher: Title, First Name, Last Name, Address Line 1, Address Line 2, City, State, and ZIP Code. This project does not use the other five field names supplied by Publisher: Company Name, Country or Region, Home Phone, Work Phone, and E-mail Address. Thus, you will delete those field names and create a new field named Category. *Why? As you create the letter, you will need to reference the category for each participant.*

The following steps customize the fields in the New Address List dialog box.

- With the New Address List dialog box displayed, click the Customize Columns button (New Address List dialog box) to display the Customize Address List dialog box.
- Click Company Name in the Field Names area to select it (Figure 7–25).

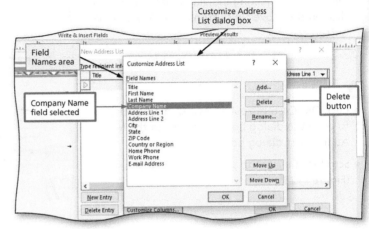

Figure 7–25

- Click the Delete button (Customize Address List dialog box). When Publisher displays a dialog box asking if you are sure you want to delete the field, click the Yes button (Microsoft Publisher dialog box) to delete the field (Figure 7–26).

Q&A What other options do I have for customization?
You can add a new field, rename a field to better describe its contents, or move fields up and down to place the fields in the desired order.

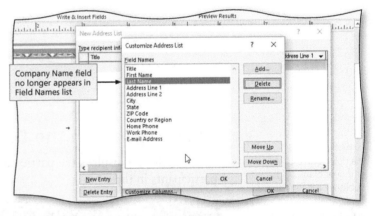

Figure 7–26

- Select, delete, and confirm the deletions of the Home Phone, Work Phone, and E-mail Address fields.
- Click 'Country or Region' in the Field Names area (Customize Address List dialog box) and then click the Rename button to display the Rename Field dialog box.
- Type **Category** in the To text box (Figure 7–27).

Q&A Can I delete multiple fields at one time?
No, you must select them and delete them individually.

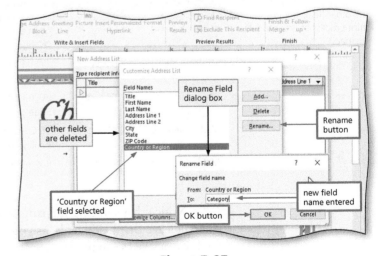

Figure 7–27

4

- Click OK (Rename Field dialog box) to close the dialog box and return to the Customize Address List dialog box (Figure 7–28).

 Experiment

- Experiment with moving the fields to different locations by selecting individual fields and then clicking the Move Up button or the Move Down button.

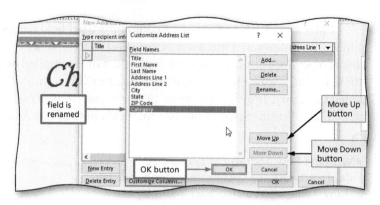

Figure 7–28

5

- Click OK (Customize Address List dialog box) to close the dialog box and return to the New Address List dialog box.

- Scroll to the right to see the new fields (Figure 7–29).

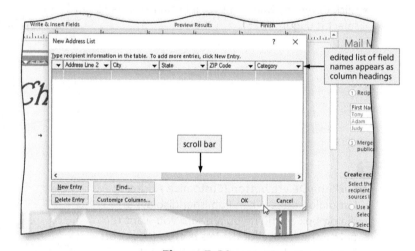

Figure 7–29

BTW
Empty Fields
If a data source contains empty or blank fields, Publisher will omit those fields when the publication is merged. For instance, if no second address line exists, Publisher will move up the other fields during the print process in order to fill the gap.

Entering Data in the Data Source

Table 7–5 displays the participant data for five people who registered as participants in the race.

Table 7–5 Participant Data								
Title	First Name	Last Name	Address Line 1	Address Line 2	City	State	ZIP Code	Category
Ms.	Deanna	Henry	649 LaGrange Avenue		Arcadia	ND	58717	Adult
Mr.	Rafael	Navas	1750 Parlay Avenue	Apt. 209	Calgary	ND	58719	Youth
Rev.	Thomas	Walters	8006 Center Street		Calgary	ND	58719	Adult
Ms.	Deborah	Winston	15 Cedar Boulevard		Calgary	ND	58719	Senior
Ms.	Lashonda	Franklin	Route 35	P.O. Box 82	Arcadia	ND	58717	Youth

Notice that some participants have no Address Line 2. For those participants, you will leave that field blank. As you enter data, do not press SPACEBAR at the end of the field. Extra spaces can interfere with the display of the merged fields.

To Enter Data in the Data Source File

The following steps enter the first record into the data source file, using the information from Table 7–5. You will use TAB to move from field to field. *Why? As it does in a Publisher table, TAB automatically moves to the next cell for data entry.*

- With the New Address List dialog box displayed, scroll as necessary to click the box in the first row below the Title heading.
- Type **Ms.** in the Title box and then press TAB.
- Type **Deanna** in the First Name box and then press TAB.
- Type **Henry** in the Last Name box and then press TAB (Figure 7–30).

Q&A What if the data is wider than the entry field?
Publisher will allow up to 256 characters in each entry field and move the text to the left, out of sight, as you type. Although it may not be visible, the text will be saved with the rest of the data.

What does the Find button (New Address List dialog box) do?
When you click the Find button, Publisher displays the Find Entry dialog box. In this dialog box, you can look for specific pieces of data that have been typed so far in the data source. The Find Entry dialog box lets you search the entire list or specific fields.

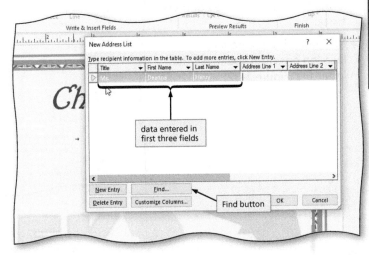

Figure 7–30

- Continue to enter data from the first row in Table 7–5. Press TAB to advance to each new entry field. Press TAB twice to leave a field empty. Do not press TAB at the end of the last row.
- Position the pointer in between the Address Line 1 and Address Line 2 fields. When the pointer is displayed as a double-headed arrow, drag to increase the width of the Address Line 1 field so that you can see the entire address. Change other column widths as necessary (Figure 7–31).

Q&A What do the other buttons do?
You can use the New Entry button (New Address List dialog box) instead of TAB to move to the next line and create a new entry. The Delete Entry button deletes the entry at the location of the insertion point.

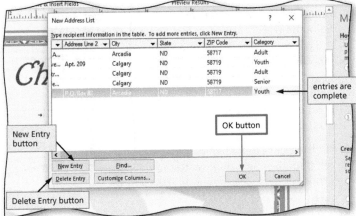

Figure 7–31

To Save the Data Source

The following steps save the data source file with the file name, SC_PUB_7_Participants. *Why? You must save the data source in order to merge it with the form letter.* It is best to save the form letter and the data source in the same directory because Publisher looks there first when performing the merge.

1

- Click OK (New Address List dialog box) to display the Save Address List dialog box.

- Type **SC_PUB_7_Participants** in the File name box. Do not press ENTER.

- Navigate to the same save location on which you saved the letter file (Figure 7–32).

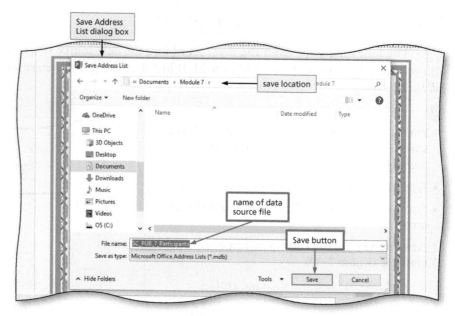

Figure 7–32

2

- Click the Save button (Save Address List dialog box) to save the file and to display the Mail Merge Recipients dialog box (Figure 7–33).

Q&A

What kinds of tasks can I perform using the Mail Merge Recipients dialog box?
You can select specific recipients, add new recipients, filter, sort, or create a new list. You will learn more about the Mail Merge Recipients dialog box later in the module.

Did the field order change?
Yes. Publisher now displays the last name field first; however, the data itself is not sorted.

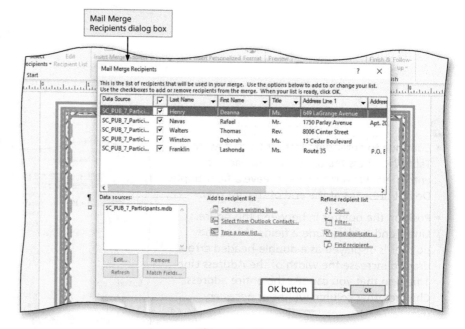

Figure 7–33

3

- Click OK (Mail Merge Recipients dialog box) to close the dialog box.

Inserting Field Codes

A publication designed for merging must be connected to its data source, and it also must contain field codes, sometimes called form fields codes, in the publication. A **field code** is placeholder text in a publication that shows Publisher where to insert the information from the data source. Once the publication is merged with the address list, the field codes are replaced with unique information. For example, a form letter may say, Thank you for your business, to every participant, but then follows it with the individual participant's name, such as John. In this case, you would type the words, Thank you for your business, insert a comma, and then insert the field code, First Name, from the data source. Publisher would insert the participant's name so that the letter would read, Thank you for your business, John.

CONSIDER THIS

What is included in the main publication for the form letter?

A main publication or document contains both the constant, or unchanging, text, as well as field codes for merged fields. Be sure the main publication for the form letter includes all essential business letter elements. A business letter should contain a date line, inside address, message, and signature block. Many business letters contain additional items such as a special mailing notation(s), an attention line, a salutation, a subject line, a complimentary close, reference initials, and an enclosure notation. It should use proper grammar, correct spelling, logically constructed sentences, flowing paragraphs, and sound ideas. Be sure to proofread it carefully.

BTW
Distributing a Document
Instead of printing and distributing a hard copy of a document, you can distribute the document electronically. Options include sending the document via email; posting it on cloud storage (such as OneDrive) and sharing the file with others; posting it on social media, a blog, or other website; and sharing a link associated with an online location of the document. You also can create and share a PDF or XPS image of the document, so that users can view the file in Acrobat Reader or XPS Viewer instead of in Publisher.

You can format, copy, move, or delete a field code just as you would regular text. Field codes need to be spaced and punctuated appropriately. For instance, if you want to display a greeting such as Dear Katie, you need to type the word, Dear, followed by a space before inserting the First Name field code. You then would type a comma or a colon after the field code to complete the greeting.

To insert a field code from the Mail Merge pane, you either can position the insertion point in the publication and click the field code, or you can drag the field code from the pane to the publication and then drop it at the appropriate location.

Publisher allows you to insert field codes from the address list into the main publication one field at a time or in predefined groups. For example, if you wanted to display the amount due from an address list, you would choose that one field from the pane. To use predefined groups, you would use a **grouped field code**, which is a set of standard fields, such as typical address fields or salutation fields, preformatted and spaced with appropriate words and punctuation. For example, instead of entering the field codes for Title, First Name, Last Name, Company Name, Address Line 1, and so on, you can choose the grouped field, Address Block, that includes all the fields displayed correctly.

To Insert Grouped Field Codes

The following steps insert grouped field codes for the address block and greeting line in the form letter. *Why? The grouped field codes contain the correct fields that are spaced and formatted appropriately.*

1
- Click in the text box to ensure that the insertion point is positioned two lines below the date in the publication and then zoom to 130%.
- In the Mail Merge pane, click the Address block link to display the Insert Address Block dialog box.
- If necessary, click each of the check boxes so that they contain check marks.
- If necessary, click the format 'Mr. Joshua Randall Jr.' in the Insert recipient's name in this format list. If necessary, click the Previous button in the Preview area until the first recipient in the data source is displayed (Figure 7–34).

Q&A | What is the difference between an Address block and Address fields?
The Address block link will include fields in the current data source. If you choose Address fields, Publisher displays a list of typical address fields that could be matched with different data sources. That way, if you choose to send a form letter to two different address lists, Publisher will try to match the fields consistently. For example, one address source might include a middle initial or company name, while another one might not.

Experiment

- One at a time, click the formats in the Insert recipient's name in this format list. View the changes in the preview. Click the Next button to view other entries from the address list. When you are finished, click the format 'Mr. Joshua Randall Jr.' again.

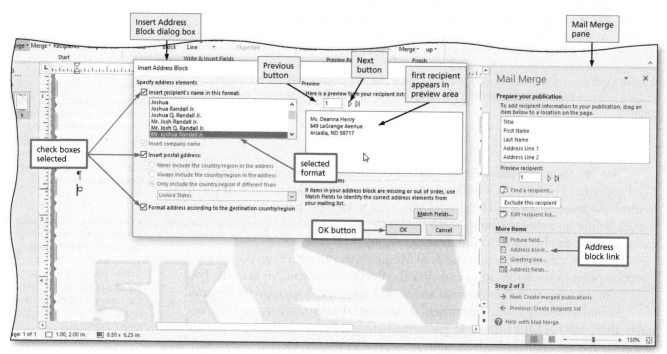

Figure 7–34

2

- Click OK (Insert Address Block dialog box) to insert the address block into the form letter.
- Click at the end of the AddressBlock grouped field code (Figure 7–35).

Q&A | What do the chevron symbols represent?
Each field code displays chevrons to let you know that it is not actual text.

Figure 7–35

3
- Press ENTER twice and then click the Greeting line link in the Mail Merge pane to display the Insert Greeting Line dialog box.
- If necessary, choose the various settings shown in Figure 7–36.

Experiment
- One at a time, click the box arrows to view the various kinds of greeting formats. Notice that the preview changes with each selection. When you are done, apply the settings shown in Figure 7–36.

Q&A What is the purpose of the Match Fields button?
Unique to grouped fields, the Match Fields button opens a dialog box where you can choose which individual fields to use in the group. If you had renamed the Title field, for example, you would have to match your new field name with the one that Publisher automatically places in the group.

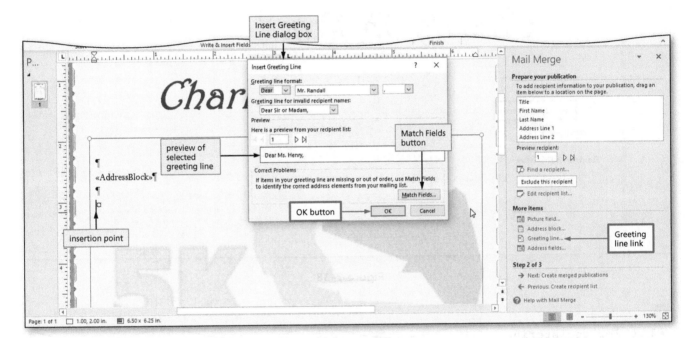

Figure 7–36

4
- Click OK (Insert Greeting Line dialog box) to insert the GreetingLine field code into the publication.
- Click after the GreetingLine field code and then press ENTER twice to move the insertion point in the publication (Figure 7–37).

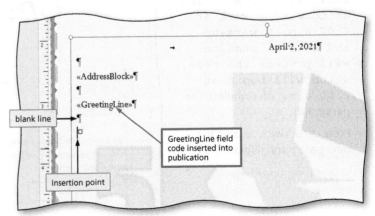

Figure 7–37

Other Ways

1. Click appropriate grouped field code button (Mailings tab | Write & Insert Fields group)

To Insert Individual Field Codes

The following steps insert individual field codes as you type the body of the form letter. *Why? Using individualized data in the body of the letter helps personalize the form letter.* Individual field codes are listed in a box near the top of the Mail Merge pane.

1

- With the insertion point positioned two lines below the greeting line (shown in Figure 7–37), type **Thank you,** and then press SPACEBAR.

- In the Mail Merge pane, click First Name to insert the field code into the publication.

- Press the COMMA key (,) and then press SPACEBAR (Figure 7–38).

Figure 7–38

2

- Type **for registering for the Charity 5K Run on Saturday, May 16, 2021. Plan on arriving at Community Park at 7:00 a.m. A warm-up and stretch session will precede the race, which will begin at 8:00 a.m.** to complete the paragraph.

- Press ENTER twice to start the next paragraph (Figure 7–39).

Q&A | Why did my line wrap differently?
Subtle differences in the width of the text box can lead to the wordwrap occurring in different locations.

Figure 7–39

❸

- Type `You will be running in the` and then press SPACEBAR.
- In the Mail Merge pane, scroll as necessary, click Category to insert the field code into the publication, and then press SPACEBAR.
- Type `category. Enclosed is your participant bib sheet. Spectators will offer water along the route. At the finish line, you will receive our appreciation gift and instructions to complete your donations.` to complete the paragraph.
- Press ENTER twice to start the next paragraph (Figure 7–40).

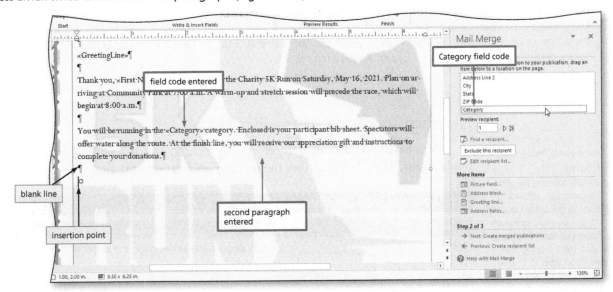

Figure 7–40

❹

- Type `Enjoy your run, and thank you for contributing to this worthy cause!` and then press ENTER twice.
- Type `Sincerely,` and then press ENTER four times to leave space for a signature.
- Type `Christina Romero, Chair` and then press ENTER.
- Type `Charity 5K Run Foundation` and then press ENTER.
- Type `Supporting the Children's Hospital` and then press ENTER twice.
- Type `Enclosure` to finish the letter (Figure 7–41).

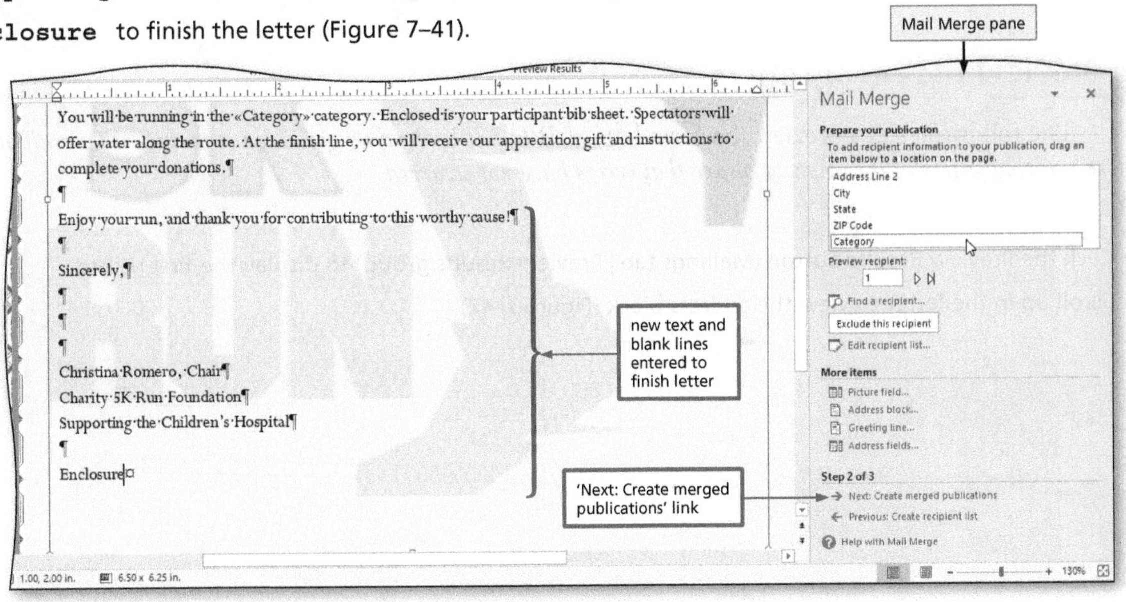

Figure 7–41

● Click the 'Next: Create merged publications' link at the bottom of the Mail Merge pane to create the merged publication.

Other Ways

1. Click 'Insert Merge Field' button (Mailings tab | Write & Insert Fields group), select field (Insert Merge Field menu)

2. Drag field from Mail Merge pane into publication

How do you merge the data source to create the form letters?

Merging is the process of combining the contents of a data source with a main publication. You can print the merged letters on the printer or place them in a new publication, which you later can edit. You also have the options of merging all data in a data source or merging just a portion of it by performing a filter or sort.

BTW

Conserving Ink and Toner

If you want to conserve ink or toner, you can instruct Publisher to print draft quality documents by clicking File on the ribbon to open Backstage view and then clicking Print in Backstage view to display the Print screen. Click the Printer Properties link and then, depending on your printer, click the Quality button and then click Draft in the list. Click OK to close the Printer Properties dialog box and then click the Print button as usual.

Managing Merged Publications

You have several choices in previewing, saving, printing, and exporting merged publications. Table 7–6 describes the merged publication options.

Table 7–6 Merged Publication Options	
Option	**Description**
Print	Print all pages with merged data, one at a time
Print preview	Preview each page of the merged pages
Merge to a new publication	Create a new publication with the merged pages, which you can edit further or print
Add to existing publication	Add the merged pages to the end of the existing publication
Print recipient list	Create a hard copy of the recipient list of the current merge for your records, including filters or sorts
Save a shortcut to recipient list	Create a shortcut to the address list used in the current merge
Export recipient list to new file	Create a new file based on the filtered or sorted address list used in the current merge
Preview Results group on Mailings tab	Traverse through each page of the merged pages; find and exclude data

To Preview the Form Letters

The following steps preview the form letters. *Why? It is always a good idea to preview the result of a merge before printing letters in the event to ensure that errors have not occurred.*

● Click the Preview Results button (Mailings tab | Preview Results group) to display the first record.

● Scroll up in the letter to view the address block (Figure 7–42).

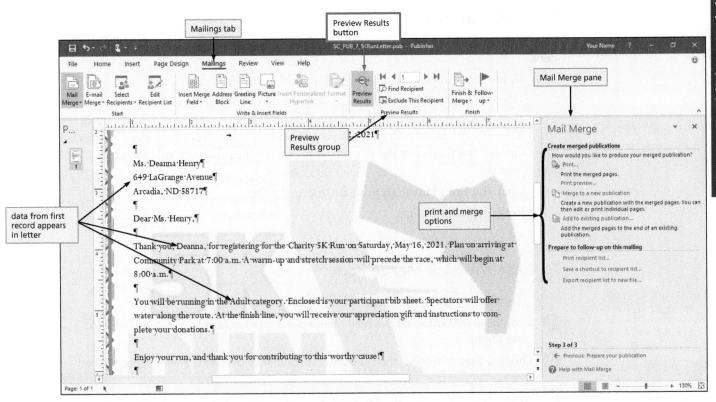

Figure 7–42

②
- Click the Next Record button (Mailings tab | Preview Results group) to display the next letter (Figure 7–43).

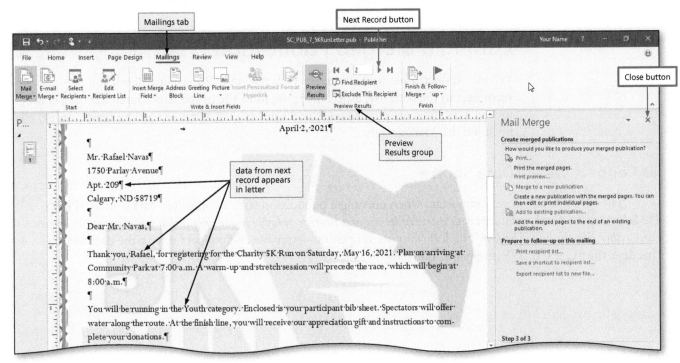

Figure 7–43

Other Ways

1. Click Print preview link (Mail Merge pane, Step 3 of 3), click Next Sheet button in Print screen

TO PRINT MERGED PAGES

If you wanted to print the merged publication, you would perform the following steps.

1. Ready the printer. Click the Print link in the Mail Merge pane.

2. When Publisher opens Backstage view, verify that the selected printer that appears on the Printer Status button will print a hard copy of the publication. If necessary, click the Printer Status button to display a list of available printer options and then click the desired printer to change the currently selected printer.

3. Click the Print button to print the merged pages.

4. Retrieve the printouts.

To Close the Mail Merge Pane

The following steps close the Mail Merge pane.

❶ Click the Close button on the Mail Merge pane title bar (shown in Figure 7–43) to close the pane.

❷ Click the Save button on the Quick Access Toolbar to overwrite the previously saved file.

❸ Open Backstage view and then click Close in the left pane to close the publication without exiting Publisher.

Break Point: If you want to take a break, this is a good place to do so. You can exit Publisher now. To resume later, start Publisher, and continue following the steps from this location forward.

Editing a Merged Publication

When you open a file with a connected data source, Publisher will ask you to reconnect to the database, especially if the form file or the data source file has been moved. Once you are connected, if you want to edit, filter, or sort the recipient list, you must use the Mailings tab.

To Connect with a Data Source

The save location is very important when opening a publication with a connected data source. *Why? Publisher searches for the connected data source in its original location, relative to the publication you are opening; if you move either file, the link is broken.* The following steps open the letter file and connect it with the data source — in this case, the SC_PUB_7_Participants.mdb data file.

1

- Open the Publisher file named SC_PUB_7_5KRunLetter.pub (Figure 7–44).

Q&A Why did Publisher display a dialog box?
Anytime a publication has been saved while connected to a data source, Publisher alerts you and verifies the connection when you open the file again.

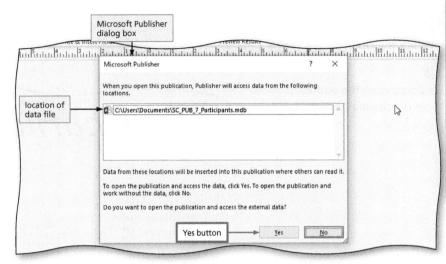

Figure 7–44

2

- Click the Yes button (Microsoft Publisher dialog box).

- If the SC_PUB_7_5KRunLetter.pub publication opens, proceed to Step 6.

Q&A What happens if I click the No button?
The publication will open with no connection to data.

3

- When Publisher displays a dialog box because the data source file is not in the expected storage location, click the 'Try to reconnect to the data source' option button to select it (Figure 7–45).

Q&A What happens if I click the 'Work without connection' option button?
The publication will open with no connection to data. The field names will appear, but you will not be able to preview any results.

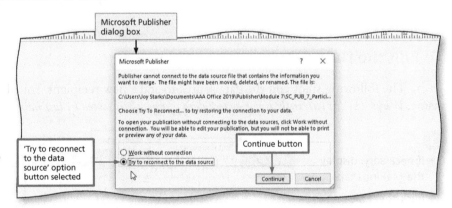

Figure 7–45

4

- Click the Continue button (Microsoft Publisher dialog box).

- When Publisher displays the Select Data Source dialog box, navigate to the location of your data source file (in this case, SC_PUB_7_Participants.mdb).

- Click the file to select it (Figure 7–46).

Q&A What is the purpose of the New Source button?
When you click the New Source button, Publisher starts a Data Connection wizard that allows you to choose from a variety of database options, including files on different servers with possible tables, network connections, passwords, and access restrictions.

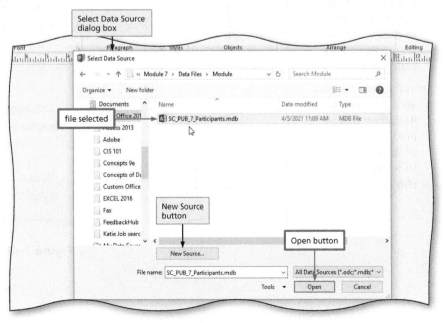

Figure 7–46

5

- Click the Open button (Select Data Source dialog box) to open the data source and connect the file.

6

- Zoom in on the address block to verify the merge (Figure 7–47).

Figure 7–47

To Edit the Data Source

The following steps edit the data source to add a new recipient. You also will sort the recipients by last name. *Why? The list currently is not sorted; data commonly is sorted by last name.*

1

- If necessary, display the Mailings tab.

- Click the 'Edit Recipient List' button (Mailings tab | Start group) to display the Mail Merge Recipients dialog box.

- In the Data sources area (Mail Merge Recipients dialog box), click the name of the data file to select it (Figure 7–48).

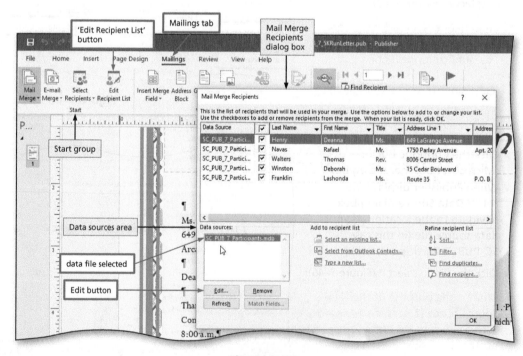

Figure 7–48

- Click the Edit button to display the Edit Data Source dialog box.

- Click the New Entry button (Edit Data Source dialog box) to create a new entry row.

- Type the following information in the new entry row. Use TAB to move from field to field. Do not press TAB after the last piece of data, as shown in Figure 7–49:

  Dr.
  Jacob
  Brimmer
  2011 N. Lapin Way
  Suite 478
  Arcadia
  ND
  58717
  Adult

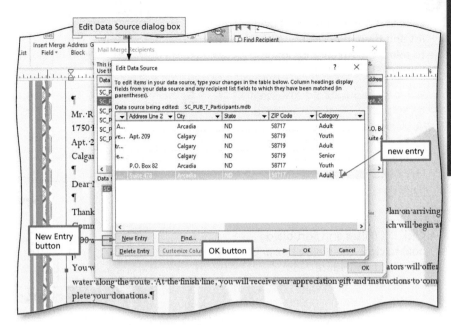

Figure 7–49

❸

- Click OK to confirm the new entry (Figure 7–50).

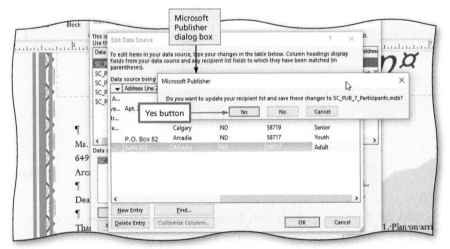

Figure 7–50

❹

- When Publisher displays a dialog box asking if you want to update the recipient list, click the Yes button to update the recipient list.

- Click the Sort link (Mail Merge Recipients dialog box) to display the Filter and Sort dialog box.

- Click the Sort by arrow (Filter and Sort dialog box) to display the field names (Figure 7–51).

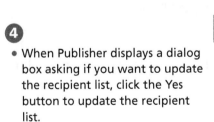
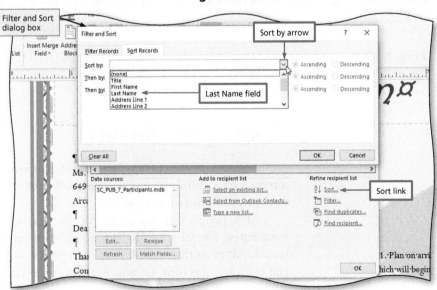

Figure 7–51

- Click Last Name in the Sort by list and then, if necessary, click to select the Ascending option button (Figure 7–52).

Q&A

What is the purpose of the Then by arrows?

You can perform a secondary sort on the data. For example, if several participants had the same last name, you could further sort by first name.

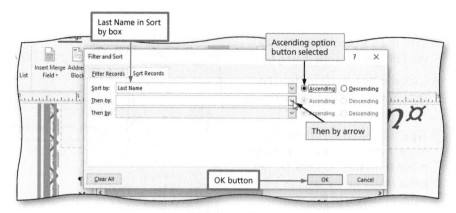

Figure 7–52

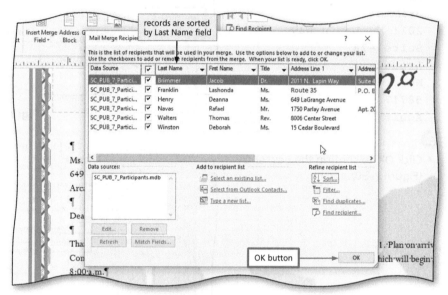

Figure 7–53

6

- Click OK (Filter and Sort dialog box) to close the dialog box and sort the data (Figure 7–53).

7

- Click OK (Mail Merge Recipients dialog box) to close the dialog box.
- Click the Save button on the Quick Access Toolbar to overwrite the previously saved file.
- Open Backstage view and then click Close to close the publication without exiting Publisher.

Break Point: If you want to take a break, this is a good place to do so. You can exit Publisher now. To resume later, start Publisher, and continue following the steps from this location forward.

Creating Bib Sheets

A bib sheet or bib is a printed sheet with a unique number used to identify a runner during a race. Bib sheets may come in all sizes and are usually attached with safety pins to the front of the runner's shirt.

The people who registered for the race will receive the bib sheet along with the form letter. The Charity 5K Run Foundation has a database of unique numbers that it uses for all races that includes four categories: senior, adult, youth, and walker. This 5K run is for runners only, so later in the module you will filter out the walker category.

The database is stored in a Microsoft Excel worksheet. This time, you will merge and insert field codes manually rather than through the wizard.

To Copy the Data Source File

Publisher recommends that the publication and its data source reside in the same folder location; therefore, the following steps copy the Microsoft Excel worksheet file from the Data Files to your storage location. To complete these steps, you will be required to use the Data Files. Please contact your instructor for information about accessing the Data Files. If you already have downloaded the Data Files to the same storage location that you are using to create files in this module, you can skip these steps.

1 Click the File Explorer button on the Windows taskbar to open a File Explorer window.

2 Navigate to the location of the Data Files.

3 Right-click the Support_PUB_7_RunnerNumbers.xlsx file to display a shortcut menu and then click Copy on the shortcut menu to copy the file.

4 Navigate to the location where you saved the files created previously in this module.

5 Right-click a blank part of the right pane in the folder to display the folder's shortcut menu and then click Paste on the shortcut menu to paste the file.

6 Close the File Explorer window.

Graphic Adjustments

The Adjust group on the Picture Tools Format tab provides many ways to edit graphics other than by changing size, position, and style (Figure 7–54).

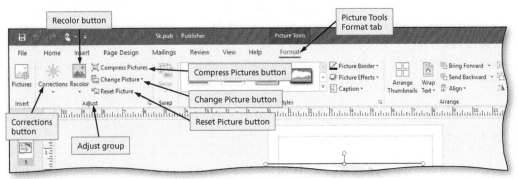

Figure 7–54

The Corrections button includes settings for brightness, contrast, and transparency. **Brightness** is the percentage of black or white added to a main color. The higher the brightness percentage, the more white the image contains. **Contrast** is the saturation or intensity of the color, such as the difference between the darkest and lightest areas of the image. The higher the contrast percentage, the more intense the color. In addition, using a command in the Corrections gallery, you can change the transparency or opacity of a graphic.

When you **recolor** a graphic, you make a large-scale color change; the color applies to all parts of the graphic, with the option of leaving the black parts black. It is an easy way to convert a color graphic to a black-and-white line drawing so that it prints more clearly. The reverse also is true: if you have a black and white graphic, you can convert it to a tint or shade of any one color.

The Change Picture button allows you to change the picture while maintaining the placement and size of the graphic in the publication. The Reset Picture button discards all of the formatting changes you might have made to the picture.

Compress means to reduce the storage size of a publication by changing the internal size of the picture. When you click the Compress Pictures button, Publisher displays the Compress Pictures dialog box. Table 7–7 describes the compression settings.

Table 7–7 Compress Pictures Settings

Setting	Description
Current combined image size	Displays the current combined size of all pictures in the publication.
Estimated combined image size after compression	Displays the estimated combined size of all pictures in the publication after compression settings.
'Delete cropped areas of pictures' check box	Deletes the pixel information that normally is stored for cropped areas of pictures.
'Remove OLE data' check box	Removes the internal part of a graphic that is used when the graphic is linked or embedded. While the picture itself appears the same, you no longer are able to open that picture by using the software in which it was created originally.
Resample pictures check box	Makes a resized picture smaller by deleting the residual data from the picture's original size. You should avoid making the picture larger after resampling as it reduces the quality of the picture.
'Convert to JPEG where appropriate' check box	Converts the picture to a JPEG file.
Commercial Printing option button	Compresses pictures to 300 pixels per inch (ppi). This option does not compress JPEG files.
Desktop Printing option button	Compresses pictures to 220 ppi and a 95 JPEG quality level.
Web option button	Compresses pictures to 96 dots per inch (dpi) and a 75 JPEG quality level.
'Apply to all pictures in the publication' option button	Applies the compression settings to all of the pictures in the publication.
'Apply to selected pictures only' option button	Applies the compression settings to only the selected picture or pictures.

To Create a Publication

The following steps create a blank publication in preparation for creating the bib sheet.

1. Start Publisher if necessary and then click the 'More Blank Page Sizes' thumbnail in the New Template gallery.

2. In the Custom area, click the 'Create new page size' thumbnail.

3. Type **Bib Sheet** in the Name text box (Create New Page Size dialog box). In the Height box, type **5.5** to set the height (Figure 7–55).

4. Click OK (Create New Page Size dialog box).

5. If necessary, click the Color scheme button and then click Office in the list. If necessary, click the Font scheme button and then click the Solstice font scheme.

6. Click the CREATE button in the template information pane to create the new publication.

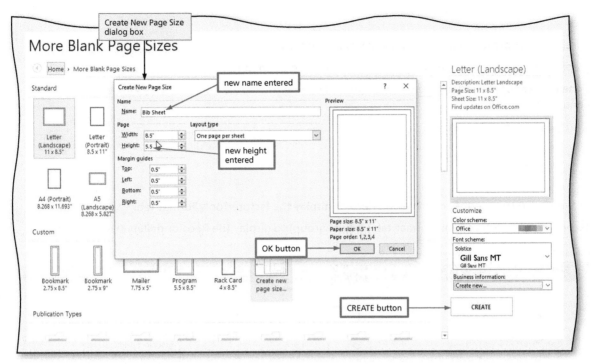

Figure 7–55

To Insert and Recolor a Picture

The following steps insert and recolor a picture. ***Why?*** *A copy of the graphic will be recolored to serve as a shadow background.* To complete these steps, you will be required to use the Data Files. Please contact your instructor for information about accessing the Data Files.

- Click the Pictures button (Insert tab | Illustrations group) and then navigate to the Data Files.
- Double-click the file named Support_PUB_7_5KRunGraphic.png to insert it into the publication (Figure 7–56).

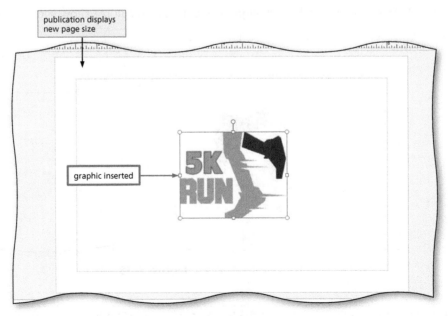

Figure 7–56

2

- Resize the graphic to approximately 3.5 inches wide by 2.5 inches tall.

- Drag the graphic to the upper margin approximately centered in the publication.

- Right-drag the picture to the scratch area on the right and release the mouse button. When Publisher displays a shortcut menu, click Copy Here.

Q&A What's the difference between drag and right-drag?

When you right-drag, Publisher gives you the choice of moving, copying, or canceling. It is a shortcut for copy and paste.

3

- If necessary, with the picture in the scratch area selected, display the Picture Tools Format tab.

- Click the Recolor button (Picture Tools Format tab | Adjust group) to display the Recolor gallery (Figure 7–57).

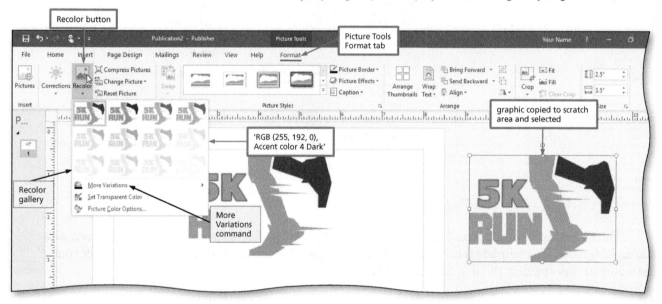

Figure 7–57

4

- Click 'RGB (255, 192, 0), Accent color 4 Dark' to change the picture to a medium yellow (Figure 7–58).

Q&A What does the More Variations command in the Recolor gallery do?

It displays the Scheme Colors gallery, where you can choose different colors than those displayed in the Recolor gallery.

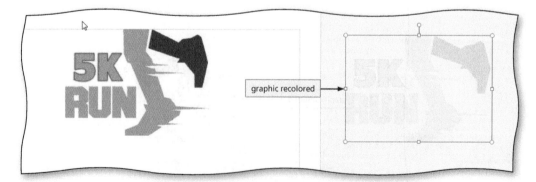

Figure 7–58

Other Ways

1. Click Recolor button (Picture Tools Format tab | Adjust group), click 'Picture Color Options' in Recolor gallery, click Color button (Format Picture dialog box | Picture tab), select color

To Edit the Brightness and Contrast

The following steps edit the brightness and contrast of the picture. *Why? Adjusting the brightness and contrast will make the features stand out, even as a shadow background.*

1

- With the picture selected, click the Corrections button (Picture Tools Format tab| Adjust group) to display the Corrections gallery (Figure 7–59).

Q&A What does the 'Picture Corrections Options' command do?

If you click 'Picture Corrections Options' in the Corrections gallery, Publisher will display the Format Picture dialog box where you can edit exact settings for brightness, contrast, and transparency.

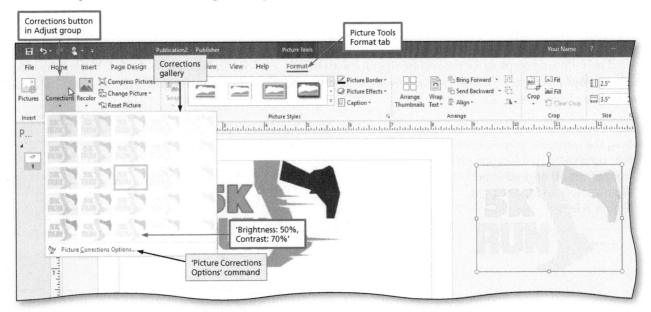

Figure 7–59

2

- Click 'Brightness: 50%, Contrast: 70%' in the Corrections gallery to change the brightness and contrast (Figure 7–60).

Experiment

- Click the Reset Picture button (Picture Tools Format tab | Adjust group) to view the picture in its original coloring, contrast, and proportion. Press CTRL+Z to undo the reset.

Q&A My gallery looks different. Did I do something wrong?

No. Depending on your screen resolution and other settings, the size of the gallery will differ, as will the placement of the gallery choices. Point to the gallery choices to verify that you are using the 'Brightness: 50%, Contrast: 70%' correction.

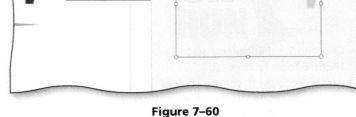

Figure 7–60

3

- Save the publication with the file name, SC_PUB_7_5KRunBib, on your storage location.

Other Ways
1. Click Corrections button (Picture Tools Format tab | Adjust group), click 'Picture Color Options' in Corrections gallery, drag Brightness or Contrast sliders (Format Picture dialog box | Picture tab), click OK   2. Right-click graphic, click Format Picture on shortcut menu, drag Brightness or Contrast sliders (Format Picture dialog box | Picture tab), click OK

Ordering

If you have multiple graphics displaying on the screen and would like them to overlap, you can change their stacking order by using the Bring Forward and Send Backward arrows (Picture Tools Format tab | Arrange group). The 'Bring to Front' command on the Bring Forward menu displays the selected object at the top of the stack, and the 'Send to Back' command on the Send Backward menu displays the selected object at the bottom of the stack. The Bring Forward and Send Backward commands each move the graphic forward or backward one layer in the stack. These commands also are available through the shortcut menu that is displayed when you right-click a graphic.

To Order Graphics

The following steps move the recolored graphic to the page layout and send it backward, behind the other graphic. *Why? Placing the recolored graphic behind and slightly offset from the original graphic will add dimension as well as a shadowed background effect.*

- Drag the recolored graphic from the scratch area to a location in front of the other graphic but slightly lower and to the right (Figure 7–61).

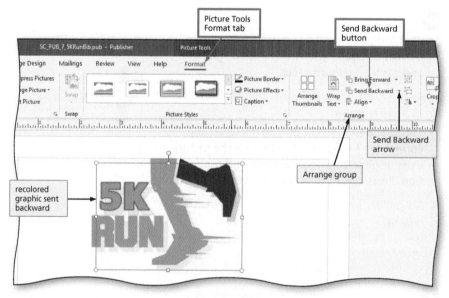

Figure 7–61

- Click the Send Backward button (Picture Tools Format tab | Arrange group) to send the recolored graphic backward one layer (Figure 7–62).

Experiment

- Click the Send Backward arrow (Picture Tools Format tab | Arrange group) to see the choices of Send Backward versus Send to Back menus. Repeat the process for the Bring Forward arrow.

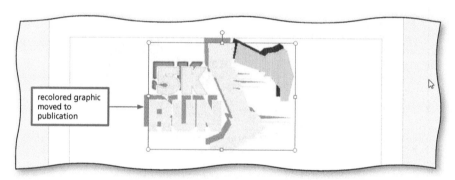

Figure 7–62

To Compress Pictures

The following steps compress the pictures. *Why?* *When you have many graphics or pictures in a publication, the physical size of the stored file increases. To reduce the file size, you will compress the pictures.* You may be familiar with Windows file compression, or zipping. In Publisher, compression includes deleting cropped areas, changing graphic file types and resolutions where necessary, and removing any extraneous data stored with the pictures.

- With either of the graphics selected, click the Compress Pictures button (Picture Tools Format tab | Adjust group) to display the Compress Pictures dialog box.

- Click to select the Desktop Printing option button in order to compress the picture for desktop printing.

- If necessary, click the 'Apply to all pictures in the publication' option button to compress all of the pictures (Figure 7–63).

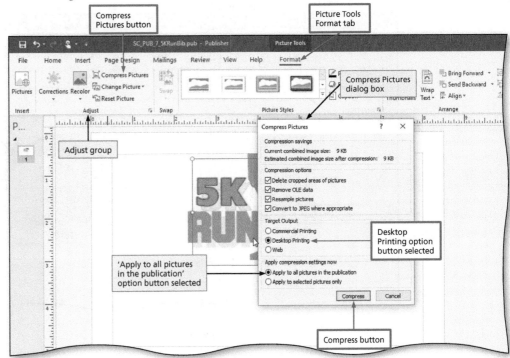

Figure 7–63

- Click the Compress button (Compress Pictures dialog box) to begin the compression process and to display a Microsoft Publisher dialog box (Figure 7–64).

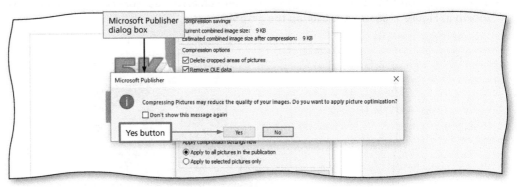

Figure 7–64

Q&A What is picture optimization?
Picture optimization involves replacing the original high-resolution pictures with a compressed version that is smaller in storage size and easier to print.

- Click the Yes button (Microsoft Publisher dialog box) to confirm the compression.

To Draw an Arrow

The following steps draw an arrow. *Why? An arrow will represent the concept of the publication and create a space for the participant ID.* You will use colors from the graphic for consistency.

- Click the scratch area to deselect any objects.
- Display the Insert tab.
- Click the Shapes button (Insert tab | Illustrations group) to display the Shapes gallery (Figure 7–65).

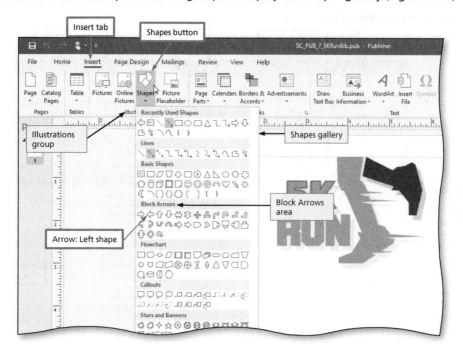

Figure 7–65

- Click the Arrow: Left shape in the Block Arrows area to select it.
- In the lower half of the publication, drag to create an arrow approximately 6.25 inches wide and 2.75 inches tall, as shown in Figure 7–66. Do not overlap the graphic.

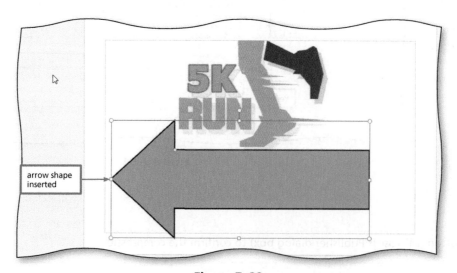

Figure 7–66

③

- Click the Shape Outline button (Drawing Tools Format tab | Shape Styles group) to display the Shape Outline gallery (Figure 7–67).

 Q&A My scheme colors look different. Did I do something wrong?
No. The default color scheme is usually Office; however, your computer may use a different default color scheme.

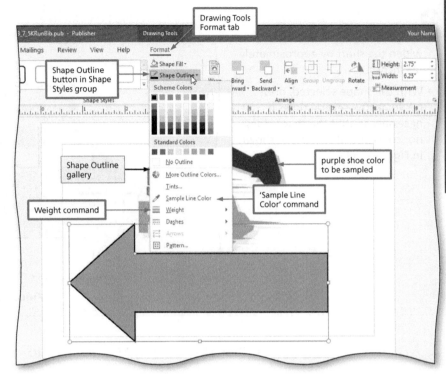

Figure 7–67

④

- Click 'Sample Line Color' in the gallery and then click the purple part of the graphic (the upper shoe).

- Click the Shape Outline button again. Point to Weight in the Shape Outline gallery and then click 3 pt on the Weight submenu (Figure 7–68).

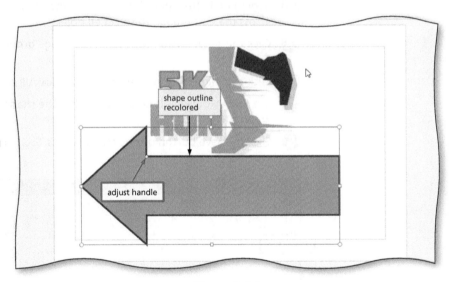

Figure 7–68

To Adjust a Shape

Many Publisher shapes display an **adjust handle** or **adjustment handle**, which is a yellow diamond on a selected shape that you can drag to change the shape's proportions without changing the overall size of the shape. In the case of an arrow, Publisher displays an adjust handle to change the width of the arrow shaft. The following step widens the arrow shaft. *Why? The arrow shaft will contain the runner ID number. It should display as prominently as possible on the bib sheet.*

1

- Drag the adjust handle up to widen the shaft by approximately .25 inches.

- With the shape selected, press DOWN ARROW several times if necessary so that the shape does not cover the blue shoe, as shown in Figure 7–69.

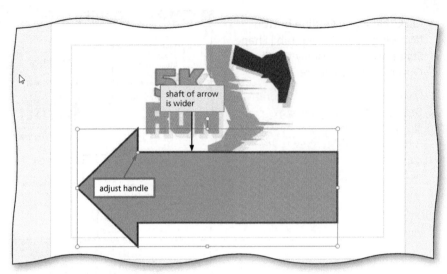

Figure 7–69

To Center the Graphics and Shape

The following steps center all of the objects horizontally on the page.

1 Beginning in the upper-left corner of the publication, drag down and to the right across the entire page to select all objects.

2 Click the Align button (Home tab | Arrange group) and then click 'Relative to Margin Guides'.

3 Click the Align button again and then click Align Center.

4 Use the ARROW keys if necessary so that the shape does not overlap the letters in the graphic (Figure 7–70).

5 Click the Save button on the Quick Access Toolbar to save the file.

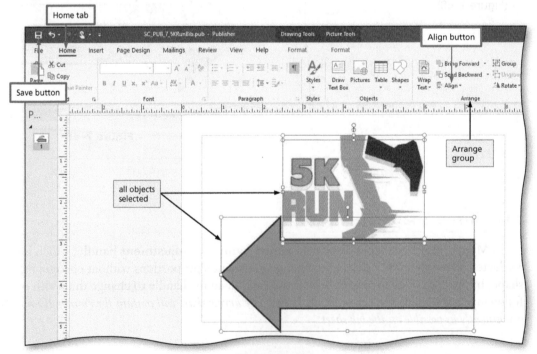

Figure 7–70

Merging with Excel

Earlier in this module, you used the Mail Merge wizard to create a recipient list saved as a database file with the extension, .mdb (Microsoft Database). While Publisher saves its data in the .mdb format, it can accept or read databases in other formats when merging. In the following sections, you will connect manually with a database stored in the Excel format. Excel files are stored with the .xlsx or .xls extension.

To Select Recipients

The following steps select recipients from the Microsoft Excel worksheet that you copied to your save location earlier. *Why? The file contains the category and participant IDs for the race.* To complete these steps, you will be required to use the Data Files. Please contact your instructor for information about accessing the Data Files.

- Click the scratch area to deselect all objects. Click Mailings on the ribbon to display the Mailings tab.

- Click the Select Recipients button (Mailings tab | Start group) to display the Select Recipients menu (Figure 7–71).

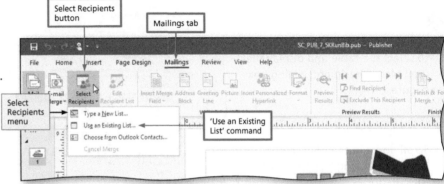

Figure 7–71

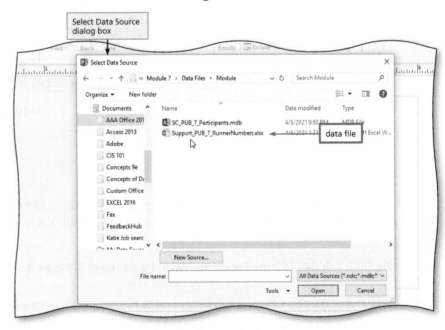

- Click 'Use an Existing List' on the Select Recipients menu to display the Select Data Source dialog box.

- Navigate to the location of the Data Files (Figure 7–72).

Figure 7–72

- Double-click the Support_PUB_7_RunnerNumbers.xlsx file to display the Select Table dialog box.

- If necessary, click the appropriate table in the list (in this case, Runners).

- If necessary, click to display a check mark in the 'First row of data contains column headers' check box (Figure 7–73).

Why does the table name have a dollar sign at the end?

Publisher appends the dollar sign to indicate that this table is from a worksheet. Imported tables without a dollar sign indicate that the table is a range.

Does the Microsoft Excel worksheet contain multiple tables?

No, but the Select Table dialog box displays for you to choose different worksheets or tables in the Excel file, should they contain any data.

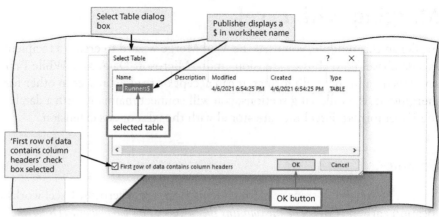

Figure 7–73

4

- Click OK (Select Table dialog box) to select the table and display the Mail Merge Recipients dialog box (Figure 7–74).

Experiment

- Scroll down in the Mail Merge Recipients dialog box to view all the categories.

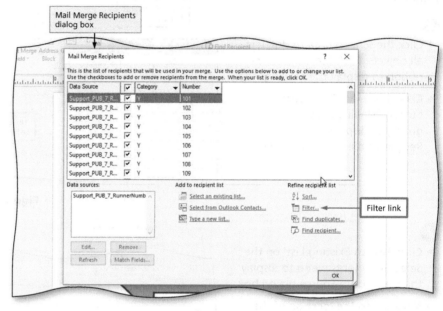

Figure 7–74

To Filter Data

The database includes ID numbers for walkers as well as the other categories. The following steps filter the data so that no numbers will be issued for walkers. *Why? This 5K race does not allow participants to walk.*

1

- Click the Filter link (Mail Merge Recipients dialog box) (shown in Figure 7–74) to display the Filter and Sort dialog box.

- If necessary, click the Filter Records tab (Filter and Sort dialog box) and then click the Field arrow to display its list.

What is the difference between filtering and sorting?

Filtering examines all records and displays only those that meet specific criteria that you specify. Sorting merely rearranges the records in a specific order but displays them all.

• Click Category in the Field list to filter by category.

• Click the Comparison arrow to display its list (Figure 7–75).

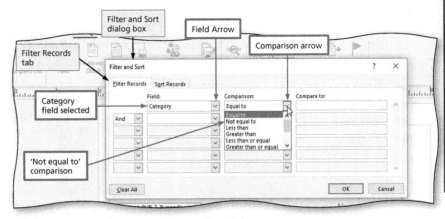

Figure 7–75

3

• Click 'Not equal to' in the Comparison list.

• Press TAB to advance to the Compare to box and then type W (which stands for Walker) to insert the Compare to value (Figure 7–76).

Q&A Will the filter delete all the Ws?

No. It selects only which categories will be used in the merge. The filter and sort links do not change the data source or mail merge permanently.

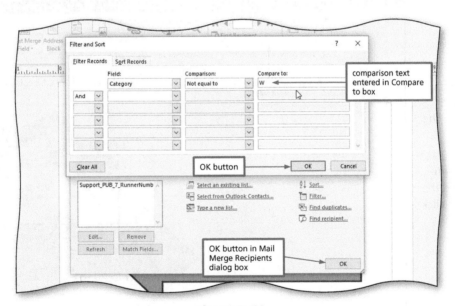

Figure 7–76

4

• Click OK (Filter and Sort dialog box) to accept the filter and return to the Mail Merge Recipients dialog box.

Q&A How did the recipient list change?

If you scroll down in the Mail Merge Recipients dialog box, you no longer will see a category for W.

5

• Click OK (Mail Merge Recipients dialog box) to close the dialog box.

To Add Text to a Shape

The following steps add text to a shape. ***Why?*** *The shape will display the category and runner number.*

- Right-click the arrow shape to display a shortcut menu (Figure 7–77).

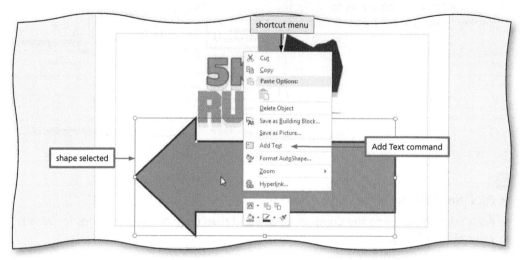

Figure 7–77

2

- Click Add Text on the shortcut menu to position the insertion point in the arrow.

- Change the font color to 'Accent 5 (White)'. Change the font size to 24.

- On the horizontal ruler, drag the Left Indent marker to the 1" mark. Do not click outside the arrow (Figure 7–78).

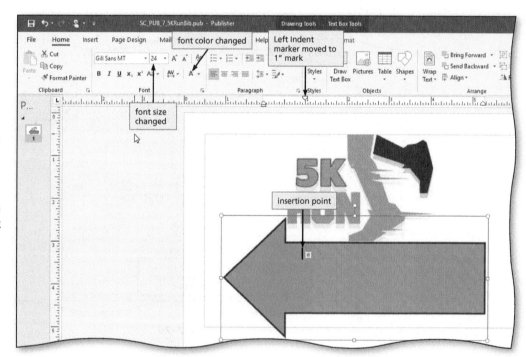

Figure 7–78

To Insert Merge Field Codes

The following steps use the ribbon to insert merge field codes. ***Why?*** *Sometimes using the Mailings tab on the ribbon is easier than using the wizard, especially if the data file has been created already.*

1

- With the insertion point positioned in the arrow, click the 'Insert Merge Field' button (Mailings tab | Write & Insert Fields group) to display the menu (Figure 7–79).

Q&A | What is the purpose of the Picture button (Mailings tab | Write & Insert Fields group)?
If your database has a field with pictures in each record, you can insert that as a field code. Publisher will display the picture.

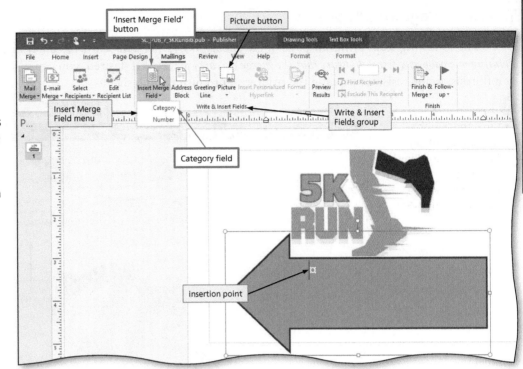

Figure 7–79

2

- Click Category in the Insert Merge Field menu to insert the field and then press SPACEBAR.

3

- Repeat Steps 1 and 2 to insert the Number field. Do not press SPACEBAR after the Number field.

- If necessary, click the Preview Results button (Mailings tab | Preview Results group) to enable it.

4

- Right-click the text and then click Best Fit on the shortcut menu to autofit the text (Figure 7–80).

- Save the file again.

 Experiment

- Click the Next Record button (Mailings tab | Preview Results group) to view subsequent numbers.

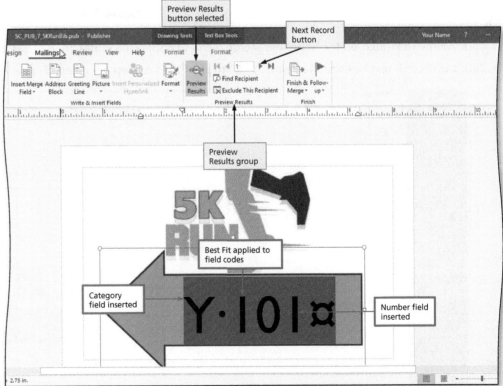

Figure 7–80

To Print a Page of Bib Sheets

The following steps print one page of bib sheets. *Why? The data source has many numbered bib sheets. Printing one page as a test will assure that the merge executed properly.* If desired, you can insert special sticker paper or a fibrous, water-resistant paper in the printer to produce the bib sheets.

1

- Click the 'Finish & Merge' button (Mailings tab | Finish group) to display the Finish and Merge menu (Figure 7–81).

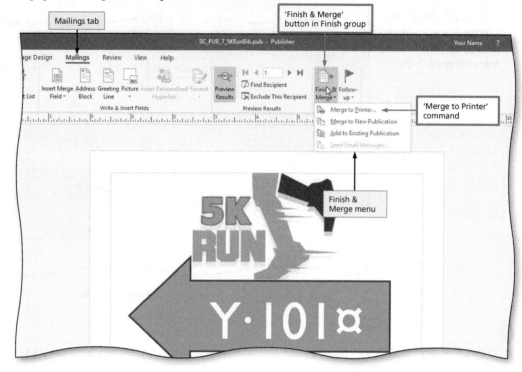

Figure 7–81

2

- Click 'Merge to Printer' on the Finish and Merge menu to display the Print screen in Backstage view.

- Click the Records text box and then type **1-2** to print the first two bib sheets (Figure 7–82).

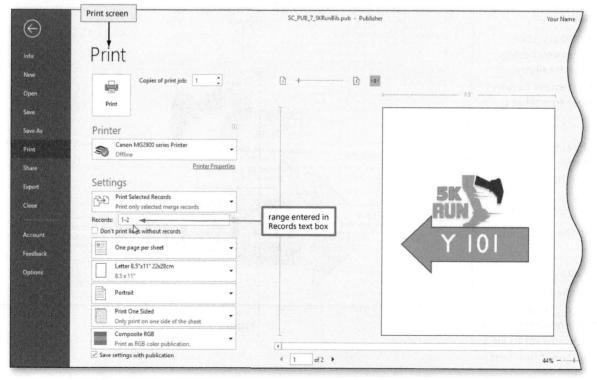

Figure 7–82

3

- Click the 'One page
per sheet' button
to display its menu
(Figure 7–83).

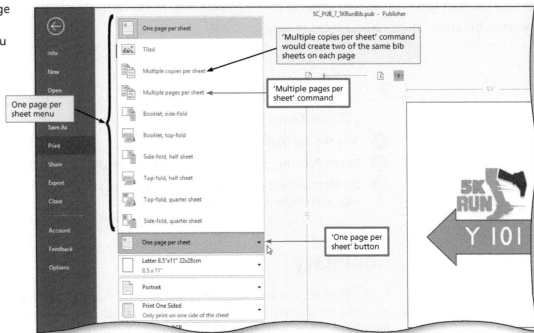

Figure 7–83

4

- Click 'Multiple pages per sheet' to choose the option.
- Verify that other settings match those shown in Figure 7–84.

Q&A What is the
difference between
'Multiple copies per
sheet' and 'Multiple
pages per sheet'
commands?
When you print more
than one copy per
page, the 'Multiple
copies per sheet'
command repeats
the record data on
all the copies on
your printed page.
The 'Multiple pages
per sheet' command
does not repeat the
data; each bib sheet
has its own category
and number.

My graphic seems
to be cut off at the
bottom. What should I do?

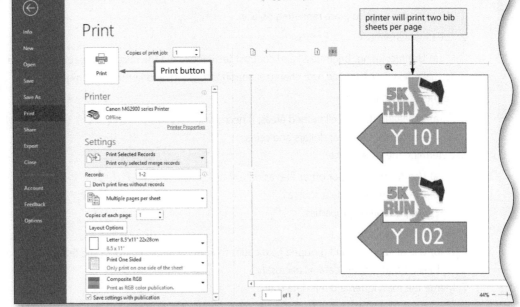

Figure 7–84

Print margins are printer dependent and vary widely. If your second bib sheet is cut off at the bottom, return to the
publication, press CTRL+A to select all text, and then press UP ARROW several times to nudge the contents upward.
Click the 'Finish & Merge' button again and then click 'Merge to Printer'.

5
- Click the Print button in the Print screen to print the publication on the currently selected printer.
- When the printer stops, retrieve the hard copy.

To Save and Exit

The final steps save the file and exit Publisher.

1 Save the file again.

2 To exit Publisher, click the Close button on the right side of the title bar.

3 If a Microsoft Publisher dialog box is displayed, click the Don't Save button so that any editing changes you have made are not saved.

Summary

In this module, you learned how to merge data files with publications. First, you created a form letter with a watermark and special character and tab formatting in the letterhead. Then, you created a Publisher data source and customized the fields. Next, you inserted field codes and merged the form letter with the data source. Finally, you created a bib sheet, used a Microsoft Excel data file to merge fields manually using the ribbon, and then printed one page of bib sheets.

CONSIDER THIS: PLAN AHEAD

What decisions will you need to make when creating your next business publication?
Use these guidelines as you complete the assignments in this module and create your own publications outside of this class.

1. Use a master page to place repeating objects.

2. Create a watermark.

   a) Use recoloring, brightness, and contrast techniques to fade necessary graphics while retaining detail.

3. To make text easier to read, use character spacing, tracking, and kerning techniques.

4. Set necessary tab stops.

   a) Use leader tabs to fill tabbed areas, if necessary.

   b) Use decimal tabs for dollars and cents.

5. Determine the data source.

   a) Use Access, Excel, or other files as data sources.

   b) Create necessary data sources.

   c) Set publication properties.

6. Create the form letter.

   a) Use fields codes and grouped field codes to insert changing parts of the letter.

   b) Filter and sort the data as necessary.

7. Merge the form letter and the data source.

   a) Proofread and check a merged copy of the publication.

Apply Your Knowledge

Reinforce the skills and apply the concepts you learned in this module.

Creating Merged Statements

Note: To complete this assignment, you will be required to use the Data Files. Please contact your instructor for information about accessing the Data Files.

Instructions: Start Publisher. If necessary, copy the data source file, Support_PUB_7_AddressList.accdb, from the Data Files to your storage location and appropriate folder. Review the section in this module titled To Copy the Data Source File for instructions on copying and pasting the file from one folder to another. The data will be merged with a publication to produce monthly statements for a company that delivers bottled water to offices and homes. You are to kern characters, set tabs, edit the address list, and then merge and print. The first merged statement is shown in Figure 7–85.

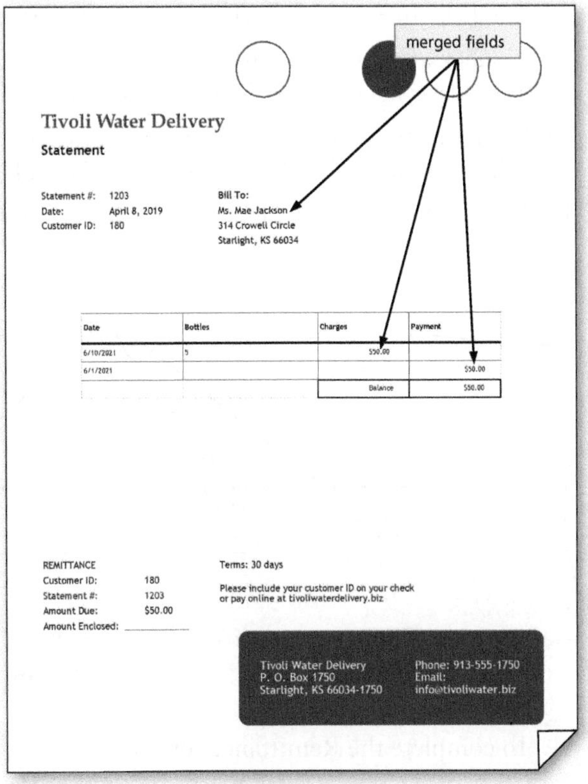

Figure 7–85

Perform the following tasks:

1. Open the publication named SC_PUB_7-2 from the Data Files. Save the publication on your storage location (in the same folder as the data source file, Support_PUB_7_AddressList.accdb) using the file name SC_PUB_7_WaterStatements.

2. Zoom in to the upper portion of the statement. Drag to select the letters, Ti, in the company name. Click the Object Size button on the Publisher status bar to open the Measurement pane. In the Kerning box, type -3 to move the two letters closer together. Repeat the process for the letters Wa in the word water. Close the Measurement pane.

3. Display the Mailings tab. Click the Mail Merge arrow (Mailings tab | Start group) and then click 'Step-by-Step Mail Merge Wizard' on the Mail Merge menu.

4. In the Mail Merge pane, if necessary, click the 'Use an existing list' option button to select it and then click the 'Next: Create or connect to a recipient list' link. When Publisher displays the Select Data Source dialog box, navigate to your storage location and then double-click the file name, Support_PUB_7_AddressList.accdb.

5. In the Mail Merge Recipients dialog box, select the file name, Support_PUB_7_AddressList.accdb, in the Data sources box and then click the Edit button (Mail Merge Recipients dialog box) to display the Edit Data Source dialog box.

6. Click the New Entry button (Edit Data Source dialog box) and then create a fictitious client with dates and payments. If requested by your instructor, enter your name and address as the new record.

7. Click OK (Edit Data Source dialog box). When Publisher asks if you want to update and save the list, click the Yes button. When the Mail Merge Recipients dialog box again is displayed, click OK.

Continued >

Apply Your Knowledge *continued*

8. To complete the text box for Statement, Date, and Customer ID:

   a. Click after the tab marker for Statement. In the Mail Merge pane, scroll in the list of fields as necessary and click Statement.

   b. Click after the tab marker for Date. Insert a date that updates automatically.

   c. Click after the tab marker for Customer ID. In the Mail Merge pane, scroll in the list of fields as necessary and click Customer Number.

9. Click the placeholder text in the 'Type address here…" box. In the Mail Merge pane, click the Address block link. Choose an appropriate address style.

10. In the statement table, insert field codes as shown in Figure 7–86.

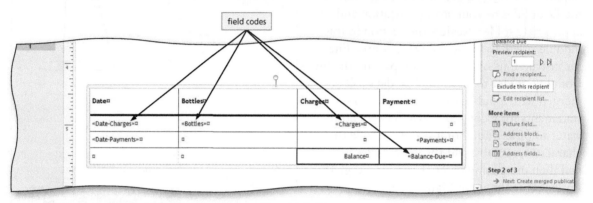

Figure 7–86

11. To complete the Remittance text box:

   a. Click after the tab marker for Customer ID. In the Mail Merge pane, scroll in the list of fields as necessary and click Customer Number.

   b. Click after the tab marker for Statement. In the Mail Merge pane, scroll in the list of fields as necessary and click Statement.

   c. Click after the tab marker for Amount Due. In the Mail Merge pane, scroll in the list of fields as necessary and click Balance Due.

12. Click the <<Charges>> field code and then click the Format button (Mailings tab | Write & Insert Fields group). Click Format Currency on the Format menu to display the Format Currency dialog box. Choose English (United States) and two decimal places. Click OK (Currency dialog box). Repeat the process for the << Payments>> and <<Balance Due>> field codes.

13. Click the 'Finish & Merge' button (Mailings tab | Finish group) and then click 'Merge to New Publication' on the Finish & Merge menu. When the new publication is displayed, save it using the file name, SC_PUB_7_WaterStatementsMerged, on your storage device. Close the file.

14. Save the SC_PUB_7_WaterStatements.pub file again.

15. Submit the files as specified by your instructor.

16. ✳ What kind of data source files would you expect to find with invoice generation? Do you think most small businesses use Access or Excel to store their invoice data? If you were asked about database options, what would you recommend for use with Publisher?

Extend Your Knowledge

Extend the skills you learned in this module and experiment with new skills. You may need to use Help to complete the assignment.

Filtering and Sorting a Recipient List

Note: To complete this assignment, you will be required to use the Data Files. Please contact your instructor for information about accessing the Data Files.

Instructions: If necessary, copy the data source file, Support_PUB_7_RecipientList.mdb, from the Data Files to your storage location and appropriate folder. Review the section in this module entitled To Copy the Data Source File for instructions on copying and pasting the file from one folder to another. Open the publication called SC_PUB_7-3.pub from the Data Files. The file you open is an envelope to which you will add addresses.

In this assignment, you will filter an address list for recipients living in two specific cities. Next, you will sort the list by last name and then by first name to create an alphabetical listing. Finally, you will apply the merged address block to an envelope publication.

Perform the following tasks:

1. Use Help to learn more about printing, exporting, filtering, and sorting recipient lists.

2. Save the publication with the file name, SC_PUB_7_EnvelopeMerge.

3. To prevent any changes to the return address and logo, move them to the master page as follows: select all (CTRL+A) and then cut (CTRL+X). Go to the master page and paste (CTRL+V) all objects to the master page. Close the master page.

4. Open the Mail Merge pane using the Step-by-Step Mail Merge wizard. Use the list named Support_PUB_7_RecipientList.mdb from your storage location.

5. In the Mail Merge Recipients dialog box, click the Filter link. Choose to filter the list with the City field equal to Eden. Click the And box arrow (Filter and Sort dialog box), click Or in the list, and then add a second filter with City equal to Griffith. Click OK to close the Filter and Sort dialog box.

6. In the Mail Merge Recipients dialog box, click the Sort link. Sort the list alphabetically first by last name and then by first name, in ascending order (Figure 7–87).

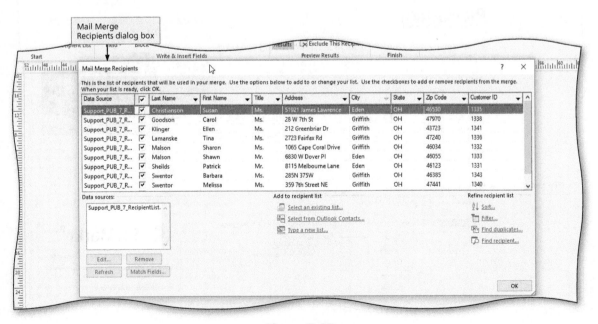

Figure 7–87

Continued >

Extend Your Knowledge *continued*

7. If instructed to do so, add your name as a new record in the file. Click OK to close the Mail Merge Recipient dialog box.

8. In the publication where the mailing address should be, draw a text box approximately 4 inches wide and 1.5 inches tall. In the Mail Merge pane, click the Address block link to display the Insert Address block dialog box. Choose an appropriate format and click OK.

9. In the publication, select the grouped field named Address block. Autofit, resize, and reposition the text box so that it creates an appropriate envelope address.

10. Return to the Mail Merge pane and proceed to the next wizard step. Click the 'Export recipient list to a new file' link (Mail Merge pane) and then save the filtered list with the file name, SC_PUB_7_EdenGriffithResidents, on your storage location.

11. Return to the Mail Merge pane and proceed to the next wizard step. Click the Print link to display the Print screen. Click the Tiled button and then click Envelope. Print the first envelope.

12. When Publisher displays the publication again, click the 'Print recipient list' link (Mail Merge pane) and include only the First Name, Last Name, Address, City, State, and Zip Code fields. Submit the copies to your instructor.

13. ✷ List two other ways you could generate envelopes if you do not have access to a printer with an envelope feed.

Expand Your World

Create a solution that uses cloud and web technologies by learning and investigating on your own from general guidance.

Creating a Watermark

Instructions: You would like to insert a watermark in a picture you have taken. You decide to try a web service called PicMarkr (Figure 7–88).

Source: picmarkr.com

Figure 7–88

Perform the following tasks:

1. Start a browser and navigate to www.PicMarkr.com.

2. Click the Browse button in the Step 1: Upload images section and navigate to a picture that you have taken. When you are finished uploading, scroll down and click the 'OK! Go to Step 2' button.

3. When PicMarkr displays Step 2, enter your name in the Text to display box in the Text watermark section and then choose a placement in the Watermark align area.

4. Click the Continue button.

5. When PicMarkr is finished, download the picture and then insert it in a publication. Submit the assignment in the format specified by your instructor.

6. ✳ How does PicMarkr compare to creating a watermark in Publisher? What steps would you have to take in Publisher to create the same effect?

In the Lab

Design and implement a solution using creative thinking and problem-solving skills.

Merging with an Excel File

Note: To complete this assignment, you will be required to use the Data Files. Please contact your instructor for information about accessing the Data Files.

Problem: A club on your campus is sponsoring a night of original one-act plays by graduate students. The club has asked you to create tickets for the production.

Part 1:   From scratch, create a new publication approximately 6 inches wide and 2.25 inches tall. Choose an appropriate color and font scheme. Insert an appropriate page border. Include the name of the production, the date and time, and the location. Track the name of the production loosely to make it more legible. Kern any character pairs that may need it. If instructed to do so, change the location of the lecture to your classroom building and number.

From the Data Files, insert the picture named Support_PUB_7_PlayGraphic.png. Recolor the picture using an Accent 2 color. Resize as necessary. Compress the picture.

Create a text box with appropriate tabbing to display the section, row, and seat. The college has given you an Excel spreadsheet that contains the seat numbers; however, due to construction, only the center section is available for the production. The spreadsheet, located in the Data Files, is named Support_PUB_7_SeatNumbers.xlsx. If necessary, copy and paste the file to your storage location. Merge the publication with the data source and place appropriate fields. Save the merged publication.

Part 2:   ✳ How can you be sure that the tickets will print correctly? What are the advantages and disadvantages to buying prescored paper to create tickets? What are the advantages and disadvantages of sending out the tickets for publication?

8 | Generating Data-Driven Catalogs

Objectives

After completing this module, you will be able to:

- Insert headers and footers
- Duplicate a master page
- Apply alternating master pages
- Use textures and number styles
- Format a picture by cropping to shape and adding a reflection
- Create catalog pages
- Use the catalog merge area
- Turn on boundaries and align objects
- Find entries
- Preview and merge catalogs
- Work with the Graphics Manager
- Translate text

Introduction

Because most businesses keep track of their inventory, data, and statistics in electronic databases, it is efficient to use that data to build custom marketing pieces, such as catalogs, for print media or for e-commerce applications on the web. A publication that is directly populated and updated from a database is considered a **data-driven publication**.

Data-driven publications can include form letters; documents with individualized data, such as tickets and envelopes; and documents linked to other applications that contain data, such as Excel data imported to Publisher tables. In this module, you will learn how to create data-driven publications by using the Catalog Tools Format tab. Many businesses customize Publisher catalogs and use customer profiling to target certain markets. While publishing a large, full-color catalog can require a significant marketing investment due to production, printing, and distribution costs, with desktop publishing, even small businesses can create external and internal publications about products, personnel, or services.

Project: Fitness Center Catalog

To introduce its equipment to the members and the community, a new local fitness center would like a catalog with pictures of the machines, descriptions, and other pieces of data about which members might be interested. The catalog contains eight half-pages, printed on both sides of two 8.5 × 11-inch pieces of paper and then folded, as shown in Figure 8–1.

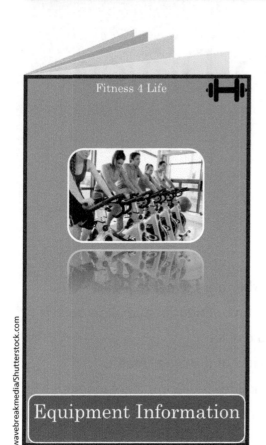

wavebreakmedia/Shutterstock.com

This catalog will be created using Publisher's catalog merge, which differs from its mail merge in two distinctive ways. The catalog merge is designed with graphics or pictures in mind. It is easy to incorporate pictures into the merge process — and the pictures can change from record to record. In addition, a catalog merge includes all records in one longer booklet publication rather than separate pages, as is the case with form letters. Toward that end, Publisher provides a unique **merge area** that desktop publishers use to design a presentation with field data that change from record to record and layout that does not.

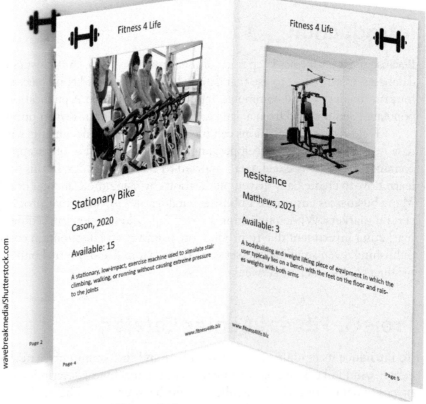

wavebreakmedia/Shutterstock.com

Figure 8–1

You will perform the following general tasks as you progress through this module:

1. Format alternating master pages with graphics, headers, footers, and page numbers.
2. Use textures and number styles.
3. Format a picture by cropping to shape and adding a reflection.
4. Create and format catalog pages, with nonrepeating text and graphics inserted.
5. Connect with a data source.
6. Insert picture and text merge fields.
7. Manage graphics.
8. Translate text, as necessary.
9. Merge to a printed publication.

Catalogs and Directories

A **catalog** is a collection of pictures and descriptive details that represent items for sale, services offered, or any data list.

Publisher has catalog templates to assist you in designing catalogs and directories. In addition, Publisher provides a catalog merge that quickly and easily populates the publication. A catalog merge is the process of combining information from a data source with a template or an original publication to create pages that display multiple records per page.

Typically, a Publisher catalog template creates eight pages of content with replaceable graphics and text boxes. You can select the page size, font scheme, and color scheme of the catalog, just as you do with other publications. In addition, with catalogs, you can choose the content layout of specific pages, selecting the number of columns, forms, calendars, featured items, or table of contents for those pages. Alternatively, you can create a catalog from scratch, designing your pages one at a time, or you can use a blank catalog template, as you will do in this project.

How do you plan the layout of a catalog?

Due to the graphical, full-color nature of catalogs and the high-quality paper that commonly is used, planning is essential to keep a catalog project on schedule and within budget. You must identify resource requirements and formulate strategies that drive business growth. Typically, a business can reuse and repurpose catalog content for other forms of advertisements, such as seasonal promotion publications. Many companies store pictures and data together in database files so that they are readily available to populate catalogs, directories, brochures, and websites. Here are some general rules to consider when you are planning a catalog's layout:

- Create your publication in a common size. It will be less costly at both the printer and the post office.
- Use an even number of pages to avoid blank pages in your catalog or directory. Check ahead of time to find out how many records of data are in the data source.
- Alternate headers and footers as necessary to create outside edge page numbers.
- Create a layout that will attract your audience. A business-to-business (B2B) catalog is different from a business-to-consumer (B2C) catalog. Catalogs for young people will have a different look than will catalogs for older people. Make the style of your catalog match the style preferences of your audience.
- Repeat layout designs or use alternating pages for consistency. Do not make the customer look for information in two places. For example, keep your prices in approximately the same place in each repeating element.
- Repeat some objects to provide consistency. Use headers and footers or a background to create a cohesive unit.
- Keep the name of the product close to any pictures or graphics.
- Limit the fonts to two or three, and use WordArt sparingly.

CONSIDER THIS

To Create a Two-Page Spread

The following steps choose a blank catalog template and set the font and color schemes for the catalog. Publisher will offer to create multiple pages, using a two-page spread. *Why? Publisher recognizes this file as a catalog template.* A **two-page spread**, or simply a **spread**, refers to the way inner pages appear as two adjacent, facing pages in a book, catalog, magazine, or other publication.

- Start Publisher.
- In the New Template gallery, click Built-In and then click Catalogs to view the available templates.
- Scroll to the middle portion of the gallery to display the Blank Sizes area.
- Click the '1/2 Letter Booklet 5.5 × 8.5"' template to select it.
- In the Customize area, select the Concourse color scheme and the Textbook font scheme.
- Click the CREATE button to display the Microsoft Publisher dialog box (Figure 8–2).

Q&A | My publication was created with a previous business information set. What should I do?
If you do not need to keep the business information set, click the Business Information button (Insert tab | Text group), click 'Edit Business Information' on the Business Information menu, click the Delete button (Business Information dialog box), click the Yes button (Microsoft Publisher dialog box), and then click the Close button (Business Information dialog box).

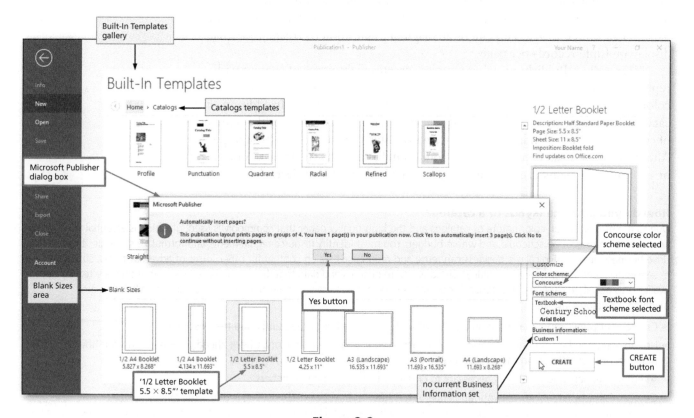

Figure 8–2

- Click the Yes button (Microsoft Publisher dialog box) to have Publisher create an even number of pages in the publication.
- If the rulers do not appear, press CTRL+R to display the rulers.

- If the Page Navigation pane does not open, click the Page Number button on the status bar.

- If necessary, click the Special Characters button to select it (Home tab | Paragraph group).

- If the Page Navigation pane is collapsed, click the 'Expand Page Navigation Pane' button at the top of the Page Navigation pane (Figure 8–3).

Q&A Why does Publisher display three thumbnails in the Page Navigation pane?

The front and back of a catalog are single pages. Pages 2 and 3 appear as a two-page spread.

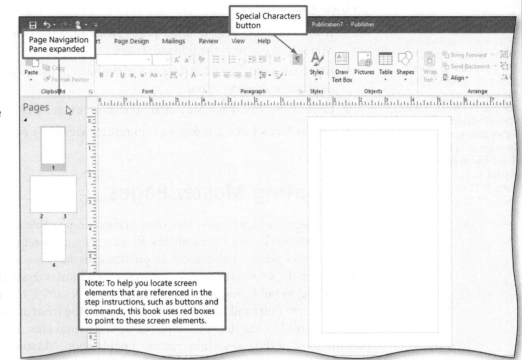

Figure 8–3

③

- Display the Page Design tab.

- Click the Margins button (Page Design tab | Page Setup group) and then click Narrow on the Margins menu to create a narrow margin (Figure 8–4).

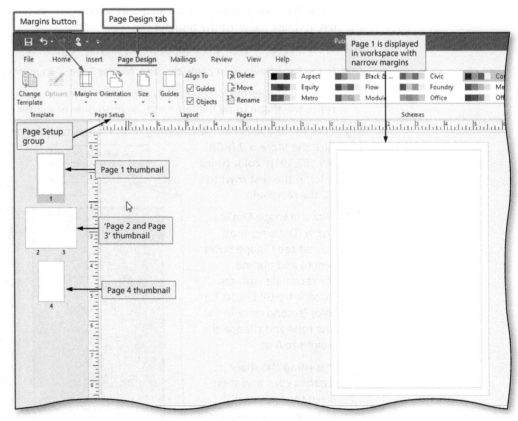

Figure 8–4

BTW

**The Ribbon and
Screen Resolution**
Publisher may change how
the groups and buttons
within the groups appear on
the ribbon, depending on the
computer or mobile device's
screen resolution. Thus, your
ribbon may look different
from the ones in this book
if you are using a screen
resolution other than
1366 × 768.

TO VIEW SINGLE PAGES

If you wanted to display single pages rather than the two-page spread for pages 2 and 3, you would perform the following steps.

1. Right-click the 'Page 2 and Page 3' thumbnail in the Page Navigation pane to display the shortcut menu.
2. Click 'View Two-Page Spread' on the shortcut menu to turn off the setting.
3. Repeat Steps 1 and 2 if you want to resume viewing a two-page spread.

Alternating Master Pages

A master page is a background area used to create repeatable elements, such as headers, footers, watermarks, and layout guides. Elements on a master page will appear on every page of a printed publication. In publications that have more than one page, you can create multiple, alternating master pages for a more versatile publication design. For example, in publications that use a spread, it is common to create multiple master pages for verso (left) and recto (right) pages or for the front and back pages.

In Publisher, the default is Normal view. **Normal view** is the view where you perform most of the tasks while creating a publication. **Master Page view** shows you the page or pages that contain the elements that you want to repeat on multiple pages.

To Create the Background on Master Page A

The following steps create a shape to use on master page A, which will appear on the first and last pages of the booklet.

1 Press CTRL+M to view the publication in Master Page view.

2 In the Page Navigation pane, click the 'Master Page A' thumbnail to select it, if necessary.

3 Click the Shapes button (Insert tab | Illustrations group), insert a rectangle, and then resize the shape to fill the left-hand, or verso, side of master page A within the margins.

4 Click the Shape Fill arrow (Drawing Tools Format tab | Shape Styles group) and then click the 'Accent 2 (RGB (45,162,191))' color (third color in the first row) to fill the rectangle.

5 Click the Shape Outline arrow (Drawing Tools Format tab | Shape Styles group) and outline the rectangle with the 'Accent 1 (RGB (70,70,70))' color (second color in the first row) and change the weight to 6 pt.

6 CTRL+drag the shape to create a copy and then place the copy on the recto side of the master page (Figure 8–5).

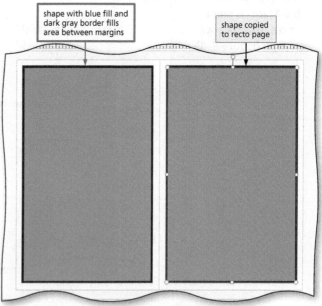

Figure 8–5

Headers and Footers

A **header** is text and graphics that print at the top of each page in a publication. Similarly, a **footer** is text and graphics that print at the bottom of every page. In Publisher, headers print one-half inch from the top margin of every page, and footers print one-half inch from the bottom margin of every page by default. In addition to text and graphics, headers and footers can include document information, such as the page number, current date, current time, and author's name.

The 'Show Header/Footer' button (Master Page tab | Header & Footer group) toggles between the header and footer areas and displays a text box in which you can insert text elements. If you want to use a graphic, you must insert the graphic and drag it to the header or footer area.

To Create a Header

The following steps create a header that will repeat across all pages of the publication. ***Why?*** *A repeating header will provide consistency and brand the look and feel of the publication.* You will add text to the header area and insert a graphic to complete the header for the verso page (left side) of master page A. To complete these steps, you will be required to use the Data Files. Please contact your instructor for information about accessing the Data Files.

- Click the shape on the verso page to select it.
- Click the 'Show Header/Footer' button (Master Page tab | Header & Footer group) to display the Header text box.
- Zoom to 100%, if necessary.
- Move the header down into the shape and then resize the height of the header text box to be approximately .5 inches tall (Figure 8–6).

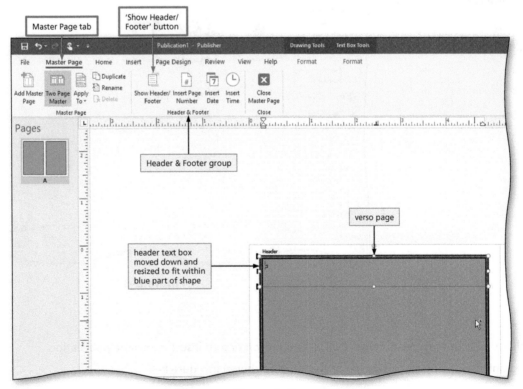

Figure 8–6

- Click the 1.5" mark on the horizontal ruler to set a tab stop.
- With the insertion point positioned in the Header text box, change the font size to 18 and then press TAB.
- Change the font color to 'Accent 5 (White)' (eighth color in the first row).
- Type **Fitness 4 Life** to complete the text (Figure 8–7).

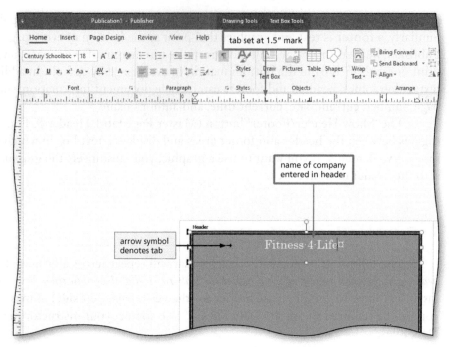

Figure 8–7

- Display the Insert tab.
- Click the Pictures button (Insert tab | Illustrations group) to display the Insert Picture dialog box.
- Navigate to the Data Files (Figure 8–8).

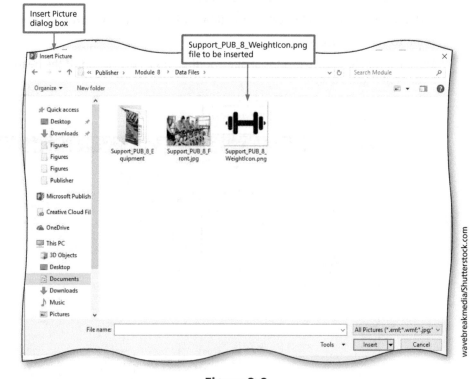

Figure 8–8

- Double-click the picture named Support_PUB_8_WeightIcon.png to insert it into the publication.
- Drag the graphic to the upper-left corner of the page, as shown in Figure 8–9.

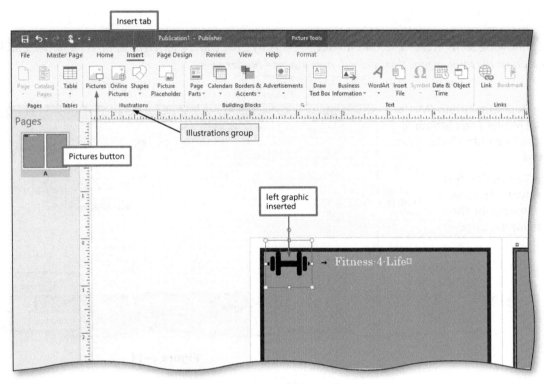

Figure 8–9

Other Ways

1. Click Header button (Insert Tab | Header & Footer group), type header text

To Create a Mirrored Header

The following steps create a mirrored header for the recto (right) pages.

1. Scroll to display the right side of master page A, which will be the recto pages in the booklet.

2. If necessary, click the header at the top of the recto page to display the text box.

3. Move the header down into the shape and then resize the height of the header text box to be approximately .5 inches tall.

4. On the horizontal ruler, click at approximately the 1.5" mark to create a tab stop.

5. Press TAB. Change the font size to 18, change the font color to 'Accent 5 (White)', and then type **Fitness 4 Life** to complete the text.

6. Select the weight icon picture and copy it. Paste the picture and then drag the copy to the upper-right corner of the recto page, as shown in Figure 8–10.

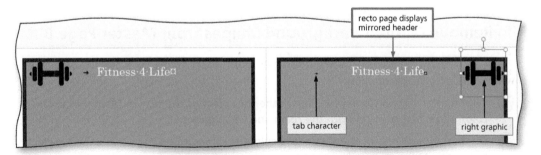

Figure 8–10

To Duplicate a Master Page

The following steps create a second master page. *Why? You will use different features on the back and front of the booklet than on the inside pages; thus, you will need a second master page.*

❶

- Click the Duplicate button (Master Page tab | Master Page group) to display the Duplicate Master Page dialog box.

- With the Description text selected, type **Inside Pages** to describe the duplicate master page (Figure 8–11).

Could I use the 'Add a Master Page' button (Master Page tab | Master Page group)?
The 'Add a Master Page' button will create a blank page. In this booklet, you would like to copy some of the features from master page A.

How does Publisher use the description that I entered?
The description appears in a ScreenTip when you point to the master page thumbnail in the Page Navigation pane.

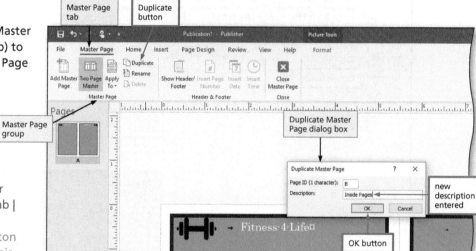

Figure 8–11

❷

- Click OK (Duplicate Master Page dialog box) to close the dialog box and create the duplicate master page.

Other Ways

1. In Master Page view, right-click master page thumbnail in Page Navigation pane, click 'Insert Duplicate Page' on shortcut menu, right-click duplicate page, click Rename on shortcut menu, enter description (Rename Master Page dialog box), click OK

TO RENAME A MASTER PAGE

If you wanted to rename a master page, you would perform the following steps.

1. In Master Page view, right-click the desired page in the Page Navigation pane, such as master page A, to display a shortcut menu.

2. Click Rename on the shortcut menu to display the Rename Master Page dialog box.

3. In the Description text box, enter a new name, such as Front and Back.

4. Click OK (Rename Master Page dialog box).

To Remove Colored Background Shapes from Master Page B

The following steps remove the shapes from master page B, as the inside pages will use a different background.

❶ With master page B displayed, change the font color of the text to Main (Black) (first color in the first row) on both the recto and verso pages.

❷ On master page B, click the shape (the colored rectangle) on the verso page to select it. Press DELETE to delete the shape.

3 Click the shape on the recto page to select it. Press DELETE to delete the shape (Figure 8–12).

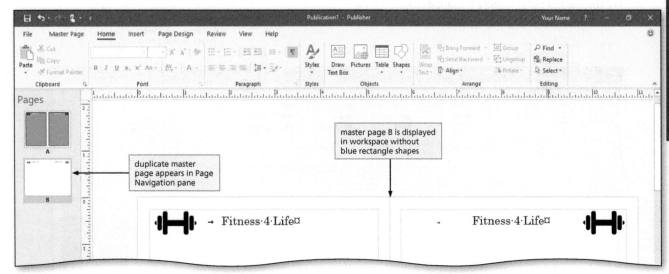

Figure 8–12

To Insert a Texture

Shape fills and Background fills include color, tints, pictures, gradients, textures, and patterns. You can use colors, pictures, and gradients to fill the background of publications; you also can use textures. A texture is a combination of color and patterns without gradual shading. Publisher's Texture gallery includes 24 images that you can use as a fill; many websites also have downloadable textures for Publisher. These textures create repeating rectangles across the page in a tiled fashion. After choosing a texture and setting a transparency, you also can select an offset. An **offset**, or **tiling option**, determines the scaling factor for the texture fill. Table 8–1 displays the offset options used to customize a texture fill.

Table 8–1 Offset Options

Setting	Purpose
Offset X	Shifts the fill to the left (negative numbers) or the right (positive numbers)
Offset Y	Shifts the fill up (negative numbers) or down (positive numbers)
Scale X	Specifies horizontal scaling of the fill by a percentage
Scale Y	Specifies vertical scaling of the fill by a percentage
Alignment	Specifies the anchor position where the picture tiling begins, such as top left or bottom right
Mirror type	Specifies that alternating horizontal or vertical tiles should appear mirrored or flipped with every other tile, horizontally, vertically, or both

The following steps add a texture to master page B. *Why? In a published directory, catalog, or booklet, a texture background will soften the look of a plain white background.*

1

- Display the Page Design tab and then click the Background button (Page Design tab | Page Background group) to display the Background gallery (Figure 8–13).

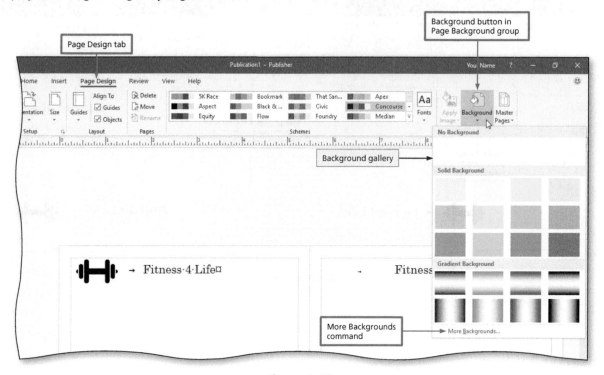

Figure 8–13

2

- Click More Backgrounds in the Background gallery to display the Format Background dialog box.

- Click the 'Picture or texture fill' option button (Format Background dialog box) to display the available settings.

- Drag the Transparency slider to 65% to increase the transparency of the texture.

- Click the Texture button to display the Texture gallery (Figure 8–14).

Experiment

- Point to each of the textures to display each texture name in a ScreenTip.

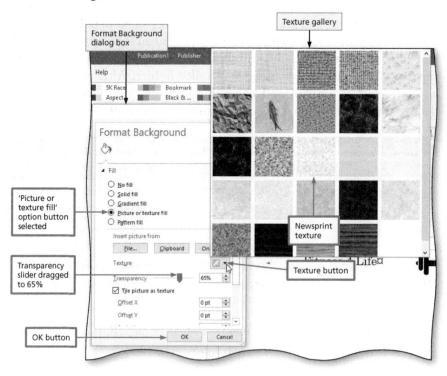

Figure 8–14

- Click the Newsprint texture in the Texture gallery to select it.

Experiment

- Scroll to and then click the Alignment arrow and the Mirror type arrow to see the choices for tiling options.

- Click OK (Format Background dialog box) to apply the background to the master page (Figure 8–15).

Q&A Could I have created the background in Normal view?
Yes, but it would have applied only to the current page. Creating the background on the master page applies it to all pages.

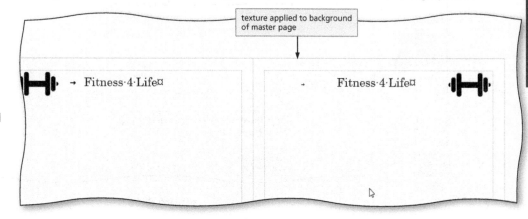

Figure 8–15

To Insert Alternating Footers

The master page for the front and back of the catalog will not display a footer. **Why?** *The first and back pages in a booklet rarely display page numbers.* The inside pages will display a footer with a page number and the company's web address.

In many publications that contain facing pages, the page number is located on the outside edges of the pages. In Publisher, you accomplish this task by specifying one type of footer for verso pages and another type for recto pages — a technique called **alternating footers**. The following steps create alternating footers for the inside pages.

- Display the Master Page tab.

- With master page B still selected, click the 'Show Header/Footer' button (Master Page tab | Header & Footer group) and then click the button again to move to the verso footer area.

- Zoom to 150%.

- Drag the footer text box up within the margin.

- Type **Page** and then press SPACEBAR.

- Click the 'Insert Page Number' button (Master Page tab | Header & Footer group) to enter the page number placeholder (Figure 8–16).

Q&A Could I have just typed the # symbol?
No. The symbol that Publisher inserts is a field code that automatically is populated with the page number when you return to Normal view.

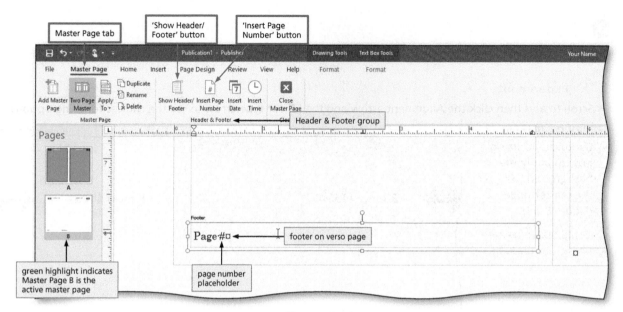

Figure 8–16

2

- Press TAB twice to move to the right side of the footer.

- Type **www.fitness4life.biz** to enter the web address (Figure 8–17).

Q&A

Were tab stops created automatically?

Yes, the footer text box has a center tab and a right tab because most users place footer information at one of those two locations or at the left margin.

Figure 8–17

3

- Click the bottom of the recto page in the two-page spread to display the footer text box for the alternating footer.

- Type **www.fitness4life.biz** to enter the web address. If Publisher capitalizes the first letter, click the AutoCorrect button and then click 'Undo Automatic Capitalization' on the menu.

- Press TAB twice. Type **Page** and then press SPACEBAR.

- Click the 'Insert Page Number' button (Master Page tab | Header & Footer group) to enter the page number placeholder.

- Move the recto footer text box up within the margin if necessary (Figure 8–18).

Q&A

What else can I insert into a header or footer?

You can type any text, insert any picture, or add an automatic date or time using the ribbon.

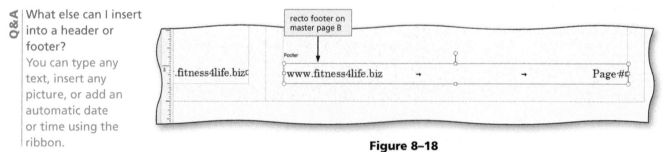

Figure 8–18

To Apply a Number Style

Along with stylistic sets, Publisher has several styles of numbers from which you may choose. The **proportional lining** style formats numbers so that the number of pixels used to create a number is proportional; for example, a 0 (zero) may be wider than a 1 (one). The **tabular style** formats numbers so that each number is the same width. **Why?** *Numbers with the same width are more precise for aligned numbers, such as those used with decimal tabs or for tables of numbers.*

Each of these two number styles has a stylistic alternative: the **lining style** will align the bottom of all numbers; the **old-style** setting will allow certain numbers, such as 3, to drop below the baseline of the other numbers. The following steps apply a number style to the page numbers on the recto page of master page B.

1

- Select the page number placeholder on the recto page and change the font to Comic Sans MS.

- Display the Text Box Tools Format tab.

- Click the Number Style button (Text Box Tools Format tab | Typography group) to display its menu (Figure 8–19).

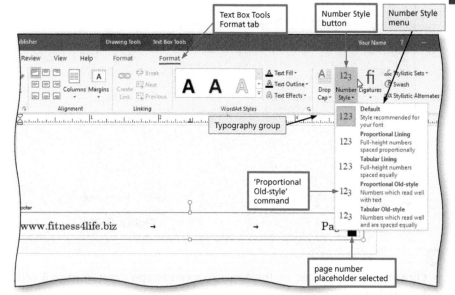

Figure 8–19

2

- Click 'Proportional Old-style' to select the number style.

◄ | Should I see a difference?
Q&A | No. You will see the number change when you leave Master Page view.

3

- Repeat Steps 1 and 2 for the page number placeholder on the verso side of master page B.

- Click outside the footer to deselect it.

To Apply Master Pages

The following steps apply master page B (with footers) to all pages in the catalog and then change the first and last pages to master page A (without footer). **Why?** *The catalog will not display a page number on the cover page or on the back page.* You can apply a master page from either Master Page view or from the Page Navigation pane shortcut menu in Normal view.

• With the 'Master Page B' thumbnail still selected in the Page Navigation pane, display the Master Page tab and then click the Apply To button (Master Page tab | Master Page group) to display the Apply To menu (Figure 8–20).

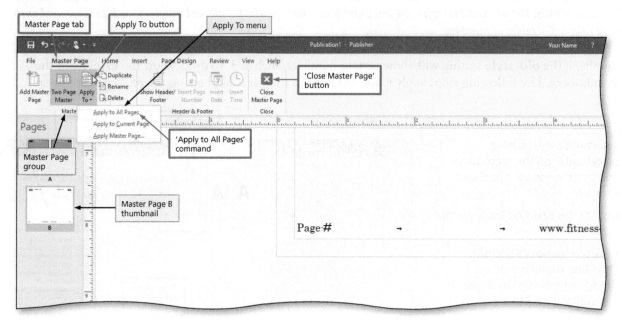

Figure 8–20

• Click 'Apply to All Pages' on the Apply To menu to apply master page B with its alternating footers to all pages in the catalog.

• Click the 'Close Master Page' button (Master Page tab | Close group) to return to Normal view (Figure 8–21).

Q&A My two-page spread did not change. Did I do something wrong?

No. Publisher sometimes separates page 2 and page 3 because they have different footers. You can right-click the 'Page 2 and Page 3' thumbnail in the Page Navigation pane and then click 'View Two-page Spread' on the shortcut menu if you want to turn off the view.

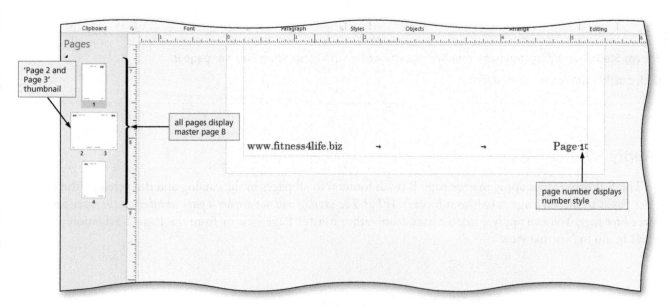

Figure 8–21

③

- In the Page Navigation pane, right-click the Page 1 thumbnail to display a shortcut menu and then point to Master Pages to display the Master Pages submenu (Figure 8–22).

Q&A What is the purpose of the 'Apply Master Page' command?

The 'Apply Master Page' command displays the Apply Master Page dialog box, where you can make additional choices about which master page to use.

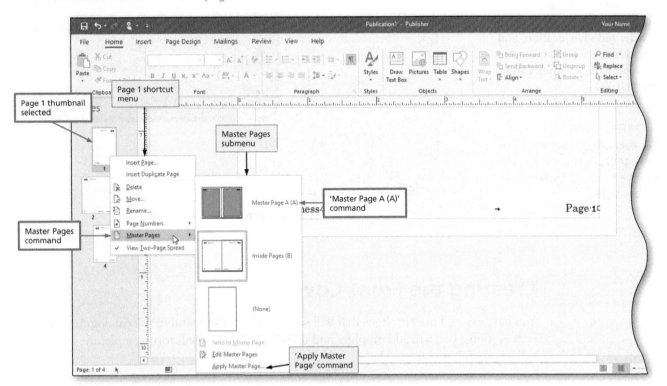

Figure 8–22

④

- Click 'Master Page A (A)' on the Master Pages submenu to apply it to page 1 of the catalog (Figure 8–23).

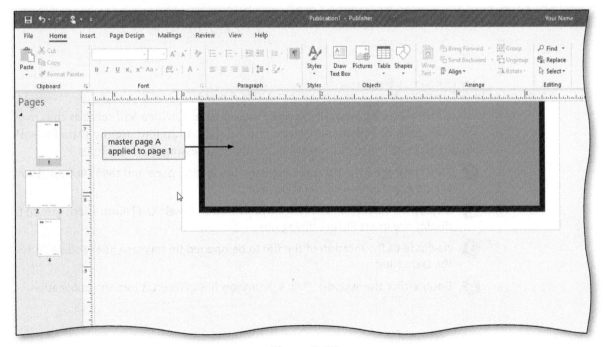

Figure 8–23

5

- Repeat Steps 3 and 4 to apply 'Master Page A (A)' to Page 4 of the publication.

- Click the Save button on the Quick Access Toolbar. Click Browse in the left pane in Backstage view, navigate to your desired save location, and then save the file using the file name, SC_PUB_8_FitnessCatalog (Figure 8–24).

Experiment

- Click each of the thumbnails in the Page Navigation pane and view the headers, footers, and number style.

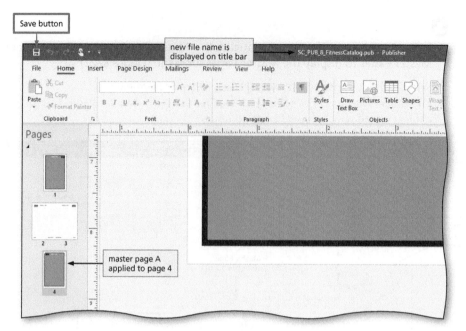

Figure 8–24

Creating the Front Cover

You have created master pages that will serve as the background in the catalog. In the next sections, you will add graphics and text to page 1. You will format a picture with a reflection and crop it to a shape.

How important is the quality of the graphics?

Catalogs are more appealing to customers when they use high-quality color pictures and graphics. Use a picture or photograph when you want to display a specific person, place, or thing. Use a graphic, such as clip art, when you do not have a photograph or when you are describing a general concept or service. Consult a graphics specialist to help choose high-resolution graphics; however, keep in mind that high-resolution images will require more memory and storage space.

To Insert a Picture

The following steps insert a picture on page 1, which will serve as the cover of the catalog. To complete these steps, you will be required to use the Data Files. Please contact your instructor for information about accessing the Data Files.

1 Click the Page 1 thumbnail in the Page Navigation pane and then click the 'Show Whole Page' button on the status bar.

2 Display the Insert tab. Click the Pictures button (Insert tab | Illustrations group) to display the Insert Picture dialog box.

3 Navigate to the location of the file to be opened (in this case, the Module 08 folder of the Data Files).

4 Double-click the Support_PUB_8_Front.jpg file to insert it into the publication.

⑤ If necessary, resize the graphic to approximately 3.00 by 2.00 and move it to the upper center of the page, as shown in Figure 8–25.

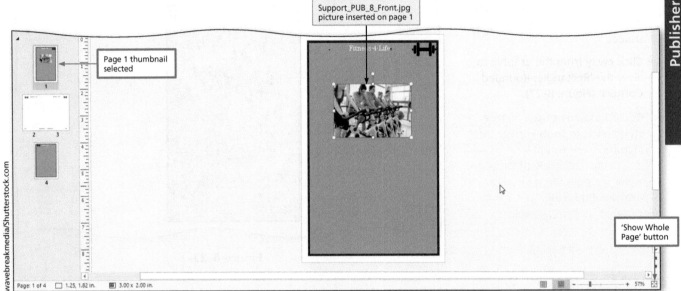

Figure 8–25

To Crop to Shape

The following steps crop a picture to fit within a certain shape. *Why? The company wants a softer look than the square corners of the current picture.* When you choose the 'Crop to Shape' command, Publisher displays the Basic Shapes gallery, from which you can choose the way the picture should be cropped.

①

- With the picture selected, click the Crop arrow (Picture Tools Format tab | Crop group) to display the Crop menu and then point to 'Crop to Shape' to display the Crop to Shape gallery (Figure 8–26).

Q&A What is the difference between the Crop button and the Crop arrow?
If you click the Crop button, which is the upper half of the button/arrow combination, Publisher

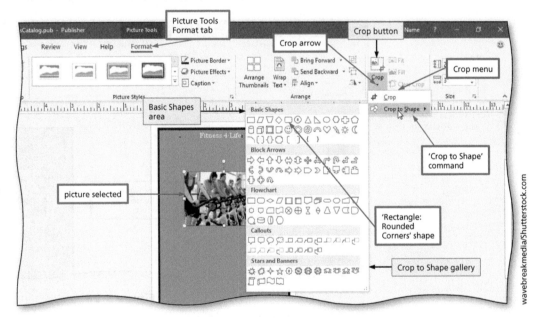

Figure 8–26

will display the picture with cropping handles and assume you want square corners. If you click the Crop arrow, which is the lower-half of the button/arrow combination, Publisher will display a menu.

2

- Click 'Rectangle: Rounded Corners' in the Basic Shapes area in the Crop To gallery to crop to shape.

- Click away from the graphic to view the 'Rectangle: Rounded Corners' (Figure 8–27).

Q&A Could I use one of the picture styles (Picture Tools Format tab | Picture Styles group)?
You could, but none of those styles matches the desired output exactly in this case, so it will be easier to crop to a shape.

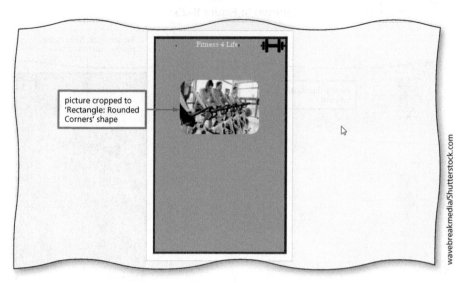

picture cropped to 'Rectangle: Rounded Corners' shape

wavebreakmedia/Shutterstock.com

Figure 8–27

To Format the Border

The following steps add a white boarder to the picture.

1 Select the picture and click the Picture Border button (Picture Tools Format tab | Picture Styles group) to display the Picture Border gallery. Click 'Accent 5 (White)' (eighth color in the first row).

2 Click the Picture Border button again. Point to Weight in the Picture Border gallery and then click 3 pt on the Weight submenu to increase the size of the border.

3 Click outside the graphic to view the formatting (Figure 8–28).

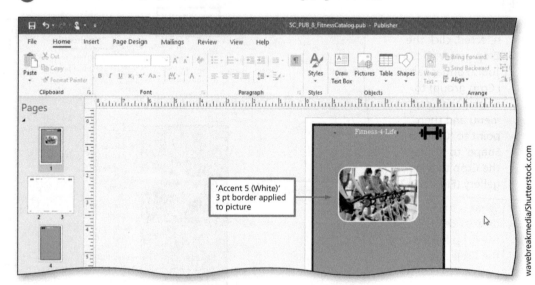

'Accent 5 (White)' 3 pt border applied to picture

wavebreakmedia/Shutterstock.com

Figure 8–28

To Create a Reflection

Shape and picture effects are similar in that they both provide options to add a bevel, glow, 3-D, and rotation, among others. In Publisher, a **reflection** is a mirrored image of the original graphic, with matching borders, to create the appearance of a partial reflection. A reflection reproduces the details of a picture or shape as opposed to a shadow, which usually is a solid color, such as gray. The Reflection gallery has many preset reflections. Table 8–2 describes other reflection settings.

Table 8–2 Reflection Settings	
Setting	**Description**
Transparency	A percentage that determines how much you see through the graphic to the background
Size	A percentage of how much of the graphic to include in the reflection
Blur	A point measurement of how much detail you can see in the reflection (a very high blur is a shadow)
Distance	A point measurement of the distance between the original graphic and its reflection (a low distance may touch the original graphic)

The following steps format the picture with a reflection. **Why?** *A reflection will add depth and interest to the front cover of the catalog.*

- Select the picture. Click the Picture Effects button (Picture Tools Format tab | Picture Styles group) to display the Picture Effects menu.
- Point to Reflection on the Picture Effects menu to display the Reflection gallery (Figure 8–29).

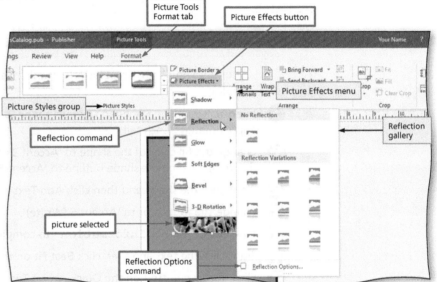

Figure 8–29

- Click Reflection Options in the Reflection gallery to display the Format Shape dialog box.
- Enter the numbers shown in Figure 8–30 to create a reflection with 50% transparency, a reduced size of 50% of the original, a 0.5 point blur, and a distance location 10 points away from the original.

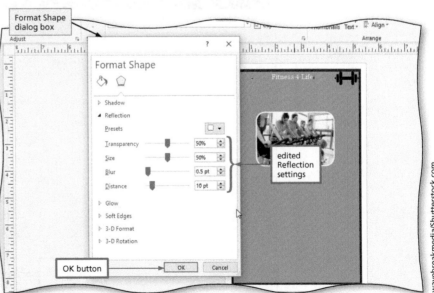

Figure 8–30

• Click OK (Format Shape dialog box) to apply the reflection settings to the picture (Figure 8–31).

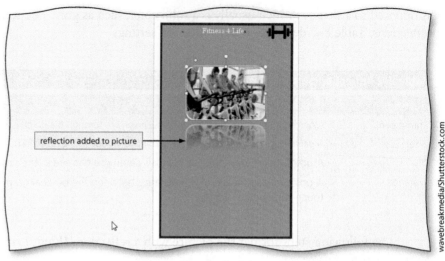

Figure 8–31

To Create a Title Graphic

The following steps create a title graphic in the lower portion of the front page of the catalog.

1 Insert a 'Rectangle: Rounded Corners' shape. Resize it to fit the bottom of page 1, approximately 1 inch tall.

2 Change the fill color of the shape to 'Accent 3 (RGB (218, 31, 40))' (fourth color in the first row). Change the shape outline to 'Accent 5 (White)' (eighth color in the first row).

3 Right-click the shape and then click Add Text on the shortcut menu.

4 Change the font color to 'Accent 5 (White)'.

5 Type **Equipment Information** to complete the text.

6 Right-click the text and then click Best Fit on the shortcut menu.

7 Click the Save button on the Quick Access Toolbar to save the publication again (Figure 8–32).

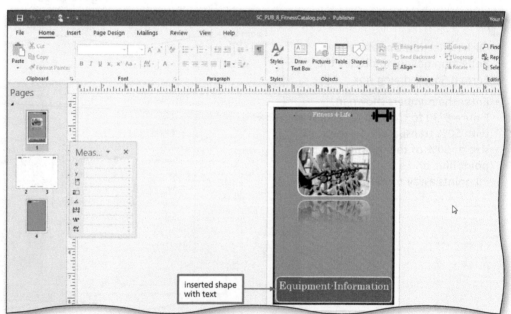

Figure 8–32

Break Point: If you want to take a break, this is a good place to do so. You can exit Publisher now. To resume later, start Publisher, open the file named SC_PUB_8_FitnessCatalog.pub, and then continue following the steps from this location forward.

Generating the Catalog Merge

The merge process requires a main publication and a data source. The main publication contains the constant (or unchanging) text, punctuation, space, and graphics, embedded with varying or changing values from the data source. The data source is a file with fields of information that will change. Catalog merges include pictures and all records commonly merged into a single publication.

The data source for Publisher's catalog merge is a called a **product list** — even if the data is not a list of products. Normally, it is a table of data that includes information about the product or service, unique product numbers or ID numbers, quantities, and paths to pictures that are used in the catalog. A **path** is the route Publisher must take through a computer's stored files to find the picture file and the file name. For example, if a .jpg picture file named Dog were located on the USB (E:) storage device in a folder named Pictures, the path would be E:\Pictures\Dog.jpg. If the file were located in the same folder as the merged publication, however, the path would be simply the file name; thus, in the previous example, the path would be Dog.jpg.

Generally, for classroom purposes, you should keep the main publication and the data source in the same folder on the same storage device. If you are using the Data Files, these data sources may be stored in a different location from the location where you saved your completed publications; thus, they should be moved or copied to your preferred storage location.

BTW
Product Lists vs. Address Lists
A product list data source differs from an address list data source in that it may contain a unique field and path to a graphics file.

To Copy the Data Source Files

Publisher recommends that the publication and its data source reside in the same folder location; therefore, the following steps copy a folder named Interns from the Data Files to your save location. To complete these steps, you will be required to use the Data Files. Please contact your instructor for information about accessing the Data Files.

If you already have downloaded the Data Files to the same location that you are using to create and save files in this module, you can skip these steps.

1 Click the File Explorer button on the Windows taskbar to open a File Explorer window.

2 In the File Explorer window, navigate to the location of the Data Files.

3 In the Module 08 folder, right-click the folder named Support_PUB_8_Equipment to display its shortcut menu and then click Copy on the shortcut menu to copy the file.

4 Navigate to your preferred storage location — in this case, the folder in which you saved the SC_PUB_8_FitnessCatalog.pub publication.

5 Right-click a blank part of the right pane in the Publisher folder to display the folder's shortcut menu and then click Paste on the shortcut menu to paste the folder.

6 Close the File Explorer window.

Catalog Pages

Catalog pages contain a unique merge area for positioning text and pictures. The **catalog merge area**, also called the **repeatable area**, is a box in the publication in which you can insert field codes. Recall that field codes are placeholders inserted in the main publication that correspond with fields from the data source. The merge area repeats for each record in the file because a catalog merge will merge all records to a single publication.

You start the catalog merge by clicking the Catalog Pages button (Insert tab | Pages group). If you start from scratch, you must insert catalog pages. Publisher then automatically adds a page or pages to your publication and inserts a catalog merge area. The merge area can be resized and adjusted for multiple records per page. You can format fields or objects added to the merge area by using normal formatting techniques.

When the merge is complete, data from the data source will populate each field, and the catalog merge area will repeat to display multiple records.

To Insert Catalog Pages

The following steps insert catalog pages. **Why?** *Because you started with a blank template, no catalog pages were inserted automatically; you must insert them.*

1

- Click the 'Page 2 and Page 3' thumbnail in the Page Navigation pane, and show the whole page if necessary.

- Display the Insert tab (Figure 8–33).

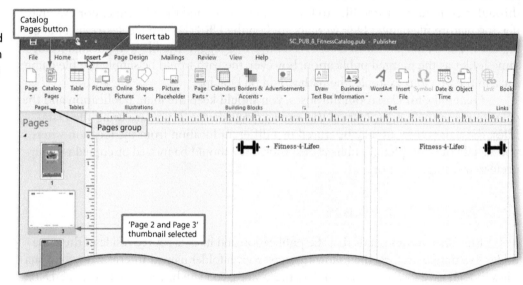

Figure 8–33

2

- Click the Catalog Pages button (Insert tab | Pages group) to insert catalog pages (Figure 8–34).

Q&A What are the new objects that appeared?
Publisher's catalog merge area is displayed in the page layout. New catalog pages are displayed in the Page Navigation pane. While you are working on catalog pages, the ribbon displays the Catalog Tools Format tab.

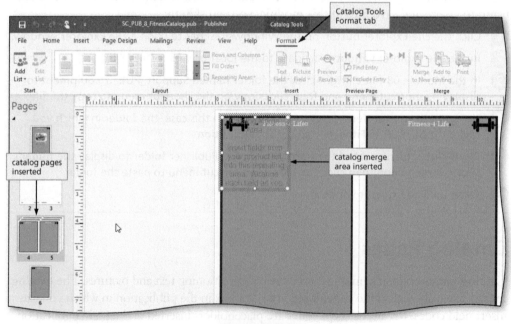

Figure 8–34

To Format the Catalog Pages

The following steps assign master page B to the catalog pages and resize the merge area.

1 Right-click the 'Page 4 and Page 5' thumbnail in the Page Navigation pane to display a shortcut menu. Point to Master Pages on the shortcut menu to display the Master Pages submenu and then click 'Inside Pages (B)' to assign the master page to the catalog pages.

2 In the publication, if necessary, select the catalog merge area. Move the catalog merge area down below the header.

3 Resize the catalog merge area to fill the area between margins and between the header and footer, as shown in Figure 8–35.

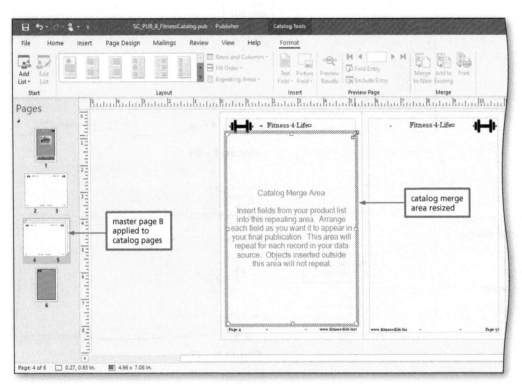

Figure 8–35

To Delete a Two-Page Spread

The following steps delete pages 2 and 3 in the publication. **Why?** *The Publisher template that you used earlier in the module created a blank page 2 and page 3. Now that you have inserted catalog pages and formatted them with the appropriate master page, you no longer need those pages. You will use only the front, back, and catalog pages in the publication.*

1

- Right-click the 'Page 2 and Page 3' thumbnail in the Page Navigation pane to display a shortcut menu (Figure 8–36).

Q&A Why does Publisher include pages that are not part of the catalog merge?

In some publications, you may want an index page or introduction to the catalog. All pages in catalogs must be in groups of two for the publication to print correctly.

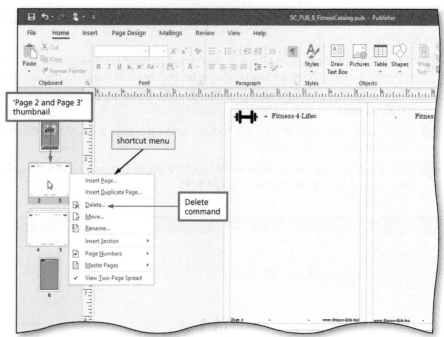

Figure 8–36

2

- Click Delete on the shortcut menu to display the Delete Page dialog box.

- If necessary, click the Both pages option button to select it (Figure 8–37).

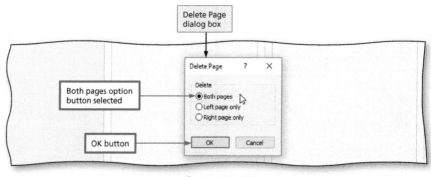

Figure 8–37

3

- Click OK (Delete Page dialog box) to delete the pages (Figure 8–38).

Q&A Did Publisher renumber the pages?

Yes. The catalog pages were moved to the page 2 and page 3 position; however, once you merge with the data source, extra pages will be created as needed, depending on the number of records in your data source. Notice that the pages appear stacked in the Page Navigation pane.

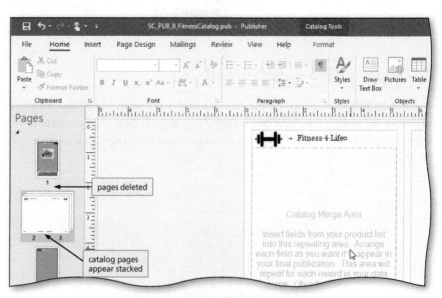

Figure 8–38

To Select the Data Source

The following steps select an existing data source. *Why? You must choose a data source to complete the merge. The data source is located in the folder that you copied to your storage location earlier in the module.*

1

• With the 'Page 2 and Page 3' thumbnail still selected, click the Add List button (Catalog Tools Format tab | Start group) to display the Add List menu (Figure 8–39).

Q&A What if I want to create a new product list?

You can choose the 'Type a New List' command. A dialog box will be displayed that allows you to customize fields and insert data.

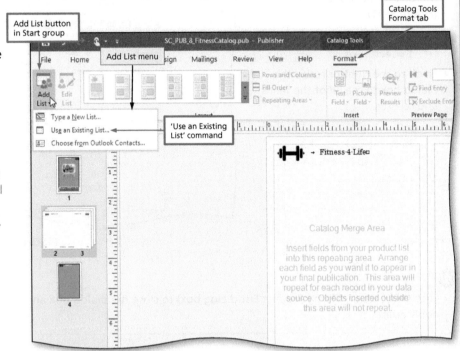

Figure 8–39

2

• Click 'Use an Existing List' on the Add List menu to display the Select Data Source dialog box.

• Navigate to your storage location and then double-click the folder named Support_PUB_8_Equipment (Figure 8–40).

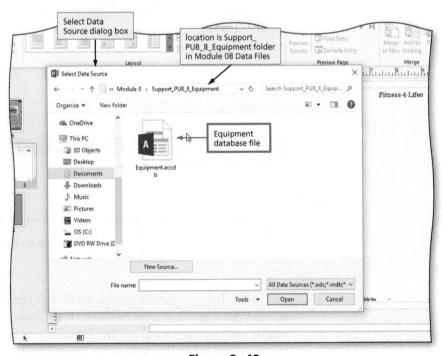

Figure 8–40

- Double-click the Equipment.accdb file to display the Catalog Merge Product List dialog box (Figure 8–41).

Experiment

- Scroll to the right or resize the dialog box to see all of the fields and records.

Q&A Do the commands in this dialog box work the same as the commands when performing a mail merge?
Yes. All of the commands in the Catalog Merge Product List dialog box work the same as the ones in the Mail Merge List dialog box.

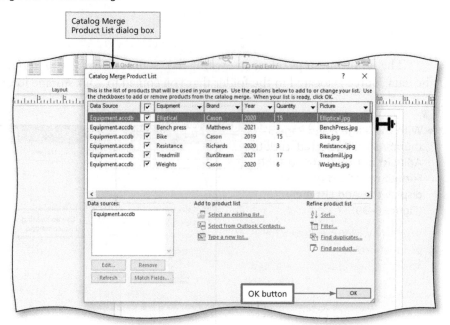

Figure 8–41

- Click OK (Catalog Merge Product List dialog box) to close the dialog box and connect the data source to the publication.

The Catalog Tools Format Tab

When performing a catalog merge, Publisher displays the Catalog Tools Format tab, which contains specialized formatting tools for catalog pages and merging (Figure 8–42). The Start group includes an Add List button used to specify or create a product list and connect it to the publication. The Edit List button is used to make changes to the catalog once it is connected.

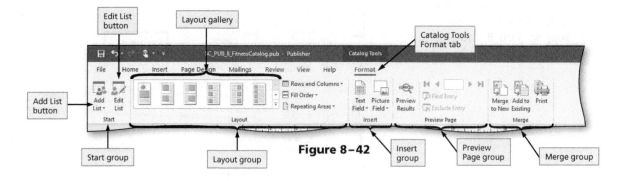

Figure 8–42

The Layout group contains a gallery of preset page layouts, formatted to a single column per page; however, Publisher has a command to create rows and columns that can be used for large catalogs. In that case, records from the database are formatted to run across and then down. You can change that setting with the Fill Order button. The Repeating Areas button allows you to specify a custom layout by row or column.

The Insert group is used to insert text and pictures manually from the data source. The Preview Page and Merge groups are similar to those on the Mailings tab.

If you choose not to use a preset layout, the merge area can be resized and adjusted for one or multiple records per page. You can format fields or objects added to the merge area using normal formatting techniques, as you will do in this module.

To Insert a Picture Field

The following steps insert the picture from the data source or product list into the catalog merge area. **Why?** *Fields or objects inserted in the catalog merge area will repeat for each record in the data source.* Objects outside the area will not repeat. You can format, resize, and reposition objects in the catalog merge area.

1

• With the catalog merge area selected, click the Picture Field button (Catalog Tools Format tab | Insert group) to display the Picture Field menu (Figure 8–43).

◄ What does the 'More Picture Options' command do?
Q&A The 'More Picture Options' command will display the Insert Picture dialog box. It is used when you have multiple picture fields in your database.

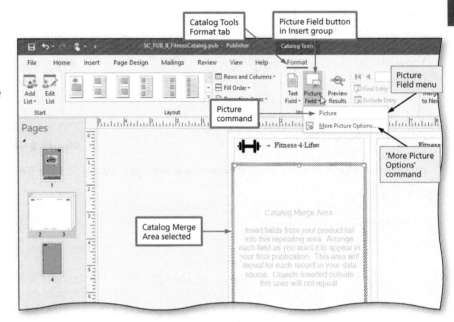

Figure 8–43

2

• Click Picture on the Picture Field menu to insert the Picture field.

• If necessary, click the Preview Results button (Catalog Tools Format tab | Preview Page group) to display the picture (Figure 8–44).

🔍 **Experiment**

• Click the More button (Catalog Tools Format tab | Layout group) to view the possible preset formats. One at a time, click each of the buttons in the Layout group to view their choices and commands. When you are finished, click the '1 entry, picture' button in the Layout group.

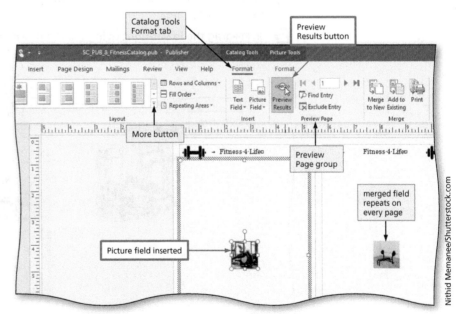

Nithid Memanee/Shutterstock.com

Figure 8–44

◄ My picture does not appear. Did I do something wrong?
Q&A No. To conserve memory resources on your computer, Publisher may not display the pictures until the file is ready to preview or print.

To View Boundaries

The following step turns on the boundaries display. **Why?** *Boundaries will assist you in placing the other fields in the catalog merge area.* A boundary is the gray, dotted line surrounding a selected object. Boundaries are useful when you want to move or resize objects on the page.

- Display the View tab.

- Click to display a check mark in the Boundaries check box (View tab | Show group) (Figure 8–45).

 **Experiment**

- Click other check boxes in the Show group on the View tab to see what objects are displayed. When you are finished, check the boxes as shown in Figure 8–45.

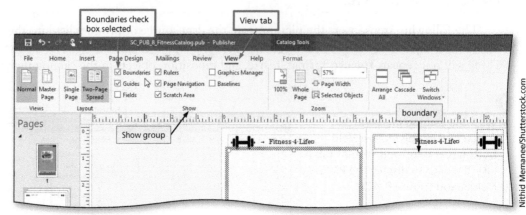

Figure 8–45

Other Ways

1. Press CTRL+SHIFT+O

To Move and Resize the Picture Field

The following steps resize the picture field and move it to the top of the page. You will place it more precisely in later steps.

1 With the picture field selected, drag the picture field to the upper-left portion of the catalog merge area.

2 SHIFT+drag the lower-right sizing handle down and to the right until the picture is approximately 3.25 inches wide and 2.7 inches tall (Figure 8–46).

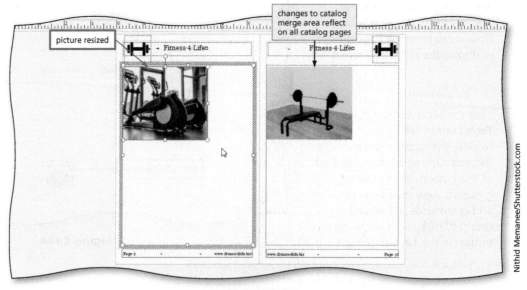

Figure 8–46

To Insert Text Fields

The following steps insert the other fields from the data source. You will create text boxes, insert fields, and then format the fields as you enter them. *Why? Formatting fields in the first merge area will apply the same formatting across all pages in the publication.* Use the Measurement pane and the rulers as necessary to help draw the text boxes. You will align the objects on the page in a later set of steps.

1

- Zoom to 130% and then scroll to the lower half of page 2.

- Display the Home tab.

- Click the 'Draw Text Box' button (Home tab | Objects group) and then draw a text box below the picture, approximately .4 inches high and 4 inches wide.

- Display the Catalog Tools Format tab. Click the Preview Results button (Catalog Tools Format tab | Preview Page group) to turn off the display so that you can see field codes as you insert them.

- With the insertion point positioned in the new text box, click the Text Field button (Catalog Tools Format tab | Insert group) to display the Text Field menu (Figure 8–47).

Q&A Could I use the Picture field and insert the picture from this list?

No. This list contains text fields. If you were to try to insert the text field code named Picture, Publisher would insert the data from the field itself, not the picture. You would see the words, Elliptical.jpg in the merge.

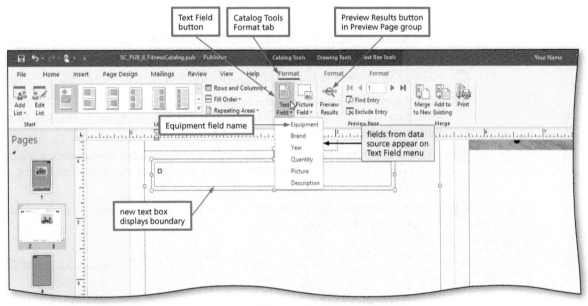

Figure 8–47

2

- Click Equipment on the Text Field menu to insert the Equipment field code into the text box.

- Select the field code and change the font size to 22 (Figure 8–48).

Q&A How are the field codes ordered in the list?

The field codes appear in the order in which they are stored in the database.

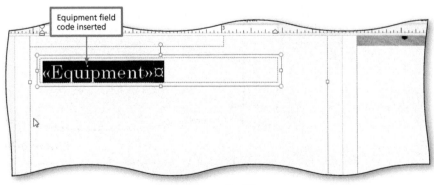

Figure 8–48

- Create a second text box below the first one.
- Click the Text Field button (Catalog Tools Format tab | Insert group) to display the Text Field menu again and then insert the Brand field code and then press the COMMA key (,).

- Press SPACEBAR to insert a space and then click the Text Field button (Catalog Tools Format tab | Insert group) to display the Text Field menu again.

- Click Year on the Text Field menu to insert the Year field code into the text box.

- Change the font size to 18 (Figure 8–49).

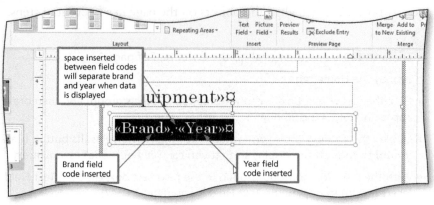

Figure 8–49

To Insert Other Text Fields

The following steps create text boxes and insert the Quantity and Description fields into the catalog merge area.

1. Draw another text box below the previous text box, approximately the same size.

2. With the insertion point inside the text box, change the font size to 18. Type **Available:** and then press SPACEBAR. Insert the Quantity field using the Text Field button (Catalog Tools Format tab | Insert group).

3. Create a fourth text box in the lower portion of the catalog merge area, 4.5 inches wide and 1.5 inch tall. Use the Measurement pane to set the width and height, if necessary.

4. With the insertion point inside the text box, change the font size to 12 and then insert the Description field (Figure 8–50).

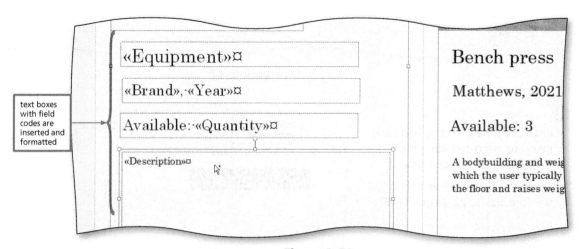

Figure 8–50

To Align Objects

In desktop publishing apps, the Home tab alignment tools refer to the text in the text box in which you are working. However, in most cases, you can align objects with each other or relative to the margins on the page. In the following steps, you will center align the picture and then left align the text boxes. *Why? Using an align command will guarantee correct placement.*

Another option is to **distribute** objects, which means to equalize the space between three or more objects vertically or horizontally.

The following steps align objects.

 1

- Click the 'Show Whole Page' button on the status bar.

- On page 2 (the verso page), select the picture placeholder and then click the Align button (Home tab | Arrange group) to display the Align menu (Figure 8–51).

- If the Align button is dimmed, drag the picture toward the center until the pink alignment guide is displayed.

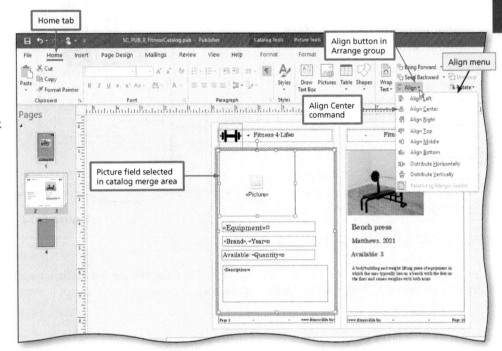

Figure 8–51

2

- Click Align Center on the Align menu to center the picture horizontally.

- On page 2, click the Equipment text box and then, one at a time, SHIFT+click the other three text boxes.

- Click the Align button (Home tab | Arrange group) to display the Align menu (Figure 8–52).

Q&A Why is the 'Relative to Margin Guides' command dimmed?

The text boxes you are working with are in the catalog merge area and will be aligned relative to that container rather than relative to the margins.

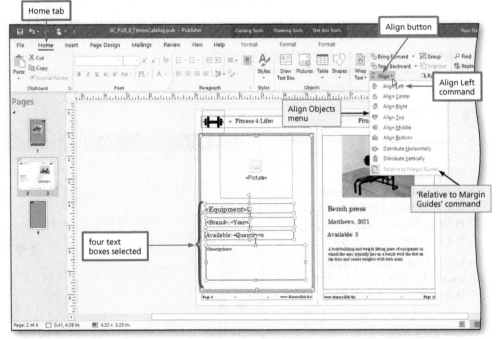

Figure 8–52

3

- Click Align Left on the Align menu to left align the three objects.

Q&A
How does Publisher decide the left position?
Publisher aligns all objects with the object that is the farthest left on the page.

- If necessary, use the ARROW keys to move the selected text boxes slightly away from the edge of the catalog merge area.

- Click the Preview Results button (Catalog Tools Format tab | Preview Page group) to display the data rather than the field codes (Figure 8–53).

4

- Click the Save button on the Quick Access Toolbar to overwrite the previously saved file.

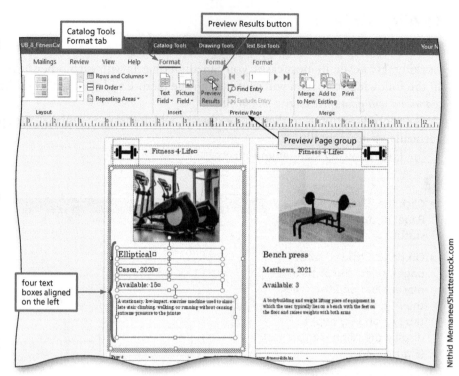

Figure 8–53

Break Point: If you want to take a break, this is a good place to do so. You can exit Publisher now. To resume later, start Publisher, open the file named SC_PUB_8_FitnessCatalog.pub, and then continue following the steps from this location forward.

To Find Entries

Publisher provides a special method for finding information in catalog entries. ***Why? The merged publication is not searchable via regular means unless you merge it to a new file.*** Using the Find Entry button (Catalog Tools Format tab | Preview Page group), Publisher looks through the data source for the keyword(s) and then navigates to that page in the catalog publication.

The following steps find an entry based on keywords. In this case, you want to determine any machines that focus on resistance training.

1

- On any catalog page, click outside any object so that nothing is selected.

- Click the Find Entry button (Catalog Tools Format tab | Preview Page group) to display the Find Entry dialog box.

- In the Find text box, type **resistance** to enter the search term (Figure 8–54).

Experiment

- Click the This field arrow to display the list of searchable fields.

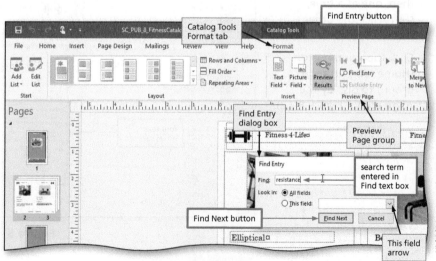

Figure 8–54

- Click the Find Next button (Find Entry dialog box) to search for the keyword (Figure 8–55).

Q&A What would happen if Publisher could not locate the search term? In such a case, Publisher would display a dialog box stating it could not find the search term you entered. You then could enter a new search term in the Find Entry dialog box.

- Click the Cancel button (Find Entry dialog box) to close the dialog box.

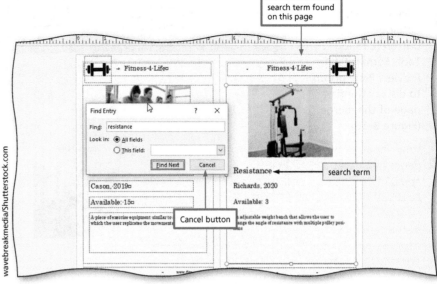

Figure 8–55

To Exclude Entries

If you wanted to exclude an entry from your data source, you would perform the following steps.

1. Navigate to the record that you want to exclude either by using the Find Entry button (described in the previous steps) or by clicking the 'Next Catalog Page' button or the 'Previous Catalog Page' button (Catalog Tools Format tab | Preview Page group).

2. When the desired record is displayed, if necessary, click the catalog merge area around that entry to select it.

3. Click the Exclude Entry button (Catalog Tools Format tab | Preview Page group) to exclude the record.

To Turn Off Boundaries

Because you are finished with the page layout, the following steps turn off the boundaries so that Publisher displays a more realistic preview.

1 Display the View tab.

2 Click to remove the check mark in the Boundaries check box (View tab | Show group).

To Preview the Merge

The following steps preview the merged publication. **Why?** *Previewing allows you to look for anomalies in the merge, such as unusual hyphenation or large fields that overlap.*

1

- Zoom to whole page.
- Display the Catalog Tools Format tab.

- Click the 'First Catalog Page' button (Catalog Tools Format tab | Preview Page group) to display the first page of the merge (Figure 8–56).

Q&A

Why are all of the pages numbered 2 and 3?
Publisher makes multiple copies of the catalog pages — enough to accommodate all of the records in the data source. When you merge to the printer, the pages will be renumbered and printed correctly.

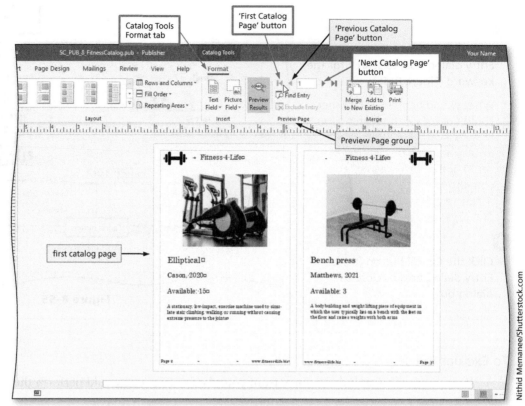

Figure 8–56

2

- Click the 'Next Catalog Page' button (Catalog Tools Format tab | Preview Page group).

- If the Description text displays incorrect hyphenation, click the 'First Catalog Page' button (Catalog Tools Format tab | Preview Pages group). Ensure that the font is Century Schoolbook, the font size is 12, and the text box is 4.5 inches wide by 1.5 inch tall. If necessary, adjust the width of the text box slightly, and check all pages.

Experiment

- Click the 'Next Catalog Page' button and the 'Previous Catalog Page' button (Catalog Tools Format tab | Preview Page group) to display other pages of the catalog.

BTW
Graphics
A file with many graphics and merged pages sometimes refreshes slowly on the screen. If you move to a new page or edit the data source, it may take several moments to open. Use the Previous Sheet button and Next Sheet button (Catalog Tools Format tab | Preview Page group) to view each record. Consider using the Graphics Manager to turn off the display of graphics and minimize the Page Navigation pane. In addition, sometimes it is better to edit a database outside a publication so that you do not have to wait for the updated screens.

The Graphics Manager

The Graphics Manager helps you manage and display all the pictures you have inserted into your publication, such as embedded pictures or linked pictures. You can change the display of the pictures so that quicker editing is possible and fewer system resources are consumed in controlling display options. You can view all the pictures related to a publication, or you can see only those pictures that are missing or have been modified since the last time you saved the publication. The Graphics Manager can display thumbnails of all graphics in the publication. You can order the pictures in the Graphics Manager pane by file name, page number, extension, or size and show the details about each one.

You can use the Graphics Manager to check the status of each picture, such as whether a picture is linked or embedded, whether it has been modified, or whether a link to an external picture is missing.

If you have many pictures in a publication with multiple pages, you can navigate quickly to a particular picture by pointing to it in the Graphics Manager pane, clicking the arrow to the right of the picture, and then clicking 'Go to this Picture' on the menu.

BTW

Embedded vs. Linked

If you want to change a picture's status from embedded to linked or vice versa, use the Graphics Manager, which offers Save As dialog boxes to assist you.

To Work with the Graphics Manager

The following steps open the Graphics Manager pane. *Why? You will view information about each of the pictures.*

- Navigate to page 1 of the publication and then display the View tab.
- Click to display a check mark in the Graphics Manager check box (View tab | Show group) and to open the Graphics Manager pane.
- Click the Sort by arrow in the Display options area in the Graphics Manager pane to display the list of picture details (Figure 8–57).

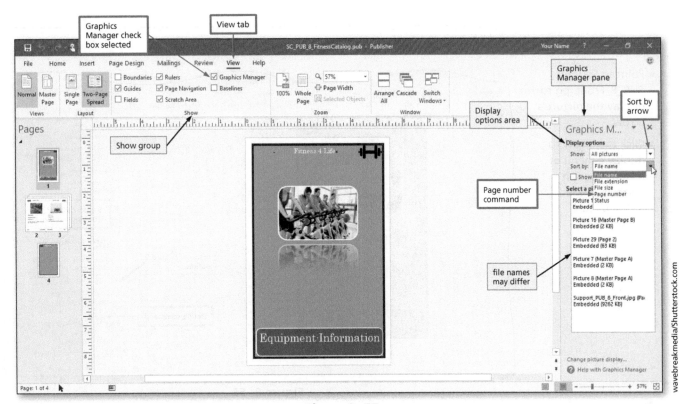

Figure 8–57

2

- Click Page number in the list to view the pictures sorted by page number (Figure 8–58).

Why is the exercise bike picture named Picture 7?
It is a random name that Publisher assigns to indirect pictures, those that are not directly inserted using the Insert Picture button on the ribbon.

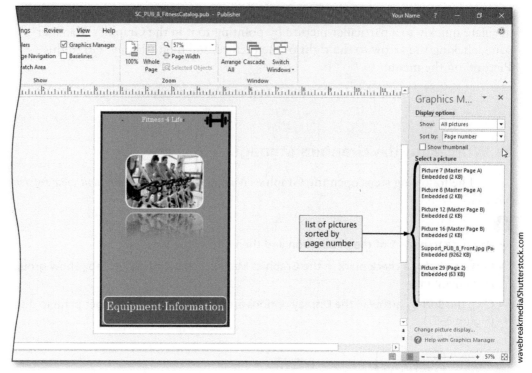

list of pictures sorted by page number

Figure 8–58

3

- Point to Support_PUB_8_Front.jpg to display the picture's arrow.
- Click the arrow to display a menu of actions you can perform related to the picture (Figure 8–59).

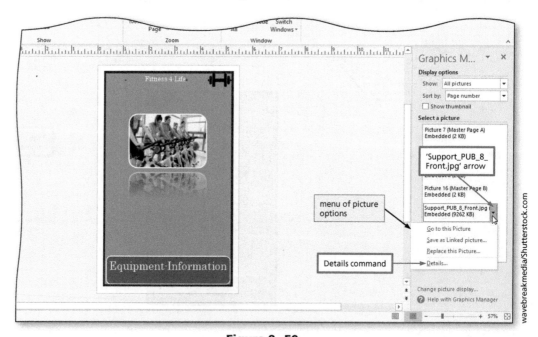

'Support_PUB_8_Front.jpg' arrow

menu of picture options

Details command

Figure 8–59

4

- Click Details on the menu to display the Details dialog box (Figure 8–60).

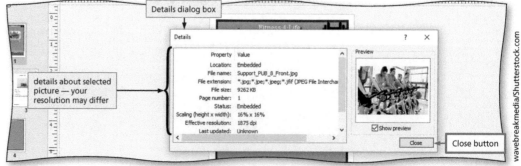

Details dialog box

details about selected picture — your resolution may differ

Close button

Figure 8–60

wavebreakmedia/Shutterstock.com

- Click the Close button (Details dialog box) to close the dialog box.

- In the lower portion of the Graphics Manager pane, click the 'Change picture display' link to display the Picture Display dialog box.

- Click the Hide pictures option button to select it (Figure 8–61).

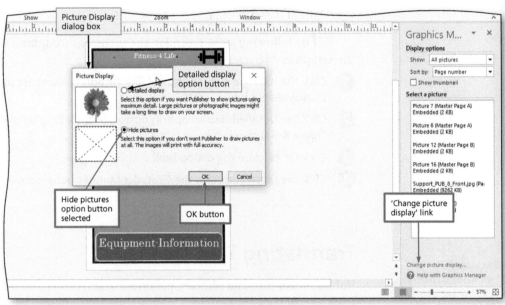

Figure 8–61

- Click OK (Picture Display dialog box) to hide the pictures in the display (Figure 8–62).

🔍 **Experiment**

- Click each of the thumbnails in the Page Navigation pane to see how quickly the pages are displayed when pictures are hidden.

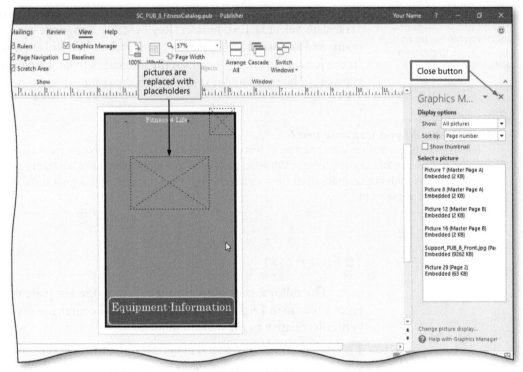

Figure 8–62

To Redisplay the Pictures and Close the Graphics Manager Pane

The following steps redisplay the pictures throughout the publication and close the Graphics Manager pane.

1 Click the 'Change picture display' link (Graphics Manager pane) to display the Picture Display dialog box.

2 Click the Detailed display option button (Picture Display dialog box) (shown in Figure 8–61) to select it.

3 Click OK to close the dialog box.

4 Click the Close button in the Graphics Manger pane (shown in Figure 8–62) to close it.

BTW
Translating
If the Research pane cannot find a translation for a word or phrase, click the Translation options link in the middle of the Research pane. Publisher will display the Translation Options dialog box. In the lower text box, choose your language pair and then click the translation service arrow to choose a different service.

Translating Text

Publisher can translate phrases, paragraphs, and individual words to a different language. Many of the modern languages are installed automatically when you install Publisher. Other languages must be installed the first time you use them. To translate text to some languages, such as right-to-left languages, you may need to satisfy certain operating system requirements.

Publisher's translation capability requires web access. When you click the 'Translate Selected Text' button (Review tab | Language group), the Research pane opens and accesses a web-based service, such as World Lingo or Microsoft Translator. In the Research pane, you can set the languages from which and to which you wish to translate. The translated text appears in the pane.

CONSIDER THIS

When should you translate text?
Use the translation tool for short passages of text or individual words in your publications. If an entire publication needs to be translated, use a professional translator. While the translation tool is not a substitute for learning the language and knowing how tone and sentence structure affect the meaning, it may be appropriate for times when you need to look up short phrases or translate a single word.

To Enter Text

The following steps create a text box on the last page in the catalog and then enter a phrase in English. In addition, you will center the text box horizontally and vertically, relative to the margin guides.

1 Navigate to page 4 in the publication and then display the Home tab.

2 Click the 'Draw Text Box' button (Home tab | Objects group) and then drag to draw a text box approximately 4.4 inches wide and 2.75 inches tall.

3 Change the font size to 18 pt. Change the font color to 'Accent 5 (White)' (eighth color in the first row).

4 Type **Fitness 4 Life is full-service gym open 24 hours a day, 7 days a week.** and then press ENTER twice.

5 Type **Visit us at www.fitness4life.biz.** and then press ENTER twice.

6 Type **For more information in Spanish please call 1-800-555-8784.** to finish the text.

7 Click the Align button (Home tab | Arrange group) and then click 'Relative to Margin Guides' on the Align menu.

8 Click the Align button (Home tab | Arrange group) again and then click Align Center on the Align menu.

9 Click the Align button (Home tab | Arrange group) again and then click Align Middle on the Align menu (Figure 8–63).

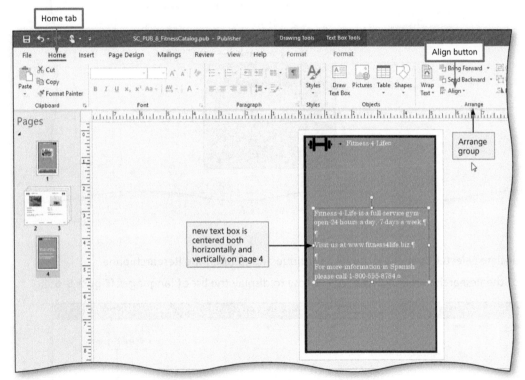

Figure 8–63

To Translate and Insert Text

The following steps translate part of the text to Spanish. *Why? The company wants to be inclusive of Spanish-speaking clients.* You must have an Internet connection to perform these steps.

- Drag to select the last sentence in the text box, excluding the phone number.
- Display the Review tab.

● Click the 'Translate Selected Text' button (Review tab | Language group) to display the Translate Selected Text dialog box (Figure 8–64).

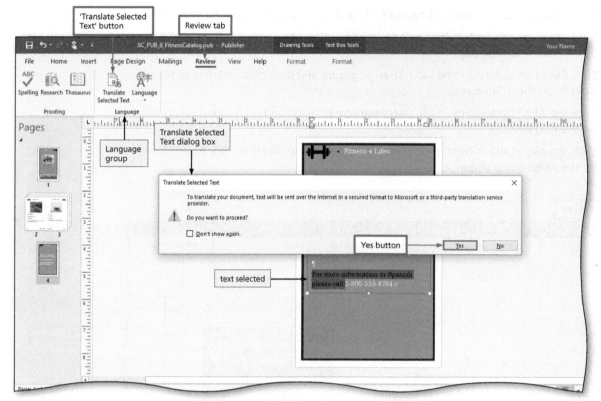

Figure 8–64

❷

● Click the Yes button (Translate Selected Text dialog box) to continue and to open the Research pane.

● In the Translation area of the Research pane, click the From arrow to display the list of languages (Figure 8–65).

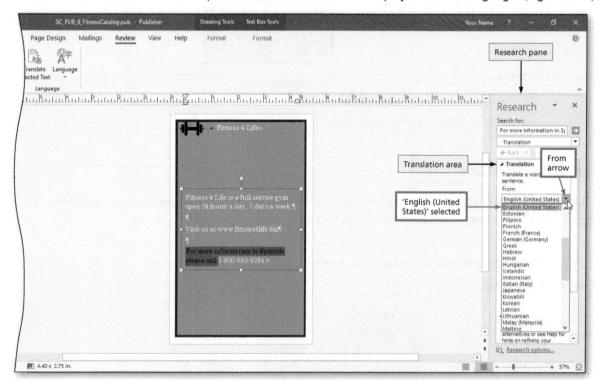

Figure 8–65

- Click the desired language you wish to translate from — in this case, 'English (United States)'.

- Click the To arrow to display the list of languages and then scroll to and click the desired language you wish to translate to — in this case Spanish (Spain) (Figure 8–66).

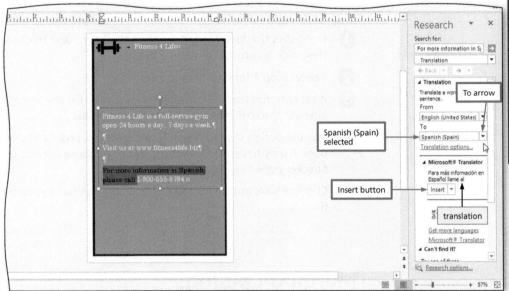

Figure 8–66

🔍 **Experiment**

- Click the To arrow and then choose other languages and view the translations. When you are finished, click the To arrow and then click Spanish (Spain).

- Click the Insert button (Research pane) to insert the translated text (Figure 8–67).

Q&A My pane does not show an Insert button. What should I do?
If a translation appears, copy and paste it into your publication. If no translation appears, see your instructor for ways to install the translation feature.

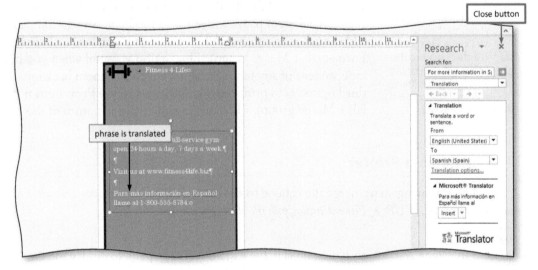

Figure 8–67

- In the text box, insert a comma after the word, Español.

- Click the Close button in the Research pane to close the pane.

Other Ways

1. To translate single word, right-click word, click Translate on shortcut menu, choose languages in Research pane, click Insert button or copy and paste translation

To Ignore Flagged Words and Check the Publication

The following steps ignore the flagged Spanish words on the last page.

1 Right-click the first flagged word on the back page to display a shortcut menu and then click Ignore All to remove the flag.

2 Repeat Step 1 for each flagged word.

3 Press F7 to run the spelling checker program. Fix any errors. Note that you will not be able use the spelling checker on merged fields.

4 Run the design checker from Backstage view, and fix any errors. Note that master page A may have empty footer text boxes; those are not errors. Close the Design Checker pane.

5 Click the Save button on the Quick Access Toolbar to overwrite the previously saved file.

BTW
Conserving Ink and Toner
If you want to conserve ink or toner, you can instruct Publisher to print draft quality documents by clicking File on the ribbon to open Backstage view, clicking Options in Backstage view to display the Publisher Options dialog box, clicking Advanced in the left pane (Publisher Options dialog box), scrolling to the Print area in the right pane, placing a check mark in the 'Use draft quality' check box, and then clicking OK. Then, use Backstage view to print the document as usual.

Merging Catalogs

You have three choices in finalizing the merge. You can merge the pages and create a new document by using the 'Merge to New' button (Catalog Tools Format tab | Merge group). In that new document, the merged pages will not need a preview, and you will not need the database connection. You will be able to edit the merged text and graphics; all eight pages will show in the Page Navigation pane. Another choice is to add the pages to another publication using the 'Add to Existing' button (Catalog Tools Format tab | Merge group). This option is useful when you have created catalog pages independent of any template and want to add them back into another publication. The third option is to print the document using the Print button (Catalog Tools Format tab | Merge group), which retains the merged nature of the catalog.

To Merge to a Printer

The following steps merge the catalog to the printer. **Why?** *The merge preview will display the collated contents of the SC_PUB_8_FitnessCatalog.pub file correctly.*

1
- Click the 'Page 2 and Page 3' thumbnail in the Page Navigation pane to display the Catalog Tools Format tab.
- If necessary, click the 'Show Whole Page' button on the status bar and then display the Catalog Tools Format tab (Figure 8–68).

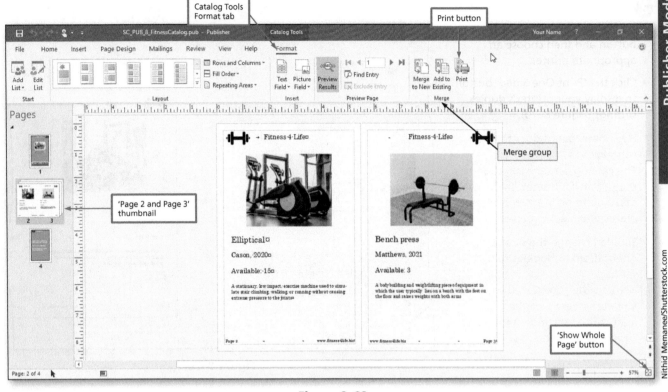

Figure 8–68

2

- Click the Print button (Catalog Tools Format tab | Merge group) to display the Print screen in Backstage view (Figure 8–69).

Q&A How are the pages displayed in Page Preview?
The pages are displayed as they will print on the paper. Once the printed pages are printed, folded, and collated correctly, they will appear in the correct order.

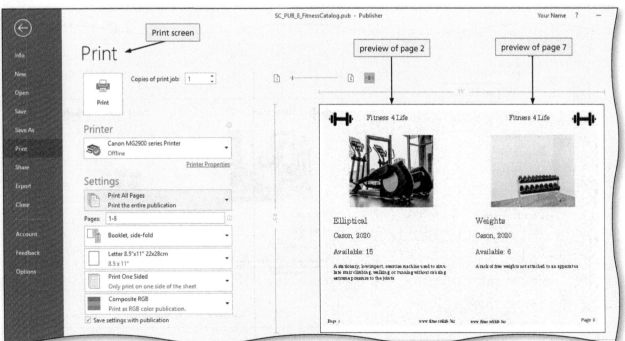

Figure 8–69

● If necessary, click the Printer button and then choose an appropriate printer.

● Click the 'Print One Sided' button to display your printer's duplex settings (Figure 8–70).

 How many pages does the catalog contain?

The catalog contains eight pages. Printed on both sides, the entire catalog can be printed using two pieces of 8.5 × 11" paper.

Should I change the page size, orientation, or booklet fold settings?

No. Because you started with a blank catalog template, many of the settings in the Print screen are preset.

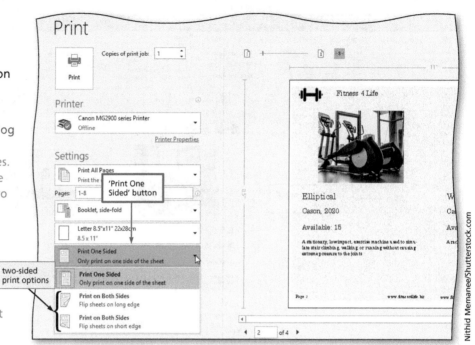

Figure 8–70

4

● If you have the choice, click the 'Print on Both Sides' option. If you do not have the option, choose an appropriate option (Figure 8–71).

 What buttons were added at the bottom of the Print screen preview area?

If you choose duplex or two-sided printing, you will see a Front button and a Back button, which allow you to preview exactly how the pages will be collated or arranged.

🔍 **Experiment**

● To preview the pages, click the Next Sheet button. Click the Front button. Click the Back button. Click the Previous Sheet button.

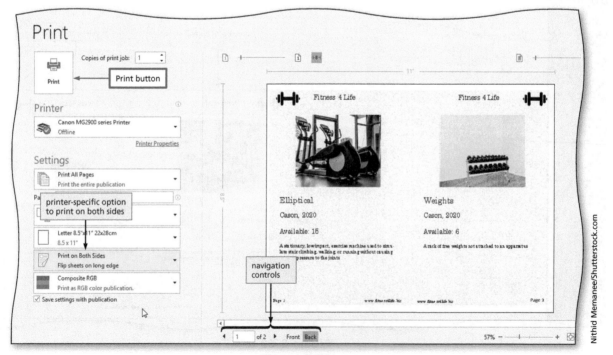

Figure 8–71

- Click the Print button in the Print screen to print the document on the currently selected printer.
- When the printer stops, retrieve the hard copy.

Q&A My printing was very slow or stopped completely. What did I do wrong?

Older printers may not have enough printer memory to handle the many graphics included in the catalog. Wait a few moments. If your printer does not continue, right-click the printer icon on the taskbar and then click your printer name to open its dialog box, right-click the file name of the document being printed, and then click Cancel on the shortcut menu. Try printing the catalog on a different printer.

Other Ways

1. Click Print in Backstage view, choose settings, click Print button

To Exit Publisher

This project is complete. The following steps exit Publisher.

1 To exit Publisher, click the Close button on the right side of the title bar.

2 If a Microsoft Publisher dialog box is displayed, click the Don't Save button so that any changes you have made are not saved.

Reopening Catalogs

When you close and then reopen a catalog, Publisher will try to reconnect to the data source and display a dialog box. If you click the No button, Publisher will open the catalog with no connected data, and the catalog pages will be blank. If you click the Yes button, Publisher will open the catalog and connect to the data; however, if the data source is not in its original location, or if you have moved the entire folder, Publisher will prompt you to reconnect. You then will need to browse to the location of the data source.

Summary

In this module, you learned how to create a data-driven catalog. You created alternating master pages with headers and footers, applied a texture to the background of a duplicate master page, and then formatted the page number with a number style. As you created catalog pages with a merge area, you inserted field codes for both text and graphics from the product list data source. You aligned objects, searched for specific data, and previewed the catalog merge. You learned how to manage and display pictures by using the Graphics Manager. On the back page, you created a text box and translated a phrase to another language by using the translation tool in Publisher. Finally, you merged the catalog and printed it.

BTW

Distributing a Document
Instead of printing and distributing a hard copy of a document, you can distribute the document electronically. Options include sending the document via email; posting it on cloud storage (such as OneDrive) and sharing the file with others; posting it on social media, a blog, or other website; and sharing a link associated with an online location of the document. You also can create and share a PDF or XPS image of the document, so that users can view the file in Acrobat Reader or XPS Viewer instead of in Publisher.

CONSIDER THIS: PLAN AHEAD

What decisions will you need to make when creating your next catalog?
Use these guidelines as you complete the assignments in this module and create your own publications outside of this class.

1. Gather the database, text, and pictures from the customer.

2. Create a catalog publication using a catalog template or blank template.

   a) Add extra pages, as necessary.

3. Create two sets of master pages.

   a) One master page will be used for the front and back of the catalog; a different master page will be used for inside pages.

   b) Use headers and footers with mirrored styles for inner pages.

   c) Consider adding a background for catalog pages so that they are not stark white.

4. Insert text and graphics for front and back pages.

5. Create the merge.

   a) Connect to the data source and filter as necessary.

   b) Choose a layout for the merge area.

   c) Insert fields and format them.

6. Use the Graphics Manager to verify graphics.

7. Translate any necessary phrases to user languages.

8. Merge to a printer or a file.

Apply Your Knowledge

Reinforce the skills and apply the concepts you learned in this module.

Using a Catalog Template

Note: To complete this assignment, you will be required to use the Data Files. Please contact your instructor for information about accessing the Data Files.

Instructions: Copy the folder, Support_PUB_8_Cactus, from the Data Files to your storage location as explained in the module. The folder contains pictures of various cacti and a data source file with the names and descriptions of the pictures. You are to use a catalog template to design a catalog that will display the pictures and descriptions of the cacti for a park district publication. A sample catalog is displayed in Figure 8–72.

Figure 8–72

Continued >

Apply Your Knowledge *continued*

1. Start Publisher. Display the built-in catalogs templates. Select the Studio template with the default size of 5.5 × 8.5 inches, the Desert color scheme, and the Versatile font scheme.

2. When the publication is displayed in the workspace, delete all but the front and back pages.

3. On page 1:

    a. Select the text in the Catalog Subtitle text box and then type `Your guide to identifying the host of the desert` as the new subtitle.

    b. Select the text in the Catalog Title text box, press CTRL+B to bold the text, and then type `Cactus Calling` to enter the new title.

    c. Right-click the graphic on page 1, point to Change Picture on the shortcut menu, and then click Change Picture on the shortcut menu. Navigate to the picture with the file named Support_PUB_8_FrontCactus.jpg, which is located in the folder named Support_PUB_8_Cactus. Double-click the file to insert it into the publication.

    d. In the bulleted list, type the following:

    `Inside`
    - `Pictures and descriptions of the most popular cacti`
    - `Size and genus`
    - `Find out which cacti are edible`
    - `Calendar of events`

    e. In the Business Name text box, type `Caleb Park District` as the name of the business.

    f. In the Date text box, type `Summer 2021` to complete the entries on page 1. If necessary, change the font color to 'Accent 5 (White)'.

4. Insert catalog pages to display the catalog merge area. Move the catalog merge area below the header.

5. Click the Add List button (Catalog Tools Format tab | Start group) and then click 'Use an Existing List' on the Add List menu. Select the file named Support_PUB_8_CactusList.mdb from the folder you copied previously. When Publisher displays the catalog merge area, change the size to approximately 4 inches wide by 2 inches tall. Drag the area to a location below the heading.

6. Use the Picture Field button (Catalog Tools Format tab | Insert group) to insert the picture field into the catalog merge area. Position the picture box in the upper-left corner of the catalog merge area.

7. Insert a table inside the catalog merge area that fills the empty space beside the picture, choosing 4 rows and 2 columns with no formatting. Align the picture and the table along the top. Resize the picture by SHIFT+dragging a corner sizing handle so that the picture fills the area beside the table.

8. In the first column of the table, enter the following row headings, making certain to press the COLON key (:) after each heading: Name, Genus, Size, and Food use. Use the Text Field button (Catalog Tools Format tab | Insert group) to enter the corresponding field codes, Name, Genus, Size, and Edible in the second column.

9. On page 4:

    a. Delete the organization logo.

    b. Click the Calendars button (Insert tab | Building blocks group) and then click More Calendars in the Calendars gallery. When Publisher displays the Building bock Library dialog box, choose the Punctuation calendar and change the date to June 2021. Click the Insert button (Building Block Library dialog box). When the calendar is displayed, select the weekday cells and then use the Fill button (Table Tools Design tab | Table Formats group) to fill the cells with Accent 2 from the color scheme. Fill the weekend cells with the Accent 3 color. Move the calendar to the top of page 4 and resize as necessary.

c. Below the calendar, insert a rectangle shape approximately .5 inches square. Fill the rectangle with the Accent 2 color. Create a text box next to the rectangle approximately 3 inches wide and .5 inches tall. Using a font of size 10 or larger, type **Open from 10 a.m. to 7 p.m.** in the text box.

d. Below the previous rectangle and text box, insert another similar rectangle shape, filled with the Accent 3 color. Create a similar text box. Using a font of size 10 or larger, type **Open from 10 a.m. to 10 p.m.** in the text box.

e. Select the text in the Business Name text box and then type **Caleb Park District** to replace the text, if necessary. If necessary change the font to Times New Roman. Change the font size to 16.7.

f. In the address text box, type:

5200 Park Drive
Caleb, AZ 85719

g. In the phone text box, type:

Phone: 520-555-4800
Fax: 520-555-4801

10. Navigate to page 2. Select the rounded rectangle shape at the top of the page. Click the Send Backward button (Home tab| Arrange group) twice. Select the text in the To Order box at the top of the page. Type **Your guide to identifying the host of the desert** to replace the synchronized text.

11. Edit master page A and create a footer with the text, Caleb Park District, on both the verso and recto pages. To create a mirrored footer, left-justify the text on the verso page, and right-justify the text on the recto page. Apply the master page A to the catalog pages only.

12. Display the View tab. Click to display a check mark in the Graphics Manager check box (View tab | Show group).When Publisher opens the Graphics Manager pane, point to SC_PUB_8_FrontCactus.jpg to display the picture's arrow. Click the arrow and then click Details to display the Details dialog box. Write down the file size and effective resolution.

13. Use the spelling checker and design checker to fix any errors. Preview the results using the Preview Results button (Catalog Tools Format tab | Preview Page group). Delete any pictures in the scratch area.

14. Save the new publication with the name SC_PUB_8_CactusCatalog. Submit the merged file in the format specified by your instructor, along with the details from the Graphics Manager.

15. ✳ What other kinds of publications might benefit from a catalog merge? Would doing a catalog merge be easier than trying to insert the pictures and details manually in a multipage, non-catalog publication?

Extend Your Knowledge

Extend the skills you learned in this module and experiment with new skills. You may need to use Help to complete the assignment.

Creating a Catalog List from Scratch

Note: To complete this assignment, you will be required to use the Data Files. Please contact your instructor for information about accessing the Data Files.

Instructions: Copy the folder, Support_PUB_8_MusicTheory, from the Data Files to your storage location as explained in the module. The folder contains a blank catalog publication and a set of pictures. Start Publisher and open the file named SC_PUB_8-1.pub, which is a publication

Continued >

Extend Your Knowledge *continued*

measuring 5.5 by 8.5 inches. You will use this publication to create a small catalog list from scratch. You will make a list of music symbols for elementary piano students. Pages 1 through 3 are shown in Figure 8–73.

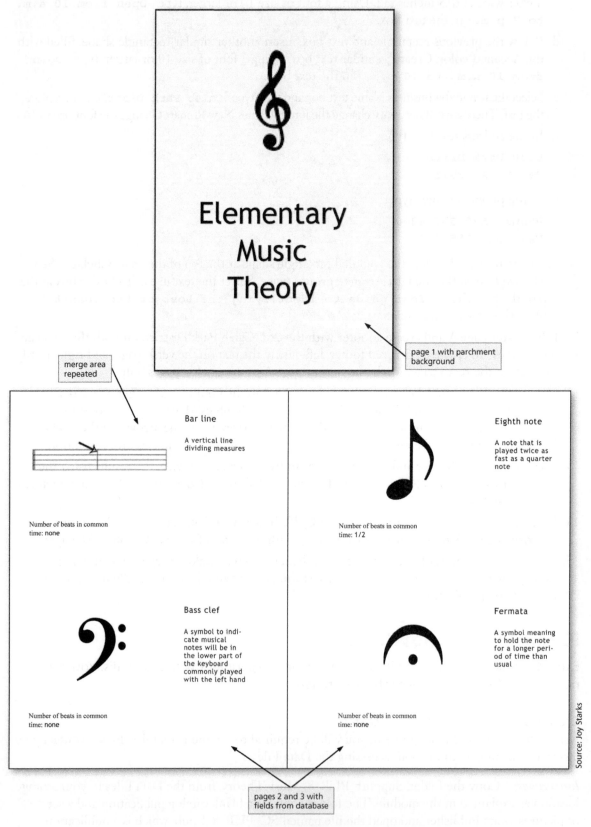

page 1 with parchment background

merge area repeated

Bar line

A vertical line dividing measures

Number of beats in common time: none

Eighth note

A note that is played twice as fast as a quarter note

Number of beats in common time: 1/2

Bass clef

A symbol to indicate musical notes will be in the lower part of the keyboard commonly played with the left hand

Number of beats in common time: none

Fermata

A symbol meaning to hold the note for a longer period of time than usual

Number of beats in common time: none

pages 2 and 3 with fields from database

Source: Joy Starks

Figure 8–73

Perform the following tasks:

1. Use Help to learn more about catalog lists, customizing columns, and catalog layouts.
2. Save the publication with the file name, SC_PUB_8_MusicTheory.
3. On page 1:
   a. Insert a Parchment background texture on page 1.
   b. Create a large text box that fills the lower third of page 1. Type **Elementary** and then press ENTER. Type **Music** and then press ENTER. Type **Theory** to complete the title. Use the Best Fit command to size the text. Center all lines of text.
   c. Insert the picture named treble.clef.png above the text box. Resize it to approximately 2 inches by 3 inches. Reposition the picture, if necessary. If the picture displays a white background, click the Recolor button (Picture Tools Format tab | Adjust group) and then click 'Set Transparent Color' on the menu. Click the white portion of the picture.
4. Navigate to page 2. To create a catalog list:
   a. Click the Add List button (Catalog Tools Format tab | Start group) and then click 'Type a new list' to display the New Product List dialog box.
   b. Click the Customize Columns button and then rename and delete field names as necessary to create four columns for data: Symbol, Description, Number of Beats in Common Time, and Picture. Click OK (New Product List dialog box). When prompted, name the database SC_PUB_8_MusicDatabase.
   c. Edit the database and enter the data from Table 8–3.

Table 8–3 Data for Music Database

Symbol	Description	Number of Beats in Common Time	Picture
Bar line	A vertical line dividing measures	none	bar line.png
Bass clef	A symbol to indicate musical notes will be in the lower part of the keyboard commonly played with the left hand	none	bass clef.png
Eighth note	A note that is played twice as fast as a quarter note	1/2	eighth note.png
Fermata	A symbol meaning to hold the note for a longer period of time than usual	none	fermata.png
Flat	A symbol that indicates the note should be played one-half step down from the original	none	flat.png
Half note	A note held twice as long as a quarter note	2	half note.png
Half rest	A symbol to indicate no sound for half the measure	2	half rest.png
Quarter note	A note representing one beat in common time signature or ¼ the time of a whole note	1	quarter note.png
Quarter rest	A symbol to indicate no sound for one beat in common time	1	quarter rest.png
Sharp	A symbol that indicates the note should be played one-half step up from the original	none	sharp.png
Sixteenth note	A note held 1/4 as long as a quarter note	1/4	sixteenth note.png
Staff	Five lines and four spaces upon which the notes are written	none	staff.png
Treble clef	A symbol to indicate musical notes will be in the upper part of the keyboard commonly played with the right hand	none	treble clef.png
Whole note	A note held 4 times as long as a quarter note, or a full measure in common time	4	whole note.png
Whole rest	A symbol to indicate no sound for four beats or a full measure in common time	4	whole rest.png

Continued >

Extend Your Knowledge *continued*

5. Click OK to close the Edit Data Source dialog box. Click OK to close the Catalog Merge Product List dialog box.

6. In the publication, select the Catalog Merge area. Click the '2 entries, picture on left' button (Catalog Tools Layout tab I Layout group). Then link data as follows:

   a. Click the picture placeholder and then choose the Picture field in the Insert Picture field dialog box.

   b. Replace the text in the text box below the picture by typing `Number of beats in common time:` and then insert the field from the database. Change the font size to 10.

   c. Select all of the text in the text box beside the picture. Insert the Symbol field and set the font size to 12. Press ENTER twice. Insert the Description field. Change the font size to 10.

7. Preview the catalog pages. Click the first picture and the use the Fit command so that the picture fits the placeholder.

8. Add the parchment texture background to page 4. If instructed to do so, create a text box with your name and course number in the lower-left corner of the page.

9. Save the publication again and print a copy for your instructor.

10. ✳ What would be an appropriate mirrored header and/or footer for the catalog pages? How does having 15 entries in the database affect the publication?

Expand Your World

Create a solution that uses cloud and web technologies by learning and investigating on your own from general guidance.

Creating a Flipbook

Problem: Flipsnack is a web publisher that will allow you to upload catalogs to the web. You decide to publish one of your catalogs on the web.

Instructions:

1. Start Publisher and open one of your catalog publications.

2. Save your catalog in the PDF format. (*Hint:* Click Export in Backstage view, click 'Create PDF/ XSP Document' in the left pane, and then click the 'Create PDF/XPS' button.) Save the file on your storage location.

3. Start a browser and navigate to https://www.flipsnack.com (Figure 8–74).

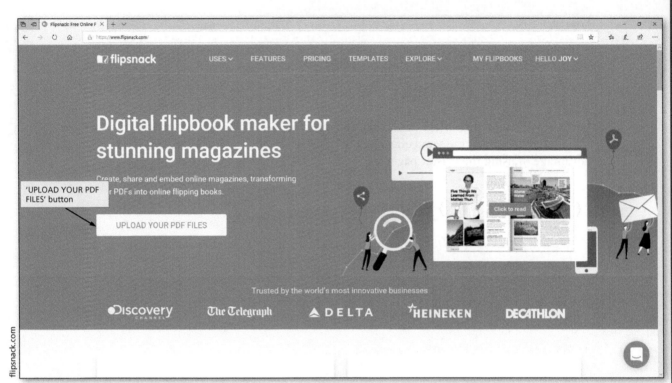

'UPLOAD YOUR PDF FILES' button

flipsnack.com

Figure 8–74

4. Click the 'UPLOAD YOUR PDF FILES' button. Sign in with your Facebook or Google account, or create a new, free account. Navigate to the location of your PDF file. Follow the instructions to upload your catalog.

5. When Flipsnack is finished creating the file, click the Publish button. Click the icon to turn the pages. If desired, click the Publish Now button and copy the web address from the Direct Link box. Send the web address to your instructor.

6. ✳ Does your flipbook look as you expected it to? What issues do you have? How can you resolve them?

In the Lab

Design and implement a solution using creative thinking and problem-solving skills.

Editing Graphics, Applying Number Styles, and Translating

Note: To complete this assignment, you will be required to use the Data Files. Please contact your instructor for information about accessing the Data Files.

Instructions: Start Publisher. Open the publication, SC_PUB_8-2.pub, from the Data Files. The publication is a three-page vacation brochure. You are to edit some of the graphics and use the thesaurus.

Part 1: On page 1, crop the picture to a shape, such as 'Flowchart: Punched Tape'. Add a reflection, such as 'Full Reflection: 4 point offset' to the picture. Use the Graphics Manager to look at the size and location of each picture in the publication. Apply the Proportional Old-Style format

Continued >

In the Lab *continued*

to the numbers on pages 2 and 3. On page 2, use the translation service to translate the word, vacation, to the language of your choice. Copy the translation and add it to the VACATION: text box. Repeat the process on page 3 for the HOLIDAY: text box. Save the file and submit it to your instructor as directed.

Part 2: Which pictures were on the master pages? Why do you think they were placed there? Would they have had the same effect had they been placed in the page background? What is the advantage of using the master page?

9 Sharing and Distributing Publications

Objectives

After completing this module, you will be able to:

- Select and format an email newsletter template
- Change the size of an email newsletter
- Set the email newsletter background to use a pattern
- Fit pictures in picture placeholders
- Insert symbols and special characters
- Use the Research pane
- Create a cited definition
- Insert a hyperlink, a mailto hyperlink, and a hot spot

- Choose options for the Design Checker
- Preview an email newsletter using Publisher
- Send an HTML-enabled email newsletter
- Send a postcard as an email attachment
- Open a Word document in Publisher and format it
- Use design accents

Introduction

Publisher makes it easy to share and distribute publications. Sending email messages and newsletters, attaching publications to email messages, using publications with social media, and uploading publications to websites are among the ways that desktop publishers can market and correspond electronically with customers, business associates, and friends.

Email, short for electronic mail, is a popular form of communication used to transmit messages and files via a computer network. For businesses, email can be an efficient and cost-effective way to keep in touch with customers and interested parties. Email is used in ways similar to traditional mail. With it, you can send correspondence, business communications, and other types of publications. An email message may display traditional correspondence-related text and graphics and may include hyperlinks similar to a webpage, as well as attachments. Many email messages sent from companies or organizations include a way for recipients to unsubscribe from the mailing list. When recipients **unsubscribe**, they remove their names and addresses from the mailing list.

Publications that sometimes are attached to an email message (or more traditionally are mailed using a postal service) include graphics, postcards, and greeting cards, among others.

Project: Distributed Publications

You may need to share and distribute Publisher files with others electronically. To ensure that others can read and/or open the files successfully, Publisher presents a variety of formats and tools to assist with sharing documents. In this module, you will create and send several publications, including an email newsletter, a postcard, and an agenda. Figure 9–1a displays an email newsletter sent to people interested in the T.R. Historical Society. Figure 9–1b displays a postcard sent to members, reminding them of an upcoming meeting. Figure 9–1c displays an agenda for that meeting. The publications include colorful headings, graphics, and directions for obtaining more information.

When you send an email message, recipients can read it using HTML-enabled email programs, such as Gmail, Yahoo! Mail, or the current versions of Microsoft Outlook and Outlook Express. **HTML-enabled email** allows the sender to include formatted text and other visuals to improve the readability and aesthetics of the message. The majority of Internet users can access HTML-enabled email. Recipients do not need to have Publisher installed to view email newsletters because the page you send will be displayed as the body of the email newsletter. Sending a one-page publication by email to a group of customers or friends is an efficient and inexpensive way to deliver a message.

Publisher provides several ways to create an email newsletter. You can use a template or create an email publication from scratch. Publisher's email templates are preformatted and use placeholder text and graphics that download quickly and are suitable for the body of an email newsletter.

A second way to create an email publication is to send a single page of another publication. This expands the use of your existing content, although you may need to adjust the width of your publication in order for it to fit in an email newsletter.

Another way is to send an entire Publisher publication as an attachment; however, this requires that the recipient have Microsoft Publisher 2002 or a later version installed to view it. When the recipient opens the attached file, Publisher automatically starts and opens the publication. Unless you convert a multipage publication into a single-page email publication, it must be sent as an email attachment.

Finally, you can create an **email merge** when you want to send a large number of messages that mostly are identical, but you also want to include some unique or personalized information in each message. An email merge, which uses the same merge techniques as a mail merge, creates personalized content for each recipient on a mailing list.

The type of publication you choose depends on the content and the needs of the recipients. Table 9–1 describes specific audiences and the appropriate kinds of email publications.

Table 9–1 Publisher Email Types

Audience Characteristic	Email Message	Email Merge	Email Attachment
Recipients definitely have Publisher installed			X
Recipients may not have Publisher installed	X	X	
Recipients need to read and print the content in its original format			X
Recipients may not have HTML-enabled email	X	X	
Recipients need personalized messages		X	

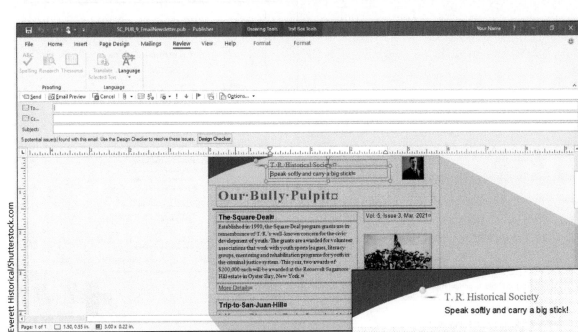

Our Bully Pulpit

The Square Deal

Established in 1990, the Square Deal program grants are in remembrance of T. R.'s well-known concern for the civic development of youth. The grants are awarded for volunteer associations that work with youth sports leagues, literacy groups, mentoring and rehabilitation programs for youth in the criminal justice system. This year, two awards of $200,000 each will be awarded at the Roosevelt Sagamore Hill estate in Oyster Bay, New York.

More Details

Vol. 5, Issue 3, Mar

Rough Rider: "a soldier
1st U.S. Volunteer Cava
recruited by T. R. ("Rou
Rider." Encarta, 2019)

Trip to San Juan Hill

In May, we will be retracing Theodore Roosevelt and the 1st United States Volunteer Cavalry's 1898 route from San Antonio, Texas to Tampa Bay, Florida then onward to Daiquiri and Santiago de Cuba. For seven days and six nights we will meet with local historians at each stop to discuss the significance of the events that helped transform the United States into the nation it is today.

This is a once-in-a-lifetime chance to understand not just how the United States views the war of 1898, but also the Cuban point of view. Make plans now to join this important event.

More Details

Member Spotlight

Renée Moreau is the ne
president of the Indiana
chapter. She is a noted
author of books about
of Indiana and has writ
several monograms ab
Theodore Roosevelt. S
currently is a lecturer a
Community College.

Around the Ring

You can purchase a Gold
Pass© at your next meeting.

The Tennessee chapter reports a successful recruiting dr
garnered 50 new members. Kudos!

The Iowa chapter is planning a trip to Medora, North Da
view the Theodore Roosevelt Maltese Cross Ranch and s
the impact the oil boom is having on the park's lands.

A big round of thanks to the New York chapter in prepar
our Square Deal Awards celebration. Their hard work w
appreciated.

Finally, the Texas chapter is hard at work keeping the 1st
teer Cavalr

a) Email Newsletter

Figure 9–1 (Continued)

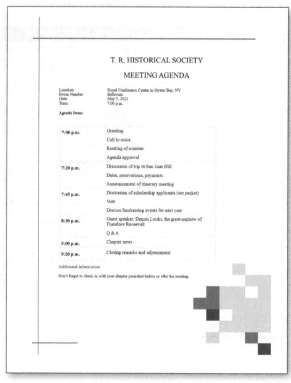

b) Postcard   c) Agenda

Figure 9–1

The following roadmap identifies general activities you will perform as you progress through this module:

1. Create an email publication, such as a newsletter.
2. Insert symbols, patterns, and special characters.
3. Use the Research pane, and create a citation.
4. Create hyperlinks and hot spots.
5. Distribute email publications.
6. Create a postcard.
7. Import a Word agenda.
8. Use design accents as appropriate.

Email Templates

Each of Publisher's design sets features several email templates, so you can create and send email communications that are consistent in design with the rest of the business communication and marketing materials that you create using Publisher. Table 9–2 lists the types of email templates and the purpose of each one.

BTW

Email Templates
Email templates contain text boxes, logos, hyperlinks, and graphics. To customize the email message, you replace the placeholder text and graphics with your own content, just as you would in any other template publication.

CONSIDER THIS

What should you keep in mind when designing an email newsletter?
Be sure to start with a Publisher email template or resize your publication to fit standard email newsletter sizes. When using a template, choose one that matches the purpose of the email newsletter, as Publisher will supply many of the necessary elements, such as text, graphics, and links. Use graphics sparingly, keeping in mind the download time. If you use wallpaper or stationery, keep it simple or a solid color.

Table 9–2 Types of Email Templates

Type	Purpose
Event/Activity	A notice of a specific upcoming activity or event containing a combination of pictures, dates, times, maps, and an agenda; provides the ability to sign up
Event/Speaker	A notice of a specific upcoming event that includes a speaker and usually contains pictures, dates, times, and a map
Featured Product	A publication that provides information about a company and a specific product or service; includes graphics and webpage links for more information
Letter	A more personalized document to correspond with one or more people; includes specific information on a single topic
Newsletter	Informs interested clientele about an organization or a business with stories, dates, contact information, and upcoming events
Product List	A sales-oriented publication to display products, prices, and special promotions, including webpage links for more information

To Select an Email Template

The following steps select an email template from the template gallery and choose color and font schemes. You do not have to be connected to the Internet or have an email program on your computer in order to create the email. You can create and save the email newsletter on any storage device rather than send it via email.

1. Start Publisher. In the template gallery, click Built-In to display the built-in templates.

2. Scroll as necessary and then click the E-mail thumbnail in the built-in templates to display the E-mail templates.

3. Scroll down to the Newsletter templates.

4. Click the Bounce thumbnail to choose the template.

5. In the Customize area, choose the Wildflower color scheme and the 'Office Classic 1' font scheme (Figure 9–2).

BTW
Touch Screen
Differences
The Office and Windows interfaces may vary if you are using a touch screen. For this reason, you might notice that the function or appearance of your touch screen differs slightly from this module's presentation.

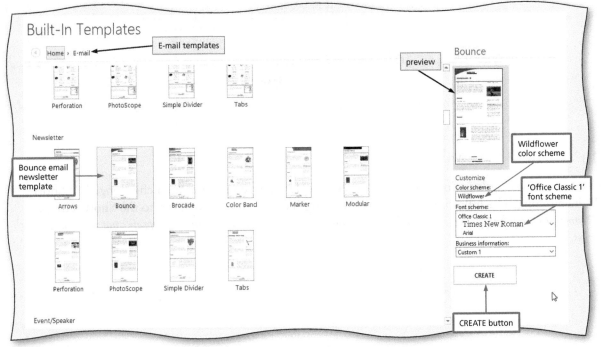

Figure 9–2

6. Click the CREATE button to create the publication with the chosen settings.

To Create the Publication and Customize the Workspace

The following steps customize the workspace.

1 Display the View tab. If necessary, click to display a check mark in the Boundaries check box (View tab | Show group).

2 Display the Home tab. If necessary, click the Special Characters button (Home tab | Paragraph group) to display paragraph marks and special characters.

3 Close the Page Navigation pane (Figure 9–3).

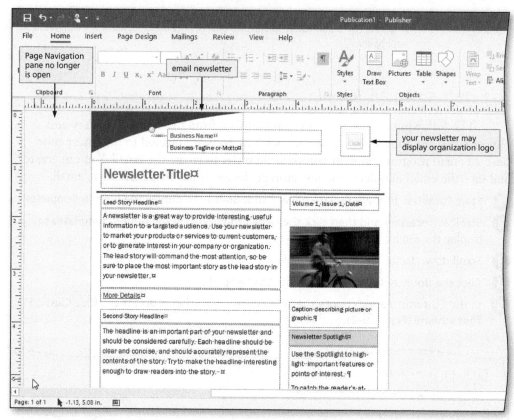

Figure 9–3

To Change the Email Newsletter Page Size

Publisher has two length settings for email newsletters. The Large setting is 66 inches long. The Short setting is 11 inches long. The following steps change the length of the email newsletter to the Short setting. **Why?** *The historical society has chosen a shorter length, as most people who read email messages prefer not to scroll through longer messages.*

1

- Display the Page Design tab.
- Click the Size button (Page Design tab | Page Setup group) to display the Size gallery.
- If necessary, scroll to the bottom of the Size gallery (Figure 9–4).

 My Size gallery is different. Did I do something wrong?
No. Your gallery may differ depending on page sizes that have been saved previously.

Can I click the Page Setup Dialog Box Launcher to customize the page size?
Yes, you can set the margins and choose various paper sizes and layouts in the Page Setting dialog box. The email sizes include the standard width of 5.818 inches but differing lengths, including a long email (up to 66 inches), a short email (up to 11 inches), or a custom size.

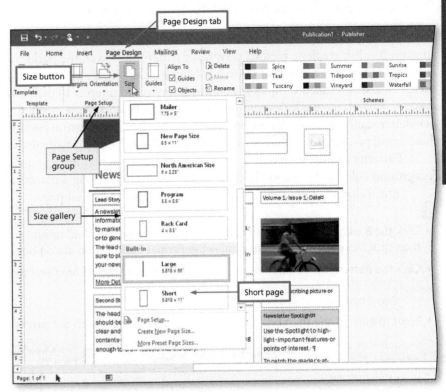

Figure 9–4

2

- Click Short in the Size gallery to specify a short page format (Figure 9–5).

 My email newsletter has a different business name listed in the publication. Did I do something wrong?
No. Your computer may be using a different business information set, or it may have an installed school or company name. You will edit the boxes later in the module.

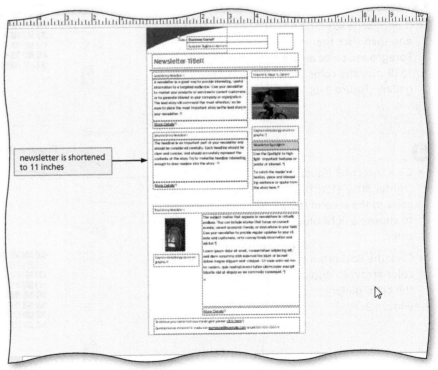

Figure 9–5

To Set the Email Background to Use a Pattern

You can add a background to an email or web publication in the same way you do for other publications — by applying a color, gradient, picture, texture, or pattern; however, the background should not be detailed or busy. *Why? Backgrounds appear behind the text and graphics and should not detract from reading the text.* People include email backgrounds, also called **wallpaper** or **stationery**, to add interest to their email messages, to convey or enhance the message, to grab the reader's attention, or to emulate business letterhead. A background also can make your email newsletter stand out from those who simply use black text on a white background. Publisher especially is useful for those email programs that do not offer wallpaper. Backgrounds usually do not increase the email download time.

Patterns include variations of repeating designs, such as lines, stripes, checks, and bricks. Publisher uses a foreground color and a second background color when creating a pattern.

The following steps set a pattern background for the email page.

1

- Click the Background button (Page Design tab | Page Background group) to display the Background gallery and then click More Backgrounds to display the Format Background dialog box.
- Click the Pattern fill option button (Format Background dialog box) and then scroll down to display the settings.

 Experiment

- Point to each of the thumbnails in the Pattern area to view each pattern name in a ScreenTip.

 My patterns are different. Did I do something wrong? No. Someone may have changed the foreground and background colors. The patterns are the same.

2

- If necessary, scroll down and then click the Foreground color arrow to display the color gallery (Figure 9–6).

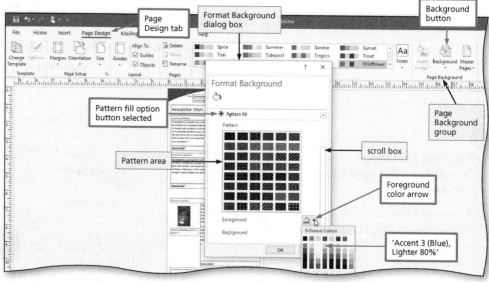

Figure 9–6

3

- Click 'Accent 3 (Blue), Lighter 80%' (fourth color in the second row) to choose a light blue color.
- Click the Background color arrow to display the color gallery (Figure 9–7).

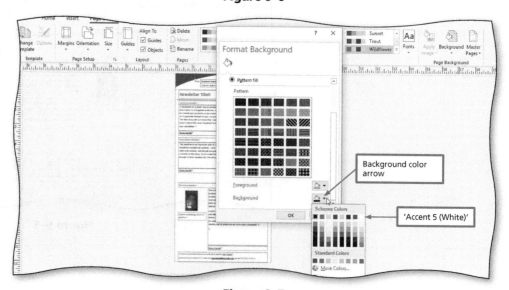

Figure 9–7

• Click 'Accent 5 (White)' (eighth color in the first row) to choose white as the background color.

• Click Dotted: 20% to specify the pattern (Figure 9–8).

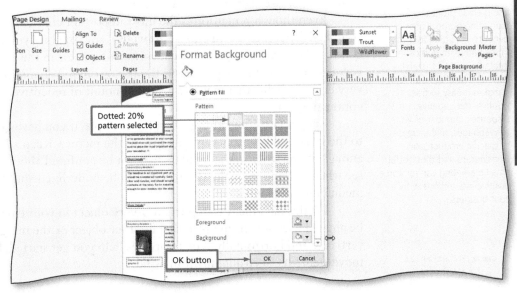

Figure 9–8

5

• Click OK (Format Background dialog box) to apply the background.

• Zoom to 150% and then scroll to the top of the page (Figure 9–9).

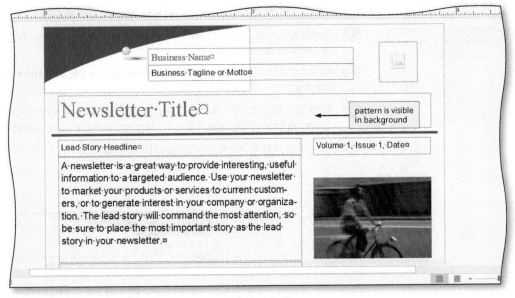

Figure 9–9

Reading Online

As with printed newsletters, when creating an email newsletter, you should pay attention to readability. A few elements, however, become very important when users are reading online. First, repetition is important. Use the same font and font size for all headings and all stories. Do not use more than three different fonts or font sizes on the page. Do not choose a third-party font that you may have downloaded. Some browsers change unknown fonts, which can cause the text to be harder to read. Use standard font sizes. In this module, you will use the Times New Roman and Arial fonts, which are easy to read, and font sizes of 10, 12, and 24. Try to use three or four colors at most. In this module, you will use red, gold, and blue from the Wildflower color scheme. Make sure you have some repeated elements, such as links for more details,

BTW
Pictures as Backgrounds
If you select a custom picture file for your background texture, make sure it is 40 KB or smaller. Large picture files will require people who are viewing your email message to wait a long time for the graphic to download.

repeated lines, or repeated colors. In this module, you will have all three. Using an element only once can look like an error.

Even though repetition is the most important consideration, make sure the color and font scheme you choose, as well as any graphics you include, provide some contrast. For example, use the most contrasting color in the scheme for headings versus stories and for shapes versus the background. You might want to include a very bright graphic that includes a small amount of repetitive color but lots of bright contrasting colors.

Keep related objects together; for example, if you have graphics, keep them close to the story and keep any caption close to the picture. Keep a More Details link close enough to the story so that readers will not be confused about what details they will see when clicking the link. All links should be underlined and use the standardized medium blue color.

Finally, alignment is important. Every object in your email publication should be aligned with something — either another object or the margin. Try to align both vertically and horizontally. The templates help you get started, but as you resize and move elements, keep alignment in mind.

To Edit the Heading

The following steps edit the heading of the newsletter.

1 Select the text, Newsletter Title, at the top of the page. Type `Our Bully Pulpit` to replace the text.

2 Select the text again, change the font size to 24, and then press CTRL+B to bold the text.

3 Click the Object Size button on the taskbar to open the Measurement pane. Use the Tracking box to change the tracking to 120% to spread the letters of the heading.

4 Click the text to remove the selection (Figure 9–10).

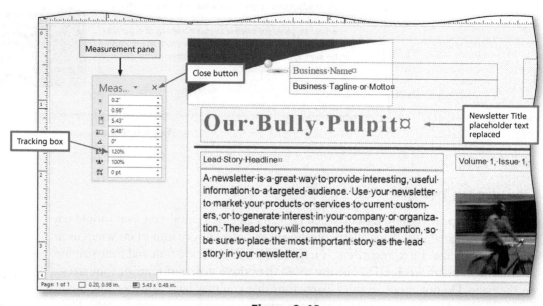

Figure 9–10

5 Click the Close button in the Measurement pane to close it.

To Edit Other Text Boxes at the Top of the Page

The following steps edit the text boxes in the upper portion of the email newsletter.

1 Select the text in the Business Name text box, change the font size to 12 if necessary, and then type **T. R. Historical Society** to replace the text.

2 Select the text in the 'Business Tagline or Motto' text box, change the font size to 10, and then type **Speak softly and carry a big stick!** to replace the text.

3 Click to select the text in the volume text box, change the font size to 10, and then type **Vol. 5, Issue 3, Mar. 2021** to replace the text (Figure 9–11).

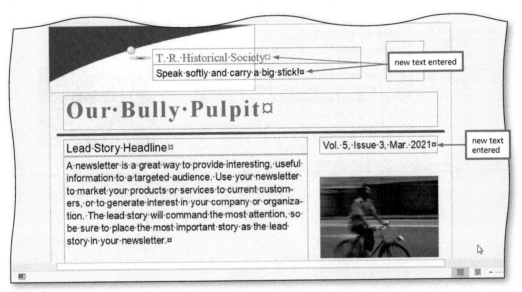

Figure 9–11

To Complete the Lead Story

The following steps edit the headline and text for the lead story. To complete these steps, you will be required to use the Data Files. Please contact your instructor for information about accessing the Data Files.

As you import this and other stories into the email newsletter, if the story is too long, Publisher will create a second page with a new text box to continue the story. If that happens, press CTRL+Z to undo the import, resize the current text box, and then import the file again.

After importing the first story, you will need to hyphenate due to the way the text wraps. Check all your stories for the need to hyphenate. You will check spelling at the end of the module.

1 Click to select the Lead Story Headline placeholder text. Change the font size to 12, change the font color to Main (Black), bold the text, and then type **The Square Deal** to replace the text.

2 Click the text in the story text box below the headline to select it.

3 Display the Insert tab.

④ Click the Insert File button (Insert tab | Text group) to display the Insert
File dialog box. Navigate to the Data Files and then double-click the file named
Support_PUB_9_GrantStory.doc to insert it in the publication (Figure 9–12).

Figure 9–12

To Complete the Second Story

The following steps edit the headline and text for the second story. Because the
second story is long, you will move and resize text boxes before importing the story.
To complete these steps, you will be required to use the Data Files. Please contact your
instructor for information about accessing the Data Files.

① Click to select the Second Story Headline placeholder text. Change the font size to 12,
change the font color to Main (Black), bold the text, and then type **Trip to San
Juan Hill** to replace the text.

② Select the More Details text box below the second story. SHIFT+drag the border of the
More Details text box straight down to a location just above the gray horizontal line.

③ Resize the second story text box to be approximately 2 inches tall.

④ Select the second story text.

⑤ Click the Insert File button (Insert tab | Text group) to display the Insert File
dialog box. Navigate to the Data Files and then double-click the file named
Support_PUB_9_SanJuanStory.doc to insert it in the publication.

⑥ Display the Text Box Tools Format tab.

⑦ Click the Hyphenation button (Text Box Tools Format tab | Text group) to display the
Hyphenate dialog box.

⑧ Click to remove the check mark in the 'Automatically hyphenate this story' check box.
Click the Manual button (Hyphenate Dialog box) to begin hyphenating the story.

⑨ When Publisher recommends hyphenating the word, Antonio, click the No button because it is a proper noun.

⑩ When Publisher recommends hyphenating the word, Daiquiri, click the No button because it is a proper noun (Figure 9–13).

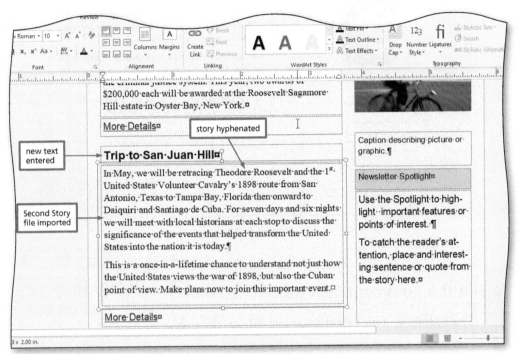

Figure 9–13

⑪ If Publisher displays a Microsoft Publisher dialog box indicating that hyphenation is complete, click OK.

To Complete the Third Story

The following steps edit the headline and text for the third story. To complete these steps, you will be required to use the Data Files. Please contact your instructor for information about accessing the Data Files.

① Click to select the Third Story Headline placeholder text. Change the font size to 12, change the font color to Main (Black), bold the text, and then type **Around the Ring** to replace the text.

② Click the text in the story text box to select it.

③ Click the Insert File button (Insert tab | Text group) to display the Insert File dialog box. Navigate to the Data Files and then double-click the file named Support_PUB_9_ChaptersStory.doc to insert it in the publication (Figure 9–14).

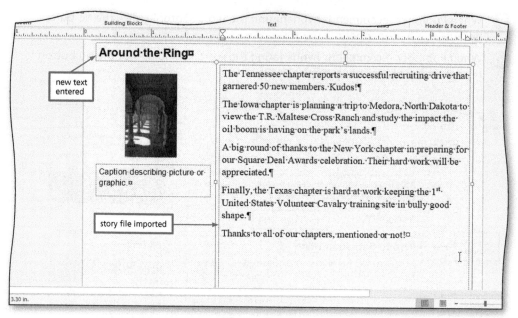

Figure 9–14

To Edit the Comment Text Box

The following steps edit the last text box on the page.

① Scroll as necessary to the bottom of the page.

② Click the email placeholder text to select it and then type `news@trhistorical.soc` to replace the text.

③ Select the last phrase and then type `or call 205-555-4900.` to replace the text (Figure 9–15).

④ Save the publication on your desired save location, using the file name, SC_PUB_9_EmailNewsletter.

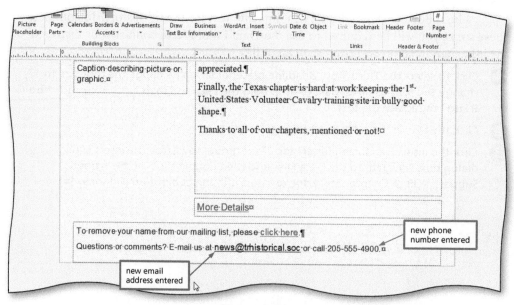

Figure 9–15

To Complete the Sidebar

The following steps edit the headline and text for the sidebar. To complete these steps, you will be required to use the Data Files. Please contact your instructor for information about accessing the Data Files.

1 Scroll to the center of the page.

2 Click to select the Newsletter Spotlight headline in the sidebar. Change the font size to 10 and then type **Member Spotlight** to replace the text.

3 Click the text in the story text box below the headline to select it.

4 Display the Insert tab.

5 Click the Insert File button (Insert tab | Text group) to display the Insert File dialog box. Navigate to the Data Files and then double-click the file named Support_PUB_9_MemberStory.doc to insert it in the publication.

6 If necessary, hyphenate the story, as described earlier in the module (Figure 9–16).

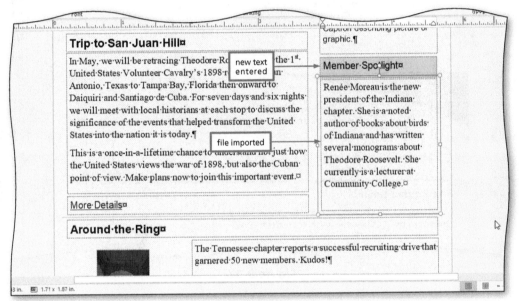

Figure 9–16

Pictures

When using pictures obtained from the web, make sure you have the legal right to use the pictures and that the owner understands that the picture will be transmitted over the web via email. Some people who do not object to their pictures being used in print are opposed to having their pictures distributed electronically.

Pictures or images used on webpages or in email newsletters should be used to draw attention, trigger emotions, and, most importantly, to enhance or add meaning to the story. Do not use pictures just to "dress up" the email. If the owner of the email newsletter or website has a logo, use it. Logos help brand the publication and let users know they are on the right page.

Check your images for quick display. Regardless of the kind of graphic or picture you include, lower ppi (points per inch) images will load faster. Use the Graphics Manager and compression techniques, when necessary.

Finally, use real people and real pictures when possible. Research has shown that clip art is not as effective in electronic publications. Publisher's email feature does not support animated graphics.

BTW
The Ribbon and Screen Resolution
Publisher may change how the groups and buttons within the groups appear on the ribbon, depending on the computer or mobile device's screen resolution. Thus, your ribbon may look different from the ones in this book if you are using a screen resolution other than 1366 × 768.

To Insert a Picture Placeholder

If you have an organization logo at the top of the page, complete these steps; otherwise, proceed to the next series of steps.

1 Scroll to the top of the page.

2 Right-click the border of the organization logo and then click Delete Object on the shortcut menu.

3 Display the Insert tab. Click the Picture Placeholder button (Insert tab | Illustrations group) to insert a picture placeholder.

4 Drag the placeholder to the upper-right corner of the page and resize as necessary, as shown in Figure 9–17.

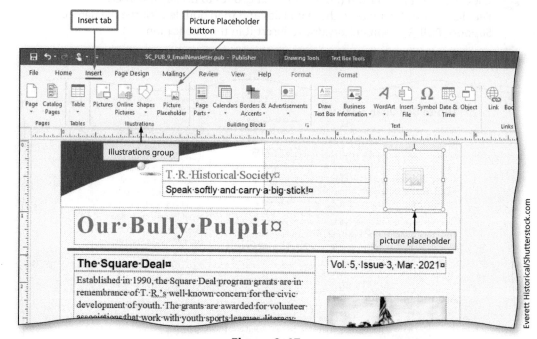

Figure 9–17

To Insert Pictures

The following steps insert pictures in the email newsletter.

1 Scroll to the top of the page.

2 Right-click the picture placeholder in the upper-right corner of the newsletter and then click Change Picture on the shortcut menu. When Publisher displays the Insert Pictures dialog box, click the 'From a file' link and navigate to the Data Files. Double-click the file named Support_PUB_9_Portrait.jpg to insert it in the placeholder.

3 Right-click the picture on the center right of the newsletter and then point to Change Picture on the shortcut menu to display the Change Picture submenu. Click Change Picture on the Change Picture submenu to display the Insert Pictures dialog box. Click the 'From a file' link and navigate to the Data Files. Double-click the file named Support_PUB_9_RoughRiders.jpg to insert it in the placeholder.

4 Click the scratch area to deselect the original picture and its replacement. Delete the original picture from the scratch area. Zoom to 150% (Figure 9–18).

Figure 9–18

To Fit a Picture

When you replace a picture in a template, you may get either excessive white space or empty space, or part of the picture may not be displayed. *Why?* *The new picture fills the picture placeholder. If the new picture is a different size, Publisher may adjust the picture, but you always should double-check it.* The following steps use the Fit button to make the picture fit the picture placeholder and then can crop any extra white space and resize.

- Right-click the picture beside the third story text box to display a shortcut menu and then point to Change Picture on the shortcut menu to display the Change Picture submenu. Click Change Picture on the Change Picture submenu to display the Insert Pictures dialog box.

- Click the 'From a file' link and navigate to the Data Files. Double-click the file named Support_PUB_9_Park.jpg to insert it in the placeholder.

- Click the scratch area to deselect the original picture and its replacement. Delete the original picture from the scratch area.

- Click the new picture to select it and then zoom to 150% (Figure 9–19).

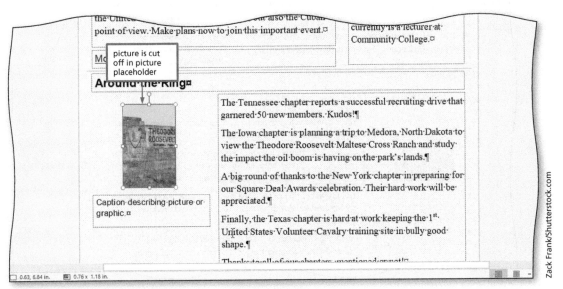

Figure 9–19

• Display the Picture Tools Format tab and then click the Fit button (Picture Tools Format tab | Crop group) to fit the picture in the picture placeholder (Figure 9–20).

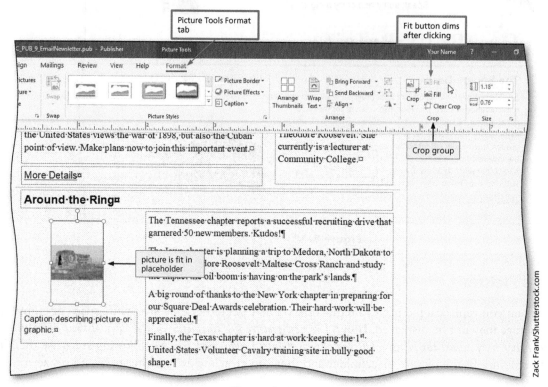

Figure 9–20

• Click the Crop button (Picture Tools Format tab | Crop group) and then drag the cropping handles toward the middle to crop out the blank space (Figure 9–21).

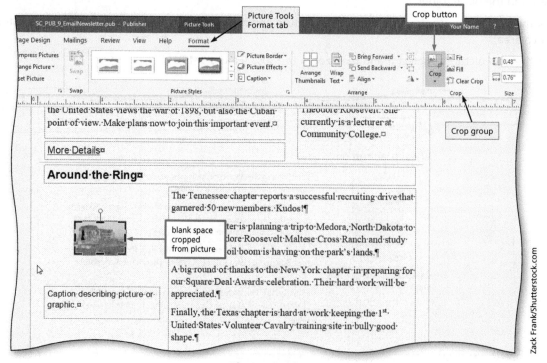

Figure 9–21

- Click the Crop button (Picture Tools Format tab | Crop group) again to turn off the cropping feature.

- SHIFT+drag corner sizing handles to resize the picture to fill the area better, as shown in Figure 9–22.

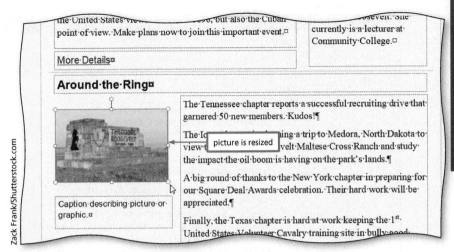

5

- Save the publication again.

Figure 9–22

Break Point: If you want to take a break, this is a good place to do so. You can exit Publisher now. To resume later, start Publisher, open the file called SC_PUB_9_EmailNewsletter.pub, and continue following the steps from this location forward.

Symbols and Special Characters

In Publisher, a **symbol** is a character that is not on your keyboard, such as ½ or ©, or a **special character**, such as an em dash (—) or ellipsis (…). Some special symbols use ASCII characters or Unicode characters. **ASCII** and **Unicode** are coding systems that represent text and symbols in computers, communications equipment, and other devices that use text.

Should you use symbols, hyperlinks, and hot spots?
Limit the use of symbols and special characters in email publications, as some may not be displayed correctly. Make sure you check for terms that may need copyright, trademark, and registration symbols. Double-check all hyperlinks for purpose and type. Create **hot spots**, or nontext hyperlinks, around graphics as necessary. Use mailto hyperlinks to help the recipient respond via email.

CONSIDER THIS

To Insert a Symbol from the Symbol Dialog Box

In the email newsletter, the second of the three lowercase letters, e, in the name Renee, should display an accent. *Why? The name contains an acute accent or diacritical mark, used in many written languages, to be punctuated correctly.* The following steps replace the letter, e, with an é in the text of the email newsletter.

1

- Zoom to 150%.

- In the sidebar story, select the second e in the name, Renee.

- Display the Insert tab.

- Click the Symbol button (Insert tab | Text group) to display the Symbol gallery (Figure 9–23).

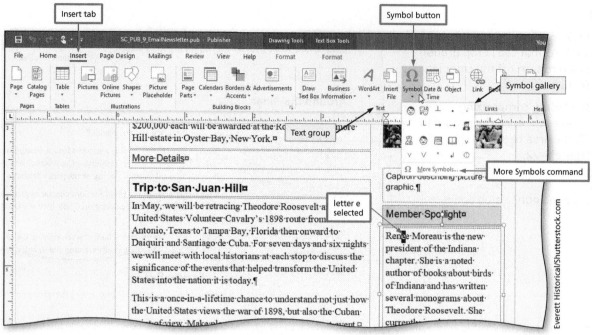

Figure 9–23

2

- Click More Symbols in the Symbol gallery to display the Symbol dialog box.

- If necessary, click the Font arrow (Symbol dialog box) and then click 'Times New Roman' in the list.

Q&A Why choose Times New Roman?
Unless you are looking for a certain graphic or web icon, it is best to start with the font used in the text itself, so that the font style will match. In this case, the font is Times New Roman.

- Scroll as necessary in the list and then click the desired symbol (in this case, é) to select it (Figure 9–24).

Q&A Does the symbol have a special name?
Publisher uses the name, Latin Small Letter E With Acute, to identify the symbol. Publisher also includes a Unicode number, 00E9, in the Character code text box to reference the é symbol.

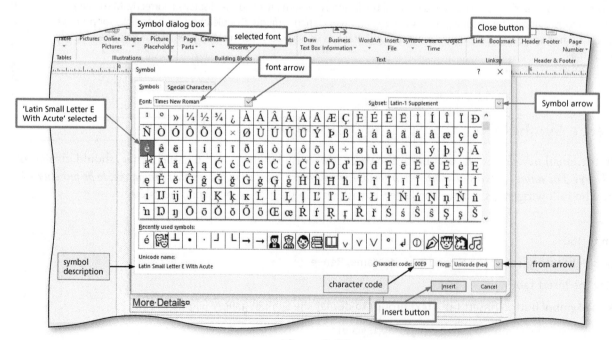

Figure 9–24

- Click the Insert button (Symbol dialog box) to place the selected symbol in the publication at the current location.

- Click the Close button to close the Symbol dialog box (Figure 9–25).

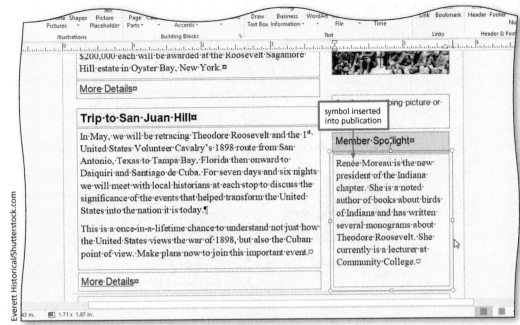

Figure 9–25

Other Ways

1. Click Symbol button (Insert tab | Text group), click More Symbols in Symbol gallery, enter Unicode number in Character code text box (Symbol dialog box), click Insert button, click Close button

---

To Insert a Special Character Using the Symbol Dialog Box

The following steps insert a copyright (©) character using the Symbol dialog box. *Why? This special character is not on the keyboard.*

- Navigate to the caption for the park picture on the left side of the newsletter.
- Click the caption to select the text and then type `You can purchase a Gold Pass` to begin the caption.
- Click the Symbol button (Insert tab | Text group) to display the Symbol gallery.
- Click More Symbols in the Symbol gallery to display the Symbol dialog box.
- Click the Special Characters tab (Symbol dialog box) to display the list of special characters.
- Click the desired special character (in this case, the © Copyright symbol) in the list of special characters (Figure 9–26).

Q&A Does the insertion point have to be inside a text box before I insert a special character?
Yes. Unlike word processing programs, Publisher uses text boxes to display text. Unless you have the symbol as a separate graphic file or can find it in clip art, you need to draw a text box first and then insert the symbol.

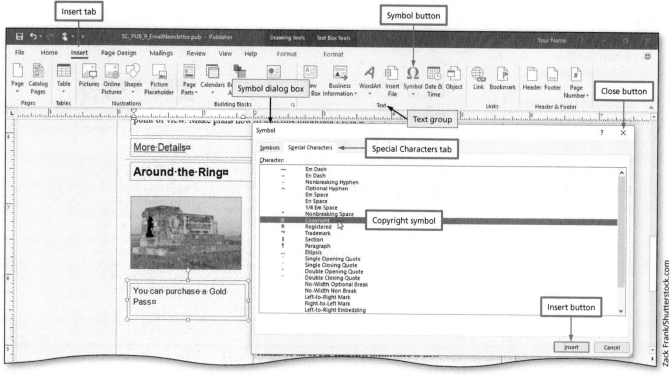

Figure 9–26

• Click the Insert button to place the selected special character in the publication.

• Click the Close button to close the dialog box (Figure 9–27).

Q&A Can I change the size of the symbol or make it a superscript?
Yes. Highlight the single character and then change the font size on the Home tab, or click the Font Dialog Box Launcher to display the Font dialog box. Click Superscript in the Effects area (Font dialog box) and then click OK.

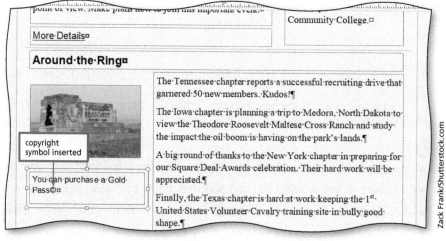

Figure 9–27

• Press SPACEBAR and then type **at your next meeting.** to complete the text (Figure 9–28).

Q&A What is the difference between a symbol and a special character?
The special character list is a subset of symbols that are used often in professional typing tasks.

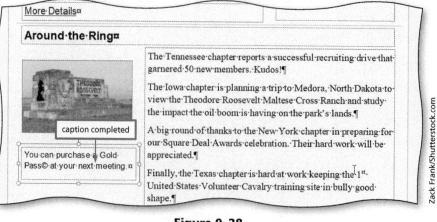

Figure 9–28

Research Pane

From within Publisher, you can search various forms of reference information. Services include a dictionary and, if you are connected to the web, an encyclopedia, a search engine, and other websites that provide information such as historical data, stock quotes, news articles, and company profiles.

Publisher's research options usually are broken down into two areas: reference books and research websites. Depending on your installation and your connection to the web, your list of reference books may include books such as the Encarta dictionary and various thesauruses. Research sites may include Bing, Factiva Works, and other search engines. The Research options link at the bottom of the Research pane allows you to add other books and websites to your list.

To Use the Research Pane

You decide to include a definition of a Rough Rider in the email newsletter. The following steps use the Research pane to look up a definition. You must be connected to the Internet to perform these steps. *Why?* *The Research tool relies on web-based dictionaries, encyclopedias, and search engines.*

- Scroll to the caption location below the picture of the Rough Riders on the center right of the newsletter.
- Resize the caption text box to fill the area between the picture and the next heading.
- Click the text to select it (Figure 9–29).

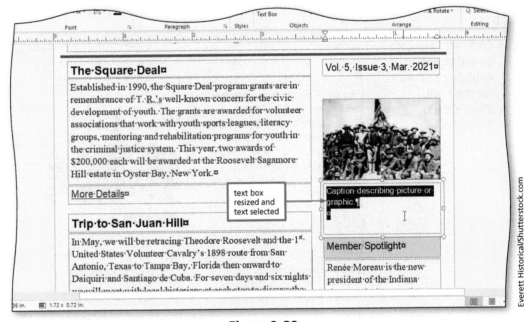

Figure 9–29

- Type, **Rough Rider: "** to begin the caption.
- Select the words, Rough Rider, and then display the Review tab.
- Click the Research button (Review tab | Proofing group) to open the Research pane.
- Click the arrow next to the word, Bing, in the Research pane to display the list of searchable locations (Figure 9–30).

Q&A How do I choose the search location?
If the term you want to research is one that you think might be in a dictionary or an encyclopedia, click the arrow next to the word, Bing, and then click 'All Reference Books.' If the term is more of a cultural item or a phrase, you may want to use Bing.

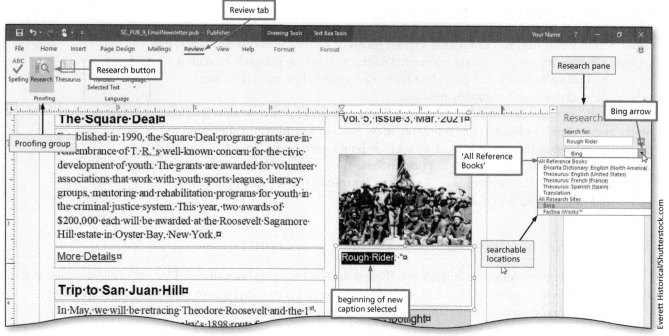

Figure 9–30

3

- Click 'All Reference Books' to instruct Publisher to search for the term (Figure 9–31).

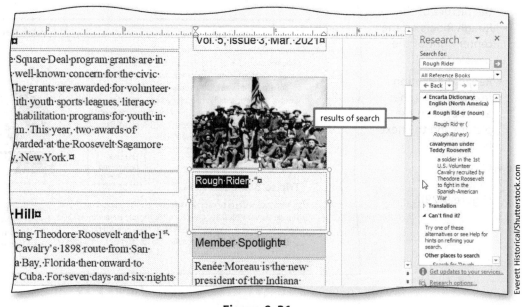

Figure 9–31

Other Ways

1. ALT+click desired word

To Create a Cited Reference

The following steps copy and paste a reference from the Research pane to the caption text box and create a citation. ***Why?*** *You always should include quotes and a citation when copying and pasting.*

1

- In the Research pane, select the text, a soldier in the 1st U.S. Volunteer Cavalry, and then press CTRL+C to copy the definition (Figure 9–32).

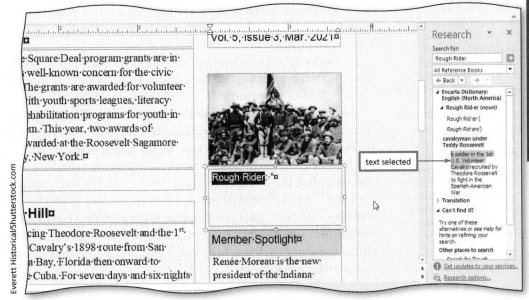

Figure 9–32

2

- Position the insertion point after the quotation mark in the caption text box and then press CTRL+V to paste the definition.

- Type **"** to complete the quote and then press SPACEBAR.

- Type **recruited by T. R. ("Rough Rider." Encarta, 2019)** to complete the citation. Resize the text box, if necessary (Figure 9–33).

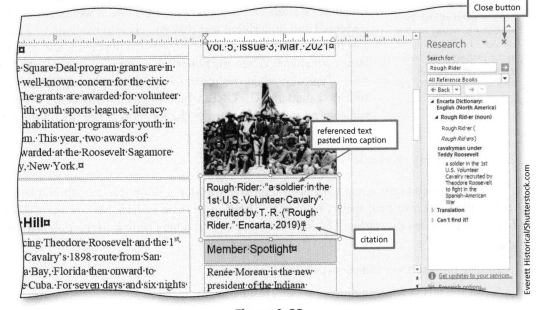

Figure 9–33

Q&A What kind of citation am I using?

The citation uses an in-text reference in **APA style**, a standard citation style in many fields.

3

- Click the Close button in the Research pane.

- Save the publication again.

Research Pane Options

When you install Publisher, it selects a series of services (reference books and websites) that it searches through when you use the Research pane. You can view, modify, and update the list of services at any time.

Clicking the Research options link at the bottom of the Research pane displays the Research Options dialog box, where you can view or modify the list of installed services. You can view information about any installed service by clicking the service in the list and then clicking the Properties button (Research Options dialog box). To activate an installed service, click the check box to its left. Likewise, to deactivate a service, click the check box to remove the check mark. To add a particular website to the list, click the Add Services button, enter the web address in the Address text box, and then click the Add button (Add Services dialog box). To update or remove services, click the Update/Remove button, select the service in the list, click the Update (or Remove) button (Update or Remove Services dialog box), and then click the Close button. You also can install parental controls through the Parental Control button (Research Options dialog box) if, for example, you want to restrict web access for minors who use Publisher.

Creating Hyperlinks and Hot Spots

Email newsletters can contain hyperlinks just as webpages do. A hyperlink usually is colored and underlined text that you click to navigate to a file, a location in a file, a webpage, or an email address; however, a hyperlink also can be a graphic, picture, button, or shape. When the hyperlink is not text, it is called a hot spot.

Typically, when you insert a hyperlink or hot spot, you must enter the web address, called a URL. **URL**, which stands for **uniform resource locator**, is the webpage address that identifies the location of the file on the Internet.

To Insert a Hyperlink

In the body of the email newsletter template, the words, More Details, should be formatted as a hyperlink that displays the historical society's webpage. *Why? In an email message, users expect to click words, such as More Details, to get more information.* The following steps insert a hyperlink into the publication.

- Display the Insert tab and zoom to 170% if necessary.
- Select the first occurrence of More Details, just below the lead story.
- Click the Link button (Insert tab | Links group) to display the Insert Hyperlink dialog box.
- If necessary, click the 'Existing File or Web Page' button in the Link to bar.
- Type **www.trhistorical.soc** in the Address box (Figure 9–34).

Q&A

Why did Publisher already list an address in the Address box?
Publisher may prefill the Address box with the most recent entry. You can replace that address as necessary.

Why did Publisher insert http:// before the web address?
The default prefix, or **protocol**, for websites is http://. While newer browsers do not require the protocol, to make sure all users can navigate to your webpage, Publisher inserts the protocol.

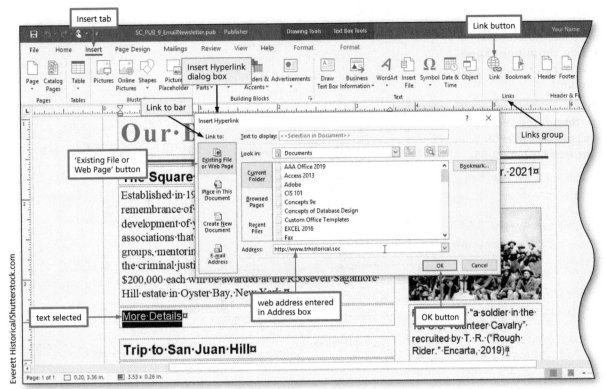

Figure 9–34

2

• Click OK (Insert Hyperlink dialog box) to apply the hyperlink.

3

• Repeat Steps 1 and 2 for the other two occurrences of the words, More Details.

Q&A How do I know for sure that the hyperlink works?
When you send the email message, users can click the link. Within Publisher, you would need to press CTRL+click to display the webpage. The web address is fictional in this example.

Other Ways

1. Select text, press CTRL+K, click 'Existing File or Web Page' in Link to bar (Insert Hyperlink dialog box), enter web address, click OK

To Insert a Mailto Hyperlink

When clicked, a **mailto** hyperlink starts the user's email program. The following steps insert a mailto hyperlink using the words, click here, in the final text box at the bottom of the page. *Why? That way, when users click the link, an email window will open, allowing them to send a message to the recipient.*

1

• In the text box at the bottom of the page, select the text, click here.

• Click the Link button (Insert tab | Links group) to display the Insert Hyperlink dialog box.

• In the Link to bar, if necessary, click the E-mail Address button.

Q&A Why did Publisher add the word, mailto, to the email address?
Because you clicked the E-mail Address button in the Link to bar, Publisher knows you want to create a mailto hyperlink and automatically creates the prefix for you.

2

- In the E-mail address text box, type `unsubscribe@trhistorical.soc` to enter the address.

- In the Subject text box, type `Unsubscribe to Newsletter` to enter a subject for the email (Figure 9–35).

Q&A How will Publisher use the text in the Subject text box?

When the user clicks the mailto link, Publisher will fill in the Subject line of the email newsletter automatically with the entered text. That way, the recipient of the email newsletter will know that the request to unsubscribe came from an email newsletter rather than from the website or another mechanism.

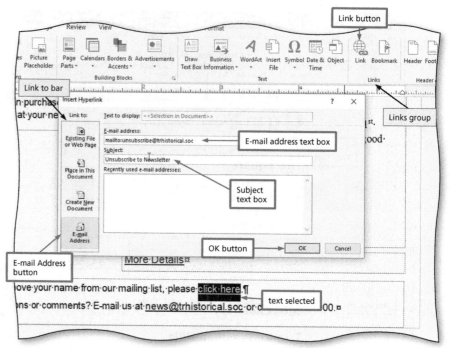

Figure 9–35

3

- Click OK (Insert Hyperlink dialog box) to close the dialog box.

- Select the text, news@trhistorical.soc.

- Press CTRL+K to display the Insert Hyperlink dialog box again.

- If necessary, click the E-mail Address button in the Link to bar (Insert Hyperlink dialog box).

- In the E-mail address text box, type `news@trhistorical.soc` as the entry.

- In the Subject text box, type `Inquiry from Website` as the entry (Figure 9–36).

4

- Click OK (Insert Hyperlink dialog box) to create the mailto hyperlink.

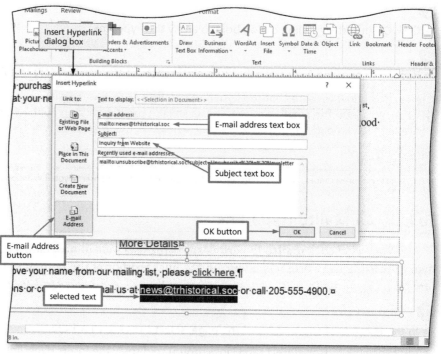

Figure 9–36

Q&A Will viewers of the email newsletter see the mailto prefix?

If users position the pointer over the link, the mailto prefix, colon, and email address may appear on their status bar.

To Create a Hot Spot

The following steps turn Theodore Roosevelt's portrait picture into a hot spot. ***Why?*** *The historical society's officials want the graphic to navigate to the society's website when clicked.*

1

- Select the graphic that you wish to use as a hot spot (in this case, the portrait at the top of the page). You may have to slowly click the graphic twice to enable the Link button.
- Click the Link button (Insert tab | Links group) to display the Insert Hyperlink dialog box.
- Click the 'Existing File or Web Page' button in the Link to bar (Insert Hyperlink dialog box).
- Click the Address arrow to display a list of recently used websites (Figure 9–37).

Q&A What does the Address arrow do?
When you click the Address arrow, Publisher displays a list of previously used hyperlinks and hot spots. You can click from the list to save time.

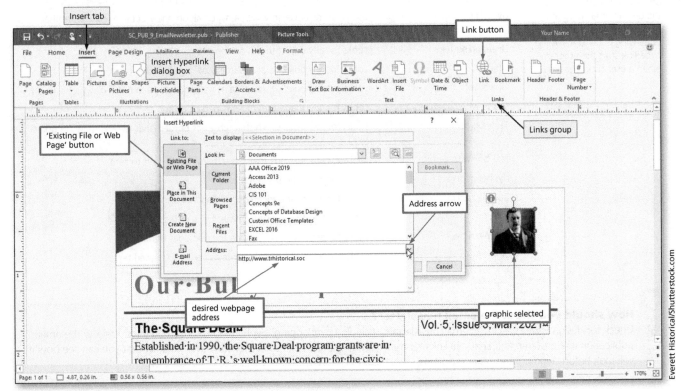

Figure 9–37

2

- Click http://www.trhistorical.soc in the Address list to select it (Figure 9–38).

3

- Click OK to create the link.

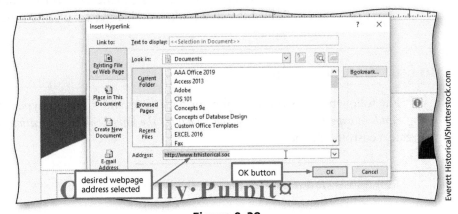

Figure 9–38

Everett Historical/Shutterstock.com

Design Issues in Email Publications

BTW
Followed Links
Followed links usually are displayed in a medium purple color and underlined.

Because email newsletters are generated electronically and are displayed in the user's email program, you must keep in mind several design issues. As with webpages, you want to make sure that the spacing, text, fonts, and hyperlinks are displayed correctly. HTML5, which is the most recent version of the scripting language, recommends that hyperlinks display in medium blue. Not all Publisher templates consistently apply that color; therefore, you may want to edit the color.

The Design Checker offers some specific checks for email publications that it does not perform with print publications. Table 9–3 displays the checks that Publisher uses to evaluate email publications.

BTW
Mailto Hyperlinks
A mailto hyperlink communicates with the operating system to discover the default email program. Publisher then creates the underlying code to make the hyperlink start the program when a user clicks the link.

Table 9–3 Design Issues

Object	Check Performed
HTML fragment	Looks for any HTML code fragment that is partially off the page
Hyperlink	Looks for instances in which a hyperlink on one webpage links to another page in a publication
Overlapping text	Looks for any object that is on top of a text box
Object	Looks for any object that is partially off a publication page
Object with text	Looks for any object that contains text and has been rotated
Shape with hyperlink	Looks for any shape that has a hyperlink on top of it
Table borders	Looks for instances in which a table has borders that are less than .75 point thick
Text box with zero margins	Looks for any text box that has a margin that is set to zero
Hyphenation	Looks for any hyphens in the text
Cell diagonal	Looks for text that is located in a diagonal table cell
Font	Looks for text that is not formatted in a web-safe font
Text overflow	Looks for any text box in which the text does not fit
Vertical text	Looks for any text box that contains vertically rotated text

CONSIDER THIS

How should you check the email newsletter?
Check for design issues specific to email newsletters, including overlapping, hyphenation, fonts, and links. Preview the email publication in a browser, and check all links. Consider sending the email newsletter to yourself first so that you can see how it will look before sending it to other recipients.

You can use the Design Checker Objects dialog box to specify which checks Publisher will use when evaluating emails and other types of publications.

To Edit the Color Scheme

The following steps edit the color for hyperlinks and followed hyperlinks (also called a visited link). *Why? Using standard hyperlink colors helps people recognize the links in your publication.* To change the colors, you will need to create a custom scheme.

1

- Display the Page Design tab.
- Click the More button (Page Design tab | Schemes group) (visible in Figure 9–40) to display the Schemes gallery (Figure 9–39).

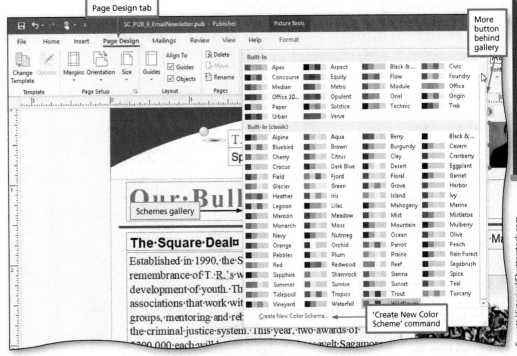

Figure 9–39

Everett Historical/Shutterstock.com

2

- Click 'Create New Color Scheme' in the Schemes gallery to display the Create New Color Scheme dialog box.
- Click the Hyperlink arrow (Create New Color Scheme dialog box) to display the color gallery and then click Blue (sixth color in the second row) to select the color (Figure 9–40).

Q&A Should I change the followed hyperlink color or the name of the color scheme?
You can. The colors will stay with the document once it is saved, no matter what the name is.

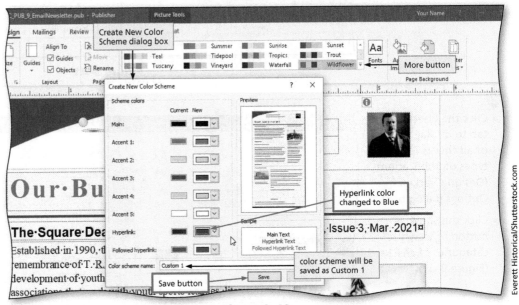

Figure 9–40

Everett Historical/Shutterstock.com

3

- Click the Save button.

 Experiment

- Scroll through the email newsletter and look at the hyperlinks to verify their new color.

To Choose Design Checker Options

The following steps display the Design Checker dialog box. *Why? You should verify which Design Checker options will be used for email publications.*

- Click File on the ribbon to open Backstage view.

- If necessary, click Info to display the Info screen and then click the 'Run Design Checker' button to open the Design Checker pane.

- Click the 'Design Checker Options' link in the Design Checker pane to display the Design Checker Options dialog box (Figure 9–41).

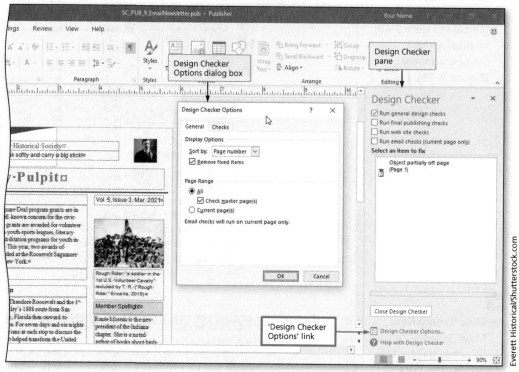

Figure 9–41

- Click the Checks tab to display a list of all checks for all types of publications (Design Checker Options dialog box).

- Click the Show button to view the categories of checks (Figure 9–42).

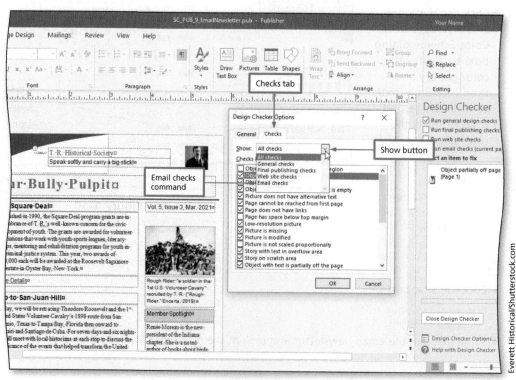

Figure 9–42

3

- Click Email checks in the list of categories to view the design issues that Publisher looks for in email publications.

- If necessary, click any check box that does not contain a check mark (Figure 9–43).

 Q&A What is the meaning of the issue, Object partially off page, in the Design Checker pane?

That error is for print publications only. Publisher is warning you about an object that is too close to or extends beyond the margin. Because this is an email publication, the warning will not affect the publication, unless the object overlaps the margin.

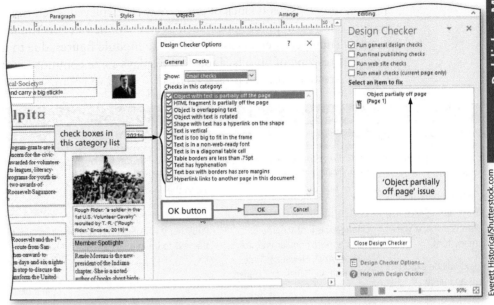

Figure 9–43

4

- Click OK to apply the changes.

To Check a Publication for Email Design Errors

The following step checks the publication for design errors specifically related to emails. You will encounter a common size error. *Why? The heading font size may be slightly larger than the text box margins will allow.* Therefore, Publisher will convert the font to a graphic so that the words will be displayed correctly.

1

- With the Design Checker pane still open, click to display a check mark in the 'Run email checks (current page only)' check box.

- Remove any other check marks in the pane to display issues related only to emails (Figure 9–44).

Experiment

- Click each issue and notice most are related to headings that will be converted to images. Click the 'Help with Design Checker' link and read about the different kinds of design issues.

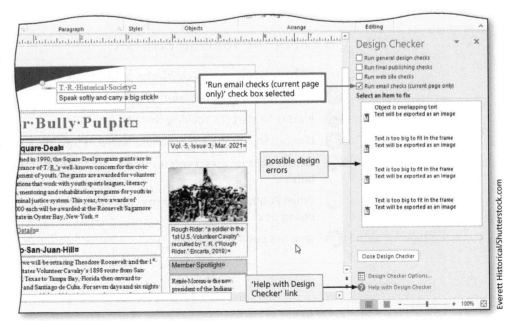

Figure 9–44

Everett Historical/Shutterstock.com

Troubleshooting Design Errors

Several kinds of errors may be displayed when running the Design Checker for email publications, such as an email newsletter. You may not see the same kind or number of errors as shown in the module figures, due to minor typing differences and resizing of objects. Table 9–4 displays some common errors in email design, possible resolutions, and pros and cons.

Table 9–4 Email Design Checker Errors

Error Message	Possible Resolution	Making the Change: Pros	Making the Change: Cons
Text is too big to fit in the frame. Text will be exported as an image.	Click the error message arrow and then click the 'Fix: Reduce font size of text to fit' command.	The page will be displayed slightly faster when someone views the email.	Reducing the font size will reduce readability slightly and may introduce many different fonts sizes, making the publication look sloppy.
Test is not in a web-ready font. Text will be exported as an image.	Change the font scheme to include more popular web fonts, such as Arial, Helvetica, Times New Roman, Times, or Courier.	Publisher will not change any of the text to images.	In newer browsers and email viewers, the fonts will not be changed to images unless the font is highly unusual. Even in that case, the fonts may be important to the branding of the company or the look and feel of the email.
Text has hyphenation. Gaps may appear in some email viewers.	Run a manual hyphenation check on the text box and choose not to hyphenate any words.	You never will have an unusual gap in the text of the email due to hyphenation.	Most email viewers can handle hyphens. You may have some unusual gaps if you do not hyphenate.
Object is partially off page.	Move the object to a location completely on the page or delete it.	You should make the change if the object overlaps the margin.	The email will not be displayed correctly and may not even transmit correctly.
Object is not visible.	Navigate to the item and bring it forward or delete it.	The email will be displayed faster.	The item never will be seen.

None of the issues listed for this publication is serious enough to elicit a change. If you want to make changes, click the arrow next to the issue, click 'Go to this Item' on the menu, and then perform the steps in the Possible Resolution column of Table 9–4. Other errors are described when you click the 'Help with Design Checker' link at the bottom of the Design Checker pane.

To Check for Spelling Errors

The following steps check the publication for spelling errors.

1 If necessary, close the Design Checker pane.

2 Press F7 to start the spelling checker.

3 If necessary, correct any problems noted in the Check Spelling dialog box.

4 When Publisher asks if you want to check the rest of the publication, click the Yes button.

5 When Publisher notifies you that the spelling check is complete, click OK in the dialog box.

6 Save the publication again.

Sending an Email Newsletter Using Publisher

Email publications can be sent to one or more people. Many organizations create a **listserv**, which is a list with email addresses of interested people who want to receive news and information email newsletters about the organization. A listserv email sends one email newsletter to everyone on the list. A listserv email newsletter should contain an unsubscribe link that allows recipients to remove their names from the list to prevent receiving future email newsletters.

When you choose to send a publication, such as a newsletter, via email, Publisher displays special text boxes to allow you to enter the email addresses and subject line. Publisher also displays special buttons for email options (Figure 9–45).

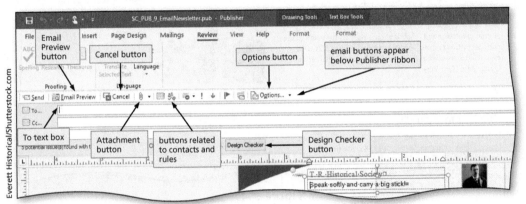

Everett Historical/Shutterstock.com

Figure 9–45

Before you send an email publication, you always should proofread it and then check it for design errors and spelling errors, as you did in the previous steps. With email publications, you also should preview the publication.

To Preview an Email Newsletter

The following steps describe how to preview an email newsletter. *Why? You want to see how it will look on the user's computer.*

1
- Click File on the ribbon to open Backstage view.
- Click Share in the left pane to display the Share screen.
- Click Email Preview in the center pane of the Share screen (Figure 9–46).

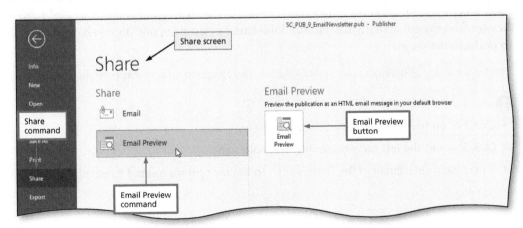

Figure 9–46

• Click the Email Preview button in the right pane to preview the email publication in your default browser. If necessary, double-click the browser title bar to maximize the window (Figure 9–47).

 Q&A My publication did not appear. Did I do something wrong? Your default browser may not be compatible with Publisher. Try using Microsoft Edge, Internet Explorer, or Chrome.

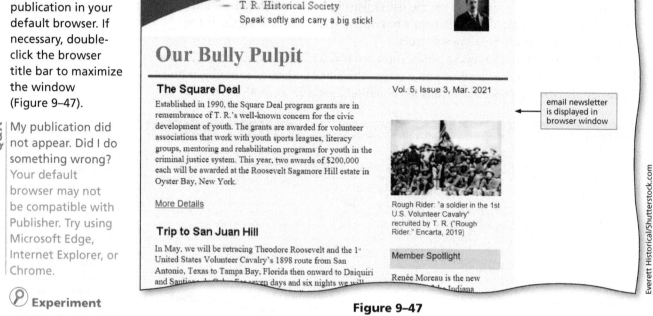

Figure 9–47

Experiment

• Scroll through the email newsletter and try clicking the other hyperlinks. The society's website is fictional and will not be displayed, but the click here hyperlink will display an email dialog box if your system is configured with an email program, such as Microsoft Outlook.

• Close all browser windows.

To Send an Email Newsletter Using Publisher

The following steps send an email newsletter using Publisher's Send Email command. *Why? Sending an email using Publisher saves the extra steps of starting an email program and copying and pasting the newsletter in the message.* You do not actually have to send the email newsletter, nor do you have to be connected to the Internet to perform the steps.

Note: If you do not have or do not want Outlook to be configured on your computer, read these steps but do not perform them.

• Click File on the ribbon to open Backstage view.

• Click Share in the left pane to display the Share screen.

• If necessary, click Email in the Share screen to display options related to email publications (Figure 9–48).

Q&A What is the purpose of the 'Send as PDF' and 'Send as XPS' buttons?
Depending on which button you click, Publisher converts the current document to either the PDF or XPS format and then attaches the PDF or XPS document to the email newsletter.

Do most people prefer to receive a publication as an email attachment?
It is not necessarily better to use attachments. For immediate viewing, such as for

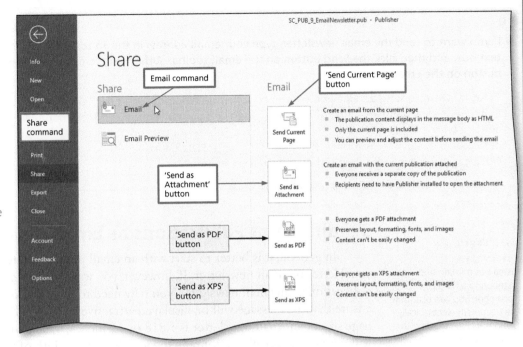

Figure 9–48

an announcement, a letter, or a card, it is better to send a single page in the body of an email newsletter. If you do send an attachment, the person receiving your email newsletter must have Publisher installed on his or her computer in order to open and view the publication. In addition, with a large attachment, you may run the risk of the email newsletter being blocked by firewalls and filters at the receiving end.

2

• Click the 'Send Current Page' button in the Share screen to display the boxes and buttons used for emailing (Figure 9–49).

Q&A What if my computer wants to configure Outlook to send an email newsletter?
If you are not sure how to configure your computer for email, or if you do not want to check your email via an email program, click the Cancel button in the Outlook dialog box and finish reading the steps in this section. Configuring your computer with an email program is not complicated, however. Windows 10 asks for your name, your email address, and your password. It then determines the type of email program and connection you need.

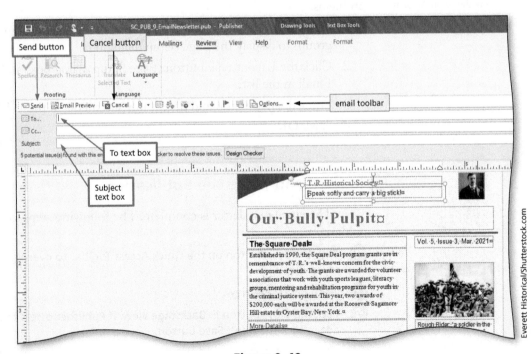

Figure 9–49

- If you want to send the email newsletter, type your email address in the To text box, enter a subject in the Subject text box, and then click the Send button on the email toolbar. Otherwise, to cancel the request, click the Cancel button on the email toolbar.

Q&A What if I want to send an email newsletter to someone who does not have Publisher installed?
Email newsletters appear in the body of the email and do not require Publisher. If you are sending an attachment and are worried that your recipient may not have Publisher installed on his or her computer, you can send your publication in a different format. Publisher can create PDF files or XPS files, which have free or inexpensive viewers. Once converted, the files then can be attached to an email.

BTW
Distributing a Document
Instead of printing and distributing a hard copy of a document, you can distribute the document electronically. Options include sending the document via email; posting it on cloud storage (such as OneDrive) and sharing the file with others; posting it on social media, a blog, or other website; and sharing a link associated with an online location of the document. You also can create and share a PDF or XPS image of the document, so that users can view the file in Acrobat Reader or XPS Viewer instead of in Publisher.

Sending Print Publications as Email Newsletters

In general, it is better to start with an email publication template, such as the email letter or email newsletter. If, however, you want to send a page of another publication as an email newsletter, you may need to modify the width and margins to ensure that the message will be displayed attractively for email recipients. The typical page size of an email newsletter is 5.818 by 11 inches, which ensures the recipients will not need to scroll horizontally to view the entire width of the message. Publisher allows only one page at a time sent as an email.

To Modify the Paper Size and Margins

If you wanted to change the page design settings of a print publication to create an email publication, you would perform the following steps. It is a good idea to send the email publication to yourself first so that you can view the publication and look for problems.

1. Click the Page Setup Dialog Box Launcher (Page Design tab | Page Setup group) to display the Page Setup dialog box.
2. Click the Layout type button (Page Setup dialog box) and then, if necessary, click Email in the list.
3. Enter the new width and height measurements in the Width and Height boxes.
4. Click OK.

To Save and Close the Publication

The email newsletter is complete. The following steps save and close the publication.

1. Click the Save button on the Quick Access Toolbar to overwrite the previously saved file.
2. Open Backstage view.
3. Click the Close button in Backstage view. If Publisher offers to save the publication again, click the Don't Save button.

Break Point: If you want to take a break, this is a good place to do so. You can exit Publisher now. To resume later, start Publisher and continue following the steps from this location forward.

Postcards

A postcard is a rectangular piece of mail intended for writing and sending without an envelope. People use postcards for greetings, announcements, reminders, and business contacts. Most postcards are rectangular and at least 3½ inches high and 5 inches long. A common size is 4 inches by 6 inches.

What should you consider when deciding to attach a Publisher file to an email message?
Publications created for print must be attached as a separate file when using email, especially when converting the publication is not possible. Remember that users must have Publisher installed in order to open a publication. If you are unsure, save the publication in the PDF or XPS format and attach it. For large publications and multipage publications, consider compressing the file.

A postcard can be an effective marketing tool to generate prospective leads at a low cost. A business or an organization can produce a postcard with a photo, graphic, advertisement, or text. Some postcards, such as picture postcards, leave space on one side to write a brief message. People purchase picture postcards to mail to friends or to serve as reminders of their vacation. Sometimes, a picture postcard is mailed to attract attention and direct people to websites or business locations. A postcard must portray its message or theme clearly in an eye-catching manner, keeping in mind the relevant audience.

Publisher has several postcard templates, including postcards for marketing, calendars, and real estate, as well as many blank templates to create postcards from scratch. In the past, postcards typically have been mailed using a postal service; however, many companies and individuals are sending **e-postcards**, or electronic postcards, electronically as attachments. An **attachment** is an electronic file sent along with an email newsletter; however, the recipient must perform some steps to open the file; it is not displayed within the body of the email newsletter. Table 9–5 displays some of the best practices for attachments.

BTW

Conserving Ink and Toner
If you want to conserve ink or toner, you can instruct Publisher to print draft quality documents by clicking File on the ribbon to open Backstage view and then clicking Print in the left pane of Backstage view to display the Print screen. Click the Printer Properties link, and then, depending on your printer, click the Print Quality button and choose Draft in the list. Close the Printer Properties dialog box and then click the Print button as usual.

Table 9–5 Best Practices for Attachments

Practice	Reasoning
Post or publish large attachments.	It is better to post large files on the web or on a shared resource when possible.
Limit your attachments to less than 5 MB.	Check with your Internet service provider (ISP) to verify the maximum allowable size of attachments.
Send multiple attachments using several email newsletters.	Some email programs have per-message limits.
Use compressed graphic file formats.	Smaller graphics are more likely to be opened and viewed.
Employ a file compression utility.	File compression, sometimes called zipping, reduces the file size and keeps files together.
Review your Sent Items folder.	Emails and attachments take up room in the sender's email as well as the recipient's. Delete older sent items as necessary.

To Open a Postcard Template

The following steps open a postcard template.

1 In the template gallery, click Built-In to display the built-in templates.

2 Scroll as necessary and then click the Postcards thumbnail in the built-in templates to display the Postcards templates.

3 Click the Bounce thumbnail to choose the template.

4 If necessary, click the Color Scheme button and choose Wildflower.

5 If necessary, click the Font Scheme button and choose 'Office Classic 1'.

6 If the Business Information box has a specified business information set, click the Business Information arrow and then click Create new. When Publisher displays the Create New business Information Set dialog box, click Cancel.

7 Click the CREATE button to create the publication using the selected template. Your postcard may display an organization logo depending on your previous use of business information sets. If a logo appears in the publication, delete it (Figure 9–50).

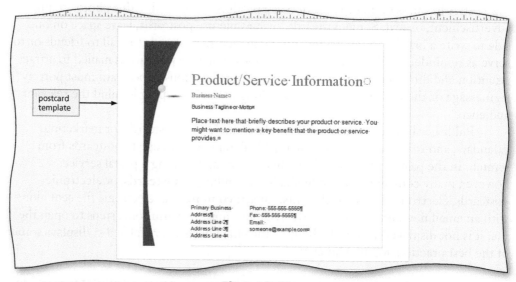

Figure 9–50

To Edit a Postcard

The following steps edit the text fields to the postcard.

1 Select the Product/Service Information placeholder text at the top of the page. Type **T. R. Historical Society** to replace the text. Select the text again and then press CTRL+B to bold the text.

2 Select the Business Name placeholder text and then type **Annual Meeting** to replace the text.

3 Select the Business Tagline or Motto placeholder text and then type **Speak softly and carry a big stick!** to replace the text.

4 Select the text in the description text box. Type **The T. R. Historical Society (National Conference) will hold its annual meeting May 5, 2021 at 7:00 p.m. at the Royal Conference Center in Oyster Bay, NY.** and then press ENTER. Type **Call 516-555-1725 or visit our website at www.trhistorical.soc for more information.** to enter the last line of text.

5 Right-click the text and then click Best Fit on the shortcut menu. Hyphenate the text if necessary.

6 Delete the lower two text boxes (Figure 9–51).

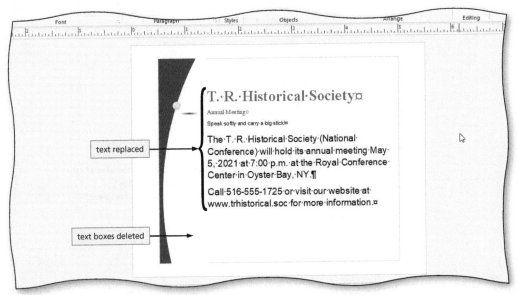

Figure 9–51

7 Save the publication on your desired save location using the file name, SC_PUB_9_Postcard.

To Switch Pages and Delete

The following steps switch to page 2 and delete it. **Why?** *Because the postcard will be sent as an attachment, there is no need for the side with the address and stamp area.* Rather than opening the Page Navigation page, you will use a shortcut key to display the Go To Page dialog box.

1
- With Page 1 still displayed, press CTRL+G to display the Go To Page dialog box.
- Type 2 in the 'Go to page' text box to enter the destination page number (Figure 9–52).

Q&A Without the Page Navigation pane, how do I know how many pages are in the publication? The page count is displayed on the left side of the Publisher status bar.

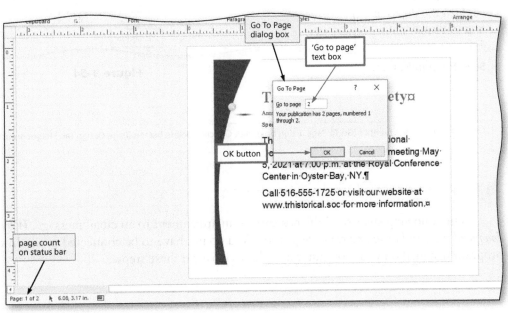

Figure 9–52

2

- Click OK (Go To Page dialog box) to go to the entered page.
- If necessary, click Page Design on the ribbon to display the Page Design tab (Figure 9–53).

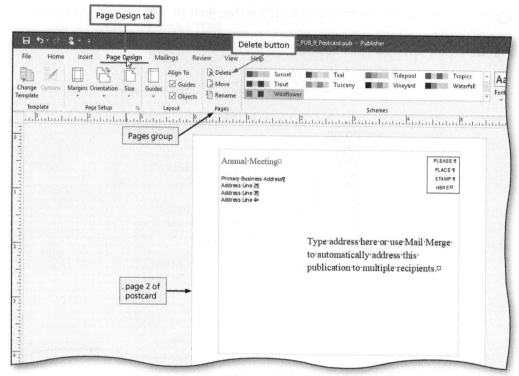

Figure 9–53

3

- Click the Delete button (Page Design tab | Pages group) to delete the current page (Figure 9–54).

4

- Click the Yes button (Microsoft Publisher dialog box) to confirm the deletion and to display page 1 again.
- Save the publication.

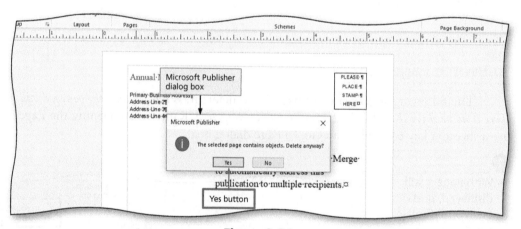

Figure 9–54

Other Ways

1. Press F5, enter page number (Go To Page dialog box), click OK, click Delete button (Page Design tab | Pages group)

To Send a Postcard as an Attachment

The following steps send the postcard as an attachment to an email message. *Why? That way, users can download the attachment and print the postcard.* You do not have to be connected to the Internet or have an email program installed on your computer in order to perform these steps.

- Open Backstage view.

- If necessary, click the Share tab in the left pane and then click Email in the Share screen.

- Click the 'Send as Attachment' button (shown in Figure 9–48) to open the Untitled Message (HTML) window (Figure 9–55).

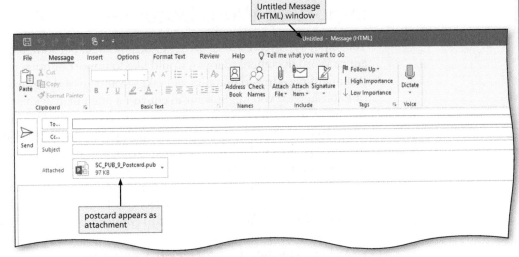

Figure 9–55

- If Publisher displays a dialog box asking you to create an Outlook account, click OK. If you decide not to create an Outlook account, simply read the rest of the steps in this section without performing them.

- In the To text box, type **listserv@trhistorical.soc** to enter the name of the historical society's mailing list.

- In the Subject text box, type **T. R. Historical Society Annual Meeting** to enter the subject.

- Click the message area. Type **Hello friends,** and then press ENTER twice.

- Type **Thank you for joining our listserv. Attached is the notice for our annual meeting. You will receive a meeting agenda in the mail.** and then press ENTER twice.

- Type **T. R. Historical Society** and press ENTER. Type **(516) 555-1725** and then press ENTER. Type **www.trhistorical.soc** to finish the message (Figure 9–56).

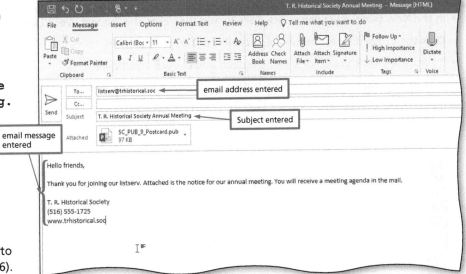

Figure 9–56

- If you want to send the email attachment, replace the email address with your own and then click the Send button to send the email message along with its attachment and to close the email window. Otherwise, close the Untitled Message (HTML) window without saving.

- Close the publication without exiting Publisher.

Break Point: If you want to take a break, this is a good place to do so. You can exit Publisher now. To resume later, start Publisher and continue following the steps from this location forward.

Importing Word Documents in Publisher

You imported several stories earlier in this module, but sometimes, you may have an entire Word document that you would like to import or open in Publisher. For example, you might need to add graphics and take advantage of the graphics-handling capabilities of Publisher. Or you might want to convert a document such as a report, resume, or statement so that it can be branded the same way as other business publications.

To import an entire document, you can use the Open command and then choose the file type. Once Publisher finishes converting the file, you will need to check the formatting, such as fonts, tables, and images, because they may have shifted or might have been lost in the conversion process. Another method is to use the Object button (Insert tab | Text group) and then select the 'Create from File' option button (Insert Object dialog box). Yet a third way is to choose a built-in template style and then import the document into the publication.

In this module, you will import a meeting agenda that was prepared in Word and then add graphics and formatting unique to Publisher.

To Import a Word Document

The following steps open a Word document template and import a Word document meeting agenda. **Why?** *Opening a template first will allow you to use the same color scheme and font scheme used for the newsletter and postcard.* To complete these steps, you will be required to use the Data Files. Please contact your instructor for information about accessing the Data Files.

 1

- In the New template gallery, click Built-In and then click the 'Import Word Documents' thumbnail.

- Click the Crossed Lines thumbnail in the list of templates.

- If necessary, click the Color scheme button and choose Wildflower.

- If necessary, click the Font scheme button and choose 'Office Classic 1'.

- If necessary, scroll to the Options area and then click the Page size button (Figure 9–57).

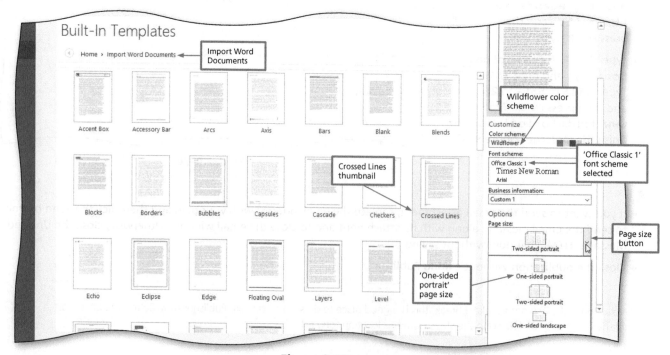

Figure 9–57

Experiment

- One at a time, click each of the layouts. Notice the changes in the thumbnails and preview. Click the Page size button again.

2

- Click the 'One-sided portrait' page size.

- If necessary, click the Columns button and then choose 1 (Figure 9–58).

Q&A When would I choose a two-sided layout?

If you anticipate the publication being long enough to need two or more pages, you can choose a two-sided layout.

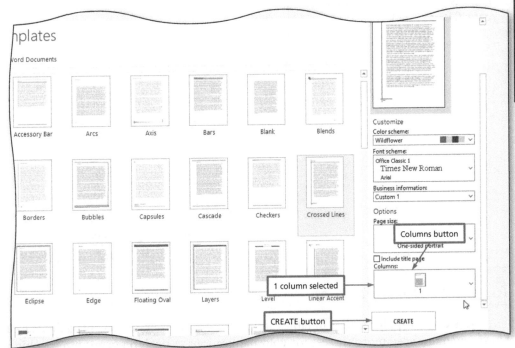

Figure 9–58

3

- Click the CREATE button.

- When Publisher displays the Import Word Document dialog box, navigate to the location of the Data Files (Figure 9–59).

Q&A Usually clicking the CREATE button causes Publisher to display a publication page. Why did it display a dialog box this time?

The template type that you chose imports a file rather than creating a new publication.

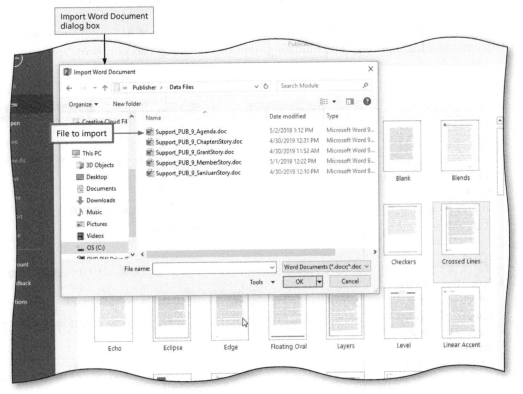

Figure 9–59

4

- Double-click the file named Support_PUB_9_Agenda.doc.

- After Publisher converts and imports the file, zoom to whole page (Figure 9–60).

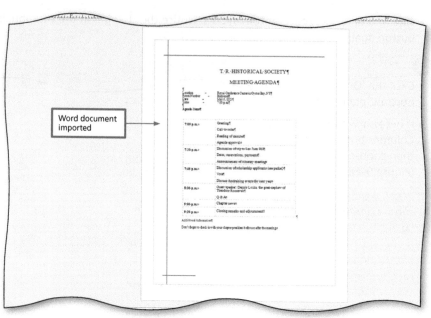

Figure 9–60

To Insert a Design Accent

It is easy to apply borders to tables and pages. The Borders & Accents gallery, part of the Building Block library, contains even more choices for your publications. A **design accent** is a graphic added for emphasis or flair, such as a bar, box, line, frame, or pattern. Some design accents are meant to fill the area; for example, line and bar accents increase the number of pattern repetitions as they are resized. Accents will display the same color scheme as your publication.

Accents are used as headers, mastheads, and in other places in a publication where the page may need some delineation or highlighting. The following steps insert a design accent. **Why?** *The page is rather plain and does not accentuate the scheme colors.*

1

- Display the Insert tab.

- Click the 'Borders & Accents' button (Insert tab | Building Blocks group) to display its gallery (Figure 9–61).

🔍 **Experiment**

- Scroll through the selections in the Borders & Accents gallery to see the different types of borders and accents.

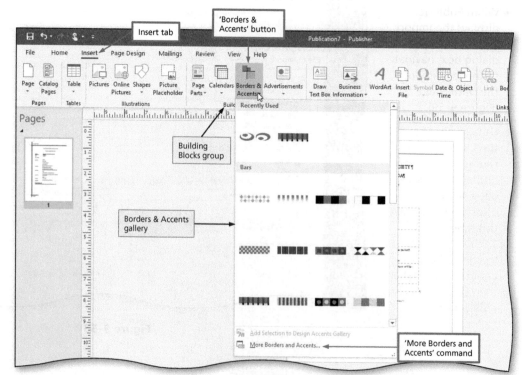

Figure 9–61

2

- Click 'More Borders and Accents' in the Borders & Accents gallery to display the Building Block Library dialog box.

- Scroll to the Patterns area and then click the Pixel Pattern thumbnail to select it (Figure 9–62).

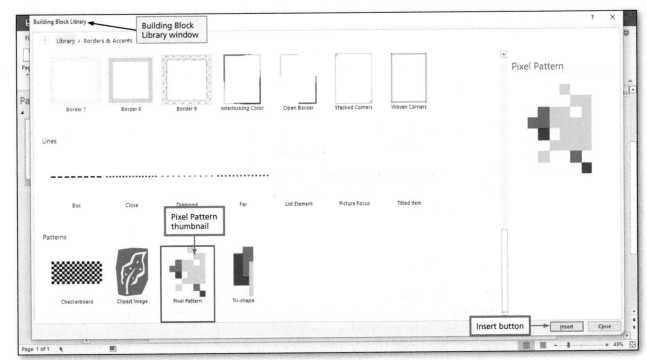

Figure 9–62

3

- Click the Insert button (Building Block Library dialog box) to insert the design accent.

- Drag the design accent to the lower-right corner of the page and resize it to approximately 2.33 by 2.67 inches (Figure 9–63).

 Q&A Why did the agenda table disappear briefly?
Publisher placed the design accent in the middle of the page, temporarily moving the table to the overflow area. When you move the design accent to the corner, the table again is displayed.

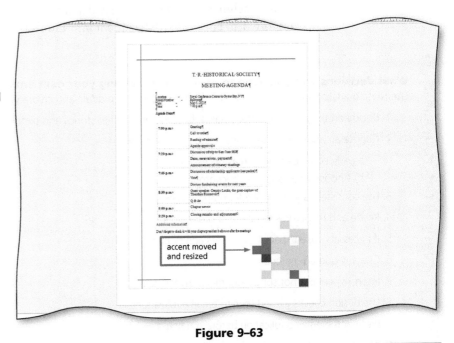

Figure 9–63

To Finish the Agenda and Save

The following steps delete unnecessary or empty boxes in the agenda, check it for errors, and save the publication.

1 At the top of the page, select the Document Title text box and then press DELETE.

2 At the bottom of the page, select the Page 1 text box and then press DELETE.

3 Check the spelling of the publication. Ignore any names that Publisher flags.

4 Design check the publication and correct any errors.

5 Save the publication with the file name, SC_PUB_9_Agenda, on your storage device.

To Delete the Custom Color Scheme and Exit Publisher

The following steps delete the custom color scheme you created earlier and then exit Publisher.

1 Display the Page Design tab.

2 Right-click the Custom 1 color scheme (Page Design tab | Schemes group) and then click Delete Scheme on shortcut menu.

3 When Publisher displays a dialog box asking if you are sure, click the Yes button.

4 Click the Close button on the Publisher title bar. If Publisher displays a dialog box, click the Don't Save button.

Summary

In this module, you learned how to create an email newsletter. First you selected and formatted an email template. Then you learned how to edit the background, text boxes, and graphics in an email publication. Next, you learned how to insert a symbol and special character. You created hyperlinks, mailto hyperlinks, and hot spots. After checking the publication for design errors and previewing the email newsletter, you sent the publication as an email newsletter. You also created a postcard and learned how to send a publication as an attachment. Finally, you created a publication for regular mail distribution as you imported an entire Word document into Publisher and added a design accent.

CONSIDER THIS: PLAN AHEAD

What decisions will you need to make when creating your next email publication?
Use these guidelines as you complete the assignments in this module and create your own publications outside of this class.

1. Decide on the purpose of the email publication and gather stories and pictures.

2. Choose an appropriate template, font, and color scheme.
   a) Adjust the page length as necessary.
   b) Choose an appropriate background.

3. Use consistent styles for headings and stories.

4. Resize and fit pictures to fill the appropriate areas.

5. If necessary, insert special characters and symbols.

6. Cite any quoted materials.

7. Insert hyperlinks, hot spots, and mailto hyperlinks.

8. Use design checks geared toward email publications.

9. Preview the email publication before sending it.

10. Attach publications, such as postcards, when appropriate.

11. When importing Word documents, customize the template.
    a) Choose an appropriate template.
    b) Choose an appropriate page layout and columns.
    c) Use a design accent where appropriate.

Apply Your Knowledge

Reinforce the skills and apply the concepts you learned in this module.

Editing an Email Newsletter

Note: To complete this assignment, you will be required to use the Data Files. Please contact your instructor for information about accessing the Data Files.

Instructions: Start Publisher and open the file named SC_PUB_9-1.pub from the Data Files. You are to add a page background, insert pictures, hyperlinks, and a symbol to create the email publication shown in Figure 9–64.

Perform the following tasks:

1. Save the publication with the file name, SC_PUB_9_MealNewsletter, on your storage device.

2. Zoom to 150% and scroll to the top of the page. Change the date to the current date. Edit the 'Top stores in this newsletter' text box to read: Featured meals in this newsletter.

3. Click the Background button (Page Design tab | Page Background group) and then click More Backgrounds in the Background gallery to display the Format Background dialog box.

4. Click the Pattern fill option button and then choose the 'Dotted diamond grid' pattern. Change the background color to 'Accent 5 (White)'. Click OK to close the Format Background dialog box.

5. One at a time, right-click each of the four pictures across the top of the email newsletter and then use the Change Picture command to insert pictures named Support_PUB_9_Meal1.tif, Support_PUB_9_Meal2.tif, Support_PUB_9_Meal3.tif, and Support_PUB_9_Meal4.tif from the Data files. Delete the original pictures from the scratch area. Copy and paste the pictures to replace the pictures down the left side.

6. For the pictures across the top of the email newsletter, one at a time, click the Fit button (Picture Tools Format tab | Crop group) to fit the picture in the picture placeholder.

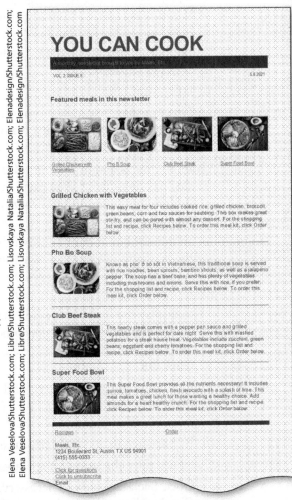

Elena Veselova/Shutterstock.com; Libre/Shutterstock.com; Lisovskaya Natalia/Shutterstock.com; Elenadesign/Shutterstock.com; Elena Veselova/Shutterstock.com; Libre/Shutterstock.com; Lisovskaya Natalia/Shutterstock.com; Elenadesign/Shutterstock.com;

Figure 9–64

7. Below each of the pictures across the top, change the text to headline text shown in Table 9–6. Edit the individual story headlines as well. Import the stories from the Data Files as listed. Format the text in each story with the Arial font, a font size of 8, and single spacing. Remove any blank lines in the stories.

Table 9–6 Text for Meal Newsletter		
Meal	**Headline**	**Story File Name**
1	Grilled Chicken with Vegetables	Support_PUB_9_GrilledChicken.doc
2	Pho Bo Soup	Support_PUB_9_PhoBoSoup.doc
3	Club Beef Steak	Support_PUB_9_ClubBeefSteak.doc
4	Super Food Bowl	Support_PUB_9_SuperFoodBowl.doc

Continued >

Apply Your Knowledge *continued*

8. In the description for Pho Bo Soup, highlight the o in the word, bo. Click the Symbol button (Insert tab | Text group). Click More Symbols in the Symbol gallery to display the Symbol dialog box. If necessary, click the Font arrow and then choose Arial. Scroll as necessary to select 'Latin Small Letter O With Grave'. Click the Insert button (Symbol dialog box) and close the dialog box.

9. In the description for Pho Bo Soup, highlight the o in the word, pho. Display the Symbol gallery again. Click the Subset arrow and the choose 'Latin Extended Additional' in the list. Scroll as necessary to select 'Latin Small Letter O With Horn And Hook Above', or enter character code 1EDF in the Character code text box. Click the Insert button to insert the symbol and then click the Close button (Symbol dialog box).

10. Edit the color scheme to make the Hyperlink color Light Blue and the Followed hyperlink color Gray.

11. One at a time, select each caption for the pictures across the top of the page. Press CTRL+K to display the Insert Hyperlink dialog box. Click the 'Place in This Document' button in the Link to bar (Insert Hyperlink dialog box) and then choose the appropriate story link.

12. In the text box at the bottom of the page, select the word Recipes and then press CTRL+K. Click the 'Existing File or Web page' button in the Link to bar (Insert Hyperlink dialog box). In the Address box, type `http://www.youcancook.biz/recipes` and then click OK to close the dialog box.

13. In the text box at the bottom of the page, select the word, Order, and then press CTRL+K. Click the 'Existing File or Web page' button in the Link to bar (Insert Hyperlink dialog box). In the Address box, type `http://www.youcancook.biz/order` and then click OK.

14. In the text box at the bottom of the page, select the text, Click to unsubscribe. Press CTRL+K to display the Insert Hyperlink dialog box. In the Link to bar, click the E-mail Address button (Insert Hyperlink dialog box). In the E-mail address text box, type `unsubscribe@YouCanCook.biz`. In the Subject text box, type `Unsubscribe to Newsletter`. Click OK.

15. In the text box at the bottom of the page, select the text, Click for questions. Repeat Step 14 to create a mailto hyperlink with questions@YouCanCook.biz as the email address and Inquiry from Newsletter as the subject.

16. If instructed to do so, enter your email address as the mailto hyperlink for email.

17. Check the publication for spelling errors.

18. Open Backstage view. If necessary, click Info in the left pane and then click the 'Run Design Checker' button in the Info screen to open the Design Checker pane.

19. Click the 'Design Checker Options' link in the Design Checker pane. Click the Checks tab (Design Checker Options dialog box) and then click the Show button. Click Email checks to view the design issues that Publisher looks for in email publications. If necessary, click any check box that does not contain a check mark. Click OK.

20. In the Design Checker pane, click to display a check mark in the 'Run email checks (current page only)' check box. Remove any other check marks in the pane. Correct any problems listed and then close the Design Checker pane.

21. Open Backstage view and then click Share in the left pane. Click Email Preview in the Share screen and then click the Email Preview button. Test the hyperlink to the fourth story about Super Food Bowl. When you are done previewing, close the browser window.

22. Save the email publication again with the same file name and then exit Publisher.

23. If you have permission, send the publication to your instructor as an email newsletter.

24. ✳ People who read email newsletters do so because of topical or visual interest. What changes could you make to the top portion of this email to make it more striking and encourage readers to open it? What words would you use in the subject line?

Extend Your Knowledge

Extend the skills you learned in this module and experiment with new skills. You may need to use Help to complete the assignment.

Creating an Appointment Postcard from Scratch

Instructions: Start Publisher. You are to create an appointment postcard for a local dentist's office that wants to be able to send the postcard via email or regular mail. You create the postcard shown in Figure 9–65.

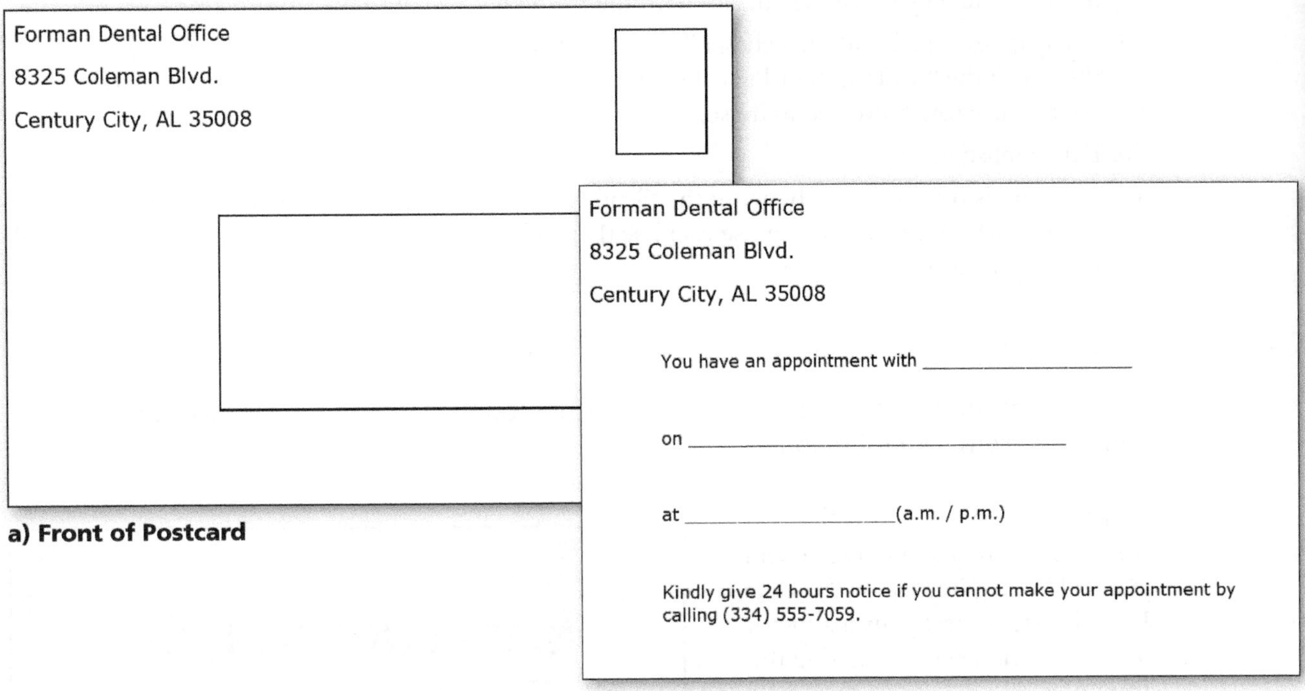

Forman Dental Office

8325 Coleman Blvd.

Century City, AL 35008

a) Front of Postcard

Forman Dental Office

8325 Coleman Blvd.

Century City, AL 35008

You have an appointment with _____

on _____

at _____(a.m. / p.m.)

Kindly give 24 hours notice if you cannot make your appointment by calling (334) 555-7059.

b) Back of Postcard

Figure 9–65

Perform the following tasks:

1. Use the New template gallery to navigate to the built-in Postcards templates. Choose the blank size labeled 'Index Card 4 × 6"'. Use the Tidepool color scheme and Online font scheme.

2. When the publication is displayed, change the orientation to Landscape.

3. Create a text box in the upper-left corner of the page, approximately 2.5 inches wide and 1 inch tall. Change the font to size 12. Type the following, pressing ENTER at the end of the first and second lines:

`Forman Dental Office`

`8325 Coleman Blvd.`

`Century City, AL 35008`

4. Use Help to learn more about duplicating pages with content in Publisher.

5. Duplicate the page.

6. If necessary, press CTRL+G to navigate to page 2. Draw a text box in the lower half of page 2, approximately 5 inches wide and 2.5 inches tall. Change the font size to 10. Type the following lines, pressing ENTER twice at the end of every line except the last. Use an underscore (_) to create the blank lines. (*Hint:* When Publisher changes the beginning of each new line to uppercase, change it back to lowercase as appropriate.)

Continued >

Extend Your Knowledge *continued*

```
You have an appointment with _____

on _____

at _____ (a.m. / p.m.)

Kindly give 24 hours notice if you cannot make your appointment by
calling (334) 555-7059.
```

7. Navigate to page 1 and insert a text box that will hold a mailing address and a shape or text box representing the location of the stamp.

8. Save the file on your storage device with the file name, SC_PUB_9_ApptPostcard.

9. Navigate to page 2 and then click File to open Backstage view. Click Share, click Email, and then click the 'Send Current Page' button. Enter your email address, or the email address of your instructor, if directed to do so.

10. Exit Publisher.

11. ✳ What is the difference between the 'Send Current Page' and 'Send as Attachment' commands? When would you use each? Is there any advantage to using a physical postcard and sending it through the mail?

Expand Your World

Create a solution that uses cloud and web technologies by learning and investigating on your own from general guidance.

Email Newsletter Analysis

Note: To complete this assignment, you will be required to use the Data Files. Please contact your instructor for information about accessing the Data files.

Instructions: Start Publisher. Open the publication called SC_PUB_9-3.pub, which is located in the Data Files. The publication you open contains a table of items related to email newsletters. You are to fill in the table using an email newsletter you find on the web (Figure 9–66).

Perform the following tasks:

1. Use the Internet to do some research about best practices in email newsletters. Use a search engine to find an example of an email newsletter, or use an email newsletter that you have received. Print a copy of the newsletter.

2. Look over the newsletter carefully with regard to the topics in the Publisher table. In the table, describe your

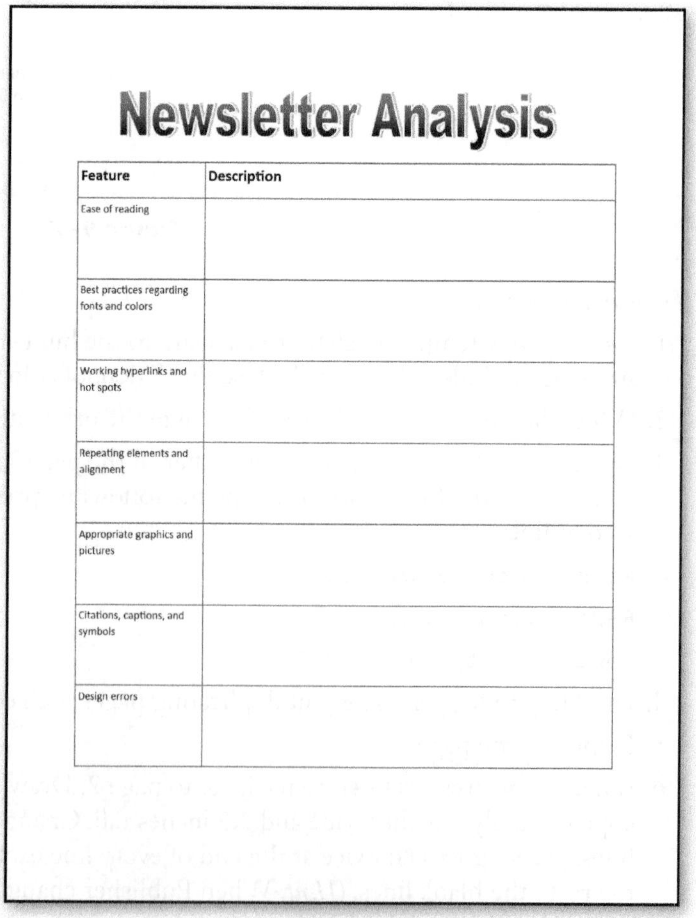

Feature	Description
Ease of reading	
Best practices regarding fonts and colors	
Working hyperlinks and hot spots	
Repeating elements and alignment	
Appropriate graphics and pictures	
Citations, captions, and symbols	
Design errors	

Figure 9–66

thoughts about each topic and how it relates to the chosen newsletter. Use full sentences. Do not insert answers such as yes, no, present, or none. Describe each topic using concepts from the module and concepts from your research.

3. When you are done, insert a design accent frame into the publication to create a border around the table. Insert a text box with your name and the name of your class. Check your publication for spelling.

4. Save the publication on your storage device.

5. Submit the publication and the printed copy of the newsletter in the format specified by your instructor.

6. ✷ Overall, do you think the creators of your chosen newsletter did a good job? Why or why not?

In the Lab

Design and implement a solution using creative thinking and problem-solving skills.

Importing a Word Letter

Note: To complete this assignment, you will be required to use the Data Files. Please contact your instructor for information about accessing the Data Files.

Problem: You need a letter of recommendation as you apply for jobs in your field. You will import a generic letter to a professor, asking for a recommendation. After importing the letter, you will use the Research pane to further research your profession.

Perform the following tasks:

Part 1: Start Publisher. Choose the 'Import Word Documents' thumbnail in the built-in templates and then choose the Quadrant template. Choose a font and color scheme. Choose the 'One-sided portrait' page size. Click the CREATE button to display the Import Word Document dialog box. Navigate to the Data Files and choose the file named Support_PUB_9_ProfLetter.doc. When the publication is displayed, delete the Document Title text box and the page number text box. Customizable fields are in gray. Change them as necessary. Highlight your job title and use the Research pane to find a good definition for your job. Insert it as appropriate into the letter. Look for any text that may need to be replaced with a symbol or special character. Email the resume as an attachment to your instructor.

Part 2: ✷ What kinds of Word documents are appropriate for importing into Publisher? What Word documents would not benefit from importing them into Publisher for editing and graphics?

10 | Editing Large-Scale Publications

Objectives

After completing this module, you will be able to:

- Insert, collapse, expand, and merge sections
- Specify starting page numbers and their associated formats
- Remove page numbers from specific pages
- Set text box and cell margins
- Use preset guide patterns
- Duplicate pages

- Link text boxes across pages
- Use the Clipboard pane
- Find and replace text
- Replace a word using the thesaurus
- Use the 'Go to Page' command
- Navigate through a publication
- Create breaks and bookmarks

Introduction

Large-scale publications — those consisting of 10 pages or more — require special techniques in editing, formatting, and printing. Planning and maintaining a consistent style is imperative. Large-scale publications require judicious use of sections, headers, footers, tables of contents, front matter, end matter, appendices, cover pages, graphics, styles, headings, and additional formatting considerations.

Examples of large-scale publications include books, booklets, magazines, catalogs, journals, and conference proceedings, among others.

Project: Creating a Booklet

The project in this module uses Publisher to create the 16-page booklet shown in Figure 10–1. This booklet, which is part of the Be Well Series published by Lightwing Outpatient Center for patients of and visitors to the center, discusses health concerns related to using technology and presents ways that users can minimize these health risks while using technology.

The first page of the booklet is the front cover page, followed by 3 pages of front matter (an abstract, a table of contents, and a blank page), then 11 content pages for the main article, and a blank back cover page. The front and back cover pages of the booklet have a green background. The front cover page displays WordArt, a graphic, and text. The inside pages of the booklet have features such as pictures, sidebars, linked text boxes, headings, and page numbers.

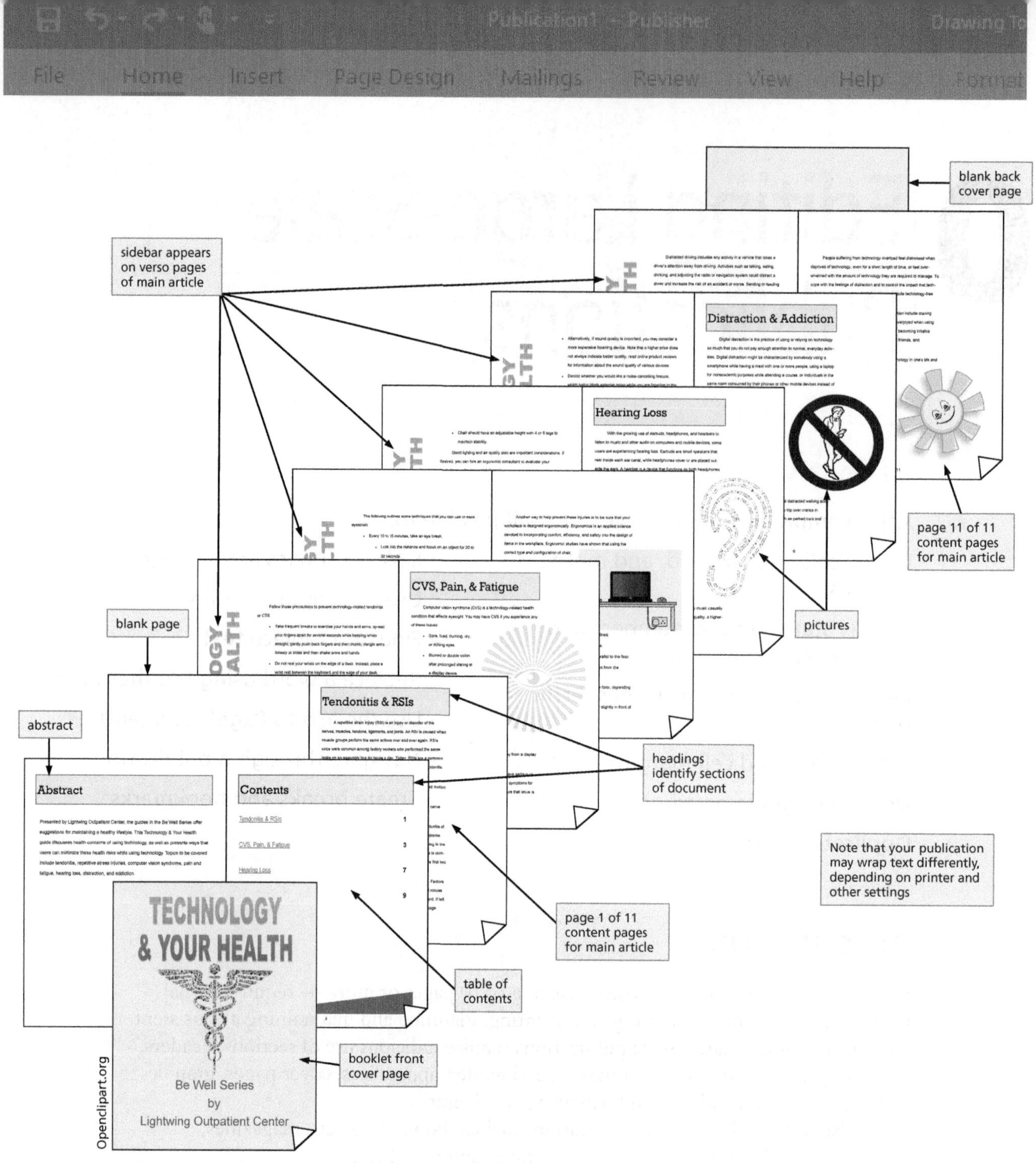

File   Home   Insert   Page Design   Mailings   Review   View   Help   Format

blank back cover page

sidebar appears on verso pages of main article

page 11 of 11 content pages for main article

pictures

page 1 of 11 content pages for main article

blank page

abstract

headings identify sections of document

Note that your publication may wrap text differently, depending on printer and other settings

Distraction & Addiction

Hearing Loss

CVS, Pain, & Fatigue

Tendonitis & RSIs

Abstract

Contents

table of contents

TECHNOLOGY & YOUR HEALTH

Be Well Series
by
Lightwing Outpatient Center

Openclipart.org

booklet front cover page

Figure 10–1

You will perform the following general tasks as you progress through this module:

1. Design the layout and create sections.
2. Insert page numbers.
3. Adjust cell margins and text box margins.
4. Display ruler guides to help place objects on the page.
5. Prepare pages for content and specify page numbers.
6. Use the Clipboard pane to copy and paste.
7. Use Find and Replace, along with the thesaurus, as necessary.
8. Navigate with bookmarks and links through a long publication.

To Start Publisher, Select a Blank Publication, and Adjust Settings

The following steps start Publisher, select an 8.5 × 11" blank print publication, choose schemes, and adjust workspace settings, such as the Page Navigation pane display and special characters.

BTW
Touch Mode
Differences
The Office and Windows interfaces may vary if you are using Touch mode. For this reason, you might notice that the function or appearance of your touch screen differs slightly from this module's presentation.

1 Start Publisher.

2 Click the 'Blank 8.5 × 11"' thumbnail in the template gallery on the Publisher start screen to create a blank publication in the Publisher window.

3 If the Publisher window is not maximized, click the Maximize button on its title bar to maximize the window.

4 If the Special Characters button (Home tab | Paragraph group) is not selected already, click it to display formatting marks on the screen.

5 Display the Page Design tab. Click the Fonts button (Page Design tab | Schemes group), scroll as necessary, and then click 'Office Classic 1' in the Fonts gallery to change the scheme fonts.

6 To change the color scheme, click the More button (Page Design tab | Schemes group) and then click Paper in the list of color schemes.

7 Display the View tab. If necessary, click the appropriate check boxes to display check marks for Boundaries, Guides, Rulers, Page Navigation, and the Scratch Area (View tab | Show group).

8 If the Page Navigation pane is expanded, click the 'Collapse Page Navigation Pane' button to collapse the pane (Figure 10–2).

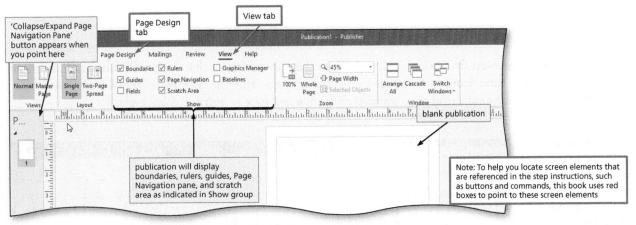

Figure 10–2

Designing the Layout

A layout is the manner in which pages, component parts, or individual items are arranged in a publication. You can use template layouts for your pages, or you can create objects on a blank page, thereby designing your own layout. When working with a large-scale publication, you need to plan for the front cover page, the back cover page, the inside of the front and back cover pages, as well as the inner pages, which sometimes are called **content pages** or **body copy**. A publication also may contain sectional elements such as front matter and end matter. **Front matter** is a term that refers to content at the beginning of a book or publication that is neither a cover page nor content pages, such as a forward, preface, or table of contents. **End matter** includes appendices, an index, reference pages, glossaries, or other lists. In the booklet in this module, you will make page-numbering decisions on front matter and content pages. Finally, you will decide on the layout of content pages, such as sidebars, headings, and tables of contents, among other elements.

CONSIDER THIS

What sections should you include in a large-scale publication?

Large-scale publications should contain some or all of the following sections:

- Front cover page: A front cover page should contain the complete title and name of the author, along with graphics or colors to encourage the reader to open the publication.

- Inside front cover page: Normally, the inside front cover page is blank, but some books use the space for author comments, references, other ancillary material, or the first page of the front matter.

- Front matter: Front matter includes a table of contents, notes from the editor or author, publication data, and other information to guide users through the content.

- Content pages: The content pages contain all of the text and graphics that constitute the book's main contents, minus the front matter and end matter.

- End matter: The end matter may contain appendices, an index, reference pages, glossaries, or other lists.

- Inside back cover page: Like the inside front cover page, the inside back cover page normally is blank, but it may contain the last page of the content, reference material, or additional information about the text or author.

- Back cover page: The back cover page may contain only graphics or color, or it may contain additional information about the content, such as a summary, online content, ISBN numbers, bar codes, and references to other pertinent publications.

To Insert Pages

The following steps insert five more blank pages into the publication so that the publication contains these six pages: one cover page, three front matter pages, one content page, and one back page. *Why? Unless you have chosen a template with the exact number of pages you wish to use, you will have to insert or delete pages.*

1

- Right-click the Page 1 thumbnail in the Page Navigation pane to display a shortcut menu (Figure 10–3).

Q&A | Can I make the Page Navigation pane bigger without expanding it to full size?
Yes, you can drag the right border of the Page Navigation pane to change its size.

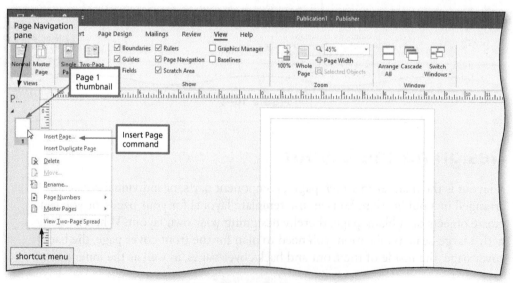

Figure 10–3

2

- Click Insert Page on the shortcut menu to display the Insert Page dialog box.
- In the 'Number of new pages' text box (Insert Page dialog box), type **5** to enter the number of pages to be inserted.

Q&A Why am I inserting only 5 pages when my publication will be 16 pages long?
In these steps, you insert only 1 content page. Later, you will add 10 more content pages so that the publication contains 11 content pages.

- If necessary, click the 'After current page' option button to select it (Figure 10–4).

Q&A Could I choose to create a new text box on the next page?
The 'Create one text box on each page' option button creates one large text box that fills the page, with no page formatting. It would not be appropriate for this module.

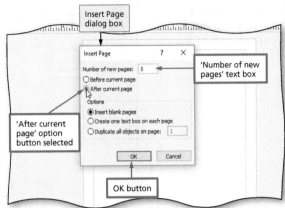

Figure 10–4

3

- Click OK to insert the blank pages in the publication (Figure 10–5).

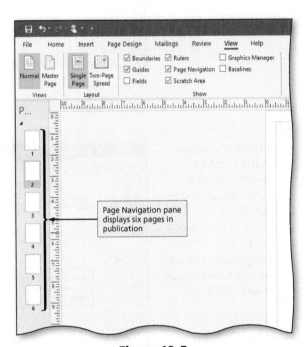

Figure 10–5

Other Ways

1. Click Page arrow (Insert tab | Pages group), click Insert Page on Page menu, enter desired number of pages (Insert Page dialog box), click OK

2. Press CTRL+SHIFT+N for each new page

To Create Sections

The front and back cover pages of the booklet will have a green background. The front matter and content pages will contain different layouts and page numbering. Publisher uses **sections**, or dividers, in the Page Navigation pane. *Why? Sections assist with pagination and organization and are used to separate the pages logically.* When you create a section, Publisher inserts a section break above the page in the Page Navigation pane. Each break contains a section button that appears as a small arrow. You click the button to expand or collapse a section. The following steps create sections for the front cover page, the front matter, the content pages, and the back cover page — a total of four sections.

• Right-click the Page 2 thumbnail in the Page Navigation pane to display a shortcut menu (Figure 10–6).

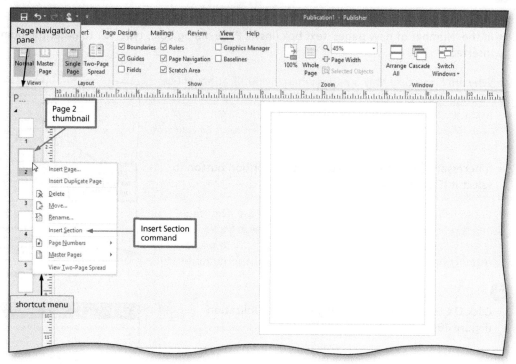

Figure 10–6

• Click Insert Section on the shortcut menu to insert a section break above page 2, which creates a separate section in the Page Navigation pane for the front cover page (Figure 10–7).

Q&A

Can I name the sections?
Publisher has no functionality to give each section a unique name.

Does the section break arrow have a name?
Yes, it is called a Collapse Section button.

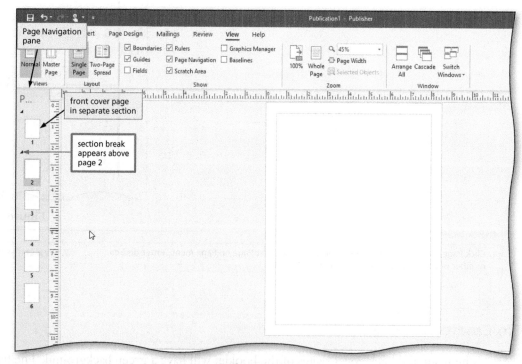

Figure 10–7

3

- Right-click the Page 5 thumbnail in the Page Navigation pane and then click Insert Section on the shortcut menu to insert a section break above page 5, which creates a section for the front matter.

- Right-click the Page 6 thumbnail in the Page Navigation pane and then click Insert Section on the shortcut menu to insert a section break above page 6, which creates a section for the current content page (Figure 10–8).

Experiment

- Right-click one of the Collapse Section buttons to view the commands related to sections on a shortcut menu. Press ESC to remove the shortcut menu from the screen.

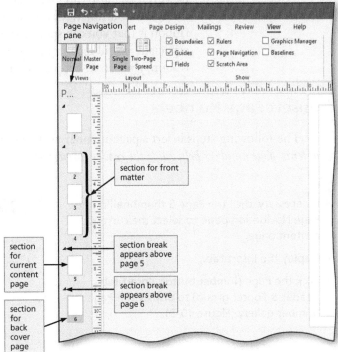

Figure 10–8

To Merge Sections

If you wanted to merge sections, you would perform the following steps.

1. In the Page Navigation pane, right-click the Collapse Section button to display a shortcut menu.

2. Click 'Merge with Previous Section' on the shortcut menu to merge the sections above and below the section break.

BTW
Expand/Collapse Section Shortcut Menu
A section title bar runs the width of the Page Navigation pane. You can right-click anywhere in that area to display the Expand/Collapse Section shortcut menu.

Pagination

Pagination refers to the way a publication applies page numbers, including the location, whether the front cover page will be included in the page numbering system, and the number with which you wish to start. When inserting page numbers in a large-scale publication, it is common for the front and back cover pages not to be numbered. If the front matter contains many pages, the pages in that section are typically numbered sequentially using lowercase Roman numerals. Page number 1 begins after the front matter.

How are pages numbered in booklets?
Using the correct pagination helps readers navigate through the sections of a booklet or large-scale publication. Decide which pages should not display page numbers, such as title pages, cover pages, and blank pages. Use lowercase Roman numerals for front matter. Use numerals for content pages. Appendices sometimes use pages numbered with letters of the alphabet. Be consistent; page numbers that change locations or styles within a publication are disconcerting to readers.

CONSIDER THIS

You can use headers and footers to place page numbers using the master page; however, you also can insert page numbers using the Insert tab on the ribbon. The information ultimately is stored on a master page, but the advantage of using the ribbon is that you can specify the number you wish to use as a starting page number, an especially useful technique for modules and sections of books. Additionally, using the ribbon, you can insert page numbers in text boxes other than the header and the footer.

To Insert Page Numbers

The following steps insert a page number at the bottom center of each page. *Why? When used with a table of contents, page numbers help guide the reader through the booklet.*

1

- If necessary, click the Page 5 thumbnail in the Page Navigation pane to select the current content page.

- Display the Insert tab.

- Click the Page Number button (Insert tab | Header & Footer group) to display the Page Number gallery (Figure 10–9).

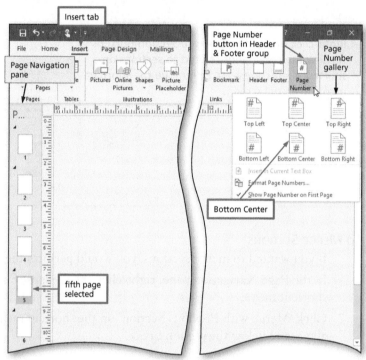

Figure 10–9

2

- Click Bottom Center in the Page Number gallery to insert page numbers at the bottom center of each page in the publication.

- Zoom to 150% and scroll to the bottom of the page to view the page number (Figure 10–10).

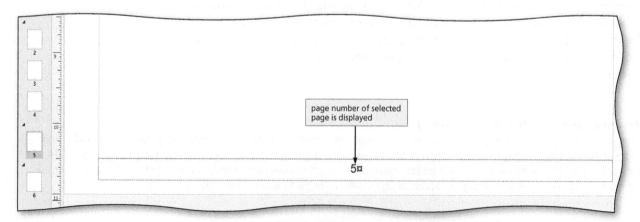

Figure 10–10

To Specify a Starting Page Number Using the Ribbon

The booklet's front matter will appear beginning on the inside front cover page. The following steps specify a starting page number, i, which will appear on the second page of the publication. *Why? It is common for front matter to use lowercase Roman numerals.*

- In the Page Navigation pane, select the second page of the publication.
- Click the Page Number button (Insert tab | Header & Footer group) to display the Page Number gallery (Figure 10–11).

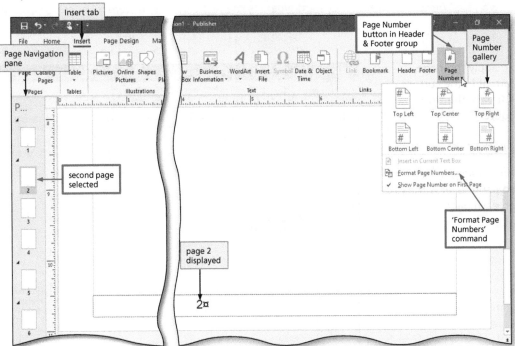

Figure 10–11

- Click 'Format Page Numbers' in the Page Number gallery to display the Page Number Format dialog box.
- Click the Number format arrow (Page Number Format dialog box) to display the available number formats in the Number format list (Figure 10–12).

Experiment

- Scroll through the Number format list and view the different kinds of page number formats, including cardinal numbers, Roman numerals, letters, ordinal numbers, and spelled out numbers (i.e., one, two, three).

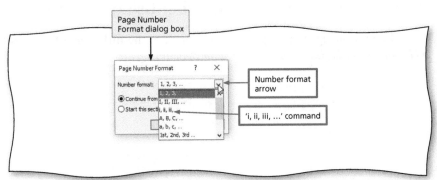

Figure 10–12

● Click 'i, ii, iii, …' in the Number format list to select the number format.

● Click the 'Start this section with' option button to select it.

● Select the text in the 'Start this section with' text box and then type **1** to specify the starting page number (Figure 10–13).

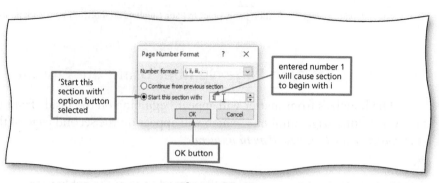

Figure 10–13

Q&A Why should I type the numeral, 1, when I want to start with page i?

The 'Start this section with' box requires an integer. The page number is page 1 of the section; the page number format is lowercase Roman numerals. You would type a numeral 1 even if you were instructing Publisher to use letters on each page.

● Click OK to apply the page number format in the current section — that is, the front matter (Figure 10–14).

🔍 **Experiment**

● Click different pages in the Page Navigation pane to view the page number on each page.

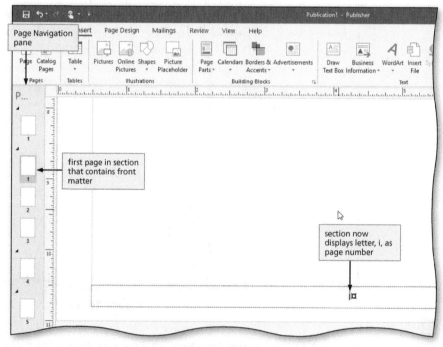

Figure 10–14

To Specify a Starting Page Number Using the Page Navigation Pane

The following steps apply the number, 1, to the fifth page of the publication. **Why?** *The fifth page of the publication is the beginning of the section for content pages.*

1

- Right-click the fifth page displayed in the Page Navigation pane, which appears as the first page in the third section to display a shortcut menu.

- Point to Page Numbers on the shortcut menu to display the Page Numbers submenu (Figure 10–15).

Q&A

How can I tell which page I am working on?

The status bar always displays a number representing the current sequential page of the overall publication. Within each section, the pages are numbered in the Page Navigation pane.

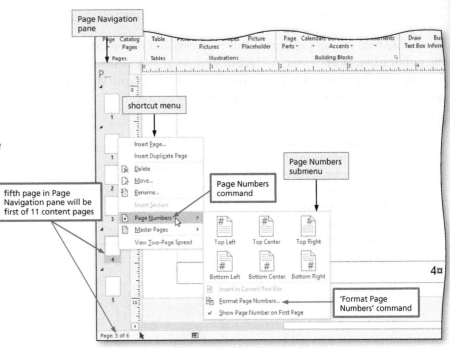

Figure 10–15

2

- Click 'Format Page Numbers' on the Page Numbers submenu to display the Page Number Format dialog box.

- If necessary, click the Number format arrow (Page Number Format dialog box) to display the Number format list and then click '1, 2, 3, …' to select the format.

- Click the 'Start this section with' option button to select it.

- Select the text in the 'Start this section with' text box and then type 1 to enter the starting page number for this section (Figure 10–16).

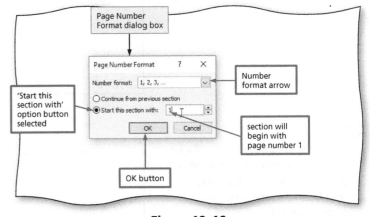

Figure 10–16

3

- Click OK to apply the page number format to the page (Figure 10–17).

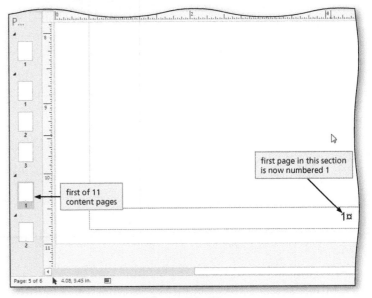

Figure 10–17

To Remove Page Numbering from Specific Pages

The final step in paginating this publication is to remove page numbers from the first and last sections of the publication. *Why? Front and back cover pages usually do not have page numbers.* Because page numbers and their formats are saved internally in a master page, the following steps remove page numbering by choosing to apply no master page to the specific pages in the publication.

1

• In the Page Navigation pane, right-click the first page of the publication (the front cover page) to display a shortcut menu and then point to Master Pages on the shortcut menu to display the Master Pages submenu (Figure 10–18).

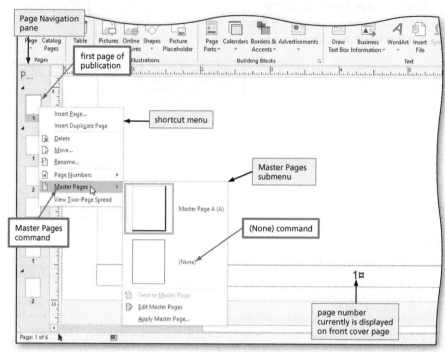

Figure 10–18

2

• Click (None) on the Master Pages submenu to remove the master page and, thus, remove page numbering from the page (Figure 10–19).

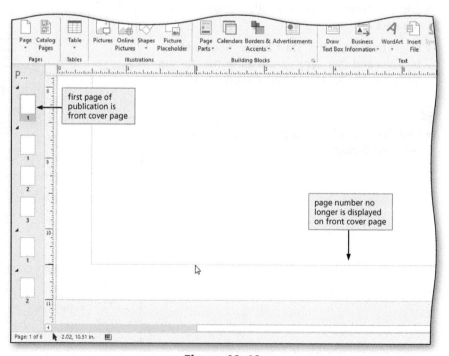

Figure 10–19

❸

- Repeat Steps 1 and 2 for the last page of the publication (the back cover page) so that page numbering will not appear on that page.

- Save the publication on your hard drive, OneDrive, or other storage location using the file name, SC_PUB_10_BeWellSeries_TechnologyBooklet.

Break Point: If you want to take a break, this is a good place to do so. Exit Publisher. To resume later, start Publisher, open the file called SC_PUB_10_BeWellSeries_TechnologyBooklet.pub, and continue following the steps from this location forward.

To Apply a Background

The following steps apply a solid green background on the first and last pages of the booklet.

❶ Select the first page of the publication in the Page Navigation pane, zoom to whole page, and display the Page Design tab.

❷ Click the Background button (Page Design tab | Page Background group) to display the Background gallery.

❸ Click '30% tint of Accent 2' (second background in the second row in the Solid Background area) in the Background gallery to apply the selected color to the page background.

❹ Repeat Steps 1 through 3 for the last page of the publication (Figure 10–20).

BTW

The Ribbon and Screen Resolution
Publisher may change how the groups and buttons within the groups appear on the ribbon, depending on the screen resolution of your computer. Thus, your ribbon may look different from the ones in this book if you are using a screen resolution other than 1366 × 768.

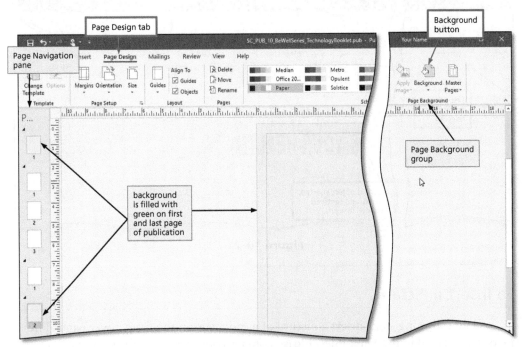

Figure 10–20

To Create the Title

The following steps create a WordArt title on the front cover page of the booklet.

1 Select the first page (the front cover page) of the publication in the Page Navigation pane.

2 Display the Insert tab.

3 Click the WordArt button (Insert tab | Text group) and then click 'Gradient Fill - Purple, Outline - White' (first WordArt style in the fourth row) in the WordArt gallery to display the Edit WordArt Text dialog box.

4 Type **TECHNOLOGY** as the first line of text (Edit WordArt Text dialog box). Press ENTER and then type **& YOUR HEALTH** as the second line of text. Click OK to close the dialog box.

5 Resize the WordArt object to approximately 6.5 inches wide and 2.58 inches tall.

6 Click the Even Height button (WordArt Tools Format tab | Text group) so that the letters in both lines of text are the same height.

7 Move the WordArt object to the top of the page, aligned at the top margin.

8 Click the Align button (WordArt Tools Format tab | Arrange group) to display the Align menu and then click 'Relative to Margin Guides' on the Align menu. Click the Align button again and then click Align Center on the Align menu to center the WordArt object between the margins (Figure 10–21).

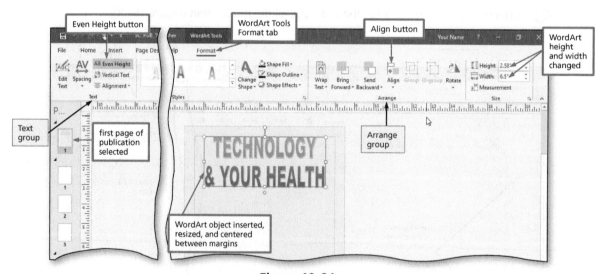

Figure 10–21

To Insert a Picture

The following steps insert a picture of a caduceus on the front cover page. The picture is located in the Data Files. Please contact your instructor for information about accessing the Data Files.

1 Insert the picture named Support_PUB_10_PrismaticCaduceus.png from the Data Files.

2 Resize the inserted picture to approximately 4.8 inches wide and 4.5 inches tall.

3 Move the picture to a location below the WordArt.

4 Click the Align button (Picture Tools Format tab | Arrange group) and then click Align Center on the Align menu to center the selected picture (Figure 10–22).

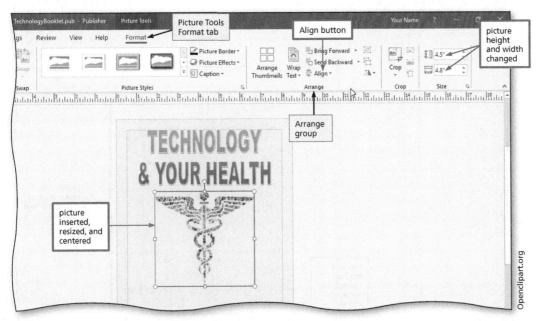

Figure 10–22

To Enter the Subtitle

The following steps add a subtitle to the front cover page of the booklet.

1 Insert a text box approximately 7.5 inches wide and 2.5 inches tall at the bottom of the page.

2 Click in the text box to position the insertion point in the text box and then change the font size to 36 point.

3 Change the font color to 'Hyperlink (RGB (130, 92, 158))' (sixth color in the first row).

4 Press CTRL+E to center the insertion point. Type **Be Well Series** and then press ENTER.

5 Type **by** and then press ENTER. Point to the small blue box below the beginning of the entered word, click the AutoCorrect Options button to display the AutoCorrect Options menu, and then click 'Undo Automatic Capitalization' on the AutoCorrect Options menu to undo the capitalization of the entered word.

6 Type **Lightwing Outpatient Center** to finish the text.

7 Right-click the name, Lightwing, to display a shortcut menu and then click Ignore All on the shortcut menu to remove the red wavy line below the name.

8 Center the text box using the Align button (Home tab | Arrange group).

9 Drag around or CTRL+click both text boxes and the picture on the page to select all three objects.

10 Click the Align button (Home tab | Arrange group) and then click Distribute Vertically on the Align menu to distribute all three objects evenly on the page from top to bottom.

11 Click the scratch area to deselect the objects (Figure 10–23).

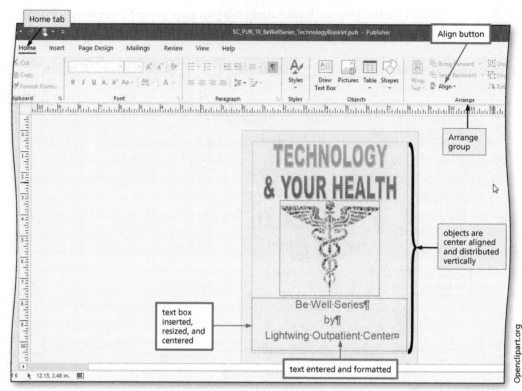

Figure 10–23

To Collapse Sections

The front and back cover pages of the booklet are complete. The following steps collapse those pages in the Page Navigation pane. **Why?** *Collapsing complete sections helps reduce the size of the Page Navigation pane and allows you to focus on pages that need to be edited.*

1

- Select the second page of the publication in the Page Navigation pane.

- In the Page Navigation pane, click the Collapse Section button above the first page of the publication to collapse the section that contains the front cover page (Figure 10–24).

Q&A What happened to the Collapse Section button that I clicked?
It changed to an Expand Section button that you can click to expand the collapsed section.

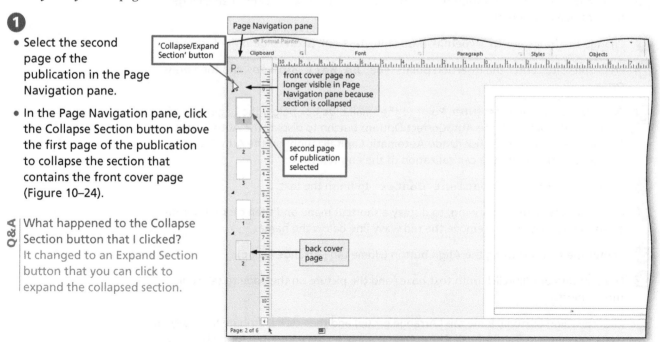

Figure 10–24

2

- Click the Collapse Section button above the last page in the Page Navigation pane to collapse the section that contains the back cover page (Figure 10–25).

3

- Save the booklet again on the same storage location with the same file name.

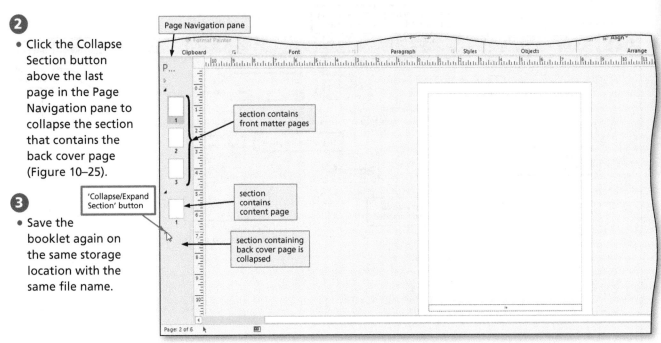

Page Navigation pane

section contains front matter pages

'Collapse/Expand Section' button

section contains content page

section containing back cover page is collapsed

Page: 2 of 6

Figure 10–25

To Insert and Format a Text Box

The following steps enter a title in a text box at the top of the first page of the front matter.

1 If necessary, click the first page of the front matter with the page number, i, to select the page.

2 Insert a text box approximately 7.5 inches wide and 1.2 inches tall at the top of the page.

3 Click the Align button (Home tab | Arrange group) to display the Align menu and then click Align Center on the Align menu to center the text box on the page.

4 If necessary, click inside the text box to display the insertion point in it. Display the Text Box Tools Format tab. Click the 'Align Center Left' button (Text Box Tools Format tab | Alignment group) to align the insertion point in the vertical center at the left edge of the text box.

5 Display the Drawing Tools Format tab. Use the Shape Fill arrow (Drawing Tools Format tab | Shape Styles group) to fill the text box with the 'Accent 2 (RGB (120, 218, 122)) Lighter 60%' color (third color in the third row).

6 Use the Shape Outline arrow (Drawing Tools Format tab | Shape Styles group) to change the outline color to 'Hyperlink (RGB (130, 92, 158))' (sixth color in the first row).

7 Change the font to Rockwell and the font size to 36 point.

8 Type **Abstract** in the text box (Figure 10-26).

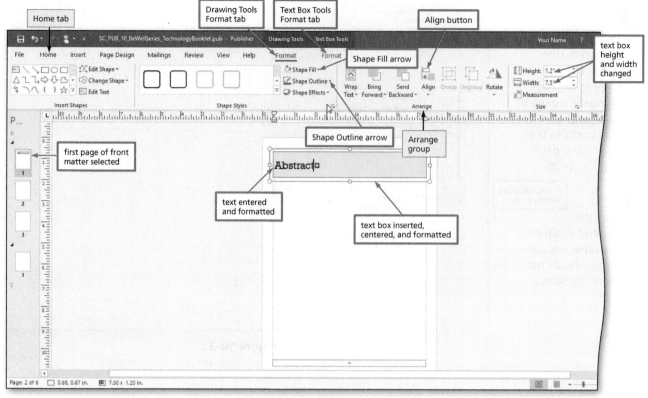

Figure 10–26

To Insert and Format Another Text Box

The following steps enter the abstract content into a text box. The text for the abstract is located in the Data Files. Please contact your instructor for information about accessing the Data Files.

1 Display the Insert tab.

2 Draw a text box below the first text box, approximately 7.25 inches wide and 3.1 inches tall.

3 With the insertion point inside the text box, click the Insert File button (Insert tab | Text group) to display the Insert Text dialog box. Navigate to the Data Files and insert the file named Support_PUB_10_Abstract.doc.

Q&A | Why is this file stored in the .doc format instead of the .docx format?
The .docx format sometimes produces an Office file validation error, especially on networked drives.

Why did Publisher display the Converting dialog box before my text appeared?
While Publisher is importing the story, you may see a message saying Publisher is converting this file. Wait until the process is complete before you continue to edit.

4 If necessary, select all of the text in the text box and then change the font size to 14 point.

5 If necessary, click the border of the text box to select it. Click the Align button (Home tab | Arrange group) and then click Align Center on the Align menu to center the text box on the page horizontally (Figure 10–27).

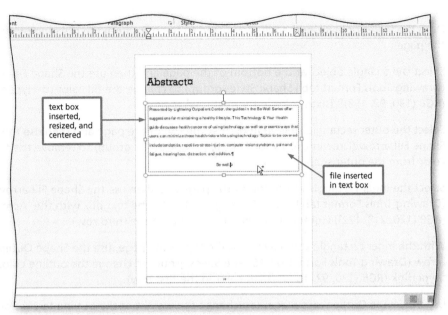

Figure 10–27

Cell and Text Box Margins

As with page margins, you can adjust the margins within table cells and within text boxes. The default margin for a text box and for a cell is approximately 0.04 inches. In some cases, that may place the text too close to the edge or border. To improve readability, you will change the margin in the table of contents cells for the booklet so that the page numbers are farther away from the margin and its border.

To Create a Table of Contents

The following steps insert a table of contents building block on the second page of the front matter.

1 In the Page Navigation pane, click the second page of the front matter with the page number, ii, to select the page.

2 Display the Insert tab.

3 Click the Building Blocks Dialog Box Launcher (Insert tab | Building Blocks group) to display the Building Block Library dialog box.

4 Click the Page Parts folder (Building Block Library dialog box) to display the available page parts building blocks.

5 Scroll to and then click the 'All Tables of Contents' folder to display the available Table of Contents building blocks.

6 Scroll to and then double-click the Tilt table of contents to insert the building block on the current page in the publication.

7 Move the building block to the upper-left corner of the page.

8 Drag the lower-right sizing handle down and to the right until the building block fills the page.

9 Select the triangle object at the bottom of the page and then use the Shape Fill arrow (Drawing Tools Format tab | Shape Styles group) to change the fill color to 'Hyperlink (RGB (130, 92, 158))' (sixth color in the first row).

10 Select the outer rectangle shaded in gray at the top of the page and then use the Shape Fill arrow (Drawing Tools Format tab | Shape Styles group) to remove the fill color from the outer shape.

11 Select the inner rectangle at the top of the page and then use the Shape Fill arrow (Drawing Tools Format tab | Shape Styles group) to fill the text box with the 'Accent 2 (RGB (120, 218, 122)) Lighter 60%' color (third color in the third row).

12 With the inner rectangle still selected at the top of the page, use the Shape Outline arrow (Drawing Tools Format tab | Shape Styles group) to change the outline color to 'Hyperlink (RGB (130, 92, 158))' (sixth color in the first row).

13 Use the Shape Outline arrow again to change the weight of the outline to 2¼ point (Figure 10–28). (Note that during these steps, the sections in the Page Navigation pane may have expanded.)

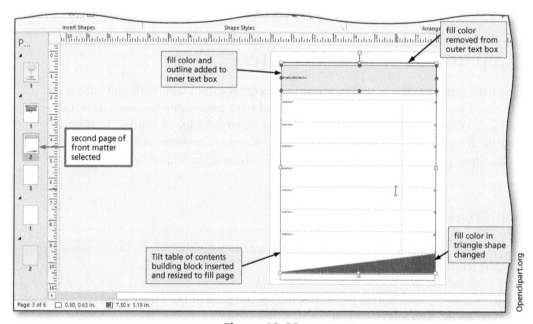

Figure 10–28

To Change Cell Margins

The following steps increase the right margin of the cells in the second column of the table of contents, where you will insert page numbers later in this module. *Why? By changing the cell margin, the page number will not appear so close to the border.*

1

- Drag through the second column of the table to select the cells.
- Display the Table Tools Layout tab.

- Click the Cell Margins button (Table Tools Layout tab | Alignment group) to display the Cell Margins gallery (Figure 10–29).

 Experiment

- Click each of the cell margin options in the Cell Margins gallery and watch the margins change in the table. When finished experimenting, redisplay the Cell Margins gallery.

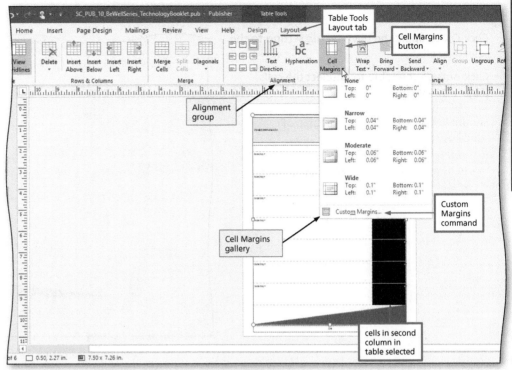

Figure 10–29

2

- Click Custom Margins in the Cell Margins gallery to display the Format Table dialog box. If necessary, click the Cell Properties tab.

- Select the text in the Right box (Format Table dialog box) and then type .3 to enter a new right margin value (Figure 10–30).

Q&A Could I use the numerical up and down buttons in the Right box?
Yes, those buttons change the text in the box by .1 inch each time you click them.

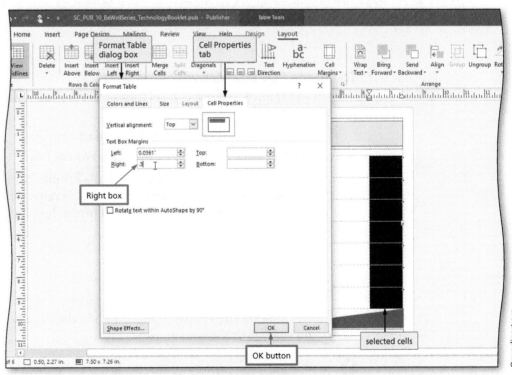

Figure 10–30

3

- Click OK to apply the new margin setting to the selected cells.

- Click outside the table to deselect the cells (Figure 10–31).

Q&A

Should I enter new text in the table of contents?

No, you will update the table of contents later in the module, after you complete all pages.

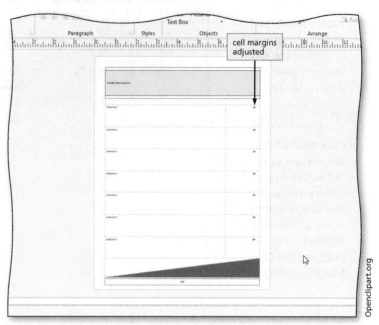

Figure 10–31

Other Ways

1. Right-click cell, click Format Table on shortcut menu, click Cell Properties tab (Format Table dialog box), enter cell margin, click OK

TO CHANGE TEXT BOX MARGINS

If you wanted to change the margins of a text box, rather than a cell, you would perform the following steps.

1. Select the text box by clicking its boundary.

2. If necessary, display the Text Box Tools Format tab.

3. Click the Margins button (Text Box Tools Format tab | Alignment group) and then either choose a preset value from the Margins gallery or click Custom Margins and enter the margin values (Format Text Box dialog box).

To Collapse the Sections

The following steps collapse all sections in the Page Navigation pane, except for the section containing the content page.

1 In the Page Navigation pane, click the first page of the content section with the page number 1.

2 Use the Collapse Section button above the sections containing the front cover page, the front matter, and the back cover page, so that all sections are collapsed except for the section containing the content page (Figure 10–32).

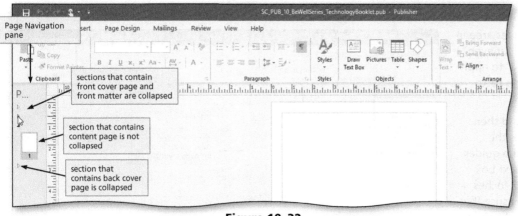

Figure 10–32

Ruler Guides

You can create individual ruler guides — green, dotted, nonprinting lines — by dragging from the rulers to help you align objects and provide visual reference. You also can choose sets of built-in ruler guides. These ruler guides are preset to contain headings, columns, and grids. Along with margin guides that are blue, the ruler guides also provide straight edges and snapping capabilities.

In this booklet, you will choose a set of ruler guides in order to display areas for text, headings, and sidebars.

To Select Ruler Guides

The following steps select a set of built-in ruler guides for the content page with the page number 1, a recto page. *Why? Ruler guides help you create objects in consistent places across pages.* After drawing a text box on page 1, you will create a second page with a mirrored set of ruler guides and a text box for page 2 of the content pages, a verso page.

1

- If necessary, select the single content page in the Page Navigation pane with the page number 1.
- Display the Page Design tab.
- Click the Guides button (Page Design tab | Layout group) to display the Guides gallery (Figure 10–33).

Q&A What does the Ruler Guides command do?
The command allows you to place ruler guides at specific measured locations.

Experiment
- Scroll in the Guides gallery to view other guides.

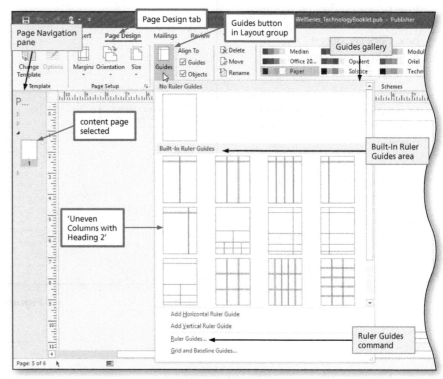

Figure 10–33

- In the Built-In Ruler Guides area in the Guides gallery, click 'Uneven Columns with Heading 2' to apply the selected guide to this recto page.

- Display the Home tab and then draw a text box that fills the lower-left area within the guides and margins, with the text box width approximately 5.5 inches and height 8.6 inches. Ensure that the text box is positioned within the margins on the left side of the page (Figure 10–34).

Q&A Can I use a different built-in ruler guide?
The 'Uneven Columns with Heading 2' ruler guide is meant to be used on recto pages. It has room on the left for a large amount of text that will appear close to the booklet binding. The outside margin provides room for sidebars.

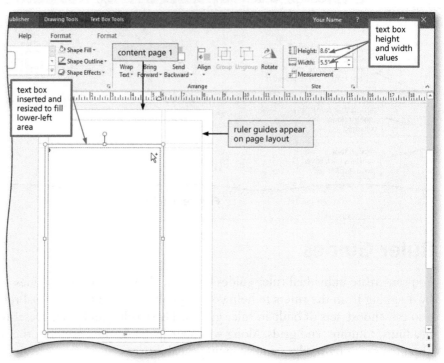

Figure 10–34

- In the Page Navigation pane, right-click the content page with the page number 1 to display a shortcut menu and then click Insert Page on the shortcut menu to display the Insert Page dialog box. Click OK (Insert Page dialog box) to accept the settings and insert the page.

- Collapse all sections in the Page Navigation pane except for the section that contains the content pages.

- If necessary, select the content page with the page number 2 in the Page Navigation pane.

- Display the Page Design tab and then click the Guides button (Page Design tab | Layout group) to display the Guides gallery (Figure 10–35).

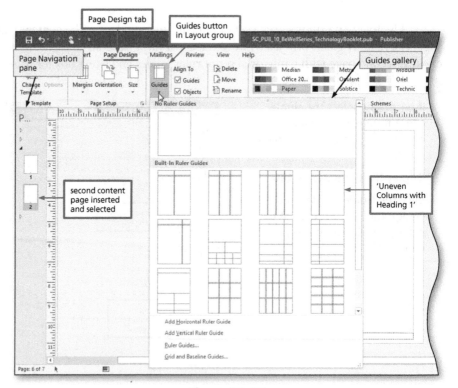

Figure 10–35

- Click 'Uneven Columns with Heading 1' in the Guides gallery to apply the selected guide to the selected verso page.

- Display the Home tab and then draw a text box that fills the lower-right area within the ruler guides and margins, with the text box width approximately 5.5 inches and height 8.6 inches. Ensure that the text box is positioned within the margins on the right side of the page (Figure 10–36).

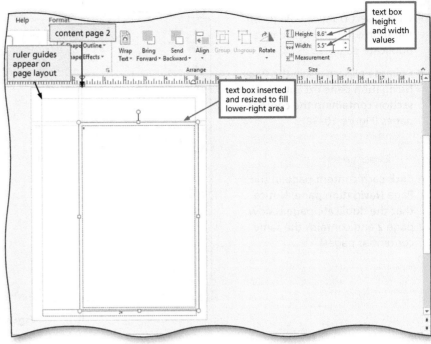

Figure 10–36

Preparing Pages for Content

Once your page numbers, layout guides, and text boxes are prepared for content, you are ready to prepare the correct number of pages for content. The number of pages is directly related to the length of your story, so you should try to create plenty of room; however, if you underestimate the number of necessary pages, Publisher will create new ones for you at the end of the publication.

The following sections duplicate pages, rearrange them as necessary, and change the view. Finally, you will link text boxes across pages so that the main article will flow correctly from beginning to end once you import it.

To Duplicate a Page

The following steps duplicate page 1, including all objects — in this case, the guides and text box. *Why? It is easier to duplicate the page than to re-create all of its elements.*

- Right-click content page 1 in the Page Navigation pane to display a shortcut menu (Figure 10–37).

Q&A Where will the duplicate page be placed?
The default setting is to place the page directly after the selected page.

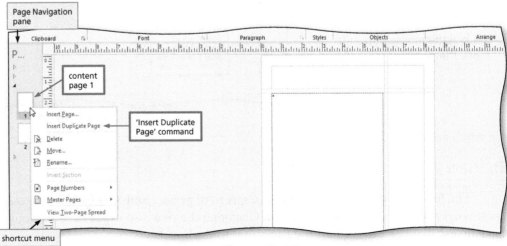

Figure 10–37

2

- Click 'Insert Duplicate Page' on the shortcut menu to create a duplicate page.

- Collapse all sections in the Page Navigation pane except for the section containing the content pages (Figure 10–38).

Experiment

- Click each content page in the Page Navigation pane. Notice that the duplicate page is now page 2 and contains the same content as page 1.

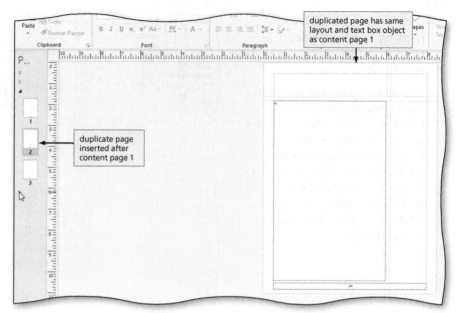

Figure 10–38

Other Ways

1. Click 'Insert Blank Page' arrow (Insert tab | Pages group), click 'Insert Duplicate Page' on Insert Blank Page menu

2. Press CTRL+SHIFT+N

To Rearrange Pages

You can use the Page Navigation pane to rearrange pages. The following steps move the newly duplicated page to position number 3 in the content section. *Why? The duplicated page is a recto page and needs to follow a verso page.*

1

- In the Page Navigation pane, drag content page 2 down below the next page until Publisher displays a horizontal bar (Figure 10–39).

Q&A

What if content page 2 will not move down?
You can move content page 3 up.

2

- Release the mouse button to move the page.

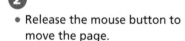
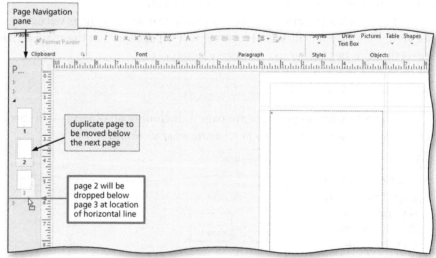

Figure 10–39

To View a Two-Page Spread

The following step views the two-page spread of pages 2 and 3. *Why? Viewing the two-page spread allows you to verify the guides and text box placement.* Changing the view also expands all sections if they are not already expanded so that you can see how the pages fit into the booklet.

1

- Display the View tab.

- Click the 'Two-Page Spread' button (View tab | Layout group) to show pages 2 and 3 together in the workspace (Figure 10–40).

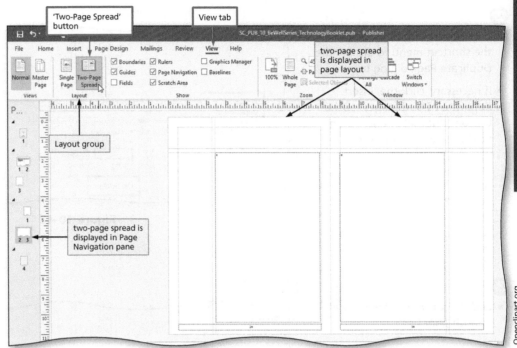

Figure 10–40

To Duplicate the Two-Page Spread

The following steps duplicate the two-page spread four times. *Why? You need a total of 11 pages for the main article — page 1 followed by five sets of two-page spreads.* As you duplicate a two-page spread, Publisher attempts to create an even number of pages per section; you sometimes need to move a page to keep a two-page spread together. In that case, Publisher will warn you of an uneven page count.

1

- In the Page Navigation pane, right-click the content page 2 and page 3 two-page spread to display a shortcut menu (Figure 10–41).

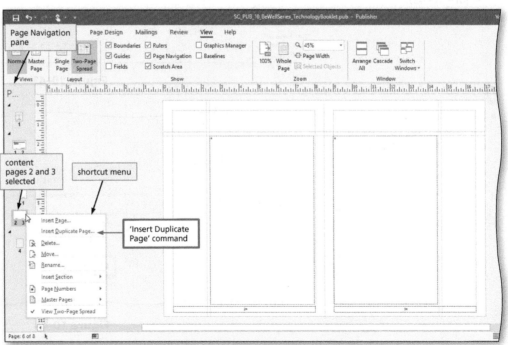

Figure 10–41

2

- Click 'Insert Duplicate Page' on the shortcut menu to display the Duplicate Page dialog box.

- If necessary, click the 'Insert duplicate of both pages' option button (Duplicate Page dialog box) to select it (Figure 10–42).

Q&A Could I use the Insert Page command and request eight more pages?
You could, but all of the pages would be recto pages. Using the Insert Duplicate Page command creates a verso page and a recto page.

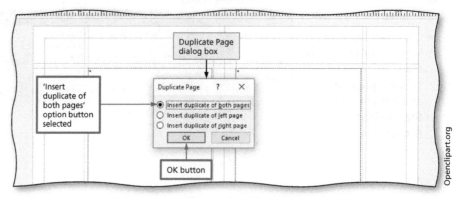

Figure 10–42

3

- Click OK to create the duplicate of both pages.

Q&A Why did Publisher split the two-page spread?
Publisher tried to make an even number of pages per section. Dragging the page corrects the problem.

- In the Page Navigation pane, drag page 6 into the previous section, above page 5, until the horizontal bar is displayed above the section break (Figure 10–43).

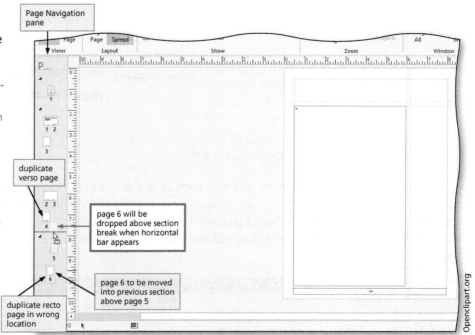

Figure 10–43

4

- Release the mouse button to move the page to the previous section (Figure 10–44).

Q&A Why did Publisher display a warning message?
Moving the page up to a new section leaves a single page in the section that contains the back cover page. Publisher warns you that the pages in the last section will be uneven.

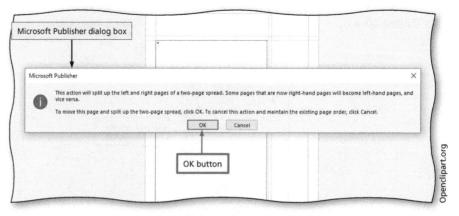

Figure 10–44

5
- Click OK (Microsoft Publisher dialog box) to accept the repagination (Figure 10–45).

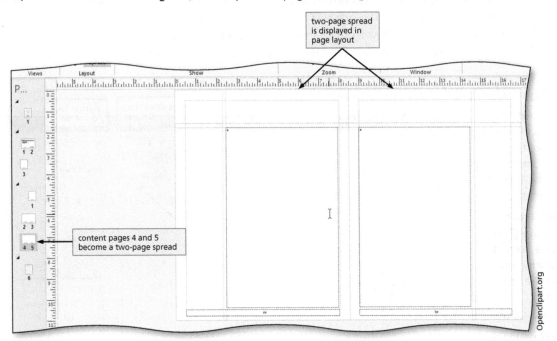

Figure 10–45

6
- In the Page Navigation pane, right-click the content page 2 and page 3 two-page spread again to display a shortcut menu and then click 'Insert Duplicate Page' on the shortcut menu to display the Duplicate Page dialog box.

- Click OK (Duplicate Page dialog box) to insert a duplicate two-page spread.

7
- Repeat Step 6 two more times to create a total of 11 content pages (Figure 10–46).

Q&A In the Page Navigation pane, my page 11 was not part of a two-page spread. Did I do something wrong?
If you copied the content page 2 and page 3 two-page spread, it should have been displayed correctly. If your page 11 is displayed individually, drag it up into the previous section, just below page 10.

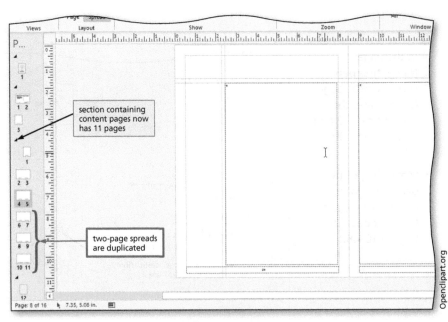

Figure 10–46

Opendipart.org

To Link Text Boxes Using the Menu

One way to link content from one text box to another after inserting text is to use the 'Text in Overflow' button when the content does not fit in the first text box. The following steps, however, link text boxes using the ribbon, so that text inserted later will flow from one to the other. *Why? If you link text boxes before importing or typing the text, the Text Box Tools Format tab contains several tools to help you create, break, and move between linked text boxes.*

1

- In the Page Navigation pane, click content page 1 to select it.

- Click the text box on content page 1 in the workspace to select the text box and then display the Text Box Tools Format tab.

- Click the Create Link button (Text Box Tools Format tab | Linking group) to start the linking process.

- Move the pointer over the text box (Figure 10–47).

Q&A Why does my pointer look like a pitcher?
Publisher uses a pitcher icon to indicate a link is about to take place. The pitcher is upright when you move it over the original text box. The pitcher will tip when you move it over any other text box, as if it is pouring in the text.

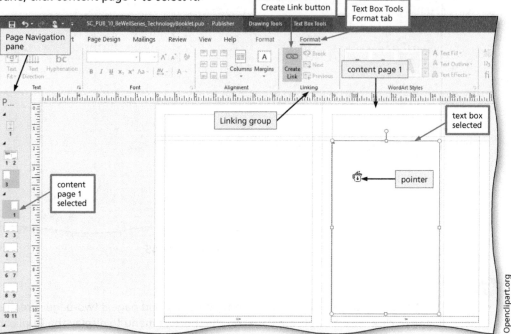

Figure 10–47

2

- In the Page Navigation pane, click the next page (in this case, the content page 2 and page 3 spread) to select it.

- Move the pointer over the text box on the verso page (content page 2) (Figure 10–48).

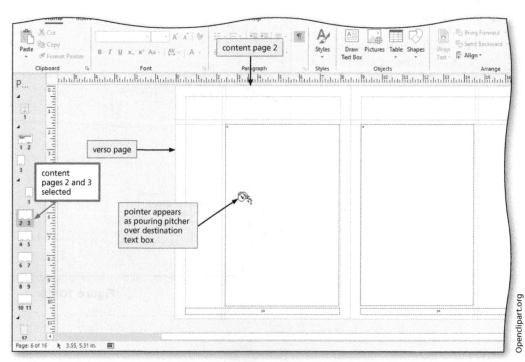

Figure 10–48

3

- Click the text box to link it to the previous text box (Figure 10–49).

How can I be sure that I have linked correctly?
If you have linked correctly, Publisher will display a Previous button on the text box border and also will enable the Previous button on the ribbon.

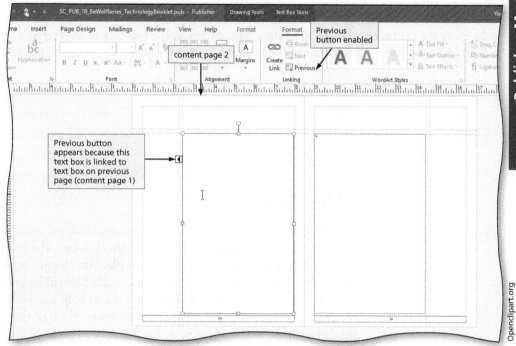

Figure 10–49

4

- To link the text box on content page 2 to the text box on content page 3, with the page 2 text box still selected, click the Create Link button (Text Box Tools Format tab | Linking group) and then click the recto page text box to link the two text boxes.

- With the text box on page 3 selected, repeat this process to link page 3 to page 4.

- Click the Previous button on page 4 to display pages 2 and 3 and select the text box on page 3 (Figure 10–50).

- Click the Next button on page 3 of the content section to display pages 4 and 5 and select the text box on page 4.

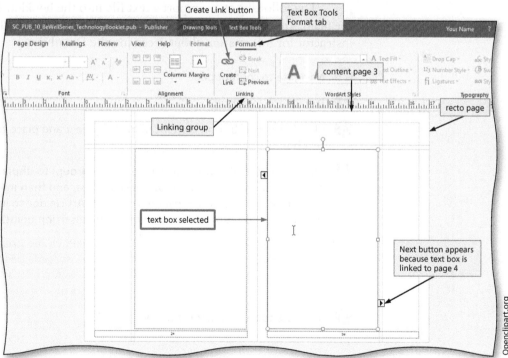

Figure 10–50

- Repeat the process to link all pages up to and including page 11.

- To verify the connections, begin at content page 1, click in the text box to select it and then click the Next button located on the lower-right border of the text box. Repeat on each page until you get to page 11.

Q&A Is an easier way available to connect boxes for really long publications?
The only other way is to import the text first. Publisher will create extra pages with connected text boxes. You then would have to format the pages, create guides, and resize the text boxes on each page.

Adding Content

Content for publications such as newsletters, catalogs, email messages, and booklets may come from a variety of sources. For this booklet, the text for the Technology & Your Health main article is in one Word file. You already have linked the text boxes across the content pages, so importing a single file will be convenient. After importing the text file, you will use the Clipboard pane to help keep track of objects as you insert them across pages. A page may display a picture. Each of the verso pages will display a sidebar with the name of the main article. As you place pictures, text will wrap around them. Later in the module, some content pages will need section headings, similar to chapter headings.

To Import Text

The following steps import a text file into the booklet. The text file that contains the main article for the booklet is located in the Data Files. Please contact your instructor for information about accessing the Data Files.

1 Navigate to content page 1.

2 Display the Insert tab.

3 Click in the text box on content page 1 to select and place the insertion point in the text box.

4 Click the Insert File button (Insert tab | Text group) to display the Insert Text dialog box, navigate to the location of the Data Files, and then insert the file named Support_PUB_10_TechnologyandYourHealthArticle.doc to insert the contents of the file in the publication at the location of the insertion point.

Q&A Why is page 11 of the content section displayed on my screen?
Because you linked text boxes together across multiple pages, the text inserted from the file spans the linked text boxes. Word displays the location of end of the inserted content, which is on page 11 of the content section.

5 Navigate to content page 1 (Figure 10–51).

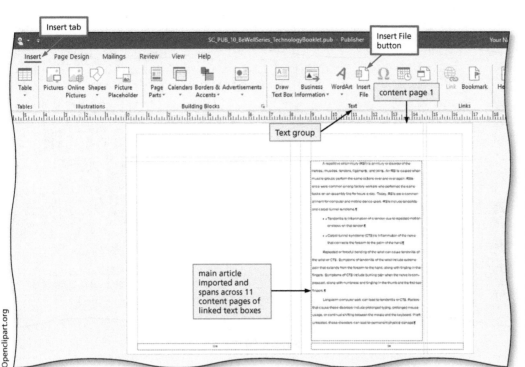

Figure 10–51

BTW

Show Office Clipboard Icon

While using the Office Clipboard, the Windows 10 taskbar displays a Clipboard icon. Right-clicking the icon displays a shortcut menu with commands to help you manage the Clipboard. If you do not see it, click the Options button (Clipboard pane) and then click 'Show Office Clipboard Icon on Taskbar' on the Options menu. Alternately, you may need to click the 'Show hidden icons' button (Windows taskbar).

To Use the Clipboard Pane

The **Clipboard pane** allows you to cut and paste multiple items from the Office Clipboard. The Office Clipboard holds up to 24 items and is different from the Windows Clipboard, which holds only 1. The following steps use the Clipboard pane to copy the WordArt title from the front cover page for use on other pages. *Why? Using the Clipboard pane to store the WordArt allows you to paste conveniently across pages while making other edits.*

1

- Navigate to the first page of the publication and then display the Home tab.

- Click the Clipboard Dialog Box Launcher to open the Clipboard pane. If any previously copied items appear in the Click an Item to Paste area, click the Clear All button in the Clipboard pane (Figure 10–52).

 Experiment

- Click the Options button (Clipboard pane) to view the choices regarding the display of the pane. Click the scratch area to close the menu.

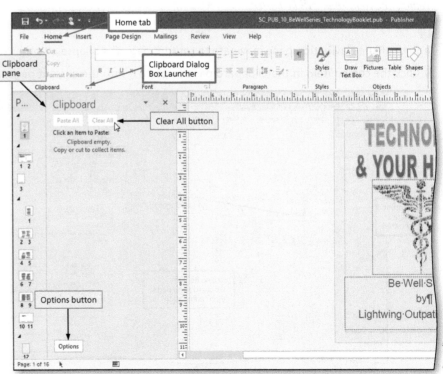

Figure 10–52

- Select and then right-click the WordArt title, TECHNOLOGY AND YOUR HEALTH, on the front cover page to display a shortcut menu and then click Copy on the shortcut menu to copy the WordArt to the Clipboard pane (Figure 10–53).

Q&A What is the purpose of the yellow box that was displayed briefly when I pasted?
Publisher displays a yellow status box when pasting to the Clipboard pane. It reminds you how many paste items you still have room for on the Clipboard.

If I am going to paste the object in the next step, do I have to use the Clipboard pane?
If you are sure that you will make no other edits until you paste the object, then you do not need to use the Clipboard pane; however, if you are making changes to various pages, it is a good idea to keep the pane open so that you do not lose the copy.

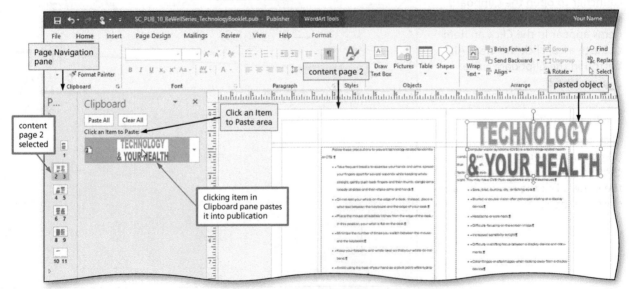

Figure 10–53

To Paste from the Clipboard Pane

The following step pastes from the Clipboard pane. *Why? Pasting from the Clipboard pane allows you to preview the item that will be pasted.*

- In the Page Navigation pane, navigate to content page 2. Collapse all other sections in the Page Navigation pane.

- Click the copied item in the Clipboard pane to paste it into the current pages in the publication (Figure 10–54).

Figure 10–54

Other Ways

1. Click button attached to right edge of item in Clipboard pane, click Paste on menu

To Edit the WordArt

The following steps rotate, move, resize, and align the WordArt to create a sidebar.

1 With the pasted WordArt still selected, click the Rotate button (Home tab | Arrange group) and then click 'Rotate Left 90°' in the Rotate gallery.

2 Display the WordArt Tools Format tab.

3 Resize the WordArt object to approximately 8 by 1.25 inches.

4 Move the WordArt object to a location left of the text box on page 2. For horizontal alignment, click the Align button (WordArt Tools Format tab | Arrange group) and then click Align Left on the Align menu to align the object with the left edge of the page. For vertical alignment, use the pink alignment guide to center it with the text box (Figure 10–55).

BTW

Clipboard Options
You can turn on a shortcut key to display the Office Clipboard. Click the Options button at the bottom of the Clipboard pane and then click 'Show Office Clipboard When CTRL+C Pressed Twice' on the Options menu. You then can access the Office Clipboard while copying by pressing CTRL+C twice.

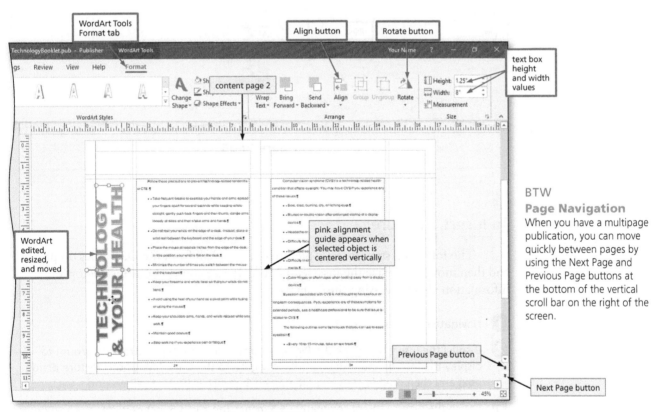

Figure 10–55

BTW

Page Navigation
When you have a multipage publication, you can move quickly between pages by using the Next Page and Previous Page buttons at the bottom of the vertical scroll bar on the right of the screen.

To Copy and Paste the Sidebar

The following steps copy the sidebar from content page 2 and paste it to each of the verso content pages. Pasting from the Clipboard keeps the exact size, shape, and location of the object for each page.

1 With the WordArt object still selected, press CTRL+C to copy it to the Clipboard pane.

2 Navigate to content page 4.

3 In the Clipboard pane, click the newly copied object to paste it on the current page.

4 Repeat this process for pages 6, 8, and 10 (Figure 10–56). (Note that depending on your printer and other settings, your page 10 may display a different amount of text.)

5 Close the Clipboard pane.

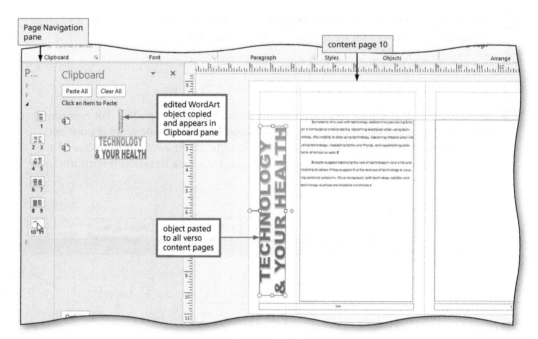

Figure 10–56

To Insert a Picture

The following steps insert a picture of an eyeball from the Data Files on page 3 and then move and resize the inserted picture. Please contact your instructor for information about accessing the Data Files.

1 Navigate to content page 3.

2 Display the Insert tab. Click the Pictures button (Insert tab | Illustrations group) to display the Insert Picture dialog box. Navigate to the Data Files (Insert Picture dialog box) and then double-click the file named Support_PUB_10_EyeRays.png.

3 Resize the picture to approximately 4.5 inches tall and 4.5 inches wide.

4 Display the Picture Tools Format tab, if necessary. Click the Recolor button (Picture Tools Format tab | Adjust group) to display the Recolor gallery and then click 'RGB (174, 233, 175), Accent color 2 Light' (second color in the third row) to change the color of the selected picture to a shade of green.

5 Move the picture vertically on page 3 as shown in Figure 10–57 and then use the Align button (Picture Tools Format tab | Arrange group) to align the picture on the right edge of the page.

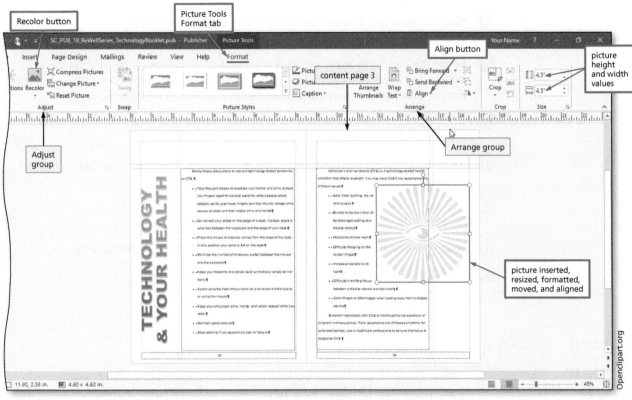

Figure 10–57

To Insert More Pictures

The following steps insert pictures from the Data Files on the other recto pages. As you resize and move the pictures, use the Measurement pane as necessary. Please contact your instructor for information about accessing the Data Files.

1 Navigate to content page 5 and then insert the picture named Support_PUB_10_ComputerWorkspace.png.

2 Resize the picture to approximately 3.33 inches tall by 4.3 inches wide.

Q&A What if I cannot get the height and width values to match exactly?
You can display the Size sheet in the Format Picture dialog box by clicking the Size Dialog Box Launcher (Picture Tools Format tab | Size group) and then remove the check mark from the 'Lock aspect ratio' check box (Format Picture dialog box). Then, try to set the height and width values again.

3 Align the picture with the right margin and position it vertically so that four lines of text appear above it.

4 Navigate to content page 7 and then insert the picture named Support_PUB_10_MusicalEar.png.

5 Resize the picture to approximately 5 inches tall by 3 inches wide. (If necessary, remove the check mark from the 'Lock aspect ratio' check box (Format Picture dialog box) so that you can specify the exact height and width measurements.)

6 Align the picture with the right margin and position it vertically so that five lines of text appear above it.

7 Navigate to content page 9 and then insert the picture named Support_PUB_10_DistractedWalking.png.

8 Resize the picture to approximately 4 inches tall by 4 inches wide. (If necessary, remove the check mark from the 'Lock aspect ratio' check box (Format Picture dialog box) so that you can specify the exact height and width measurements.)

9 Use the Recolor button (Picture Tools Format tab | Adjust group) to change the color of the picture to Grayscale.

10 Align the picture with the right margin and position it vertically so that six lines of text appear above it.

11 Navigate to content page 11 and then insert the picture named Support_PUB_10_HappySun.png.

12 Resize the picture to approximately 4.14 inches tall and 4.25 inches wide.

13 Align the picture with the lower-right margins of the page.

To Change Text Wrapping Options

The Wrap Text gallery enables you to change how text wraps around a picture, including options such as tight, top and bottom, and square wrapping. The following steps increase the distance between the text and picture using text wrapping layout options. **Why?** *With large pictures and small text, the normal wrapping distance may seem too close.*

- Navigate to content page 3 and select the picture of the eye.

- Display the Picture Tools Format tab, if necessary. Click the Wrap Text button (Picture Tools Format tab | Arrange group) to display the Wrap Text gallery (Figure 10–58).

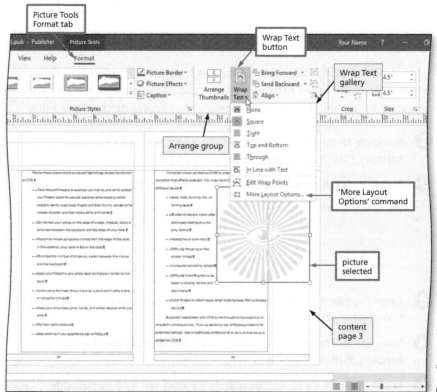

Figure 10–58

Openclipart.org

- Click 'More Layout Options' in the Wrap Text gallery to display the Format Picture dialog box.

- In the Distance from text area in the Layout sheet, remove the check mark from the Automatic check box (Format Picture dialog box).

- Click the Left up arrow as many times as necessary to increase the distance to 0.24 inches (Figure 10–59).

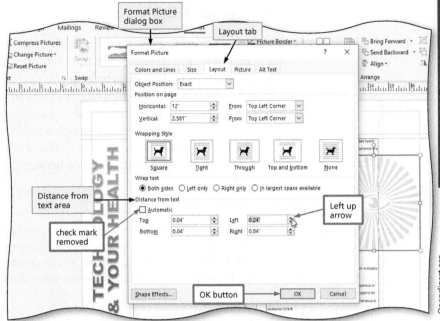

Figure 10–59

Openclipart.org

- Click OK to apply the setting to the selected picture (Figure 10–60).

Experiment

- Click the Undo button on the Quick Access Toolbar to view the text wrapping before the change. Click the Redo button on the Quick Access Toolbar to compare the text wrapping after the change.

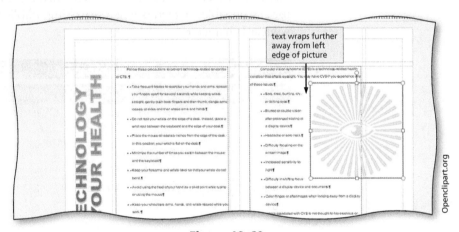

Figure 10–60

Openclipart.org

- Repeat this process of increasing the distance from the left to 0.24 inches for the pictures on pages 5, 7, and 9.

Q&A Why not format the picture on page 11 also?
No text appears on page 11 to the left of the picture.

Break Point: If you want to take a break, this is a good place to do so. You can exit Publisher now. To resume later, start Publisher, open the file called SC_PUB_10_BeWellSeries_TechnologyBooklet.pub, and continue following the steps from this location forward.

Find and Replace

Many applications provide you the capability to find or search for specific characters. Most also allow you to search for and then replace text. Publisher's Find and Replace commands use a pane to help you determine search parameters and how the replacement will be made. For example, you can search for matches that use whole words only or occurrences that match in case (i.e., uppercase or lowercase). You also can search forward or backward through a publication, as well as search the publication in its entirety. In Publisher, you have to find a search string one occurrence at a time. The Replace command offers a choice between replacing one occurrence at a time or replacing all occurrences.

CONSIDER THIS

What are global tools?

Publisher tools that help you locate information in large-scale publications are called global tools. Use find and search techniques to make consistent corrections. Replace overused words or find better terms with synonyms from the built-in thesaurus. Create manual page breaks to make content flow better and keep paragraphs together. Insert bookmarks at logical places in the publication that you may need to locate frequently. Bookmarks are discussed later in this module.

You can search for individual characters, symbols, spaces, formatting marks, or entire words and phrases. Table 10–1 displays some of the wildcard and formatting marks for which you can search. A **wildcard** is a character that may be substituted for any possible characters when searching. Publisher uses the ? (question mark) as a wildcard character.

Table 10–1 Wildcard and Format Searching			
Search Characters	**Searches For**	**Example**	**Finds**
?	wildcard	s?t	sat, sit, subset, stalwart, etc.
^^	caret	^^	next occurrence of ^
^?	question mark	^?	next occurrence of a question mark
^n	soft return	^n	next occurrence of a soft return
^(number)	search for ASCII character	^233	next occurrence of é
^p	hard return	^pTo	new line that begins with the word To, Today, etc.
^t	tab character	^t^t	two tabs together
^w	white space	^w	next occurrence of any kind of white space, including tabs

To Use the Find Command

Sometimes, you may want to find an occurrence of a certain character or phrase in a long publication. *Why? Using the Find feature in Publisher is faster than reading through the entire publication and attempting to locate text manually.* The following steps use the Find command to locate the word, follow.

- Navigate to content page 1.
- Display the Home tab.
- Click the Find button (Home tab | Editing group) to open the Find and Replace pane.

Q&A What if the Find menu is displayed?
You clicked the Find arrow instead of the Find button. Click Find on the Find menu to open the Find and Replace pane.

- In the Search for box in the Find and Replace pane, type **follow** to enter the search text (Figure 10–61).

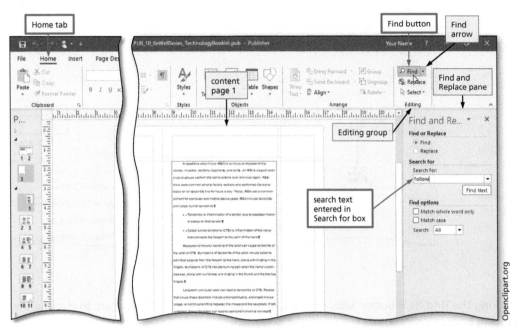

Figure 10–61

②

- Click the Find Next button in the Find and Replace pane to display the first occurrence of the search text in the publication.

- Press F9 to zoom to 100% (Figure 10–62).

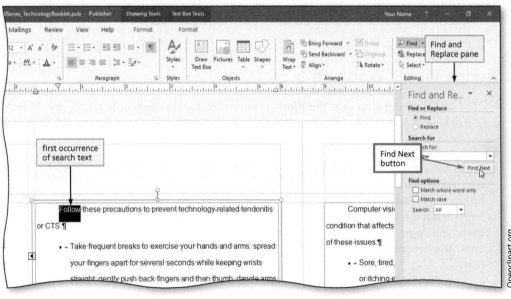

Figure 10–62

③

- Click the Find Next button again to display the next occurrence of the search text in the publication (Figure 10–63).

Q&A

Why did Publisher find the word, following?

With none of the check boxes selected in the Find and Replace pane, Publisher looks for any sequence of the letters, follow. For example, it also would find the words, follows or followed, with any combination of lowercase and uppercase letters.

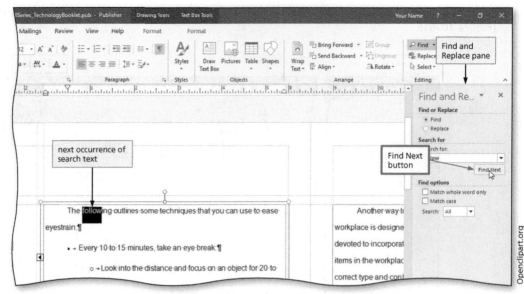

Figure 10–63

 4

- Continue clicking the Find Next button until no more occurrences of the search text are found and then click OK (Publisher dialog box) to indicate that the searching is finished.

 **Experiment**

- Enter some of the examples from Table 10–1 to search for formatting characters and to use wildcards.

Other Ways
1. Press CTRL+F, enter search text in Find and Replace pane, click Find Next button

To Find Whole Words Only

The following step uses the Find command to locate the whole word, eye. **Why?** *Searching for the whole word will omit any of its other forms, such as eyes or eyesight.*

1

- Select the current text in the Search for box in the Find and Replace pane and then type **eye** to enter the new search text.

- Select the 'Match whole word only' check box so that it displays a check mark.

- Click the Find Next button to locate the first occurrence of the whole word of the search text (Figure 10–64).

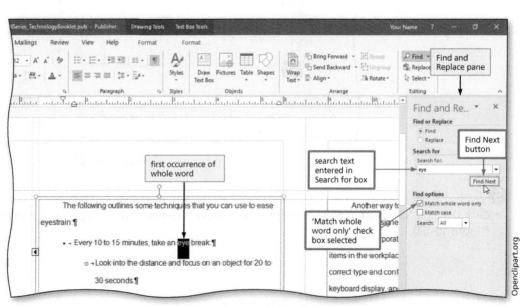

Figure 10–64

Q&A Do I need to start at the first page of my publication?
No, Publisher will search from the current location and continue searching all text boxes on all pages. For this reason, your screen may display a different occurrence of the search text.

To Use the Replace Command

Sometimes, you may want to make changes to a character or set of characters across multiple locations in a publication. *Why? A date or place may change, and you need to make sure you locate and change all of the occurrences, or you may have misused a word throughout the publication.* In the Technology & Your Health main article, you notice that the word, addition, was used instead of 'addiction' in the phrase, technology addiction. The following steps use the Replace command to replace occurrences of the text, technology addition, with the text, technology addiction.

- In the Find and Replace pane, click the Replace option button to display the Replace with settings.

- Select the current text in the Search for box and then type `technology addition` to enter the new search text.

- Press TAB to move to the Replace with text box.

- Type `technology addiction` in the Replace with box to specify the replacement text.

- If necessary, click to place a check mark in the 'Match whole word only' check box.

- Click the Find Next button (Figure 10–65).

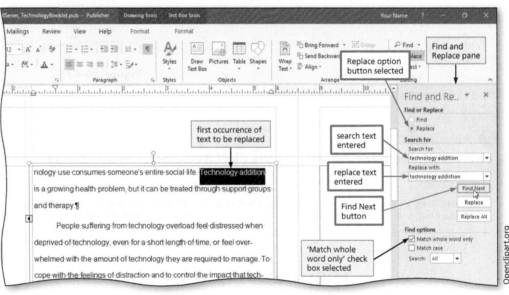

Figure 10–65

- Click the Replace button to replace the current selection and locate the next occurrence of the search text (Figure 10–66).

Q&A What does the Match case check box do?
When you select the Match case check box, Publisher will find only the exact capitalization of the occurrence. For example, it would differentiate between School and school.

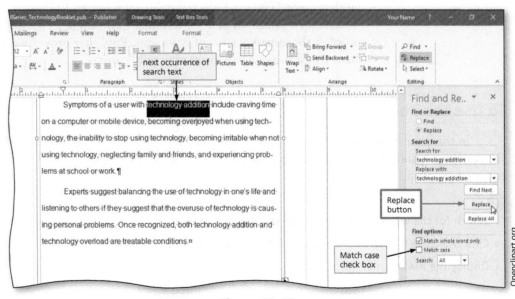

Figure 10–66

Openclipart.org

3

- Click the Replace All button to replace all of the other occurrences in the publication (Figure 10–67).

Can I always use the Replace All button? No. You must be extremely careful about specifying exact text and parameters in the Find and Replace pane. Do not click the Replace All button unless you absolutely are sure that your search term will not be misinterpreted.

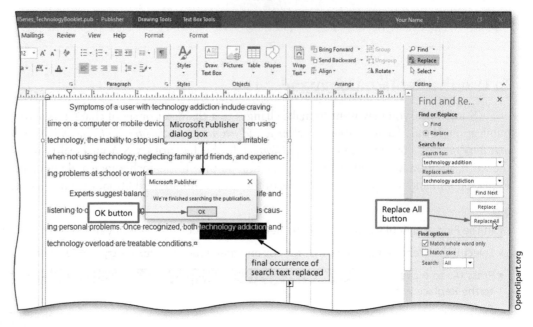

Figure 10–67

4

- When Publisher finishes replacing the text, click OK (Microsoft Publisher dialog box) to close the dialog box.

Other Ways

1. Press CTRL+H, enter search text, enter replacement text, click Replace button in Find and Replace pane
2. Click Replace button (Home tab | Editing group), enter search text, enter replacement text, click Replace button in Find and Replace pane

Thesaurus

When writing, you may discover that you used the same word in multiple locations or that a word you used was not quite appropriate. In these instances, you will want to look up a **synonym** or a word similar in meaning to the duplicate or inappropriate word. A **thesaurus** is a list of synonyms. Publisher provides a thesaurus so that you have a tool to assist you in creating publications.

To Use the Thesaurus

In this project, you would like to find a synonym for the word, fixed, in the second paragraph on page 9 of the content section. *Why? You would like to find a more suitable and descriptive term.* The following steps show how to find an appropriate synonym.

1

- Search for the word, fixed, in the Find and Replace pane.
- Click the Close button in the Find and Replace pane to close the pane.
- Display the Review tab.

Publisher Module 10

- With the word, fixed, selected, click the Thesaurus button (Review tab | Proofing group) to open the Thesaurus pane (Figure 10–68).

 Experiment

- Scroll in the Thesaurus pane to display more synonyms.

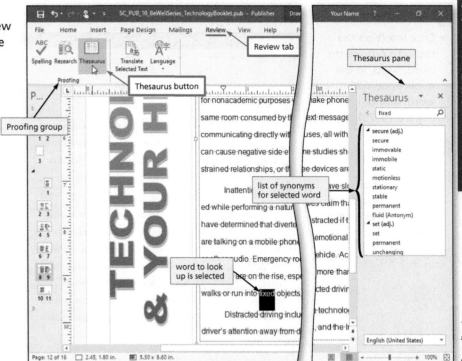

Figure 10–68

2

- In the Thesaurus pane, point to the word, motionless, to display an arrow and then click the arrow to display a menu of options (Figure 10–69).

Q&A What if the synonyms menu does not display a suitable word?

The Thesaurus pane displays many synonyms; however, if you do not find a suitable word, you can click any word in the pane to look up other synonyms. You also can look up an **antonym**, or a word with an opposite meaning.

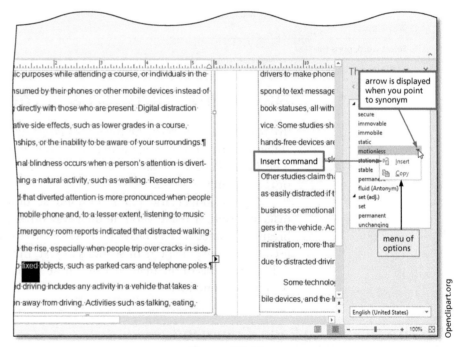

Figure 10–69

- Click Insert on the menu to replace the word, fixed, in the publication with the word, motionless (Figure 10–70).

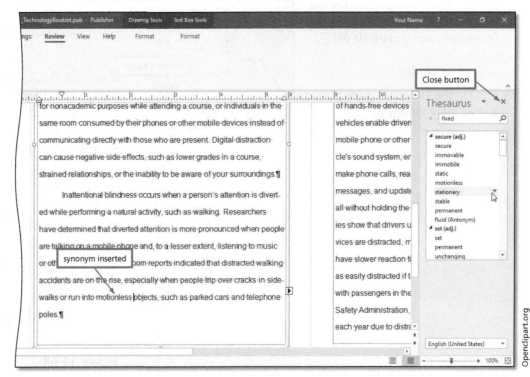

Figure 10–70

- Click the Close button in the Thesaurus pane title bar to close the pane.

Other Ways

1. Select word, press SHIFT+F7

Navigating through a Large-Scale Publication

To make it easier to navigate through a large publication and check pagination, Publisher provides commands that help both designers and viewers of the publication. The 'Go to Page' command allows you to move quickly to a given page number to edit or read the information.

By breaking a large publication into sections, chapters, or modules, you also make it easier for readers to find their way through the publication. You can insert breaks in connected text boxes to move text to the next page. Breaks sometimes are used to delineate chapters or sections of text. In this module, you will create breaks to indicate sections of the main article. Those sections, with new headings, will be used in the table of contents.

To Use the 'Go to Page' Command

In longer publications, you may find the Page Navigation pane cumbersome, especially if you have to scroll through many sections and pages. The 'Go to Page' command displays a dialog box that allows you to enter the desired page number in the publication; however, you must use sequential page numbers related to the overall publication. *Why?* *Many publications have duplicate page numbers, such as a page 1 for each section; therefore, you must use the page number as shown on the Publisher status bar.*

The following steps use the 'Go to Page' command to move quickly to the sixth page of the publication.

- Display the Home tab.

- Click the Find arrow (Home tab | Editing group) to display the Find menu (Figure 10–71).

Q&A

What if the Find and Replace pane opens?

You clicked the Find button instead of the Find arrow. Close the Find and Replace pane and then click the Find arrow.

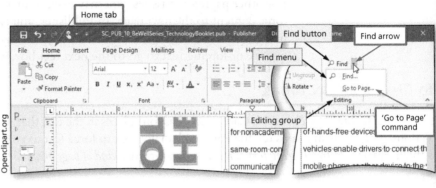

Figure 10–71

- Click 'Go to Page' on the Find menu to display the Go To Page dialog box.

- Type 10 to replace the text in the 'Go to page' text box (Go To Page dialog box) (Figure 10–72).

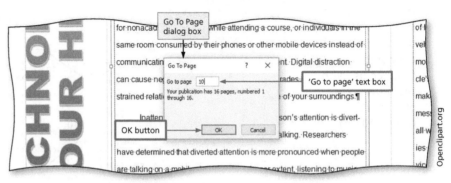

Figure 10–72

3

- Click OK to go to the entered page.

- Scroll to the bottom of the page (Figure 10–73).

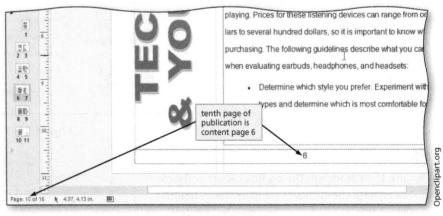

Figure 10–73

Other Ways

1. Press CTRL+G, enter page number, click OK (Go To Page dialog box)

Page Breaks

It is important to look at large-scale publications with an eye for appropriate page or column breaks. You do not want a heading to be displayed without its subordinate content. In some booklets, such as a schedule, you may want mornings, afternoons, or days all on the same page. You might decide a column should not break in the middle of a short paragraph.

Widow and orphan control is turned on automatically for connected text boxes. A **widow** is the last line of a paragraph appearing by itself at the top of a page. An **orphan** is the first line of a paragraph appearing by itself at the bottom of a page.

For other pagination issues, you may need to manually break a page or column to force content to the next page. In Publisher, you can make decisions about keeping paragraphs together, such as bulleted lists; keeping lines together, such as for extended quotes; or forcing text to go to the next text box, which is similar to a page break.

To Create a Text Break

The Technology & Health Care article has four places in the text that would be better positioned as new sections. The following steps use the Paragraph dialog box to force text to go to the next text box, which in this case is the next page. *Why? Forcing text to the next page creates a kind of page break as you create sections within the main article.*

- Scroll up the current page and then position the insertion point at the beginning of the paragraph that begins, With the growing use of earbuds... (Figure 10–74).

Q&A Will the setting apply before or after the insertion point?
The setting applies to the entire paragraph at the position of the insertion point, in this case following the insertion point.

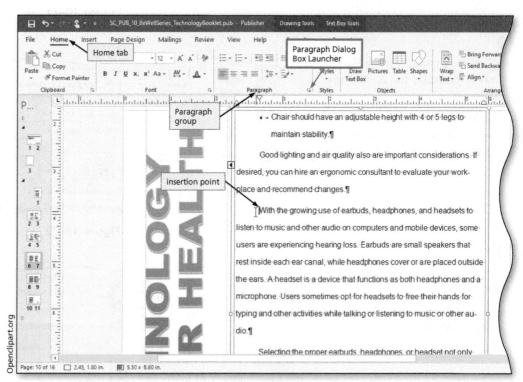

Figure 10–74

- Click the Paragraph Dialog Box Launcher (Home tab | Paragraph group) to display the Paragraph dialog box.

- Click the Line and Paragraphs Breaks tab (Paragraph dialog box) to display the commands related to breaks.

- Select the 'Start in next text box' check box so that it contains a check mark (Figure 10–75).

Q&A Could I press CTRL+ENTER to insert a section or page break as I do in word processing programs?
Pressing CTRL+ENTER inserts a new page and a break in the publication. In this case, you only want to move the paragraph to the next text box.

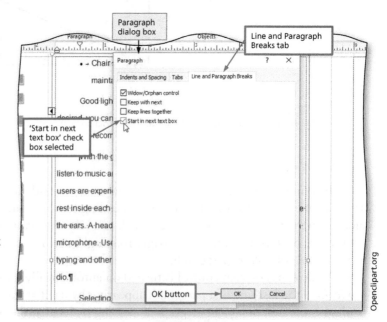

Figure 10–75

3

- Click OK to apply the setting, which moves the text at the location of the insertion point to the next text box.

- Zoom to whole page to view the pagination (Figure 10–76).

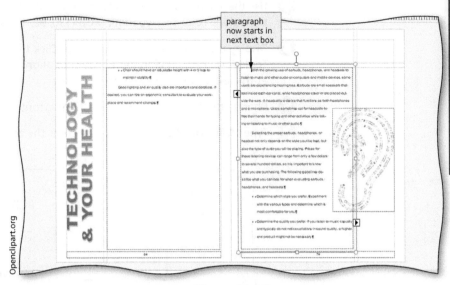

Openclipart.org

Figure 10–76

To Insert Another Break

The following steps create one more break within the main article by using the Paragraph dialog box.

1 Press CTRL+G to display the Go To Page dialog box. Type   12   in the 'Go to page' box (Go To Page dialog box). Click OK to navigate to page 12.

2 Position the insertion point immediately to the left of the last paragraph on the page that begins with the phrase, Digital distraction is the practice of.

3 Click the Paragraph Dialog Box Launcher (Home tab | Paragraph group) and then click the Line and Paragraph Break tab (Paragraph dialog box) to display the commands related to breaks.

4 Select the 'Start in next text box' check box and then click OK to apply the setting.

To Create a Section Heading

The following steps create a text box to use as a section heading for the main article in the content pages.

1 Navigate to content page 1.

2 Draw a text box at the top of the page. Resize it to fit the blank area between the margin guides with dimensions of approximately 1.1 inches tall by 5.5 inches wide, as shown in Figure 10–77.

3 Display the Drawing Tools Format tab. Use the Shape Fill arrow (Drawing Tools Format tab | Shape Styles group) to fill the text box with the 'Accent 2 (RGB (120, 218, 122)) Lighter 60%' color (third color in the third row).

④ Use the Shape Outline arrow (Drawing Tools Format tab | Shape Styles group) to change the outline color to 'Hyperlink (RGB (130, 92, 158))' (sixth color in the first row).

⑤ Display the Text Box Tools Format tab. Click the 'Align Center Left' button (Text Box Tools Format tab | Alignment group) to align the insertion point in the vertical center at the left edge of the text box.

⑥ Change the font size to 36 point and the font to Rockwell.

⑦ Type **Tendonitis & RSIs** to enter the text in the text box (Figure 10–77).

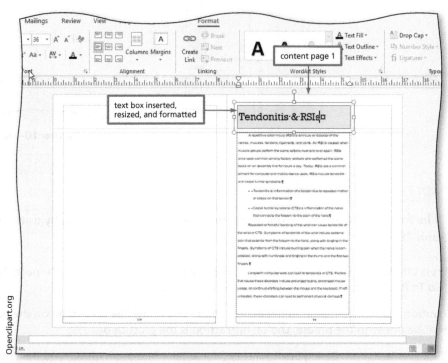

Figure 10–77

To Copy and Paste the Section Heading

The following steps copy the section heading to other pages in the main article.

① Click the border of the section heading on content page 1 to select the entire text box.

② If desired, open the Clipboard pane. Press CTRL+C to copy the shape.

③ Navigate to content page 3 and then press CTRL+V to paste the heading. Change the text to CVS, Pain, & Fatigue.

④ Navigate to content page 7 and then paste the heading. Change the text to Hearing Loss.

⑤ Navigate to content page 9 and then paste the heading. Change the text to Distraction & Addiction (Figure 10–78).

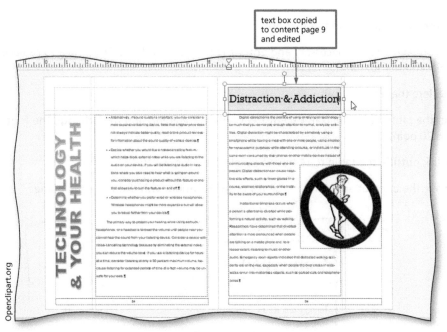

text box copied
to content page 9
and edited

Figure 10–78

Updating the Table of Contents

Table 10–2 displays the table of contents for the main article, based on the headings you inserted.

Item	Page Number
Table 10–2 Table of Contents	
Tendonitis & RSIs	1
CVS, Pain, & Fatigue	3
Hearing Loss	7
Distraction & Addiction	9

To Update the Table of Contents

The following steps update the table of contents on the second page of the front matter, which is the third physical page in the publication.

1 Press CTRL+G to display the Go To Page dialog box.

2 Type 3 in the Go to page box (Go To Page dialog box), click OK to display page 3, zoom to approximately 80%, and then scroll to the top of the page.

3 In the top row of the table, select the text and then click the Font Dialog Box Launcher to display the Font dialog box.

4 In the Font dialog box, change the font to Rockwell and the font size to 36, remove the bold format by clicking Regular in the Font style list, remove the check mark from the All caps check box in the Effects area, and then click OK to specify formatting for text to be entered.

5 Type **Contents** in the text box.

6 Zoom and scroll as necessary and enter the information from Table 10–2 to replace the placeholder text in the table.

7 Delete the unused rows.

8 In the table, select all cells except the Contents heading and then change the font size to 20 point.

9 Click outside the table to remove the selection (Figure 10–79).

10 Save the booklet again in the same storage location with the same file name.

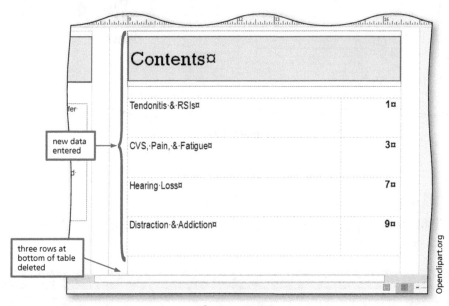

Figure 10–79

Bookmarks

A **bookmark** is a physical location in a publication that you name for reference purposes. Used to organize large publications, a named bookmark allows you to display its associated text quickly, instead of scrolling through the publication pages to locate an object or text. Bookmarks display as small flags in page layout only; they do not appear when you print publications. Bookmarks are saved, however, when the publication is saved. They serve as a searchable reference when viewing the publication online and can be referenced as a link within the Publisher publication and when converting the publication to the PDF format.

To Create a Bookmark

The following steps create a bookmark for the Tendonitis & RSIs heading in the main article. *Why? When you link the table of contents to that part of the publication, bookmarks will help.*

- Navigate to content page 1.

- Display the Insert tab.

- Click the Bookmark button (Insert tab | Links group) to display the Bookmark dialog box.
- Type **Tendonitis & RSIs** in the Bookmark name text box (Bookmark dialog box) (Figure 10–80).

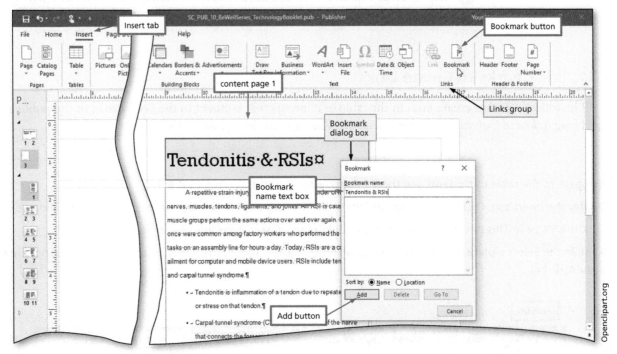

Figure 10–80

Q&A What is the best way to navigate to content page 1?

It depends on your personal preference. You can use the Page Navigation pane or press CTRL+G to display the Go To Page dialog box. If you use the dialog box, remember to enter the page number related to the entire publication, not the content page number.

2

- Click the Add button to insert the bookmark in the publication.
- Drag the bookmark to a location just to the left of the heading (Figure 10–81).

Q&A Can I edit a bookmark?

You can double-click a bookmark to redisplay to the Bookmark dialog box. From there, you can add, delete, sort, rename, or navigate to other bookmarks.

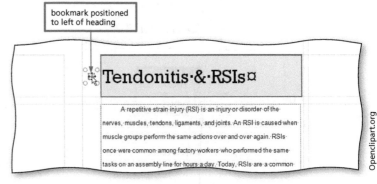

Figure 10–81

To Create More Bookmarks

The following steps create additional bookmarks for each portion of the publication that is referenced in the table of contents.

1 Navigate to content page 3.

2 Click the Bookmark button (Insert tab | Links group) to display the Bookmark dialog box. Type **CVS, Pain, & Fatigue** in the Bookmark name text box (Bookmark dialog box) and then click the Add button to insert the bookmark.

3 Drag the bookmark to a location just left of the heading.

4 Repeat Steps 1 through 3 to add bookmarks for Hearing Loss on content page 7 and Distraction & Addiction on content page 9.

To Use Bookmarks to Create Links

The following steps create links in the table of contents that connect to the bookmarks in the publication. *Why? Using links and bookmarks together provide quick navigation through long publications.*

- Navigate to the table of contents and then drag to select the text, Tendonitis & RSIs.
- Display the Insert tab. Click the Link button (Insert tab | Links group) to display the Insert Hyperlink dialog box.
- Click the 'Place in This Document' button in the Link to bar (Insert Hyperlink dialog box).
- Scroll in the Select a place in this document area and then click 'Tendonitis & RSIs' to select the desired bookmark (Figure 10–82).

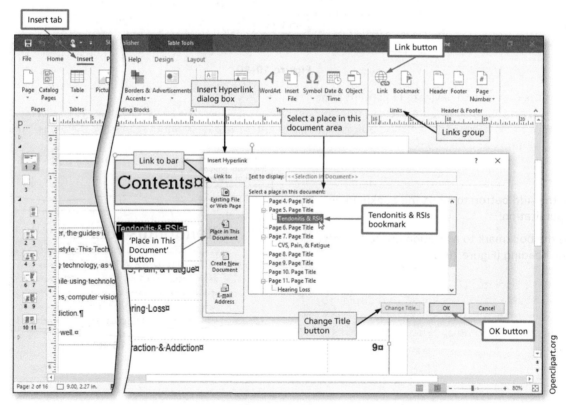

Figure 10–82

Q&A What is the purpose of the Change Title button?

Each page of a publication has an internal bookmark initially named Page Title. You can edit that name by selecting the Page Title in the list and then clicking the Change Title button. That bookmark name also would appear in the title bar of a browser should the publication be used on the web.

2

- Click OK to create the link for the selected text (Figure 10–83).

3

- Repeat Steps 1 and 2 for each of the entries in the table of contents. Link each item to its corresponding bookmark name in the Insert Hyperlink dialog box.

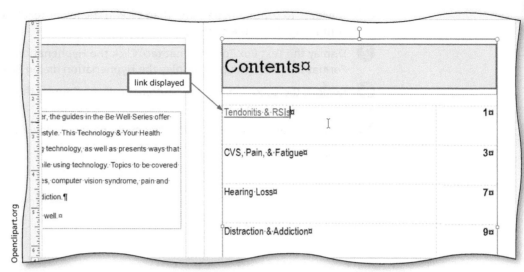

Figure 10–83

Other Ways

1. Select text, press CTRL+K, click 'Place in This Document' button (Insert Hyperlink dialog box), select bookmark, click OK

To Test a Link

The following step tests one of the links. ***Why?*** *You always should test your links to make sure they navigate to the correct location.*

1

- In the table of contents, CTRL+click the Hearing Loss link to jump to the bookmark (Figure 10–84).

Q&A Why did the pointer shape change to a hand when I pressed CTRL? When positioned over a link, the pointer changes to a hand as soon as you press CTRL.

Experiment

- Redisplay to the table of contents and check the other links.

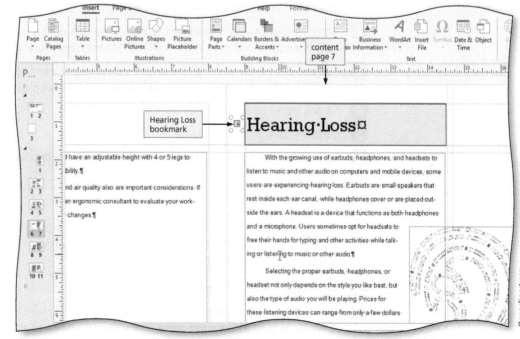

Figure 10–84

To Hyphenate the Publication

Long stories connected across text boxes need to be checked for proper hyphenation. While you should apply all of the hyphenation rules, you particularly should check the publication to avoid hyphenating the first or last line of a paragraph.

The following steps check the publication for hyphenation.

1 Navigate to content page 1 and then click in the lower text box to select the text box containing the article content.

2 Display the Text Box Tools Format tab. Click the Hyphenation button (Text Box Tools Format tab | Text group) to display the Hyphenation dialog box.

3 Remove the check mark in the 'Automatically hyphenate this story' check box (Hyphenate dialog box).

4 Click the Manual button to begin the hyphenation, following hyphenation rules.

Q&A What are the hyphenation rules?
Some of the most common rules include the following:
- Hyphenate only at standard syllable breaks.
- Do not change the hyphen location in a word that already is hyphenated.
- Avoid hyphenating words in the first or last line of a paragraph.
- Avoid hyphenations that leave only two letters at the beginning or ending of a line.
- Avoid hyphenating two lines in a row.
- Avoid hyphenating a line across text boxes or pages.
- Avoid hyphenating proper nouns.

5 When the hyphenation process is complete, click OK (Microsoft Publisher dialog box).

To Check the Publication for Spelling and Design Errors

The following steps check the publication for spelling and design errors and then save it.

1 Display the Review tab. Click the Spelling button (Review tab | Proofing group) to start checking the spelling in the publication. Choose to ignore names and acronyms.

2 When Publisher asks if you want to check the rest of the publication, click the Yes button and finish checking the spelling. If necessary, close the Master Page view.

3 Run the Design Checker. Ignore any design errors related to too much space at a margin or objects that may approach a nonprintable region.

4 Fix any other errors found by the Design Checker.

5 Close the Design Checker pane.

6 Save the booklet again in the same storage location with the same file name.

BTW
Distributing a Document
Instead of printing and distributing a hard copy of a document, you can distribute the document electronically. Options include sending the document via email; posting it on cloud storage (such as OneDrive) and sharing the file with others; posting it on social media, a blog, or other website; and sharing a link associated with an online location of the document. You also can create and share a PDF or XPS image of the document, so that users can view the file in Acrobat Reader or XPS Viewer instead of in Publisher.

To Save in the PDF Format

To review and test the links in a different application, the following steps save the Publisher file in the PDF format.

1 Click File on ribbon to open Backstage view.

2 Click Export in Backstage view to display the Export screen and then click the 'Create PDF/XPS' button in the right pane in the Export screen to display the Publish as PDF or XPS dialog box.

3 Navigate to the desired save location.

4 If necessary, type `SC_PUB_10_BeWellSeries_TechnologyBooklet` in the File name box (Publish as PDF or XPS dialog box) as the file name.

5 Click the Publish button to save the publication in PDF format.

To Navigate with Bookmarks in a PDF File

The bookmarks and links you created in the Publisher file automatically are created in the PDF file. PDF files open using an application such as Adobe Reader or Adobe Acrobat. The following steps open the PDF file and display the table of contents in the PDF file. **Why?** *The table of contents retains the links you created in Publisher.*

- Open a File Explorer window and then navigate to the location of your saved files.

- Double-click the PDF file named SC_PUB_10_BeWellSeries_ TechnologyBooklet.pdf to open it in the Adobe app.

- If necessary, click the Maximize button in the Adobe window to maximize the window. Note that your screen may differ, depending on your version of Adobe.

- Zoom to view the entire page (Figure 10–85).

Q&A

My reader does not have a 'Show next page' button. What is the best way to navigate in the PDF file? Your application may use the RIGHT ARROW key to move down through the document, page by page.

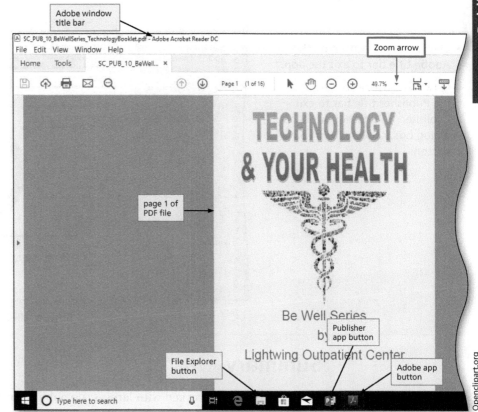

Figure 10–85

Openclipart.org

- Navigate to page 3 in the 16-page publication (Figure 10–86).

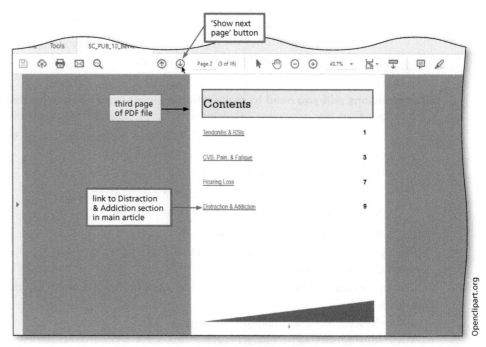

Figure 10–86

Openclipart.org

3

- Click the Distraction & Addiction link on the table of contents page to navigate to that page in the booklet (Figure 10–87).

4

- Click the Close button on the Adobe title bar to exit the app.

- Click the Close button on the Publisher title bar to exit Publisher. If Publisher displays a dialog box, click the Don't Save button.

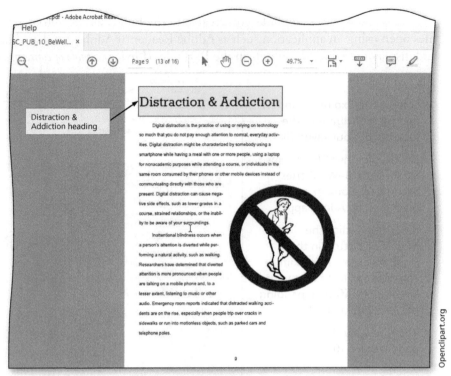

Figure 10–87

Summary

In this module, you worked with large-scale publications by inserting and duplicating pages, assigning page number formatting, set beginning page numbers, and paginating page parts. You learned how to create and work with sections in the Page Navigation pane. After inserting the front matter, you created ruler guides and linked text boxes for the content pages of the booklet. Next, you used global editing tools, such as find and replace, the thesaurus, and the 'Go to Page' command. You created breaks in the publication. Finally, you created bookmarks and links to help viewers navigate from the table of contents to various pages.

CONSIDER THIS: PLAN AHEAD

What decisions will you need to make when creating your next large-scale publication?

Use these guidelines as you complete the assignments in this chapter and create your own publications outside of this class.

1. After deciding on the purpose and audience of a large-scale publication, design the layout, insert pages, and create sections.
2. Use appropriate pagination and be consistent in its placement.
   a) Use lowercase Roman numerals for the front matter.
   b) Use standard Arabic numerals for the content pages.
   c) Decide on page numbering for any end matter material.
3. Apply BorderArt sparingly and purposefully.
4. Ruler guides may be used to help alignment of objects on each page.
5. Insert content and thoroughly proofread.
6. Employ the Find and Replace commands to make consistent changes throughout the publication.
7. Use the thesaurus as necessary.
8. Create bookmarks and links to help with navigation.
9. Proofread again and use the Design Checker.
10. Convert to a PDF file, if necessary.

Apply Your Knowledge

Reinforce the skills and apply the concepts you learned in this module.

Paginating a Large-Scale Publication Template

Note: To complete this assignment, you will be required to use the Data Files. Please contact your instructor for information about accessing the Data Files.

Instructions: Start Publisher. Open the publication, SC_PUB_10-1.pub, which is located in the Data Files. The publication contains 18 blank pages. You are to add sections, page numbering, a border, and section headings to create a template that will be used to for your company's five-year plan. Table 10–3 displays the sections to create and the page numbering formats.

Table 10–3 Pagination for Five-Year Plan Template		
Publication Pages	**Section**	**Page Numbering**
1 – 2	Front cover and inside front cover pages	none
3 – 4	Front matter	i, ii, iii, …
5 – 14	Content pages	1, 2, 3, …
15 – 16	End matter	continuing 1, 2, 3, …
17 – 18	Inside back cover and back cover pages	none

A sample two-page spread is shown in Figure 10–88, along with the Page Navigation pane.

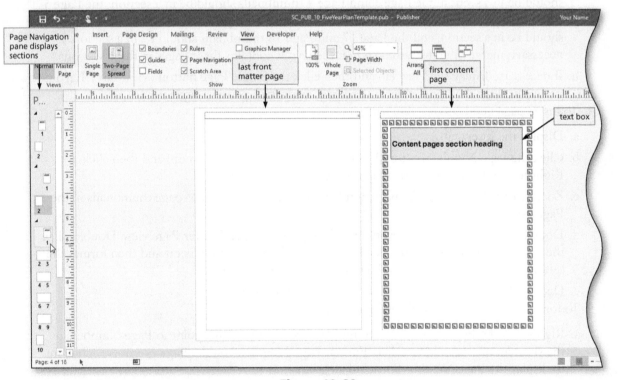

Figure 10–88

Continued >

Apply Your Knowledge *continued*

Perform the following tasks:

1. Click File on the ribbon to open Backstage view, click Save As, and then save the publication using the new file name, SC_PUB_10_FiveYearPlanTemplate.

2. If necessary, display boundaries, rulers, guides, page navigation, and the scratch area by selecting the appropriate check boxes (View tab | Show group).

3. Create sections in the publication as follows:

   a. To create a section for the front cover page and inside front cover page, right-click the Page 3 thumbnail in the Page Navigation pane and then click Insert Section on the shortcut menu.

   b. To create a section for the two front matter pages, right-click the Page 5 thumbnail in the Page Navigation pane and then click Insert Section on the shortcut menu.

   c. To create a section for the 10 content pages, right-click the Page 15 thumbnail in the Page Navigation pane and then click Insert Section on the shortcut menu.

   d. To create a section for the two end matter pages, right-click the Page 17 thumbnail in the Page Navigation pane and then click Insert Section on the shortcut menu.

   e. Practice collapsing and expanding the sections. When finished practicing, be sure that all sections are expanded.

   f. If necessary, display the View tab and then click the 'Two-Page Spread' button (View tab | Layout group) to show the thumbnails in the Page Navigation pane as two-page spreads, if applicable.

   g. Review the thumbnails in the Page Navigation pane. The Page 1 and Page 2 thumbnails should be in a section; the Page 3 and Page 4 thumbnails should be in a section; the Page 5 through Page 14 thumbnails should be in a section; the Page 15 and Page 16 thumbnails should be in a section; and the Page 17 and Page 18 thumbnails should be in a section. If necessary, merge or add sections so that the layout contains these pages in these sections.

   h. If necessary, display the View tab and then click the Single Page button (View tab | Layout group) to show the thumbnails in the Page Navigation pane as single pages.

4. To insert page numbers on every page:

   a. Display the Insert tab.

   b. Click the Page Number button (Insert tab | Header & Footer group) and then click Top Right to insert page numbers in that location on every page.

   c. Zoom to 100% and view the page numbers by clicking the various page thumbnails in the Page Navigation pane.

   d. Double-click the page number on one of the pages to open Master Page view. Double-click the page number format in the header in Master Page view to select it and then format the selected page number format to be bold and use a font size of 12.

   e. Display the Master Page tab and then close Master Page view.

5. To format page numbers for the front matter:

   a. Right-click the Page 3 thumbnail in the Page Navigation pane, point to Page Numbers on the shortcut menu, and then click 'Format Page Numbers' on the Page Numbers submenu to display the Page Number Format dialog box.

   b. Click the Number format arrow (Page Number Format dialog box) and then click 'i, ii, iii, …' in the Number format list.

   c. Click the 'Start this section with' option button and then specify 1 as the starting page number.

   d. Click OK to apply the selected page number format to the pages in the current section.

6. To format page numbers for the content pages:

a. Right-click the fifth page in the Page Navigation pane (which is the first page in the third section), point to Page Numbers on the shortcut menu, and click 'Format Page Numbers' on the Page Numbers submenu to display the Page Number Format dialog box.

b. Click the Number format arrow (Page Number Format dialog box) and then click '1, 2, 3, …' in the list.

c. Click the 'Start this section with' option button and then specify 1 as the starting page number.

d. Click OK to apply the selected page number format to the pages in the current section.

7. To remove page numbers from the section containing the front cover page and inside front cover page and the section containing the inside back cover page and back cover page:

a. Right-click the first page in the Page Navigation pane, point to Master Pages on the shortcut menu, and click None on the Master Pages submenu to remove page numbers from the front cover page.

b. Repeat the previous step for the second page in the Page Navigation pane to remove page numbers from the inside front cover page.

c. Right-click the next-to-the-last page in the Page Navigation pane (which is the seventeenth page), point to Master Pages on the shortcut menu, and then click None on the Master Pages submenu to remove page numbers from the inside back cover page.

d. Repeat the previous step for the last page in the Page Navigation pane (which is the eighteenth page) to remove page numbers from the back cover page.

8. Access Master Page view by clicking the Master Page button (View tab | Views group). If necessary, click the 'Show Whole Page' button on the status bar.

9. Click the Duplicate button (Master Page tab | Master Page group) and name the page, BorderArt, in the Description box (Duplicate Master Page dialog box). Click OK to create a duplicate master page in the Page Navigation pane.

10. To create a border for the content pages, on the duplicate master page:

a. With the duplicate master page selected in the Page Navigation pane, display the Insert tab. Click the Shapes button (Insert tab | Illustrations group) and then click the Rectangle shape.

b. Drag the pointer to draw a rectangle that fills the entire page from the upper-left margin to the lower-right margin. Do not include the page number area.

c. Right-click the rectangle and then click Format AutoShape on the shortcut menu to display the Format AutoShape dialog box.

d. Click the BorderArt button (Format AutoShape dialog box) to display the BorderArt dialog box and then scroll as necessary through the Available Borders list (BorderArt dialog box) to select the 'Eclipsing Squares 2' border.

e. Click OK to select the border and close the BorderArt dialog box.

f. In the Line area (Format AutoShape dialog box), change the color to 'Accent 2 (RGB (192, 80, 77))' (third color in the first row).

g. Click OK to apply the border to the duplicate page.

11. Display the Master Page tab and then close Master Page view.

12. In the Page Navigation pane, collapse all sections except for the third section that includes the 10 content pages.

13. In the Page Navigation pane, right-click the first content page, point to Master Pages on the shortcut menu to display the Master Pages submenu, and click BorderArt (B) on the Master Pages submenu to apply the BorderArt to the current page.

14. Repeat Step 13 for each of the remaining nine content pages.

Continued >

Apply Your Knowledge continued

15. Expand all sections in the Page Navigation pane.

16. To create headings:

    a. On the first page in the Page Navigation pane, draw a text box at the top of the page that is 6.5 inches wide by 1.5 inches tall.

    b. If necessary, display the Drawing Tools Format tab. Use the Shape Fill arrow (Drawing Tools Format tab | Shape Styles group) to fill the text box with the 'Accent 2 (RGB (192, 80, 77)) Lighter 80%' color (third color in the second row).

    c. Use the Shape Outline arrow (Drawing Tools Format tab | Shape Styles group) to change the outline color to 'Accent 1 (RGB (31, 73, 125))' (second color in the first row).

    d. Use the Align button (Drawing Tools Format tab | Arrange group) to align the text box with the top center of the page. (You may need to use the 'Relative to Margin Guides' command on the Align menu first in order to center the text box at the top of the page.)

    e. Display the Text Box Tools Format tab. Click the 'Align Center Left' button (Text Box Tools Format tab | Alignment group) to align the insertion point in the vertical center at the left edge of the text box.

    f. Change the font size to 26 point and the font to Arial Rounded MT Bold.

    g. Type **Front cover page** as the text in the text box.

    h. Click an edge or corner of the text box containing the section heading to select the entire shape. Press CTRL+C to copy the shape. Navigate to the third page in the Page Navigation pane and then paste the heading on the first page of the front matter. If necessary, align the text box with the top center of the page. Change the text in the text box to Front matter section heading.

    i. Navigate to the fifth page in the Page Navigation pane (which is the first content page) and then paste the heading on the first content page. Position the text box below the BorderArt and, if necessary, center it between the margins. Change the text in the text box to Content pages section heading.

    j. Navigate to the fifteenth page in the Page Navigation pane (which is the first end matter page) and then paste the heading on the first page of the end matter. If necessary, align the text box with the top center of the page. Change the text in the text box to End matter section heading.

    k. Navigate to the last page in the Page Navigation pane and then paste the heading on the back cover page. If necessary, align the text box with the top center of the page. Change the text in the text box to Back cover page.

    l. If requested by your instructor, navigate to the second page in the Page Navigation pane, paste the heading on the inside front cover page, and change the text in the text box to your name.

    m. Display the View tab and then click the 'Two-Page Spread' button (View tab | Layout group) to show the thumbnails in the Page Navigation pane as two-page spreads, if applicable.

17. Save the publication again with the same file name and then submit it in the format specified by your instructor.

18. If requested by your instructor, send the publication to your instructor as an email message attachment. Close the publication and exit Publisher.

19. ✺ What are some advantages to creating a template like this one? What other features might you add to make the template even more useful?

Extend Your Knowledge

Extend the skills you learned in this module and experiment with new skills. You may need to use Help to complete the assignment.

Using Baseline Guides

Note: To complete this assignment, you will be required to use the Data Files. Please contact your instructor for information about accessing the Data Files.

Instructions: Start Publisher. Open the publication, SC_PUB_10-2.pub, which is located in the Data Files. You will edit the publication, which discusses baseline guides, to align the text in the two text boxes (Figure 10–89).

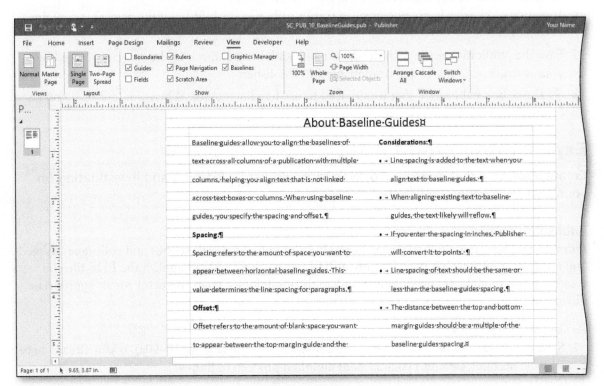

Figure 10–89

Perform the following tasks:

1. Use Help to learn more about baseline guides in Publisher.

2. Click File on the ribbon, click Save As, and then save the template using the new file name, SC_PUB_10_BaselineGuides.pub.

3. To set the baseline guides:

   a. Display the Page Design tab.

   b. Click the Guides button (Page Design tab | Layout group) and then click 'Grid and Baseline Guides' in the Guides gallery to display the Layout Guides dialog box.

   c. Click the Baseline Guides tab. Enter 14 in both the Spacing and Offset boxes (Layout Guides dialog box).

   d. Click OK to close the dialog box.

4. To align the text:

   a. Select all the text in the left text box.

   b. Display the Paragraph dialog box and then, if necessary, click the Indents and Spacing tab.

Continued >

Extend your knowledge *continued*

    c. In the Line spacing area (Paragraph dialog box), change the value in the After paragraphs box to 0.

    d. Select the 'Align text to baseline guides' check box and then click OK to apply the settings to the selected text and close the dialog box.

    e. Drag the bottom of the text box down to resize it so that all its text appears on the page.

    f. Select all the text in the right text box. Repeats Steps 4b, 4c, 4d, and 4e. Click outside the text box to deselect the text.

5. To view the baseline guides:

    a. Display the View tab.

    b. Select the Baselines check box (View tab | Show group).

6. If requested by your instructor, create a third text box at the bottom of the page that contains your name.

7. Save the publication again with the same name and then submit it in the format specified by your instructor. Close the publication and exit Publisher.

8. ✺ Describe a publication that would need to use baseline guides. When would it be better to create linked text boxes? Why?

Expand Your World

Create a solution that uses cloud or web technologies by learning and investigating on your own from general guidance.

Publishing Online

Instructions: You would like to post your publication online for your friends and colleagues to see. You notice that most web services require a PDF file, so you decide to publish the PDF file you created in this module. If you did not complete the module, see your instructor for an appropriate file to use.

Perform the following tasks:

1. Start a browser and then navigate to the issuu.com website (Figure 10–90a). If you already have an issuu account, sign into your account and then proceed to Step 4.

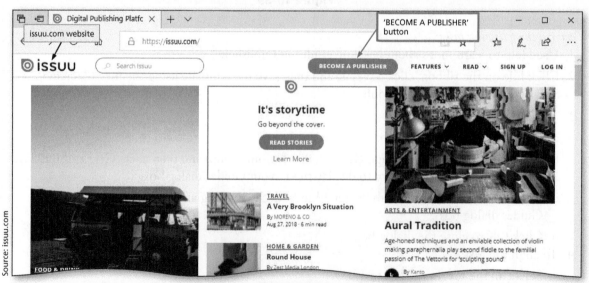

Figure 10–90a

2. Click the 'BECOME A PUBLISHER' button to display a webpage with publishing options, including a starter free trial, a premium free trial, or a free plan.

3. Scroll to the bottom of the webpage and then click the free plan link to display a page requesting information (such as your email address) for a free account. Enter the required information and then click the 'CREATE FREE ACCOUNT' button.

4. Once you have created or signed in to your account, click the 'SELECT FILE TO UPLOAD' button, navigate to the location in which you stored the files for this module, and then double-click the PDF file named SC_PUB_10_BeWellSeries_TechnologyBooklet.pdf.

5. Enter a title for your publication in the Title text box (Figure 10–90b). If desired, enter a description of the publication in the Description text box. Scroll through and fill in other options about the publication, as desired.

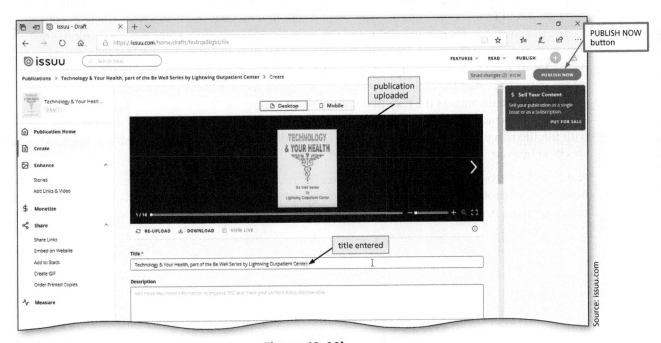

Figure 10–90b

6. Click the PUBLISH NOW button to publish your PDF file online.

7. If requested by your instructor, click the SHARE or Share Links button, copy the web address of the published publication, and send the web address to your instructor.

8. Click the View Live button in the right pane of the issuu.com webpage and then flip through the pages of your published publication.

9. Close the browser window.

10. ✷ What are the advantages of sharing a publication via a web service such as issuu.com? Could friends and customers navigate through the publication easier than if it were emailed or posted on a social media site? What are the disadvantages?

In the Lab

Design and implement a solution using creative thinking and problem-solving skills.

Creating an Ebook Template

Problem: Because your company often writes and publishes ebooks as a tool to inform the market and generate new business, you decide it would be convenient to have a template into which you can type or import text for various ebooks. You want the body copy for each ebook content to fit in five content pages.

Part 1: Start Publisher and open a blank 8.5 × 11" publication. Set the font scheme and the color scheme to selections of your choice. Duplicate the page in the Page Navigation pane. On the second page, create a large text box that fills the page. Set the margin of the text box to 0.5 inches. Duplicate the content page several times to create a total of six pages in the publication (one for the cover page and five content pages). Go to page 2 (the first content page) and then create a section so that the cover page is in one section and the content pages are in another section. Link the text box on the second page to the one on the third page and then link the text boxes on remaining pages. Insert page numbering on every page except the title page. Create a heading in a text box on the cover page that contains the text, cover page, and another heading in a text box on the first content page that contains the text, first content page.

Use the concepts and techniques presented in this module. Save the finished template with the file name, SC_WD_10_EbookTemplate, and then submit the assignment in the format specified by your instructor.

Part 2: ✳ Microsoft Word contains templates for research papers and includes citation tools. Make a list of three publications that are easier to create in Word and three publications that are easier to create in Publisher. How does familiarity with the software affect your list?

11 | Advanced Publisher Features

Objectives

After completing this module, you will be able to:

- Create and print a folded invitation card
- Insert a design accent
- Create and print a banner
- Convert a graphic to a Microsoft drawing object
- Fill a graphic with a custom RGB color
- Download an online template
- Install a new font
- Customize ruler guides

- Specify macro security settings
- Create a macro
- Add commands and macros as buttons on the Quick Access Toolbar
- Delete buttons from the Quick Access Toolbar
- Use VBA to create and edit an event procedure

Introduction

Publisher has some advanced features that you may not use every day; however, knowing about these features is important for a full understanding of the app. These include creating folded invitations and banners, working with online templates, installing fonts, working with macros, and using VBA to create event procedures and edit macros and event procedures. This module discusses the tools used to perform these tasks.

Project: Party Publications

To illustrate some of the advanced features of Publisher, this module presents a series of steps to create the three separate retirement party publications shown in Figure 11–1: a folded invitation card, a banner, and a menu. The folded invitation card and the banner are created from built-in templates, and the menu is created using an online template. The invitation card and the menu include a design accent, the banner contains a custom RGB color, and the menu uses a new font.

Although Publisher has many buttons and commands, it does not include a command or button for every possible task. Thus, Publisher includes **Visual Basic for Applications** (**VBA**), which is a powerful programming language that allows users to customize and extend the capabilities of Publisher to suit their needs.

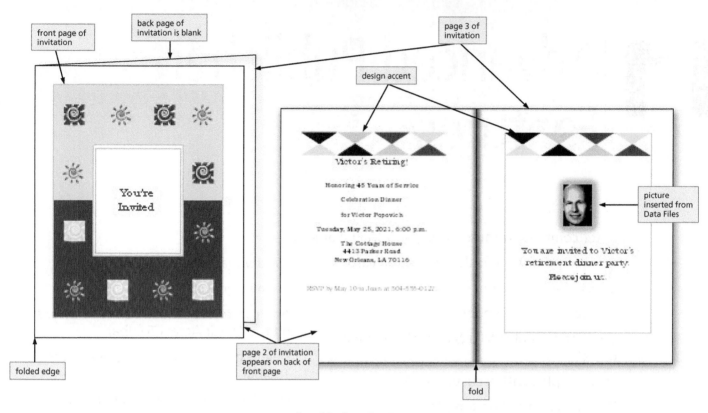

a) Folded Invitation

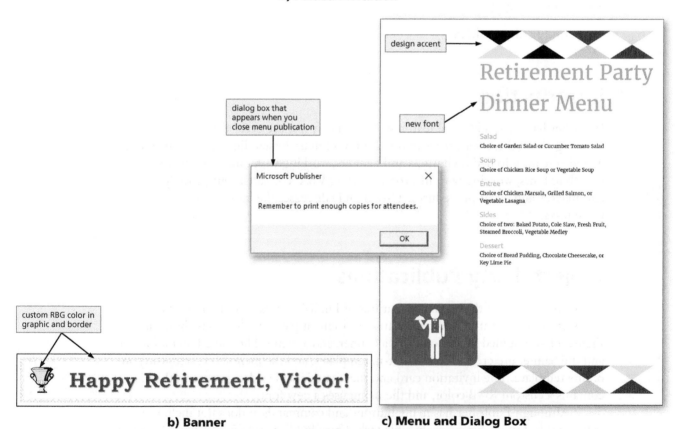

b) Banner

c) Menu and Dialog Box

Figure 11–1

In this project, the menu publication also includes a macro and an event procedure. A **macro** is a named set of instructions, written in VBA, that performs tasks automatically in a specified order. The macro in this project changes the zoom to page width. An **event procedure**, similar to a macro, is written in VBA but occurs only when a specific event occurs. The event procedure for the menu in this project, which runs when a user closes the publication, displays a dialog box that reminds the user to print copies for attendees (Figure 11–1c). The event procedure for the menu also contains an instruction that removes personal information from the publication file.

In this module, you will learn how to create the party publications shown in Figure 11–1. You will perform the following general tasks as you progress through this module:

1. Create an invitation card.
2. Create a banner.
3. Create a menu.
4. Add a macro and an event procedure to the menu.

Creating a Folded Invitation

An invitation card in Publisher is a folded card that usually includes pictures or illustrations and that requests the recipient's presence or participation at an event, a place, a gathering, or some other occasion. Invitation cards often are mailed using the postal service, or they can be sent as e-cards using web services or an email program. In Publisher, the invitation card templates include categories such as birthdays, holidays, and occasions and events. The invitation card can be folded in half or in quarters and may contain a variety of layouts, in addition to the usual color and font schemes. Publisher also contains blank invitation card templates.

Creating an invitation card is no different from creating other publications. You need to be mindful only of how the pages and folds are organized. In the Publisher workspace, page 1 is the front of the card, pages 2 and 3 are the inside of the card, and page 4 is the back of the card. When you print the invitation card from this module using a standard paper size, all four pages will print on a single side of one piece of paper. The two inside pages of the invitation card will print upside down in comparison to the front and the back pages; however, once the pages are folded, all pages appear right-side up. Another option is to purchase special invitation card paper and direct Publisher to print pages 1 and 4 on the front and pages 2 and 3 on the back. These choices are available in the Print screen in Backstage view.

The following sections create an invitation card for a retirement party.

To Customize an Invitation Card Template

The following steps open an invitation card template and make changes to the layout. **Why?** *Publisher offers several different layouts for each kind of invitation card. Selecting a different layout will create a unique card.*

- Start Publisher and then click Built-In in the template gallery to display the built-in templates.

- Scroll as necessary and then click the Invitation Cards thumbnail to display the invitation card templates.

- In the section labeled Event, click the All Event folder to open it.

- Scroll to the Celebration area and then click the Retirement thumbnail to select it.
- Click the Color scheme button in the template information pane to display a list of color schemes. Scroll as necessary and then click Ivy to select the color scheme.
- Click the Font scheme button in the template information pane to display a list of font schemes. Scroll as necessary and then click Literary to select the font scheme.
- Ensure that 'Quarter-sheet side fold' is selected in the Options area. If it is not, click the Page size button and then click 'Quarter-sheet side fold' (Figure 11–2).

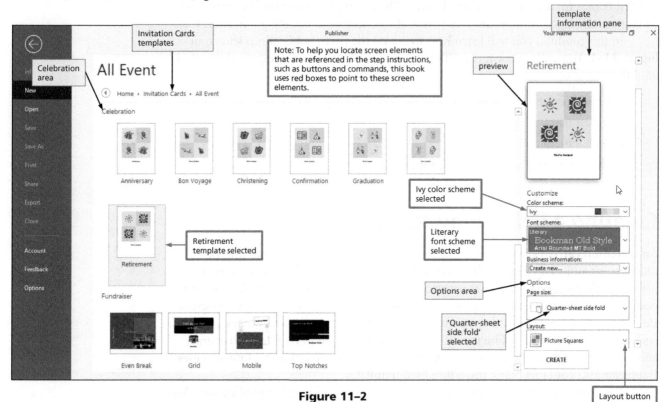

Figure 11–2

2

- If necessary, scroll in the Options area and then click the Layout button to display the Layout menu (Figure 11–3).

🔍 **Experiment**

- Click one of the layouts on the Layout menu and notice the changes in the thumbnails and preview. Practice clicking other layouts on the Layout menu. When finished, click the Layout button again to display the Layout menu.

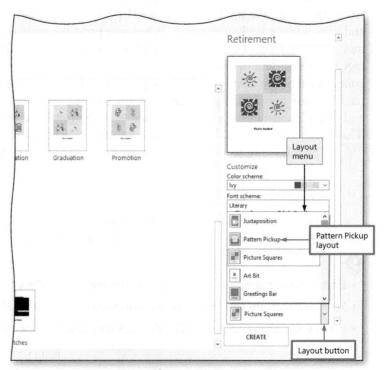

Figure 11–3

3

- Scroll to the top of the Layout menu and then, even if it is selected already, click Pattern Pickup on the Layout menu to select that layout (Figure 11–4).

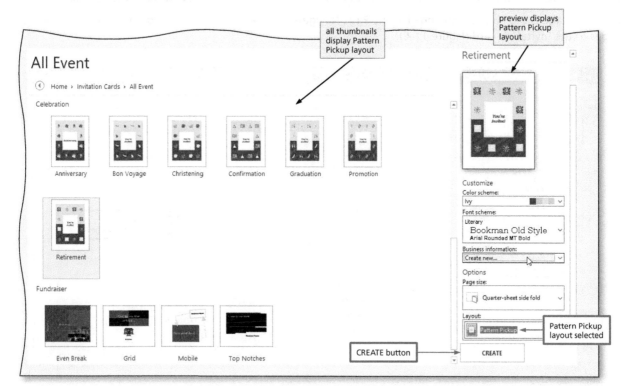

Figure 11–4

4

- Click the CREATE button at the bottom of the template information pane to create the specified invitation card template.

- If the Special Characters button (Home tab | Paragraph group) is not selected already, click it to display formatting marks on the screen.

- If the Page Navigation pane is not open, click the Page Number button on the status bar to open it.

- If necessary, display the View tab and then click the 'Two-Page Spread' button (View tab | Layout group) to display facing pages in the publication as a two-page spread (Figure 11–5).

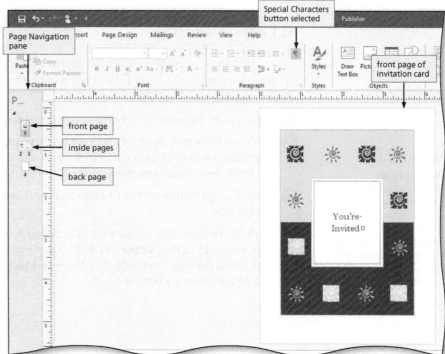

Figure 11–5

5

- Click the Page 4 thumbnail in the Page Navigation pane to display the blank back page of the invitation card.
- Click the Page 1 thumbnail in the Page Navigation pane to display the front page of the invitation card.
- Click the 'Page 2 and Page 3' thumbnail in the Page Navigation pane to display the two-page spread of the inside pages of the invitation card (Figure 11–6).

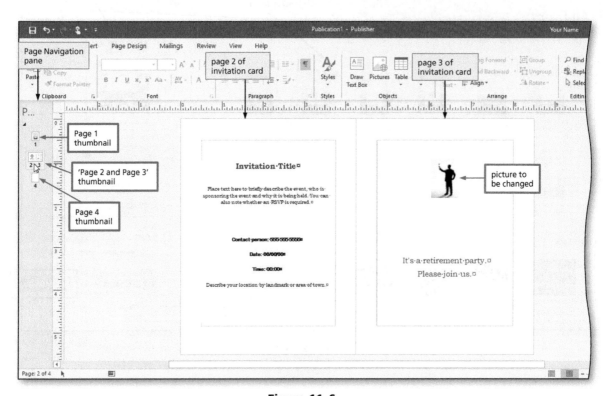

Figure 11–6

To Change a Picture

The following steps change the picture on page 3 of the invitation card. The picture is located in the Data Files. Please contact your instructor for information about accessing the Data Files.

1 If necessary, navigate to the two-page spread for pages 2 and 3.

2 Right-click the picture to be changed (in this case, the picture on page 3 of the invitation card) to display a shortcut menu and then point to Change Picture on the shortcut menu to display the Change Picture submenu.

3 Click Change Picture on the Change Picture submenu to display the Insert Pictures dialog box.

4 Click 'From a file' in the Insert Pictures dialog box to display the Insert Picture dialog box, navigate to the Support_PUB_11_FaceShot.png file in the Data Files (Insert Picture dialog box), and then click the Insert button to replace the selected image with the new picture file (Figure 11–7).

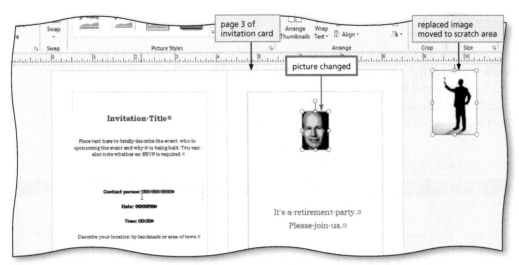

Figure 11–7

To Delete a Picture from the Scratch Area and Format a Picture

The following steps remove the picture from the scratch area because you no longer need that image. You also move the picture on page 3 in the invitation card down and apply a glow effect to the new picture.

1. Click anywhere to deselect the pictures.

2. Right-click the picture in the scratch area to display a shortcut menu and then click Delete Object on the shortcut menu to remove the picture from the scratch area.

3. Drag the new picture on page 3 of the invitation card down a bit so that it is top-aligned with the paragraph of text on page 2 of the invitation card.

4. With the picture still selected, if necessary, display the Picture Tools Format tab. Click the Picture Effects button (Picture Tools Format tab | Picture Styles group) to display the Picture Effects menu.

5. Point to Glow on the Picture Effects menu to display the Glow gallery and then click 'Accent 1, 18 pt glow' in the Glow gallery (first effect in the last row) to apply the selected glow effect to the picture (Figure 11–8).

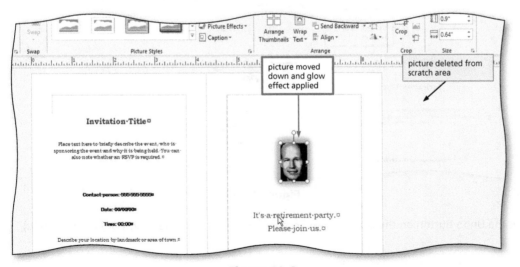

Figure 11–8

To Insert a Design Accent

A design **accent** is a graphic added for emphasis or flair, such as a bar, box, line, frame, or pattern. Unlike other graphics, accents are meant to fill the area; line and bar accents may increase the number of pattern repetitions as they are resized. Accents will be displayed in the same color scheme as the publication.

Accents are used as headers, mastheads, and in other places in a publication where the page may need some delineation or highlighting. The following steps insert a design accent on page 3. *Why? The page is rather plain for a party invitation.*

1

- Display the Insert tab and then click the 'Borders & Accents' button (Insert tab | Building Blocks group) to display the Borders & Accents gallery (Figure 11–9).

Experiment

- Scroll through the selections in the Borders & Accents gallery to see the different types of borders and accents.

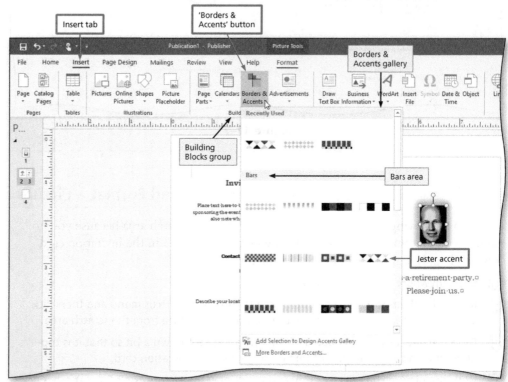

Figure 11–9

2

- In the Bars area in the Borders & Accents gallery, click the Jester accent to insert it into the publication.

- Drag the accent to the top of page 3 and then resize it to 3.25 inches wide by .5 inches tall so that the accent fills the area between margins on the page (Figure 11–10). (If your height and width boxes are dimmed after moving the accent, click the Undo button on the Quick Access Toolbar and then resize the accent before moving it.)

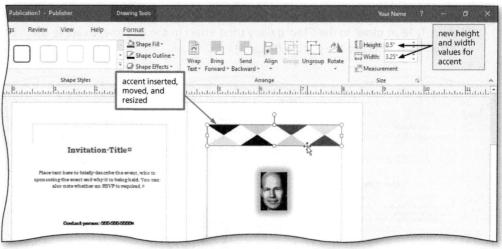

Figure 11–10

Q&A

The number of triangles in my pattern increased. Why?

Accents contain repeating patterns, and depending on how you resize the accent, Publisher may fill the resized shape with additional repeating patterns. For example, additional patterns may fill the accent if you drag the edges of the accent to resize it instead of using the Height and Width boxes (Drawing Tools Format tab | Size group) to resize it.

To Copy a Design Accent

The following steps copy the design accent from the top of page 3 to the top of page 2.

1 With the accent selected, press CTRL+C to copy the accent to the Clipboard.

2 Press CTRL+V to paste the accent on the current page.

3 Drag the copied accent to the top of page 2 in the invitation card (Figure 11–11).

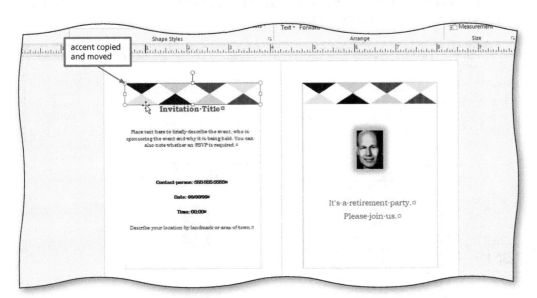

Figure 11–11

To Edit Text on Page 2 of the Invitation Card

The following steps edit the text on page 2 of the invitation card.

1 Point to the Contact person text to display the text box surrounding this text, click the text box to select it, and then press DELETE to delete this text box and its text.

2 Point to the Date text to display the text box surrounding this text, click the text box to select it, and then press DELETE to delete this text box and its text.

3 Point to the Time text to display the text box surrounding this text, click the text box to select it, and then press DELETE to delete this text box and its text.

4 Select the text, Invitation Title, at the top of page 2 and then type `Victor's Retiring!` as the title.

5 Select the paragraph of text below the title, change the font size to 10 point, and then bold the text.

6 Type `Honoring 45 Years of Service` to replace the selected text and then press ENTER.

7 Type `Celebration Dinner` and then press ENTER.

8 Type `for Victor Popovich` and then press ENTER. (If Publisher automatically capitalized the f in for, point to the small blue box below the beginning of the entered word, click the AutoCorrect Options button to display the AutoCorrect Options menu, and then click 'Undo Automatic Capitalization' on the AutoCorrect Options menu to undo the capitalization of the entered word.)

⑨ Type **Tuesday, May 25, 2021, 6:00 p.m.** and then press ENTER.

⑩ Drag the bottom sizing handle in the text box down to the top of the text below it.

⑪ Type **The Cottage House** and then press SHIFT+ENTER to insert a line break so that the blank space below this line is not as large.

⑫ Type **4413 Parker Road** and then press SHIFT+ENTER to insert a line break.

⑬ Type **New Orleans, LA 70116** as the last line in this text box.

⑭ Select the text in the bottom text box that begins, Describe your location…, and then type **RSVP by May 10 to Joan at 504-555-0127.** to replace the text in the bottom text box (Figure 11–12).

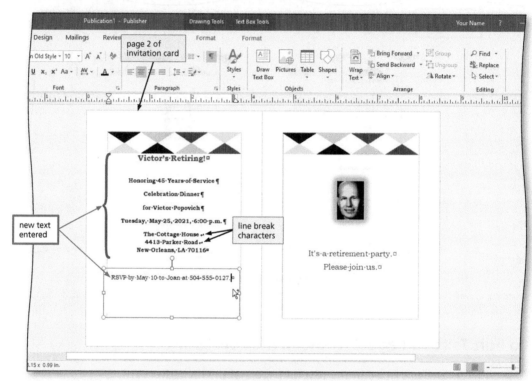

Figure 11–12

BTW

The Ribbon and Screen Resolution
Publisher may change how the groups and buttons within the groups appear on the ribbon, depending on the screen resolution of your computer. Thus, your ribbon may look different from the ones in this book if you are using a screen resolution other than 1366 × 768.

To Send a Shape Backward

The following steps send the outer rectangle shape on page 3 of the invitation card backward so that you can edit text in the text boxes on the page. (Note that you should skip these steps if you are able to edit the text in the text boxes on page 3.)

① Try to click the text box on page 3 that contains the text, It's a retirement party. If you are able to select this text, skip Steps 2 and 3.

② Select the outer rectangle shape on page 3 of the invitation card.

③ Display the Home tab and then click the Send Backward button (Home tab | Arrange group) to send the selected shape backward, which allows you to select the text boxes on the page so that you can edit their contents (Figure 11–13).

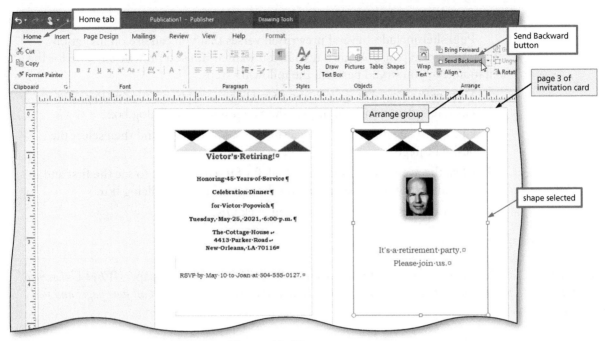

Figure 11–13

To Edit Text on Page 3 of the Invitation Card

The following steps insert text on page 3 of the invitation card.

1️⃣ Select the text in the first text box on page 3 of the invitation card and then bold the text.

2️⃣ Type **You are invited to Victor's retirement dinner party.** to replace the text (Figure 11–14).

Figure 11–14

To Save the Invitation Card

The following steps save the invitation card.

1️⃣ Save the publication on your hard drive, OneDrive, or other storage location using SC_PUB_11_RetirementPartyInvitation as the file name.

TO USE A PREWRITTEN VERSE FOR INVITATION TEXT

Publisher includes several prewritten verses that you can use on invitation cards instead of typing your own text. If you wanted to use a prewritten verse for the invitation text, you would perform the following steps.

1. Display the Page Design tab and then click the Options button (Page Design tab | Template group) to display the Suggested Verse dialog box.
2. Click the Category arrow (Suggested Verse dialog box) and then select the desired category.
3. Click the available messages on the left of the dialog box to see the first and second part of the message text on the right side of the dialog box.
4. Select the desired message and then click OK.

To Print a Folded Publication

The following steps print the invitation card using a single sheet of 8.5 × 11-inch paper. *Why? Unless you have special invitation card paper, using an 8.5 × 11-inch piece of paper is the easiest way to print all four pages and fold them for an invitation card.*

- Open Backstage view and then click Print to display the Print screen.
- Make sure your printer is displayed as the current printer.
- If necessary, click the first button in the Settings area and then click 'Print All Pages'.
- If necessary, type **1-4** in the Pages text box.
- If necessary, click the second button in the Settings area and then click 'Side-fold, quarter sheet' (Figure 11–15).

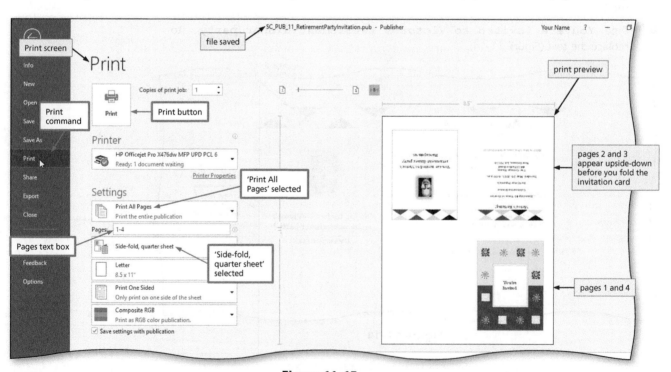

Figure 11–15

- Click the Print button in the Print screen to print the publication.
- Retrieve the printout and fold the invitation card.
- Close the publication. Do not exit Publisher.

Break Point: If you want to take a break, this is a good place to do so. To resume later, start Publisher and continue following the steps from this location forward.

Creating a Banner

A **banner** in Publisher is a horizontal publication that is longer or taller than a standard 8½ × 11-inch piece of paper that hangs on a wall, door, or other part of a building at an event, a gathering, or some other occasion. Publisher prints a banner across several sheets of paper with an extra margin between pages to allow for taping the pages together. In Publisher, you can create banners with a size up to 240 × 240 inches. The following sections create a banner for a retirement party.

To Customize a Banner Template

The following steps open a banner template and make changes to the layout. *Why? Publisher offers several different layouts for banners. Selecting a different layout will create a unique banner.*

- If necessary, start Publisher.
- Click File on the ribbon to open Backstage view and then, if necessary, click New in Backstage view to display the template gallery in the New screen.
- Click Built-In in the template gallery to display the built-in templates.
- Scroll as necessary and then click the Banners thumbnail to display the banner templates.
- In the section labeled Congratulations, if your screen displays an All Congratulations folder, click the All Congratulations folder to open it.
- Click the 'To the Best' thumbnail to select that banner template.

Q&A Why not select the Retirement thumbnail?
You prefer the graphic on the 'To the Best' thumbnail for this banner.

- If the color scheme displayed is not Ivy, click the Color scheme button in the template information pane to display a list of color schemes. Scroll as necessary and then click Ivy to select the color scheme.
- If the font scheme displayed is not Literary, click the Font scheme button in the template information pane to display a list of font schemes. Scroll as necessary and then click Literary to select the font scheme (Figure 11–16).

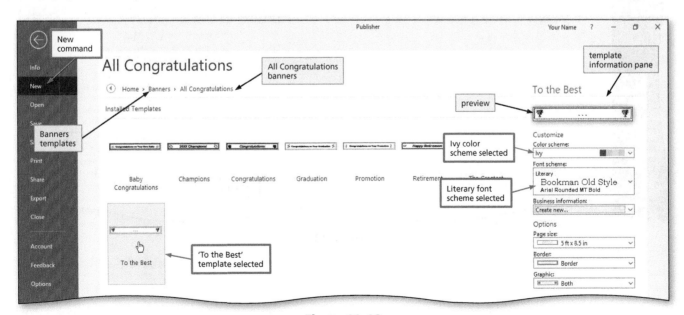

Figure 11–16

- Ensure that the page size in the Options area is 5 ft × 8.5 in. If it is not, select the Page size button and then click '5 ft × 8.5 in'.

 Experiment

- Click the Page Size button to display various banner sizes on the Page Size menu. When finished looking at the options, be sure to select '5 ft × 8.5 in' on the Page size menu.

- Ensure that Border is selected. If it is not, select the Border button and then click Border on the Border menu.

- Click the Graphic button to display the Graphic menu (Figure 11–17).

Experiment

- Click one of the options on the Graphic menu and notice the changes in the thumbnails and preview. Practice clicking other options on the Graphic menu. When finished, click the Graphic button again to display the Graphic menu.

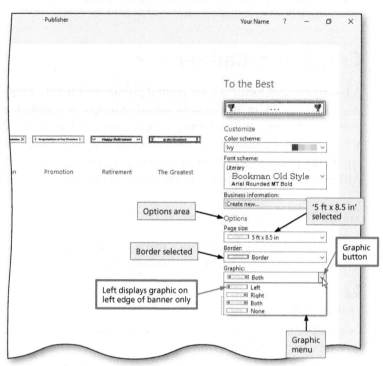

Figure 11–17

- Click Left on the Graphic menu so that the graphic appears on the left edge of the banner only (Figure 11–18).

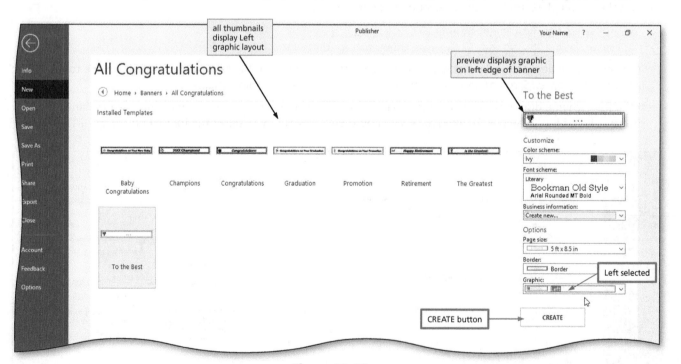

Figure 11–18

- Click the CREATE button at the bottom of the template information pane to create the specified banner template.
- If the Special Characters button (Home tab | Paragraph group) is not selected already, click it to display formatting marks on the screen.
- If the Page Navigation pane is not open, click the Page Number button on the status bar to open it.
- If necessary, display the View tab and then click the Single Page button (View tab | Layout group) to display the banner on a single page.
- Change the zoom to 22% so that the banner fills the page (Figure 11–19).

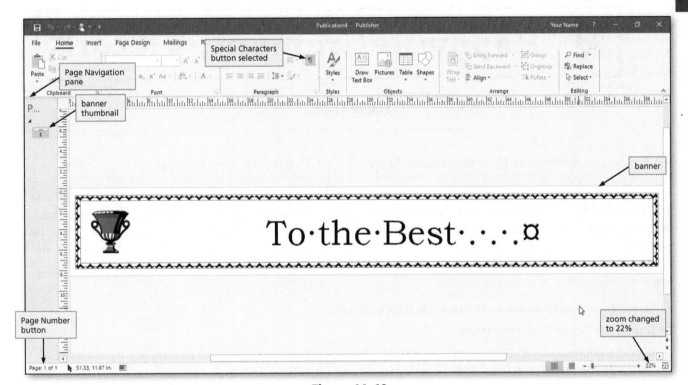

Figure 11–19

To Edit Text on the Banner

The following steps edit the text the banner.

1. Select all text in the text box on the banner and then type **Happy Retirement, Victor!** as the new banner text.

2. Select the entered text, bold the selected text, and then use the Font Color button (Home tab | Font group) to change its color to 'Accent 1, RGB (51, 102, 0))' (second color in the first row).

3. Apply a WordArt style to the selected text by displaying the Text Box Tools Format tab, clicking the More button (Text Box Tools Format tab | WordArt Styles group), and then clicking 'Fill - Accent 1, Outline - Accent 5, Hard Shadow - Accent 1' (third style in the last row).

4. Click anywhere in the text box to deselect the text (Figure 11–20).

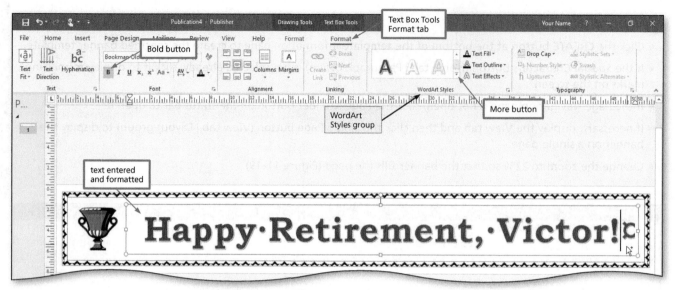

Figure 11–20

To Convert a Picture to a Drawing Object and Ungroup the Object

You would like to change all the red colors in the trophy image in the banner to a shade of yellow, but you still want the black outlines to remain. To do this, you need to ungroup the picture; however, the trophy picture is not a grouped object. Thus, the following steps convert the picture to a Microsoft drawing object as part of the ungroup procedure. *Why? After converting and ungrouping, you will have access to each part of the picture and can use tools on the Drawing Tools Format tab to format individual elements of the picture.*

1

• Select the picture to format (in this case, the trophy picture).

• Display the Picture Tools Format tab.

• Click the Ungroup button (Picture Tools Format tab | Arrange group) to ungroup the picture, which will display a Microsoft Publisher dialog box (Figure 11–21).

Q&A Can I convert every picture this way?

No. Conversion is limited to a few file types, such as the Windows Metafile Format (WMF) format and some GIF, PNG, and BMP files.

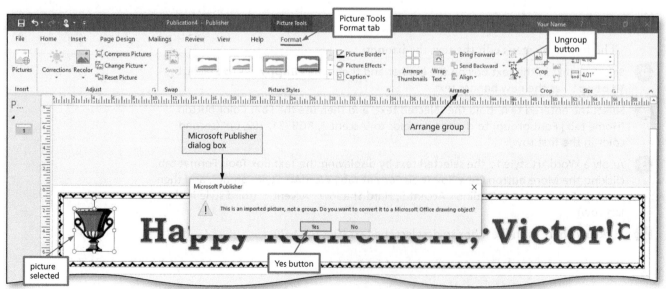

Figure 11–21

2

- Click the Yes button (Microsoft Publisher dialog box) to convert the picture to a grouped drawing object and display the Drawing Tools tab instead of the Picture Tools tab on the ribbon (Figure 11–22).

Q&A What do all of the dots mean?
The dots represent the corners of each shape within the grouped shape.

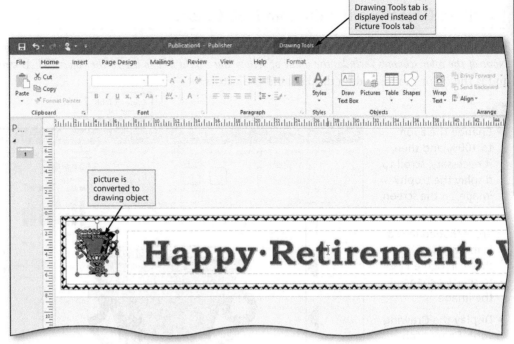

Figure 11–22

3

- Click the Ungroup button (Drawing Tools Format tab | Arrange group) to ungroup the drawing object (Figure 11–23).

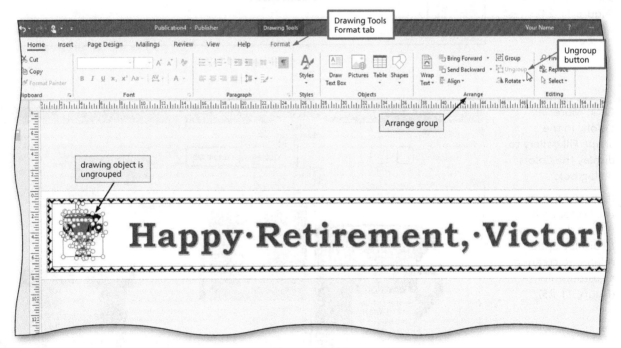

Figure 11–23

4

- Click outside of the drawing object to deselect it.

To Fill an Object with a Custom RGB Color

The following steps fill portions of the image with a unique color created by using RGB settings. *Why?* *None of the color schemes includes the shade of yellow you would like to use in the object.* RGB stands for red, green, blue and is the color mode used on displays and projectors.

1

• Change the zoom to 100% and then, if necessary, scroll to display the trophy image on the screen.

• Click one of the areas shaded in red in the trophy, as shown in Figure 11–24, to select a shape in the image.

• Display the Drawing Tools Format tab.

• Click the Shape Fill arrow (Drawing Tools Format tab | Shape Styles group) to display the Shape Fill gallery (Figure 11–24).

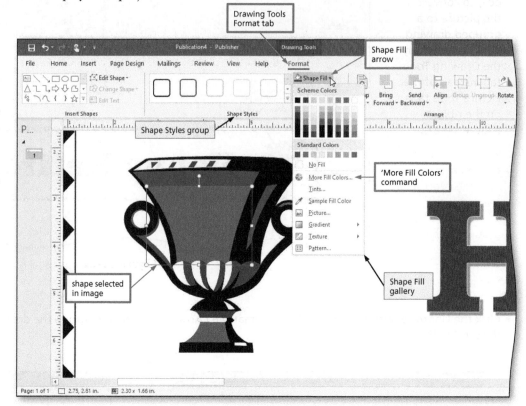

Figure 11–24

2

• Click 'More Fill Colors' in the Shape Fill gallery to display the Colors dialog box.

• If necessary, click the Custom tab (Colors dialog box) to display options related to creating a custom color (Figure 11–25).

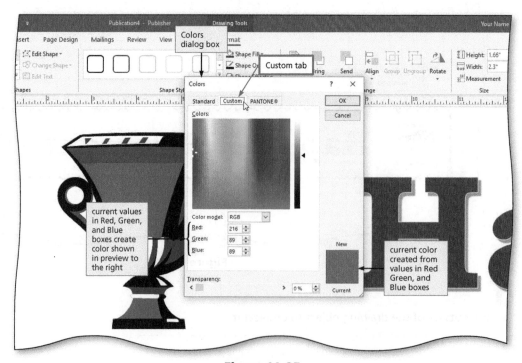

Figure 11–25

3

- Type 245 in the Red box, type 245 in the Green box, and type 27 in the Blue box (Figure 11–26).

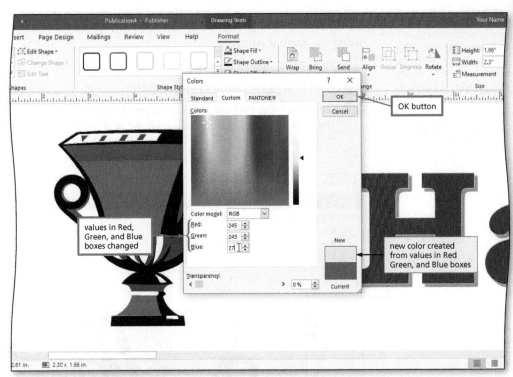

Figure 11–26

4

- Click OK to apply the color to the selected shape (Figure 11–27).

Q&A Why does my color look different? Subtle color differences occur between colors printed on paper in the CMYK mode and the colors you see on your screen in RGB mode.

Figure 11–27

BTW
Color Modes
A color mode describes the way in which colors combine to create other colors. The most commonly used color modes are RGB (used with displays and projectors), CMYK (used in color printing), and LAB (used in photographic retouching and color correction).

To Copy Formatting

The following steps copy the new yellow fill color to other parts of the picture using the format painter.

1 With the shape still selected, display the Home tab.

2 Double-click the Format Painter button (Home tab | Clipboard group).

3 One at a time, click each of the other red portions of the trophy graphic to change them to yellow. If you make a mistake and click the wrong area, press CTRL+Z and then click again (Figure 11–28).

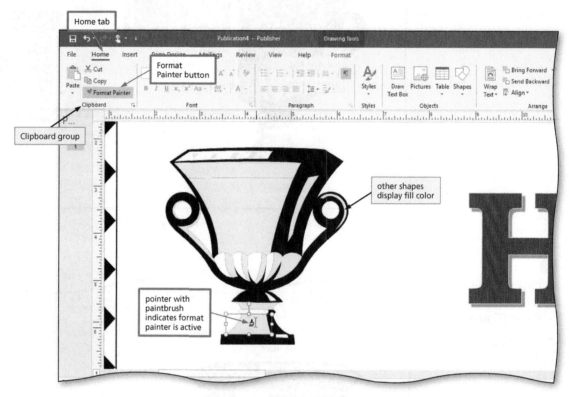

Figure 11–28

4 Click the Format Painter button again to deselect it.

5 Click outside the graphic to deselect any shape.

BTW
JPEG File Format
The JPEG file format is optimal when you need to keep the size of an image file small. JPEG format is a good option for photos but is not as good for logos, line art, or wide areas of flat color.

Picture Formats

Pictures or graphic files are created and stored using many different file types and extensions. The type of file sometimes is determined by the hardware or software used to create the file. Other times, the user has a choice in applying a file type and makes the decision based on the file size, the intended purpose of the picture file, or the desired color mode. Table 11–1 outlines a few common picture file types.

Table 11–1 Picture File Types

File Extension	File Type	Description
BMP	Bitmap	BMP is a standard Windows image format used with Windows-compatible computers. BMP format supports many different color modes.
EMF	Enhanced Metafile	EMF is an improved version of the standard Windows-based graphic format that provides for scaling, built-in descriptions, and device independence.
EPS	Encapsulated PostScript	EPS files can contain both bitmap and vector graphics. Almost all graphics, illustration, and page-layout programs support the EPS format, which can be used to transfer PostScript artwork between applications.
GIF	Graphics Interchange Format	GIF commonly is used to display graphics and images on webpages. It is a compressed format designed to minimize file size and electronic transfer time.
JPG or JPEG	Joint Photographic Experts Group	JPEG format supports many different color modes and retains all color information in an RGB image, unlike GIF format. Most digital cameras produce JPEG files.
PDF	Portable Document Format	PDF is a flexible file format based on the PostScript imaging model that is cross platform and cross application. PDF files accurately display and preserve fonts, page layouts, and graphics. PDF files can contain electronic document search and navigation features, such as links.
PNG	Portable Network Graphics	PNG is a format that does not lose data when compressed or zipped. This format can display millions of colors and supports transparency.
PSD	Photoshop Document	PSD format is the default file format in Photoshop and is the only format that supports all Photoshop features. Other Adobe applications can import PSD files directly and preserve many Photoshop features due to the tight integration among Adobe products.
RAW	Photoshop Raw	RAW format is a flexible file format used for transferring images among applications and computer platforms. This format has no pixel or file size restrictions. Files saved in the Photoshop Raw format cannot contain layers, which are effects or images placed over or under another image.
TIF or TIFF	Tagged Image File Format	TIF is a flexible bitmap image format supported by almost all paint, image-editing, and page-layout applications. This format often is used for files that are to be exchanged among applications or computer platforms. Most desktop scanners can produce TIF images.
WMF	Windows Metafile Format	WMF is a format portable across Office applications, composed of drawn graphics and shapes.

Publisher can import, save, and perform minor editing on most of the picture file types in Table 11–1, except the PDF, PSD, and RAW formats.

To Regroup and Save as a Picture

The following steps regroup the shapes in the picture and then save the trophy picture as a picture file.

1. Display the entire banner in the window.

2. With the pointer positioned outside of the top-left corner of the banner, drag into the banner to select all of the objects in the trophy picture (Figure 11–29).

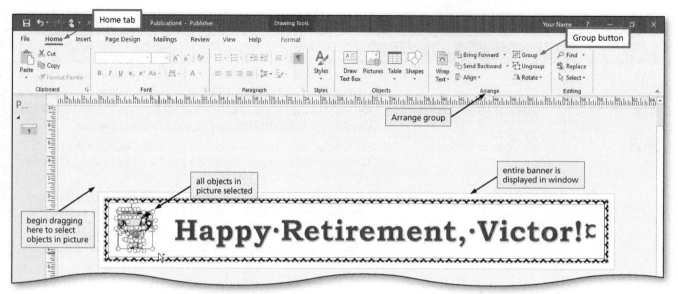

Figure 11-29

BTW
GIF File Format
The GIF file format is used with animated effects and is a good option for clip art, flat graphics, and images that use minimal colors and precise lines, such as logos or blocks of colors.

3 Click the Group button (Home tab | Arrange group) to group the selected shapes into a single drawing object.

4 Right-click the grouped picture to display a shortcut menu and then click 'Save as Picture' on the shortcut menu to display the Save As dialog box.

5 Type `SC_PUB_11_TrophyPicture` in the File Name box (Save As dialog box) and then navigate to the desired save location on your hard drive, OneDrive, or other storage location.

6 Click the Save button to save the picture in the specified save location.

To Change the Picture Resolution while Saving

When printing a picture, you might want to increase the picture's resolution. If you wanted to change a picture's resolution while saving it, you would perform the following steps:

1. Right-click the picture to display a shortcut menu and then click 'Save as Picture' on the shortcut menu to display the Save As dialog box.

2. Click the Change button (Save As dialog box) to display the Change Resolution dialog box, select the desired resolution (Change Resolution dialog box), and then click OK.

3. Enter a name in the File name box (Save As dialog box) and then navigate to the desired save location on your hard drive, OneDrive, or other storage location.

4. Click the Save button to save the picture.

To Change the Banner Outline

The following steps change the color of the banner outline to the newly defined RGB color.

1 If necessary, zoom the page to view the banner outline and then click the outline on the banner to select it.

2 If necessary, display the Drawing Tools Format tab.

3 Click the Shape Outline arrow (Drawing Tools Format tab | Shape Styles group) to
display the Shape Outline gallery (Figure 11–30).

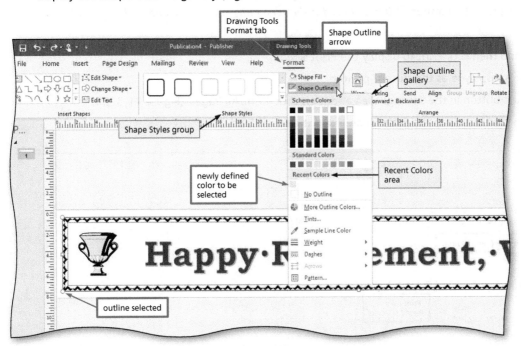

Figure 11–30

4 Click the newly defined yellow color in the Recent Colors area in the Shape Outline
gallery to apply that color to the selected outline on the banner (shown in Figure 11–31).

To Save the Banner

The following step saves the banner.

1 Save the publication on your hard drive, OneDrive, or other storage location using
SC_PUB_11_RetirementPartyBanner as the file name (Figure 11–31).

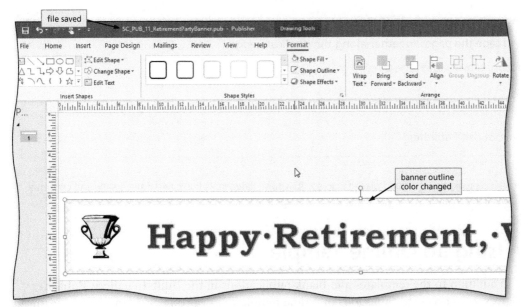

Figure 11–31

To Print a Banner

The following steps print the banner. ***Why?*** *You are finished designing the banner and wish to print it.*

- Open Backstage view and then click Print to display the Print screen.
- Make sure your printer is displayed as the current printer.
- If necessary, click the first button in the Settings area and then click 'Print All Pages' (Figure 11–32).
- If necessary, click the second button in the Settings area and then click Tiled.

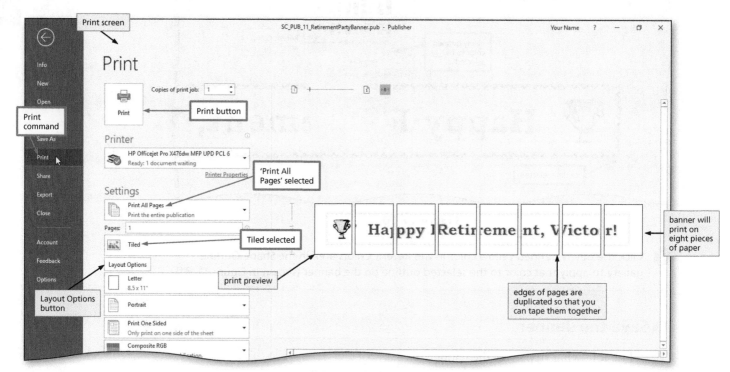

Figure 11–32

- Click the Print button in the Print screen to print the publication.
- Retrieve the printout and tape the pages together along the duplicate edges.

◄ | What if I wanted more margin overlap on the pages?
Ơ | You would click the Layout Options button in the Print screen to display the Layout Options dialog box,
 | enter the desired overlap value in the appropriate boxes (Layout Options dialog box), and then click the
 | Close button.

- Close the publication. Do not exit Publisher.

Break Point: If you want to take a break, this is a good place to do so. To resume later, start Publisher, if necessary, and continue following the steps from this location forward.

Using an Online Template

In addition to the templates and blank publications in the Built-In gallery, Publisher gives users access to thousands of online templates in various categories. Some featured online templates appear when you start Publisher or when you click New in Backstage view. Other online templates can be located by entering search terms in the 'Search for online templates' box. You can enter terms, such as business, industry, holiday, or illustrations, among others. In addition, you can enter the type of publication you are looking for, such as invoice, newsletter, brochure, and so on.

To Search for an Online Template

The following steps search for an online menu template. ***Why?*** *You searched through the menu templates in the Built-In gallery and could not locate a template that will work for your needs, so you search through the online templates to see if a more suitable template exists online.* Note that you must be connected to the Internet in order to search for online templates.

1

- If necessary, start Publisher.
- Click File on the ribbon to open Backstage view and then, if necessary, click New in Backstage view to display the template gallery in the New screen.

 Experiment

- Scroll through the featured online templates.
- Type **menu** in the 'Search for online templates' box to enter the search text (Figure 11–33).

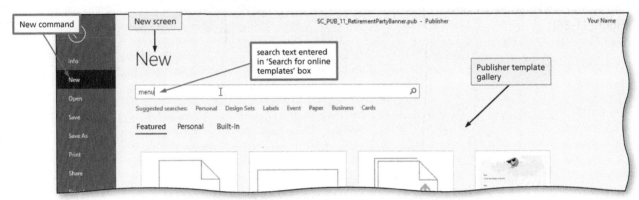

Figure 11–33

2

- Press ENTER to display online templates related to the search text (Figure 11–34).

 Experiment

- Scroll through the online templates.

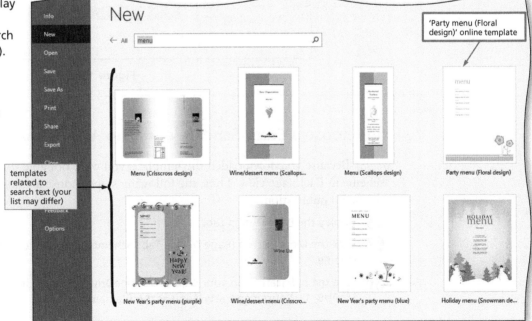

Figure 11–34

3

- Click the 'Party menu (Floral design)' online template to select it and display a dialog box (Figure 11–35).

Q&A What if I cannot locate the same menu template?

Close Backstage view, open the publication called Support_PUB_11_MenuTemplate.pub from the Data Files (please contact your instructor for information about accessing the Data Files), and then skip Step 4.

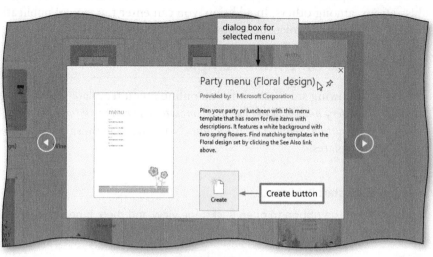

Figure 11–35

4

- Click the Create button to download the template and to display it in the Publisher window (Figure 11–36).

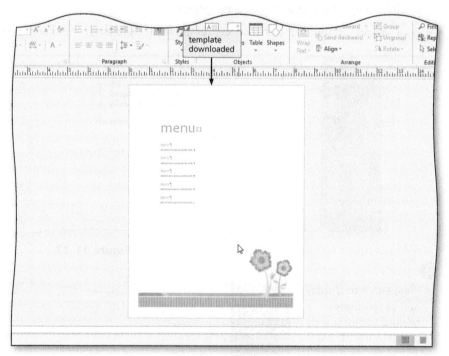

Figure 11–36

To Choose a Color Scheme and Save the Menu Publication

Because you downloaded the template, you were not able to select a color scheme in Backstage view. Thus, the following steps choose a color scheme and save the menu publication.

1 Display the Page Design tab.

2 Click the More button (Page Design Tab | Schemes group) and then click the Ivy color scheme.

3 Save the publication on your hard drive, OneDrive, or other storage location using SC_PUB_11_RetirementPartyMenu as the file name.

To Delete Objects from the Template

The following steps delete all the graphic images at the bottom of the template.

1 With the pointer positioned outside of the middle-left edge of the menu, drag across to the right side of the menu and then down to the bottom of the menu to select all of the objects at the bottom of the menu.

2 Press DELETE to delete the selected objects from the menu (Figure 11–37).

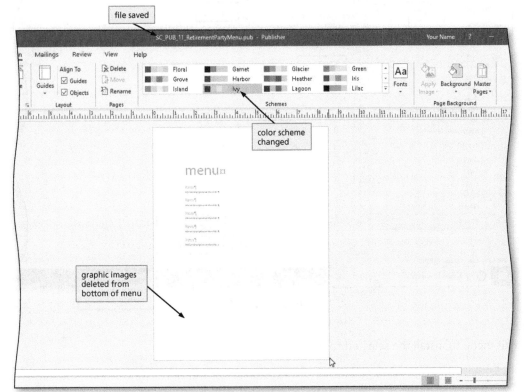

Figure 11–37

BTW
Storing Font Files
Most installed fonts are stored in a folder named C:\Windows\Fonts on your hard drive.

To Install a New Font

While many fonts are installed when you install Microsoft Office 2019, sometimes you need a specialized font to provide a certain look and feel for your publication. You can purchase some fonts commercially, while others are available as shareware or for free. In addition, a business may have developed a personalized font. In any of these cases, you may need to download and install that font on your computer. Installing fonts is a function of the operating system and provides access to that font across publications and across apps.

The following steps install a new font on your computer. If you are in a lab environment, check with your instructor before performing these steps. *Why? Some lab settings are restricted to starting apps and prohibit making changes to the installation.* To complete these steps, you will be required to use the Data Files. Please contact your instructor for information about accessing the Data Files.

1

- Click the File Explorer button on the Windows taskbar to open a File Explorer window.

- Navigate to the location of your font file, in this case the Data Files.

- Right-click the file named Support_PUB_11_ Merriweather-Regular.ttf to display a shortcut menu (Figure 11–38).

Q&A How would I install a downloaded font?
Most downloaded fonts are stored in a compressed file. You must extract the files, read and agree to the license agreement, if any, and then use these steps to install the font.

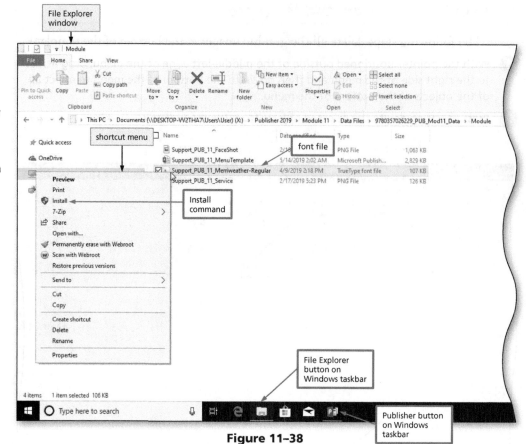

Figure 11–38

2
- Click Install on the shortcut menu to install the selected font.

Q&A How do I know if the font installed correctly?
You can look in the font list in any of the Office apps.

Where are fonts stored?
Fonts are stored in the registry of your computer, but they can be viewed and manipulated via the Control Panel app.

To Format a Text Box to Shrink Text on Overflow

The following steps format the text box containing the menu title to shrink text on overflow so that all text entered in the text box is resized automatically to fit in the text box.

1 Click the Publisher button on the Windows taskbar to display the Publisher window with the Retirement Party Menu publication.

2 Change the zoom to 100% and display the menu title in the Publisher window.

3 Click in the text box containing the text, menu, and then display the Text Box Tools Format tab.

4 Click the Text Fit button (Text Box Tools Format Tab | Text group) to display the Text Fit menu (Figure 11–39).

5 Click 'Shrink Text On Overflow' on the Text Fit menu to apply the selected format to the text box so that future text entered in this text box automatically will be resized to fit in the borders of the text box.

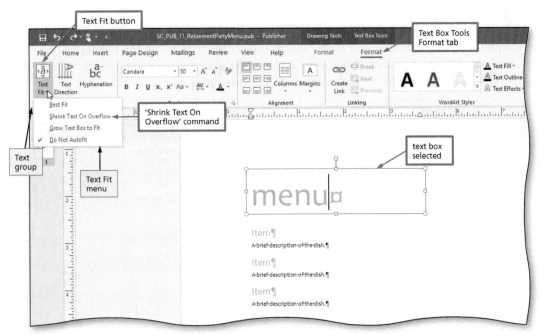

Figure 11–39

To Format and Enter Text in a Text Box

The following steps resize the text box containing the menu title and enter text in the text box using the new font.

1. Resize the text box containing the menu title to 1.75 inches tall and 5 inches wide.

2. Select the text, menu, in the text box and then change the font to Merriweather.

3. Type **Retirement Party Dinner Menu** to replace the text in the text box (Figure 11–40).

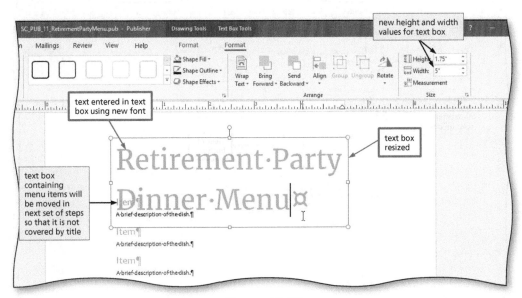

Figure 11–40

To Create Custom Ruler Guides

Built-in ruler guides for publication pages help you align objects and create dividers on the page. In this menu publication, you will create custom ruler guides. *Why? With custom ruler guides, you can align objects at specific locations on a page.* The following steps create vertical and horizontal ruler guides.

• Display the Page Design tab.

• Click the Guides button (Page Design tab | Layout group) to display the Guides gallery (Figure 11–41).

Q&A What do the Add commands in the Guides gallery do?
They create a horizontal or vertical line in the middle of the page, which you then can move to any location.

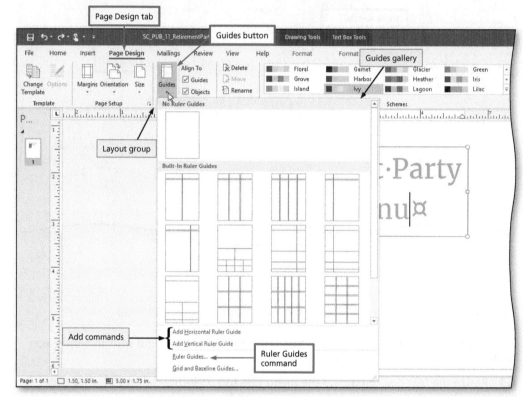

Figure 11–41

• Click Ruler Guides in the Guides gallery to display the Ruler Guides dialog box.

• If necessary, click the Horizontal tab (Ruler Guides dialog box) to display the current positions of the horizontal ruler guides (Figure 11–42).

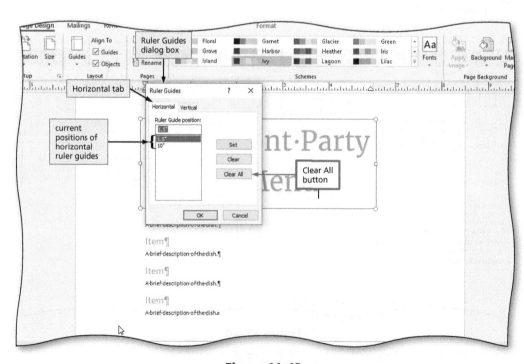

Figure 11–42

- Click the Clear All
  button to clear all
  current horizontal
  ruler guides
  (Figure 11–43).

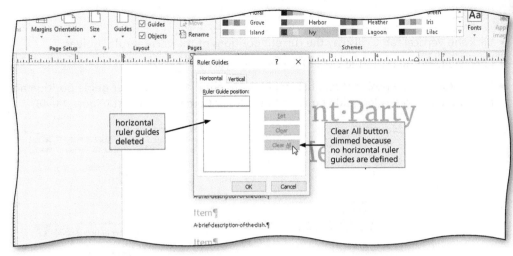

Figure 11–43

- In the 'Ruler Guide
  position' text box,
  type 2 to enter
  a horizontal ruler
  guide position and
  then click the Set
  button to add the
  entered ruler guide
  position to the Ruler
  Guide position list
  (Figure 11–44).

Q&A
Could I drag from
the ruler to create
ruler guides?
Yes, but often it is
difficult to drag the
ruler guides to an exact location.

Figure 11–44

- In the 'Ruler Guide position' text box, type 3 to enter a horizontal ruler guide position and then click the Set
  button to add the entered ruler guide position to the Ruler Guide Position list.

- In the 'Ruler Guide
  position' text box,
  type 3.25 to
  enter a horizontal
  ruler guide position
  and then click the
  Set button to add
  the entered ruler
  guide position to the
  Ruler Guide Position
  list (Figure 11–45).

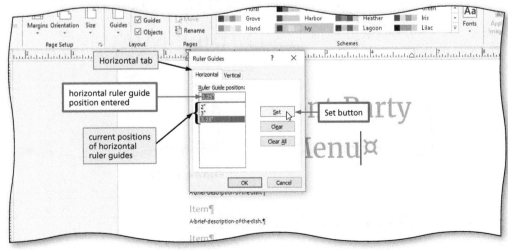

Figure 11–45

6

- Click the Vertical tab to display the current positions of the vertical ruler guides.

- Click the Clear All button to clear all current vertical ruler guides.

- In the 'Ruler Guide position' text box, type   3   to enter a vertical ruler guide position and then click the Set button to add the entered ruler guide position to the Ruler Guide position list (Figure 11–46).

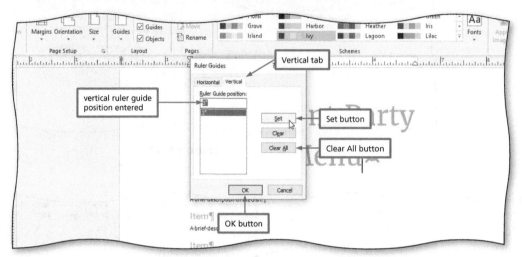

Figure 11–46

7

- Click OK to create the specified horizontal and vertical ruler guides (Figure 11–47).

 Experiment

- Point to a ruler guide. When the pointer changes to a double-headed arrow, drag the ruler guide to move it. Click the Undo button on the Quick Access Toolbar to move the ruler guide back.

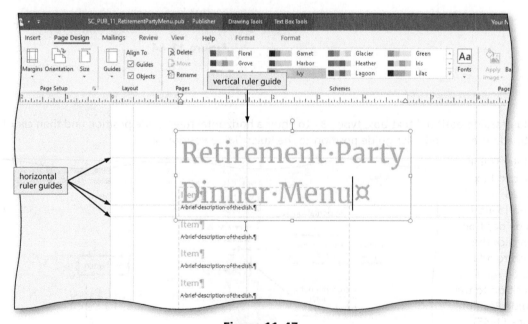

Figure 11–47

Other Ways

1. Drag from horizontal or vertical ruler to desired ruler guide position

To Position Text Boxes at New Ruler Guides

The following steps position the two text boxes on the menu at the location of the new ruler guides.

1 Change the zoom to whole page.

2 Drag the text box containing the menu items so that its top-left corner rests at the horizontal ruler guide positioned at 3.25 inches and the vertical ruler guide positioned at 3 inches.

3 Drag the text box containing the menu title so that its bottom-left corner rests at the horizontal ruler guide positioned at 3 inches and the vertical ruler guide positioned at 3 inches (Figure 11–48).

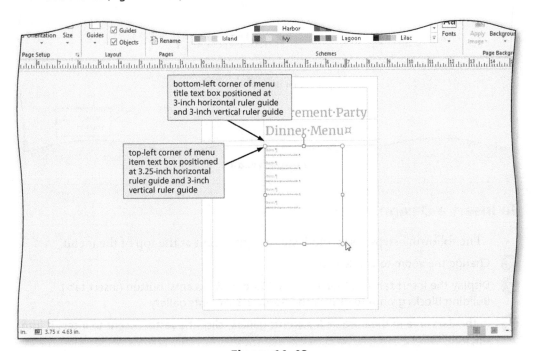

Figure 11–48

To Enter and Format Text in a Text Box

The following steps enter and format the menu items text in the lower text box.

1 Change the zoom to 100%.

2 In the bottom text box, change each of the Item headings to the following from top to bottom: Salad, Soup, Entree, Sides, Dessert.

3 In the bottom text box, change each placeholder text, A brief description of the dish., to the Merriweather font, 10-point font size, and the following text from top to bottom (Figure 11–49):

Choice of Garden Salad or Cucumber Tomato Salad
Choice of Chicken Rice Soup or Vegetable Soup
Choice of Chicken Marsala, Grilled Salmon, or Vegetable Lasagna
Choice of two: Baked Potato, Cole Slaw, Fresh Fruit, Steamed Broccoli, Vegetable Medley
Choice of Bread Pudding, Chocolate Cheesecake, or Key Lime Pie

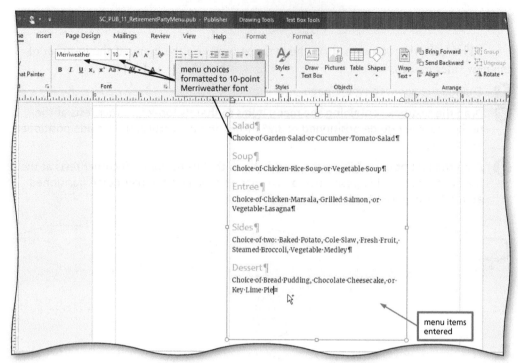

Figure 11–49

To Insert a Design Accent

The following steps insert the Jester design accent at the top of the menu.

1 Change the zoom to whole page.

2 Display the Insert tab and then click the 'Borders & Accents' button (Insert tab | Building Blocks group) to display the Borders & Accents gallery.

3 In the Bars area in the Borders & Accents gallery, click the Jester accent to insert it into the publication.

4 Drag the accent to the top of the page above the menu title, resize it to 5 inches wide by .77 inches tall, and then move it, if necessary, so that the accent fills the area to the right of the vertical ruler guide (Figure 11–50). (If your height and width boxes are dimmed after moving the accent, click the Undo button on the Quick Access Toolbar and then resize the accent before moving it.)

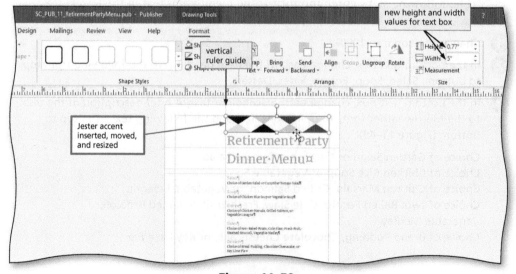

Figure 11–50

To Copy a Design Accent

The following steps copy the design accent from the top of the page to the bottom of the page.

1 With the accent selected at the top of the page, press CTRL+C to copy the accent to the Clipboard.

2 Press CTRL+V to paste the accent on the current page.

3 Drag the copied accent to the bottom of the page (shown in Figure 11–51).

To Insert and Format a Picture

The following steps insert and format a picture that will appear at the bottom of the menu. The picture is located in the Data Files. Please contact your instructor for information about accessing the Data Files.

1 Insert the picture named Support_PUB_11_Service.png from the Data Files.

2 Resize the picture to a height of approximately 1.7 inches and a width of 2.4 inches.

3 Use the Recolor button (Picture Tools Format tab | Adjust group) to change the color of the picture to 'RGB (51, 102, 0), Accent color 1 Dark' (first color in the second row).

4 Move the picture to the left of vertical ruler guide near the bottom of the page, as shown in Figure 11–51.

5 Save the menu again on the same storage location with the same file name.

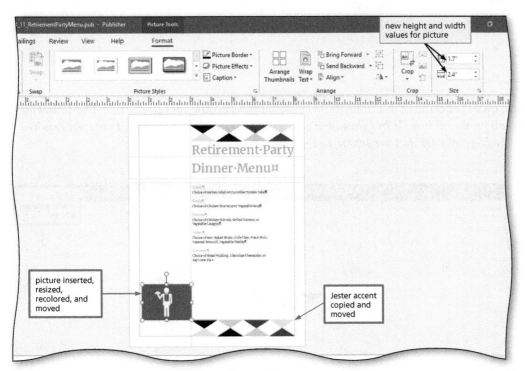

Figure 11–51

Break Point: If you want to take a break, this is a good place to do so. To resume later, start Publisher, open the file called SC_PUB_11_RetirementPartyMenu.pub, and continue following the steps from this location forward.

Using Macros, Event Procedures, and VBA to Automate Tasks

VBA (Visual Basic for Applications) is a powerful tool used to program how Publisher and other apps perform while creating documents. In Publisher, VBA provides you with the ability to create macros and write procedures.

A macro consists of a named set of Publisher commands or instructions, written in VBA, that acts as a shortcut so that you can execute those instructions at a later time. Macros provide a convenient way to automate a difficult or lengthy task. In Publisher, you can run macros created elsewhere or create macros yourself. An event procedure, similar to a macro, is written in VBA but executes only when a specific event occurs.

In this project, the menu publication includes a macro and an event procedure. The macro changes the zoom to page width. The event procedure, which executes when a user closes the menu publication, displays a dialog box that reminds the user to print copies for attendees (shown in Figure 11–1c at the beginning of this module). The event procedure for the menu also contains an instruction that removes personal information from the publication file. The following sections show how to create this macro and event procedure.

CONSIDER THIS

Should you customize applications with macros and event procedures?

Many casual Microsoft Office users are not aware that this type of customization is available. Creating macro and event procedures can save time and reduce errors. If you understand how to work with macros and event procedures, this type of customization can be an excellent productivity tool.

To Show the Developer Tab

To create macros and event procedures in Publisher, you use buttons on the Developer tab. The following steps show the Developer tab on the ribbon. *Why? Because it allows you to perform more advanced tasks not required by everyday Publisher users, the Developer tab does not appear on the ribbon by default.*

1

- Right-click an empty area on the ribbon to display a shortcut menu (Figure 11–52).

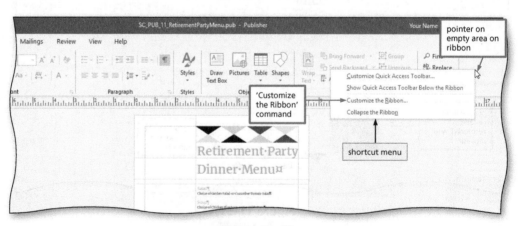

Figure 11–52

2

- Click 'Customize
  the Ribbon' on the
  shortcut menu to
  display the Publisher
  Options dialog box.

- In the Main Tabs list
  (Publisher Options
  dialog box), place a
  check mark in the
  Developer check box
  (Figure 11–53).

Q&A
What are the plus
symbols to the left
of the tab names?
Clicking the plus
symbol expands to
show groups.

Can I show or hide
any tab in this list?
Yes. Place a check
mark in the check
box to show the tab
and remove the check
mark to hide the tab.

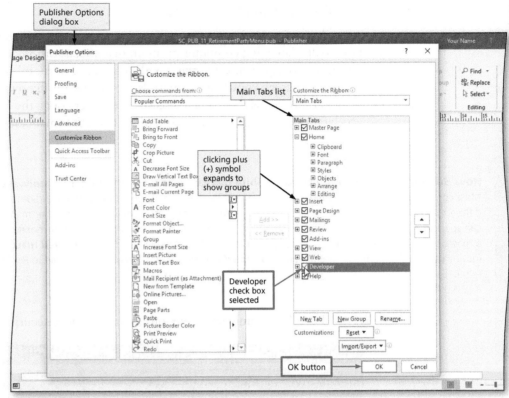

Figure 11–53

3

- Click OK to show the Developer tab on the ribbon.

Q&A
How do I remove the Developer tab from the ribbon?
Follow these same steps, except remove the check mark from the Developer check box (Publisher Options
dialog box).

- Click Developer on
  the ribbon to display
  the Developer tab
  (Figure 11–54).

Figure 11–54

Other Ways

1. Click File on ribbon, click Options in Backstage view, click Customize Ribbon (Publisher Options dialog box), select Developer check box, click OK

Macro Security Levels

A **computer virus** is a type of malicious software, or malware, which is a potentially damaging computer program that affects, or infects, a computer or mobile device negatively by altering the way the computer or mobile device works, usually without the user's knowledge or permission. Millions of known viruses and other malicious programs exist. The increased use of networks, the Internet, and email has accelerated the spread of computer viruses and other malicious programs.

CONSIDER THIS

How do you protect a computer or mobile device from viruses and other malware?

Most computer users run an **antivirus program** that locates viruses and other malware and destroys the malicious programs before they infect a computer or mobile device. Macros are known to carry viruses and other malware. For this reason, you can specify a macro security level in Publisher to reduce the chance that your computer or mobile device will be infected with a macro virus. The macro security levels allow you to enable or disable macros. An **enabled macro** is a macro that Publisher (or any other Office app) will execute, and a **disabled macro** is a macro that is unavailable to Publisher (or any other app).

Table 11–2 summarizes the four available macro security levels in Publisher.

Table 11–2 Publisher Macro Security Levels	
Macro Security Level	**Condition**
Very high	Publisher will execute only macros installed in trusted locations. All other signed and unsigned macros are disabled when the publication is opened.
High	Publisher will execute only macros that are digitally signed. All other macros are disabled when the publication is opened.
Medium	Upon opening a publication that contains macros from an unknown source, Publisher displays a dialog box asking if you want to enable the macros.
Low	Publisher turns off macro virus protection. The publication is opened with all macros enabled, including those from unknown sources.

If Publisher's macro security level is set to very high or high and you include a macro in a publication, Publisher will disable the macro when you open the publication. If the macro security level is set to medium, each time you open the Publisher publication or any other document that contains a macro from an unknown source, Publisher will display a dialog box warning that a macro is attached and allows you to enable or disable the macros. If you are confident of the source (author) of the publication and macros, you should click the Enable Macros button in the dialog box. If you are uncertain about the reliability of the source of the publication and macros, you should click the Disable Macros button.

To Set the Security Macro Level in Publisher

The following steps set Publisher's macro security level. *Why? When you open the completed menu in this module, you want the macros to be enabled. At the same time, your computer or mobile device should be protected from potentially harmful macros. Thus, you will specify a macro setting that allows you to enable macros each time you open this module's menu or any publication that contains a macro from an unknown source.*

1

- Click the Macro Security button (Developer tab | Code group) to display the Trust Center dialog box.
- If necessary, click Macro Settings in the left pane (Trust Center dialog box) to display the macro settings options.
- If it is not selected already, click the 'Disable all macros with notification' option button, which causes Publisher to alert you when a publication contains a macro so that you can decide whether to enable the macro(s) (Figure 11–55).

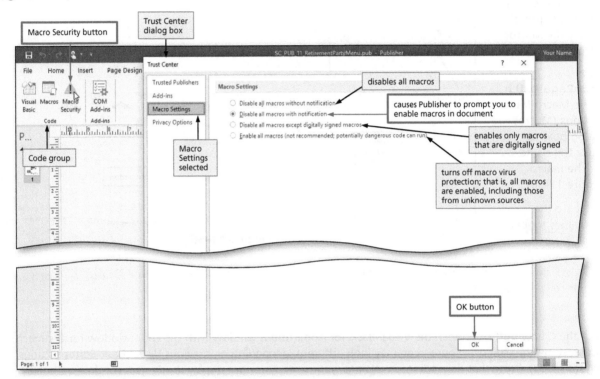

Figure 11–55

2

- Click OK to apply the settings and close the dialog box.

Other Ways

1. Click File on ribbon, click Options in Backstage view, click Trust Center in left pane (Publisher Options dialog box), click 'Trust Center Settings' button, click Macro Settings in left pane (Trust Center dialog box), select desired macro security setting, click OK button in each dialog box

Visual Basic Editor

The **Visual Basic Editor** is a full-screen editor that allows you to enter macro and event procedure instructions by typing lines of VBA code, called code statements, in a code window as if you were using word processing software. Because the code window is similar to a text box or word processing software window, at the end of a line, you press ENTER or use the DOWN ARROW key to move to the next line. If you make a mistake in a code statement, you can use the arrow keys and DELETE or BACKSPACE to correct it. You also can move the insertion point to lines requiring corrections.

To Create a Macro

The following steps create a macro that changes the zoom to page width. *Why? Assume that you find you are repeatedly changing the zoom to page width. To simplify this task, the macro in this project changes the zoom to page width.*

1

- Click the Macros button (Developer tab | Code group) to display the Macros dialog box.

- Type **ZoomPageWidth** in the Macro Name text box (Macros dialog box) to enter the name for the macro (Figure 11–56).

Q&A What are the guidelines for macro names?
Macro names can be up to 255 characters in length and can contain only numbers, letters, and the underscore character. A macro name cannot contain spaces or other punctuation.

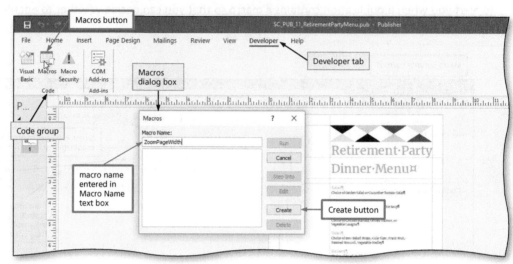

Figure 11–56

2

- Click the Create button to open the Visual Basic for Applications window with the code window for the macro displayed on the screen — your screen may look different, depending on previous Visual Basic Editor settings (Figure 11–57). (Note that depending on settings, your screen may not display the Project window or Properties panel.)

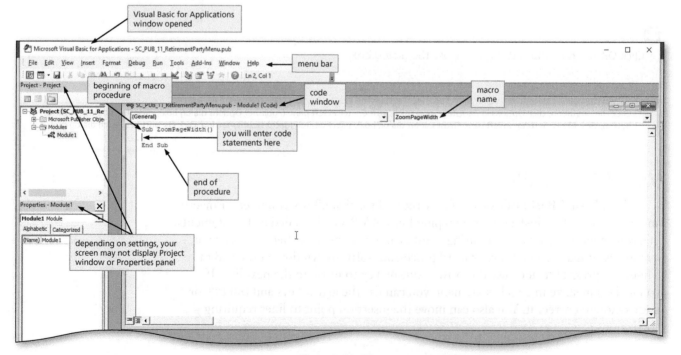

Figure 11–57

- Press TAB. Type **' Changes the zoom to page width** and then press ENTER to enter the comment line.

Q&A Why press TAB?

Pressing TAB indents the lines of code and has no effect on how the code executes; it merely aids in readability.

My comment is not green. Why not?

Be sure you entered an apostrophe before typing the comment text.

- Type **ActiveDocument.ActiveView.Zoom = pbZoomPageWidth** to enter the code statement that changes the zoom to page width (Figure 11–58).

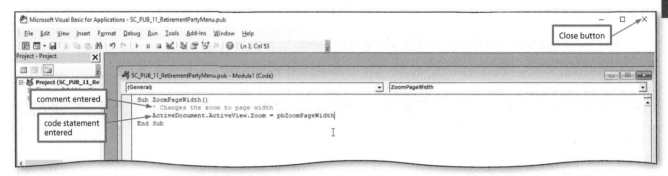

Figure 11–58

Q&A I did not have to press ENTER to indent the second line of code. Why not?

The indent format is carried forward automatically when you press ENTER. If you wanted to move the insertion point back to the left margin, you would press SHIFT+TAB before typing.

④

- Click the Close button on the right edge of the Visual Basic for Applications window title bar to close the window.

VBA

As shown in the previous steps, a VBA procedure begins with a Sub statement and ends with an End Sub statement. The Sub statement is followed by the name of the procedure, which in this case is the macro name (ZoomPageWidth). The parentheses following the macro name in the Sub statement are required. They indicate that arguments can be passed from one procedure to another. Passing arguments is beyond the scope of this module, but the parentheses still are required. The End Sub statement signifies the end of the procedure and returns control to Publisher.

Comments often are added to a procedure to help you remember the purpose of the macro (or other procedure) and its code statements at a later date. Comments begin with an apostrophe (') and appear in green in the code window. Comments have no effect on the execution of a procedure; they simply provide information about the procedure, such as its name and description.

For readability, code statement lines are indented. Table 11–3 explains the various elements of VBA code statements.

BTW

Naming Macros
If you give a new macro the same name as an existing built-in command in Publisher, the new macro's actions will replace the existing actions. Thus, you should be careful not to assign a macro a name that is reserved for an event procedure (see Table 11-4) or for any Publisher command. To view a list of Publisher commands, open Backstage view, click Options to display the Publisher Options dialog box, click Customize Ribbon in the left pane (Publisher Options dialog box), click the 'Choose commands from' arrow, and then click All Commands in the Choose commands from list. When finished scrolling through the list, close the dialog box.

Table 11–3 Elements of a Code Statement

Code Statement		
Element	Definition	Examples
Keyword	Recognized by Visual Basic as part of its programming language; keywords appear in blue in the code window	Sub End Sub
Variable	An item whose value can be modified during program execution	ActiveDocument.ActiveView.Zoom = pbZoomPageWidth
Constant	An item whose value remains unchanged during program execution	False
Operator	A symbol that indicates a specific action	=

To Run a Macro

The following steps run the macro that changes the zoom to page width. *Why? You want to test the macro to be sure it works properly.*

1

- If necessary, change the zoom to whole page.

- Click the Macros button (Developer tab | Code group) to display the Macros dialog box.

- If necessary, click the ZoomPageWidth macro in the Macro Name list (Macros dialog box) to select the macro (Figure 11–59).

Figure 11–59

2

- Click the Run button run the macro, which changes the zoom to page width of the publication on the screen (Figure 11–60). (Note that, depending on settings, your zoom percentage may differ from this figure.)

- Change the zoom back to whole page.

Figure 11–60

Other Ways

1. Press ALT+F8, select macro in list (Macros dialog box), click Run button

To Add a Command and a Macro as Buttons on the Quick Access Toolbar

Publisher allows you to add buttons to and delete buttons from the Quick Access Toolbar. You also can assign a command, such as a macro, to a button on the Quick Access Toolbar. The following steps add an existing command to the Quick Access Toolbar and assign a macro to a new button on the Quick Access Toolbar. *Why? This module shows how to add the New File command to the Quick Access Toolbar and also shows how to create a button for the ZoomPageWidth macro so that instead of using the Macros dialog box, you can click the button to change the zoom to page width.*

1

- Click the 'Customize Quick Access Toolbar' button on the Quick Access Toolbar to display the Customize Quick Access Toolbar menu (Figure 11–61).

Q&A
What happens if I click the commands listed on the Customize Quick Access Toolbar menu?
If the command does not have a check mark beside it and you click it, Publisher places the button associated with the command on the Quick Access Toolbar. If the command has a check mark beside it and you click (deselect) it, Publisher removes the command from the Quick Access Toolbar.

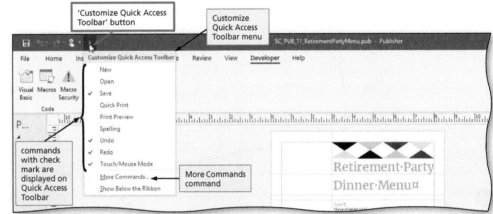

Figure 11–61

2

- Click More Commands on the Customize Quick Access Toolbar menu to display the Publisher Options dialog box with Quick Access Toolbar selected in the left pane.

- Scroll through the list of popular commands (Publisher Options dialog box) and then click New File to select the command.

- Click the Add button to add the selected command (New File, in this case) to the Customize Quick Access Toolbar list (Figure 11–62).

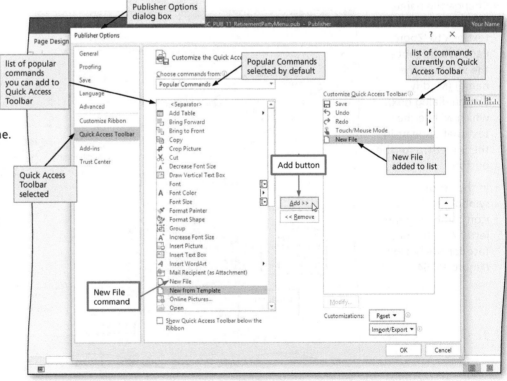

Figure 11–62

- Click the 'Choose commands from' arrow to display a list of categories of commands you can add to the Quick Access Toolbar (Figure 11–63).

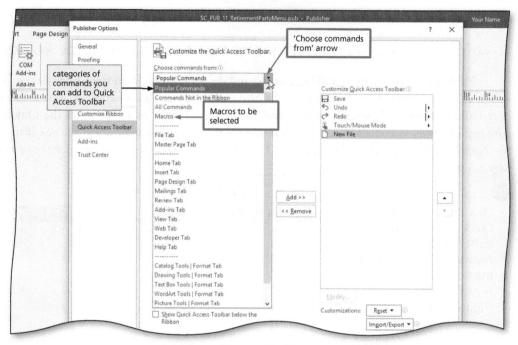

Figure 11–63

- Click Macros in the Choose commands from list to display the macro in this document.
- If necessary, click the macro to select it.
- Click the Add button (Publisher Options dialog box) to display the selected macro in the Customize Quick Access Toolbar list.
- Click the Modify button to display the Modify Button dialog box.
- Change the name in the Display name text box to 'Zoom Page Width' (note the spaces in the name) (Modify Button dialog box), which will be the text that appears in the ScreenTip for the button.
- In the list of symbols, click the icon containing the letter A as the new face for the button (Figure 11–64).

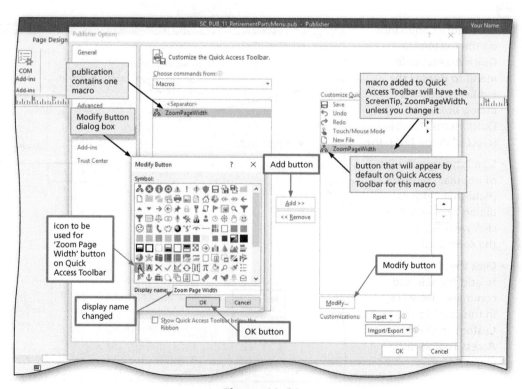

Figure 11–64

• Click OK (Modify Button dialog box) to change the button characteristics in the Customize Quick Access Toolbar list (Figure 11–65).

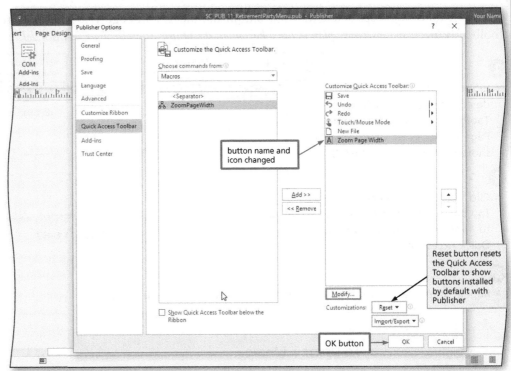

Figure 11–65

• Click OK (Publisher Options dialog box) to add the buttons to the Quick Access Toolbar (Figure 11–66).

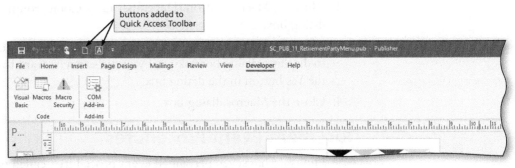

Figure 11–66

Other Ways

1. Right-click Quick Access Toolbar, click 'Customize Quick Access Toolbar' on shortcut menu

To Use the New Buttons on the Quick Access Toolbar

The next step is to test the new buttons on the Quick Access Toolbar — that is, the New button and the 'Zoom Page Width' button, which will execute, or run, the macro that changes the zoom to page width. The following steps use buttons on the Quick Access Toolbar.

1 Click the New button on the Quick Access Toolbar to display a new blank publication window. Close the new blank publication window.

2 If necessary, change the zoom to whole page.

3 Click the 'Zoom Page Width' button on the Quick Access Toolbar, which causes Publisher to perform the instructions stored in the ZoomPageWidth macro — that is, to change the zoom to page width.

To Delete Buttons from the Quick Access Toolbar

The following steps delete the New button and the 'Zoom Page Width' button from the Quick Access Toolbar. ***Why?*** *If you no longer plan to use a button on the Quick Access Toolbar, you can delete it.*

- Right-click the button to be deleted from the Quick Access Toolbar, in this case the 'Zoom Page Width' button, to display a shortcut menu (Figure 11–67).

- Click 'Remove from Quick Access Toolbar' on the shortcut menu to remove the button from the Quick Access Toolbar.

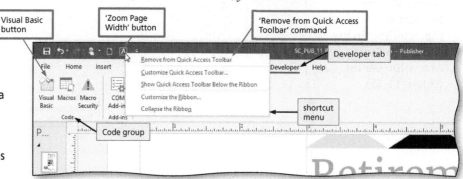

Figure 11–67

3

- Repeat Steps 1 and 2 for the New button on the Quick Access Toolbar.

To Delete a Macro

If you wanted to delete a macro, you would perform the following steps.

1. Display the Developer tab.
2. Click the Macros button (Developer tab | Code group) to display the Macros dialog box.
3. Click the macro to delete and then click the Delete button (Macros dialog box) to display a dialog box asking if you are sure you want to delete the macro. Click the Yes button in the dialog box.
4. Close the Macros dialog box.

Document Event Procedures

Publisher has seven prenamed event procedures, called **document events**, that execute automatically when certain events occur. Table 11–4 lists the name of each of these document events and when it runs.

Table 11–4 Document Events	
Document Event	**When It Runs**
BeforeClose	Immediately before any open publication closes
ShapesAdded	When one or more new shapes are added to a publication; this event occurs whether shapes are added manually or via program code
Undo	When a user undoes the last action performed
Redo	When reversing the last action that was undone
Open	When you open a publication containing the macro
ShapesRemoved	When a shape is deleted from a publication
WizardAfterChange	After the user chooses an option in the wizard pane that changes any of the following settings in the publication: page layout (page size, fold type, orientation, label product), print setup (paper size or print tiling), adding or deleting objects, adding or deleting pages, or object or page formatting (size, position, fill, border, background, default text, text formatting)

The name you use for a document event procedure depends on when you want certain actions to occur. The following sections illustrate how to create a BeforeClose event procedure using VBA because when a user closes the Retirement Party Menu publication in Publisher, you want a message box to appear that reminds the user to print enough copies of the menu for retirement party attendees.

To Open the Visual Basic for Applications Window

The following step opens the Visual Basic for Applications window. *Why? You use Visual Basic for Applications to create event procedures.*

- If necessary, display the Developer tab.
- Click the Visual Basic button (Developer tab | Code group) (shown in Figure 11–67) to open the Visual Basic for Applications window.
- If necessary, double-click the Visual Basic for Applications title bar to maximize the window.
- If the Project window does not open, click View on the menu bar and then click Project Explorer on the View menu. If the Properties panel appears below the Project window, click its Close button.
- In the Project window, if a plus sign appears next to Project (SC_PUB_11_RetirementPartyMenu.pub), click the plus sign to expand the group.
- If a plus sign appears next to Microsoft Publisher Objects, click the plus sign to expand the group.
- Double-click ThisDocument to open a code window for the event procedure (Figure 11–68).

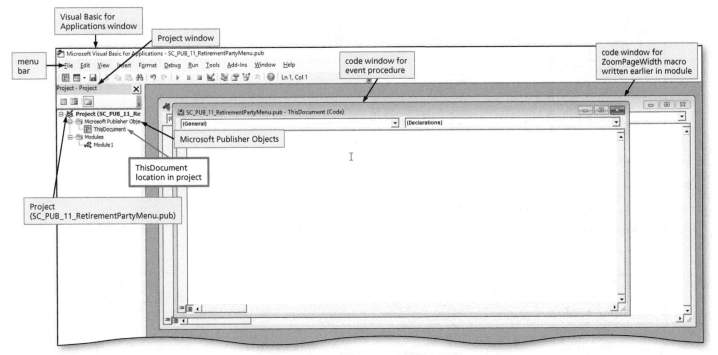

Figure 11–68

Other Ways

1. Press ALT+F11

BTW
VBA
VBA includes many more statements beyond those presented in this module. You may need to have a background in programming if you plan to write VBA code instructions in macros you develop and if the VBA code instructions are beyond the scope of the instructions presented in this module.

VBA Functions

The BeforeClose event in the Retirement Party Menu publication includes a code statement that calls, or executes, a function. A **function** is a keyword, already programmed in VBA, that activates a procedure. You will use the **MsgBox function**, which displays a message in a dialog box and then waits for the user to click a button. In its simplest forms, the code statement includes the function keyword, MsgBox, and the text that will appear in the message box enclosed in quotation marks. VBA programmers use a message box to display copyright information about a publication, remind users to perform a certain action, and so forth.

To Create a BeforeClose Event Procedure Using VBA

The following steps create a BeforeClose event procedure using VBA. *Why? In this project, when a Publisher user closes the Retirement Party Menu publication, you want a message box to appear, reminding the user to print enough copies of the menu for retirement party attendees.* This document event will apply only to the current publication; other publications will not have access to the code in this publication.

- In the event procedure code window, click the Object arrow to display the Object menu (Figure 11–69).

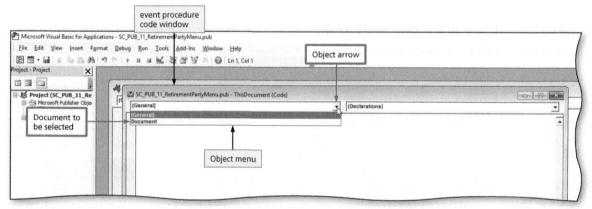

Figure 11–69

2
- Click Document on the Object menu to select a document event procedure.
- Click the Procedure arrow to display the Procedure menu (Figure 11–70).

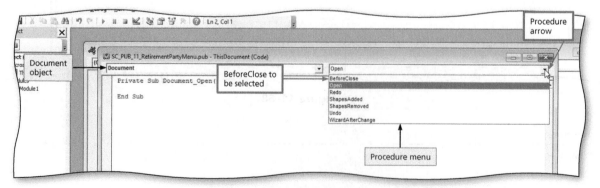

Figure 11–70

3

- Click BeforeClose on the Procedure menu to select the BeforeClose event procedure (Figure 11–71).

Q&A **Why did Publisher create two procedures?**
The beginning and ending code statements for the BeforeClose and Open procedures appear in the code window. Publisher automatically displays the Open procedure by default, but it will have no effect on this publication.

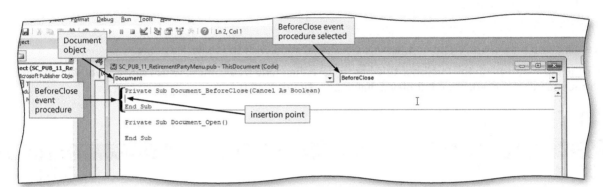

Figure 11–71

4

- With the insertion point positioned in the BeforeClose event procedure, as shown in Figure 11–71, press TAB to indent the insertion point. Type **' Displays a message when Publisher closes** and then press ENTER to enter the comment line.

- Type **MsgBox "Remember to print enough copies for attendees."** to enter the code statement. If necessary, press ESC to remove the ScreenTip (Figure 11–72).

Q&A **What are the lists that appear in the Visual Basic Editor as I enter code statements?**
The lists present valid statement elements to assist you with entering code statements. Because they are beyond the scope of this module, ignore them.

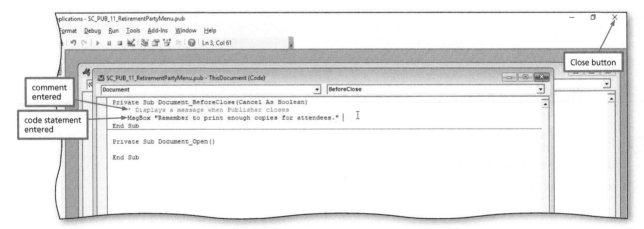

Figure 11–72

5

- Click the Close button on the Visual Basic for Applications title bar to close the window.

Q&A **How do I test an event procedure?**
Activate the event that causes the procedure to execute. For example, the BeforeClose event procedure runs whenever you close the publication.

To Save and Then Run the BeforeClose Event Procedure

The next step is to execute, or run, the BeforeClose event procedure to ensure that it works. To run the BeforeClose event procedure, you need to close the Retirement Party Menu publication. *Why? The BeforeClose event procedure executes when you close the publication, so you will close the publication to be sure the event procedure executes as intended.* The following steps save the publication and then close the publication to run the BeforeClose event procedure.

- Save the menu publication again on the same storage location with the same file name.
- Click the Close button on the Publisher title bar to close the menu publication, which causes Publisher to run the BeforeClose event procedure and display a dialog box (Figure 11–73).

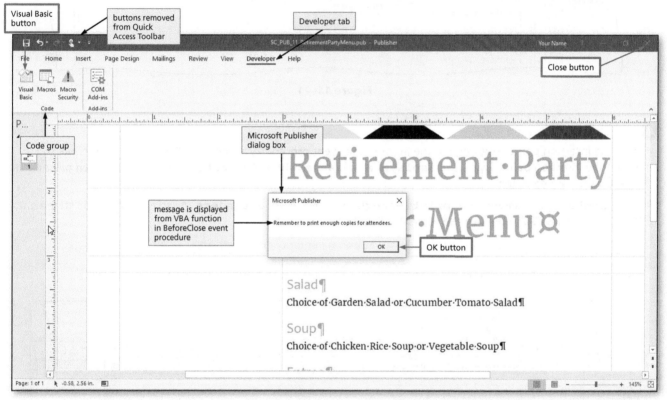

Figure 11–73

- Click OK to close the dialog box and the publication.
- If necessary, exit Publisher.

To Open a Publication with Macros

The following steps start Publisher again and open the Retirement Party Menu publication, which contains macros.

1. Start Publisher and open the file just closed, called SC_PUB_11_RetirementPartyMenu.pub, which causes the Microsoft Publisher Security Notice dialog box to be displayed because the publication contains macros (Figure 11–74).

2. Click the Enable Macros button to close the dialog box and open the publication.

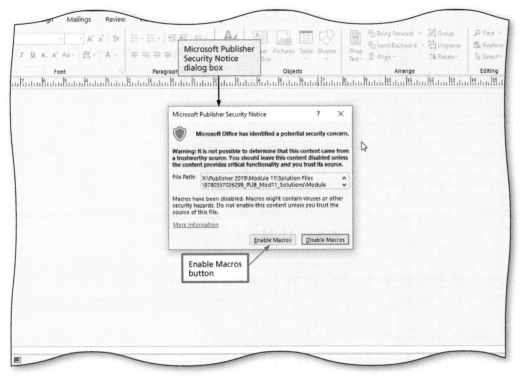

Figure 11–74

To Edit the BeforeClose Event Procedure Using VBA

The following steps edit the BeforeClose event procedure. *Why? You want to add a code statement to the procedure that removes any personal information from the file when you close the publication.*

1

- If necessary, display the Developer tab.

- Click the Visual Basic button (Developer tab | Code group) (shown in Figure 11–73) to open the Visual Basic for Applications window.

- If necessary, double-click the Visual Basic for Applications title bar to maximize the window.

- If the Project window does not open, click View on the menu bar and then click Project Explorer on the View menu. If the Properties panel appears below the Project window, click its Close button.

- In the Project window, if a plus sign appears next to Project (SC_PUB_11_RetirementPartyMenu.pub), click the plus sign to expand the group.

- If a plus sign appears next to Microsoft Publisher Objects, click the plus sign to expand the group.

- If necessary, double-click ThisDocument to open a code window with the event procedures in this document.

2

- Position the insertion point at the end of the MsgBox code statement and then press ENTER.

- Type **' Removes personal information from publication** and then press ENTER to enter the comment line.

- Type **ActiveDocument.RemovePersonalInformation = True** to enter the code statement. If necessary, press ESC to remove the ScreenTip (Figure 11–75).

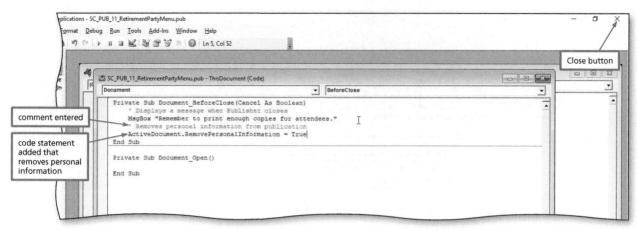

Figure 11–75

- Click the Close button on the Visual Basic for Applications title bar to close the window.

To Hide the Developer Tab

The following steps hide the Developer tab so that it no longer appears on the ribbon.

1. Open Backstage view and then click Options in the left pane of Backstage view to display the Publisher Options dialog box.

2. Click Customize Ribbon in the left pane (Publisher Options dialog box).

3. Remove the check mark from the Developer check box in the Main Tabs list.

4. Click OK to hide the Developer tab from the ribbon.

BTW
Distributing a Document
Instead of printing and distributing a hard copy of a document, you can distribute the document electronically. Options include sending the document via email; posting it on cloud storage (such as OneDrive) and sharing the file with others; posting it on social media, a blog, or other website; and sharing a link associated with an online location of the document. You also can create and share a PDF or XPS image of the document, so that users can view the file in Acrobat Reader or XPS Viewer instead of in Publisher.

To Save, Print, and Run the BeforeClose Event Procedure

The final steps in this project save the publication, print it, and run the BeforeClose event procedure to ensure that it works as intended.

1. Save the menu again on the same storage location with the same file name.

2. Print the publication.

3. Click the Close button on the Publisher title bar to close the menu publication, which causes Publisher to run the BeforeClose event procedure and display a dialog box.

4. Click OK to close the dialog box and the publication.

5. If necessary, exit Publisher.

Summary

In this module, you were introduced to some advanced Publisher features. You created a folded invitation card, inserted a design accent, created a banner, converted a picture to a Microsoft drawing object, created a custom RGB fill color, downloaded an online template, installed a new font, created custom ruler guides, set macro security levels, created a macro, added buttons for commands and macros to the Quick Access Toolbar, and created and edited an event procedure using VBA.

What decisions will you need to make when creating your party publications?
Use these guidelines as you complete the assignments in this module and create your own publications outside of this class.

1. Select and customize an appropriate invitation card template.

2. Select and customize an appropriate banner template.

3. Download any additional online templates you might need.

4. Format the templates as necessary.

    a) Insert design accents.

    b) Convert pictures to drawing objects, if needed.

    c) Create desired custom RGB colors.

    d) Install any specific fonts.

    e) Create custom ruler guides as needed.

5. Add macros to automate tasks.

    a) Set security levels to run macros.

    b) Add buttons for the macros to the Quick Access Toolbar.

    c) If you are familiar with computer programming, consider adding VBA code to the macro to extend its capabilities.

    d) Test the macros to be sure they work as intended.

6. Add document event procedures, if appropriate.

    a) If you are familiar with computer programming, consider adding VBA code to the macro to extend its capabilities.

    b) Test the document event procedures to be sure they work as intended.

BTW
Web Tools and Development
Microsoft does not recommend Publisher for web development, which is the reason Publisher no longer includes web templates in the template gallery. While Publisher still includes web tools, this format is not supported by many web servers. Thus, web tools and web development are beyond the scope of this book and no longer covered in this module.

Apply Your Knowledge

Reinforce the skills and apply the concepts you learned in this module.

Creating a Folded Invitation

Note: To complete this assignment, you will be required to use the Data Files. Please contact your instructor for information about accessing the Data Files.

Instructions: You have been hired as an intern for a local branch of Scenic Horizons Travel. Your branch will be hosting a bon voyage party for all customers of an upcoming cruise. You are to create a folded invitation card that will be sent to each customer (Figure 11–76).

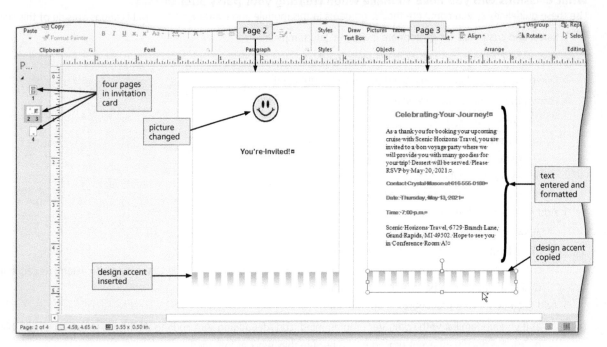

Figure 11–76

Perform the following tasks:

1. Start Publisher and then click Built-In in the template gallery to display the built-in templates. Scroll as necessary and then click the Invitation Cards thumbnail to display the Invitation Card templates. In the section labeled Event, click the All Event folder to open it. If necessary, scroll to the Celebration area and then click the Bon Voyage thumbnail to select it.

2. In the template information pane, do the following:

   a. Click the Color scheme button to display a list of color schemes. Scroll as necessary and then click Island to select the color scheme.

   b. Click the Font scheme button to display a list of font schemes. Scroll as necessary and then click Galley to select the font scheme.

   c. Ensure that 'Quarter-sheet side fold' is selected in the Options area. If it is not, select the Page size button and then click 'Quarter-sheet side fold'.

   d. If necessary, scroll in the Options area and then click the Layout button to display the Layout menu. Scroll to and then click Retro Orbits on the Layout menu to select that layout.

   e. Click the CREATE button to create the specified invitation card template in a Publisher window.

3. If the Page Navigation pane is not open, click the Page Number button on the status bar to open it.

4. If necessary, display the View tab and then click the 'Two-Page Spread' button (View tab | Layout group) to display facing pages in the publication as a two-page spread. Click through the thumbnails in the Page Navigation pane and review the contents of the pages in the invitation card.

5. To reverse pages 2 and 3, display the View tab and then click the Single Page button (View tab | Layout group) to display single pages. Click the Page 2 thumbnail in the Page Navigation pane to select it and then drag the Page 2 thumbnail in the Page Navigation pane down below the Page 3 thumbnail. Click the 'Two-Page Spread' button (View tab | Layout group) to display facing pages in the publication as a two-page spread.

6. Change the verse in the invitation card by displaying the Page Design tab and then clicking the Options button (Page Design tab | Template group) to display the Suggested Verse dialog box. Be sure the Category displays Bon Voyage Party (Suggested Verse dialog box) and then click the fourth verse in the Available messages list that begins with the text, We're saying, to select a new verse for the first page of the card. Click OK.

7. If necessary, navigate to the two-page spread for pages 2 and 3. Right-click the picture on page 2 to display a shortcut menu, point to Change Picture on the shortcut menu to display the Change Picture submenu, and then click Change Picture on the Change Picture submenu to display the Insert Pictures dialog box. Click 'From a file' in the Insert Pictures dialog box to display the Insert Picture dialog box, navigate to the Support_PUB_11_HappyFace.png file in the Data Files (Insert Picture dialog box), and then click the Insert button to replace the selected image with the new picture file. Click anywhere on page 2 to deselect the pictures. Next, select the inserted picture of the happy face on page 2 of the invitation card so that only that picture is selected and then click the Fit button (Picture Tools Format tab | Crop group) to resize the picture so that it displays in its entirety inside the picture area. Resize the picture to an approximate height of 1 inch and a width of 0.63 inches and then position it at the top of the page centered between the margins.

8. In the text box on page 2, add an exclamation point at the end of the sentence so that it reads: You're Invited!

9. Change the text on page 3 of the invitation card as follows:
   a. In the top text box, change the text, Invitation Title, to the text, Celebrating Your Journey!, for the title. Bold the entered text and change the font color to 'Accent 1 (RGB (51, 153, 255)), Darker 25%' (second color in the fifth row).
   b. In the second text box, change the paragraph of text to the following:
      As a thank you for booking your upcoming cruise with Scenic Horizons Travel, you are invited to a bon voyage party where we will provide you with many goodies for your trip! Dessert will be served. Please RSVP by May 10, 2021.
   c. In the third text box, change the text, Contact person: 555-555-5555, to the text, Contact Crystal Mason at 616-555-0188, for the contact. Change the font color of all text in this text box to 'Accent 1 (RGB (51, 153, 255)), Darker 25%' (second color in the fifth row).
   d. In the fourth text box, change the text, 00/00/00, to the text, Thursday, May 13, 2021, for the date. Change the font color of all text in this text box to 'Accent 1 (RGB (51, 153, 255)), Darker 25%' (second color in the fifth row).
   e. In the fifth text box, change the text, 00:00, to the text 7:00 p.m., for the time. Change the font color of all text in this text box to 'Accent 1 (RGB (51, 153, 255)), Darker 25%' (second color in the fifth row).
   f. In the last text box, change the location to the following: Scenic Horizons Travel, 6729 Branch Lane, Grand Rapids, MI 49502. Hope to see you in Conference Room A!

10. Insert a design accent on page 2 of the invitation card by displaying the Insert tab, clicking the 'Borders & Accents' button (Insert tab | Building Blocks group) to display the Borders &

Continued >

STUDENT ASSIGNMENTS

Apply Your Knowledge *continued*

Accents gallery, and then clicking the Awning Stripes accent in the Bars area. Position the accent at the bottom of page 2 and then resize it to a height of 0.5 inches and width of 3.55 inches. (If your height and width boxes are dimmed after moving the accent, click the Undo button on the Quick Access Toolbar and then resize the accent before moving it.)

11. Copy the design accent and then paste it at the bottom of page 3 of the invitation card, as shown in Figure 11–76.

12. Navigate to page 4 of the invitation card. Right-click the picture in the circle at the bottom of page 4 and then change the picture to the Support_PUB_11_Suitcases.png file, which is located in the Data Files. Click anywhere to deselect the picture.

13. Delete the pictures in the scratch area by selecting them, right-clicking the selection, and then clicking Delete Object on the shortcut menu.

14. If requested by your instructor, navigate to page 3 of the invitation card and change the contact name to your name and the contact phone number to your phone number.

15. Save the publication on your hard drive, OneDrive, or other storage location using SC_PUB_11_BonVoyageInvitation as the file name.

16. Print the publication and then fold it so that it looks like the finished invitation card.

17. Submit the completed publication in the format specified by your instructor. Exit Publisher.

18. ✷ Thank you cards are a type of greeting card template in Publisher, which are similar to invitation cards because they are a folded publication. If you wanted to create thank you cards for those who attended the bon voyage party, how would you design the thank you cards? Why?

Extend Your Knowledge

Extend the skills you learned in this module and experiment with new skills. You may need to use Help to complete the assignment.

Creating a Banner

Instructions: You have been hired as an intern for a local branch of Scenic Horizons Travel. Your branch will be hosting a bon voyage party for all customers of an upcoming cruise. You are to create a banner for the bon voyage party (Figure 11–77).

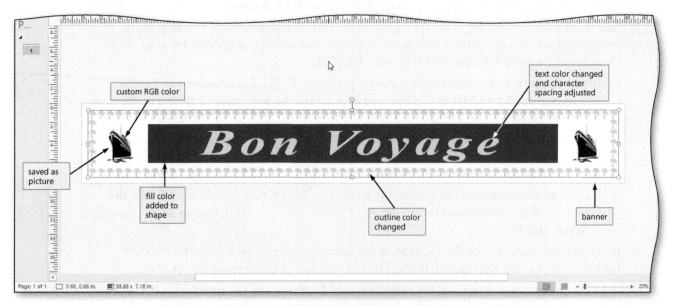

Figure 11–77

Perform the following tasks:

1. Use Help to learn more about banners, character spacing, grouping and ungrouping objects, custom RGB colors, and saving pictures.

2. Start Publisher and then click Built-In in the template gallery to display the built-in templates. Scroll as necessary and then click the Banners thumbnail to display the Banners templates. In the section labeled Event, if your screen displays an All Event folder, click the All Event folder to open it. Click the Bon Voyage thumbnail to select it.

3. In the template information pane,

    a. Click the Color scheme button to display a list of color schemes. Scroll as necessary and then click Island to select the Island color scheme.

    b. Click the Font scheme button to display a list of font schemes. Scroll as necessary and then click Galley to select the Galley font scheme.

    c. Ensure that the page size in the Options area is set to 5 feet × 8.5 inches. If it is not, select the Page size button and then click '5 ft × 8.5 in'.

    d. Ensure that Border is selected. If it is not, select the Border button and then click Border on the Border menu.

    e. Ensure that Both is selected. If it is not, click the Graphic button to display the Graphic menu and then click Both so that the graphic appears on both edges of the banner.

    f. Click the CREATE button to create the specified banner template in a Publisher window.

4. Select the text box surrounding the Bon Voyage text and then use the Shape Fill arrow (Drawing Tools Format tab | Shape Styles group) to change the fill in the text box to the color 'Accent 1 (RGB (51, 153, 255)), Darker 50%' (second color in the last row).

5. Select the text, Bon Voyage, and bold it. Change its color to 'Accent 2 (RGB (204, 255, 0))' (third color in the first row).

6. With the text selected, click the Character Spacing button (Text Box Tools Format tab | Font group) to display the Character Spacing menu and then click Very Loose on the Character Spacing menu. Display the Character Spacing menu again and then click More Spacing on the menu to display the Character Spacing dialog box. Change the value in the Scaling box to 150% (Character Spacing dialog box) and then click OK to adjust the spacing as specified.

7. Select the cruise ship picture on the left side of the banner, display the Picture Tools Format tab, and then click the Ungroup button (Picture Tools Format tab | Arrange group) to ungroup the picture, which will display a Microsoft Publisher dialog box. Click the Yes button (Microsoft Publisher dialog box) to convert the picture to a grouped drawing object and display the Drawing Tools tab on the ribbon. Click the Ungroup button (Drawing Tools Format tab | Arrange group) to ungroup the drawing object. Click outside of the drawing object to deselect it.

8. Change the zoom to 100% and display the cruise ship picture on the left side of the banner. Click to select the entire ship, click the Shape Fill arrow (Drawing Tools Format tab | Shape Styles group) to display the Shape Fill gallery, click 'More Fill Colors' in the Shape Fill gallery to display the Colors dialog box, click the Custom tab (Colors dialog box) to display options related to creating a custom color, type **40** in the Red box, type **62** in the Green box, and type **46** in the Blue box, and then click OK to apply the defined color to the ship.

Continued >

Extend Your Knowledge *continued*

9. One at a time, click each of the waves below the ship and use the Shape Fill arrow (Drawing Tools Format tab | Shape Styles group) to change their color to 'Accent 1 (RGB (51, 153, 255)), Darker 50%' (second color in the last row).

10. Change the zoom to whole page. With the pointer positioned outside of the top-left corner of the banner, drag into the banner to select all of the objects in the cruise ship picture and then click the Group button (Home tab | Arrange group) to group the selected shapes into a single drawing object.

11. Right-click the grouped picture to display a shortcut menu and then click 'Save as Picture' on the shortcut menu to display the Save As dialog box and then save the picture on your hard drive, OneDrive, or other storage location using SC_PUB_11_CruiseShip as the file name.

12. Right-click the black-and-white cruise ship picture on the right side of the banner and then use the Change Picture command on the shortcut menu to change the picture to the SC_PUB_11_CruiseShip file that you saved in Step 9.

13. Delete the picture in the scratch area by selecting it, right-clicking the selection, and then clicking Delete Object on the shortcut menu.

14. Click the banner outline to select it. Use the Shape Outline arrow (Drawing Tools Format tab | Shape Styles group) to change the color of the palm trees in the outline to 'Hyperlink (Teal), Lighter 60%' (sixth color in the third row).

15. If requested by your instructor, replace the cruise ship image on the right side of the banner with a picture of yourself.

16. Save the publication on your hard drive, OneDrive, or other storage location using SC_PUB_11_BonVoyageBanner as the file name.

17. If requested by your instructor, print the publication and then tape it together so that it looks like a banner.

18. Submit the completed publication in the format specified by your instructor. Exit Publisher.

19. ✹ If you wanted to create a banner to print vertically instead of horizontally, what setting would you change before you started designing the banner?

Expand Your World

Create a solution that uses cloud or web technologies by learning and investigating on your own from general guidance.

Searching for an Online Template and Using an Online Photo Editor

Instructions: As an assistant to the marketing manager at Wedding Solutions, you have been asked to create a new line of wedding publications. You look through available online wedding templates and download one to use for this project. You then use an online photo editor to enhance an image in the downloaded template. Be creative — the modified image shown in the online photo editor in Figure 11–78 is only a sample solution. Your image, even if it is the same one, should look different.

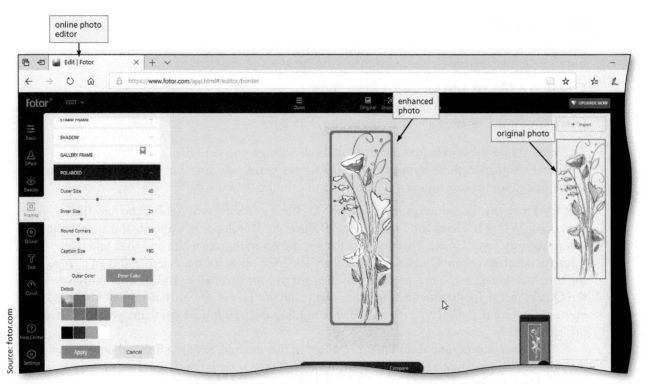

Figure 11–78

Perform the following tasks:

1. Start Publisher. Type **wedding** in the 'Search for online templates' box to enter the search text and then press ENTER to display online templates related to the search text. Scroll through the templates, select one that contains a picture or an image, and then click the Create button to download the selected template and display it in the Publisher window.

2. Right-click the picture or image in the template to display a shortcut menu and then click 'Save as Picture' on the shortcut menu to display the Save As dialog box and then save the picture on your hard drive, OneDrive, or other storage location using SC_PUB_11_OnlineTemplatePicture as the file name.

3. Use File Explorer to locate the saved picture file on your computer or mobile device and then double-click the file to open it. In what program did it open?

4. Start a browser. Search for the text, online photo editor, using a search engine. Visit several of the online photo editors and determine which you would like to use to edit an image. Navigate to the desired online photo editor.

5. In the photo editor, open the SC_PUB_11_OnlineTemplatePicture image that you created in Step 2. Use the photo editor to enhance the image. Apply at least five enhancements. Which enhancements did you apply?

6. If requested by your instructor, add your name as a text element to the photo.

7. Save the revised image with the file name, SC_PUB_11_OnlineTemplatePictureEnhanced. In what format did the online photo editor save the file? Submit the original and enhanced images in the format specified by your instructor.

8. ✱ Answer the questions posed in #3, #5, and #7. Which online photo editors did you evaluate? Which one did you select to use, and why? Do you prefer using the online photo editor or Publisher to enhance images?

In the Lab

Design and implement a solution using creative thinking and problem-solving skills.

Creating a Macro and an Event Procedure

Note: To complete this assignment, you will be required to use the Data Files. Please contact your instructor for information about accessing the Data Files.

Problem: As customer relations manager at Knoll Springs, you send thank you cards to all volunteers. You created the layout and content for the thank you cards but want to add a macro and event procedure because others will be using and printing these cards.

Part 1:   Open the file named called SC_PUB_11-1.pub and then save it using the new file name, SC_WD_11_ThankYouCardComplete. Show the Developer tab. Specify the appropriate macro security level. Create a macro that changes the zoom to page width and then add that macro as a button on the Quick Access Toolbar. Test the button for the macro and then change the text, VolunteerFirstName, on page 2 of the card to your first name. Add another button to the Quick Access Toolbar for any Publisher command not on the ribbon. Create a BeforeClose event procedure that displays a message box reminding the user to fold the thank you card after printing it.

Use the concepts and techniques presented in this module. Save the finished publication on the same storage location with the same file name and then submit the assignment in the format specified by your instructor.

Part 2:   ☀ Think of other messages that designers might want to include in print publications. Make a list of when the message should appear and what it needs to tell the user of the publication.

Index

Note: Page references in **bold** indicate defined terms.